Lecture Notes in Computer Science 14257

Founding Editors

Gerhard Goos
Juris Hartmanis

Editorial Board Members

The series Lecture Notes in Computer Science (LNCS), including its subseries Lecture Notes in Artificial Intelligence (LNAI) and Lecture Notes in Bioinformatics (LNBI), has established itself as a medium for the publication of new developments in computer science and information technology research, teaching, and education.

LNCS enjoys close cooperation with the computer science R & D community, the series counts many renowned academics among its volume editors and paper authors, and collaborates with prestigious societies. Its mission is to serve this international community by providing an invaluable service, mainly focused on the publication of conference and workshop proceedings and postproceedings. LNCS commenced publication in 1973.

Lazaros Iliadis · Antonios Papaleonidas ·
Plamen Angelov · Chrisina Jayne
Editors

Artificial Neural Networks and Machine Learning – ICANN 2023

32nd International Conference on Artificial Neural Networks
Heraklion, Crete, Greece, September 26–29, 2023
Proceedings, Part IV

 Springer

Editors
Lazaros Iliadis (iD)
Democritus University of Thrace
Xanthi, Greece

Antonios Papaleonidas (iD)
Democritus University of Thrace
Xanthi, Greece

Plamen Angelov (iD)
Lancaster University
Lancaster, UK

Chrisina Jayne (iD)
Teesside University
Middlesbrough, UK

ISSN 0302-9743   ISSN 1611-3349 (electronic)
Lecture Notes in Computer Science
ISBN 978-3-031-44215-5   ISBN 978-3-031-44216-2 (eBook)
https://doi.org/10.1007/978-3-031-44216-2

This Springer imprint is published by the registered company Springer Nature Switzerland AG
The registered company address is: Gewerbestrasse 11, 6330 Cham, Switzerland

Paper in this product is recyclable.

Preface

The European Neural Network Society (ENNS) is an association of scientists, engineers and students, conducting research on the modelling of behavioral and brain processes, and on the development of neural algorithms. The core of these efforts is the application of neural modelling to several diverse domains. According to its mission statement ENNS is the European non-profit federation of professionals that aims at achieving a worldwide professional and socially responsible development and application of artificial neural technologies.

The flagship event of ENNS is ICANN (the International Conference on Artificial Neural Networks) at which contributed research papers are presented after passing through a rigorous review process. ICANN is a dual-track conference, featuring tracks in brain-inspired computing on the one hand, and machine learning on the other, with strong crossdisciplinary interactions and applications.

The response of the international scientific community to the ICANN 2023 call for papers was more than satisfactory. In total, 947 research papers on the aforementioned research areas were submitted and 426 (45%) of them were finally accepted as full papers after a peer review process. Additionally, 19 extended abstracts were submitted and 9 of them were selected to be included in the front matter of ICANN 2023 proceedings. Due to their high academic and scientific importance, 22 short papers were also accepted.

All papers were peer reviewed by at least two independent academic referees. Where needed, a third or a fourth referee was consulted to resolve any potential conflicts. Three workshops focusing on specific research areas, namely Advances in Spiking Neural Networks (ASNN), Neurorobotics (NRR), and the challenge of Errors, Stability, Robustness, and Accuracy in Deep Neural Networks (ESRA in DNN), were organized.

The 10-volume set of LNCS 14254, 14255, 14256, 14257, 14258, 14259, 14260, 14261, 14262 and 14263 constitutes the proceedings of the 32nd International Conference on Artificial Neural Networks, ICANN 2023, held in Heraklion city, Crete, Greece, on September 26–29, 2023.

The accepted papers are related to the following topics:

Machine Learning: Deep Learning; Neural Network Theory; Neural Network Models; Graphical Models; Bayesian Networks; Kernel Methods; Generative Models; Information Theoretic Learning; Reinforcement Learning; Relational Learning; Dynamical Models; Recurrent Networks; and Ethics of AI.

Brain-Inspired Computing: Cognitive Models; Computational Neuroscience; Self-Organization; Neural Control and Planning; Hybrid Neural-Symbolic Architectures; Neural Dynamics; Cognitive Neuroscience; Brain Informatics; Perception and Action; and Spiking Neural Networks.

Neural applications in Bioinformatics; Biomedicine; Intelligent Robotics; Neuro-robotics; Language Processing; Speech Processing; Image Processing; Sensor Fusion; Pattern Recognition; Data Mining; Neural Agents; Brain-Computer Interaction; Neuro-morphic Computing and Edge AI; and Evolutionary Neural Networks.

September 2023

Lazaros Iliadis
Antonios Papaleonidas
Plamen Angelov
Chrisina Jayne

Organization

General Chairs

Iliadis Lazaros   Democritus University of Thrace, Greece
Plamen Angelov   Lancaster University, UK

Program Chairs

Antonios Papaleonidas   Democritus University of Thrace, Greece
Elias Pimenidis   UWE Bristol, UK
Chrisina Jayne   Teesside University, UK

Honorary Chairs

Stefan Wermter   University of Hamburg, Germany
Vera Kurkova   Czech Academy of Sciences, Czech Republic
Nikola Kasabov   Auckland University of Technology, New Zealand

Organizing Chairs

Antonios Papaleonidas   Democritus University of Thrace, Greece
Anastasios Panagiotis Psathas   Democritus University of Thrace, Greece
George Magoulas   University of London, Birkbeck College, UK
Haralambos Mouratidis   University of Essex, UK

Award Chairs

Stefan Wermter   University of Hamburg, Germany
Chukiong Loo   University of Malaysia, Malaysia

Communication Chairs

Sebastian Otte   University of Tübingen, Germany
Anastasios Panagiotis Psathas   Democritus University of Thrace, Greece

Steering Committee

Stefan Wermter   University of Hamburg, Germany
Angelo Cangelosi   University of Manchester, UK
Igor Farkaš   Comenius University in Bratislava, Slovakia
Chrisina Jayne   Teesside University, UK
Matthias Kerzel   University of Hamburg, Germany
Alessandra Lintas   University of Lausanne, Switzerland
Kristína Malinovská (Rebrová)   Comenius University in Bratislava, Slovakia
Alessio Micheli   University of Pisa, Italy
Jaakko Peltonen   Tampere University, Finland
Brigitte Quenet   ESPCI Paris, France
Ausra Saudargiene   Lithuanian University of Health Sciences,
                                            Lithuania
Roseli Wedemann   Rio de Janeiro State University, Brazil

Local Organizing/Hybrid Facilitation Committee

Aggeliki Tsouka   Democritus University of Thrace, Greece
Anastasios Panagiotis Psathas   Democritus University of Thrace, Greece
Anna Karagianni   Democritus University of Thrace, Greece
Christina Gkizioti   Democritus University of Thrace, Greece
Ioanna-Maria Erentzi   Democritus University of Thrace, Greece
Ioannis Skopelitis   Democritus University of Thrace, Greece
Lambros Kazelis   Democritus University of Thrace, Greece
Leandros Tsatsaronis   Democritus University of Thrace, Greece
Nikiforos Mpotzoris   Democritus University of Thrace, Greece
Nikos Zervis   Democritus University of Thrace, Greece
Panagiotis Restos   Democritus University of Thrace, Greece
Tassos Giannakopoulos   Democritus University of Thrace, Greece

Program Committee

Abraham Yosipof	CLB, Israel
Adane Tarekegn	NTNU, Norway
Aditya Gilra	Centrum Wiskunde & Informatica, Netherlands
Adrien Durand-Petiteville	Federal University of Pernambuco, Brazil
Adrien Fois	LORIA, France
Alaa Marouf	Hosei University, Japan
Alessandra Sciutti	Istituto Italiano di Tecnologia, Italy
Alessandro Sperduti	University of Padua, Italy
Alessio Micheli	University of Pisa, Italy
Alex Shenfield	Sheffield Hallam University, UK
Alexander Kovalenko	Czech Technical University in Prague, Czech Republic
Alexander Krawczyk	Fulda University of Applied Sciences, Germany
Ali Minai	University of Cincinnati, USA
Aluizio Araujo	Universidade Federal de Pernambuco, Brazil
Amarda Shehu	George Mason University, USA
Amit Kumar Kundu	University of Maryland, USA
Anand Rangarajan	University of Florida, USA
Anastasios Panagiotis Psathas	Democritus University of Thrace, Greece
Andre de Carvalho	Universidade de São Paulo, Brazil
Andrej Lucny	Comenius University, Slovakia
Angel Villar-Corrales	University of Bonn, Germany
Angelo Cangelosi	University of Manchester, UK
Anna Jenul	Norwegian University of Life Sciences, Norway
Antonios Papaleonidas	Democritus University of Thrace, Greece
Arnaud Lewandowski	LISIC, ULCO, France
Arul Selvam Periyasamy	Universität Bonn, Germany
Asma Mekki	University of Sfax, Tunisia
Banafsheh Rekabdar	Portland State University, USA
Barbara Hammer	Universität Bielefeld, Germany
Baris Serhan	University of Manchester, UK
Benedikt Bagus	University of Applied Sciences Fulda, Germany
Benjamin Paaßen	Bielefeld University, Germany
Bernhard Pfahringer	University of Waikato, New Zealand
Bharath Sudharsan	NUI Galway, Ireland
Binyi Wu	Dresden University of Technology, Germany
Binyu Zhao	Harbin Institute of Technology, China
Björn Plüster	University of Hamburg, Germany
Bo Mei	Texas Christian University, USA

Brian Moser	Deutsches Forschungszentrum für künstliche Intelligenz, Germany
Carlo Mazzola	Istituto Italiano di Tecnologia, Italy
Carlos Moreno-Garcia	Robert Gordon University, UK
Chandresh Pravin	Reading University, UK
Chao Ma	Wuhan University, China
Chathura Wanigasekara	German Aerospace Centre, Germany
Cheng Shang	Shanghai Jiaotong University, China
Chengqiang Huang	Huawei Technologies, China
Chenhan Zhang	University of Technology, Sydney, Australia
Chenyang Lyu	Dublin City University, Ireland
Chihuang Liu	Meta, USA
Chrisina Jayne	Teesside University, UK
Christian Balkenius	Lund University, Sweden
Chrysoula Kosma	Ecole Polytechnique, Greece
Claudio Bellei	Elliptic, UK
Claudio Gallicchio	University of Pisa, Italy
Claudio Giorgio Giancaterino	Intesa SanPaolo Vita, Italy
Constantine Dovrolis	Cyprus Institute, USA
Coşku Horuz	University of Tübingen, Germany
Cunjian Chen	Monash, Australia
Cunyi Yin	Fuzhou University, Singapore
Damien Lolive	Université Rennes, CNRS, IRISA, France
Daniel Stamate	Goldsmiths, University of London, UK
Daniel Vašata	Czech Technical University in Prague, Czech Republic
Dario Pasquali	Istituto Italiano di Tecnologia, Italy
David Dembinsky	German Research Center for Artificial Intelligence, Germany
David Rotermund	University of Bremen, Germany
Davide Liberato Manna	University of Strathclyde, UK
Dehao Yuan	University of Maryland, USA
Denise Gorse	University College London, UK
Dennis Wong	Macao Polytechnic University, China
Des Higham	University of Edinburgh, UK
Devesh Jawla	TU Dublin, Ireland
Dimitrios Michail	Harokopio University of Athens, Greece
Dino Ienco	INRAE, France
Diptangshu Pandit	Teesside University, UK
Diyuan Lu	Helmholtz Center Munich, Germany
Domenico Tortorella	University of Pisa, Italy
Dominik Geissler	American Family Insurance, USA

DongNyeong Heo	Handong Global University, South Korea
Dongyang Zhang	University of Electronic Science and Technology of China, China
Doreen Jirak	Istituto Italiano di Tecnologia, Italy
Douglas McLelland	BrainChip, France
Douglas Nyabuga	Mount Kenya University, Rwanda
Dulani Meedeniya	University of Moratuwa, Sri Lanka
Dumitru-Clementin Cercel	University Politehnica of Bucharest, Romania
Dylan Muir	SynSense, Switzerland
Efe Bozkir	Uni Tübingen, Germany
Eleftherios Kouloumpris	Aristotle University of Thessaloniki, Greece
Elias Pimenidis	University of the West of England, UK
Eliska Kloberdanz	Iowa State University, USA
Emre Neftci	Foschungszentrum Juelich, Germany
Enzo Tartaglione	Telecom Paris, France
Erwin Lopez	University of Manchester, UK
Evgeny Mirkes	University of Leicester, UK
F. Boray Tek	Istanbul Technical University, Turkey
Federico Corradi	Eindhoven University of Technology, Netherlands
Federico Errica	NEC Labs Europe, Germany
Federico Manzi	Università Cattolica del Sacro Cuore, Italy
Federico Vozzi	CNR, Italy
Fedor Scholz	University of Tuebingen, Germany
Feifei Dai	Chinese Academy of Sciences, China
Feifei Xu	Shanghai University of Electric Power, China
Feixiang Zhou	University of Leicester, UK
Felipe Moreno	FGV, Peru
Feng Wei	York University, Canada
Fengying Li	Guilin University of Electronic Technology, China
Flora Ferreira	University of Minho, Portugal
Florian Mirus	Intel Labs, Germany
Francesco Semeraro	University of Manchester, UK
Franco Scarselli	University of Siena, Italy
François Blayo	IPSEITE, Switzerland
Frank Röder	Hamburg University of Technology, Germany
Frederic Alexandre	Inria, France
Fuchang Han	Central South University, China
Fuli Wang	University of Essex, UK
Gabriela Sejnova	Czech Technical University in Prague, Czech Republic
Gaetano Di Caterina	University of Strathclyde, UK
George Bebis	University of Nevada, USA

Gerrit Ecke	Mercedes-Benz, Germany
Giannis Nikolentzos	Ecole Polytechnique, France
Gilles Marcou	University of Strasbourg, France
Giorgio Gnecco	IMT School for Advanced Studies, Italy
Glauco Amigo	Baylor University, USA
Greg Lee	Acadia University, Canada
Grégory Bourguin	LISIC/ULCO, France
Guillermo Martín-Sánchez	Champalimaud Foundation, Portugal
Gulustan Dogan	UNCW, USA
Habib Khan	Islamia College University Peshawar, Pakistan
Haizhou Du	Shanghai University of Electric Power, China
Hanli Wang	Tongji University, China
Hanno Gottschalk	TU Berlin, Germany
Hao Tong	University of Birmingham, UK
Haobo Jiang	NJUST, China
Haopeng Chen	Shanghai Jiao Tong University, China
Hazrat Ali	Hamad Bin Khalifa University, Qatar
Hina Afridi	NTNU, Gjøvik, Norway
Hiroaki Aizawa	Hiroshima University, Japan
Hiromichi Suetani	Oita University, Japan
Hiroshi Kawaguchi	Kobe University, Japan
Hiroyasu Ando	Tohoku University, Japan
Hiroyoshi Ito	University of Tsukuba, Japan
Honggang Zhang	University of Massachusetts, Boston, USA
Hongqing Yu	Open University, UK
Hongye Cao	Northwestern Polytechnical University, China
Hugo Carneiro	University of Hamburg, Germany
Hugo Eduardo Camacho Cruz	Universidad Autónoma de Tamaulipas, Mexico
Huifang Ma	Northwest Normal University, China
Hyeyoung Park	Kyungpook National University, South Korea
Ian Nabney	University of Bristol, UK
Igor Farkas	Comenius University Bratislava, Slovakia
Ikuko Nishikawa	Ritsumeikan University, Japan
Ioannis Pierros	Aristotle University of Thessaloniki, Greece
Iraklis Varlamis	Harokopio University of Athens, Greece
Ivan Tyukin	King's College London, UK
Iveta Bečková	Comenius University in Bratislava, Slovakia
Jae Hee Lee	University of Hamburg, Germany
James Yu	Southern University of Science and Technology, China
Jan Faigl	Czech Technical University in Prague, Czech Republic

Jan Feber	Czech Technical University in Prague, Czech Republic
Jan-Gerrit Habekost	University of Hamburg, Germany
Jannik Thuemmel	University of Tübingen, Germany
Jeremie Cabessa	University Paris 2, France
Jérémie Sublime	ISEP, France
Jia Cai	Guangdong University of Finance & Economics, China
Jiaan Wang	Soochow University, China
Jialiang Tang	Nanjing University of Science and Technology, China
Jian Hu	YiduCloud, Cyprus
Jianhua Xu	Nanjing Normal University, China
Jianyong Chen	Shenzhen University, China
Jichao Bi	Zhejiang Institute of Industry and Information Technology, China
Jie Shao	University of Electronic Science and Technology of China, China
Jim Smith	University of the West of England, UK
Jing Yang	Hefei University of Technology, China
Jingyi Yuan	Arizona State University, USA
Jingyun Jia	Baidu, USA
Jinling Wang	Ulster University, UK
Jiri Sima	Czech Academy of Sciences, Czech Republic
Jitesh Dundas	Independent Researcher, USA
Joost Vennekens	KU Leuven, Belgium
Jordi Cosp	Universitat Politècnica de Catalunya, Spain
Josua Spisak	University of Hamburg, Germany
Jozef Kubík	Comenius University, Slovakia
Junpei Zhong	Hong Kong Polytechnic University, China
Jurgita Kapočiūtė-Dzikienė	Vytautas Magnus University, Lithuania
K. L. Eddie Law	Macao Polytechnic University, China
Kai Tang	Independent Researcher, China
Kamil Dedecius	Czech Academy of Sciences, Czech Republic
Kang Zhang	Kyushu University, Japan
Kantaro Fujiwara	University of Tokyo, Japan
Karlis Freivalds	Institute of Electronics and Computer Science, Latvia
Khoa Phung	University of the West of England, UK
Kiran Lekkala	University of Southern California, USA
Kleanthis Malialis	University of Cyprus, Cyprus
Kohulan Rajan	Friedrich Schiller University, Germany

Koichiro Yamauchi   Chubu University, Japan
Koloud Alkhamaiseh   Western Michigan University, USA
Konstantinos Demertzis   Democritus University of Thrace, Greece
Kostadin Cvejoski   Fraunhofer IAIS, Germany
Kristína Malinovská   Comenius University in Bratislava, Slovakia
Kun Zhang   Inria and École Polytechnique, France
Laurent Mertens   KU Leuven, Belgium
Laurent Perrinet   AMU CNRS, France
Lazaros Iliadis   Democritus University of Thrace, Greece
Leandro dos Santos Coelho   Pontifical Catholic University of Parana, Brazil
Leiping Jie   Hong Kong Baptist University, China
Lenka Tětková   Technical University of Denmark, Denmark
Lia Morra   Politecnico di Torino, Italy
Liang Ge   Chongqing University, China
Liang Zhao   Dalian University of Technology, China
Limengzi Yuan   Shihezi University, China
Ling Guo   Northwest University, China
Linlin Shen   Shenzhen University, China
Lixin Zou   Wuhan University, China
Lorenzo Vorabbi   University of Bologna, Italy
Lu Wang   Macao Polytechnic University, China
Luca Pasa   University of Padova, Italy
Ľudovít Malinovský   Independent Researcher, Slovakia
Luis Alexandre   Universidade da Beira Interior, Portugal
Luis Lago   Universidad Autonoma de Madrid, Spain
Lukáš Gajdošech Gajdošech   Comenius University Bratislava, Slovakia
Lyra Puspa   Vanaya NeuroLab, Indonesia
Madalina Erascu   West University of Timisoara, Romania
Magda Friedjungová   Czech Technical University in Prague,
                                 Czech Republic
Manuel Traub   University of Tübingen, Germany
Marcello Trovati   Edge Hill University, UK
Marcin Pietron   AGH-UST, Poland
Marco Bertolini   Pfizer, Germany
Marco Podda   University of Pisa, Italy
Markus Bayer   Technical University of Darmstadt, Germany
Markus Eisenbach   Ilmenau University of Technology, Germany
Martin Ferianc   University College London, Slovakia
Martin Holena   Czech Technical University, Czech Republic
Masanari Kimura   ZOZO Research, Japan
Masato Uchida   Waseda University, Japan
Masoud Daneshtalab   Mälardalen University, Sweden

Mats Leon Richter	University of Montreal, Germany
Matthew Evanusa	University of Maryland, USA
Matthias Karlbauer	University of Tübingen, Germany
Matthias Kerzel	University of Hamburg, Germany
Matthias Möller	Örebro University, Sweden
Matthias Müller-Brockhausen	Leiden University, Netherlands
Matus Tomko	Comenius University in Bratislava, Slovakia
Mayukh Maitra	Walmart, India
Md. Delwar Hossain	Nara Institute of Science and Technology, Japan
Mehmet Aydin	University of the West of England, UK
Michail Chatzianastasis	École Polytechnique, Greece
Michail-Antisthenis Tsompanas	University of the West of England, UK
Michel Salomon	Université de Franche-Comté, France
Miguel Matey-Sanz	Universitat Jaume I, Spain
Mikołaj Morzy	Poznan University of Technology, Poland
Minal Suresh Patil	Umea universitet, Sweden
Minh Tri Lê	Inria, France
Mircea Nicolescu	University of Nevada, Reno, USA
Mohamed Elleuch	ENSI, Tunisia
Mohammed Elmahdi Khennour	Kasdi Merbah University Ouargla, Algeria
Mohib Ullah	NTNU, Norway
Monika Schak	Fulda University of Applied Sciences, Germany
Moritz Wolter	University of Bonn, Germany
Mostafa Kotb	Hamburg University, Germany
Muhammad Burhan Hafez	University of Hamburg, Germany
Nabeel Khalid	German Research Centre for Artificial Intelligence, Germany
Nabil El Malki	IRIT, France
Narendhar Gugulothu	TCS Research, India
Naresh Balaji Ravichandran	KTH Stockholm, Sweden
Natalie Kiesler	DIPF Leibniz Institute for Research and Information in Education, Germany
Nathan Duran	UWE, UK
Nermeen Abou Baker	Ruhr West University of Applied Sciences, Germany
Nick Jhones	Dundee University, UK
Nicolangelo Iannella	University of Oslo, Norway
Nicolas Couellan	ENAC, France
Nicolas Rougier	University of Bordeaux, France
Nikolaos Ioannis Bountos	National Observatory of Athens, Greece
Nikolaos Polatidis	University of Brighton, UK
Norimichi Ukita	TTI-J, Japan

Oleg Bakhteev	EPFL, Switzerland
Olga Grebenkova	Moscow Institute of Physics and Technology, Russia
Oliver Sutton	King's College London, UK
Olivier Teste	Université de Toulouse, France
Or Elroy	CLB, Israel
Oscar Fontenla-Romero	University of A Coruña, Spain
Ozan Özdenizci	Graz University of Technology, Austria
Pablo Lanillos	Spanish National Research Council, Spain
Pascal Rost	Universität Hamburg, Germany
Paul Kainen	Georgetown, USA
Paulo Cortez	University of Minho, Portugal
Pavel Petrovic	Comenius University, Slovakia
Peipei Liu	School of Cyber Security, University of Chinese Academy of Sciences, China
Peng Qiao	NUDT, China
Peter Andras	Edinburgh Napier University, UK
Peter Steiner	Technische Universität Dresden, Germany
Peter Sutor	University of Maryland, USA
Petia Georgieva	University of Aveiro/IEETA, Portugal
Petia Koprinkova-Hristova	Bulgarian Academy of Sciences, Bulgaria
Petra Vidnerová	Czech Academy of Sciences, Czech Republic
Philipp Allgeuer	University of Hamburg, Germany
Pragathi Priyadharsini Balasubramani	Indian Institute of Technology Kanpur, India
Qian Wang	Durham University, UK
Qinghua Zhou	King's College London, UK
Qingquan Zhang	Southern University of Science and Technology, China
Quentin Jodelet	Tokyo Institute of Technology, Japan
Radoslav Škoviera	Czech Technical University in Prague, Czech Republic
Raoul Heese	Fraunhofer ITWM, Germany
Ricardo Marcacini	University of São Paulo, Brazil
Riccardo Renzulli	University of Turin, Italy
Richard Duro	Universidade da Coruña, Spain
Robert Legenstein	Graz University of Technology, Austria
Rodrigo Clemente Thom de Souza	Federal University of Parana, Brazil
Rohit Dwivedula	Independent Researcher, India
Romain Ferrand	IGI TU Graz, Austria
Roman Mouček	University of West Bohemia, Czech Republic
Roseli Wedemann	Universidade do Estado do Rio de Janeiro, Brazil

Rufin VanRullen	CNRS, France
Ruijun Feng	China Telecom Beijing Research Institute, China
Ruxandra Stoean	University of Craiova, Romania
Sanchit Hira	JHU, USA
Sander Bohte	CWI, Netherlands
Sandrine Mouysset	University of Toulouse/IRIT, France
Sanka Rasnayaka	National University of Singapore, Singapore
Sašo Karakatič	University of Maribor, Slovenia
Sebastian Nowak	University Bonn, Germany
Seiya Satoh	Tokyo Denki University, Japan
Senwei Liang	LBNL, USA
Shaolin Zhu	Tianjin University, China
Shayan Gharib	University of Helsinki, Finland
Sherif Eissa	Eindhoven University of Technology, Afghanistan
Shiyong Lan	Independent Researcher, China
Shoumeng Qiu	Fudan, China
Shu Eguchi	Aomori University, Japan
Shubai Chen	Southwest University, China
Shweta Singh	International Institute of Information Technology, Hyderabad, India
Simon Hakenes	Ruhr University Bochum, Germany
Simona Doboli	Hofstra University, USA
Song Guo	Xi'an University of Architecture and Technology, China
Stanislav Frolov	Deutsches Forschungszentrum für künstliche Intelligenz (DFKI), Germany
Štefan Pócoš	Comenius University in Bratislava, Slovakia
Steven (Zvi) Lapp	Bar Ilan University, Israel
Sujala Shetty	BITS Pilani Dubai Campus, United Arab Emirates
Sumio Watanabe	Tokyo Institute of Technology, Japan
Surabhi Sinha	Adobe, USA
Takafumi Amaba	Fukuoka University, Japan
Takaharu Yaguchi	Kobe University, Japan
Takeshi Abe	Yamaguchi University, Japan
Takuya Kitamura	National Institute of Technology, Toyama College, Japan
Tatiana Tyukina	University of Leicester, UK
Teng-Sheng Moh	San Jose State University, USA
Tetsuya Hoya	Independent Researcher, Japan
Thierry Viéville	Domicile, France
Thomas Nowotny	University of Sussex, UK
Tianlin Zhang	University of Manchester, UK

Tianyi Wang	University of Hong Kong, China
Tieke He	Nanjing University, China
Tiyu Fang	Shandong University, China
Tobias Uelwer	Technical University Dortmund, Germany
Tomasz Kapuscinski	Rzeszow University of Technology, Poland
Tomasz Szandala	Wroclaw University of Technology, Poland
Toshiharu Sugawara	Waseda University, Japan
Trond Arild Tjostheim	Lund University, Sweden
Umer Mushtaq	Université Paris-Panthéon-Assas, France
Uwe Handmann	Ruhr West University, Germany
V. Ramasubramanian	International Institute of Information Technology, Bangalore, India
Valeri Mladenov	Technical University of Sofia, Bulgaria
Valerie Vaquet	Bielefeld University, Germany
Vandana Ladwani	International Institute of Information Technology, Bangalore, India
Vangelis Metsis	Texas State University, USA
Vera Kurkova	Czech Academy of Sciences, Czech Republic
Verner Ferreira	Universidade do Estado da Bahia, Brazil
Viktor Kocur	Comenius University, Slovakia
Ville Tanskanen	University of Helsinki, Finland
Viviana Cocco Mariani	PUCPR, Brazil
Vladimír Boža	Comenius University, Slovakia
Vojtech Mrazek	Brno University of Technology, Czech Republic
Weifeng Liu	China University of Petroleum (East China), China
Wenxin Yu	Southwest University of Science and Technology, China
Wenxuan Liu	Wuhan University of Technology, China
Wu Ancheng	Pingan, China
Wuliang Huang	ICT, China
Xi Cheng	NUPT, Hong Kong, China
Xia Feng	Civil Aviation University of China, China
Xian Zhong	Wuhan University of Technology, China
Xiang Zhang	National University of Defense Technology, China
Xiaochen Yuan	Macao Polytechnic University, China
Xiaodong Gu	Fudan University, China
Xiaoqing Liu	Kyushu University, Japan
Xiaowei Zhou	Macquarie University, Australia
Xiaozhuang Song	Chinese University of Hong Kong, Shenzhen, China

Xingpeng Zhang	Southwest Petroleum University, China
Xuemei Jia	Wuhan University, China
Xuewen Wang	China University of Geosciences, China
Yahong Lian	Nankai University, China
Yan Zheng	China University of Political Science and Law, China
Yang Liu	Fudan University, China
Yang Shao	Hitachi, Japan
Yangguang Cui	East China Normal University, China
Yansong Chua	China Nanhu Academy of Electronics and Information Technology, Singapore
Yapeng Gao	Taiyuan University of Technology, China
Yasufumi Sakai	Fujitsu, Japan
Ye Wang	National University of Defense Technology, China
Yeh-Ching Chung	Chinese University of Hong Kong, Shenzhen, China
Yihao Luo	Yichang Testing Technique R&D Institute, China
Yikemaiti Sataer	Southeast University, China
Yipeng Yu	Tencent, China
Yongchao Ye	Southern University of Science and Technology, China
Yoshihiko Horio	Tohoku University, Japan
Youcef Djenouri	NORCE, Norway
Yuan Li	Military Academy of Sciences, China
Yuan Panli	Shihezi University, China
Yuan Yao	Tsinghua University, China
Yuanlun Xie	University of Electronic Science and Technology of China, China
Yuanshao Zhu	Southern University of Science and Technology, China
Yucan Zhou	Institute of Information Engineering, Chinese Academy of Sciences, China
Yuchen Zheng	Shihezi University, China
Yuchun Fang	Shanghai University, China
Yue Zhao	Minzu University of China, China
Yuesong Nan	National University of Singapore, Singapore
Zaneta Swiderska-Chadaj	Warsaw University of Technology, Poland
Zdenek Straka	Czech Technical University in Prague, Czech Republic
Zhao Yang	Leiden University, Netherlands
Zhaoyun Ding	NUDT, China
Zhengwei Yang	Wuhan University, China

Zhenjie Yao	Chinese Academy of Sciences, Singapore
Zhichao Lian	Nanjing University of Science and Technology, China
Zhiqiang Zhang	Hosei University, Japan
Zhixin Li	Guangxi Normal University, China
Zhongnan Zhang	Xiamen University, China
Zhongzhan Huang	Sun Yat-sen University, China
Zi Long	Shenzhen Technology University, China
Zilong Lin	Indiana University Bloomington, USA
Zuobin Xiong	Georgia State University, USA
Zuzana Cernekova	FMFI Comenius University, Slovakia

Invited Talks

Developmental Robotics for Language Learning, Trust and Theory of Mind

Angelo Cangelosi

University of Manchester and Alan Turing Institute, UK

Growing theoretical and experimental research on action and language processing and on number learning and gestures clearly demonstrates the role of embodiment in cognition and language processing. In psychology and neuroscience, this evidence constitutes the basis of embodied cognition, also known as grounded cognition (Pezzulo et al. 2012). In robotics and AI, these studies have important implications for the design of linguistic capabilities in cognitive agents and robots for human-robot collaboration, and have led to the new interdisciplinary approach of Developmental Robotics, as part of the wider Cognitive Robotics field (Cangelosi and Schlesinger 2015; Cangelosi and Asada 2022). During the talk we presented examples of developmental robotics models and experimental results from iCub experiments on the embodiment biases in early word acquisition and grammar learning (Morse et al. 2015; Morse and Cangelosi 2017) and experiments on pointing gestures and finger counting for number learning (De La Cruz et al. 2014). We then presented a novel developmental robotics model, and experiments, on Theory of Mind and its use for autonomous trust behavior in robots (Vinanzi et al. 2019, 2021). The implications for the use of such embodied approaches for embodied cognition in AI and cognitive sciences, and for robot companion applications, was also discussed.

Challenges of Incremental Learning

Barbara Hammer

CITEC Centre of Excellence, Bielefeld University, Germany

Smart products and AI components are increasingly available in industrial applications and everyday life. This offers great opportunities for cognitive automation and intelligent human-machine cooperation; yet it also poses significant challenges since a fundamental assumption of classical machine learning, an underlying stationary data distribution, might be easily violated. Unexpected events or outliers, sensor drift, or individual user behavior might cause changes of an underlying data distribution, typically referred to as concept drift or covariate shift. Concept drift requires a continuous adaptation of the underlying model and efficient incremental learning strategies. Within the presentation, I looked at recent developments in the context of incremental learning schemes for streaming data, putting a particular focus on the challenge of learning with drift and detecting and disentangling drift in possibly unsupervised setups and for unknown type and strength of drift. More precisely, I dealt with the following aspects: learning schemes for incremental model adaptation from streaming data in the presence of concept drift; various mathematical formalizations of concept drift and detection/quantification of drift based thereon; and decomposition and explanation of drift. I presented a couple of experimental results using benchmarks from the literature, and I offered a glimpse into mathematical guarantees which can be provided for some of the algorithms.

Reliable AI: From Mathematical Foundations to Quantum Computing

Gitta Kutyniok[1,2]

[1]Bavarian AI Chair for Mathematical Foundations of Artificial Intelligence, LMU Munich, Germany
[2]Adjunct Professor for Machine Learning, University of Tromsø, Norway

Artificial intelligence is currently leading to one breakthrough after the other, both in public life with, for instance, autonomous driving and speech recognition, and in the sciences in areas such as medical diagnostics or molecular dynamics. However, one current major drawback is the lack of reliability of such methodologies.

In this lecture we took a mathematical viewpoint towards this problem, showing the power of such approaches to reliability. We first provided an introduction into this vibrant research area, focussing specifically on deep neural networks. We then surveyed recent advances, in particular concerning generalization guarantees and explainability methods. Finally, we discussed fundamental limitations of deep neural networks and related approaches in terms of computability, which seriously affects their reliability, and we revealed a connection with quantum computing.

Intelligent Pervasive Applications for Holistic Health Management

Ilias Maglogiannis

University of Piraeus, Greece

The advancements in telemonitoring platforms, biosensors, and medical devices have paved the way for pervasive health management, allowing patients to be monitored remotely in real-time. The visual domain has become increasingly important for patient monitoring, with activity recognition and fall detection being key components. Computer vision techniques, such as deep learning, have been used to develop robust activity recognition and fall detection algorithms. These algorithms can analyze video streams from cameras, detecting and classifying various activities, and detecting falls in real time. Furthermore, wearable devices, such as smartwatches and fitness trackers, can also monitor a patient's daily activities, providing insights into their overall health and wellness, allowing for a comprehensive analysis of a patient's health. In this talk we discussed the state of the art in pervasive health management and biomedical data analytics and we presented the work done in the Computational Biomedicine Laboratory of the University of Piraeus in this domain. The talk also included Future Trends and Challenges.

Content – Part IV

Advancing Brain Tumor Detection with Multiple Instance Learning on Magnetic Resonance Spectroscopy Data

Diyuan Lu[1]([✉]) [ID], Gerhard Kurz[2] [ID], Nenad Polomac[3], Iskra Gacheva[3],
Elke Hattingen[3], and Jochen Triesch[1] [ID]

[1] Frankfurt Institute for Advanced Studies, 60438 Frankfurt am Main, Germany
`elu@fias.uni-frankfurt.de`
[2] 76131 Karlsruhe, Germany
[3] Hospital of the Goethe University Frankfurt Institute of Neuroradiology,
60528 Frankfurt am Main, Germany

Abstract. Magnetic resonance spectroscopy (MRS) is a clinical procedure that reveals the biochemical composition of brain tissue and can be used to detect tumors therein. However, accurate brain tumor diagnosis is challenging because: 1) data is corrupted with noise, 2) data is relatively scarce, 3) patient representation is unbalanced, i.e., the number of spectra per patient varies, 4) visual inspection of the MRS data suffers from large inter-rater variability and is time-consuming. Here, we propose an algorithm for automatic brain tumor detection with MRS. We address the above challenges by considering the task as a multiple instance learning (MIL) problem. Specifically, we aggregate multiple spectra from the same patient into a "bag" and apply data augmentation to enlarge the training set. To achieve permutation invariance during the process of bagging, we propose two modules: 1) concatenation of min-, max-, and average-pooling of the features, and 2) a self-attention mechanism. We evaluate the proposed method on multiple neural network architectures in a five-fold leave-patient-out cross-validation scheme and also against human experts on a withheld data set. We find that classification performance is significantly improved due to MIL. Furthermore, we demonstrate that our proposed model outperforms human experts.

Keywords: Brain Tumor Detection · Magnetic Resonance Spectroscopy · Self-attention · Multiple Instance Learning · Permutation Invariant

1 Introduction

We study the problem of brain tumor detection from MRS data, which is a common non-invasive diagnostic tool used to characterize the brain tissue biochemical composition because it can be easily acquired alongside commonplace

G. Kurz—Independent Researcher.

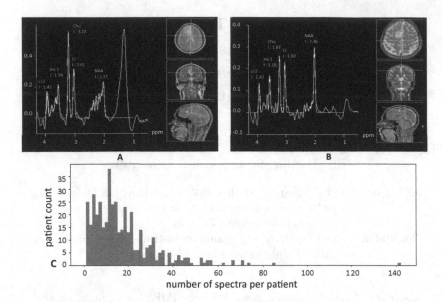

Fig. 1. Overview of the MRS data used in this paper. Each spectrum is a data array with 288 data points with the x-axis indicating the position of different metabolites and the y-axis indicating the intensity of the corresponding metabolites. Several spectra may stem from the same patient. **A.** An example of a **tumor** MR spectrum. **B.** An example of a **non-tumor** MR spectrum. **C.** Histogram of the number of spectra per patient (17 ± 15, mean $\pm$ standard deviation).

MR imaging procedures and it uniquely reflects the biochemical composition of the brain tissue *in situ*. There has been increasing interest in MRS for clinical use because of the semiautomatic data acquisition, processing, and quantification [1–5]. However, the interpretation of MRS spectra is traditionally performed by human radiologists based on the concentration ratios of certain metabolites. In contrast, we train a model to learn informative features from the spectra as a whole. MRS data are often corrupted by noise from head movements and baseline distortions of the spectrum. Also, labels are only provided per patient and not per instance, which introduces labeling noise as spectra from the tumor-affected hemisphere can be falsely labeled as "tumor" even though they contain healthy brain tissue.

Our contributions can be summarized as follows. (1) We present a multiple-instance-learning (MIL)-based framework for MRS-based tumor detection that performs patient-wise classification, thus avoiding the laborious manual effort for instance-level labeling. (2) We propose two permutation-invariant modules for processing bags of instances simultaneously, i.e., an attention module and the concatenation of max-, min-, and average-pooling, which we refer to as the "3Pool" module. (3) We demonstrate that our proposed modules can be easily plugged into any given DNN-based model and improve the classification performance. (4) We evaluate the proposed method with a leave-patient-out cross-validation scheme, which tests the trained model on data from unseen patients.

We also show that our method is even able to outperform human neuroradiologists. To the best of the authors' knowledge, this is the first work applying MIL-based methods to MRS data in brain tumor detection.

2   Related Work

Modern machine learning approaches based on deep neural networks (DNNs) have recently obtained impressive results in a range of classification tasks, sometimes even outperforming human experts. This has motivated a range of applications in oncology such as tumor detection, tumor segmentation, tumor progression estimation [1,6,7], tumor grade classification [1], etc. However, acquiring the required labeled data is often difficult or expensive in certain medical applications where the number of patients is small. Multiple instance learning (MIL) is a framework to handle scenarios where detailed annotations for each individual instance is noisy, laborious to obtain, or simply not available. It tries to make a decision based on a set of single instances instead of a decision for each single instance. MIL has been widely used in medical applications such as breast cancer detection [8–10] and other forms of computer-assisted diagnosis [11,12].

Applying machine learning methods to medical applications with MRS data is gaining more and more momentum, for example in brain tumor detection [3,5,13], brain tumor segmentation [7,14], breast tumor detection [15,16], and tumor motion prediction [6]. There is also work to investigate the effect of the length of the echo time used to perform MR spectroscopy for tumor detection [3]. In [4], the authors proposed to use a generative-adversarial-network-based model to synthesize MRS data with real-world appearance and features for deep model training. A variant of generative topographic mapping method for diagnostic discrimination between different brain tumor pathology and the outcome prediction was proposed in [5].

Multiple instance learning (MIL) is a framework to combat the problems, where detailed annotation for each single instance is noisy, or is laborious to obtain, or simply not available. Single-Instance Learning is a "naive" approach that assigns all instances in one bag the same label as its bag, which might lead to mislabeling negative instances in positive bags [17]. Support vector machines (SVMs) with the multiple-instance assumption that at least one instance in each bag is positive have been proposed in [17–19], where SVMs are implemented on top of projected whole-bag-level features. MIL has been widely used in medical applications such as breast cancer detection [8,9], computer assist diagnosis [11], brain disease diagnosis [12], lung cancer diagnosis [20], blood cell disorder analysis [10], etc. Our work represents the pioneering application of MIL-based methods to MRS data for brain tumor detection, as far as the authors are aware.

3   Materials and Methods

3.1   Data Acquisition and Processing

We use 1H-MR-spectroscopy data collected from 435 patients recorded in the Institute for Neuroradiology of the University Hospital in Frankfurt between

01/2009 to 3/2019. They were reviewed retrospectively and have been completely anonymized for this study. The patients were suffering from either glial or glioneuronal first diagnosed tumors (the *tumor* group, 266 patients) or other non-neoplastic lesions, e.g., demyelination, gliosis, focal cortical dysplasia, enlarged Virchow-Robin spaces or similar (the *non-tumor* group, 156 patients). The tumor group included all spectra from the tumor-affected hemisphere. The non-tumor group consisted of spectra from both hemispheres of the patients.

As a result, 7442 spectra (3388 non-tumor and 4054 tumor) were selected for further analysis. The obtained MRS examples are saved as 1-d arrays with 288 data points, i.e., in shape (288 × 1), shown in Fig. 1A, B, where the y-axis shows signal intensities of different metabolites, and the x-axis represents the chemical shift positions in ppm indicating various metabolites. The indices correspond to the position of metabolites and the values indicate signal intensities of corresponding metabolites. We normalize each spectrum to zero mean and unit variance. All spectra from the same patient are labeled with the patient's diagnosis, i.e., all spectra from one tumor patient will be labeled as *tumor*, and all spectra from one non-tumor patient would be labeled as *non-tumor*.

There is a huge variance in the number of spectra per patent in our data set – some patients have dozens of spectra and some have just a few spectra or even just a single one (see Fig. 1C). Due to the fairly limited number of patients, machine learning methods trained on this data set are prone to overfitting, therefore applying out-of-the-box methods would not yield satisfactory results. Each spectrum describes the biochemical composition of one voxel of brain tissue. We propose to perform classification not on a single spectrum, but on a bag of spectra from this patient. Specifically, we create bags of spectra from each patient for training and validation.

Patient-Wise Data Preparation. We have MRS spectra from a total number of P patients, the total number of spectra for patient p is N_p. We generate bags of spectra consisting of a fixed number $M \in \mathbb{N}$ of spectra from each patient by sampling from all spectra of the patient with replacement during training. Each bag is in shape $M \times 288$. The bags from patient p are denoted as $\mathbf{X}^p = \{\mathbf{x}_1^p, \ldots, \mathbf{x}_{p_b}^p\}$, where p_b is the total number of bags generated for patient p. Since this is a combinatorial problem, we could potentially generate millions of samples. This could be viewed as a data augmentation (DA) process. However, the more bags we generate from one patient, the less diversity we introduce through the DA and the worse the network is at generalization. Empirically, we set the number of generated bags of one patient to three times their single spectra count. Of course, further exploration of the optimum number of spectra to use might be beneficial in the future. Each training bag is provided a class label $y^p \in \{tumor, non\text{-}tumor\}$ based on the diagnosis of the patient. More formally, our goal is to learn a function f, which takes a set of spectra $\mathbf{x}^p = \{x_i^p, \ldots, x_N^p\}$ from patient p, and output the classification decision $\hat{y}^p$. The function f processes all spectra at the same time and generates a final predicted label $\hat{y}$. The training objective is the classic cross-entropy loss:

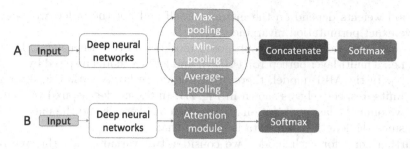

Fig. 2. Overview of the proposed framework with two proposed permutation invariant modules, which can be plugged into any DNN-based models. **A.** The proposed "3Pool" module. **B.** The proposed attention module.

$$\min_{\theta} \mathbb{E}_{P(\mathbf{x},\hat{y})}[-\log P_{\theta}(y = \hat{y}|\mathbf{x})], \tag{1}$$

where θ refers to the parameters of the function f.

The ability of the classifier to generalize to new previously unseen patients is of great clinical importance. Therefore, we apply a 5-fold **leave-patients-out** cross-validation scheme. To be specific, we divide the patient list into 5 sub-lists, each with around 80 patients. In each cross-validation set, we withhold the data from the patients of one sub-list, while we train and validate using the data from the other sub-lists. During training and validation, we adopt a 4:1 split ratio of all generated bags. During testing, we switch off the data augmentation strategy and only allow the minimal repetition of the spectra to fill up the last bag, which may be only partially filled otherwise. This makes sure that the number of bags to generate for patient p follows.

$$p_b = \begin{cases} 1, & \text{if } N_p \le M, \\ \lceil N_p/M \rceil, & \text{if } N_p > M. \end{cases} \tag{2}$$

3.2 Network Structure

When working with bags of MRS spectra, we note that the order of the stacked spectra is randomly chosen and should not affect the result of the network. Being invariant to the order of the spectra can either be achieved by augmenting with shuffled data, which is an approximation, or by designing the network architecture in such a way that the output of the network is independent of the order of the spectra in the input. For the former, we have described the data augmentation that we use to generate bags of training samples in Sect. 3.1. For the latter, we proposed two modules that can be easily plugged into any DNN-based models: (1) to aggregate the minimum-, maximum- and mean-pooling of the feature maps which yields exact order invariance, (2) to leverage attention mechanism [10,21], where different instances in the bag are assigned with different attention weights, which can be learned by the neural network. The schematic of the proposed method is shown in Fig. 2. The final extracted feature is a weighted average of features from all the instances in one bag. Since the attention weights depend on the instance itself and not the order, we can also achieve exact permutation invariance.

In this work, we test the two proposed modules on two other network structures, i.e., a multi-layer perceptron (MLP), and a CNN model inspired by Hatami et al. [2]. In the MLP model, there are three dense layers with 128, 32, and 2 dense units, respectively, as shown in Fig. 2B. In the model inspired by Hatami et al., we omit the last convolutional layer with 512 kernels and the max-pooling layer, since the length of our data is smaller than theirs.

Furthermore, for each model, we consider two variants, i.e., the one with concatenated max-, min-, and average-pooling, denoted "3Pool", and the other with an attention module, denoted "Att". Note that the feature extraction in each dense layer is performed on the single instance level, i.e., the convolution is only done horizontally with the kernel height as one. The feature maps are then either pooled and concatenated in a "3Pool" branch or processed by the attention module.

3.3   Attention Module

In order to weigh the different samples contained in a bag, we make use of the attention mechanism proposed by [21]. The idea is to introduce a layer whose output z is a weighted average $z = \sum_{k=1}^{M} a_k h_k$ of the inputs h_k with weights

$$a_k = \frac{\exp\left(w^T \tanh(V h_k^T)\right)}{\sum_{k=1}^{M} \exp\left(w^T \tanh(V h_k^T)\right)}, \tag{3}$$

where $w \in \mathbb{R}^{1 \times N_{att}}$ and $V \in \mathbb{R}^{N_{att} \times L_{h_k}}$ are learned parameters of the layer. N_{att} is the number of attention heads and L_{h_k} is the dimension of the hidden feature h_k. As each a_k depends on the values inside h_k, the weights are different in each bag and can take the concrete values inside the input bag into account. Note that the output z is independent of the order of the inputs h_k

The network is trained with randomly initialized weights using the Adam optimizer with default parameters and a mini-batch size of 32. The model is trained on a Windows machine with an Intel(R) Core i7-4770 CPU, 16 GB RAM, and a GeForce GTX1060 GPU with 6 GB of memory. The training takes less than 3 min for 30 training epochs.

4   Result

Overall Performance with Ablation. To evaluate performance, we use the area under the receiver operating characteristic (ROC) curve, the F1-Score, precision, the Matthews correlation coefficient (MCC), and the patient-level accuracy. The ROC curve is constructed by varying the classification threshold and calculating the true positive (TP), false positive (FP), true negative (TN), and false negative (FN) rates. We report classification accuracy, area under the ROC curve (AUC), F1-score $= \frac{2\text{TP}}{2\text{TP}+\text{FP}+\text{FN}}$,

Table 1. Performance matrices averaged across five-fold cross-validation data sets of the proposed method compared to other baseline methods. The results are shown in **mean ± standard deviation**. MCC: Matthews correlation coefficient, AUC: area under ROC curve. SI: single instance. Baseline MIL models: MI-SVM [18], Ray-MISVM [17], and NSK [19]. MLP: multi-layer perceptron. +DA: with data augmentation.

	Bag AUC	Patient AUC	F1-score	MCC	Precision	Patient ACC	# Trainables
Ray-MISVM [17] (SI)	0.71 ± 0.03	0.78 ± 0.04	0.67 ± 0.02	0.30 ± 0.06	0.72 ± 0.07	0.32 ± 0.06	~600
Ray-MISVM [17]	0.73 ± 0.08	0.73 ± 0.07	0.78 ± 0.03	0.26 ± 0.07	0.66 ± 0.06	0.44 ± 0.07	~600
Ray-MISVM [17] + DA	0.73 ± 0.09	0.73 ± 0.08	0.78 ± 0.03	0.25 ± 0.07	0.66 ± 0.06	0.45 ± 0.06	~600
MI-SVM [18] (SI)	0.71 ± 0.04	0.78 ± 0.05	0.67 ± 0.03	0.29 ± 0.07	0.72 ± 0.07	0.32 ± 0.05	~600
MI-SVM [18]	0.69 ± 0.07	0.69 ± 0.07	0.19 ± 0.09	0.10 ± 0.12	0.80 ± 0.16	0.34 ± 0.06	~600
MI-SVM [18] + DA	0.69 ± 0.08	0.69 ± 0.07	0.14 ± 0.10	0.08 ± 0.12	0.82 ± 0.22	0.35 ± 0.06	~600
NSK [19] (SI)	0.71 ± 0.04	0.78 ± 0.05	0.67 ± 0.03	0.29 ± 0.06	0.72 ± 0.07	0.32 ± 0.06	~600
NSK [19]	0.70 ± 0.06	0.69 ± 0.06	0.69 ± 0.05	0.27 ± 0.10	0.73 ± 0.05	0.54 ± 0.02	~600
NSK [19] + DA	0.74 ± 0.04	0.74 ± 0.04	0.73 ± 0.03	0.33 ± 0.07	0.76 ± 0.05	0.57 ± 0.03	~600
MLP (SI)	0.71 ± 0.03	0.78 ± 0.04	0.66 ± 0.02	0.29 ± 0.07	0.72 ± 0.07	0.69 ± 0.05	41,314
MLP-3Pool	0.74 ± 0.07	0.74 ± 0.07	0.70 ± 0.10	0.31 ± 0.15	0.76 ± 0.09	0.65 ± 0.09	41,314
MLP-3Pool + DA	0.74 ± 0.11	0.73 ± 0.10	0.66 ± 0.19	0.35 ± 0.13	0.78 ± 0.06	0.65 ± 0.13	41,314
MLP-Att	0.79 ± 0.06	0.78 ± 0.05	0.68 ± 0.08	0.38 ± 0.11	0.82 ± 0.10	0.66 ± 0.08	41,220
MLP-Att + DA	0.79 ± 0.08	0.78 ± 0.08	0.68 ± 0.14	0.38 ± 0.16	0.81 ± 0.11	0.66 ± 0.10	41,220
CNN (SI)	0.68 ± 0.03	0.73 ± 0.02	0.67 ± 0.03	0.24 ± 0.05	0.68 ± 0.06	0.69 ± 0.03	488,514
CNN-3Pool	0.82 ± 0.07	0.82 ± 0.05	0.76 ± 0.05	0.44 ± 0.15	0.82 ± 0.08	0.72 ± 0.06	488,514
CNN-3Pool + DA	$\mathbf{0.82 \pm 0.07}$	$\mathbf{0.82 \pm 0.06}$	$\mathbf{0.77 \pm 0.07}$	$\mathbf{0.46 \pm 0.20}$	$\mathbf{0.83 \pm 0.09}$	$\mathbf{0.74 \pm 0.08}$	488,514
CNN-Att	0.81 ± 0.05	0.81 ± 0.04	0.73 ± 0.04	0.43 ± 0.07	0.82 ± 0.08	0.70 ± 0.04	507,012
CNN-Att + DA	0.81 ± 0.06	0.81 ± 0.05	0.74 ± 0.02	0.39 ± 0.12	0.80 ± 0.08	0.69 ± 0.03	507,012

and $\text{MCC} = \dfrac{\text{TP} \times \text{TN} - \text{FP} \times \text{FN}}{\sqrt{(\text{TP+FP})(\text{TP+FN})(\text{TN+FP})(\text{TN+FN})}}$. The MCC is generally considered as a balanced measure that takes into account TP, TN, FP, and FN, and it can be used even if the classes are not balanced. The patient-wise accuracy is computed as follows. (1) Average the network's output for all the bags from the same patient, (2) obtain the predicted label by the index of the highest averaged value, (3) compute the patient-wise accuracy by (number of correct diagnoses/total number of patients). We also conducted ablation studies on the effectiveness of data augmentation on different network structures. Moreover, we compared our method to three other baseline methods, i.e., the support vector machine approaches by Ray-MISVM [17], MI-SVM [18], and NSK [19]. For this purpose, we used the implementation from [22].

Empirically, we found that using 31 spectra per bag yields relatively good results. Therefore, we report the averaged performance metrics with the default $M = 31$ across all cross-validation sets. The results averaged across all leave-subjects-out cross-validation sets are shown in Table 1. In addition to the comparison on multiple instances learning, we also ran all the models (1) with single instances, denoted with "(SI)", (2) with the oversampling data augmentation, denoted with " + DA". From Table 1, we made the following observations and possible explanations. Firstly, the CNN network with the proposed "3Pool" module has overall superior performance compared to that of the MLP model. Secondly, when grouping multiple instances into bags for training without any data augmentation, models with low complexity, indicated by the number of

Table 2. Performance averaged on withheld neuroradiologist-labeled data set of all cross-validation models. SI: single-instance classification. MCC: Matthews correlation coefficient, AUC: area under ROC curve. SI: single instance.

	Bag AUC	Patient AUC	F1-score	MCC	Precision	Patient ACC
Neuroradiologists (SI)	0.68 ± 0.00	0.71 ± 0.00	0.58 ± 0.00	0.37 ± 0.00	0.62 ± 0.00	0.69 ± 0.00
MLP (SI)	0.71 ± 0.03	0.78 ± 0.04	0.66 ± 0.02	0.29 ± 0.07	0.72 ± 0.07	0.69 ± 0.05
MLP-3Pool	0.74 ± 0.07	0.74 ± 0.07	0.70 ± 0.10	0.31 ± 0.15	0.76 ± 0.09	0.65 ± 0.09
MLP-Att	0.79 ± 0.06	0.78 ± 0.05	0.68 ± 0.08	0.38 ± 0.11	$\mathbf{0.82 \pm 0.10}$	0.66 ± 0.08
CNN (SI)	0.79 ± 0.07	0.76 ± 0.04	0.65 ± 0.09	0.43 ± 0.14	0.66 ± 0.12	0.66 ± 0.07
CNN-3Pool	0.82 ± 0.07	$\mathbf{0.82 \pm 0.05}$	$\mathbf{0.76 \pm 0.05}$	0.44 ± 0.15	$\mathbf{0.82 \pm 0.08}$	$\mathbf{0.72 \pm 0.06}$
CNN-Att	$\mathbf{0.86 \pm 0.02}$	0.80 ± 0.03	$\mathbf{0.76 \pm 0.03}$	$\mathbf{0.55 \pm 0.04}$	0.78 ± 0.04	$\mathbf{0.72 \pm 0.03}$

trainable parameters, show a performance deterioration and models with a large number of trainable parameters still show an improvement in the performance. One contributing factor might be that the number of total training samples is significantly reduced when changing from the SI learning case to MI learning, thus the generalization ability is not fully explored. Thirdly, of the two proposed modules to achieve permutation invariance, i.e., 3Pool and the Attention modules, we found that the performance difference is marginal.

Human vs. Machine. We compared the performance of implemented DNN models to that of human neuroradiologists on one randomly selected test set, which has 844 spectra from around 42 patients (see Table 2). For the collection of the classification results of neuroradiologists, we divided the test set into eight subsets, and each subset was assigned to one of eight neuroradiologists. The neuroradiologists' performance, therefore, represents the collective effort of eight individuals. The data shows that the performance of our proposed method is better on almost all performance metrics except the MCC. The reason is that the neuroradiologists achieved a specificity of 0.88 but at a cost of low sensitivity of 0.54. This may reflect that neuroradiologists assign different "costs" to false positive vs. false negative classifications.

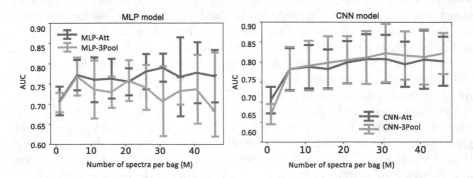

Fig. 3. Averaged ROC-AUC as a function of the number of instances per bag across five leave-patients-out cross-validation sets for proposed methods. The error bars represent one standard deviation.

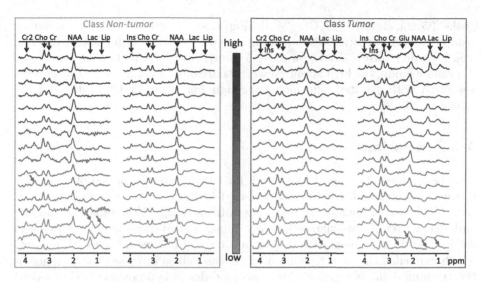

Fig. 4. Exemplar bags (column) of MRS spectra with attention, color-coded with shades in descending order. Red arrows in instances with relatively low attention show the features from the opposite class. (Color figure online)

Varying the Bag Size. To investigate the effect of the number of samples per bag, we vary the value from one (i.e., single instance classification) to 51. The AUC as a function of the number is shown in Fig. 3. We observe that learning from the bags of multiple instances is better than learning from a single instance for all models. The performance is significantly improved when M increases from one to six, and then this improvement attenuated after $M = 6$. Additionally, the performance with the attention module did not show deterioration with an increasing M in all models. However, in the MLP model, the performance degraded after $M = 6$ with the "3Pool" module.

Attention Visualization. Further, we show two bags of samples from each class with color-coded attention during testing, shown in Fig. 4. We can see that features of spectra in one bag are very heterogeneous exhibiting different peak ratios, peak positions, etc. Note that, samples with high attention might be stereotypical of that class or raise a red flag for that class decision. One benefit of visualizing the attention assignment is that it provides not only a final classification result but also contextual information about the same patient's brain tissue. This could provide more information for the MRS data interpretation. The common metabolites from left to right in our data are creatine2 (Cr2, 3.9 ppm), myoinositol and glycine (MI/Gly, ~3.5 ppm), Myo-inositol (Ins, 3.61 ppm), choline (Cho, 3.19 ppm), creatine (Cr, 3.03 ppm), Glutamine (Glu, 2.2–2.4 ppm), N-acetyl aspartate (NAA, 2.01 ppm), lactate (Lac, 1.4 ppm), and Lipids (Lip, 0.9 ppm) [23,24]. There are several indicative features in MRS data that are clinically relevant. For example, in tumor spectra, there are weakened Cr and Ins [23], reduced NAA concentration [23], elevated Cho, Glu, Lac, Lip peaks [25, 26], elevated MI/Gly [24]. In Fig. 4, we can see that in the *non-tumor* group, the high attention weights are assigned to samples with flat Lip, flat Lac [25], high and narrow NAA (low 2.0–2.5 ppm), clear Cr/Cho ratio > 1, etc. For the *tumor* group, the high attention weights are often assigned to instances with low NAA with elevated Glu, high Lac, high Lip, clear Cr/Cho ratio < 1, as shown in [23–26].

5   Conclusion

This paper presents a novel framework for tumor detection based on multiple-instance learning (MIL) with noisily-labeled MRS data. We proposed two modules to achieve permutation-invariance within each bag: (1) an attention module and (2) a "3Pool" module with max-, min-, and average-pooling. Moreover, we applied data augmentation to generate bags of instances from each patient, which expanded the total training data size as well as increased the variance in the training data. We applied these two modules to two popular DNN models, i.e., an MLP and a CNN model inspired by Hatami et al. [2]. We conducted a thorough comparison between the different models as well as three conventional SVM-based MI methods. We also carried out an ablation study regarding the effect of data augmentation for all models. We observed the MI SVMs do not perform well on our data set. The data augmentation almost always improved the performance compared to the counterpart without augmentation, except in the case of [18]. In the CNN model, the proposed "3Pool" module achieved slightly better performance than the "Att" module. However, in the MLP model, the proposed "Att" module was superior. We also demonstrate that the proposed method outperforms human radiologists in terms of the F1-score while achieving a similar MCC. The limitation of this work is that the results are obtained from a data set collected from a single site. Due to the factors such as the variability of data acquisition procedures, and the diverse patient populations, the generalization ability of the proposed method to other MRS data sets is not demonstrated. Furthermore, so far we only experimented with a very simple data augmentation method. Further exploration of other data augmentation strategies such as mixup, adding noise, scaling amplitude, etc., might be interesting in the future. Adding explainable machine learning methods is also beneficial for promoting the approach for clinical practice. Finally, we would like to investigate the behavior of the proposed approaches on further data sets collected at other sites.

Acknowledgments. This work is supported by the China Scholarship Council (No. [2016]3100), the State of Hesse with a LOEWE-Grant to the CePTER-Consortium (www.uni-frankfurt.de/67689811), and the Johanna Quandt Foundation. We thank Charles Wilmot for inspiring discussions and Marija Radović for her ideas on automating data export procedures.

References

1. Ranjith, G., Parvathy, R., Vikas, V., Chandrasekharan, K., Nair, S.: Machine learning methods for the classification of gliomas: initial results using features extracted from MR spectroscopy. Neuroradiol. J. **28**(2), 106–111 (2015)
2. Hatami, N., Sdika, M., Ratiney, H.: Magnetic resonance spectroscopy quantification using deep learning. In: Frangi, A.F., Schnabel, J.A., Davatzikos, C., Alberola-López, C., Fichtinger, G. (eds.) MICCAI 2018. LNCS, vol. 11070, pp. 467–475. Springer, Cham (2018). https://doi.org/10.1007/978-3-030-00928-1_53
3. González-Navarro, F.F., Belanche-Muñoz, L.A.: Using machine learning techniques to explore 1H-MRS data of brain tumors. In: 2009 Eighth Mexican International Conference on Artificial Intelligence, pp. 134–139. IEEE (2009)
4. Olliverre, N., Yang, G., Slabaugh, G., Reyes-Aldasoro, C.C., Alonso, E.: Generating magnetic resonance spectroscopy imaging data of brain tumours from linear, non-linear and deep learning models. In: Gooya, A., Goksel, O., Oguz, I., Burgos, N. (eds.) SASHIMI 2018. LNCS, vol. 11037, pp. 130–138. Springer, Cham (2018). https://doi.org/10.1007/978-3-030-00536-8_14
5. Cruz-Barbosa, R., Vellido, A.: Semi-supervised analysis of human brain tumours from partially labeled MRS information, using manifold learning models. Int. J. Neural Syst. **21**(01), 17–29 (2011)
6. Lin, H., Zou, W., Li, T., Feigenberg, S.J., Teo, B.-K.K., Dong, L.: A super-learner model for tumor motion prediction and management in radiation therapy: development and feasibility evaluation. Sci. Rep. **9**(1), 1–11 (2019)
7. Pereira, S., Pinto, A., Alves, V., Silva, C.A.: Brain tumor segmentation using convolutional neural networks in MRI images. IEEE Trans. Med. Imaging **35**(5), 1240–1251 (2016)
8. Sudharshan, P.J., Petitjean, C., Spanhol, F., Oliveira, L.E., Heutte, L., Honeine, P.: Multiple instance learning for histopathological breast cancer image classification. Expert Syst. Appl. **117**, 103–111 (2019)
9. Conjeti, S., Paschali, M., Katouzian, A., Navab, N.: Deep multiple instance hashing for scalable medical image retrieval. In: Descoteaux, M., Maier-Hein, L., Franz, A., Jannin, P., Collins, D.L., Duchesne, S. (eds.) MICCAI 2017. LNCS, vol. 10435, pp. 550–558. Springer, Cham (2017). https://doi.org/10.1007/978-3-319-66179-7_63
10. Sadafi, A., et al.: Attention based multiple instance learning for classification of blood cell disorders. In: Martel, A.L., et al. (eds.) MICCAI 2020. LNCS, vol. 12265, pp. 246–256. Springer, Cham (2020). https://doi.org/10.1007/978-3-030-59722-1_24
11. Fung, G., Dundar, M., Krishnapuram, B., Bharat Rao, R.: Multiple instance learning for computer aided diagnosis. In: Advances in Neural Information Processing Systems, vol. 19, p. 425 (2007)
12. Liu, M., Zhang, J., Adeli, E., Shen, D.: Landmark-based deep multi-instance learning for brain disease diagnosis. Med. Image Anal. **43**, 157–168 (2018)
13. Rao, V., Sarabi, M.S., Jaiswal, A.: Brain tumor segmentation with deep learning. MICCAI Multimodal Brain Tumor Segmentation Challenge (BraTS) **59**, 1–4 (2015)
14. Dvořák, P., Menze, B.: Local structure prediction with convolutional neural networks for multimodal brain tumor segmentation. In: Menze, B., et al. (eds.) MCV 2015. LNCS, vol. 9601, pp. 59–71. Springer, Cham (2016). https://doi.org/10.1007/978-3-319-42016-5_6

15. Tavolara, T.E., Niazi, M.K.K., Arole, V., Chen, W., Frankel, W., Gurcan, M.N.: A modular cGAN classification framework: application to colorectal tumor detection. Sci. Rep. **9**(1), 1–8 (2019)
16. Ren, S., He, K., Girshick, R., Sun, J.: Faster R-CNN: towards real-time object detection with region proposal networks. arXiv preprint arXiv:1506.01497 (2015)
17. Ray, S., Craven, M.: Supervised versus multiple instance learning: an empirical comparison. In: Proceedings of the 22nd International Conference on Machine Learning, pp. 697–704 (2005)
18. Andrews, S., Tsochantaridis, I., Hofmann, T.: Support vector machines for multiple-instance learning. In: Advances in Neural Information Processing Systems, vol. 15, pp. 561–568 (2002)
19. Gärtner, T., Flach, P.A., Kowalczyk, A., Smola, A.J.: Multi-instance kernels. In: ICML, vol. 2, p. 7 (2002)
20. Ozdemir, O., Russell, R.L., Berlin, A.A.: A 3D probabilistic deep learning system for detection and diagnosis of lung cancer using low-dose CT scans. IEEE Trans. Med. Imaging **39**(5), 1419–1429 (2019)
21. Ilse, M., Tomczak, J.M., Welling, M.: Attention-based deep multiple instance learning. CoRR, abs/1802.04712 (2018)
22. Doran, G.: MISVM: multiple-instance support vector machines (2019)
23. Faghihi, R., et al.: Magnetic resonance spectroscopy and its clinical applications: a review. J. Med. Imaging Radiat. Sci. **48**(3), 233–253 (2017)
24. Hattingen, E., Lanfermann, H., Quick, J., Franz, K., Zanella, F.E., Pilatus, U.: 1 H MR spectroscopic imaging with short and long echo time to discriminate glycine in glial tumours. Magn. Reson. Mater. Phys. Biol. Med. **22**(1), 33 (2009)
25. Rae, C.: RE: magnetic resonance spectroscopy of the brain: review of metabolites and clinical applications. Clin. Radiol. **64**(10), 1042–1043 (2009)
26. Fan, G.: Magnetic resonance spectroscopy and gliomas. Cancer Imaging **6**(1), 113–115 (2006)

An Echo State Network-Based Method for Identity Recognition with Continuous Blood Pressure Data

Ziqiang Li[1](✉)(iD), Kantaro Fujiwara[1](iD), and Gouhei Tanaka[1,2](iD)

[1] International Research Center for Neurointelligence, The University of Tokyo,
Tokyo 113-0033, Japan
{ziqiang-li,kantaro}@g.ecc.u-tokyo.ac.jp
[2] Department of Computer Science, Graduate School of Engineering,
Nagoya Institute of Technology, Nagoya 466-8555, Japan
gtanaka@nitech.ac.jp

Abstract. With the development of Continuous Blood Pressure (CBP) monitoring devices, we can collect real-time blood pressure non-invasively and accurately. Since CBP data can reflect the unique dynamical characteristics of the cardiovascular system for each person, it is reasonable to develop an identity recognition method based on these data. In this study, we propose an Echo State Network-based identity recognition method with CBP data. In the proposed method, we divide each CBP series data into several CBP segments. Then we use a Bidirectional Echo State Network to transform the input segments into high-dimensional reservoir states. Finally, we compute the identity recognition results in an aggregation mode. To evaluate the proposed method, we performed person identification tasks using ten sub-datasets sampled from a large-scale CBP dataset. Our proposed method achieved higher recognition accuracy than other relevant methods in spite of its relatively low computational cost on segment-by-segment and aggregated recognition tasks, respectively.

Keywords: Machine Learning · Reservoir Computing · Biometric Information

1 Introduction

Identity Recognition (IR) is one of the highly-demanded machine learning techniques which can automatically identify different people by using various information [13]. This technology plays a fundamental role in many applications such as access control systems [11], personal recommendation systems [12], and so on. The accuracy of IR results directly affects the quality of follow-up services provided by the above identity-based systems. In some studies about IR [13,17], appearance information (such as the face, irises, and gait information) is widely considered as input data due to convenience in data collection. However, the

L. Iliadis et al. (Eds.): ICANN 2023, LNCS 14257, pp. 13–25, 2023.
https://doi.org/10.1007/978-3-031-44216-2_2

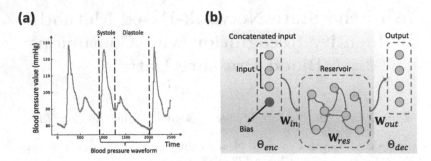

Fig. 1. (a) An example of continuous blood pressure data with the sampling rate 1000 HzHz [15]. (b) An example of a standard Echo State Network [7]. Two matrices $\mathbf{W}_{in}$ and $\mathbf{W}_{res}$ are fixed, and only the matrix $\mathbf{W}_{out}$ is trainable.

effectiveness of the corresponding IR systems is easily affected by many factors, such as camera positions, lighting conditions, and data resolutions. Moreover, additional efforts are required to preserve the collected appearance information due to the relatively high requirement for privacy protection. Other studies choose voices and handwritings as input data [13]. However, existing proposals for IR are difficult to be applied in the real world since those data are easily imitated. The direction widely considered to be the most promising is to use biometric information for constructing IR systems [10,13]. This kind of data can reflect the unique biological characteristics of each person, which are ideal input data for an IR system. Most of the related studies focus on using palmprints or fingerprints as inputs. However, people who have limb defects hardly provide high-quality data. Continuous Blood Pressure (CBP) data are one kind of bio-metric information that can reflect the dynamics of the cardiovascular system for each person. With the development of continuous blood pressure monitoring devices, CBP data can be easily collected in a non-invasive mode. We show an example of CBP data in Fig. 1(a).

In the data processing models used for IR systems, Convolutional Neural Networks (CNNs) [8] and Recurrent Neural Networks (RNNs) [14] are the two most commonly used ones for extracting features from various biometric inputs. Although these models trained by the BackPropagation (BP) method have pow-erful representative abilities, relatively long training times are unavoidable for building a well-trained recognition model. Moreover, it is necessary to obtain a large number of bio-signal samples corresponding to each person, causing diffi-culty in data collection. Extra efforts may be necessary to deal with the over-fitting problem [3] if only a relatively small amount of training data is used.

Randomized neural networks [6] are a special class of neural networks where connection weights of hidden layers are randomly determined rather than tuned by the BP method. The Echo State Network [7] is a representative approach for building a randomized recurrent neural network where a predetermined dynam-ical system (reservoir) is adopted to form the recurrent layer. We show the standard architecture of an ESN in Fig. 1(b). We notice that a standard ESN

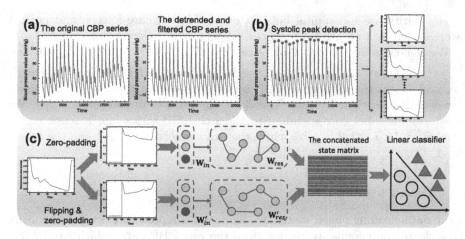

Fig. 2. Three processing phases of our proposed method. (a) The data-cleaning phase, (b) the segment-determination phase, and (c) the recognition phase.

comprises two modules, a fixed encoding module Θ_{enc} and a trainable decoding module Θ_{dec} [9]. This setup makes the training time of an ESN extremely low. One variant of the standard ESN, called the Bidirectional-ESN (Bi-ESN), can perform better than the standard ESN on some benchmark time-series classification tasks by encoding both the original and flipped sequential inputs with a bidirectional architecture [1]. In this work, we propose a new ESN-based IR system with CBP data. Our method can transform the raw CBP series into CBP segments composed of sequential data between two maxima of adjacent blood pressure waveforms, and generate accurate identity recognition results by a Bi-ESN. Simulation results show that our proposed method can achieve high IR accuracy rates with relatively low computational costs, indicating that it is a possible practical option for fast identity recognition from biometric features.

The rest of this paper is organized as follows: The proposed method is described in Sect. 2. The details of the experiments are introduced in Sect. 3. The conclusion of this work is given in Sect. 4.

2   The Proposed Method

We present three main phases of our method in Fig. 2. In the data-cleaning phase shown in Fig. 2(a), we remove the polynomial trend and high-frequency fluctuations from the raw CBP series. In the segment-determination phase displayed in Fig. 2(b), we detect the local maxima in every blood pressure waveform and then divide the detrended and filtered CBP series into CBP segments. In the recognition phase presented in Fig. 2(c), We feed the zero-padded CBP segments and flipped those into two encoding modules respectively, and then compute the final recognition results by using a linear classifier. The details about the above-mentioned three phases will be introduced in Sects. 2.1–2.3.

For clarity, we use capital bold letters, bold lowercase letters, and normal lowercase letters to represent matrices, vectors, and scalers, respectively.

We denote a set of raw CBP series by $\mathcal{S} = \{\mathbf{s}^{(i)} | i = 1, 2, ..., N_S\}$ where $\mathbf{s}^{(i)} = \left[s^{(i)}(1), s^{(i)}(2), ..., s^{(i)}(N_T)\right]^{\top} \in \mathbb{R}^{N_T}$ is the i-th CBP series with length N_T, and N_S is the number of CBP series. We assume that each CBP series corresponds to each individual. Therefore, the number of categories is N_S. We transform the label corresponding to the i-th CBP series into a score vector $\mathbf{y}^{(i)} \in \mathbb{R}^{N_S}$, for $i = 1, 2, \ldots, N_S$ where the i-th element of $\mathbf{y}^{(i)}$ is 1 and the others are -1.

2.1   Data-Cleaning Phase

In the data-cleaning phase, we remove the trend components calculated by using the k-degree polynomial regression from the raw CBP data, which can be formulated as follows:

$$\check{\mathbf{s}}^{(i)} = \mathbf{s}^{(i)} - \mathbf{r}^{(i)}, \tag{1}$$

where $\check{\mathbf{s}}^{(i)} \in \mathbb{R}^{N_T}$ is the i-th detrended CBP series with length N_T, and $\mathbf{r}^{(i)} \in \mathbb{R}^{N_T}$ is the corresponding trend component. The trend component $\mathbf{r}^{(i)} = \mathbf{S}^{(i)}\mathbf{v}^{(i)}$ where $\mathbf{S}^{(i)} \in \mathbb{R}^{N_T \times k}$ is a Vandermonde matrix whose columns are the element-wise powers of $\mathbf{s}^{(i)}$, which can be represented as

$$\begin{bmatrix} 1 & s^{(i)}(1) & \cdots & \left(s^{(i)}(1)\right)^{k-1} \\ 1 & s^{(i)}(2) & \cdots & \left(s^{(i)}(2)\right)^{k-1} \\ \vdots & \vdots & \vdots & \vdots \\ 1 & s^{(i)}(N_T) & \cdots & \left(s^{(i)}(N_T)\right)^{k-1} \end{bmatrix},$$

and $\mathbf{v}^{(i)}$ is the coefficient vector for mapping $\mathbf{S}^{(i)}$ into the trend component $\mathbf{r}^{(i)}$. Since the target of the polynomial regression is to minimize the objective function $\left\|\mathbf{s}^{(i)} - \mathbf{S}^{(i)}\mathbf{v}^{(i)}\right\|^2$, the estimated coefficient vector corresponding to the i-th trend, $\hat{\mathbf{v}}^{(i)} \in \mathbb{R}^k$, can be calculated as follows:

$$\hat{\mathbf{v}}^{(i)} = \left(\left(\mathbf{S}^{(i)}\right)^{\top}\mathbf{S}^{(i)}\right)^{-1}\left(\mathbf{S}^{(i)}\right)^{\top}\mathbf{s}^{(i)}. \tag{2}$$

We use a band-pass filter to smooth the detrended $\check{\mathbf{s}}^{(i)} \in \mathbb{R}^{N_T}$, which can be formulated as

$$\bar{\mathbf{s}}^{(i)} = \mathrm{BPF}\left(\check{\mathbf{s}}^{(i)}, l, h\right), \tag{3}$$

where $\mathrm{BPF}(\cdot, l, h)$ stands for the band-pass filter that passes signals with the frequency band of $[l, h]$ Hz. In this work, a third-order digital Butterworth band-pass filter [16] is applied.

2.2   Segment-Determination Phase

As shown in Fig. 1(a), a CBP series comprises blood pressure waveforms that appear one after another. Therefore, it is reasonable to use these waveforms as inputs for the IR system. However, since it is relatively difficult to accurately detect the starting point of the systolic period and the ending point of the diastolic period, we divide a CBP series into several CBP segments whose starting and ending points are the two adjacent systolic peak points, as shown in Fig. 2(b). In order to find these peaks, we leverage a simple method originally proposed for the peak detection of PPG signals [4]. Since the systolic peaks are only located at the positive parts of $\bar{\mathbf{s}}^{(i)}$, we transform $\bar{\mathbf{s}}^{(i)}$ into a new series $\mathbf{z}^{(i)} = \left[z^{(i)}(1), z^{(i)}(2), \ldots, z^{(i)}(N_T) \right]^{\top} \in \mathbb{R}^{N_T}$, which can be formulated as follows:

$$\mathbf{z}^{(i)} = \left(\text{ReLU}\left(\bar{\mathbf{s}}^{(i)} \right) \right)^2, \tag{4}$$

where ReLU $(\cdot)$ stands for the Rectified Linear Unit function and $(\text{ReLU}(\cdot))^2$ represents the element-wise function. To determine the systolic zone in the series, we compute two decision series for the i-th CBP series,

$$\mathbf{m}^{(i)} = \left[m^{(i)}(1), m^{(i)}(2), \ldots, m^{(i)}(N_T) \right]^{\top} \in \mathbb{R}^{N_T},$$
$$\mathbf{n}^{(i)} = \left[n^{(i)}(1), n^{(i)}(2), \ldots, n^{(i)}(N_T) \right]^{\top} \in \mathbb{R}^{N_T},$$

by using the first-order moving average method with a peak window of size ω_m and a beat window of size ω_n, respectively. The corresponding values at time t can be formulated as follows:

$$m^{(i)}(t) = \frac{z^{(i)}(t-(\omega_m+1)/2)+\cdots+z^{(i)}(t)+\ldots z^{(i)}(t+(\omega_m+1)/2)}{\omega_m},$$

$$n^{(i)}(t) = \frac{z^{(i)}(t-(\omega_n+1)/2)+\cdots+z^{(i)}(t)+\ldots z^{(i)}(t+(\omega_n+1)/2)}{\omega_n} + \beta \frac{1}{N_T} \sum_{t=1}^{N_T} z^{(i)}(t), \tag{5}$$

where β is a parameter that controls the ratio of the offset. We assume that a systolic zone having a period of time indexes $[t_p, t_p + 1, \ldots, t_q]$ which satisfies $m^{(i)}(t_p) > n^{(i)}(t_p)$, $m^{(i)}(t_p + 1) > n^{(i)}(t_p + 1)$, ..., $m^{(i)}(t_q) > n^{(i)}(t_q)$, and $(t_q - t_p + 1) > \theta$, where θ is a length threshold of the systolic zone. We can detect the peak point in the systolic zone by satisfying the following two conditions simultaneously: 1) the maximum of $\left[\bar{s}^{(i)}(t_p), \bar{s}^{(i)}(t_p + 1), \ldots, \bar{s}^{(i)}(t_q) \right]$, and 2) the distance from the previous peak should be larger than ϵ.

2.3   Recognition Phase

In the recognition phase, we leverage the Bi-ESN to generate classification results. The two reservoir encoders of the Bi-ESN symbolized by $\Theta_{enc} = \{ \mathbf{W}_{in}, \mathbf{W}_{res} \}$ and $\Theta'_{enc} = \{ \mathbf{W}'_{in}, \mathbf{W}'_{res} \}$, are designed for encoding CBP segments and flipped CBP segments, respectively. Since the initialization of Θ_{enc} is the same as that of Θ'_{enc}, we describe Θ_{enc} and the linear decoder Θ_{dec} in detail.

We assume that a set of CBP segments corresponding to the i-th CBP series can be represented by $\mathcal{G}^{(i)} = \left\{ \mathbf{g}_j^{(i)} | j = 1, 2, \ldots, N_J \right\}$, where $\mathbf{g}_j^{(i)}$ is the j-th CBP segment corresponding to the i-th CBP series and N_J is the number of segments. Since the length of each segment is probably different, we add the zero-paddings at the beginning of each CBP segment so that all CBP segments have the same length as that of the longest CBP segment in $\mathcal{G}^{(i)}$ for $i = 1, 2, \ldots, N_S$. We represent the set of zero-padded CBP segments corresponding to the i-th CBP series as $\widetilde{\mathcal{G}}^{(i)} = \left\{ \widetilde{\mathbf{g}}_j^{(i)} | j = 1, 2, \ldots N_J \right\}$, where $\widetilde{\mathbf{g}}_j^{(i)} = \left[g_j^{(i)}(1), g_j^{(i)}(2), \ldots, g_j^{(i)}(N_T^{\max}) \right] \in \mathbb{R}^{N_T^{\max}}$ and $\mathbb{R}^{N_T^{\max}}$ symbolizes the length of the longest CBP segment among $\mathcal{G}^{(i)}$ for $i = 1, 2, \ldots, N_S$.

We feed CBP segments into Θ_{enc} for generating reservoir states. The reservoir state of the j-th segment corresponding to the i-th CBP series at time t, which is represented by $\mathbf{x}_j^{(i)}(t) \in \mathbb{R}^{N_R}$, can be calculated as follows:

$$\mathbf{x}_j^{(i)}(t) = \tanh \left(\mathbf{W}_{in} \mathbf{u}_j^{(i)}(t) + \mathbf{W}_{res} \mathbf{x}_j^{(i)}(t-1) \right), \qquad (6)$$

where $\mathbf{u}(t) = \left[1; g_j^{(i)}(t) \right] \in \mathbb{R}^2$ is the concatentated input vector at time t. The element values of $\mathbf{W}_{in} \in \mathbb{R}^{N_R \times 2}$ are randomly chosen from a uniform distribution with the range of $[-\eta, \eta]$. We randomly determine the element values of $\mathbf{W}_{res} \in \mathbb{R}^{N_R \times N_R}$ by using the uniform distribution with the range of $[-1, 1]$ and then rescale the spectral radius of $\mathbf{W}_{res}$ symbolized by ρ to be an appropriate value. Likewise, the reservoir state calculated by feeding the data point at time t of the flipped and zero-padded $\mathbf{g}_j^{(i)}$ into Θ_{enc}' can be represented by $\check{\mathbf{x}}_j^{(i)}(t)$.

The recognition score vector of the j-th segment corresponding to the i-th CBP series, $\hat{\mathbf{y}}_j^{(i)}$, can be calculated as follows:

$$\hat{\mathbf{y}}_j^{(i)} = \mathbf{W}_{out} \mathbf{c}_j^{(i)}, \qquad (7)$$

where $\mathbf{c}_j^{(i)} \in \mathbb{R}^{2N_R N_T^{\min}}$ is the collected state vector formed by concatenating $\mathbf{x}_j^{(i)}(t)$ and $\check{\mathbf{x}}_j^{(i)}(t)$ for $t = N_T^{\max} - N_T^{\min} + 1, N_T^{\max} - N_T^{\min} + 2, \ldots, N_T^{\max}$, and $N_T^{\min}$ is the length of the shortest CBP segment among $\mathcal{G}^{(i)}$ for $i = 1, 2, \ldots, N_S$. The symbol $\mathbf{W}_{out} \in \mathbb{R}^{N_S \times 2N_R N_T^{\min}}$ is the readout weight matrix. We assume that there are N_{tr} training segments for each CBP series. The estimated readout weight matrix can be calculated as follows:

$$\hat{\mathbf{W}}_{out} = \mathbf{Y}_{tr} \mathbf{C}^\top \left(\mathbf{C} \mathbf{C}^\top + \gamma \mathbf{I} \right)^{-1}, \qquad (8)$$

where $\mathbf{Y}_{tr} \in \mathbb{R}^{N_S \times N_{tr} N_S}$ is the label score matrix corresponding to $N_{tr} N_S$ training segments, $\mathbf{C} \in \mathbb{R}^{2N_R N_T^{\min} \times N_{tr} N_S}$ is the collected state matrix corresponding to $N_{tr} N_S$ training segments, $\mathbf{I} \in \mathbb{R}^{2N_R N_T^{\min} \times 2N_R N_T^{\min}}$ is the identity matrix, and γ is the L_2 regularization factor. The aggregated IR score vector for the i-th CBP series can be calculated as follows:

$$\mathbf{y}^{(i)} = \sum_{j=1}^{N_{te}} \mathbf{y}_j^{(i)}, \qquad (9)$$

where N_{te} is the number of testing segments for each CBP series. The aggregated IR output for the i-th CBP segment can be decided by the index of the maximum element in $\mathbf{y}^{(i)}$.

3   Experiments

We describe the dataset, the task and metrics, the experimental settings, and the experimental results in Sects. 3.1, 3.2, 3.3, and 3.4, respectively.

3.1   Dataset Description

In this work, we use a dataset containing 1121 continuous blood pressure series non-invasively recorded from 1121 volunteers [15]. The recording length of each CBP series ranges from 8 min to 45 min, and the sampling frequency is 1000 Hz Hz. We use the 500 CBP series marked by 1 in the column "device" of the description file. For stability, we randomly select 100 CBP series and discard the serial data in the first 20 s. We divide these 100 CBP series equally into ten sub-datasets and execute the experiments on each of those. We report the average performances of the tested models over ten sub-datasets.

3.2   Tasks and Metrices

We consider two kinds of tasks in the following evaluations. One of the tasks is the Segment-by-segment Recognition (SR) task. The corresponding metrics can be formulated as follows:

$$\text{Acc}_{\text{SR}} = \frac{\text{The number of correct recognized segments}}{\text{The number of total recognized segments}} \times 100\%. \tag{10}$$

The other one is the Aggregated Recognition (AR) task. The corresponding metrics can be formulated as follows:

$$\text{Acc}_{\text{AR}} = \frac{\text{The number of correct aggregated outputs}}{\text{The number of categories}} \times 100\%. \tag{11}$$

3.3   Experiment Settings

We set the degree k, the low-cut frequency l, and the high-cut frequency h at 5, 0.5, and 8, respectively. We fixed the offset ratio β, and the distance threshold ϵ at 0.2 and 300, respectively. We searched the size of the peak window ω_m and the size of the beat window ω_n in the ranges of [61, 111, ..., 261], and [567, 617, ..., 817], respectively. In the recognition phase, we set the values of reservoir sizes, the spectral radius, and the input scalings of Θ_{enc} and Θ'_{enc} to be the same for simplicity. The hyperparameters and corresponding search ranges are listed in Table 1. We use a parameter symbolized by N_R^{total} to represent the total reservoir size. We searched the total reservoir size N_R^{total}, the spectral radius ρ,

Table 1. Hyperparameter settings of the ESN-based models used in the recognition phase.

Parameter	Symbol	Search range
Spectral radius	ρ	$[0.8, 0.9,, \ldots, 1.3]$
Reservoir size	N_R^{total}	$[10, 20, 50, 100, 200]$
Input scaling	η	$[1\mathrm{E}{-}03,\ 1\mathrm{E}{-}02,\ \ldots,\ 1\mathrm{E}{+}02]$
Regularization	γ	$[1\mathrm{E}{-}02,\ 5\mathrm{E}{-}02,\ \ldots,\ 1\mathrm{E}{+}01]$

and the input scaling η in the ranges of $[10, 20, 50, 100, 200]$, $[0.8, 0.9, \ldots, 1.3]$, and $[1\mathrm{E}{-}03,\ 1\mathrm{E}{-}02,\ \ldots,\ 1\mathrm{E}{+}02]$, respectively. We searched the regularization factor γ in the range of $[1\mathrm{E}{-}2,\ 5\mathrm{E}{-}2,\ \ldots,\ 1\mathrm{E}{+}01]$.

To evaluate the computational ability of the model used in the recognition phase, we compared the IR performances of the Bi-ESN with those of the standard Echo State Network (ESN) [7], the Deep Echo State Network (DeepESN) [5], and the stacked Gate Recurrent Unit (stacked GRU) [2]. The hyperparameters of the ESN and the DeepESN are set to be the same as those listed in Table 1. We set the number of layers at two for the DeepESN. For the hyperparameter settings of the stacked GRU, we configured two stacked GRU layers, each of which has 64 hidden neurons. We used a softmax classifier with L_2 regularization factor $1\mathrm{E}{-}04$ and the Adam optimizer with learning rate $1\mathrm{E}{-}03$. All the models were implemented with Pytorch 1.8, and the corresponding programs are executed on a machine with Intel (R) Core i9-7900X CPU, 96GB RAM of DDR4 2666 MHz.

We randomly sampled (without replacement) N_{tr}, N_{val}, and N_{te} CBP segments corresponding to each CBP series for composing the training set, the validation set, and the testing set, respectively. We varied N_{tr} in the range of $[10, 20, 40, 60, 80]$ and set N_{val} and N_{te} to be ten. We executed the abovementioned sampling procedure ten times and randomly initialized each tested model ten times.

3.4   Experimental Results

We show a heatmap of the average recognition performances of our method on the SR task under different window size combinations of ω_m and ω_n in Fig. 3. In this evaluation, we fixed ρ, N_R^{total}, η, and γ at 1.3, 200, 1, and $5\mathrm{E}{-}01$, respectively. Our method yields the best average recognition accuracy rate when $\omega_n = 767$ and $\omega_m = 261$.

In searching for appropriate hyperparameters of the Bi-ESN, we can see that the spectral radius and the input scaling jointly affect the encoding ability of reservoirs. We show a heatmap of the average recognition performances of the Bi-ESN on the SR task under different combinations of ρ and η in Fig. 4(a). We can notice that the input scaling plays a more important role than the spectral radius in affecting the recognition performances of the Bi-ESN. The

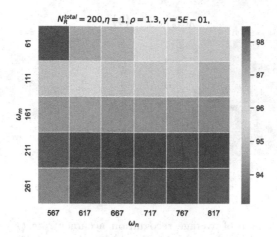

Fig. 3. The heatmap of average recognition accuracy rates (%) obtained by varying values of ω_m and ω_n on the SR task under the parameter settings of $N_R^{\text{total}} = 200$, $\rho = 1.3$, $\eta = 1$, and $\gamma = 5\text{E}{-}01$. We set the number of training samples N_{tr} at 80.

best performance is obtained when $\rho = 1.3$ and $\eta = 1$. On the other hand, we present average recognition accuracy rates under different combinations of N_R^{total} and γ in Fig. 4(b). When $N_R^{\text{total}} = 200$ and $\gamma = 5\text{E}{-}01$, the Bi-ESN reaches the highest recognition accuracy rate. We keep these best hyperparameter settings in the following performance comparisons.

We report the average IR performances of different tested models used in the recognition phase on the SR tasks in Table 2. We can see that the Bi-ESN outperforms the other tested models for different numbers of training samples. Observing the overall performances, we notice that the model that can encode bidirectional inputs performs better than the models that can only encode unidirectional inputs. Moreover, not only the Bi-ESN but also the ESN and the DeepESN have better accuracy rates than the stacked GRUs when N_{tr} is lower than 80, which indicates that ESN-based models can show better representation abilities when the amount of training samples are relatively small. We show the training times of all the tested models in Table 3. We can see that the computational time for training a Bi-ESN is much lower than that for training stacked GRUs.

Finally, we present the IR results of the Bi-ESN on the AR task in Fig. 5. We can notice that, for $N_{tr} = 40$, 60, and 80, our proposed method can reach 100% recognition rate when the testing numbers N_{te} are larger than 6, 5, and 3, respectively. Since a blood pressure waveform normally lasts around one second, the above results imply that our model only needs training samples collected from the CBP series lasting around 40 s to achieve very accurate IR.

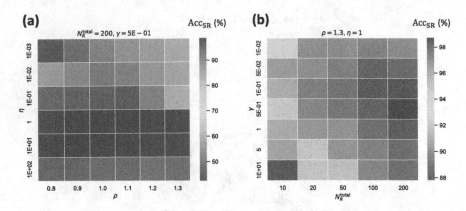

Fig. 4. (a) The heatmap of average recognition accuracy rate (%) on the SR task obtained by varying values of ρ and η jointly. (b) The heatmap of average recognition accuracy rate (%) on the SR task obtained by varying values of N_R^{total} and γ jointly.

Table 2. The best average recognition accuracy rates (%) for all tested models on the SR tasks under different N_{tr}.

N_{tr}	ESN	DeepESN	Stacked GRUs	Bi-ESN
10	$83.04 \pm (7.95)$	$86.54 \pm (6.07)$	$65.85 \pm (10.83)$	$92.54 \pm (4.16)$
20	$84.90 \pm (6.20)$	$87.35 \pm (5.95)$	$72.70 \pm (8.41)$	$94.46 \pm (2.62)$
40	$87.45 \pm (5.68)$	$88.01 \pm (5.86)$	$82.36 \pm (7.59)$	$96.70 \pm (2.42)$
60	$88.05 \pm (6.93)$	$88.97 \pm (6.50)$	$85.63 \pm (6.59)$	$97.43 \pm (1.75)$
80	$88.51 \pm (6.20)$	$89.76 \pm (6.92)$	$90.93 \pm (7.18)$	$98.30 \pm (1.63)$

Table 3. The average training times (second) of the tested models when $N_{tr} = 80$.

	ESN	DeepESN	Stacked GRUs	Bi-ESN
Training time	$100.70 \pm (14.40)$	$173.60 \pm (18.20)$	$4437.09 \pm (300.51)$	$146.53 \pm (11.99)$

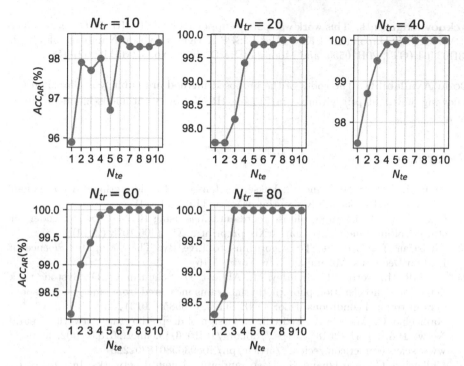

Fig. 5. The average recognition accuracy rates (%) obtained by varying N_{te} from 1 to 10 on the AR task under the searched best hyperparameter settings with $N_{tr} = 10$, 20, 40, 60, and 80.

4   Conclusion

Identity recognition systems are a crucial part of many identity-based applications. In this paper, the ESN-based method has been proposed for identity recognition with CBP data. This method can divide the CBP series data into CBP segments and leverage these segments for generating recognition results. We have experimentally demonstrated that the proposed method can generate accurate identity recognition results on randomly selected CBP datasets with a relatively small amount of training CBP segments. Also, by comparing both the recognition results and the training times of the Bi-ESN with those of some other models used in the recognition phase, we have found that using the Bi-ESN can ensure high effectiveness with relatively low training costs. These results manifest that the proposed method has the potential to be applied to real-world identity recognition tasks.

Some remaining issues should be dealt with in the future. The effectiveness of our proposed method on datasets with more categories needs to be evaluated. Since the performances of our method are sensitive to many hyperparameters, the problem of how to efficiently optimize the hyperparameters still remains to be tackled.

Acknowledgments. This work was partly supported by JST CREST Grant Number JPMJCR19K2, Japan (ZL, FK, GT) and JSPS KAKENHI Grant Numbers 20K11882, 23H03464 (GT), 20H00596, and Moonshot R&D Grant No. JPMJMS2021(KF).

Code Availability. The codes of the proposed method are publicly available on the following URL: https://github.com/Ziqiang-IRCN/ESN-Continuous-blood-pressure-data.

References

1. Bianchi, F.M., Scardapane, S., Løkse, S., Jenssen, R.: Bidirectional deep-readout echo state networks. arXiv preprint arXiv:1711.06509 (2017)
2. Cho, K., et al.: Learning phrase representations using RNN encoder-decoder for statistical machine translation. arXiv preprint arXiv:1406.1078 (2014)
3. Christian, B., Griffiths, T.: Algorithms to Live By: The Computer Science of Human Decisions. Macmillan, New York (2016)
4. Elgendi, M., Norton, I., Brearley, M., Abbott, D., Schuurmans, D.: Systolic peak detection in acceleration photoplethysmograms measured from emergency responders in tropical conditions. PLoS ONE **8**(10), e76585 (2013)
5. Gallicchio, C., Micheli, A., Pedrelli, L.: Design of deep echo state networks. Neural Netw. **108**, 33–47 (2018). https://doi.org/10.1016/j.neunet.2018.08.002. https://www.sciencedirect.com/science/article/pii/S0893608018302223
6. Gallicchio, C., Scardapane, S.: Deep randomized neural networks. In: Oneto, L., Navarin, N., Sperduti, A., Anguita, D. (eds.) Recent Trends in Learning From Data. SCI, vol. 896, pp. 43–68. Springer, Cham (2020). https://doi.org/10.1007/978-3-030-43883-8_3
7. Jaeger, H.: Tutorial on training recurrent neural networks, covering BPPT, RTRL, EKF and the "echo state network" approach (2002)
8. Li, Z., Liu, F., Yang, W., Peng, S., Zhou, J.: A survey of convolutional neural networks: analysis, applications, and prospects. IEEE Trans. Neural Netw. Learn. Syst. (2021)
9. Li, Z., Tanaka, G.: Multi-reservoir echo state networks with sequence resampling for nonlinear time-series prediction. Neurocomputing **467**, 115–129 (2022)
10. Mekruksavanich, S., Jitpattanakul, A.: Biometric user identification based on human activity recognition using wearable sensors: an experiment using deep learning models. Electronics **10**(3), 308 (2021)
11. Norman, T.L.: Foundational security and access control concepts, Chapter 2. In: Norman, T.L. (ed.) Electronic Access Control, 2nd edn., pp. 21–42. Butterworth-Heinemann (2017). https://doi.org/10.1016/B978-0-12-805465-9.00002-6. www.sciencedirect.com/science/article/pii/B9780128054659000026
12. Ochoa, J.G.D., Csiszár, O., Schimper, T.: Medical recommender systems based on continuous-valued logic and multi-criteria decision operators, using interpretable neural networks. BMC Med. Inform. Decis. Mak. **21**, 1–15 (2021)
13. Qin, Z., Zhao, P., Zhuang, T., Deng, F., Ding, Y., Chen, D.: A survey of identity recognition via data fusion and feature learning. Inf. Fusion **91**, 694–712 (2023)
14. Salehinejad, H., Sankar, S., Barfett, J., Colak, E., Valaee, S.: Recent advances in recurrent neural networks. arXiv preprint arXiv:1801.01078 (2017)
15. Schumann, A., Bär, K.J.: Autonomic aging–a dataset to quantify changes of cardiovascular autonomic function during healthy aging. Sci. Data **9**(1), 95 (2022)

16. Selesnick, I.W., Burrus, C.S.: Generalized digital Butterworth filter design. IEEE Trans. Signal Process. **46**(6), 1688–1694 (1998)
17. Szymkowski, M., Jasiński, P., Saeed, K.: Iris-based human identity recognition with machine learning methods and discrete fast Fourier transform. Innov. Syst. Softw. Eng. **17**, 309–317 (2021)

Analysis and Interpretation of ECG Time Series Through Convolutional Neural Networks in Brugada Syndrome Diagnosis

Alessio Micheli[1], Marco Natali[1], Luca Pedrelli[1(✉)], Lorenzo Simone[1], Maria-Aurora Morales[2], Marcello Piacenti[3], and Federico Vozzi[2]

[1] Department of Computer Science, University of Pisa, Pisa, Italy
luca.pedrelli@di.unipi.it
[2] Institute of Clinical Physiology, IFC-CNR, Pisa, Italy
[3] Fondazione Toscana Gabriele Monasterio, Pisa, Italy

Abstract. In this research, we present a novel approach to evaluate and interpret Convolutional Neural Networks (CNNs) for the diagnosis of Brugada Syndrome (BrS), a rare heart rhythm disease, from the electrocardiogram (ECG) time series. First, the model is assessed on the ECG classification of type-1 BrS. Then, we define a method to interpret the BrS prediction through Gradient-weighted Class Activation Mapping (Grad-CAM) applied to continuous time series. Finally, the proposed approach provides a tool to analyze the main areas of the ECG time series responsible for the BrS diagnosis through CNNs. In experimental assessments we use an original dataset of 306 ECGs collected from several clinical centers within the BrAID (Brugada syndrome and Artificial Intelligence applications to Diagnosis) project.

Keywords: Time series analysis · Health Informatics · Brugada Syndrome · Convolutional Neural Networks

1 Introduction

The Brugada Syndrome (BrS) is a rare heart rhythm disorder first reported in 1992 that can lead to sudden cardiac death, accounting for 4% to 12% of such events [3]. BrS is a channelopathy that arises from a modification of trans-membrane currents of the cardiomyocyte, which are essential for cardiac action potential to function correctly [13]. Research has confirmed that around 20% of Brugada syndrome cases are connected to mutations in the SCN5A gene that encodes for the sodium ion channel in the cardiac cells. Individuals suffering from this syndrome are more likely to develop ventricular tachyarrhythmias, which can lead to fainting, cardiac arrest, or sudden cardiac death. The clinical onset of the disease usually occurs in adulthood, with a mean age of onset of 40 years. However, it can also affect children and adolescents.

Three BrS patterns [13] have been identified as: Type-1, characterized by ST-segment elevation (>2 mm) followed by a negative T wave in leads V1 and

L. Iliadis et al. (Eds.): ICANN 2023, LNCS 14257, pp. 26–36, 2023.
https://doi.org/10.1007/978-3-031-44216-2_3

V2; Type 2, showing a similar ST-segment elevation but followed by a positive T wave; and Type 3, presenting a right precordial ST-segment elevation (≤ 1 mm) followed by a saddleback morphology. However, identifying these patterns is time-consuming and challenging for the clinicians, since electrocardiograms (ECGs) may show dynamic changes thus impairing a definite diagnosis. In doubtful situations, to unmask the BrS pattern, patients were subjected to infusion with Sodium channel blockers, such as ajmaline or flecainide, able to provoke type-1 BrS ECG patterns. In conclusion, Brugada Syndrome is a rare but potentially life-threatening genetic disorder. Its early diagnosis, risk stratification, and appropriate management are crucial for preventing sudden cardiac death in affected individuals and their families.

Since ECG interpretation depends on the individual experience of the clinician, the use of machine learning (ML) approaches may represent a supportive tool for the ECG analysis in these patients. Several ML applications focus on detecting cardiac arrhythmias [2]. In the literature, few works are focused on BrS classification with ML approaches. Preliminary works that use recurrent neural networks to classify BrS were presented in [4,15]. Other works are focused on the use of CNNs [9,10]. However, to the best of our knowledge, no approaches face the interpretability of the model in the classification of BrS ECG patterns.

This paper presents a novel approach for ECG time series to interpret temporal data analysis in BrS Type 1 diagnosis based on Convolutional Neural Networks (CNNs). In particular, (i) we use an original dataset composed of 306 ECGs (123 of positive class and 183 of negative class) collected from several clinical centers within the BrAID project [1], a funded project by the Health Research Fundings established as part of the Tuscany Region initiatives. Then, (ii) in order to address low data volume we experimentally assess the CNN model in classifying BrS through a double cross-validation (DCV) approach. Finally, (iii) we implement an interpretation of the ECG time-series analysis through Grad-CAM [12] adapted to time series. Overall, the approach provides a support tool to discover and analyze the main areas of the ECG time series that are important to make the BrS diagnosis. Differently from previous works [4,15], in this research we propose a 1-dimensional CNN for temporal data, a novel dataset composed by more data with respect to [4] and single heart beat with respect to [15]. Moreover, we introduce a novel approach to analyze the CNN prediction in temporal data through Grad-CAM adapted to time series. Other works exploit CNN but with a different dataset, validation approach and without interpretation [9,10].

The paper is organized as follows. In Sect. 2, the BrAID project is presented and the dataset used in the study is described. In Sect. 3, the CNN model for time-series classification is introduced. Section 4 describes the experimental assessment for the classification of BrS. Section 5 presents our approach to interpreting the model predictions in BrS analysis. Section 6 shows the quantitative and qualitative results obtained from our approach. Finally, in Sect. 7, conclusions are drawn.

2   BrAID Project and BrS Dataset

The BrAID project [1] was initiated in September 2020 with the primary objective of creating a clinical tool supporting clinicians in the diagnosis of type 1 BrS. The main objectives of BrAID focused on: developing a novel approach to disease management through the implementation of standardized procedures across clinical centers; an Electronic Health Record (EHR) system for data management and the construction of a supervised Machine Learning (ML) model for ECG analysis.

The project consists of three incremental phases: (1) The first phase involves setting standard clinical procedures and data collection protocols for BrS patients. (2) The second phase focuses on organizing a retrospective study with the development of ML models for ECG analysis, which is being tested in the collected population. (3) In the final phase, a prototype platform based on an electronic health record (EHR) system integrated with the proposed model is being released, and later validated by clinical centers.

Before conducting experiments, the process of creating the dataset was characterized by a multitude of technical hurdles to address for having an input suitable for a machine learning model following a pre-processing pipeline defined in [4]. Among these issues we noticed inconsistencies in ECG recordings from various clinical centers, differences in the type of data collected (electronic ECGs or scanned paper ECGs), and the presence of noise or signal artifacts. We addressed these challenges through the following pre-processing steps:

- Paper format ECGs were scanned by the clinical center before analysis. Then, several image processing filters were applied to reduce the source of noise from manual procedures.
- To limit the loss of information during the extraction process, a second-order spline interpolation was utilized in combination with a 50 Hz Butterworth filter of order 2.
- Each recording has been resampled to a frequency of 500 Hz with a single beat selected as suggested by clinicians to maintain a time window within a 1-second duration.

The original dataset is composed of 306 time series pre-processed from ECGs. Among these recordings 123 were positive class (87 Spontaneous BrS and 36 Positive *provocative test*) and 183 were negative class (169 Controls and 14 Negative *provocative test*). In particular, *provocative test* samples are related to the administration of sodium blocker channels under medical supervision in the Electrophysiology Lab. In Spontaneous BrS and Positive provocative cases the BrS is diagnosed, while in Control and Negative provocative cases the BrS is not diagnosed. Table 1 presents the distribution of samples across the four original cases. These four original cases are combined into two classes, considering *Spontaneous BrS* and *Positive provocative* as the positive class, while *Control* and *Negative provocative* as the negative class.

Figures 1a) and 1b) show two time series pre-processed from ECG lead V2. Figure a) shows an example of a positive class while Figure b) shows an example of a negative class.

3   Convolutional Neural Networks

A convolutional neural network (CNN) is a type of neural network characterized by the usage of convolutional operators, which apply filters to an input image or signal to extract features, and pool layers reducing the size of the feature maps [8,16]. The model optimizes its weights through backpropagation in order to minimize a predefined supervised loss function. Recently, CNNs have been successfully adapted to processing temporal data, such as audio signals or time series. They have shown great potential in the classification of heart arrhythmias due to their ability to extract local patterns or subtle changes in the morphology of ECGs, which is crucial for an accurate diagnosis [6]. In Fig. 2, we provide a summary of our CNN-based workflow specifically designed for Brugada syndrome prediction from ECG recordings.

In this work, we consider a CNN composed of N_b convolutional blocks with varying temporal window sizes (also referred to as kernel) and number of filters to capture a hierarchical representation across the signal. Each convolutional block consists of a 1D convolutional layer followed by a batch normalization [7] and a rectified linear unit (ReLU) activation function. More formally, considering the input signal $\mathbf{A}^{(0)} = \mathbf{X}$, a convolutional layer at depth $m > 0$ receives as input $\mathbf{A}^{(m-1)}$ producing the output $\mathbf{A}_k^{(m)}$ also referred to as a feature map and computed as:

$$\mathbf{A}_k^{(m)} = ReLU(BN(\sum_{i=1}^{K} \mathbf{W}_{ki}^{(m)} * \mathbf{A}_i^{(m-1)} + b_k^{(m)})), \tag{1}$$

where $\mathbf{W}$ and b refer respectively to weight and bias matrices, BN denotes the batch normalization layer and $*$ the 1D convolutional operator.

A dropout regularization mask [14] is also applied in between each convolutional block, while on top of the architecture there is a fully connected output layer with sigmoid activation function. Lastly, the initial weights are set following Glorot uniform initialization [5] and the model is trained from scratch using stochastic gradient descent (SGD) optimizing the binary cross-entropy loss function $\mathcal{L}(y, \hat{y}) = -[y \log(\hat{y}) + (1 - y) \log(1 - \hat{y})]$, given a label y and the model prediction $\hat{y}$.

4   Experimental Assessment (BrS Classification)

First, we started with the classification task of evaluating the CNN model in BrS diagnosis. We perform a model selection considering CNN configurations with a number of convolutional blocks $N_b = 3, 4, 5, 6, 7$ with V1 lead (5 hyperparameter configurations) and V2 lead (5 hyperparameter configurations) in input. The

Table 1. Distribution of the original four cases, later merged into two distinctive classes for the binary classification task.

Total	Positive Class		Negative Class	
	Spontaneous BrS	Positive provocative	Control	Negative provocative
306	87	36	169	14

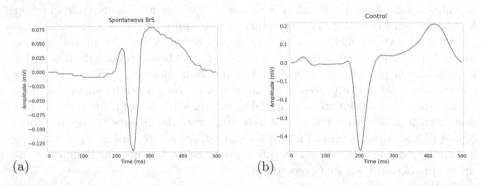

Fig. 1. An example of two time series of the dataset pre-processed from ECG lead V2. A positive class (a) and a negative class (b).

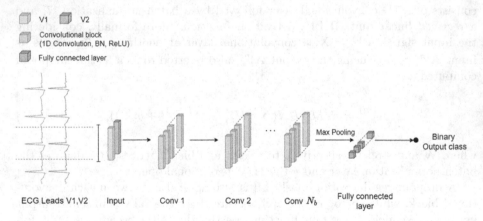

Fig. 2. Visual summary of our CNN-based classifier used in the experimental assessment for Brugada syndrome prediction from ECG recordings.

model selection is performed through a DCV approach with 5 external and 4 internal folds. Accordingly, the dataset is randomly shuffled with uniform distribution and then split into 5 test outer folds. The hyper-parameters of each convolutional block configuration were selected in validation folds through a random search by using a range of values shown in Table 2.

As metrics to evaluate the model we use accuracy (rate of correctly classified ECG), sensitivity (true positive rate) and specificity (true negative rate). The

Table 2. Ranges of hyperparameters used in the random search for the model selection.

	Hyperparameters
filter	$[5, 10, 15]$
kernel	$[5, 10, 15, 20, 30, 40]$
weight decay	$[5 \cdot 10^{-6}, 1 \cdot 10^{-5}, 1 \cdot 10^{-3}, 5 \cdot 10^{-3}]$
dropout	$[0, 0.1, 0.2, 0.3, 0.4, 0.5]$
learning rate	$[0.01, 0.005, 0.004, 0.003]$

validation accuracy is evaluated for each outer fold by averaging the accuracy achieved in the inner folds. Then, for each outer fold, the test results are evaluated considering the hyperparameters that obtained the best validation accuracy in the inner folds. The test results are computing averaging the results obtained in the outer folds of the DCV. Finally, the best configuration is considered to apply the proposed approach presented in Sect. 5.

5   Interpretation of ECGs Analysis in BrS Diagnosis

In this section, we describe the proposed approach used for the interpretation of time-series analysis in the case of BrS classification. Initially, we employed the Pan-Tompkins algorithm [11] to accurately identify R-peaks in each ECG recording proceeding with a beat alignment process. To ensure a higher precision of quantitative results we manually refined borderline cases. To capture the relevant electrical activity, we utilized a fixed time window of 1 s, comprising 250 timesteps before and after each R-peak. The signal was then processed by averaging each sample from the dataset within respective classes computing their gradient class activation mappings (Grad-CAM [12]) adapted for the temporal case as detailed in this section.

Gradient class activation mappings allowed us to point out highly contributing regions from an input ECG starting from a prediction, while identifying the features negatively or positively impact the outcome. The original idea is preserved but reformulated for a 1D input scenario; using the gradients of the final convolutional layer's output with respect to the class score to generate a region heatmap.

Technically, we can define $L(c)$ as the final convolutional layer in the CNN and $A_k^L(p)$ as the output for the k-th feature map in the layer at position p. The global average pooling of the gradient of the output class score y^c with respect to the feature maps A_k^L is computed as $\alpha_k^c = \frac{1}{Z} \sum_p \frac{\partial y^c}{\partial A_k^L(p)}$, where Z

is the number of spatial positions in the feature map. Afterwards, we compute a weighted combination of the activation maps A_k^L using the coefficients α_k^c as weights $L^c(p) = \sum_k \alpha_k^c A_k^L(p)$. Differently from the original formulation, our importance coefficients $L^c(p) \in \mathbb{R}$ do not rule out negative values, since we avoided the usage of the outer ReLU activation. This allowed for a more comprehensive interpretation of the binary prediction enclosing positive and negative contributions.

6   Experimental Results

In this section, we show the classification results of model interpretation. Table 3 shows the test results obtained by the CNN model using $N_b = 3, 4, 5, 6, 7$ convolutional blocks, weight decay, dropout and leads V1 and V2. The results highlight that using V2 lead obtains better results than V1 lead. In particular, the use of 6 convolutional blocks with the use of V2 achieves the best test result with accuracy, sensitivity and specificity of 90.53%, 87.73% and 92.34%, respectively. Considering the configuration with 6 convolutional blocks, we evaluated the model with the use of both V1 and V2 leads achieving accuracy, sensitivity and specificity of 89.87%, 89.43% and 90.20%, respectively. In this case, the configuration achieved a slightly low accuracy of 89.87% w.r.t. the best configuration that achieved 90.53.%. However, the use of 6 convolutional and both V1 and V2 leads allowed us to obtain a better sensitivity of 89.43% w.r.t. best configuration that obtained 87.73%. The results obtained in the BrS classification task are generally competitive with the recent literature approach [10] in which the model obtains a sensitivity of 88.4% and a specificity of 89.1% (although evaluated with a different dataset). Moreover, the results obtained in this paper significantly outperforms the results achieved in preliminary works [15] [4] (up to a maximum of 80% accuracy).

After the model selection, the architecture mentioned above (6 convolutional blocks) have been employed for the interpretability assessment focusing on lead V2. Following the principles detailed in Sect. 5, we computed the importance coefficients $L^c(p)$ averaged over each test fold from the double-CV. A bar plot visualization of the coefficients is showcased in the bottom row in Fig. 3 (red bars stands for positive class contribution, while blue bars for negative class contribution). For instance, in the left column (BrS patterns) each coefficient greater than zero supports the actual prediction, thus being colored in red. Mutually, negative coefficients refer to timesteps disowning the ground truth label, thus favoring a control-like prediction instead. Additionally, we provide the outcome of a manual ECG wave annotation phase performed by clinicians to identify the different ECG segments and better comprehend the correlation between interpretability outcomes and clinical practice (top row). The middle row depicts an

Table 3. Test accuracy (Acc), Sensitivity, Specificity and the standard deviation inside the brackets obtained by the CNN model with the use of $N_b = 3, 4, 5, 6, 7$ convolutional blocks, weight decay (wd), dropout and leads V1 and V2.

Architecture	Test Accuracy (%)	Sensitivity	Specificity
3 blocks V1	83.65(3.90)	80.50(0.078)	85.84(0.067)
4 blocks V1	85.28(7.40)	87.00(0.015)	84.22(0.120)
5 blocks V1	86.91(0.049)	88.67(0.058)	85.78(0.063)
6 blocks V1	85.62(0.020)	85.36(0.001)	85.81(0.032)
7 blocks V1	83.00(0.033)	76.43(0.069)	87.50(0.064)
3 blocks V2	83.65(3.90)	80.50(0.078)	85.84(0.067)
4 blocks V2	87.28(0.060)	82.77(0.094)	90.24(0.103)
5 blocks V2	87.31(0.007)	86.99(0.001)	82.52(0.010)
6 blocks V2	**90.53(0.028)**	**87.73(0.083)**	**92.34(0.011)**
7 blocks V2	87.59(0.012)	83.73(0.057)	90.17(0.037)
6 blocks V1, V2	89.87(0.028)	89.43(0.078)	90.20(0.032)

average ECG beat for positive and negative classes and their standard deviation (translucent region). Interestingly, we can infer how the saddleback pattern typical of Type 1 BrS ECG is associated with the syndrome in the left pane, which can be distinguished from the average morphology of healthy subjects (V2 lead, right column). In Fig. 3, the grey dashed lines represent the focal areas for a correct model prediction. In both positive and negative cases, there is a noticeable concentration of coefficients throughout the ST segment (from S wave offset to T onset), a portion heedful to healthcare practitioners to identify patterns to establish a BrS diagnosis. Furthermore, the model leverages the waves S and T in the positive case, as shown by the two distinct points defining average beat contribution. Conversely, for the averaged morphology of patients without the disease the network examines mainly the QRS segment. Although, it should be acknowledged that the multitude of overlapping opposite sign coefficients (visible over time regions in bottom row plots) results from the aggregation of various ECG recordings from diverse patients in the test set. Thus, the presence of noise is attributable to the process of joining singular variations in signal morphology across various patients, which is consistent with the complexity of the task.

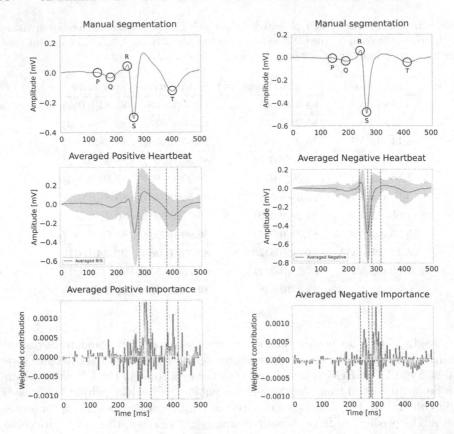

Fig. 3. (Top row) Outcome of a manual wave annotation process performed by clinicians. (Middle row) Averaged amplitude plot from ECGs including positive (left) and negative (right) class. (Bottom row) Weighted importance coefficients averaged over test folds. The areas highlighted by the grey dashed lines represent the signal ranges where the model is focused on making the prediction. (Color figure online)

7   Conclusions

In this paper, we proposed a predictive approach supporting BrS diagnosis and a post hoc interpretability assessment leveraging CNNs. The dataset has been collected from several clinical centers within the BrAID project [1]. It comprises of 306 ECGs (123 of positive class and 183 of negative class) obtained from scanned paper and digital format. An extensive pre-processing pipeline was performed to produce the dataset through a multitude of technical hurdles (such as different clinical centers and various ECG formats) to address having a temporal input suitable for a machine learning model.

Initially, we performed an experimental assessment employing a double cross-validation approach to evaluate the model in BrS type-1 classification task. Within model selection, we considered several model configurations by varying the number of convolutional blocks and the input leads (V1 and V2). Specifically, a configuration with 6 convolutional blocks using the lead V2 obtained the best test result with an accuracy, sensitivity, and specificity of 90.53%, 87.73%, and 92.34%, respectively. Accordingly, we used V2 to analyze the model in the BrS classification from the ECG time series.

Finally, we computed the important areas of the ECG time series which allow the model to make the prediction. First, we computed two plots, one averaged from the values of positive beats and the other from negative beats. Analyzing the plots of the averaged beats we can note the typical saddleback pattern in Type 1 BrS. Moreover, by interpreting the predictions on lead V2, we found a higher correlation in the ST segment amongst importance coefficients and positive output class, confirming the suggestion from healthcare clinicians. Overall, the interpretability results are consistent with the patterns analyzed by clinicians to perform diagnosis of BrS. We were able to display through the application of our framework the impact on the decision-making process of the predictions for positive and negative test samples. The approach offers a way to improve the transparency and accountability of the classifier, potentially allowing clinicians to revise the output class based on the interpretability outcome.

Our research highlighted that the proposed predictive model based on convolutional neural networks is comparable with the results provided by state-of-the-art approaches for BrS classification. The results of the proposed method based on the interpretation of the relevant input areas in the BrS classification show that this architecture could potentially support clinicians in the early diagnosis of a rare ECG pattern. Through the insights provided on the focal signal regions, clinicians can better evaluate its suitability for making informed decisions in clinical practice.

In conclusion, we believe the proposed approach can contribute to and stimulate the development of novel approaches in future works to interpret model predictions on time-series applications.

Acknowledgements. The project BrAID was funded within the "Regione Toscana Bando Ricerca Salute 2018" (Decreto n. 15397, 26/09/2018). Moreover we would like to acknowledge all of the clinical centers part of BrAID who has collected the data used in this paper. In particular: Clinical Physiology Institute (IFC) of the Italian National Research Council (CNR), Fondazione Toscana Gabriele Monasterio per la Ricerca Medica e di Sanità Pubblica (FTGM), Azienda Sanitaria Toscana Sud Est - U.O.C Cardiologia ASL 8 Arezzo (AUTSE), Azienda Sanitaria Toscana Nord Ovest - U.O.C. Cardiologia, Ospedale Versilia (AUTNO), Azienda Ospedaliera Universitaria Careggi - SOD Aritmologia - Firenze (AOUC), Azienda Ospedaliero Universitaria Pisana - Cardiologia 2 Cisanello (AOUP).

References

1. Braid.   https://www.ifc.cnr.it/index.php/en/news/685-kick-off-del-progetto-braid. Accessed 03 Apr 2023
2. Ahsan, M.M., Siddique, Z.: Machine learning-based heart disease diagnosis: a systematic literature review. Artif. Intell. Med. 102289 (2022)

3. Brugada, P., Brugada, J.: Right bundle branch block, persistent ST segment elevation and sudden cardiac death: a distinct clinical and electrocardiographic syndrome: a multicenter report. J. Am. Coll. Cardiol. **20**(6), 1391–1396 (1992)
4. Dimitri, G.M., Gallicchio, C., Micheli, A., Morales, M.A., Ungaro, E., Vozzi, F.: A preliminary evaluation of Echo State Networks for Brugada syndrome classification. In: 2021 IEEE SSCI, pp. 01–08. IEEE (2021)
5. Glorot, X., Bengio, Y.: Understanding the difficulty of training deep feedforward neural networks. In: Proceedings of the Thirteenth AISTATS, pp. 249–256. JMLR Workshop and Conference Proceedings (2010)
6. Hannun, A.Y., et al.: Cardiologist-level arrhythmia detection and classification in ambulatory electrocardiograms using a deep neural network. Nat. Med. **25**(1), 65–69 (2019)
7. Ioffe, S., Szegedy, C.: Batch normalization: accelerating deep network training by reducing internal covariate shift. In: ICML, pp. 448–456. PMLR (2015)
8. LeCun, Y., et al.: Backpropagation applied to handwritten zip code recognition. Neural Comput. **1**(4), 541–551 (1989)
9. Liao, S., et al.: Use of wearable technology and deep learning to improve the diagnosis of Brugada syndrome. Clin. Electrophysiol. **8**(8), 1010–1020 (2022)
10. Liu, C.M., et al.: A deep learning-enabled electrocardiogram model for the identification of a rare inherited arrhythmia: Brugada syndrome. Can. J. Cardiol. **38**(2), 152–159 (2022)
11. Pan, J., Tompkins, W.J.: A real-time QRS detection algorithm. IEEE Trans. Biomed. Eng. **BME-32**(3), 230–236 (1985)
12. Selvaraju, R.R., Cogswell, M., Das, A., Vedantam, R., Parikh, D., Batra, D.: Grad-CAM: visual explanations from deep networks via gradient-based localization. In: Proceedings of the IEEE ICCV, pp. 618–626 (2017)
13. Sheikh, A.S., Ranjan, K.: Brugada syndrome: a review of the literature. Clin. Med. **14**(5), 482 (2014)
14. Srivastava, N., Hinton, G., Krizhevsky, A., Sutskever, I., Salakhutdinov, R.: Dropout: a simple way to prevent neural networks from overfitting. J. Mach. Learn. Res. **15**(1), 1929–1958 (2014)
15. Vozzi, F., et al.: Artificial intelligence algorithms for the recognition of Brugada type 1 pattern on standard 12-leads ECG. Europace **24**(Suppl._1), euac053–558 (2022)
16. Waibel, A., Hanazawa, T., Hinton, G., Shikano, K., Lang, K.J.: Phoneme recognition using time-delay neural networks. IEEE Trans. Acoust. Speech Signal Process. **37**(3), 328–339 (1989)

Analysis of Augmentations in Contrastive Learning for Parkinson's Disease Diagnosis

Shuangyi Wang, Tianren Zhou, Zhaoyan Shen, and Zhiping Jia[(✉)]

School of Computer Science and Technology, Shandong University, Qingdao, China
{shuangyiwang,trzhou}@mail.sdu.edu.cn, {shenzhaoyan,jzp}@sdu.edu.cn

Abstract. Parkinsons disease (PD) is a neurodegenerative disease that causes a movement disorder. Early diagnosis of PD is critical for patients to receive proper treatment, such as levodopa/carbidopa, which are more effective when administered early on at the beginning stage of the disease. However, due to a shortage of experts in the field, a considerable volume of unlabeled data remains unexplored in the existing supervised learning-based PD diagnosis. To fully utilize the available data, we propose a framework to thoroughly evaluate the effect of different data augmentation settings for contrastive learning (CL)-based PD diagnosis. We also provide PD datasets with three modalities (i.e., hand-drawing, speech, and gait) to comprehensively evaluate the detection performance and make them publicly available. Experimental results demonstrate that different augmentation approaches and parameters have a large impact on PD detection performance, and CL could outperform the existing unsupervised deep learning method with proper data augmentation settings. Our study provides insights for researchers in choosing the proper data augmentation and corresponding parameters for CL-based PD diagnosis.

Keywords: Unsupervised learning · Contrastive learning · Parkinson's disease detection · Data augmentation

1 Introduction

Parkinsons disease (PD) is a long-lasting, progressively worsening neurodegenerative condition that detrimentally affects patients' quality of life by compromising their motor and cognitive abilities, ultimately resulting in death [24]. Currently, there is no cure for PD but the medications and treatments can provide symptomatic relief [24]. Initiating treatment in the early stages can help manage symptoms more effectively, improving the patient's quality of life and potentially slowing the progression of PD [8,24].

Supervised machine learning algorithms have been applied to conduct the early diagnosis of PD [2,14,25]. These algorithms require extensive labeled data provided by domain experts as training material. However, labeling a sufficient amount of training data is not sustainable due to the limited domain expertise. In

L. Iliadis et al. (Eds.): ICANN 2023, LNCS 14257, pp. 37–50, 2023.
https://doi.org/10.1007/978-3-031-44216-2_4

addition, inter-observer variability would lead to a different diagnostic conclusion on the same input data since there is no definitive diagnostic test for PD [24]. To address this, self-supervised learning is proposed to fully utilize unlabeled data by learning the intrinsic structure and patterns of the data to discover underlying representations. Among self-supervised learning paradigms, contrastive learning (CL) has gained growing attention in recent years. The main idea of CL is to compare the similarity between two or more samples to learn a model. This process entails learning an encoder that can effectively encode data of the same type while maximizing the differences in encoding outcomes between distinct data classes. Representative works such as MoCo [10], SimCLR [1], and BYOL [8] are proposed and achieve state-of-the-art performances in various tasks.

In this paper, we devise a self-supervised CL framework to distinguish Parkinson's patients from normal individuals with unlabeled data. The choice of data augmentation and the corresponding parameter value in CL play a crucial role in the performances [1,22]. This paper comprehensively analyzes the effect of different enhancements (e.g., random rotation and random cropping) and the corresponding parameters (e.g., rotation range and crop size) of CL on Parkinson's detection performances. The proposed framework evaluates the effect of data augmentation and the corresponding parameter of CL using datasets from three distinct modalities, namely hand-drawing, speech, and gait, to provide a comprehensive assessment of the parameter settings of data augmentations. The hand-drawing dataset contains spirals and meanders pictures of the subjects while the speech dataset contains the subject's audio recordings. The gait dataset records the vertical ground reaction force of the subject while walking. The main contributions are summarized as follows:

- We are the first study to thoroughly investigate the impact of various data augmentation and corresponding parameter settings in CL for self-supervised PD detection over three different modalities, offering valuable insights for future research in the field.
- The deep model trained under the classic CL method with the proper data augmentation approach outperforms the existing self-supervised learning methods such as AutoEncoder in terms of various PD detection metrics.
- We collect data from multiple Parkinson's disease public dataset and reorganize the dataset based on three modalities for future research in the field. The datasets are made open-source[1].

2   Related Works

Patients with PD exhibit speech disorders that manifest in various aspects of voice, including articulation, phonation, prosody, and speech fluency. Deep learning has been widely used in the medical field [12], such as medical image segmentation [27], cardiac monitoring [23], PD detection [5], etc. Supervised learning methods based on deep models such as convolutional neural networks (CNN) are

---

[1] https://drive.google.com/drive/folders/1XGnz6KfrbQsSsNEgPGKONC70jn4r-oIX.

proposed to extract these speech features of PD patients and diagnose PD [2]. Time-frequency representations of speech signals (i.e., Mel-spectrograms) are utilized as the input to the deep model [25]. Some studies combine CNN with LSTM for speech sequence modeling [13,16]. For the hand-drawing dataset, authors in [14] use CNNs to learn features from spiral images drawn by patients to distinguish Parkinsons patients from healthy individuals. Authors in [3] devise the deep model based on Bidirectional Gated Recurrent Units (BiGRUs) and one-dimensional convolution to conduct PD diagnosis. For the gait dataset, 1D-CNN [5] and attention-enhanced long and short-term memory (LSTM) [29] are used to analyze gait information, respectively. However, these methods are supervised learning, which requires training using a large amount of labeled data, it needs to be labeled by professional doctors and consumes a lot of human and material resources.

As for unsupervised learning, authors in [32] propose a clustering approach for PD detection, but the magnitude of plantar bend data collected in the experiments has not been used. In [15], authors devise a novel unsupervised two-step sparse transfer learning. They used CSC to learn efficient speech structure and designed JLSDA to eliminate the discrepancy between the training set and test set. In [21] processed the collected inertial data through a feature extraction algorithm and then used three unsupervised learning algorithms (Self-organizing maps (SOM), K-means, and hierarchical clustering) for multiple comparisons and analysis to distinguish different levels of PD. The most related work [8] proposes a tree-structure-guided graph convolutional network with CL scheme to conduct PD assessment using only video-based hand movements. But this study requires recording videos, which have certain limitations when applied in practice. These methods all use unlabeled data for Parkinson's diagnosis, but the accuracy is lower compared to the supervised approach and the results do not meet the desired goals.

3   Method

3.1   Contrastive Learning Framework for Parkinson Detection

We propose a framework to thoroughly evaluate the effect of data augmentation and corresponding parameters based on the classic CL method MoCo [10] for PD detection. The overview of the proposed framework is shown in Fig. 1. We define the training dataset of CL as $X = \{x_1, x_2, x_3, ...x_n\}$, which contains n inputs. In the framework, we first apply data augmentation over each input $x_i \in X$ to get x_{i1}, x_{i2} respectively. We then choose one image as an anchor. For example, as shown in Fig. 1, x_{i1} is set as the anchor, x_{i2} is the positive sample for x_{i1}, and $\{x_{12}, x_{22}, ..., x_{(i-1)2}, x_{(i+1)2}, ...x_{n2}\}$ are negative simples for x_{i1}. The input anchor sample x_{i1} into an encoder (E^+) to get feature f_{i1}, and input positive sample x_{i2} into the same structure of encoder (E^-) to get feature f_{i2}. f_{i1} is used as a query (q), f_{i2} is used as the positive sample key (k^+). Other negative samples to get $\{f_{12}, f_{22}, f_{32}, ...\}$ constitute a set of encoded samples $\{k_1, k_2, k_3, ...\}$ that are the keys of a dictionary. In the beginning, a queue of size K is generated

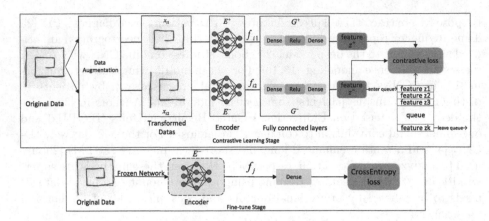

Fig. 1. MoCo Method Framework.

to store the keys, and the features inside are randomly initialized. The newly generated feature key is added to the queue at each iteration of training, and the first feature added to the queue is allowed to leave the queue. Next, the features f_{i1} and f_{i2} are passed through some fully connected layers (G^+ and G^-) to generate the final outputs z^+ and z^-, respectively, and then passed to the loss function to compute the overall model contrast loss. Our task is to train these encoders to perform a dictionary lookup task, where the encoded query f_{i1} is as similar as possible to the key f_{i2} that it matches, and as far away as possible from the other negative sample keys ($f_{12}, f_{22}, f_{32}, ...$).

We use InfoNCE [17] as the loss function, which takes the dot product values as similarity values. The loss function is formulated as:

$$L_q = -log \frac{exp(q \cdot k^+/\tau)}{\sum_{i=0}^{K} q \cdot k_i/\tau)}, \qquad (1)$$

where τ is a temperature hyper-parameter [28]. When the query is similar to its positive sample pair k^+ and different from all other keys, the loss value is low. The sum is over one positive and K negative samples.

For both encoders E^+ and E^-, we use the part before the last fully connected layer in resnet18. For the fully connected layer part, G^+ and G^- both use a fully connected layer + Relu + fully connected layer. Although the structures of E^+ and E^-, G^+ and G^- are the same, weights are different. For E^+ and G^+ the weights are updated by backpropagation, while the weights of E^- and G^- are updated by the Momentum update method with the following equation:

$$\theta \leftarrow m\theta_k + (1 - m)\theta_q, \qquad (2)$$

where m is the artificially set weights range of $[0, 1)$.

The weights of E^- are used after training and frozen for the downstream task. G^- is replaced with a fully connected layer with an output dimension of 2. The final classification is obtained by fine-tuning the downstream task using labeled samples (x_i, y_i) to distinguish Parkinson's patients from healthy individuals, where x_i is the sample and y_i is the label. In the fine-tuning process, we use supervised training, and the loss function uses the Cross Entropy loss.

3.2 Data Augmentation for Different Datasets

The type of data augmentation and the choice of parameters in contrastive learning would greatly affect final PD detection performance. For each dataset with one modality, we use different data augmentation approaches and try a wide range of parameter values.

Hand-Drawing. For the hand-drawing dataset, we used six data augmentation methods: 1) *Random Crop and Restore:* A value is randomly sampled in the interval $[s, 1] (s \in (0, 1])$, and then the image is cropped with the ratio of the cropping region's area to the original image's area. Finally restored to the original image size; 2) *Color Jitter:* Randomly change the brightness, contrast, saturation and hue of an image; 3) *Gaussian Blur:* Select a random number in the range $[0.1, k)$ as the standard deviation of the Gaussian kernel, add Gaussian blur to the image; 4) *Random Horizontal Flip:* There is a half chance that the image will be flipped horizontally; 5) *Random Vertical Flip:* There is a half chance that the image will be flipped vertically; 6) *Random Rotation:* Rotate the image according to the given rotation range.

Speech. For the sound signal, we also used six data augmentation methods: 1) *Add Scaling Noise:* Generate a normal distribution N_1 with a mean value of 1, a standard deviation of σ, and the same length as the original signal. The input sound signal is multiplied by the normal distribution N_1 to obtain $\tilde{x}(t) = N_1 \times x(t)$; 2) *Add Write Noise:* Generate a normal distribution N_2 with a mean value of 0, a standard deviation of 1, and the same length as the original signal. Then, given the parameter β, the augmented speech signal is calculated using $\tilde{x}(t) = x(t) + \beta \times N_2$: 3) *Right Shift:* Scroll the elements along the first dimension at the given scale; 4) *Time Stretch:* Time-stretch an audio series by a fixed rate R; 5) *Pitch Shift:* Shift the pitch of a waveform by N steps; 6) *Horizontal Flip:* The input signal is flipped Horizontally across as $\tilde{x}(t) = x(-t + L)$ where L is the length of input signal x(t).

Gait. For the gait signal, we use the same several data augmentation methods as for the voice, namely *Add Scaling Noise, Add Write Noise, RightShift,* and *Horizontal Flip.* Since the shape of the gait signal is $T \times 18$, where T represents the length and 18 represents the width of the signal, we perform the data augmentation methods on every single column of the data segment.

4   Experiments

4.1   Dataset

For the hand-drawing domain, we found two public datasets, described as follows:

HandPD [18]. This dataset was collected at Botucatu Medical School, containing 92 subjects, divided into 18 healthy people (6 males, 12 females) and 74 PD patients (56 males, 15 females). Eight images of two types (spirals and meanders), four for each type, were drawn by each subject. A total of 144 healthy images and 592 Parkinson's images were included.

NewHandPD [19]. This dataset is the extension of the HandPD dataset. 66 subjects were included, 35 of them were healthy and 31 were PD patients. Each person draws 4 spirals, 4 meanders, and 1 circle. That is, there are 9 images for each person, a total of 315 healthy images and 279 Parkinson's images.

Kaggle [31]. Images of spirals and waves were drawn for each subject. For both spirals and waves, there are 51 healthy images and 51 images for PD.

For the speech domain, we found two public datasets, described as follows:

ItalianVoice [4]. The dataset consisted of 65 native Italian speakers, including 15 young (age 20.8 ± 2.65), 22 elderly (age 67.09 ± 5.16) healthy individuals, and 28 elderly Parkinson's patients (age 67.21 ± 8.73). All recordings were performed in a quiet, echo-free room with a professional microphone. Participants were asked to perform a set of tasks including reading phonologically balanced text, performing the pronunciation of syllables /pa/ and /ta/, vowels /a/, /e/, /i/, /o/, /u/, reading phonologically balanced word lists, and finally reading phonologically balanced sentence lists. The sampling frequency is 16kHz.

MDVR-KCL [11]. It consists of voice recordings from 16 PD patients and 21 healthy subjects. The dataset contains a total of 73 audio samples, ranging from 1 to 3 min. The collecting process was recorded by the microphone of a mobile phone with a sample rate of 44.1 kHz and a bit depth of 16 bits.

For the gait data, we used an open dataset [7], which consists of three different sub-datasets from three different experiments [6,9,30], called Ga, Ju, and Si, respectively, where the subjects in the Si sub-dataset were walking on a treadmill. Each subject wore a pair of shoes with a powerful sensor and walked for approximately 2 min at his/her usual pace. It includes 18 columns of data, which consist of 16 sensors located under the sole of each foot, 8 per foot, and the total force under the left foot and right foot. The entire dataset consisted of 93 PD patients and 73 healthy control subjects.

4.2   Data Preparation

We performed a selective merging for datasets of the same type and open-sourced them. Then the different types of datasets were processed differently.

For the hand-drawing dataset, we used spirals and meanders graphs from all datasets to make sure the graph types are consistent, excluding circle images from NewHandPD and wave graphs from Kaggle. Since they have different image sizes, we rescaled them to RGB images of size 224 * 224. Then we normalized the data. Finally, because they have different background colors, we converted them to grayscale images.

For ItalianVoice in the speech dataset, we excluded data from all healthy young people and two older healthy people with murmurs. Then three tasks with longer time were selected: reading speech-balanced text, sentences, and words. For the MDVR-KCL dataset, we used data from all people, but the voice recordings of the dataset contain white space and the voice of the staff, which interfere with the learning of the model. To only retain information that is valid for training, we cropped the irrelevant audio segments. Since the ItalianVoice dataset is sampled at 16 kHz, the MDVR-KCL voice signals were downsampled to 16 kHz before merging the datasets. Then all data were normalized. Since all sound data is long and varies in length, each data is segmented. We set the segment length to 64005 and the overlap to 50% of the segment length. Finally, we converted the original sound signal into a 256 * 256 Meier spectrum to reduce the effects of noise and distortion, improve the generalization of the model.

For the gait dataset, we only used two sub-datasets: *Ga* and *Ju*. Because the *Si* dataset was tested on a treadmill, merging it in would affect the results. The first 10 s and last 10 s of each data were removed to eliminate the transient effect. Like the speech dataset, we segmented the gait data and set the segment length to 1000 with an overlap of 50% of the segment length.

4.3 Implementation Details

To convert speech data into Mel-spectrograms, we used 128 Mel filters with an FFT window length of 2048, and the number of samples between successive frames was 251. Finally, the number of Mel bands was set to 256.

Since each type of data set is unbalanced, we add weighting paramcters to the loss function and set the weight values to (2.0, 1.0), (1.3, 1.0), and (3.0, 1.0) for the drawing data, speech data, and gait data, respectively.

For all datasets, we set the batch size to 64 and the length of the queue k in contrastive learning to 1024. We trained the model for 200 epochs and set the temperature parameter t to 0.07. A cosine annealing learning rate decay strategy was used, and the initial learning rate was set to 0.03 for training the encoder. The fine-tuning process is the same as in MoCo [10], the initial learning rate was set to 0.1, and 100 epochs were trained.

We used a five-fold cross-validation for all types of databases, dividing the data into five equal parts to ensure that the same subject's data would only be in the same fold. One fold of each experiment was used for testing and the rest for training. The final experiment was averaged over 5 times.

Finally, we use Accuracy (ACC), Sensitivity (SEN), Specificity (SPE), and F1-score to evaluate our method.

4.4 Experimental Results

As described in Sect. 3, we apply different data augmentations based on the type of datasets. For each augmentation in the drawing dataset, we use various

Table 1. Augmentation parameters of contrastive learning in hand-drawing dataset.

Augmentation Method	Data Points
Random Crop and Restore(s)	[0.1, 0.2, 0.3, 0.4, 0.5,0.6, 0.7, 0.8, 0.9]
Color Jitter({C,I})	[{0.2, 0.1}{0.4, 0.3}{0.6, 0.5}{0.8, 0.1} {0.2, 0.1}{0.4, 0.3} {0.6, 0.5}{0.8, 0.1} {0.2, 0.1}{0.4, 0.3}{0.6, 0.5}{0.8, 0.1}]
Gaussian Blur(k)	[1, 2, 5, 10, 15, 20, 30]
Random Horizontal Flip	————
Random Vertical Flip	————
Random Rotation({n,x})	[{0, 90}{0, 180}{0, 270}{0, 360}{90, 180} {90, 270}{90, 360}{180, 270}{180, 360}{270, 360}]

Table 2. Inference performance after fine-tuning using hand-drawing datasets.

Augmentation Method	Best Parameter	ACC	SEN	SPE	F
Random Crop and Restore(s)	**0.9**	**89.42**	**91.08**	**86.48**	**91.62**
Color Jitter({C,I})	{0.8, 0.5}	84.08	84.79	82.87	87.15
Gaussian Blur(k)	1	85.25	88.99	78.65	88.45
Random Horizontal Flip	–	87.92	89.65	84.87	90.41
Random Vertical Flip	–	87.58	89.38	84.43	90.15
Random Rotation({n,x})	{0, 360}	89.33	89.92	88.32	91.47

parameters that are detailed in Table 1. For *Random Crop and Restore* augmentation, we randomly select a value in the range of $[s, 1]$ as the cropping ratio. For *Gaussian Blur*, we simplify the process by setting the same value C for brightness, contrast, and saturation, and I for hue. We set the maximum value of the Gaussian kernel in *Gaussian blur* to k. The min value in *Random Rotation* is set to n, and the max value is set to x.

Table 2 shows the optimal parameters and results of each data augmentation after fine-tuning on the hand-drawing dataset. It is seen that the best parameter is 0.9 for *Random Crop and Restore*, {0,8, 0.5} for *Color Jitter*, 1 for *Gaussian Blur*, and {0, 360} for the *Random Rotation* method. The most effective technique for data augmentation is *Random Crop and Restore*, which inference performance of accuracy, sensitivity, specificity, and F1-score reaching 89.42%, 91.08%, 86.48%, and 91.62%, respectively. On the other hand, the *Color Jitter* method proved to be the least favorable.

For each augmentation applied on the speech dataset, we used various parameters as shown in Table 3. We set the scaling factor of *Add Scaling Noise* to σ, the product factor of *Add Write Noise* to β, the shift ratio of *Right Shift* to L (e.g., $L = 80$ means 80% shift), the rate stretch of *Time Stretch* to R, and the offset step of *Pitch Shift* to N.

Table 3. Augmentation parameters of contrastive learning in speech dataset.

Augmentation Method	Data Points
Add Scaling Noise(σ)	[0.01, 0.02, 0.03, 0.05, 0.08, 0.1, 0.15, 0.2, 0.3, 0.5, 0.8]
Add Write Noise(β)	[0.01, 0.02, 0.03, 0.05, 0.08, 0.1, 0.15, 0.2, 0.3, 0.5, 0.8]
Right Shift(L)	[20, 30, 40, 50, 60, 70, 80]
Time Stretch(R)	[0.5, 0.7, 0.8, 0.85, 0.9,0.95, 1.1, 1.3, 1.5, 1.7, 2]]
Pitch Shift(N)	$[-10, -5, -3, -2, -1, 1, 2, 3, 5, 10]$
Horizontal Flip	———————

Table 4. Inference performance after fine-tuning using the speech dataset.

Method	Para	ACC	SEN	SPE	F1	ACC^P	SEN^P	SPE^P	$F1^P$
Scaling Noise(σ)	0.2	89.42	89.33	89.53	90.49	90.59	89.00	92.20	90.26
Write Noise(β)	0.01	88.16	88.47	87.74	89.38	90.12	85.24	94.70	89.34
Right Shift(L)	**80**	**91.16**	**92.22**	**89.77**	**92.15**	**92.26**	**92.99**	**91.63**	**92.17**
Time Stretch(R)	1.7	90.04	91.38	88.31	91.18	92.13	90.14	94.02	91.78
Pitch Shift(N)	10	89.50	89.06	90.04	90.52	92.26	90.14	94.02	91.78
Horizontal Flip	–	88.43	88.74	88.02	89.63	89.92	86.67	92.88	89.92

Table 5. Inference performance after fine-tuning using the gait dataset.

Method	Para	ACC	SEN	SPE	F1	ACC^P	SEN^P	SPE^P	$F1^P$
Scaling Noise(σ)	0.02	70.69	71.27	69.18	77.62	77.41	79.55	74.44	79.69
Write Noise(β)	0.3	73.61	73.80	72.89	80.21	78.41	81.21	74.44	80.92
Right Shift(L)	**60**	**74.56**	**74.54**	**74.62**	**80.69**	**79.32**	**79.55**	**78.89**	**81.31**
Horizontal Flip	–	76.96	69.93	68.58	73.93	77.11	76.06	78.61	79.19

Since the sound signal was divided into several segments, we calculated the inference performance each segment and then combined all segments for each subject to calculate each subject's inference performance. Table 4 shows the optimal parameters and the results for each data augmentation after fine-tuning on the speech dataset. The second column displays the best parameters found in the optional parameters. Columns three to six exhibit the inference performance for each segment, while the last four columns show the inference performance for each subject, where 'P' indicates the results by subject. According to Table 4, the optimal parameters for *Add Scaling Noise, Add Write Noise, Right Shift, Time Stretch,* and *Pitch Shift* methods are 0.2, 0.01, 80, 1.7, and 10, respectively. *Right Shift* is the best method for all data augmentation, with accuracy, sensitivity, specificity, and F1-score for each segment at 91.16%, 92.22%, 89.77%, 92.15%, and for each subject at 92.26%, 92.99%, 91.63%, and 92.17%, respectively.

For the gait dataset, we applied the same *Add Scaling Noise, Add Write Noise, Right Shift,* and *Horizontal Filp* data augmentation methods as we did to

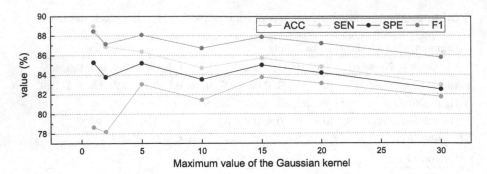

Fig. 2. Inference results for different parameters when using the *Gaussian Blur* augmentation method in hand-drawing dataset.

Table 6. Inference performances on hand-drawing dataset.

	ACC	SEN	SPE	F1
Supervise Resnet18	90.92	91.33	90.12	92.74
Contrastive Learning	89.42	91.08	86.48	91.62
AutoEncoder	87.08	89.77	82.32	89.82
DCGAN	85.58	85.83	84.99	88.33

the speech dataset with the same specific parameter choices. Table 5 shows the optimal parameters and results for each data augmentation as with Table 4 after fine-tuning on the gait dataset. According to the Table, the optimal parameters for *Add Scaling Noise*, *Add Write Noise*, and *Right Shift* methods are 0.01, 0.3, and 60, respectively. The accuracy, sensitivity, specificity, and F1-score of each segment are 74.56%, 74.54%, 74.62%, and 80.69%, respectively, while those for each subject are 79.32%, 79.55%, 78.89%, and 81.31%, respectively.

According to Table 4 and Table 5, we find that the *Right Shift* augmentation method is always the best in two different types of datasets, but the corresponding optimal parameter values are not the same. the *Horizontal Flip* method is worse in both. Accordingly, we speculate that the data augmentation methods have certain generalizations in data sets of similar types. However, since different data types cannot use the same augmentation methods, there are limitations to exploring the problem in depth, further research can be conducted in future work.

To demonstrate that different parameters of data augmentation have different effects on the results, Fig. 2 shows the inference performance of the *Gaussian Blur* augmentation method on the and-drawing dataset. The figure clearly highlights the significant impact of different parameter choices on the results. For example, the best F1-score can reach 88.45%, while the worst can only reach 85.78%. Due to space constraints, we have not listed the parameters for other augmentation methods and datasets. But same as in Fig. 2, different parameters have an impact on the results.

Table 7. Inference performances on speech dataset.

	ACC	SEN	SPE	F1	ACC^P	SEN^P	SPE^P	$F1^P$
Supervise Resnet18	94.63	94.15	95.25	95.18	93.53	91.84	95.27	93.33
Contrastive Learning	91.16	92.22	89.77	92.15	92.26	92.99	91.63	92.17
AutoEncoder	88.33	88.30	88.33	89.46	86.11	83.32	88.86	85.26
DCGAN	88.00	88.47	87.37	89.18	87.65	84.48	90.95	86.84

Table 8. Inference performances on gait dataset.

	ACC	SEN	SPE	F1	ACC^P	SEN^P	SPE^P	$F1^P$
Supervise Resnet18	74.12	73.84	75.20	80.79	81.02	81.06	81.11	82.98
Contrastive Learning	74.56	74.54	74.62	80.69	79.32	79.55	78.89	81.31
AutoEncoder	63.24	61.24	68.92	70.16	73.41	72.42	74.72	75.09
DCGAN	66.98	65.39	74.09	70.16	72.40	71.06	74.72	74.13

Finally, to demonstrate the superiority of the contrastive learning method we used, we compared it with other popular unsupervised methods in deep learning, namely AutoEncoder [26] and DCGAN [20]. We also tested supervised learning that employed resnet18 as the network architecture. The results for the three types of datasets are shown in Table 6, Table 7, and Table 8. It can be seen that although contrastive learning is slightly worse than supervised learning, it outperforms the AutoEncoder and DCGAN significantly. The F1-score of contrastive learning on hand-drawing dataset, speech dataset, and gait dataset is higher than AutoEncoder by 1.8%, 6.91%, 6.22%, and 3.29%, 5.33%, 7.18% higher than DCGAN. This proves the excellence of the contrastive learning method we used.

5 Conclusion

In this paper, we propose a framework to explicitly explore the effect of data augmentations of CL for PD diagnosis. PD datasets with three modalities (i.e., hand-drawing, speech, and gait) are collected to comprehensively evaluate the effect of different parameters on PD detection performance. Experimental results show that the best data augmentation approach for hand-drawing dataset, speech dataset, and gait dataset are *Random Crop and Restore* with parameter 0.9, *Right Shift* with parameter 80, and *Right Shift* with parameter 60, respectively. The datasets will be made open-source to provide valuable references and insights for future research in the field of CL-based PD diagnosis.

Acknowledgment. The work described in this paper is partially supported by the Natural Science Foundation of Shandong Province under Grant ZR2022LZH010, and the National Natural Science Foundation of China under Grant 92064008.

References

1. Chen, T., Kornblith, S., Norouzi, M., Hinton, G.: A simple framework for contrastive learning of visual representations. In: International Conference on Machine Learning, pp. 1597–1607. PMLR (2020)
2. Correia, J., Trancoso, I., Raj, B.: In-the-wild end-to-end detection of speech affecting diseases. In: 2019 IEEE Automatic Speech Recognition and Understanding Workshop (ASRU), pp. 734–741. IEEE (2019)
3. Diaz, M., Moetesum, M., Siddiqi, I., Vessio, G.: Sequence-based dynamic handwriting analysis for Parkinson's disease detection with one-dimensional convolutions and BiGRUs. Expert Syst. Appl. **168**, 114405 (2021)
4. Dimauro, G., Di Nicola, V., Bevilacqua, V., Caivano, D., Girardi, F.: Assessment of speech intelligibility in Parkinson's disease using a speech-to-text system. IEEE Access **5**, 22199–22208 (2017)
5. El Maachi, I., Bilodeau, G.A., Bouachir, W.: Deep 1D-Convnet for accurate Parkinson disease detection and severity prediction from gait. Expert Syst. Appl. **143**, 113075 (2020)
6. Frenkel-Toledo, S., Giladi, N., Peretz, C., Herman, T., Gruendlinger, L., Hausdorff, J.M.: Treadmill walking as an external pacemaker to improve gait rhythm and stability in Parkinson's disease. Mov. Disorders Official J. Mov. Disorder Soc. **20**(9), 1109–1114 (2005)
7. Goldberger, A.L., et al.: PhysioBank, PhysioToolkit, and PhysioNet: components of a new research resource for complex physiologic signals. Circulation **101**(23), e215–e220 (2000)
8. Guo, R., Li, H., Zhang, C., Qian, X.: A tree-structure-guided graph convolutional network with contrastive learning for the assessment of parkinsonian hand movements. Med. Image Anal. **81**, 102560 (2022)
9. Hausdorff, J.M., Lowenthal, J., Herman, T., Gruendlinger, L., Peretz, C., Giladi, N.: Rhythmic auditory stimulation modulates gait variability in Parkinson's disease. Eur. J. Neurosci. **26**(8), 2369–2375 (2007)
10. He, K., Fan, H., Wu, Y., Xie, S., Girshick, R.: Momentum contrast for unsupervised visual representation learning. In: Proceedings of the IEEE/CVF Conference on Computer Vision and Pattern Recognition, pp. 9729–9738 (2020)
11. Jaeger, H., Trivedi, D., Stadtschnitzer, M.: Mobile device voice recordings at King's College London (MDVR-KCL) from both early and advanced Parkinson's disease patients and healthy controls. Zenodo (2019)
12. Jia, Z., Wang, Z., Hong, F., Ping, L., Shi, Y., Hu, J.: Learning to learn personalized neural network for ventricular arrhythmias detection on intracardiac EGMs. In: Zhou, Z.H. (ed.) Proceedings of the Thirtieth International Joint Conference on Artificial Intelligence, IJCAI 2021, pp. 2606–2613. International Joint Conferences on Artificial Intelligence Organization (2021). https://doi.org/10.24963/ijcai.2021/359. Main Track
13. Karan, B., Mahto, K., Sahu, S.S.: Detection of Parkinson disease using variational mode decomposition of speech signal. In: 2018 International Conference on Communication and Signal Processing (ICCSP), pp. 0508–0512. IEEE (2018)
14. Khatamino, P., Cantürk, İ., Özyılmaz, L.: A deep learning-CNN based system for medical diagnosis: an application on Parkinson's disease handwriting drawings. In: 2018 6th International Conference on Control Engineering & Information Technology (CEIT), pp. 1–6. IEEE (2018)

15. Li, Y., Zhang, X., Wang, P., Zhang, X., Liu, Y.: Insight into an unsupervised two-step sparse transfer learning algorithm for speech diagnosis of Parkinson's disease. Neural Comput. Appl. **33**, 9733–9750 (2021)
16. Mallela, J., et al.: Voice based classification of patients with amyotrophic lateral sclerosis, Parkinson's disease and healthy controls with CNN-LSTM using transfer learning. In: 2020 IEEE International Conference on Acoustics, Speech and Signal Processing (ICASSP), ICASSP 2020, pp. 6784–6788. IEEE (2020)
17. van den Oord, A., Li, Y., Vinyals, O.: Representation learning with contrastive predictive coding. arXiv preprint arXiv:1807.03748 (2018)
18. Pereira, C.R., et al.: A new computer vision-based approach to aid the diagnosis of Parkinson's disease. Comput. Methods Programs Biomed. **136**, 79–88 (2016)
19. Pereira, C.R., Weber, S.A., Hook, C., Rosa, G.H., Papa, J.P.: Deep learning-aided Parkinson's disease diagnosis from handwritten dynamics. In: 2016 29th SIBGRAPI Conference on Graphics, Patterns and Images (SIBGRAPI), pp. 340–346. IEEE (2016)
20. Radford, A., Metz, L., Chintala, S.: Unsupervised representation learning with deep convolutional generative adversarial networks. arXiv preprint arXiv:1511.06434 (2015)
21. Rovini, E., Fiorini, L., Esposito, D., Maremmani, C., Cavallo, F.: Fine motor assessment with unsupervised learning for personalized rehabilitation in Parkinson disease. In: 2019 IEEE 16th International Conference on Rehabilitation Robotics (ICORR), pp. 1167–1172. IEEE (2019)
22. Soltanieh, S., Etemad, A., Hashemi, J.: Analysis of augmentations for contrastive ECG representation learning. In: 2022 International Joint Conference on Neural Networks (IJCNN), pp. 1–10. IEEE (2022)
23. Suresh, P., Narayanan, N., Pranav, C.V., Vijayaraghavan, V.: End-to-end deep learning for reliable cardiac activity monitoring using seismocardiograms. In: 2020 19th IEEE International Conference on Machine Learning and Applications (ICMLA), pp. 1369–1375 (2020). https://doi.org/10.1109/ICMLA51294.2020.00213
24. Thomas, B., Beal, M.F.: Parkinson's disease. Hum. Mol. Genet. **16**(R2), R183–R194 (2007)
25. Vásquez-Correa, J.C., Arias-Vergara, T., Orozco-Arroyave, J.R., Eskofier, B., Klucken, J., Nöth, E.: Multimodal assessment of Parkinson's disease: a deep learning approach. IEEE J. Biomed. Health Inform. **23**(4), 1618–1630 (2018)
26. Vincent, P., Larochelle, H., Lajoie, I., Bengio, Y., Manzagol, P.A., Bottou, L.: Stacked denoising autoencoders: learning useful representations in a deep network with a local denoising criterion. J. Mach. Learn. Res. **11**(12) (2010)
27. Wang, C., Zhang, J., Liu, S.: Medical ultrasound image segmentation with deep learning models. IEEE Access **11**, 10158–10168 (2023). https://doi.org/10.1109/ACCESS.2022.3225101
28. Wu, Z., Xiong, Y., Yu, S.X., Lin, D.: Unsupervised feature learning via non-parametric instance discrimination. In: Proceedings of the IEEE Conference on Computer Vision and Pattern Recognition, pp. 3733–3742 (2018)
29. Xia, Y., Yao, Z., Ye, Q., Cheng, N.: A dual-modal attention-enhanced deep learning network for quantification of Parkinson's disease characteristics. IEEE Trans. Neural Syst. Rehabil. Eng. **28**(1), 42–51 (2019)
30. Yogev, G., Giladi, N., Peretz, C., Springer, S., Simon, E.S., Hausdorff, J.M.: Dual tasking, gait rhythmicity, and Parkinson's disease: which aspects of gait are attention demanding? Eur. J. Neurosci. **22**(5), 1248–1256 (2005)

31. Zham, P., Kumar, D.K., Dabnichki, P., Poosapadi Arjunan, S., Raghav, S.: Distinguishing different stages of Parkinson's disease using composite index of speed and pen-pressure of sketching a spiral. Front. Neurol. 435 (2017)
32. Zhao, H., Xie, J., Cao, J.: Early detection of Parkinson's disease by unsupervised learning from plantar bend data. In: 2022 IEEE 9th International Conference on Computational Intelligence and Virtual Environments for Measurement Systems and Applications (CIVEMSA), pp. 1–5. IEEE (2022)

BF-Net: A Fine-Grained Network for Identify Bacterial and Fungal Keratitis

Kangyu Lin[1], Jianwei Zhang[1], Xiuying Jiang[3], Jianxin Liu[1],
and Shiyou Zhou[2]([✉])

[1] School of Computer Science and Engineering,
South China University of Technology, Guangzhou 510006, China
[2] State Key Laboratory of Ophthalmology, Zhongshan Ophthalmic Center,
Sun Yat-sen University, Guangdong Provincial Key Laboratory of Ophthalmology
and Visual Science, Guangzhou 510006, China
zhoushiy@mail.sysu.edu.cn
[3] Department of Ophthalmology, Affiliated Foshan Hospital,
Southern Medical University, Foshan 528000, China

Abstract. Infectious keratitis is the leading cause of blindness in the word where bacteria keratitis (BK) and fungi keratitis (FK) are common causes of infection. As an ophthalmic emergency, BK and FK need to be treated correctly as soon as possible to prevent irrecoverable damage to vision, but the early correct diagnosis between them is challenging. Some research have shown that even trained ophthalmologists have less than 80% accuracy in correctly diagnosing FK from BK. In this paper, a Fine-Grained model called BF-Net is proposed to improve the accuracy of automatic diagnosis of keratitis, with consideration of the characteristics of keratitis images. We build a keratitis dataset containing 1433 Slit-Lamp images of BK or FK from 458 patients and conducted detailed experiments to prove the effectiveness of our method. The Precision, Recall, Accuracy, AUC and F1 score of our method are 82.34%, 87.20%, 83.12%, 0.85 and 0.85 respectively, which has achieved the best effect compared with other classification methods. Furthermore, visualization technique Grad-CAM++ is used to provide interpretability for the validity of our model.

Keywords: Infectious keratitis · Deep Learning · Fine-Grained Classification · Metric Learning

1 Introduction

Globally, infectious keratitis is the fifth leading cause of blindness [1], which can be classified as microbial keratitis (bacteria, fungi or parasites), or viral keratitis (herpes viruses) [2]. According to the latest epidemiological data, microbial keratitis (MK) may be epidemic in parts of the world, moreover, bacterial keratitis (BK) and fungal keratitis (FK) are the most common causes of MK [2]. As an ocular emergency, MK may result in sight loss for which the prospect of visual recovery is often poor, therefore the early diagnosis is critical to avoid destructive vision threatening results.

L. Iliadis et al. (Eds.): ICANN 2023, LNCS 14257, pp. 51–62, 2023.
https://doi.org/10.1007/978-3-031-44216-2_5

However, the diagnosis between FK and BK is challenging. Slit-Lamp examination of the ocular surface is widely applied for the diagnosis of MK. In addition, polymerase chain reaction (PCR) tests, in vivo confocal microscopy and clinical features can contribute to the diagnosis of ophthalmologists, while the culture of corneal infiltration is the gold standard for distinguishing BK from FK [3,4]. But the Culture-Based methods, which are Time-Consuming and Labor-Costly, may result in patients missing the optimal duration of treatment and thus lead to impaired vision. Early diagnosis of keratitis depends heavily on the personal experience and clinical knowledge of the diagnostician, while even well trained corneal professionals have more than 30% chance of making mistakes [4]. This aroused researchers' attention about building an automatic diagnosis system for keratitis based on deep learning.

In recent years, deep learning (DL) based artificial intelligence (AI) has shown amazing power in the field of image processing. In the past few years, DL has been applied to diagnostic tasks related to ocular. Given the strong capability exhibited by DL in medical diagnosis task, AI appears to be an excellent tool to aid disease diagnosis, especially in places where medical resources are poor. Recently, several studies have probed the possibility of automated diagnosis of keratitis. Kuo et al. [5] used DenseNet [6] to automatically recognize FK from the cornea photos, with an average accuracy of about 70% in five-fold cross validation. Xu et al. [7] proposed a deep learning model base on Sequential-Level to effectively differentiate infectious keratitis by manually segmenting the infectious regions of Slit-Lamp images. But the manual segmentation of corneal areas is a Time-Consuming task. Hung et al. [5] using 1330 Slit-Lamp images from 580 patients to construct a deep learning algorithm, which consists of a segmentation model for detecting areas rich in information and a classification model, with an accurate of 80%. Mayya et al. [8] proposed a model called MS-CNN for accurate segmentation of the corneal region. Their method achieved 88.96% accuracy on the dataset containing 540 keratitis images.

The researches mentioned above proves that getting more accurate diseased areas through image segmentation is helpful to improve the performance of classification diagnosis of keratitis. However, training a segmentation model requires manual annotation, which is Low-Efficient and Labor-Intensive. Different from this two-stage strategy combining segmentation and classification, we propose a Fine-Grained classification model called BF-Net by reason of the characteristics of keratitis. The experimental results show that our method has better performance in the classification of keratitis compared to other classification methods.

2   Materials and Methods

In this section, we introduce the dataset used in this study and a Fine-Grained network (see Fig. 2) for keratitis classification using Slit-Lamp images. In Sect. 2.1 and 2.2, we introduce the dataset and the process of image preprocessing. Then the difficulties of this classification task summarized by the characteristics of keratitis images are described in Sect. 2.3. Finally, we introduce the overall architecture of the proposed BF-Net in Sect. 2.4.

2.1 Images Collection

We obtained a Slit-Lamp images dataset of FK and BK keratitis infection provided by the Zhongshan Ophthalmic Center at Sun Yat-sen University. Furthermore, for fairness, only up to five images per patient can be retained in the dataset. After filtering, our dataset contains 1433 images. Among them, 666 images (201 patients) were marked as BK and 767 images (257 patients) were labeled as FK. All samples have been diagnosed by professional corneal doctors and ensure that only one corneal infection is affected (BK or FK). The collected dataset was divided into five equally in order to perform Five-Fold Cross-Valid. The specific distribution of data is shown in Table 1. Each time, one of them is used as the verification set, and the rest is used as the training set.

Table 1. The data are divided into five parts on average.

Dataset	BK (patients#)	BK (images)	FK (patients#)	FK (images)	Total (images)
part1	41	127	52	156	283
part2	40	132	52	152	284
part3	40	144	51	145	289
part4	40	124	51	155	279
part5	40	139	51	159	298

2.2 Data Preprocessing and Augmentation

These images are processed into an appropriate format before being input to the classification network. All pictures were filled into squares and then resized to $3 \times 512 \times 512$. When training the model, some methods are used for image augmentation, including vertical and horizontal flipping, random brightness and saturation adjustment, Random Erasing [9] and cropping ($3 \times 448 \times 448$). Moreover, considering that the diseased area is generally near the image center, we have the alternative of random cropping or center cropping during training, where the former is to enhance sample diversity, and the latter can retain useful information at the maximum range. Furthermore, in the testing, only center cropping is used. Finally, we normalized and standardized images which can make the model converge rapidly and the distribution of input data is more uniform,

$$x = \frac{x/255 - \mu}{\sigma} \qquad (1)$$

where $x \in R^{3 \times 448 \times 448}$ represents the pixel value of the image, $\mu \in R^3$, $\sigma \in R^3$ denotes the mean value, standard deviation on each channel of the images respectively. In practice, we used the and calculated by a large dataset ImageNet [10].

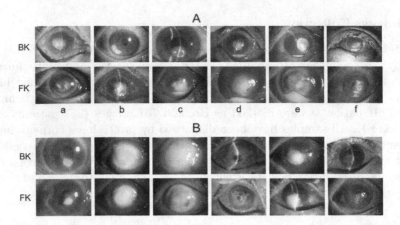

Fig. 1. Examples of BK and FK in the dataset. (A) There are some differences between FK and BK. The ulcer margin of BK is usually continuous while that of FK is rough (see a–c). Hypopyon may occur in various pathogenic keratitis. The plane of hypopyon of FK may be convex or horizontal while that of BK may be horizontal as shown in d–f; (B) Some samples with high intra class and low inter class variance problems in the dataset. It is difficult to find the characteristics that can distinguish these samples.

2.3   Difficulties in Classifying BK and FK

We carefully observed the characteristics of images in our dataset. For the classification of keratitis, we must solve the following three key problems. To begin with, the biggest problem is the large Intra-class gap and the small Inter-class gap between FK and BK. In most cases, FK and BK have some differences in clinical symptoms as shown in Fig. 1A, but this is not absolute. As we can see from Fig. 1B, there are no obvious difference between BK and FK, but the symptoms are very different in the same infectious disease. It is difficult for even ophthalmologists to distinguish these pictures correctly. In the second place, region of infection difficult to be localized. The complex backgrounds and tiny ulcer areas in keratitis images make neural network difficult to capture these important areas. And the presence of noise in the image due to the Slit-Lamp also increases the difficulty of classification. Finally, data is one of the keys to the success of deep learning algorithm [11]. However, data on keratitis are difficult to collect. We have tried our best to collect data from the eye center of Sun Yat sen University which is one of the largest eye centers in China, but the data is still insufficient. Therefore, the Over-fitting [12] caused by the limited data is also one of the problems to be solved.

The methods proposed in this paper are dedicated to solving these problems. More details will be provided in Sect. 2.4.

2.4   Network Architecture

The whole network architecture of our method is shown in Fig. 2. This model consists of two sub-modules: a feature extractor called SERes50 and a fine-

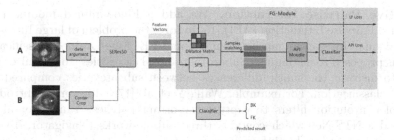

Fig. 2. BF-Net architecture used for classify BK from FK based on Slit-Lamp image. (A) Training process of BF-Net; (B) Testing process of BF-Net.

grained module (FG-Module) which includes three parts: API, LS Loss and SPS. FG-Module is the most important part of our method which is proposed to learn Fine-Grained features to distinguish highly similar samples. We first introduce the meanings of some variables. SERes50 is described in further detail ensued. Next, we provide detailed description for the Sub-components of FG-Module. A brief description of the differences between training and testing is introduced in last.

Problem Definition. Given a dataset $D = \{(x_i, y_i)\}_{i=1}^{n}$, where n is the number of samples, x_i and y_i denote Slit-Lamp image after data augmentation and One-Hot label vector respectively. If x_i belongs to BK, $y_i = [1, 0]^T$; when x_i belongs to FK, $y_i = [0, 1]^T$. For each image x_i, we use SERes50 to obtain a t-dimensional feature vector f_i. $S \in R^{(m \times m)}$ is a matrix used to represent the distance (or similarity) in a batch, where m refers to the number of samples for each batch and $S_{ij} = \|f_i - f_j\|_2$ denotes the similarity between sample x_i and x_j. Finally, we use $p_i \in R^2$ to represent the final classification results.

The Architecture of SERes50. Attention mechanism, which is inspired by the fact that human beings can focus on important regions in complex backgrounds, is used to locate information of interest and suppress useless information. In practice, we apply SE Block proposed by SENet [13] to accurately distinguish the lesion location in the complex background as much as possible. It is an implementation of channel attention mechanism which can explicitly model the interdependence between feature channels and give different weights to channels. We insert a SE Block after the last convolution layer of ResNet50 [14] to form our feature extractor SERes50. The input of SERes50 is x_i, and the output is a feature vector which can be expressed as follow:

$$f_i = g(x_i) \tag{2}$$

where $g(x_i)$ is a function that maps x from the original space to the feature space.

Attentive Pairwise Interaction. We add a Fine-Grained module called Attentive Pairwise Interaction (API) [15] to solve the problem of large Intra-class gap and small Inter-class gap between BK and FK. Fine-Grained classification, which is proposed to distinguish Subordinate-Level categories [16], requires more effort to discover the subtle differences between subcategories compared with general classification. For example, Wang Y et al. [17] additionally introduced a set of convolution filters to capture important patches. Yang Z et al. [18] proposed a NTS-Net which contains three Sub-networks (Navigator, Teacher, Scrutinizer) to find highly informative regions.

API is introduced into our methods to solve the identification problem between highly similar samples, it accepts a pair of inputs then through progressive comparison to identify them based on the fact that when humans distinguish highly similar images, they will put them together for comparison. The specific details can be seen in the original paper [15] because we haven't made any changes to it. For convenience, we use L_{api} to represent the total loss caused by the API module while it contains two parts (L_{rk} and L_{ce}) actually. By optimizing L_{api}, our network can find some features which is contributed to the classification results and give them priority which is helpful to discover the subtle differences between different classes.

Lifted Structured Feature Learning. Not only Fine-Grained classification but also metric learning is applied to solve the problem of high Intra-class and low Inter-class variance between BK and FK. Considering the relationship between classes and within classes, we add Lifted Structured (LS) Loss [19] to the training. LS Loss, which was first proposed in the field of deep metric learning [20], is aim at making the distance between each sample in this positive sample pair and all other negative samples greater than the given threshold, where positive, negative sample pair means that this pair of samples belongs to the same, different category respectively. LS Loss can make use of the information in a batch because it considers all the paired distances,

$$L_{i,j} = log(\sum_{(i,k)\in N} exp\{\alpha - S_{i,k}\} + \sum_{(j,l)\in N} exp\{\alpha - S_{j,l}\} + S_{(i,j)}) \qquad (3)$$

$$L_{ls} = \frac{1}{2|P|} \sum_{(i,j)\in P} max(0, L_{i,j}) \qquad (4)$$

where P, N denotes the set of positive, negative pairs in a batch respectively. When $L_{l,s}$ is minimized, the distance of Intra-class samples will be smaller and the distance of Inter-class samples will be larger.

Stochastic Partial Swap. Stochastic Partial Swap (SPS) [21] is added to solve the problem of Over-fitting. The design principle of SPS is similar to Dropout [22]. But the difference between them is that dropout uses manually designed noise to replace some elements in the features while SPS randomly exchange some elements between all samples in a batch. SPS can enhance the robustness of the model by expanding the diversity of input samples. For example, when SPS occurs within intra class, the classifier can see more combinations of class patterns. On the contrary, when SPS occurs between classes, it can simulate noise samples with other classes of patterns. This noise is more consistent with real world noise because it comes from other real samples.

Training and Testing. The training process of BF-Net is shown in Fig. 2A. We train the model efficiently by optimizing L_{total} consists of L_{api} and L_{ls}.

It should be noted that during the training period, the FG-Module can summarize the comparison clues of a pair of images, gradually improving the SERes50's ability to extract individual image representations. Therefore, in the testing phase, one can simply unload FG-Module for single-input test image, without much loss of generalization. Expressed as:

$$p_i = f_c(g(x_i)) \tag{5}$$

where f_c represents a classifier, which is essentially a full-connection layer. So our method has similar computational complexity to ResNet50 during testing.

3   Experimental Results

In this Section, we describe our experiments to evaluate the effectiveness of the proposed methods. We first introduce the experimental setup for infectious keratitis classification. Then we introduce the metrics used to evaluate the performance of the model. Finally, we compare our method with some existing methods.

3.1   Experiment Setup

Our project was running on Ubuntu OS with NVIDIA TiTan X GPU. For the implementation and training of the BF-Net, we employed Python 3.6.13 with the PyTorch 1.6.0. We used the standard SGD (momentum = 0.9, weight decay = 0.05) to update the weights of the network. The batch size is set to 8, taking four samples from each of the two categories and the model is trained for 80 epochs. We use 0.0001 as the initial learning rate in this paper except EfficientNet (0.001). The parameters of API and LS Loss are consistent with the original paper [15,19]. For each batch, we performed 0–4 SPS operations randomly, in which the proportion of swapped elements is 0.0–0.2.

3.2   Evaluation Metrics

Some standard metrics were used for validating the proposed approach, including Precision, Recall, Accuracy, AUC and F1 score. Note that the metrics we ultimately used were the mean and standard values based on Five-Fold cross validation. Precision indicates the proportion of true positive samples among the predicted positive samples and Recall denotes the probability of being predicted as positive in positive samples. Accuracy refers to the proportion of correctly classified samples by the classifier to the total number samples. F1 score is viewed as a harmonic mean of model precision and recall. The AUC is defined as the area under the ROC (receiver operating characteristic) curve. The metrics are defined as follows:

$$Accuracy = \frac{TP + FP}{TP + TN + FP + FN} \tag{6}$$

$$Precision = \frac{TP}{TP + FP}; Recall = \frac{TP}{TP + FN} \tag{7}$$

$$F_1 = \frac{2 \times Precision \times Recall}{Precision + recall} \tag{8}$$

where TP and TN represent the correctly predicted numbers of FK and BK respectively. FP represents the number of BK wrongly classified as FK; FN denotes the numbers of FK wrongly classified as BK.

3.3   Performances of Different Models

We compare our method with some general classification models [6,14,23–27]. Besides, we also make a comparison with several excellent Fine-Grained classification model in recent years [15,18,28]. Notably, all general models and the backbone of fine-grained model were pre-trained with ImageNet [10]. Table 2 lists the experimental results of our method and the models mentioned above. It is obvious from Table 2 that the proposed BF-Net achieved the state-of-the-art result as it achieves the highest mean in all indicators while maintaining a relatively small variance. The Precision, Recall, Accuracy, F1 score of our proposed BF-NET is 82.34%, 87.20%, 83.15%, 0.85, outperformed the second place by a margin of 1.04%, 0.80%, 1.95%, 0.02, but there is no obvious gap in AUC of all models. Compared to general models, Fine-Grained models achieved better results but they have more parameters and require more computation. Furthermore, according to Table 2, Our BF-Net is superior to ResNet50 in all aspects although the complexity and computation of our model is similar to ResNet50.

The dominant classification areas decided by the model to identify BK from FK are visualized using Grad-CAM++ [29]. Figure 3 shows the Grad-CAM++ visualization for the correctly classified images. It is patently obvious that our model is more accurate in locating the lesion area.

3.4   Ablation Study

We performed an ablation study to probe into the contribution of various independent modules in the FG-Module. The accuracy obtained from Five-Fold was used as a standard for comparison. API, SPS, LSLoss were used for ablation

Table 2. Classification results of different classification models.

Method	Param. (M)	FLOPs (G)	Mean values ± Standard values				
			Precision	Recall	Accuracy	AUC	F1
Resnet18* [14]	11.2	7.3	80.39±0.51	85.01±2.03	80.89±0.69	0.84±0.015	0.83±0.010
Resnet50* [14]	23.5	16.6	80.38±1.84	84.90±1.92	80.82±1.27	0.84±0.019	0.83±0.013
DenseNet121* [6]	7.0	11.6	80.01±1.95	85.22±3.42	80.60±1.20	0.85±0.023	0.82±0.010
DenseNet121* [6]	12.5	13.8	80.10±2.23	86.00±4.23	80.96±0.93	0.85±0.020	0.83±0.010
MobileNetV2* [24]	2.2	1.3	77.68±1.37	**87.21±2.96**	79.70±1.29	0.85±0.017	0.82±0.011
GoogLeNet* [25]	13.0	6.1	79.28±1.13	85.60±3.66	80.35±1.41	0.85±0.012	0.82±0.019
EfficientNet_b0 [23]	4.0	1.68	80.42±1.73	82.82±1.80	79.99±1.14	0.84±0.032	0.82±0.010
EfficientNet_b4 [23]	17.6	6.37	79.94±2.79	84.59±4.07	80.27±1.07	0.85±0.018	0.82±0.013
SwinT_t [26]	27.5	18.0	69.51±1.61	72.48±5.48	68.28±3.20	0.73±0.039	0.71±0.034
ConNeXt_t [27]	27.8	17.9	66.14±1.93	69.14±4.91	64.51±2.90	0.66±0.030	0.68±0.029
API-Net [15] (ResNet101*)	45.7	31.5	80.58±0.96	85.37±1.68	81.14±0.79	0.85±0.020	0.83±0.007
WS-DAN [28] (ResNet50*)	23.7	33.2	80.30±2.90	86.40±6.13	81.17±1.30	0.85±0.020	0.83±0.017
NTS-Net [18] (ResNet50*)	26.2	16.6	81.30±3.05	84.15±3.84	81.05±2.10	0.85±0.029	0.83±0.019
BF-Net (ResNet50*)	27.2	16.6	**82.34±1.29**	87.20±1.00	**83.12±0.96**	0.85±0.027	**0.85±0.008**

We use * to represent that the pre-trained weights of the model are provided by the torchvision toolkit, and the rest of the model pre-trained weights are provided by the original paper.

experiment, all results are summarized in the Table 3. In addition, we also compared the performance of SPS and Dropout. From the experimental results, we can see that each part has contributed to the improvement of classification effect.

Table 3. Ablation study of our proposed method.

Method	API	SPS	LSLoss	Mean Accuracy (%)
SERes50				81.67
SERes50+API	✓			82.23
SERes50+SPS		✓		82.16
SERes50+LSLoss			✓	81.82
SERes50+API+SPS	✓	✓		81.67
SERes50+API+LSLoss	✓		✓	82.14
SERes50+SPS+LSLoss		✓	✓	82.30
SERes50+API+SPS/Dropout+LSLoss	✓	✓	✓	83.12/82.84

4   Discussion

Overall, our work establishes a Fine-Grained model called BF-Net to identify BK and FK. Furthermore, our method only uses Slit-Lamp images, with an average accuracy of 83.12%. As far as I know, this work is the first to apply Fine-Grained classification algorithm to the diagnosis of keratitis. Compared with other existing work, we have achieved better classification results while maintaining efficiency. For example, Kuo et al. [30] developed a DenseNet to automatically recognize FK from the photo while BF-Net performs better than DenseNet in our dataset (refer to Table 2). At the same time, we save time in making labels and training segmentation models, when compared with those methods containing segmentation.

But how to accurately classify BK and FK is a challenging task not only for ophthalmologists, but also for depth learning algorithms. Even though our proposed method has certain advantages over other classification methods, it still cannot achieve very satisfactory results. So this work on automatic diagnosis of keratitis has a long way to go before it can be truly applied. First, the data we collected is not enough to represent the actual data, which may lead to insufficient generalization of the trained model in practical applications. Second, only Slit-Lamp images are used for diagnosis in our study while the patient's medical history is also important supplementary information. Finally, our work is just to classify BK and FK while infectious keratitis also includes parasitic keratitis and viral keratitis. In the future, we will try to collect a dataset containing multiple categories of keratitis, and then build a multi category keratitis classification system to make this work more practical.

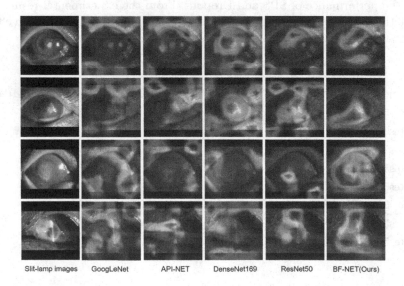

Fig. 3. Sample Grad-CAM++ visualizations generated by the models that correctly classified bacterial keratitis from fungal keratitis.

5   Conclusion

Early correct diagnosis of MK is crucial for patients with keratitis and can avoid visual impairment. In this work, we proposed a Fine-Grained model called BF-Net to classify BK from FK only using Slit-Lamp images. The experimental results proved that our method performed relatively well in terms of performance. The lower variance of experimental metrics proved that our model has better generalization ability. In addition, the visualization technology Grad cam++ also provide interpretability for our model. The proposed pipeline can be used as an auxiliary tool for early diagnosis. It can also combine other medical data, such as medical history, to improve the diagnostic accuracy and provide a core framework for building a complete keratitis diagnosis system.

References

1. Cabrera-Aguas, M., Khoo, P., Watson, S.L.: Infectious keratitis: a review. Clin. Exp. Ophthalmol. **50**(5), 543–562 (2022)
2. Durand, M.L., Barshak, M.B., Chodosh, J.: Infectious keratitis in 2021. JAMA **326**(13), 1319–1320 (2021)
3. Ibrahim, Y.W., Boase, D.L., Cree, I.A.: Epidemiological characteristics, predisposing factors and microbiological profiles of infectious corneal ulcers: the portsmouth corneal ulcer study. Br. J. Ophthalmol. **93**(10), 1319–1324 (2009)
4. Dalmon, C., et al.: The clinical differentiation of bacterial and fungal keratitis: a photographic survey. Invest. Ophthalmol. Vis. Sci. **53**(4), 1787–1791 (2012)
5. Hung, N., et al.: Using slit-lamp images for deep learning-based identification of bacterial and fungal keratitis: model development and validation with different convolutional neural networks. Diagnostics **11**(7), 1246 (2021)
6. Huang, G., Liu, Z., Van Der Maaten, L., Weinberger, K.Q.: Densely connected convolutional networks. In: Proceedings of the IEEE Conference on Computer Vision and Pattern Recognition, pp. 4700–4708 (2017)
7. Xu, Y., et al.: Deep sequential feature learning in clinical image classification of infectious keratitis. Engineering **7**(7), 1002–1010 (2021)
8. Mayya, V., Kamath Shevgoor, S., Kulkarni, U., Hazarika, M., Barua, P.D., Acharya, U.R.: Multi-scale convolutional neural network for accurate corneal segmentation in early detection of fungal keratitis. J. Fungi **7**(10), 850 (2021)
9. Zhong, Z., Zheng, L., Kang, G., Li, S., Yang, Y.: Random erasing data augmentation. In: Proceedings of the AAAI Conference on Artificial Intelligence, vol. 34, pp. 13001–13008 (2020)
10. Deng, J., Dong, W., Socher, R., Li, L.J., Li, K., Fei-Fei, L.: ImageNet: a large-scale hierarchical image database. In: 2009 IEEE Conference on Computer Vision and Pattern Recognition, pp. 248–255. IEEE (2009)
11. Sun, C., Shrivastava, A., Singh, S., Gupta, A.: Revisiting unreasonable effectiveness of data in deep learning era. In: Proceedings of the IEEE International Conference on Computer Vision, pp. 843–852 (2017)
12. Ying, X.: An overview of overfitting and its solutions. In: Journal of Physics: Conference Series, vol. 1168, p. 022022. IOP Publishing (2019)
13. Hu, J., Shen, L., Sun, G.: Squeeze-and-excitation networks. In: Proceedings of the IEEE Conference on Computer Vision and Pattern Recognition, pp. 7132–7141 (2018)

14. He, K., Zhang, X., Ren, S., Sun, J.: Deep residual learning for image recognition. In: Proceedings of the IEEE Conference on Computer Vision and Pattern Recognition, pp. 770–778 (2016)
15. Zhuang, P., Wang, Y., Qiao, Y.: Learning attentive pairwise interaction for fine-grained classification. In: Proceedings of the AAAI Conference on Artificial Intelligence, vol. 34, pp. 13130–13137 (2020)
16. Zhao, B., Feng, J., Wu, X., Yan, S.: A survey on deep learning-based fine-grained object classification and semantic segmentation. Int. J. Autom. Comput. **14**(2), 119–135 (2017)
17. Wang, Y., Morariu, V.I., Davis, L.S.: Learning a discriminative filter bank within a CNN for fine-grained recognition. In: Proceedings of the IEEE Conference on Computer Vision and Pattern Recognition, pp. 4148–4157 (2018)
18. Yang, Z., Luo, T., Wang, D., Hu, Z., Gao, J., Wang, L.: Learning to navigate for fine-grained classification. In: Proceedings of the European Conference on Computer Vision (ECCV), pp. 420–435 (2018)
19. Oh Song, H., Xiang, Y., Jegelka, S., Savarese, S.: Deep metric learning via lifted structured feature embedding. In: Proceedings of the IEEE Conference on Computer Vision and Pattern Recognition, pp. 4004–4012 (2016)
20. Kaya, M., Bilge, H.Ş: Deep metric learning: a survey. Symmetry **11**(9), 1066 (2019)
21. Huang, S., Wang, X., Tao, D.: Stochastic partial swap: enhanced model generalization and interpretability for fine-grained recognition. In: Proceedings of the IEEE/CVF International Conference on Computer Vision, pp. 620–629 (2021)
22. Srivastava, N., Hinton, G., Krizhevsky, A., Sutskever, I., Salakhutdinov, R.: Dropout: a simple way to prevent neural networks from overfitting. J. Mach. Learn. Res. **15**(1), 1929–1958 (2014)
23. Tan, M., Le, Q.: EfficientNet: rethinking model scaling for convolutional neural networks. In: International Conference on Machine Learning, pp. 6105–6114. PMLR (2019)
24. Sandler, M., Howard, A., Zhu, M., Zhmoginov, A., Chen, L.C.: MobileNetv 2: inverted residuals and linear bottlenecks. In: Proceedings of the IEEE Conference on Computer Vision and Pattern Recognition, pp. 4510–4520 (2018)
25. Szegedy, C., et al.: Going deeper with convolutions. In: Proceedings of the IEEE Computer Society Conference on Computer Vision and Pattern Recognition (2015)
26. Liu, Z., et al.: Swin transformer: hierarchical vision transformer using shifted windows. In: Proceedings of the IEEE/CVF International Conference on Computer Vision, pp. 10012–10022 (2021)
27. Liu, Z., Mao, H., Wu, C.Y., Feichtenhofer, C., Darrell, T., Xie, S.: A convnet for the 2020s. In: Proceedings of the IEEE/CVF Conference on Computer Vision and Pattern Recognition, pp. 11976–11986 (2022)
28. Hu, T., Qi, H., Huang, Q., Lu, Y.: See better before looking closer: weakly supervised data augmentation network for fine-grained visual classification. arXiv preprint arXiv:1901.09891 (2019)
29. Chattopadhay, A., Sarkar, A., Howlader, P., Balasubramanian, V.N.: Grad-CAM++: generalized gradient-based visual explanations for deep convolutional networks. In: 2018 IEEE Winter Conference on Applications of Computer Vision (WACV), pp. 839–847. IEEE (2018)
30. Kuo, M.T., et al.: A deep learning approach in diagnosing fungal keratitis based on corneal photographs. Sci. Rep. **10**(1), 14424 (2020)

Bilateral Mammogram Mass Detection Based on Window Cross Attention

Hua Yuan, YiMao Yan[✉], and Shoubin Dong

School of Computer Science and Engineering, Guangdong Provincial Key Laboratory
of Communication and Computer Network, South China University of Technology,
Guangzhou 510006, China
202121045675@mail.scut.edu.cn

Abstract. Breast cancer is the most common cancer in the world. Mammogram mass detection aids in the early detection of breast cancer and increases patient survival rates. Because the bilateral breasts of the same patient are similar and symmetrical, information fusion of bilateral mammogram images is advantageous in improving the detection rate of masses. However, existing mass detection methods use pixel-level corresponding feature fusion methods, which are sensitive to image registration errors. In this paper, we propose WCA-RCNN, a novel mass detection framework that uses window cross attention to fuse information from bilateral mammogram images. The window cross attention module eliminates pixel-level correspondence and significantly improves mass detection accuracy. In addition, we propose a mass deformation data augmentation method to address the issue of insufficient mass samples. We evaluate the proposed method on the publicly available mammography dataset DDSM, demonstrating that it outperforms state-of-the-art mass detection methods.

Keywords: Mammography · Mass detection · Cross attention · Data Augment

1 Introduction

Breast cancer has become the leading cause of death among women [4, 29, 30]. Early detection and treatment can significantly improve the survival rate of patients. Mammography, which generates multiple mammogram images for the same patient, is considered the most effective mass detection method [12]. Breast mass is a common symptom of breast cancer, but detecting it is difficult for professional radiologists because the mass in mammogram images has low contrast and looks similar to normal breast tissue [3, 7]. As a result, the automated mass detection method can aid radiologists in diagnosis by increasing the detection rate and decreasing the false positive rate, which has significant application value.

This work is supported by the National Natural Science Foundation of China General Program 61976239.

Despite the fact that mass detection methods have been developed for many years, most methods only consider information from a single breast, ignoring radiologists' clinical experience in comparing bilateral mammogram images. A few methods emphasize the significance of multi-view information, but they use a simple feature concatenation method that cannot effectively fuse information from bilateral mammogram images. In light of Transformer's [31] outstanding performance on multimodal tasks and relation modeling tasks [11], we considered applying cross attention to the replace simple feature concatenation method. However, due to the high resolution of pixels in images, the attention mechanism introduces unaffordable computation. Given that bilateral mammogram images are symmetrical and have a natural region-level correspondence, we solve the problem by fusing regional features instead of global features. We propose a mass detection framework WCA-RCNN with an excellent performance by replacing the pixel-level corresponding feature fusion method with a novel window cross attention module.

Our method differs from previous bilateral mammogram mass detection methods in that we fuse bilateral mammogram image features using a novel window cross attention module. To the best of our knowledge, this is the first bilateral mammogram mass detection framework to exploit attention to improve the accuracy of mass detection. In addition, we propose a mass deformation data augmentation method to deal with the problem of insufficient mass samples. Experimental results on the public mammography dataset DDSM [10] demonstrate that the proposed method outperforms existing bilateral mammogram mass detection methods.

2   Related Works

Mass detection methods can be roughly divided into the traditional detection method and the deep learning-based detection method. Traditional detection methods are typically limited to shallow features such as mass shape and edge. Although the calculation speed is fast, shallow features struggle to represent masses of varying sizes and shapes. Deep learning has advanced rapidly in recent years, making significant contributions to the field of medical image analysis [16, 33]. Various object detection methods have been used for mass detection [1,2,6, 13]. However, these methods are mostly based on unilateral mammogram images, ignoring the relationship between bilateral mammogram images and limiting mass detection rate improvement.

The similarity and symmetry of the same patient's bilateral breasts can be used to screen out false positives and improve the detection rate. In recent years, mass detection methods that take into account bilateral mammogram images have gradually gained traction. For example, Liu et al. [20] proposed a mass detection framework CBN based on Mask RCNN [8] and designed a logic guided bilateral module based on radiologists' domain knowledge to fuse information from bilateral mammogram images. CBN replaces image feature fusion with ROI (region of interest) feature fusion to reduce the impact of the systematic error caused by image registration. However, this method ignores image information from non-ROI regions and relies on ROI quality. Since image registration errors have a significant impact on performance, some researchers have improved the image registration method. Li et al. [14] thought that the rigid transformation was too simple to represent the deformation state of the squeezed breast, so they used threshold segmentation to obtain the binary image of bilateral breasts, and trained a fully convolutional neural network [22] to learn the space transformation to implement the alignment of bilateral mammogram images. Yang et al. [32] first detected and aligned the nipple positions of bilateral mammogram images, and then performed affine transformation on the auxiliary view based on the breast contour of the main view. Furthermore, some researchers are not limited to the improvement of image registration methods. For example, Liu et al. [19] used a multi-scale kernel pooling module to aggregate the spatial information, which improves the model's tolerance to image registration errors.

Although these methods have improved in image registration and other modules, they still rely on pixel-level corresponding feature fusion methods like feature concatenation and feature subtraction based on channel dimensions. These pixel-level corresponding feature fusion methods are sensitive to image registration error, which causes these methods to extract and fuse information from bilateral mammogram images ineffectively.

3   Proposed Method

3.1   Mass Detection Framework WCA-RCNN

Our detection framework WCA-RCNN is based on Faster RCNN [26] and contains a novel window cross attention module. As shown in Fig. 1, firstly, the features of the main view and the auxiliary view are extracted through the weight-shared backbone. Then, the bilateral mammogram image features are fused by the window cross attention module, and the enhanced feature of the main view is output. Finally, the detection result is obtained via the RPN (region proposal network) module and the detection heads.

3.2   Image Pre-processing

The images must be preprocessed before being fed into the network in order to reduce noise in the original mammogram image and roughly align the bilateral mammogram images. Pre-processing consists primarily of three steps: removal of background information, extraction of breast regions, and image alignment. First, the breast is separated from the background using OTSU threshold segmentation [24], which removes irrelevant text information and reduces interference factors. Second, the breast mask obtained through threshold segmentation is used to crop the minimum rectangular area containing the breast. This step can reduce the computation cost by removing the redundant black background. Finally, to achieve a rough alignment of the bilateral mammogram images, the auxiliary view is flipped horizontally and scaled to the same size as the main view.

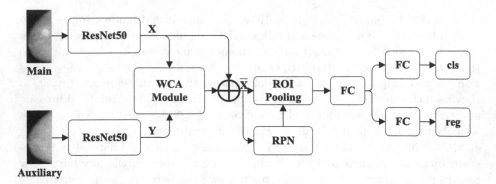

Fig. 1. The architecture of our WCA-RCNN framework.

3.3   Window Cross Attention Module

The window cross attention module is designed to efficiently fuse information from bilateral mammogram images. Existing bilateral mammogram image fusion methods use feature concatenation or feature subtraction, which are pixel-level correspondence fusion methods. However, due to the inherent differences in bilateral breasts, pixel-level alignment cannot be achieved and the improvement of mass detection accuracy is limited. To avoid the one-to-one pixel-level correspondence, we considered using the attention mechanism to connect all pixels in bilateral mammogram image features. The problem is that the computational complexity of this method is unaffordable. But is it necessary to connect all pixels? Bilateral breasts have a certain similarity and symmetry, which means that bilateral mammogram images have a natural region-level correspondence. Therefore, we only need to connect all pixels in the corresponding area, and pixels that are far away don't need to be connected. Inspired by Swin Transformer [21], we divide bilateral mammogram image features into windows of the same size and use cross attention to fuse the corresponding window information. In this way, the huge amount of calculation is reduced and the information of bilateral mammogram images is effectively fused.

As shown in Fig. 1, the window cross attention module takes the main view feature $\mathbf{X} \in \mathbf{R}^{W \times H \times C}$ and auxiliary view feature $\mathbf{Y} \in \mathbf{R}^{W \times H \times C}$ as input, and outputs the enhanced main view feature $\overline{\mathbf{X}} \in \mathbf{R}^{W \times H \times C}$, where W and H represent the height and width of the feature, respectively, and C represents the channel dimension. Before fusion, the features of the main view and the auxiliary view will be divided into equal-sized and disjoint windows. The feature of a single window in the main view can be expressed as $\mathbf{X_w} \in \mathbf{R}^{S^2 \times C}$, and the feature of a single window in the auxiliary view can be expressed as $\mathbf{Y_w} \in \mathbf{R}^{S^2 \times C}$, where S represents the side length of the window. Subsequently, the pairwise window features at the corresponding positions of the main view and the auxiliary view will be fused by cross attention, and the fused window features will be recombined into a complete main view feature. The feature dimension of the main view remains unchanged before and after enhancement.

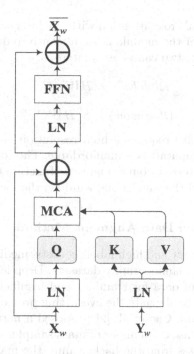

Fig. 2. Fusion block based on cross attention.

The fusion module is shown in Fig. 2, and the calculation process can be expressed as:

$$\overline{\mathbf{X_w}} = Attention(Q, K, V) + \mathbf{X_w} \qquad (1)$$

$$\overline{\mathbf{X_w}} = FFN(LN(\overline{\mathbf{X_w}})) + \overline{\mathbf{X_w}} \qquad (2)$$

where LN represents layer normalization, which can improve the stability of model training; FFN represents a feed-forward neural network, which consists of two layers of fully connected layers and activation function GELU to form a nonlinear operation to improve expression ability; MCA represents multi-head cross attention. Specifically, the window feature of the main view will generate the Query of the attention mechanism through the fully connected layer, which can be expressed as $Q \in \mathbf{R}^{S^2 \times C}$, and the window feature of the auxiliary view will generate the corresponding Key and Value, which can be expressed as $K \in \mathbf{R}^{S^2 \times C}$ and $V \in \mathbf{R}^{S^2 \times C}$, respectively. Then, the generated Query, Key, and Value will be calculated for attention:

$$Attention(Q, K, V) = softmax(\frac{QK^T}{\sqrt{C}} + P)V \qquad (3)$$

Considering that the pixels between the two windows have a similar position relationship, the relative position encoding P in the attention calculation is retained, which is the same as Swin Transformer.

By replacing the global cross attention with the inter-window cross attention, the calculation amount of the module is significantly reduced, and the computational complexity of the two can be estimated as:

$$\Omega(global) = (HW)^2C \tag{4}$$

$$\Omega(window) = S^2HWC \tag{5}$$

The object detection model requires a high resolution of the input image, and global cross attention computation is unaffordable. The computational complexity can be effectively converted from a quadratic function to a linear function by dividing the window, and the smaller the window, the lower the complexity.

3.4 Mass Deformation Data Augment Method

Due to issues such as privacy and high labeling costs, medical image datasets are usually small, and so are mammography datasets. Deep learning-based methods rely on a large amount of data for training, and insufficient data will have an impact on performance. To alleviate the overfitting problem that may be caused by a small amount of data, Cao et al. [2] proposed a natural deformation data augment method to increase the number of mass samples. However, because this method separates the mass from the background, the mass after data augment has an unnatural edge that must be smoothed by an image restoration algorithm. The proposed mass deformation data augmentation method utilizes the elastic deformation operation [27] to generate new mass samples simply and naturally. The method flow is shown in Fig. 3. First, the displacement in horizontal and vertical directions is generated for each pixel in the mass area according to the mass mask. The displacement fields Δx and Δy are between $-\alpha$ and α, where α is a coefficient controlling the degree of deformation. Then, a Gaussian of standard deviation σ is used to smooth the displacement matrix, so that close pixels have similar displacement. The visual displacement matrix is shown in Fig. 3(c). Finally, the displacement fields are applied to move each pixel to a new position, and the pixel values at integer coordinates are obtained by bilinear interpolation. From Fig. 3(e), it can be seen intuitively that the deformed mass is natural and has no separation from the background. A new mass sample is generated by simulating the natural changes of the mass while maintaining sample quality.

4   Experiments

4.1   Experimental Setup

Dataset. The experiment is conducted on the public mammography dataset DDSM (Digital Database for Screening Mammography). Other datasets such as INBreast [23], MIAS [28], etc. are not used, because these datasets are too small to evaluate the effectiveness of the model [18]. DDSM contains information on

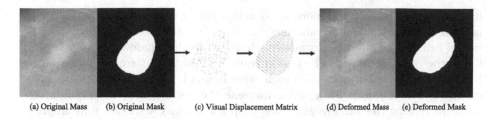

(a) Original Mass   (b) Original Mask   (c) Visual Displacement Matrix   (d) Deformed Mass   (e) Deformed Mask

Fig. 3. Flow chart of mass deformation.

2620 patient cases, and each case contains 4 breast images (two for the left breast and two for the right breast). After removing incomplete or damaged data, a total of 2580 cases are used for the experiment. Similar to the previous mass detection methods [17,19,20,32], the dataset is divided into the training, validation, and test sets by 8: 1: 1 at the case level. After division, each set contains 8256, 1032, and 1032 mammogram images respectively. The experimental evaluation metric adopts the general Recall@FPPI of the mass detection task, where FPPI means the average number of false positives per mammogram image. If the IoU of the ground truth box and the predicted output box is greater than 0.2, the mass is assumed as successfully identified.

Training Details. The implementation of the proposed WCA-RCNN is based on PyTorch deep learning framework [25] and maskrcnn-benchmark framework. The backbone network uses ResNet50 [9] pre-trained on ImageNet [5], combined with the feature pyramid FPN [15], which is also the baseline used by many mass detection methods. The mammogram image is uniformly scaled and padded to 1280×640. Considering that the number of masses in the mammogram image is small and the distribution is sparse, the NMS threshold in the post-processing step is reduced to 0.2, and the maximum number of detections is set to 5. To retain more positive samples for the two-stage training, the NMS threshold of RPN post-processing is increased to 0.8. The window cross attention module uses 8 attention heads, the default window size is set to 5×5. The number of modules is 2, and the second module uses the same window shift operation as Swin Transformer. The experiment is conducted on two NVIDIA GeForce GTX 1080 Ti GPUs. We adopt SGD with a learning rate of 0.0005, weight decay of 10^{-4}, and momentum of 0.9. The whole training procedure takes 9000 steps.

4.2 Effect of Window Size

Window size is the core parameter of the window cross attention module. In this section, we investigated the effect of window size on model performance. As shown in Table 1, when the window size is set to 1×1, window cross attention can only establish a one-to-one pixel-level correspondence, which is sensitive to bilateral mammogram image registration errors. As the window size is gradually increased, the overall recall rate steadily increases because each pixel transmits information with more and more surrounding pixels, effectively fusing the information of bilateral mammogram images. When the window size is set to 5×5, the model achieves the best performance. However, as the window size increases to 6 × 6, the recall decreases. The reason could be that the information correlation between the pixels far away from each other is small, which has a negative effect on the fusion of information. If we increase the resolution of the input image while increasing the window size, the accuracy of mass detection may improve further, but the computational complexity is too high. As a result, 5 × 5 was used as the default window size in the experiment.

Table 1. Effect of window size in the window cross attention module.

Window Size	R@0.5	R@1.0	R@2.0
1 × 1	78.0%	84.7%	90.2%
2 × 2	78.8%	85.1%	91.0%
3 × 3	79.2%	85.5%	90.2%
4 × 4	79.2%	**87.1%**	**91.8%**
5 × 5	**80.8%**	**87.1%**	**91.8%**
6 × 6	78.8%	85.5%	91.0%

4.3   Comparison with Pixel-Level Corresponding Fusion Methods

To highlight the advantages of the window cross attention module, We compared it with several representative pixel-level corresponding feature fusion methods. In Table 2, 'None' indicate detecting mass with Faster RCNN based on a single mammogram image without fusing the information of bilateral mammogram images. 'ROI Feature Concatenation' and 'Feature Concatenation' indicate that both of them concatenate features based on channel dimension and use 1×1 convolution to reduce the number of channels. The difference is that the concatenation operation is located before or after the RPN module. 'Feature Subtraction' means subtracting the bilateral backbone features and taking the absolute value. The comparison demonstrates that fusion methods are better than the method based on a single mammogram image. This suggests that combining the information of the auxiliary view is beneficial to improve the mass detection accuracy of the main view.

Although several pixel-level corresponding feature fusion methods have been improved, they are greatly affected by image registration errors and have limited improvement in model performance. By connecting pixels between the two paired windows using window cross attention, our fusion method achieved the best performance and increased Recall by about 2% under each FPPI threshold. The main reason for the notable improvement should be that, by connecting close pixels between bilateral backbone features, the window cross attention module reduces the adverse effect of image registration errors and integrates more effective information.

Table 2. Comparisons with different fusion methods.

Fusion Methods	R@0.5	R@1.0	R@2.0
None	76.5%	83.1%	88.2%
ROI Feature Concatenation	76.9%	84.0%	90.1%
Feature Subtraction	76.5%	85.7%	89.6%
Feature Concatenation	77.3%	85.1%	90.2%
Window Cross Attention	**80.8%**	**87.1%**	**91.8%**

4.4 Comparison with State-of-the-Art

The proposed method was further compared with state-of-the-art methods to justify its effectiveness. To ensure fairness, we compared the performance of each method on DDSM. The comparison results in Table 3 clearly show that our proposed method outperforms the state-of-the-art methods for bilateral mammogram mass detection, suggesting that window cross attention is a better choice for information fusion of bilateral mammogram images.

Table 3. Comparison with state-of-the-art methods.

Methods	DDSM (train/validate/test)	R@0.5	R@1.0	R@2.0
CBN [20]	8384/1048/1048	78.8%	84.2%	89.0%
MKP (3, 5) [19]	1640/204/204	79.1%	84.9%	89.6%
MKP (3, 5, 9) [19]	1640/204/204	78.4%	85.6%	88.5%
BiDualNet-v2 [32]	8256/1020/1036	80.1%	85.3%	89.1%
IGN [17]	8256/1020/1036	79.1%	86.3%	91.4%
Proposed Method	**8256/1032/1032**	**80.8%**	**87.1%**	**91.8%**

In the Table 3, CBN is a method of fusing ROI feature information, but it does not consider the role of global information, and the accuracy is slightly lower than the method of fusing bilateral backbone features. BiDualNet-v2 uses the nipple position to align bilateral mammogram images more accurately but still uses the pixel-level corresponding feature concatenation method. MKP first fuses the information of surrounding pixels through a multi-scale kernel pooling module and then performs feature fusion. The numbers in parentheses represent the size of the kernels. IGN [17] uses graph convolution to integrate regional information into graph nodes, and then propagates information of bilateral mammogram images through graph nodes. Both MKP and IGN effectively reduce the adverse effect of image registration errors by integrating regional information before fusing features, but the fusion of regional information is coarse-grained. Different from MKP and IGN, the window cross attention module achieves fine-grained information fusion by many-many pixels correspondence. The best performance obtained by the proposed method demonstrates that the interaction between pixels improves the accuracy of mass detection.

5   Conclusion

In this work, we proposed a mass detection framework WCA-RCNN by combining the Faster RCNN with a novel window cross attention module. Compared with pixel-level corresponding feature fusion methods, the window cross attention module fuses the information of bilateral mammogram images more effectively. The way of dividing the window also effectively reduces the computation introduced by the attention mechanism. In addition, we propose a mass deformation data augment method to increase the number of mass samples. To verify the effectiveness of the proposed method, we compared it to the state-of-the-art method on the public dataset DDSM, the comparison results demonstrated that the proposed framework achieves the best performance. In the future, we will investigate how to effectively integrate the information from four mammogram images and design a model with better performance.

References

1. Aly, G.H., Marey, M., El-Sayed, S.A., Tolba, M.F.: YOLO based breast masses detection and classification in full-field digital mammograms. Comput. Methods Programs Biomed. **200**, 105823 (2021)
2. Cao, H., Pu, S., Tan, W., Tong, J.: Breast mass detection in digital mammography based on anchor-free architecture. Comput. Methods Programs Biomed. **205**, 106033 (2021)
3. Cao, Z., et al.: DeepLIMa: deep learning based lesion identification in mammograms. In: Proceedings of the IEEE/CVF International Conference on Computer Vision Workshops, pp. 362–370 (2019)
4. Debelee, T.G., Schwenker, F., Ibenthal, A., Yohannes, D.: Survey of deep learning in breast cancer image analysis. Evol. Syst. **11**, 143–163 (2020)
5. Deng, J., Dong, W., Socher, R., Li, L.J., Li, K., Fei-Fei, L.: ImageNet: a large-scale hierarchical image database. In: 2009 IEEE Conference on Computer Vision and Pattern Recognition, pp. 248–255 (2009). https://doi.org/10.1109/CVPR.2009.5206848
6. Dhungel, N., Carneiro, G., Bradley, A.P.: A deep learning approach for the analysis of masses in mammograms with minimal user intervention. Med. Image Anal. **37**, 114–128 (2017)
7. Gardezi, S.J.S., Elazab, A., Lei, B., Wang, T.: Breast cancer detection and diagnosis using mammographic data: systematic review. J. Med. Internet Res. **21**(7), e14464 (2019)

8. He, K., Gkioxari, G., Dollár, P., Girshick, R.: Mask R-CNN. In: Proceedings of the IEEE International Conference on Computer Vision, pp. 2961–2969 (2017)

9. He, K., Zhang, X., Ren, S., Sun, J.: Deep residual learning for image recognition. In: Proceedings of the IEEE Conference on Computer Vision and Pattern Recognition (CVPR) (2016)

10. Heath, M., et al.: Current status of the digital database for screening mammography. In: Karssemeijer, N., Thijssen, M., Hendriks, J., van Erning, L. (eds.) Digital Mammography. Computational Imaging and Vision, vol. 13, pp. 457–460. Springer, Dordrecht (1998). https://doi.org/10.1007/978-94-011-5318-8_75

11. Hu, H., Gu, J., Zhang, Z., Dai, J., Wei, Y.: Relation networks for object detection. In: Proceedings of the IEEE Conference on Computer Vision and Pattern Recognition, pp. 3588–3597 (2018)

12. Jalalian, A., Mashohor, S.B., Mahmud, H.R., Saripan, M.I.B., Ramli, A.R.B., Karasfi, B.: Computer-aided detection/diagnosis of breast cancer in mammography and ultrasound: a review. Clin. Imaging **37**(3), 420–426 (2013)

13. Jung, H., et al.: Detection of masses in mammograms using a one-stage object detector based on a deep convolutional neural network. PLoS ONE **13**(9), e0203355 (2018)

14. Li, Y., Zhang, L., Chen, H., Cheng, L.: Mass detection in mammograms by bilateral analysis using convolution neural network. Comput. Methods Programs Biomed. **195**, 105518 (2020)

15. Lin, T.Y., Dollar, P., Girshick, R., He, K., Hariharan, B., Belongie, S.: Feature pyramid networks for object detection. In: Proceedings of the IEEE Conference on Computer Vision and Pattern Recognition (CVPR) (2017)

16. Litjens, G., et al.: A survey on deep learning in medical image analysis. Med. Image Anal. **42**, 60–88 (2017)

17. Liu, Y., Zhang, F., Chen, C., Wang, S., Wang, Y., Yu, Y.: Act like a radiologist: towards reliable multi-view correspondence reasoning for mammogram mass detection. IEEE Trans. Pattern Anal. Mach. Intell. **44**(10), 5947–5961 (2022). https://doi.org/10.1109/TPAMI.2021.3085783

18. Liu, Y., Zhang, F., Zhang, Q., Wang, S., Wang, Y., Yu, Y.: Cross-view correspondence reasoning based on bipartite graph convolutional network for mammogram mass detection. In: Proceedings of the IEEE/CVF Conference on Computer Vision and Pattern Recognition (CVPR) (2020)

19. Liu, Y., et al.: Compare and contrast: detecting mammographic soft-tissue lesions with C2-Net. Med. Image Anal. **71**, 101999 (2021)

20. Liu, Y., et al.: From unilateral to bilateral learning: detecting mammogram masses with contrasted bilateral network. In: Shen, D., et al. (eds.) MICCAI 2019, Part VI. LNCS, vol. 11769, pp. 477–485. Springer, Cham (2019). https://doi.org/10.1007/978-3-030-32226-7_53

21. Liu, Z., et al.: Swin transformer: hierarchical vision transformer using shifted windows. In: Proceedings of the IEEE/CVF International Conference on Computer Vision, pp. 10012–10022 (2021)

22. Long, J., Shelhamer, E., Darrell, T.: Fully convolutional networks for semantic segmentation. In: Proceedings of the IEEE Conference on Computer Vision and Pattern Recognition, pp. 3431–3440 (2015)

23. Moreira, I.C., Amaral, I., Domingues, I., Cardoso, A., Cardoso, M.J., Cardoso, J.S.: INbreast: toward a full-field digital mammographic database. Acad. Radiol. **19**(2), 236–248 (2012). https://doi.org/10.1016/j.acra.2011.09.014, https://www.sciencedirect.com/science/article/pii/S107663321100451Xhttps://www.sciencedirect.com/science/article/pii/S107663321100451X

24. Otsu, N.: A threshold selection method from gray-level histograms. IEEE Trans. Syst. Man Cybern. **9**(1), 62–66 (1979)
25. Paszke, A., et al.: PyTorch: an imperative style, high-performance deep learning library. In: Wallach, H., Larochelle, H., Beygelzimer, A., d'Alché-Buc, F., Fox, E., Garnett, R. (eds.) Advances in Neural Information Processing Systems, vol. 32. Curran Associates, Inc. (2019). https://proceedings.neurips.cc/paper/2019/file/bdbca288fee7f92f2bfa9f7012727740-Paper.pdf
26. Ren, S., He, K., Girshick, R., Sun, J.: Faster R-CNN: towards real-time object detection with region proposal networks. In: Advances in Neural Information Processing Systems, vol. 28 (2015)
27. Simard, P.Y., Steinkraus, D., Platt, J.C., et al.: Best practices for convolutional neural networks applied to visual document analysis. In: ICDAR, vol. 3. Edinburgh (2003)
28. Suckling, J.: The mammographic images analysis society digital mammogram database. In: Exerpta Medica. International Congress Series 1994. vol. 1069, pp. 375–378 (1994)
29. Sun, Y.S., et al.: Risk factors and preventions of breast cancer. Int. J. Biol. Sci. **13**(11), 1387 (2017)
30. Sung, H., et al.: Global cancer statistics 2020: GLOBOCAN estimates of incidence and mortality worldwide for 36 cancers in 185 countries. CA: Cancer J. Clin. **71**(3), 209–249 (2021)
31. Vaswani, A., et al.: Attention is all you need. In: Advances in Neural Information Processing Systems, vol. 30 (2017)
32. Yang, Z., et al.: MommiNet-v2: mammographic multi-view mass identification networks. Med. Image Anal. **73**, 102204 (2021)
33. Zhao, Z.Q., Zheng, P., Xu, S.T., Wu, X.: Object detection with deep learning: a review. IEEE Trans. Neural Netw. Learn. Syst. **30**(11), 3212–3232 (2019)

Boundary Attentive Spatial Multi-scale Network for Cardiac MRI Image Segmentation

Ran You$^{(\boxtimes)}$, Qing Zhu, and Zhiqiang Wang

Faculty of Information Technology, Beijing University of Technology, Beijing, China
youran@emails.bjut.edu.cn, {ccgszq,wzqcg}@bjut.edu.cn

Abstract. Accurate automatic segmentation of cardiac MRI images can be used for clinical parameter calculation and provide visual guidance for surgery, which is important for both diagnosis and treatment of cardiac diseases. Existing automatic segmentation methods for cardiac MRI are based on U-shaped network structure introducing global pooling, attention and etc. operations to extract more effective features. These approaches, however, suffer from a mismatch between sensing receptive field and resolution and neglect to pay attention to object boundaries. In this paper, we propose a new boundary attentive multi-scale network based on U-shaped network for automatic segmentation of cardiac MRI images. Effective features are extracted based on channel attention for shallow features. With the goal of increasing segmentation accuracy, multi-scale features are extracted using densely coupled multi-scale dilated convolutions. In order to improve the ability to learn the precise boundary of the objects, a gated boundary-aware branch is introduced and utilized to concentrate on the object border region. The effectiveness and robustness of the network are confirmed by evaluating this method on the ACDC cardiac MRI dataset to produce segmentation predictions for the left ventricle, right ventricle, and myocardial. Comparative studies demonstrate that our suggested method produces superior segmentation outcomes when compared to other cardiac MRI segmentation methods.

Keywords: Image Segmentation · Cardiac MRI Image · Dilated Convolutions · Multi-Scale

1 Introduction

The heart is one of the most vital organs in the human body, and various cardiovascular diseases (CVDs) are characterized by high incidence rates, high disability rates and high mortality rates, which have become a major cause of death. The method of automated segmentation of cardiac MRI images is based on the accurate mapping of the Right and Left Ventricular Cavities and Myocardium to give precise segmentation results of cardiac MRI images. Applying automated segmentation methods can save doctors' time in manual segmentation while eliminating ambiguities from human intervention. However, cardiac MRI images are characterized by blurred boundaries, low contrast and difficult feature recognition due to their imaging methods and equipment. Therefore, it is a critical and challenging job to present automatic cardiac segmentation methods that meet clinical accuracy requirements.

With the development of deep learning technology, deep learning-based methods have received wide attention in the field of medical image segmentation. The significant research include the full convolutional neural network (FCN) [6], U-Net [8] architecture, and attention based segmentation methods. However, when it comes to high-precision medical image segmentation tasks, the single U-shaped network needs to be improved because it lacks the ability to comprehend the image's global contextual information. While CPFNet [1] fuses global/multi-scale contextual information by introducing self-learning, SA-UNet [10] introduces a spatial attention mechanism to stack multi-scale features to improve network representation. These approaches seek to improve the performance of pixel-level classification by extracting more useful features in a manner that ensures precise segmentation. Nevertheless, they fail to take into consideration the inherent shape information of the heart tissue and overlook the output image's structure.

In this work, we propose a new end-to-end segmentation network for cardiac MRI images. This approach is proposed based on two assumptions. First, since cardiac MRI images contain different momentary states in the heartbeat sequence and suffer from class imbalance, extracting and fusing effective features at different scales is important to enhance the network representation capability to perform cardiac image segmentation with high accuracy. Secondly, the cardiac tissue has its inherent shape characteristics, and the attention for object boundaries can enhance the segmentation results. On the basis of these two presumptions, we propose our approach.

The main contributions of this paper are as follows: (1) We propose a boundary-attentive spatial multi-scale network based on the U-shape network architecture. The network performs multi-scale feature extraction and fusion in the encoder, while introducing additional supervision for boundary learning. The network is used to segment the left and right ventricles as well as the myocardial regions, achieving improved segmentation accuracy; (2) the multi-scale feature extraction module (D-ASPP) fuses multi-scale features in a densely connected manner to enhance network representation and effectively improve segmentation accuracy; (3) adaptive gated convolution(AGC) is introduced in the encoder to emphasize effective features and reduce the negative impact of irrelevant features; (4) the gated boundary attention stream (GBA-Stream) extracts boundary features from texture features and introduces additional supervision for boundary learning. This enables the network to effectively extract image boundary information and output accurate object boundaries.

2   Method

2.1   Overall Structure

As shown in the previous section, the U-shaped network structure is suitable for medical image segmentation, but it is difficult to achieve the accuracy requirement because it lacks the understanding of global contextual information. In view of this, we propose boundary-attentive spatial multi-scale network (Fig. 1). The convolution block in U-Net is replaced with adaptive gated convolution block to enhance the ability to focus on valid features and filter non-semantic features. A D-ASPP module is added to enhance the understanding of multi-scale features, thus improving the network representation capability. In addition, a gated boundary-aware Stream(GBA-Stream) is added, which introduces additional constraints to enhance the network's ability to learn boundaries. The details of each part of the structure will be described in the next three subsections. More specifically, the D-ASPP is described in Sect. 2.2, the adaptive gated convolution is described in Sect. 2.3, the GBA-Stream is described in Sect. 2.4.

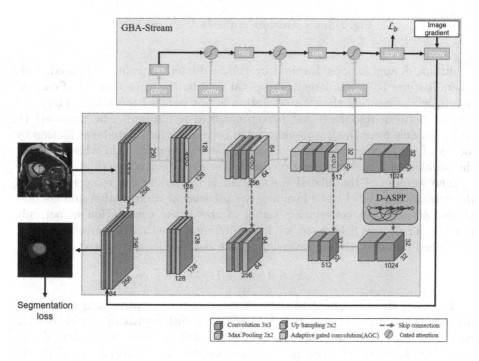

Fig. 1. The illustration of the overall architecture.

2.2   D-ASPP Module

The D-ASPP module is used to extract multi-scale features to cover a larger receptive field and obtain global information. Generally, using larger convolution kernels or larger strid during pooling operations is required to account for the aim to obtain features with larger receptive fields. Both methods have shortcomings, though, with the former adding a lot of work and the latter losing

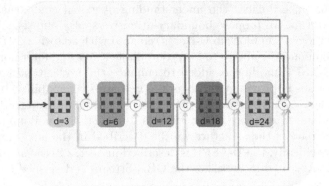

Fig. 2. Inner structure of the D-ASPP module.

resolution in applications. Inspired by [12], a dilated convolution is used. This allows features to have a larger perceptual field by the same amount of computation, while ensuring that the resolution is not reduced too much. Thus, the conflict between resolution and perceptual field is resolved. The proposed D-ASPP module fuses the features extracted by multi-scale dilated convolution by means of dense concatenation, covering a larger receptive field while avoiding the problem of kernel degeneration due to the expansion of the dilated rate.

The purpose of the dilated convolution is to expand the receptive field of the convolution kernel while avoiding the increase of computation and the loss of resolution. For a convolution kernel of size k the convolution kernel only provides a receptive field of size k * k. Improving it to a dilated convolution with an dilated rate of d, the equivalent receptive field size is represented as:

$$k' = d \times (k-1) + 1 \tag{1}$$

However, there is a limit to the expansion of the receptive field by a single dilated convolution. When applying dilated convolution with an extremely large rate, only the center filter weight is effective due to image boundary effects. Therefore this convolution cannot capture long distance information and degenerates to a 1×1 convolution. The stacking of multiple convolution kernels can be used to capture larger receptive field effectively. When connecting two convolutions with size k_1 and k_2 receptive fields, the new receptive field size is represented as:

$$k = k_1 + k_2 - 1 \tag{2}$$

The D-ASPP module can simultaneously compose a much denser and larger feature pyramid using only a few Atrous Convolution layers. Specifically, as shown in Fig. 2, the D-ASPP module densely connects five different scales of dilated convolution, with the dilation rate set to 3, 6, 12, 18, and 24, respectively. The input of each layer is a stack of features at each scale of the prior. The output of the new features with larger receptive fields is then stacked to the input of the posterior layer-by-layer. The feature y_i extracted in layer i of D-ASPP can be expressed as:

$$y_i = D_{k_i,d_i}([y_{i-1}, y_{i-2}, ..., y_0])\tag{3}$$

where $D_{k,d}(...)$ represents an dilated convolution, k_i and d_i represents the kernel size and dilation rate of layer i, and $[\cdot \cdot \cdot]$ denotes the concatenation operation. $[y_{i-1}, y_{i-2}, ..., y_0]$ means the feature map formed by concatenating the outputs from all previous layers.

2.3   Adaptive Gated Convolution (AGC)

Based on the convolution block proposed by U-Net, our proposed adaptive gated convolution(AGC) block introduces a parameter-learnable gating mechanism. As shown in Fig. 3, AGC sets learnable gating weights to the feature map in the channel direction and reactivates the feature map according to the weights. This improvement can selectively emphasize the effective features and suppress the invalid features, thus enhancing the network representation and improving the segmentation quality.

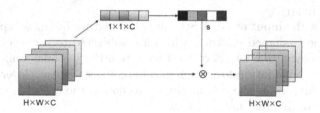

Fig. 3. Structure of the adaptive gated convolution.

Specifically, for the feature map $X \in R^{H \times W \times C}$, the feature representation is extracted in the channel dimension using the global average pooling operation, and the output is $t = [t_1, t_2, ..., t_C] \in R^C$. Where the feature representation of the c-th channel is computed as:

$$t_c = \frac{1}{H \times W}\sum_{i=0}^{H}\sum_{j=0}^{W} x_c(i, j)\tag{4}$$

After obtaining the feature representation t for each channel, there is a need to further capture channel-wise dependencies. The inter-dependencies between channels are modeled by the method f() consisting of Fully Connected Layers as well as Activation Function, which parameterize the gating mechanism for the channel direction features. This is a process of adaptively learning channel-level feature weight s:

$$s = \sigma(W_2\delta(W_1 t))\tag{5}$$

where W_1 and W_2 denote the parameters of the two Fully Connected Layers, respectively; δ refers to the ReLU function, denoting the sigmoid normalization operation. Finally, the channel direction features are weighted according to the weights s. The features are reactivated to obtain the new features after channel-level attention enhancement. The feature map is denoted as X = $[x_1, x_2, ..., x_C]$ in the channel direction, and gating is performed for the c-th channel feature as follows:

$$x_c' = s_c \cdot x_c \tag{6}$$

2.4   GBA-Stream

Gated boundary attention stream learns boundary features in a gated convolution, based on texture features extracted from the u-shaped network structure. To improve the learning for object edges, the boundary features are gradually fused with the texture features. It improves the network's attention to border information and, as a result, the network's segmentation of the object boundary. Our suggested gating unit uses the boundary features extracted from each layer as a gating, filters out other texture information in it that does not belong to the object boundary, and then generates a boundary prediction that only focuses on the object boundary.

Specifically, the input of GBA-Stream is the texture features captured layer by layer by the U-shaped network, which are subjected to a convolution operation with a convolution kernel of 1×1 to obtain the boundary information of each scale. The boundary information of different sizes in each layer is up sampled to the same size as the original image to obtain the object boundary cues corresponding to different fields of view.

$$b_i = F(C_{1 \times 1}(t_i)) \tag{7}$$

where $C_{1 \times 1}(...)$ refers to the 1×1 convolution operation and F(...) refers to the up sampling to the original image size.

After that, a gated convolution block is constructed to connect the boundary attention feature maps obtained from the shallow features and the boundary cues extracted from each layer to computationally generate a boundary attention map α_i:

$$\alpha_i = \sigma(C_{1 \times 1}(B_i \parallel b_i)) \tag{8}$$

where $\parallel$ denotes the channel-wise concatenation of feature maps, $\sigma(...)$ is the sigmoid function. The boundary feature map B_i is generated layer by layer by filtering out the boundary irrelevant information from the boundary attention feature map:

$$B_{i+1} = R(B_i \otimes \alpha_i) \tag{9}$$

where $\otimes$ is the Hadamard product, R(...) denote the residual block function.

To obtain more accurate boundary information, the canny edge information of the original image is calculated based on the image gradient. It is connected with the boundary features obtained by GBA-Stream to output the final boundary prediction.

GBA-Stream provides boundary supervision for the network and constructs an objective function expressed as the binary cross-entropy loss between the boundary prediction map generated by GBA-Stream and the GT boundary map of the image:

$$\mathcal{L}_b = \mathcal{L}_{BCE}(B_n, B_{GT}) \tag{10}$$

where B_n denotes predicted boundary maps, n denotes the number of U-shaped network feature extraction layers, and B_{GT} denotes GT boundaries.

3   Experiments

In this section, we first introduce the cardiac MRI dataset used and the evaluation metrics for the cardiac MRI image segmentation task, secondly describe the details of our experimental implementation specifically, and finally show the segmentation results of our proposed method in the cardiac MRI image segmentation task in a qualitative and quantitative manner, respectively, to illustrate the superiority of our method compared to existing methods.

3.1   Datasets and Metrics

Cardiac MRI segmentation experiments using the ACDC (Automated Cardiac Diagnosis Challenge) dataset. The ACDC dataset is from the MICCAI 2017 Automated Cardiac Diagnosis Challenge. The ACDC dataset contains sequential MRI images of the heart from 150 different patients, with 100 in the training set and 50 in the test set. The patients were divided into five subgroups based on medically reported cardiac physiological parameters to ensure a uniform distribution of patient categories. The data set is labeled with information where 0 indicates background, 1 indicates right ventricle, 2 indicates myocardium, and 3 indicates left ventricle.

To evaluate the segmentation effectiveness of the network, the Dice coefficient (DICE) between the automatic segmentation results of the network and the GT at end-diastole (ED) and end-systole (ES) of the ventricle, respectively, was calculated as a quantitative evaluation index of the algorithm performance.

In addition, since one of the goals of our method is to predict high-quality boundaries, another evaluation metric, Contour Accuracy, is introduced to evaluate the segmentation quality of semantic boundaries. Specifically, this metric computes the F-score along the boundary of the predicted mask, given a small slack in distance. In our experiments, the thresholds are set to 0.002, 0.0075, and 0.03, which correspond to 1, 3, and 9 pixels respectively.

3.2   Implementation Details

All experiments performed in our work were implemented on an RTX 3080 GPU with 10G of memory. The experiments were performed with batch size set to 4 and epoch set to 300. The training process was performed using stochastic gradient descent (SGD) optimizer with hyper parameters set to: initial learning rate (0.03), momentum (0.9), weight decay (0.0001).

In the data pre-processing stage, for the 2D segmentation network, we slice the 3D MRI data, convert it to a 2D image matrix whose size is cropped or filled to 256 × 256, and perform data enhancement (replication and rotation).

3.3   Experimental Results

We compared our proposed method with several popular segmentation methods (UNet [8], SENet [3], CPFNet [1], SA-UNet [10]). UNet is the most popular method in the field of medical image segmentation, and most medical image segmentation methods are based on the U-shaped structure proposed by UNet; SENet is an advanced attention model; CPFNet and SA-UNet are typical to enhance the accuracy of medical image segmentation by obtaining spatial contextual information, which provides inspiration for our method. The experiment results are shown in Table 1, our proposed method performs better than other medical image segmentation methods in cardiac MRI image segmentation task. The segmentation results are shown in Fig. 4, and it can be seen that the comparison group predicted incomplete labels (rows 1, 2) as well as blurred boundaries (rows 3, 4, 5). And our prediction results are closer to the GT labels.

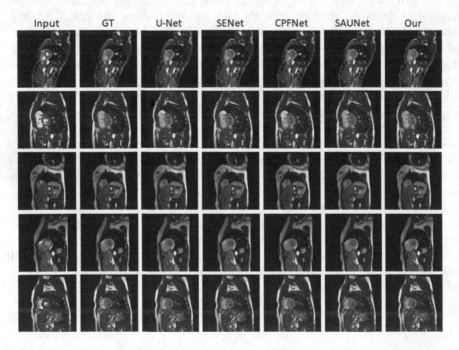

Fig. 4. Comparison of the segmentation results.

Table 1. Dice Scores for LV, RV and MYO.

Method	LV		RV		MYO	
	ED	ES	ED	ES	ED	ES
UNet [8]	0.93	0.86	0.91	0.85	0.85	0.87
SENet [3]	0.94	0.87	0.91	0.83	0.84	0.86
CPFNet [1]	0.94	0.86	0.90	0.80	0.83	0.86
SA-Unet [10]	**0.95**	0.91	0.92	0.88	**0.86**	**0.88**
Our	**0.95**	**0.92**	**0.93**	**0.89**	**0.86**	**0.88**

Next we compare the proposed method with the state-of-the-art methods at the ACDC challenge. These state-of-the-art methods can be divided into two categories, which are end-to-end segmentation and multi-stage segmentation. We note that multi-stage segmentation methods obtain high quality segmentation results by introducing complex data pre-processing and post-processing operations. However, in applications, end-to-end segmentation methods are able to predict directly from the input image, which greatly simplifies the segmentation process and is more efficient. So it is significant to improve the performance of end-to-end segmentation method so that it can approach the accuracy level of multi-stage segmentation methods. As shown in Table 2, the segmentation performance of our proposed method surpasses the existing advanced end-to-end segmentation methods (rows 5–7 in Table 2), especially for the myocardial region where the performance improvement is more obvious. Meanwhile, our method achieves a performance level close to the multi-stage segmentation methods for the left ventricle and myocardium (the first 4 rows in Table 2). It even surpasses the method of Khened [5] in the segmentation of the myocardial region. It can be seen that our method, as an end-to-end segmentation network, achieves advanced segmentation levels without introducing complex preprocessing of ROI and various post-processing operations.

Table 2. Comparison with state-of-the-art methods, testing dataset Dice scores for ACDC-17 segmentation on the challenge testing data.

Method	LV		RV		MYO	
	ED	ES	ED	ES	ED	ES
Isensee [4]	**0.967**	**0.928**	**0.946**	**0.904**	**0.896**	**0.919**
Khened [5]	0.964	0.917	0.935	0.879	0.889	0.898
Simantiris [9]	**0.967**	**0.928**	0.936	0.889	0.891	0.904
Zotti [13]	0.964	0.912	0.934	0.885	0.886	0.902
Jain [7]	0.955	0.885	0.911	0.819	0.882	0.897
Wolterink [11]	0.961	0.918	0.928	0.872	0.875	0.894
Ilias [2]	0.948	0.848	0.887	0.767	0.799	0.784
Our	0.963	0.913	0.926	0.859	0.891	0.901

In addition, we conduct ablation experiments for each module in the architecture. Table 3 demonstrates the effect of each module in the proposed method on the segmentation result. The results demonstrate the effectiveness of our proposed 3 modules for segmentation performance improvement.

Table 3. Ablation experiments for each module of the network.

Method	LV		RV		MYO	
	ED	ES	ED	ES	ED	ES
w/o D-ASPP	**0.96**	0.87	0.92	0.87	0.85	0.87
w/o GBA-Stream	0.95	0.88	0.92	0.88	**0.86**	**0.88**
w/o AGC	0.95	0.89	0.92	0.88	**0.86**	**0.88**
Our	0.95	**0.92**	**0.93**	**0.89**	**0.86**	**0.88**

Table 4 demonstrates the effect of different dilation rates of the dilation convolution in the D-ASPP module on the segmentation result of the model. The experiment results prove that our chosen dilation rates (3, 6, 12, 18, 24) can obtain the best segmentation results, especially in the segmentation of the left and right ventricles. Table 5 shows the segmentation quality of the semantic boundaries. Our method improves the F-score for boundary alignment due to the boundary attention module added. We illustrate its effect at three different thresholds. All of the 1, 3, and 9 pixel regions adjacent to the semantic boundary result in higher quality segmentation results. Specifically, we see up to 2.1% improvement at the strictest regime.

Table 4. Effect of network segmentation with different dilatation rates.

Method	LV		RV		MYO	
	ED	ES	ED	ES	ED	ES
d = 3, 6, 12	0.95	0.89	0.91	0.86	0.86	0.88
d = 3, 12, 18	0.95	0.90	0.91	0.86	0.86	0.88
d = 3, 6, 12, 18, 24	0.95	**0.92**	**0.93**	**0.89**	0.86	0.88

Table 5. Effect of proposed method at difference thresholds in terms of boundary quality (F-score).

Method	th = 1 px	th = 3 px	th = 9 px
UNet [8]	81.6	89.8	93.1
ours	**83.7**	**91.4**	**94.5**

4 Conclusion

To meet the requirement of high-accuracy segmentation of cardiac MRI images, we propose an end-to-end segmentation network based on a U-shaped network structure. The network achieves the understanding of spatial global information through densely connected multi-scale dilated convolution, which enhances the network expression capability. Based on the high requirement of tissue boundary accuracy in cardiac segmentation applications, adding the shape boundary module to the network makes the segmentation model pay more attention to the boundary features and thus obtains better segmentation of the boundary. Experimental results show that our proposed method achieves advanced segmentation performance on the ACDC dataset.

Acknowledgments. This work is supported by Beijing Natural Science Foundation (4232017).

References

1. Feng, S., et al.: CPFNet: context pyramid fusion network for medical image segmentation. IEEE Trans. Med. Imaging **PP**(99), 1 (2020)
2. Grinias, E., Tziritas, G.: Fast fully-automatic cardiac segmentation in MRI using MRF model optimization, substructures tracking and B-spline smoothing. In: Pop, M., et al. (eds.) STACOM 2017. LNCS, vol. 10663, pp. 91–100. Springer, Cham (2018). https://doi.org/10.1007/978-3-319-75541-0_10
3. Hu, J., Shen, L., Albanie, S., Sun, G., Wu, E.: Squeeze-and-excitation networks. IEEE Trans. Pattern Anal. Mach. Intell. **42**(8), 2011–2023 (2020). https://doi.org/10.1109/TPAMI.2019.2913372
4. Isensee, F., Jaeger, P.F., Full, P.M., Wolf, I., Engelhardt, S., Maier-Hein, K.H.: Automatic cardiac disease assessment on cine-MRI via time-series segmentation and domain specific features. In: Pop, M., et al. (eds.) STACOM 2017. LNCS, vol. 10663, pp. 120–129. Springer, Cham (2018). https://doi.org/10.1007/978-3-319-75541-0_13
5. Khened, M., Alex, V., Krishnamurthi, G.: Fully convolutional multi-scale residual DenseNets for cardiac segmentation and automated cardiac diagnosis using ensemble of classifiers. Med. Image Anal. **51**, 21–45 (2018)
6. Long, J., Shelhamer, E., Darrell, T.: Fully convolutional networks for semantic segmentation. IEEE Trans. Pattern Anal. Mach. Intell. **39**(4), 640–651 (2015)
7. Patravali, J., Jain, S., Chilamkurthy, S.: 2D-3D fully convolutional neural networks for cardiac MR segmentation. In: Pop, M., et al. (eds.) STACOM 2017. LNCS, vol. 10663, pp. 130–139. Springer, Cham (2018). https://doi.org/10.1007/978-3-319-75541-0_14
8. Ronneberger, O., Fischer, P., Brox, T.: U-net: convolutional networks for biomedical image segmentation. CoRR abs/1505.04597 (2015). http://arxiv.org/abs/1505.04597
9. Simantiris, G., Tziritas, G.: Cardiac MRI segmentation with a dilated CNN incorporating domain-specific constraints. IEEE J. Sel. Top. Signal Process. **14**(6), 1235–1243 (2020). https://doi.org/10.1109/JSTSP.2020.3013351

10. Sun, J., Darbehani, F., Zaidi, M., Wang, B.: SAUNet: shape attentive U-net for interpretable medical image segmentation. In: Martel, A.L., et al. (eds.) MICCAI 2020, Part IV. LNCS, vol. 12264, pp. 797–806. Springer, Cham (2020). https://doi.org/10.1007/978-3-030-59719-1_77

11. Wolterink, J.M., Leiner, T., Viergever, M.A., Išgum, I.: Automatic segmentation and disease classification using cardiac cine MR images. In: Pop, M., et al. (eds.) STACOM 2017. LNCS, vol. 10663, pp. 101–110. Springer, Cham (2018). https://doi.org/10.1007/978-3-319-75541-0_11

12. Yang, M., Yu, K., Zhang, C., Li, Z., Yang, K.: DenseASPP for semantic segmentation in street scenes. In: Proceedings of the IEEE Conference on Computer Vision and Pattern Recognition, pp. 3684–3692 (2018)

13. Zotti, C., Luo, Z., Lalande, A., Jodoin, P.M.: Convolutional neural network with shape prior applied to cardiac MRI segmentation. IEEE J. Biomed. Health Inform. **23**(3), 1119–1128 (2018)

Clinical Pixel Feature Recalibration Module for Ophthalmic Image Classification

JiLu Zhao[1], Xiaoqing Zhang[1,2](✉), Xiao Wu[1], ZhiXuan Zhang[1], Tong Zhang[1], Heng Li[1], Yan Hu[1](✉), and Jiang Liu[1,2](✉)

[1] Research Institute of Trustworthy Autonomous Systems and Department of Computer Science and Engineering, Southern University of Science and Technology, Shenzhen 518055, China
11930927@mail.sustech.edu.cn
[2] Guangdong Provincial Key Laboratory of Brain-Inspired Intelligent Computation, Department of Computer Science and Engineering, Southern University of Science and Technology, Shenzhen 518055, China

Abstract. Ophthalmic image examination has become a commonly-acknowledged way for ocular disease screening and diagnosis. Clinical features extracted from ophthalmic images play different roles in affecting clinicians making diagnosis results, but how to incorporate these clinical features into convolutional neural network (CNN) representations has been less studied. In this paper, we propose a simple yet practical module, *Clinical Pixel Feature Recalibration Module (CPF)*, aiming to exploit the potential of clinical features to improve the ocular disease recognition performance of CNNs. CPF first extracts clinical pixel features from each spatial position of all feature maps by clinical cross-channel pooling, then estimates each spatial position recalibration weight in a pixel-independent clinical fusion. By infusing the relative importance of clinical features into feature maps at the pixel level, CPF is supposed to enhance the representational ability of CNNs. Our CPF is easily inserted into existing CNNs with negligible overhead. We conduct comprehensive experiments on two publicly available ophthalmic image datasets and CIFAR datasets, and the results show the superiority and generation ability of CPF over advanced attention methods. Furthermore, this paper presents an in-depth weight visualization analysis to investigate the inherent behavior of CPF, aiming to improve the interpretability of CNNs in the decision-making process.

Keywords: Ophthalmic image · CPF · interpretability · attention · classification

1 Introduction

According to World Health Organization (WHO) [11], it is estimated that approximately 2.2 billion people have vision impairment caused by various ocular diseases. Especially, 1 billion people with vision impairment can improve

---

J. Zhao and X. Zhang—Equal Contribution.

L. Iliadis et al. (Eds.): ICANN 2023, LNCS 14257, pp. 87–98, 2023.
https://doi.org/10.1007/978-3-031-44216-2_8

their vision loss and life quality through early prevention and surgery treatments. Ophthalmic image examination has become a widely-used way to detect ocular diseases [20]. This is mainly because clinical features extracted from ophthalmic images significantly affect clinicians' diagnosis decisions. Over the past decades, researchers have achieved promising progress in developing computer-aided (CAD) techniques for automatic ocular disease diagnosis. Zhang et al. [22] proposed an adaptive feature squeeze network to classify cataract and retinal diseases. Fu et al. [2] presented a multilevel deep network to detect angle-closure. Kurma et al. [9] proposed a hybrid deep neural network for diabetic retinopathy classification. Raghavendra et al. [14] proposed a deep convolutional neural network (CNN) to recognize glaucoma. However, these methods have not fully leveraged the potential of clinical features to enhance feature representations of deep CNNs.

Recently, attention mechanism has widely incorporated into CNNs to improve their representational capability. One of the most successful attention methods is squeeze-and-excitation (SE) [7], which emphasizes significant channels and suppresses redundant ones by constructing long-range dependencies among channels. Efficient channel attention (ECA) [15] models the local-range dependencies among channels. Clinical-aware attention (CCA) [23] adaptively estimates the relative importance of each channel. Furthermore, we find that these attention methods often apply spatial pooling methods to aggregate spatial context features across the spatial dimensions, which may not be viewed as other forms of clinical features well. This is because these spatial context features are global statistics information, but clinical features are usually extracted from lesion regions that are local statistics information. And these clinical features which are strongly related to ocular diseases play an indispensable role in ophthalmic image classification. Given this, a question arises: can we view clinical features as clinical pixel features and then exploit the potential of them to enhance the representational power of a CNN?

Motivated by this question, this paper proposes an efficient attention module, Clinical Pixel Feature Recalibration Module (CPF), which explicitly infuses the clinical pixel features into feature map representations of a CNN through the pixel feature recalibration form. CPF adaptively estimates the relative significance of each clinical pixel feature and then recalibrates spatial positions independently, allowing a CNN to highlight lesion regions and ignore redundant ones. Figure 1 presents a general framework of CPF, consisting of two major components: clinical cross-channel pooling and clinical fusion. The well-designed clinical cross-channel pooling extracts clinical pixel features for each spatial position along the channel axis. It is followed the clinical fusion, which dynamically fuses clinical pixel features at the channel dimension to generate spatial position attention weights with an independent position manner, which are utilized to recalibrate spatial position. Our CPF is lightweight and can be easily plugged into modern CNNs. To demonstrate the effectiveness and efficiency of our CPF, we conduct extensive experiments on two publicly available medical image datasets (OCTMNIST and RETINAMNIST [19]) and CIFAR

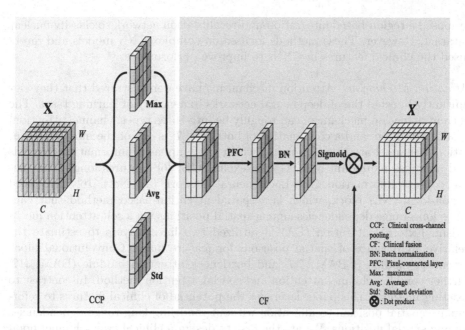

Fig. 1. A clinical pixel feature recalibration module (CPF). The module has two main components: clinical cross-channel pooling (CCP) and clinical fusion (CF). CPF infuses the clinical features into feature maps at the pixel level based on the relative significance of clinical features and clinical fusion.

datasets. The results show that CPF achieves a better balance between performance and model complexity than state-of-the-art attention methods. Our CPF achieves over 0.07%–7.6% of accuracy with similar or fewer parameters through comparisons to other advanced attention methods on two publicly available medical image datasets (OCTMNIST and RETINAMNIST) and CIFAR datasets. Furthermore, this paper also provides visual analysis to explain the relative contributions of clinical pixel features in guiding a CNN to focus on significant lesion regions and suppress redundant ones.

2   Related Work

Computer-Aided Ocular Disease Diagnosis Techniques. Deep neural networks have achieved promising progress in computer-aided ocular disease diagnosis in recent years. Perdomo et al. [13] proposed a customized CNN to classify diabetes-related retinal diseases. Hao et al. [4] proposed a hybrid variation-aware network to assess anterior chamber angles. Xu et al. [18] proposed a global-local CNN to recognize fundus-based cataract. Li et al. [10] designed an annotation-free restoration network for cataract diagnosis. Das et al. [1] developed a multi-scale deep feature fusion network to classify macular pathologies. Fu et al. [2] proposed a deep learning system for automated angle-closure detection. Zhang et al. [21]

proposed a region-based integration-and-recalibration network to classify nuclear cataract. However, These methods focused on complex CNN models and rarely fused the clinical features in CNNs to improve performance.

Attention Mechanism. Attention mechanisms have demonstrated that they significantly boosted the of deep neural networks in a variety of learning tasks. The current attention mechanism can roughly be into three types: channel attention, spatial attention, and a combination of both. SE [7] is one of the most representational channel attention methods, which can emphasize informative channels and suppress redundant ones. Gather-excite (GE) [6] captures long-range spatial context information. Non-Local neural network (NL-Net) [16] introduced a non-local (NL) block, which is a spatial attention-based method that captures long-range dependencies among spatial positions via a self-attention mechanism. External attention (EA) [3] utilized two linear layers to estimate the relative significance of spatial positions for feature maps. Convolutional block attention module (CBAM) [17] and bottleneck attention module (BAM) [12] further combine channel attention and spatial attention method. In contrast to existing methods, this paper leverages the potential of clinical features to reformulate spatial position recalibration without modeling long-range dependencies among spatial positions. We are the first to design a clinical cross-channel pooling method to extract three clinical pixel features at the channel dimension, which is superior to average or maximum cross-channel pooling methods.

3   Method

3.1   Clinical Pixel Feature Recalibration Module

The clinical pixel feature recalibration module (CPF) can be viewed as an effective architectural unit, aiming to improve the representational power of a CNN. It takes the intermediate feature tensor $X \in R^{C \times H \times W}$ as inputs and generates the augmented feature tensor $X' \in R^{C \times H \times W}$. Our CPF can be divided into the following two components: clinical cross-channel pooling and clinical fusion (as shown in Fig. 1), which will be described step by step.

Clinical Cross-Channel Pooling. Existing efforts have widely applied spatial pooling methods to extract global context features. However, rare research has utilized cross-channel pooling methods to extract pixel context features, which is vital for highlighting local lesion regions. Hence, we propose a well-design clinical cross-channel pooling (CCP) to extract three clinical pixel features along the channel axis: average (Avg), maximum (Max), and standard deviation (Std). Specifically, three clinical pixel features at per spatial position $p(i,j)$ can be computed by:

$$\mu(i,j) = \frac{1}{C} \sum_{k=1}^{C} x(k,i,j) \tag{1}$$

$$m(i,j) = max(x(1,i,j), \ldots, x(C,i,j)) \tag{2}$$

$$\sigma(i,j) = \sqrt{\frac{1}{C}\sum_{k=1}^{C}(x(k,i,j) - \mu(i,j))^2} \tag{3}$$

$$t(i,j) = [m(i,j), \mu(i,j), \sigma(i,j)], \tag{4}$$

where $\mu(i,j)$, $m(i,j)$, and $\sigma(i,j)$ indicate Avg, Max, and Std pixel features of $p(i,j)$ accordingly. $t \in R^3$ is served as a summary descriptor of the clinical pixel feature information.

Clinical Fusion. Following the clinical cross-channel pooling, we propose a clinical fusion operator to convert the clinical pixel features into spatial position attention weights. The clinical fusion operator is supposed to adjust the relative importance of clinical pixel features associated with per spatial position so as to focus on or ignore them, respectively. To implement this purpose, we construct a simple yet practical combination of a pixel-connected layer (PFC), a batch normalization layer (BN) and a sigmoid activation function. Given the clinical pixel feature representation $T \in R^{3 \times H \times W}$ as the input, the feature fusion operator performs the pixel-wise encoding with learnable parameters $R^{3 \times H \times W}$:

$$Z = W \cdot T, \tag{5}$$

$Z \in R^{N \times HW}$ is the encoded clinical pixel features for each pixel location where N , H and W indicate batch size , height of the feature map and width of the feature map. Then we apply BN to facilitate training and the sigmoid function as the gating mechanism to generate the spatial position attention weights:

$$G = \sigma(BN(Z)), \tag{6}$$

where G denotes the spatial position attention weights and σ denotes the sigmoid function.

Finally, the original input tensor X is augmented by multiplying attention weights G in a dot product manner, thus the output tensor $X' \in R^{C \times H \times W}$ is obtained by the following formula:

$$X' = X \cdot G \tag{7}$$

3.2   Implementation

As the key goal of this paper is to enhance the representational power of CNNs by exploring clinical pixel features, here we adopt classical ResNet18 and ResNet50 to demonstrate the advantages of CPF over state-of-the-art attention methods. We combine the CPF module with the residual block to form the Residual-CPF module. Commonly-used softmax function and cross-entropy loss function are used as the classifier and the loss function, respectively.

4   Datasets and Experiment Settings

4.1   Datasets

OCTMNIST Dataset: It is a publicly available dataset of retinal diseases. The dataset contains four retinal disease types: normal, drusen, choroidal neovascularization (CNV), and diabetic macular edema (MDE). It contains 109,309 optical coherence tomography (OCT) images, and the size of the images is 28×28. To ensure a fair comparison, we follow the same dataset splitting method [19], which has three subsets: training, validation, and testing.

RETINAMNIST Dataset: It is a fundus image dataset for diabetic retinopathy grading, which contains 1600 images (the image size of 28×28). Literature [19] splits it into three subsets: training (1080), validation (120), and testing (400), and this paper adopts this dataset-splitting method.

4.2   Experiment Settings

Evaluation Metrics: In this paper, we use the following evaluation metrics to verify the overall performance of the method: accuracy (ACC), F1, and kappa coefficient value.

Comparable Baselines: we use CBAM, BAM, SE, GE, NL and EA to examine the effectiveness of CPF.

Implementation Detail: We implement CPF and other attention methods with the PyTorch tool and train all methods with a stochastic gradient descent (SGD) optimizer using default settings. The initial learning rate and training epochs are set to 0.0025 and 150 correspondingly. In training, the learning rate is reduced by a factor of 5 every 20 epochs. Moreover, we follow standard data augmentation methods to augment training data, such as the random flipping method and random cropping method. We run all methods on a workstation equipped with NVIDIA A6000 GPUs.

5   Results and Discussion

5.1   Comparisons with State-of-the-art Attention Methods

Performance Comparison on OCTMNIST Dataset: We first compare the proposed CPF with SOTA attention methods on the OCTMNIST dataset by taking ResNet18 and ResNet50 as backbones, as listed in Table 1. CPF consistently improves the performance than competitive attention methods under less model complexity. We see that our CPF shares almost the total parameters with the ResNet18, which obtains absolute over **3.0%** on three evaluation measures. Remarkably, CPF outperforms NL by over **14%** of accuracy, while NL is 90% larger in parameters. With less complexity than CBAM and BAM, our CPF achieves over 2.0% of accuracy, demonstrating the superiority of the clinical fusion manner of different clinical pixel context features to local fusion manner.

Table 1. Performance comparison and complexity comparison of CPF and state-of-the-art attention methods on the OCTMNIST dataset when taking ResNet18 and ResNet50 as backbones.

Method	ACC	F1	Kappa	Params
ResNet18 [5]	76.20	73.61	68.27	11.18M
+ CBAM [17]	76.60	73.90	68.80	11.26M
+ BAM [12]	77.00	74.15	69.33	11.18M
+ SE [7]	72.50	67.79	63.33	11.27M
+ GE [6]	78.60	76.07	71.47	11.45M
+ NL [16]	75.60	72.26	67.47	11.91M
+ EA [3]	77.20	74.76	69.60	11.42M
+ CPF	**79.40**	**76.81**	**72.53**	11.18M
ResNet50 [5]	78.00	75.82	70.67	23.50M
+ CBAM [17]	77.80	75.11	70.40	26.04M
+ BAM [12]	78.10	75.10	70.81	23.70M
+ SE [7]	72.50	67.69	63.33	26.05M
+ GE [6]	78.30	75.44	71.07	27.46M
+ NL [16]	65.80	58.78	54.4	44.76M
+ EA [3]	78.30	75.60	71.10	25.44M
+ CPF	**80.10**	**77.67**	**73.47**	23.52M

Performance Comparison on RETINAMNIST Dataset: Table 2 presents the classification results of our CPF and other SOTA attention methods on retinal images. We can see that CPF achieves a better balance between the performance and the model complexity than competitive attention methods by adopting ResNet18 and ResNet50 as backbones. By taking ResNet18 as the backbone, CPF outperforms GE by above **5%** on F1 score and by above **4%** on kappa value under similar parameters. Remarkably, CPF achieves over **2.34%** gain of kappa and **1.75%** gains of accuracy than NL based on ResNet18 and ResNet50, although NL is 6.6% larger in parameters. The results demonstrate the effectiveness of our method by incorporating pixel-based context information into feature maps.

5.2 Visualization and Interpretability

Clinical Pixel Feature Value Map and Weight Map Visualization: Figure 2(b) plots three clinical pixel feature value maps (first row) and their corresponding pixel feature weight maps (second row) on OCT images at the high stage of ResNet50. We can observe that pixel feature value distributions of avg and std pixel features are similar: pixel feature values in upper regions are larger than those in lower regions. In contrast, max pixel feature values on boundary regions are larger than on center regions. Furthermore, pixel feature weight distributions of three clinical pixel features differ from clinical pixel feature maps, indicating that CPF can adaptively set different weights for clinical pixel features at the per-pixel position, which is beneficial to guide a CNN focus on lesion regions.

Attention Weight Map Visualization: Figure 2(c) presents the attention weight maps of CPF at three stages of ResNet50. It can be seen that when the network goes deep, the difference among attention weight values becomes obvious. It is worth noting that attention weight distribution of CPF at the high stage agrees with lesion distribution, proving our CPF can allow a CNN to emphasize significant regions and ignore redundant ones.

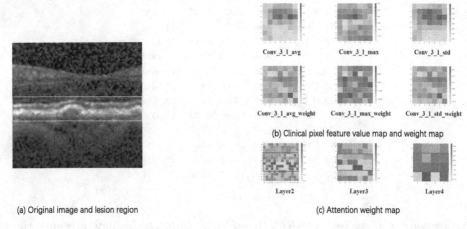

(a) Original image and lesion region

(c) Attention weight map

Fig. 2. (a) Original image and lesion region marked by the red box; (b) Clinical pixel feature value distribution and weight distribution of CPF at third stage of ResNet50 on OCTMNIST dataset; (c) Attention weight distribution of CPF at three stages of ResNet50 on OCTMNIST dataset. (Color figure online)

5.3   Ablation Study

Clinical Cross-Channel Pooling: We validate the benefit of the proposed clinical cross-channel pooling through comparisons to other pooling methods. We adopt the ResNet50 as the backbone and address retinal disease classification on the OCTMNIST dataset by following the same experiment setting in Sect. 4.2. Table 3 lists the classification results of different pooling methods under the CPF except for the backbone. We can observe that each individual pooling method brings valuable performance improvements, and combinations of two pooling methods further enhance the performance. Our proposed clinical cross-channel pooling gets the best performance, which demonstrates the superiority of our method by taking advantage of three clinical pixel features.

Validation: To demonstrate the generalization capability of CPF on natural images, Table 4 offers the results of our CPF and SOTA attention methods on CIFAR benchmarks. CIFAR benchmarks consist of CIAFAR-10 (10 labels) and CIAFAR-100 (100 labels). They contain 50,000 training images and 10,000 test

Table 2. Performance comparison and complexity comparison of CPF and state-of-the-art attention methods on the RETINAMNIST dataset when taking ResNet18 and ResNet50 as backbones.

Method	ACC	F1	Kappa	Params
ResNet18 [5]	52.00	31.99	29.45	11.17M
+ CBAM [17]	52.25	34.81	31.73	11.27M
+ BAM [12]	53.00	38.27	32.93	11.19M
+ SE [7]	51.00	36.43	31.05	11.27M
+ GE [6]	50.00	33.27	29.46	11.45M
+ NL [16]	51.75	34.03	31.51	11.92M
+ EA [3]	51.75	32.61	31.89	11.41M
+ CPF	**53.50**	**38.30**	**33.85**	11.18M
ResNet50 [5]	51.50	33.76	31.15	23.51M
+ CBAM [17]	51.50	33.95	32.29	26.04M
+ BAM [12]	50.25	33.08	29.78	23.69M
+ SE [7]	47.75	31.65	26.16	26.05M
+ GE [6]	53.25	35.51	33.04	27.45M
+ NL [16]	52.50	30.21	30.75	44.77M
+ EA [3]	50.75	32.51	30.42	25.43M
+ CPF	**53.50**	**32.36**	**34.34**	23.51M

Table 3. Comparison of different pooling methods on OCTMNIST dataset.

Method	ACC	F1	Kappa
ResNet50	78.00	75.82	70.67
+ Max	78.40	75.94	71.21
+ Avg	79.10	76.90	72.13
+ Std	78.90	77.06	71.87
+ Max + Avg	79.50	77.34	72.67
+ Max + Std	79.60	77.48	72.81
+ Avg + Std	79.50	77.60	72.67
+ Avg + Std+ Max(CPF)	**80.10**	**77.67**	**73.47**

images of 32×32 pixels, respectively. We adapt the same data augmentation strategy in [8]. We set training epochs and batch size to 200 and 128 accordingly. The initial learning rate is set to 0.1, which is decreased by a factor of 10 every 40 epochs. It can be observed that CPF achieves the best classification performance. At the same time, it increases the minimal parameter through comparisons to other attention methods under ResNet18 and ResNet50, proving that the effectiveness of CPF is not limited to medical images.

Table 4. Accuracy on CIFAR benchmarks with ResNet18 and ResNet50 as backbones and complexity comparison.

Method	CIFAR-10		CIFAR-100	
	ACC	Params	ACC	Params
ResNet18 [5]	93.02	11.17M	74.56	11.22M
+ CBAM [17]	95.19	11.26M	77.82	11.31M
+ BAM [12]	95.20	11.20M	78.09	11.24M
+ SE [7]	94.84	11.27M	75.19	11.32M
+ GE [6]	95.14	11.55M	77.64	11.56M
+ NL [16]	93.38	11.96M	71.97	12.01M
+ EA [3]	93.16	11.47M	72.05	11.50M
+ CPF	**95.26**	11.18M	**78.51**	11.23M
ResNet50 [5]	93.62	23.52M	78.51	23.71M
+ CBAM [17]	95.70	26.05M	80.13	26.24M
+ BAM [12]	95.54	23.88M	80.00	24.06M
+ SE [7]	95.35	26.06M	79.28	26.64M
+ GE [6]	95.44	27.87M	79.54	28.05M
+ NL [16]	94.00	46.17M	72.15	46.36M
+ EA [3]	93.98	25.64M	71.85	25.80M
+ CPF	**95.87**	23.53M	**80.26**	23.71M

6   Conclusions

In this paper, we proposed a lightweight yet efficient architectural unit, clinical pixel feature recalibration module (CPF), which dynamically recalibrates spatial position responses based on clinical pixel feature importance. By infusing the clinical pixel features into spatial positions of feature maps, CPF significantly improves the representational capability of CNNs. The extensive experiments on two ophthalmic image datasets and CIFAR datasets demonstrate that our CPF keeps a better trade-off between effectiveness and efficiency than state-of-the-art attention methods. Furthermore, we verify the ability of CPF to guide the CNN to focus on the significant spatial positions and suppress redundant ones. We hope our work may shed light on better exploiting the potential of clinical features to improve both the interpretability and representational power of CNNs from the spatial position perspective.

References

1. Das, V., Dandapat, S., Bora, P.K.: Multi-scale deep feature fusion for automated classification of macular pathologies from OCT images. Biomed. Signal Process. Control **54**, 101605 (2019). https://doi.org/10.1016/j.bspc.2019.101605, https://www.sciencedirect.com/science/article/pii/S1746809419301867
2. Fu, H., et al.: Angle-closure detection in anterior segment oct based on multilevel deep network. IEEE Trans. Cybern. **50**(7), 3358–3366 (2019)
3. Guo, M.H., Liu, Z.N., Mu, T.J., Hu, S.M.: Beyond self-attention: external attention using two linear layers for visual tasks. T-PAMI 1–13 (2022). https://doi.org/10.1109/TPAMI.2022.3211006
4. Hao, J., et al.: Hybrid variation-aware network for angle-closure assessment in AS-OCT. TMI **41**(2), 254–265 (2021)
5. He, K., Zhang, X., Ren, S., Sun, J.: Deep residual learning for image recognition. In: CVPR, pp. 770–778 (2016)
6. Hu, J., Shen, L., Albanie, S., Sun, G., Vedaldi, A.: Gather-excite: exploiting feature context in convolutional neural networks. In: Proceedings of the 32nd International Conference on Neural Information Processing Systems, NIPS 2018, pp. 9423–9433. Curran Associates Inc., Red Hook (2018)
7. Hu, J., Shen, L., Sun, G.: Squeeze-and-excitation networks. In: 2018 IEEE/CVF Conference on Computer Vision and Pattern Recognition, pp. 7132–7141 (2018). https://doi.org/10.1109/CVPR.2018.00745
8. Krizhevsky, A.: Learning multiple layers of features from tiny images (2009)
9. Kumar, G., Chatterjee, S., Chattopadhyay, C.: DRISTI: a hybrid deep neural network for diabetic retinopathy diagnosis. Signal Image Video Process. **15**(8), 1679–1686 (2021). https://doi.org/10.1007/s11760-021-01904-7, https://europepmc.org/articles/PMC8051933
10. Li, H., et al.: An annotation-free restoration network for cataractous fundus images. TMI **41**, 1699–1710 (2022)
11. World Health Organization, et al.: World report on vision (2019)
12. Park, J., Woo, S., Lee, J.Y., Kweon, I.S.: A simple and light-weight attention module for convolutional neural networks. IJCV **128**(4), 783–798 (2020)
13. Perdomo, O., et al.: Classification of diabetes-related retinal diseases using a deep learning approach in optical coherence tomography. Comput. Methods Program. Biomed. **178**, 181–189 (2019)
14. Raghavendra, U., Fujita, H., Bhandary, S.V., Gudigar, A., Tan, J.H., Acharya, U.R.: Deep convolution neural network for accurate diagnosis of glaucoma using digital fundus images. Inf. Sci. **441**, 41–49 (2018)
15. Wang, Q., Wu, B., Zhu, P., Li, P., Zuo, W., Hu, Q.: ECA-net: efficient channel attention for deep convolutional neural networks. In: CVPR, pp. 11531–11539 (2020). https://doi.org/10.1109/CVPR42600.2020.01155
16. Wang, X., Girshick, R., Gupta, A., He, K.: Non-local neural networks. In: 2018 IEEE/CVF Conference on Computer Vision and Pattern Recognition, pp. 7794–7803 (2018). https://doi.org/10.1109/CVPR.2018.00813
17. Woo, S., Park, J., Lee, J.Y., Kweon, I.S.: CBAM: convolutional block attention module. In: ECCV, pp. 3–19 (2018)
18. Xu, X., Zhang, L., Li, J., Guan, Y., Zhang, L.: A hybrid global-local representation CNN model for automatic cataract grading. IEEE J. Biomed. Health Inform. **24**(2), 556–567 (2020). https://doi.org/10.1109/JBHI.2019.2914690

19. Yang, J., et al.: MedMNIST v2: a large-scale lightweight benchmark for 2D and 3D biomedical image classification. arXiv preprint arXiv:2110.14795 (2021)
20. Zhang, X.Q., Hu, Y., Xiao, Z.J., Fang, J.S., Higashita, R., Liu, J.: Machine learning for cataract classification/grading on ophthalmic imaging modalities: a survey. Mach. Intell. Res. **19**(3), 184–208 (2022)
21. Zhang, X., et al.: Attention to region: region-based integration-and-recalibration networks for nuclear cataract classification using AS-OCT images. Med. Image Anal. **80**, 102499 (2022)
22. Zhang, X., et al.: Adaptive feature squeeze network for nuclear cataract classification in AS-OCT image. JBI **128**, 104037 (2022). https://doi.org/10.1016/j.jbi.2022.104037, https://www.sciencedirect.com/science/article/pii/S1532046422000533
23. Zhang, X., et al.: CCA-net: clinical-awareness attention network for nuclear cataract classification in AS-OCT. KBS **250**, 109109 (2022)

CopiFilter: An Auxiliary Module Adapts Pre-trained Transformers for Medical Dialogue Summarization

Jiaxin Duan[✉] and Junfei Liu

School of Software and Microelectronics, Peking University, Beijing, China
duanjx@stu.pku.edu.cn, liujunfei@pku.edu.cn

Abstract. To relieve doctors from trivial recording, medical dialogue summarization (MDS) aims at automatically generating electronic health records (EHR) from the dialogues between doctors and patients. Having seen their remarkable performance on text/document summarization tasks, we naturally expect to fine-tune pre-trained language models for MSD. However, most of the models have no special interfaces for exploiting the characteristics of dialogue (e.g., speaker's role) and have trouble dealing with the unique features of the task. Therefore, we propose a CopiFilter module to adapt pre-trained Transformers for medical dialogue summarization. The module consists of a filter and a copier. Specifically, the filter refines the coarse features of dialogue by incorporating the query and speaker information, and the copier implements a copy mechanism to help correctly generate the medical terminologies that are not contained in the predefined vocabulary. Furthermore, we propose a local correlation detecting (LCD) task and fine-tune the augmented Transformers in a multi-task fashion. Extensive experiments on two public datasets show that the augmented Transformers significantly outperform their baselines w.r.t. ROUGE (average) and entity matching rate (up to 5.01/3.64 on IMCS-MRG and 7.29/3.26 on SUM2).

Keywords: Text summarization · Medical dialogue summarization · Pre-trained language models

1 Introduction

With the rapid development of digital health, online medical consultation platforms have gradually emerged in recent years. It allows doctors to communicate with patients on the Internet, diagnose and provide treatment suggestions, thus facilitating patients a lot. However, doctors are required to summarize patients' health conditions into an electronic health record (EHR) during each consultation [5], which heavily limits their work efficiency. Therefore, medical dialogue summarization (MDS) takes its goal as automatically generating EHRs according to the dialogues between doctors and patients to relieve doctors from trivial recording.

L. Iliadis et al. (Eds.): ICANN 2023, LNCS 14257, pp. 99–114, 2023.
https://doi.org/10.1007/978-3-031-44216-2_9

Despite the remarkable success of pre-trained Transformers like T5 [16], BART [9], and PEGASUS [25] in text/document summarization, directly fine-tuning them for dialogue summarization still faces substantial obstacles. Note that the majority of the models are designed for general purposes. They struggle to directly take advantage of the distinctive qualities of dialogue due to their rigid structure and prescribed training schema. Several academics suggest pre-training algorithms specifically designed for analyzing dialogue to address the issue. For the purpose of summarizing lengthy dialogue, Zhong et al. [29] develop a window-based denoising task and train a Transformer with limited attention. To summarize meetings, Qi et al. [14] propose a hierarchical Transformer and train it concurrently on three carefully crafted tasks. Yet, training such complex models from scratch is expensive, time-consuming, and often impossible in data-limited scenarios. Contrarily, it makes more sense to build a fresh model using a published Transformer as the foundation. According to Liu et al. [11], the BERT's segment embedding [3] represents the speakers' roles and is outfitted with an additional decoder for abstractive summarization. They start the decoder training from scratch, which results in a mismatch between the two modules.

In addition, MDS is query-oriented. A typical EHR (see Fig. 1) fundamentally contains elements like the main complaint, illness histories, diagnosis, suggestions, etc. Each element corresponds to a certain topic and needs to be gathered independently. On the other hand, MDS is also domain-specific. A medical dialogue frequently uses many medical terminologies, the majority of which are not included in a pre-trained model's predefined vocabulary. Unfortunately, the limited number of samples makes it challenging to fine-tune the models to comprehend complex terminologies or appropriately produce terminologies they have never encountered.

The purpose of this work is to make full use of the pre-training advantages in medical dialogue summarization. Therefore, we take the pre-trained Transformers with the encoder-decoder structure as our object and propose a CopiFilter module which consists of a filter and a copier to augment them without changing their natures. In the augmented Transformer, the filter serves as an extended structure of the encoder. It incorporates the encoder's output with speaker embedding and query embedding to obtain refined features. Then, the copier calculates the generating probability and attention score for each token in dialogue to implement a copy mechanism [17], preventing the decoder from generating misused terminologies. Moreover, inspired by the two-stage fine-tuning [11] and the locality hypothesis [6], we define a local correlation detecting (LCD) task and fine-tune the augmented Transformers with a multi-task strategy to alleviate the mismatch between each component.

In summary, our contributions are as follows:

- We propose a plug-and-play module CopiFilter to adapt pre-trained Transformers for medical dialogue summarization.
- We define a local correlation detecting task and propose a multi-task strategy to fine-tune the augmented Transformers.

PT: How to treat iritis with **"blurred vision"**? (Male, 33 years old)   **DR:** Hello! How long have you been in this situation? You need to go to the hospital. To what extent do you need medication now?   **PT: Half a month**   **DR:** Oh, it's been too long. Have you seen a doctor?   **PT:** I have treated **blurred vision** with tobramycin and dexamethasone and compound topicamide, headache now   **DR:** Is the inflammation eliminated now? Headache, do you have high intraocular pressure?   **PT:** The intraocular pressure is unknown. Is this disease cured quickly? How to treat? My eyes are not red anymore, but **my vision is blurry**   **DR:** Well, this disease is troublesome and easy to recur. Well, do you have arthritis or other similar diseases?   **PT:** No   **DR:** You have to **go to the hospital for examination** once your eyes are uncomfortable. **If you get inflamed**, you should **take medicine in time**. If you **get it repeatedly**, it can cause cataracts or glaucoma.
Chief complaint: Blurred vision for more than **half a month** with **headache.**   **Suggestions:** In case of **blurred vision, go to the hospital for examination** immediately. **If you get inflamed, take medicine in time** to avoid **recurrent disease.**

Fig. 1. A case in SUM2 to illustrate the locality of medical dialogue summarization. Note that the majority of tokens in the suggestion are contained in certain sentences of the dialogue. PT: patient. DR: doctor. The original language is Chinese, we here translate it to English.

- We conduct a lot of experiments on two datasets to validate the effectiveness of our proposals and find that the augmented models consistently outperform their baselines w.r.t. various evaluation metrics.
- To the best of our knowledge, this is the first work to adapt the pre-trained Transformers for medical dialogue summarization.

2   Related Work

2.1   Pre-trained Transformer Models

Recently, a lot of generative pre-trained language models have shown reliable performance on sequence-to-sequence tasks. Most of them have the same encoder-decoder structure as the standard Transformer [22], while they differ in terms of the volume and the pre-training tasks. Song et al. [19] propose masked sequence-to-sequence pre-training (MASS) for language generation. Lewis et al. [9] introduce denoising sequence-to-sequence tasks to pre-train bidirectional and auto-regressive Transformers (BART) for text generation. T5 [16] regards all the natural language processing (NLP) tasks as text-to-text generation and further introduces relative position embeddings. Further more, PEGASUS [25] is designed especially for abstractive text summarization and introduces a novel self-supervised objective called Gap Sentences Generation (GSG). Despite all of their state-of-the-art performance on various benchmarks, as for dealing with medical dialogue summarization, they neither have any available interfaces for incorporating the characteristics of dialogue nor are able to ensure the generation of accurate medical terminologies. The CopiFilter in this paper is therefore designed to break these limits.

2.2 Dialogue Summarization

Different from well-explored text summarization (meeting or chat summarization), there are only a limited number of existing works on medical dialogue summarization, which can be roughly divided into two branches. The first branch takes the goal as summarizing a medical dialogue for certain aspects. For example, Liu et al. [12] extend the pointer generator network (PGN) [17] with a topic-level attention mechanism to summarize the nurse-to-patient conversations. Similarly, Joshi et al. [6] also modify the PGN by incorporating medical knowledge, and aim to gather medical histories of patients. Zhang et al. [27] resort to graph convolution network and propose a question-focused dual attention to generate the summarizations of medical answers. Their tasks are all query-free and thus can be solved by universal models. Another branch is about generating medical text like EHR, which is query-oriented because more than one item is contained in a record and each of them should be generated independently. Existing researches deal with the problem by pipelines [7,8] or Seq2Seq models [4]. They are either non-end-to-end approaches or require external annotations. Besides, as far as we know, few relevant researches propose to benefit from pre-trained models, which is however the theme of this work.

3   Methodology

3.1   Problem Definition

We define the medical dialogue summarization task as a sequence-to-sequence problem, where the source sequence is a medical dialogue $\mathbf{X} = (x_1, x_2, \cdots, x_n)$ contains n tokens and the target sequence is the corresponding medical record $\mathbf{Y} = (y_1, y_2, \cdots, y_n)$. The objective is to generate the target sequence by modeling conditional probability $P(y_1, y_2, \cdots, y_m | x_1, x_2, \cdots, x_n)$. As previously mentioned, a medical record includes l segments $\mathbf{Y}_1, \mathbf{Y}_2, \cdots, \mathbf{Y}_l$, each of which is about a certain aspect. We correspondingly introduce l queries $Q_1, Q_2, \cdots, Q_l$ to describe all these aspects. Besides, as there are two speakers involved in a medical dialogue (one doctor and one patient), we further introduce the speaker's role $R_i \in (0, 1)$ to indicate whether the token x_i is uttered by doctor ($R_i = 0$) or patient ($R_i = 1$). After that, we rewrite the medical dialogue as $\mathbf{X} = ((x_1, R_1), (x_2, R_2), \cdots, (x_n, R_n))$, and split a training pair $(\mathbf{X}, \mathbf{Y})$ into l sub-pairs $(\mathbf{X}, \mathbf{Y}_1), (\mathbf{X}, \mathbf{Y}_2), \cdots, (\mathbf{X}, \mathbf{Y}_l)$. The goal of the MDS task can in turn be rewritten as:

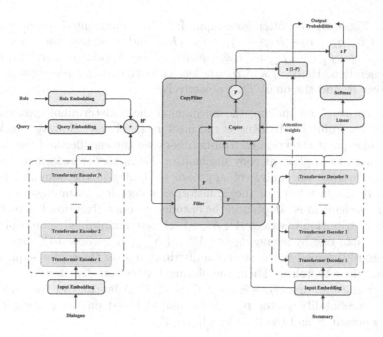

Fig. 2. The structure of the augmented Transformer with our CopiFilter.

$$\prod_{k=1}^{l} P\left(\mathbf{Y}_k | \left(x_1, R_1\right), \left(x_2, R_2\right), \cdots, \left(x_n, R_n\right), Q_k\right), \tag{1}$$

where each sub-task $P\left(\mathbf{Y}_k | \left(x_1, R_1\right), \left(x_2, R_2\right), \cdots, \left(x_n, R_n\right), Q_k\right)$ is solved individually. For the convenience of our illustration, we fix the query as Q_k and thus the target sequence is the segment $\mathbf{Y}_k$ in the following parts of this section.

3.2 CopiFilter

Our proposed CopiFilter serves as an auxiliary component and needs to be attached to a pre-trained Transformer with the encoder-decoder structure. Therefore, the augmented Transformer with a CopiFilter module consists of an encoder, a filter, a copier and a decoder as depicted in Fig. 2.

Filter: Procedurally, tokens in the dialogue $\mathbf{X}$ are first fed into the encoder simultaneously, producing encoder hidden states $H = [\boldsymbol{h}_1, \boldsymbol{h}_2, \cdots, \boldsymbol{h}_n]$, which are usually regarded as the semantic features. However, according to previous studies [6], not all the tokens are necessary for generating medical records. Intuitively, depressing noise tokens helps to make the obtained features more informative. Speaker's role and query's induction are the directly available prompt for this matter. Therefore, we construct a filter by stacking L Transformer blocks (each block consists of a multi-head attention layer followed by a feed forward layer) and connect it to the encoder. As shown in Fig. 3(a), the filter gets input from the augmented features $\boldsymbol{H}' = [\boldsymbol{q}_k + \boldsymbol{r}_1 + \boldsymbol{h}_1, \boldsymbol{q}_k + \boldsymbol{r}_2 + \boldsymbol{h}_2, \cdots, \boldsymbol{q}_k + \boldsymbol{r}_n + \boldsymbol{h}_n]$ and produces the refined features $\boldsymbol{F} = [\boldsymbol{f}_1, \boldsymbol{f}_2, \cdots, \boldsymbol{f}_n]$ for the copier and the decoder to carry on subsequent generation. Here, $\boldsymbol{r}_i$ and $\boldsymbol{q}_k$ are learnable embedding representations of the speaker R_i and the query Q_k, respectively.

Copier: To avoid misspelling the uncommon medical terminologies, copying them directly from the dialogue is the most rational way. However, lacking a unique and explicit attention distribution between the encoder and the decoder makes it hard to implement copy mechanism [17] in the Transformer. Inspired by [2], we leverage an equivalent approach to analogize the standard pointer network. In the last layer of the Transformer's decoder, assuming the h-head attention mechanism is adapted in the encoder-decoder attention layers, then h attention distribution matrices $\boldsymbol{A}^1, \boldsymbol{A}^2, \cdots, \boldsymbol{A}^h$ are maintained. The copier first fuses them into one by averaging i.e. $\boldsymbol{A}^* = \frac{1}{h} \sum_{i=1}^{h} \boldsymbol{A}^i$, whose t-th row $\boldsymbol{A}_t^*$ can be analogously seemed as the attention distribution over the source sequence for generating the t-th token. Then, the obtained attention distribution is further used to produce an analogous context $\boldsymbol{C} = \boldsymbol{A}^* \boldsymbol{F}$. Adapting the idea from [17] and [2], a probability vector $\boldsymbol{p}_{gen}$ is calculated based on the context $\boldsymbol{C}$, the decoder's output $\boldsymbol{S}$ and the decoder's input $\boldsymbol{Z}$:

$$\boldsymbol{p}_{gen} = \sigma\left(\boldsymbol{w}_c^T \boldsymbol{C} + \boldsymbol{w}_s^T \boldsymbol{S} + \boldsymbol{w}_z^T (\boldsymbol{M}\boldsymbol{Z}) + b_{ptr}\right), \tag{2}$$

where vectors $\boldsymbol{w}_c, \boldsymbol{w}_s, \boldsymbol{w}_z$ and scalar b_{ptr} are all learnable parameters. σ represents the sigmoid activation, '$\odot$' means element-level multiplication and $\boldsymbol{M}$ is a unit lower triangular matrix for masking purpose. For each step t, we use the produced $\boldsymbol{p}_{gen}$ to decide whether the decoder generates a token from the vocabulary, or the copier copies a token from the source sequence. Therefore, the following probability distribution is obtained:

$$P_t(w) = p_{gen,t} P_{vocab}(w) + (1 - p_{gen,t}) \sum_{i:x_i=w} A_{ti}^*, \tag{3}$$

where $p_{gen,t}$ means the t-th element of the vector $\boldsymbol{p}_{gen}$, and the vocabulary distribution $P_{vocab}(w)$ is produced by the decoder.

In our intention, the terminologies in the generated medical record must be copied from the dialogue. As illustrated in Fig. 3(c), we further split the sequence-to-sequence generation problem into delexicalized record generation and terminologies generation. The first task requests the model to generate a delexicalized record, where all the terminologies are represented as a special token [TERM]. And for the second task, the model needs to decide which terminology the [TERM] represents according to following probability distribution:

$$P_t^*(e) = \sum_{i:x_i=e} A_{ti}^*, \tag{4}$$

where $e \in \mathbf{E}$, and $\mathbf{E}$ is the set of all terminologies contained in the dialogue.

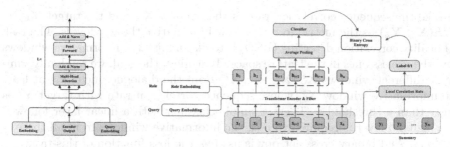

(a) The structure of the filter.

(b) The illustration of local correlation detecting task.

(c) The illustration of delexicalization.

Fig. 3. The illustration of our proposals.

3.3 Locality Correlation Detecting

Even equipping the backbone Transformer with our CopiFilter, there are still two latent dangers. Firstly, experimental results in Sect. 4.7 show that the refined features are not as informative as we hope once without any interventions. In addition, the Transformer has been pre-trained before augmenting while the CopiFilter is constructed from scratch, thus causing a mismatch problem [11] between the two components. To mitigate these negative impacts, we introduce another Locality Correlation Detecting (ICD) task and propose to fine-tune the augmented Transformer in a multi-task fashion (Sect. 3.4).

Locality: Locality is first proposed by Joshi et al. [6], that is, the majority of the information needed in a summary is presented in the dialogue with some novel words introduced to stitch them together. As shown in Fig. 1, we find that the locality is also suitable for medical dialogue summarization.

Sequence Correlation Rate: Given a source string $S = (s_1, s_2, ..., s_n)$ and a query string $T = (t_1, t_2, ..., t_m)$, we define the correlation rate of the two strings as:

$$SCR(S,T) = \frac{LCQ(S,T)}{\min(n,m)}, \quad (5)$$

where $LCQ(S,T)$ means the length of the longest common subsequence of S and T.

Locality Correlation Detecting: As illustrated in Fig. 3(b), a series of consecutive tokens are selected from the dialogue $\mathbf{X}$ and compose a fix sized window $\mathbf{X}_w = (x_i, x_{i+1}, \cdots, x_{i+w})$, whose refined feature is $\boldsymbol{f}_w = \frac{1}{w} \sum_{i=0}^{w} \boldsymbol{f}_{i+w}$. Besides, we take the sequence correlation rate of the window $\mathbf{X}_w$ and the target $\mathbf{Y}_k$ i.e. $SCR(\mathbf{X}_w, \mathbf{Y}_k)$ as the metric to reflect how informative the window is. The task of Locality correlation detecting (LCD) is to distinguish the informative windows from the useless ones in the feature space. To achieve the goal, we randomly sample N different windows $\mathbf{X}_w^1, \mathbf{X}_w^2, \cdots, \mathbf{X}_w^N$ from the dialogue, including at least one informative window $\mathbf{X}_w^j$ whose sequence correlation rate with target $\mathbf{Y}_k$ is larger than a threshold γ. Then, a simple classifier with a linear layer followed by a sigmoid layer is required to pick the informative windows from all these N windows. And binary cross entropy is used as the loss function of this task:

$$w_j = \sigma\left(\boldsymbol{w}^T \boldsymbol{f}_j^w + b\right)$$
$$\text{loss}_{lcd} = -\frac{1}{N}\sum_{j=1}^N \bar{w}_j \log w_j + (1 - \bar{w}_j)\log(1 - w_j), \tag{6}$$

where $\boldsymbol{f}_i^w$ is the feature of the window $\mathbf{X}_w^i$, and $\bar{w}_j \in (0,1)$ is the unsupervised label to indicate whether the window $\mathbf{X}_w^i$ is an informative window. We suppose that the fewer mistakes the weak classifier makes, the greater the difference between informative windows and useless windows, and in turn the easier it is for the decoder to attend to the key tokens contained in the informative windows for the generation. Empirically (see Sect. 4.7), training with LCD enables the filter to refine the coarse features more targeted.

3.4   Multi-task Fine-Tuning

Following previous works, we use a negative log likelihood loss as the training objective of the primary summarization task, that is:

$$loss_{gen} = -\sum_{t=1}^{|\mathbf{Y}_k|} logP(y_t|\mathbf{X}, Q_k, y_{1:t}), \tag{7}$$

where

$$P(y_t|\mathbf{X}, Q_k, y_{1:t}) = P_t(y_t') + m_t P_t^*(y_t), \tag{8}$$

where y_t' is a delexicalized token (i.e. if y_t is a terminology, then y_t' is [TERM]), and $m_t \in (0,1)$ is used to indicate whether y_t is a terminology. Besides, following the standard PGN [17], we further use a coverage loss to avoid the repetition problem, which is calculated as follows:

$$loss_{cov} = \sum_t \sum_i A_{ti}^* C_{ti}^*, \tag{9}$$

where the t-th row of the coverage matrix $\boldsymbol{C}^*$ is defined as $\boldsymbol{C}_t^* = \sum_{t'=0}^t \boldsymbol{A}_{t'}^*$. Therefore, the overall loss to fine-tune the augmented Transformer is:

$$loss_k = loss_{gen} + \lambda_1 loss_{cov} + \lambda_2 loss_{lcd}, \tag{10}$$

where λ_1 and λ_2 are two hyperparameters. In practice, λ_2 can be set larger than 1 to speed up the overall convergence. During training, we obtain the loss of the training pair $(\mathbf{X}, \mathbf{Y})$ by accumulating the loss of each sub-pair i.e. $\sum_{k=1}^l loss_k$.

4 Experiment

4.1 Datasets

IMCS-MRG [26]: is an abstractive dataset and defines a task to generate electronic medical records (EMR) from dialogue between doctors and patients. Each EMR needs to be generated containing 6 items, namely chief complaint, present illness history, past illness history, auxiliary examination, diagnosis, and suggestion. 1824, 616, and 612 samples are used for training, evaluating, and testing, respectively.

SUM2 [20]: is a dataset collected from the Internet, whose task is to summarize doctors' suggestions and patients' chief complaints from medical dialogues. It contains nearly 45K samples, but only 3375 of them are used for extractive summarization. In our experiments, we randomly select 2700 samples (80%) for training and the remaining 675 samples (20%) for evaluation.

4.2 Baselines

Seq2Seq [1]: an RNN based encoder-decoder model with attention mechanisms, leverages a bidirectional LSTM as the encoder and an LSTM as the decoder. **Transformer**: standard Transformer [22] with encoder-decoder structure and without any pre-training. **Pointer Generator (PGNet)** [17]: a strong baseline for document summarization, which modifies standard Seq2Seq model by introducing the copy mechanism. **SPNet** [24]: incorporates the scaffolds of speaker role, semantic slot and dialog domain into PGNet for abstractive dialogue summarization[1]. **ProphetNet** [15]: a Transformer pre-trained with future n-gram prediction and introduces an n-stream self-attention mechanism into the decoder. It shows the powerful performance on text summarization. **PEGASUS**: the 'Randeng-Pegasus-238M-Summary-Chinese' version [23] is used in our experiment. **T5**: the 'mengzi-t5-base' version [28] is used in our experiment. **BART**: the 'bart-base-chinese' version [18] is used in our experiment.

4.3 Implement Details

For all experiments, we set the max length of the dialogue text to 1024 and the max length of the corresponding summary to be generated to 256. All the pre-trained transformers (augmented by our CopiFilter or not) are implemented with Huggingface Transformer repository[2], while other models (Seq2Seq, Transformer and pointer networks) are implemented with OpenNMT[3]. Besides, the filter with 3 layers is adapted in our CopiFilter. When generating, the greedy search strategy is adapted for all the models. More details about the optimizer, learning scheme and the settings of the locality correlation detecting task are provided in Appendix A.

---

[1] The domain scaffold is ignored in our implementation because MSD is a single-domain summarization task.

[2] https://huggingface.co/models.

[3] https://opennmt.net.

4.4   Evaluation Metrics

ROUGE [10]: we adapt the conventionally used average of F1 scores for ROUGE-1, ROUGE-2 and ROUGE-L as one of our metrics.

Entity Matching Rate (EMR): drawing the lessons from [30], we also define an entity matching rate to reflect the ability of a model to generate faithful medical records that contain correct terminologies. We first use a BERT-CRF [21] to recognize terminologies contained in the ground-truth and the generated record, respectively. Then, suppose the set of the terminologies in the ground-truth is E_s and the set of the terminologies in the generated record is E_a, the EMR is calculated as:

$$EMR = 100 \times \frac{|E_s \cap E_a|}{|E_s \cup E_a|} \tag{11}$$

4.5   Main Results

We report the comparison results in Table 1. Note that the evaluation of IMCS-MRG is carried out on the test set and the results are produced by the official program[4] automatically (the same as below). It is obvious that on both datasets, pre-trained Transformers significantly outperform Seq2Seq models and pointer networks (PGNet, SPNet), and augmented Transformers with our CopiFilter (CF) consistently surpass their baselines. The CopiFilter has the most significant effect on BART. The average ROUGE score of BART-CF is 5.01 higher than that of BART on IMCS-MRG and is 7.29 higher than that of BART on SUM2. The CopiFilter also increased T5's EMR score by 3.64 and 3.26 respectively on the two datasets. On the whole, PEGASUS-CF achieves the best performance on IMCS-MRG and T5-CF achieves the best performance on SUM2. These results prove that our CopiFilter is a simple-designed but effective plug-and-play module (Table 2).

4.6   Human Evaluation Results

We randomly sample 50 cases from the evaluation set of IMCS-MRG and SUM2 respectively. Then, referring to the ground truth, we ask three volunteers majoring in clinical medicine to score each of the generated medical records from the perspective of readability, integrality and authenticity on a scale of 1 to 10. The results are shown in Table 3, and one case coupled with the generated records corresponding to it is shown in Fig. 6. Not surprisingly, pre-trained Transformers can generate fluent sentences with few grammar and logic mistakes (sometimes suffer from repetition problems). But in terms of integrality, they ignore some adverbial words and adjectives of time. Even if it does not harm semantic integrality, the incomplete content is one of the reasons that drop their ROUGE scores. Most importantly, pre-trained Transformers tend to produce hallucinatory terminologies, which are common but irrelevant to the dialogue. Therefore,

---

[4] https://tianchi.aliyun.com/dataset/95414/submission.

Table 1. Main evaluation results. The best results are in bold.

Model	IMCS-MRG				SUM2			
	R-1	R-2	R-L	EMR	R-1	R-2	R-L	EMR
Seq2Seq	56.29	47.15	55.36	25.03	59.48	50.68	56.43	28.85
PGNet	61.54	55.23	60.60	35.90	64.62	58.30	62.68	37.77
Transformer	61.34	49.57	58.87	33.68	63.14	51.36	62.70	39.70
SPNet	62.21	56.76	60.75	36.75	64.88	58.71	62.66	39.91
ProphetNet	65.21	51.69	61.08	35.56	68.09	56.04	64.38	39.87
BART	64.24	50.17	59.87	35.29	65.78	54.65	61.12	38.69
T5	65.55	51.73	61.21	35.22	67.99	56.11	64.21	39.32
PEGASUS	65.46	52.47	62.06	36.10	67.95	56.73	64.95	39.33
BART+CF	69.02	55.62	64.66	38.03	73.24	59.71	70.46	41.37
T5+CF	**69.58**	57.03	65.99	38.86	**73.94**	**60.98**	**71.49**	**42.58**
PEGASUS+CF	69.28	**57.24**	**66.07**	**39.06**	73.38	60.66	71.47	42.02

Table 2. Human evaluation results. Read. is the abbr. of readability, Int. is the abbr. of integrality and Aut. is the abbr. of authenticity. The best results are in bold.

Model	IMCS-MRG			SUM2		
	Read.	Int.	Aut.	Read.	Int.	Aut.
Seq2Seq	5.7	3.1	4.2	6.9	4.8	5.0
Pointer Generator	7.8	5.9	6.6	7.8	5.9	6.3
Transformer	7.9	3.7	6.2	7.8	5.5	5.7
SPNet	7.9	6.2	6.8	7.9	6.9	6.5
ProphetNet	8.6	6.1	6.3	8.5	6.9	6.5
BART	8.5	5.9	6.4	8.4	6.8	6.8
T5	8.6	6.1	6.5	8.5	6.7	6.9
PEGASUS	8.7	6.0	6.2	8.5	7.1	6.7
BART+CF	8.7	**7.1**	**7.5**	8.6	7.4	7.5
T5+CF	**8.8**	6.7	7.1	**8.6**	7.5	7.5
PEGASUS+CF	8.7	6.9	7.2	8.5	**7.9**	**7.6**

their authenticity is relatively low (another reason that drops their ROUGE scores). After being augmented, their integrality score and authenticity score are improved. On the whole, the results of the human evaluation are consistent with the automatic evaluation, revealing that our CopiFilter is capable of helping the pre-trained Transformers to generate faithful and readable medical records.

Table 3. Ablation study using BART with different augmentation strategies.

filter	copier	MTF	IMCS-MRG				SUM2			
			R-1	R-2	R-L	EMR	R-1	R-2	R-L	EMR
+	−	−	66.50	52.42	61.53	36.05	68.36	57.40	66.44	39.07
+	+	−	67.65	55.83	64.21	37.32	69.90	58.35	66.43	39.90
+	−	+	67.49	55.09	64.12	36.77	69.96	58.58	66.59	39.28
−	+	−	64.91	54.60	60.91	37.11	68.08	57.01	65.14	39.65
−	+	+	67.15	55.85	65.02	37.87	70.94	58.66	65.71	40.41
−	−	+	66.55	53.98	63.19	36.47	70.98	57.67	65.31	39.25

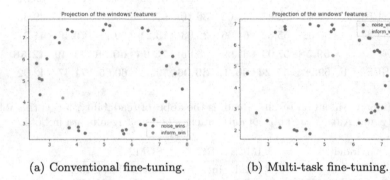

(a) Conventional fine-tuning.   (b) Multi-task fine-tuning.

Fig. 4. An informative window and 31 unless windows is 2D space. The windows are sampled from a case in IMCS-MRG. (a) is produced by fine-tuning the BART+filter conventionally and (b) is produced by fine-tuning the BART+filter with the multi-task strategy.

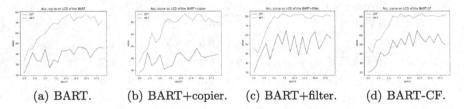

(a) BART.   (b) BART+copier.   (c) BART+filter.   (d) BART-CF.

Fig. 5. Accuracy of LCD during fine-tuning. The evaluation is carried out on the evaluation set of IMCS-MRG. MTF in the figures means the proposed multi-task fine-tuning, while CTF means the conventional fine-tuning on MSD.

4.7   Ablation Study

Augmenting Transformers only with the Filter: To explore whether the query and speaker information contribute to the over improvement, we augment the pre-trained BART only with the filter and fine-tune the augmented model in both single-task and multi-task fashion. According to the evaluation results in Table 3, simply adding coarse features (also can be seen as the token embed-

Ground-truth: (1) Chief complaint: vomit half an hour after milk sleep. (2) Current medical history: The child vomited 3 times half an hour after sleeping with milk for 6 months, and was mentally ill. (3) Auxiliary examination: stool routine: fatty acid++; Blood routine test: "virus infection". (4) Past history: unknown. (5) Diagnosis: upper respiratory tract infection. (6) Suggestion: Get medical attention in time.

Seq2Seq: (1) Chief complaint: fever. (2) Current medical history: The child has fever. (3) Auxiliary inspection:. (4) Past History:. (5) Diagnosis: fever in children. (6) Suggestion: It is recommended to take take take take take take take Mummy orally and go to the doctor go to the doctor go to the doctor go to the doctor go to the doctor go to the doctor go to the doctor.

Transformer: (1) Chief complaint: vomiting. (2) Current medical history: the child vomited, had runny nose, sneezed, sneezed, and his lips turned white. Now take Mommy Love. (3) Auxiliary inspection:. (4) Past History:. (5) Diagnosis: Consider virus infection. (6) Suggestion: Take Mommy Love orally.

PGNet: (1) Chief complaint: vomiting. (2) Current medical history: Vomiting and fell asleep. (3) Auxiliary inspection: . (4) Past history: . (5) Diagnosis: cold. (6) Suggestion: Take Mumi'ai orally.

SPNet: (1) Chief complaint: vomiting. (2) Current medical history: The child vomited and fell asleep. (3) Auxiliary inspection: . (4) Past history: unknown. (5) Diagnosis: common cold. (6) Suggestion: Take Mumi'ai orally and observe the changes of the condition.

BART: (1) Chief complaint: vomiting. (2) Current medical history: the child vomited, had runny nose, sneezed, sneezed, and his lips turned white. Now take Mommy Love. (3) Auxiliary inspection:. (4) Past History:. (5) Diagnosis: Consider virus infection. (6) Suggestion: Take Mommy Love orally.

T5: (1) Chief complaint: vomiting. (2) Current medical history: the child vomited, had runny nose, sneezed, sneezed, sneezed, sneezed, coughed with phlegm. Now take Mommy Love. (3) Auxiliary inspection: temporarily unavailable. (4) Past history: unknown. (5) Diagnosis: Consider viral cold. (6) Suggestion: Take Mommy Love orally.

PEGASUS: (1) Chief complaint: fever. (2) Current medical history: fever and diarrhea. (3) Auxiliary inspection: temporarily unavailable. (4) Past history: unknown. (5) Diagnosis: common cold. (6) Suggestion: Take Mommy Love and Smecta orally and observe the changes of the condition.

BART-CF: (1) Chief complaint: vomiting. (2) Current medical history: The child suffered from diarrhea and cold, and took Mommy Love orally. At present, the symptoms have not improved significantly. (3) Auxiliary inspection: temporarily unavailable. (4) Past history: unknown. (5) Diagnosis: respiratory tract infection. (6) Suggestion: See a doctor in the hospital and test the blood routine test.

T5-CF: (1) Chief complaint: vomiting, diarrhea. (2) Current medical history: The child vomited. (3) Auxiliary examination: blood routine examination, stool routine examination. (4) Past history: history of enteritis. (5) Diagnosis: viral cold, catching cold. (6) Suggestion: Take yeast powder orally, and add complementary food and iron.

PEGASUS-CF: (1) Chief complaint: Frequent vomiting. (2) Current medical history: The 6-month old child vomited three times an hour. (3) Auxiliary inspection: temporarily unavailable. (4) Past history: history of enteritis. (5) Diagnosis: viral cold. (6) Suggestion: Get medical attention in time and take yeast powder orally.

Fig. 6. Case study results. The case is sampled from IMCS-MRG.

dings produced by a pre-trained BERT-like model), speaker embedding, and query embedding can improve the upper limit of the model on the MDS task, but it is still a little hard for the pre-trained decoder to understand the refined features (as can be seen in Fig. 5, the augmented encoders need nearly 10 epochs to converge on LCD task or even can not converge with conventional fine-tuning). Then we project the refined features which achieved the best performance in 2D space with umap [13] (see Fig. 4) and find that compared with the multi-task approach, regularly fine-tuning the augmented BART can not obtain highly informative features. Our proposed multi-task fine-tuning makes it easier to recognize informative segments from useless ones. Theoretically, it is also easier for the decoder and the filter to match each other.

Augmenting Transformers only with the Copier: As shown in Table 3, augmenting BART only with the copier can also improve the overall performance. Although the ROUGE scores are not improved markedly, the copier significantly enhances BART w.r.t. entity matching rate. Subsequently, we add the filter further in the augmented BART, and the situation continues to improve. That is to say, generating correct terminologies is one of the most critical issues in adapting pre-trained Transformers for MSD, moreover, informative features are necessary for the copier and the decoder to work better.

Fine-Tuning with Local Correlation Detecting: Finally, we fine-tune the standard BART and the augmented BARTs (with only the filter, only the copier, and the whole CopiFlter) with our multi-task strategy. Row 3 and rows 6–8 in Table 3 show that compared with the conventional method, multi-task fine-tuning is a better choice. This result is identical to the findings in [11] that fine-tuning the pre-trained language model first on discriminant tasks facilitates the subsequent fine-tuning on the generative task. It can be seen from Fig. 5 that BART+CopiFilter and BART+filter also perform better than standard BART on the sub-task (LCD). From the perspective of LCD, it needs only a few epochs for the BARTs (in fact, the encoders or the augmented encoders) to converge. In the later stage of fine-tuning, the training loss caused by the LCD task is relatively small. Therefore, the decoder (and the copier) is trained more targeted, and the overfitting is alleviated or delayed. Since fine-tuning with LCD makes the extracted dialogue features more informative, the performance of the main task (MDS) is also improved.

5   Conclusion

In this paper, we augment pre-trained Transformers with the proposed CopiFilter module to adapt them for medical dialogue summarization tasks. The augmented Transformers extract dialogue features under the prompt of the speaker's role and query's induction and copy relevant terminologies directly from the dialogue to avoid hallucinatory generation. Moreover, we define a local correlation-detecting task and use a multi-task strategy to fine-tune the augmented models. Extensive experiments and analyses show that our proposals are simple-designed, effective, and plug-and-play, improving the pre-trained Transformers (BART, T5, and PEGASUS) without changing their natures.

A   Experiment Settings

On both IMCS-MRG and SUM2, we set the width of the window w to 12, the number of windows that need to be sampled to 32, and the standard value of the threshold γ to 0.5. When sampling, we slide the window on each dialogue with the stride of 1. To ensure there is at least one informative window, the window has the largest LCR with the ground-truth record first selected, and the remaining 31 windows are randomly selected from the other obtained windows. Once a sample has no informative window, we reduce the threshold but no smaller than 0.3. Otherwise, we do not perform multi-task tuning over this sample.

All pre-trained Transformers are fine-tuned by an Adam optimizer with an initial learning rate of 1e-4 for 15 epochs. We set the batch size to 16 and decay the learning rate every 50 optimization steps with a decay rate of 0.9. We fine-tune the augmented Transformers for 20 epochs with $\lambda_1 = 1$, $\lambda_2 = 1.5$ and adapt a 3-layer filter in the CopiFilter module. We train other models (Seq2Seq, standard Transformer and pointer networks) also for 20 epochs with the initial learning rate 2.5e-4 and batch size 64, other parameters remain unchanged. In our experiments, we train all the models at least 10 times and report their best performance on the evaluation sets (or test sets).

References

1. Cho, K., et al.: Learning phrase representations using RNN encoder-decoder for statistical machine translation. In: EMNLP 2014, pp. 1724–1734 (2014)
2. Deaton, J., Jacobs, A., Kenealy, K., See, A.: Transformers and pointer-generator networks for abstractive summarization (2019)
3. Devlin, J., Chang, M., Lee, K., Toutanova, K.: BERT: pre-training of deep bidirectional transformers for language understanding. In: NAACL-HLT 2019, pp. 4171–4186 (2019)
4. Enarvi, S., et al.: Generating medical reports from patient-doctor conversations using sequence-to-sequence models. In: Proceedings of the First Workshop on Natural Language Processing for Medical Conversations, pp. 22–30 (2020)
5. Feng, X., Feng, X., Qin, B.: A survey on dialogue summarization: recent advances and new frontiers. In: IJCAI 2022, pp. 5453–5460 (2022)
6. Joshi, A., Katariya, N., Amatriain, X., Kannan, A.: Dr.summarize: global summarization of medical dialogue by exploiting local structures. In: EMNLP 2020, pp. 3755–3763 (2020)
7. Kazi, N., Kahanda, I.: Automatically generating psychiatric case notes from digital transcripts of doctor-patient conversations. In: Proceedings of the 2nd Clinical Natural Language Processing Workshop, pp. 140–148 (2019)
8. Krishna, K., Khosla, S., Bigham, J.P., Lipton, Z.C.: Generating SOAP notes from doctor-patient conversations using modular summarization techniques. In: ACL/IJCNLP 2021, pp. 4958–4972 (2021)

9. Lewis, M., Liu, Y., et al.: BART: denoising sequence-to-sequence pre-training for natural language generation, translation, and comprehension. In: ACL 2020, pp. 7871–7880 (2020)
10. Lin, C.Y.: Rouge: a package for automatic evaluation of summaries. In: Text Summarization Branches Out, pp. 74–81 (2004)
11. Liu, Y., Lapata, M.: Text summarization with pretrained encoders. In: EMNLP-IJCNLP 2019, pp. 3728–3738 (2019)
12. Liu, Z., Ng, A., Guang, S.L.S., Aw, A.T., Chen, N.F.: Topic-aware pointer-generator networks for summarizing spoken conversations. In: ASRU 2019, pp. 814–821 (2019)
13. McInnes, L., Healy, J., Saul, N., Grossberger, L.: UMAP: uniform manifold approximation and projection. J. Open Source Softw. **3**(29), 861 (2018)
14. Qi, M., Liu, H., Fu, Y., Liu, T.: Improving abstractive dialogue summarization with hierarchical pretraining and topic segment. In: EMNLP 2021, pp. 1121–1130 (2021)
15. Qi, W., et al.: ProphetNet: predicting future n-gram for sequence-to-sequence pre-training. In: EMNLP 2020, pp. 2401–2410 (2020)
16. Raffel, C., et al.: Exploring the limits of transfer learning with a unified text-to-text transformer. CoRR abs/1910.10683 (2019)
17. See, A., Liu, P.J., Manning, C.D.: Get to the point: summarization with pointer-generator networks. In: ACL 2017, pp. 1073–1083 (2017)
18. Shao, Y., et al.: CPT: a pre-trained unbalanced transformer for both Chinese language understanding and generation. arXiv preprint arXiv:2109.05729 (2021)
19. Song, K., Tan, X., Qin, T., Lu, J., Liu, T.: MASS: masked sequence to sequence pre-training for language generation. In: ICML 2019, pp. 5926–5936 (2019)
20. Song, Y., Tian, Y., Wang, N., Xia, F.: Summarizing medical conversations via identifying important utterances. In: COLING 2020, pp. 717–729 (2020)
21. Souza, F., Nogueira, R., Lotufo, R.: Portuguese named entity recognition using BERT-CRF. arXiv preprint arXiv:1909.10649 (2019)
22. Vaswani, A., et al.: Attention is all you need. In: NeurIPS 2017, pp. 5998–6008 (2017)
23. Wang, J., et al.: Fengshenbang 1.0: being the foundation of Chinese cognitive intelligence. CoRR abs/2209.02970 (2022)
24. Yuan, L., Yu, Z.: Abstractive dialog summarization with semantic scaffolds. CoRR abs/1910.00825 (2019). http://arxiv.org/abs/1910.00825
25. Zhang, J., Zhao, Y., Saleh, M., Liu, P.J.: PEGASUS: pre-training with extracted gap-sentences for abstractive summarization. In: ICML 2020, pp. 11328–11339 (2020)
26. Zhang, N., Chen, M., Bi, Z., Liang, X., et al.: CBLUE: a Chinese biomedical language understanding evaluation benchmark. In: ACL 2022, pp. 7888–7915 (2022)
27. Zhang, N., Deng, S., Li, J., Chen, X., Zhang, W., Chen, H.: Summarizing Chinese medical answer with graph convolution networks and question-focused dual attention. In: EMNLP 2020, pp. 15–24 (2020)
28. Zhang, Z., et al.: Mengzi: towards lightweight yet ingenious pre-trained models for Chinese (2021)
29. Zhong, M., Liu, Y., Xu, Y., Zhu, C., Zeng, M.: DialogLM: pre-trained model for long dialogue understanding and summarization. In: AAAI, pp. 11765–11773 (2022)
30. Zhu, C., et al.: Enhancing factual consistency of abstractive summarization. In: NAACL-HLT 2021, pp. 718–733 (2021)

IESBU-Net: A Lightweight Skin Lesion Segmentation UNet with Inner-Module Extension and Skip-Connection Bridge

Cunhao Lu[1], Huahu Xu[2(✉)], Minghong Wu[1], and Yuzhe Huang[2]

[1] School of Environmental and Chemical Engineering, Shanghai University, Shanghai, China
[2] School of Computer Engineering and Science, Shanghai University, Shanghai, China
huahuxu@shu.edu.cn

Abstract. Skin disease is one of the most common human diseases. In order to improve the segmentation of automatic skin lesions, some pioneering work often uses more complex modules to improve the segmentation performance. However, the models with high computational complexity are difficult to be applied to the realistic medical scenarios with limited computational resources. To solve this problem, we propose a light-weight model, IESBU-Net. It achieves a balance between cost of parameters and computational complexity in the segmentation of skin lesions. Briefly, we propose three modules: (1) the introduction of depth-wise separable convolutions by LSR in shallow encoders reduces computational complexity and expands the receptive field for protecting primary feature information. (2) CA collects dense global feature information in the context-rich encoder bottleneck layer. (3) SCB adds a bridge in the process of feature fusion between encoder and decoder, which is used to smooth the semantic gap between encoder and decoder caused by skip-connection. We evaluated the proposed model on the ISIC 2017 and ISIC 2018 datasets. The experimental results show that the model achieves a good balance between the number of parameters, computational complexity and performance, and improves the performance of skin lesion segmentation significantly.

Keywords: Light-weight model · Skin lesion segmentation · Feature protection · Contextual aggregation · Skip-connection

1 Introduction

With the development of computer vision technology, people begin to apply it to medical image segmentation. Medical image segmentation model can help doctors to segment and locate the pathological tissue, help them to eliminate subjective factors and greatly improve the efficiency of them. Segmentation of skin lesions is an important field in medical image segmentation. Skin is the largest organ of the human body, is the human body's first physiological line of defense. It covers about 16 percent of a person's body weight. It is in direct contact with the external environment, more susceptible to lesions, including lesions on the skin and skin accessories [1]. There are many kinds of skin diseases, early detection and timely prevention can greatly reduce the probability of cancerization.

© The Author(s), under exclusive license to Springer Nature Switzerland AG 2023
L. Iliadis et al. (Eds.): ICANN 2023, LNCS 14257, pp. 115–126, 2023.
https://doi.org/10.1007/978-3-031-44216-2_10

Deep learning-based image segmentation methods are greatly superior to traditional image processing methods [2]. Most of the medical image segmentation methods are based on UNet [3]. It is an Encoder-Decoder based U-shaped structure model, similar to Seg-Net [4]. The difference is that the skip-connection are added between the encoder and decoder in each layer except the last layer of the encoder. Due to the advantages of its simple structure and easy scalability, many improved UNet models have been proposed, such as UNet++ [5], 3D-UNet [6], UNet3+ [7], AttentionUNet [8], ResUnet [9], etc. In 2017, Vaswani et al. [10] proposed an attention mechanism-based network for application to natural language processing tasks. Due to the flexibility of the Transformer model, it has inspired computer vision scholars. Some researchers introduced the self-attention mechanism into UNet, e.g., TransUNet [11], Swin-UNet [12], TransFuse [13], DS-TransUNet [14] etc. In 2020, Jose et al. [15] projected the data to higher dimensions and achieved better segmentation results. However, it is difficult to to learn explicit long-range and global semantic information interaction, so that some studies have used atrous convolutional layers [16, 17] and image pyramids [18] to solve this problem, but these models are still limited in modeling long-range dependence. In addition, many improved architectures mostly focus on optimization algorithms in feature extraction, ignoring the loss of high-resolution information in the shallow layer and the aggregation of rich contextual information in the bottleneck layer of the encoder.

Considering that most existing methods optimize the segmented network by stacking convolutional layers into different network structures, we are going to change our thinking. Starting from the internal module of the encoder, the shallow layer and the bottleneck layer are designed to protect the high-resolution information of the head and extract the global information of the bottleneck layer. We have designed a low-level feature residuals module (LFR), which reduces computational complexity by introducing a depthwise separable convolution [19] so that a larger convolution core can be used to expand the receptive field of a shallow network. Residual connection [20] is introduced to protect the primary feature information. We designed a context aggregation module (CA) to replace the traditional UNet bottleneck stack convolution layer for better context information collection. Skip-connection bridge module (SCB) is designed to smooth the feature difference of long distance connections. The main contributions of this work can be summarized as follows:

- In order to obtain sufficient primary features from the input images, an LFR module is embedded in IESBU-Net, which can expand the receptive field of the network and improve the computational efficiency. A CA module is proposed for feature extraction of encoder bottleneck layer, which improves the extraction of global information of deep network.
- The SCB module is designed to allow fine-grained computation in long-distance connections between encoders and decoders by means of a spatial feature selection unit and a channel feature selection unit.
- Extensive experiments were conducted on the ISIC2017 [21] and ISIC2018 [22] datasets. Evaluation results demonstrate that our proposed IESBU-Net balances parameters, computational complexity and segmentation performance and is more suitable for realistic medical scenarios.

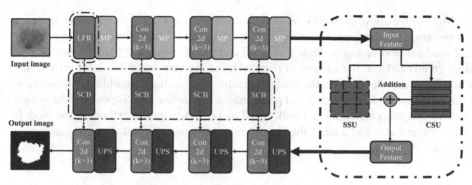

Fig. 1. The illustration of IESBU-Net architecture. LFR and CA modules are applied in the shallow and bottleneck layers of the encoder, respectively, SCB modules are applied in the layers other than the bottleneck layer.

2 Related Works

Most of the previous segmentation methods of skin lesions are based on traditional image processing techniques. Including threshold-based methods, edge detection-based methods, active contour-based methods, region-based and morphological methods, and classifier-based methods [23–26]. But these methods often lack of generalizability, it is difficult to achieve accurate segmentation of skin lesions automatically, difficult to adapt to different skin lesions samples.

In recent years deep learning techniques have developed rapidly and are widely used in image segmentation. In 2015 Long et al. [27] first proposed a full convolutional neural network to implement an end-to-end image segmentation network. Based on this, UNet [3] proposed a full convolutional encoder-decoder model that is more applicable to the field of medical image segmentation, where upsampling operations are performed in the decoder to recover the resolution of the input image. In addition, it combines the features extracted from the encoder with the upsampling results through Skip-connection, achieves good segmentation performance. Zhou et al. [5] replaced the cropping and splicing operations in the skip-connection part of UNet with dense convolutional operations in order to obtain better feature information and reduce the semantic loss of feature fusion between encoder and decoder. Huang et al. [7] improved skip-connection in UNet and designed a full-scale skip-connection method to combine information from different scales. Venkatesh et al. [28] added multi-scale residual connections to UNet to preserve the information lost during downsampling and prevent the gradient disappearance and gradient explosion problems. Qamar et al. [29] introduced atrous spatial pyramid pooling (ASPP) in UNet for extracting multi-scale features. The feature maps of the encoder path and decoder path were concatenated using dense skip-connection, which improves the performance of the network for medical image segmentation. Oktay et al. [8] used the importance of a novel bottom-up attention gate in UNet to further reduce information loss and improve segmentation performance. Jha et al. [30] organized two UNet architectures into a DoubleU-Net network. Atrous spatial pyramid pooing (ASPP) are constructed at the end of each encoder downsampling layer to obtain multi-scale contextual information.

Most of the above networks are designed without considering the balance between parameters, computational complexity and performance. It is difficult to be applied for real medical environments. Jeya et al. [31] combined with MLP [32] on the basis of Unet greatly reduced the number of parameters of the network. It has been proved that while designing the network, the medical practical applications should be considered to balance the network parameters and performance. Therefore, we propose a light-weight medical image segmentation network based on previous studies, extending the module inside the encoder and adding the skip-connection bridge to ensure the segmentation performance.

3 Method

In this section, we first introduce the proposed lightweight model IESBU-Net in Subsect. 3.1, and then introduce the LFR, CA and SCB modules sequentially in Subsects. 3.2, 3.3 and 3.4.

3.1 IESBU-Net Architecture

The architecture of our proposed network is shown in Fig. 1. The architecture is based on the U-Net architecture with the addition of the SCB to transition the long-range skip-connection based on the original encoder, decoder and skip-connection. In addition, the shallow layer encoder and the bottleneck layer encoder are modified. SSU and CSU represent spatial feature selection unit and channel feature selection unit, respectively. While MP and UPS represent maxpooling and upsampling, respectively. For the shallow encoder, there is the problem of small receptive field. We propose the low-level feature residual module (LFR) to increase the receptive field of the shallow encoder by introducing depthwise separable convolution [19] to improve the computational efficiency while expanding the depthwise convolution kernel size. For the end layer of the encoder, which has rich contextual information, we propose the Context Aggregation module (CA) to enhance the collection of global information. To improve the computational efficiency, the convolution layers are reduced from two to one for the middle encoder layer and decoder layer. The loss function is BceDice loss, represented by the following metric.

$$L_{Bce} = -\frac{1}{N} \sum_{i=1}^{N} [y_i \log(p_i) + (1 - y_i)\log(1 - p_i)] \tag{1}$$

$$L_{Dice} = 1 - \frac{2|X \cap Y|}{|X| + |Y|} \tag{2}$$

$$L_{BceDice} = \lambda_1 L_{Bce} + \lambda_2 L_{Dice} \tag{3}$$

where N is the total number of samples, y_i is the real label, p_i is the prediction. |X| and |Y| represent ground truth and prediction, respectively. λ_1 and λ_2 refer to the weight of two loss functions. We will take both weights as 1.

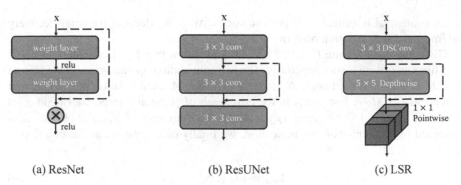

Fig. 2. Comparing our LSR module with ResNet [20] and ResUnet [9] designs used to extract the Primary semantic information from the input images.

3.2 Low-level Feature Residual

In the process of performing medical image segmentation, most segmentation models perform convolutional operations in the downsampled blocks of shallow networks, which will yield more fine-grained information and are rich in spatial information, when the receptive field is smaller and the resolution of features is higher. The original UNet [3] network architecture uses ordinary convolution for downsampling and this structure has been widely used for a variety of different segmentation models. In medical image segmentation, we need a more light-weight network in order to make the parameters and computational complexity of the segmentation network more suitable for medical application scenarios. Therefore, we choose to use a depthwise separable convolution [19] to replace the ordinary convolution. As shown in Fig. 2 (c) for the LSR module, it performs a residual skip-connection between the depthwise separable convolution and the previous convolution, which consists of a depthwise convolution and a pointwise convolution. Because in the process of downsampling in shallow networks, the receptive field is generally small and the overlap area of the receptive field corresponding to each pixel of the feature map is small. We use a larger convolution kernel to extract features without exponentially increasing the parameters and computational complexity when using depthwise seprable convolution. Considering the performance and light-weight, we use 5×5 depthwise convolution and 1×1 pointwise convolution. As shown in Fig. 2 (a) ResNet [20] was the first to propose the concept of residual connection. As shown in Fig. 2 (b) ResUNet [9] combines ResNet and UNet together. Inspired by ResNet and ResUNnet, we adopt the residual connection strategy to enhance the original low-level features and reduce the effect of potential gradient disappearance.

3.3 Context Aggregation

As the CA module shown in Fig. 3, the feature F is obtained through the upper encoder, each pixel in F has rich contextual information and is rich in high-level semantic information. As the network deepens and has a larger receptive field, the global contextual information of the feature map F is richer at this point, enabling the capture of richer and denser contextual information. It is more conducive to the decoder for detail recovery and improved segmentation performance.

Given the input feature $F \in R^{C \times H \times W}$, CA performs two 1×1 convolutions and a 1×1 filter on feature F simultaneously. The two convolution operations yield the feature $M \in R^{C_1 \times H \times W}$ and the feature $N \in R^{C_1 \times H \times W}$. For M, each position p(h, w) can get a vector $M_P \in M_{R^{c_1}}$. For pixels in the cross-path of position p in N, we obtain a set of vectors $N_P \in R^{C_1 \times H \times W}$. And $N_{P,i} \in R^{C_1}$ is the i-th vector of N_P. The two are then combined by element-wise multiplication, we finally obtain the enhanced correlation map E:

$$E_{p,i} = M_u \otimes N_{p,i}^T \tag{4}$$

where $E_{m,i} \in E$ denotes the degree of correlation brtween M_P and $N_{P,i}$, $E \in R^{(H \times W)^2}$, $i \in [1, H+W]$. "$\otimes$" denotes the element-wise multiplication. We then apply the sigmoid function to calculate the weight map W.

The different convolutional layer with 1×1 filters on F to generate feature $Q \in R^{C \times H \times W}$. Similar to M and N, we can obtain a set of vectors $Q_P \in R^{C \times H \times W}$. $Q_{P,i}$ is the i-th vector of Q_P. Next we perform element-wise multiplication with the weight map W and finally element-wise addition with the original feature F:

$$F_p' = \sum_{p=1}^{H+W} W \otimes Q_{P,i} \oplus F_P \tag{5}$$

where F_p' is the vector at position p of the output feature $F' \in R^{C \times H \times W}$. F_P denotes the vector at position p of the input feature F. "$\otimes$" denotes the element-wise multiplication. "$\oplus$" denotes the element-wise addition.

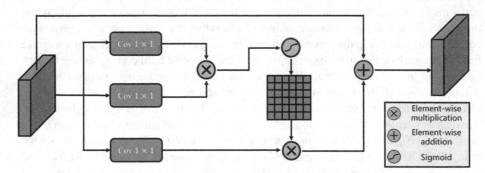

Fig. 3. Context aggregation module structure for collecting denser, richer contextual information at the bottleneck level of the encoder.

3.4 Skip-connection Bridge

Traditional U-net networks use direct skip-connection during long distance Residual connection. However, there is a large semantic gap between encoder and decoder features. We propose a SCB module, as shown in Fig. 4, which aims to alleviate the semantic gap between encoder and decoder features to some extent. The SCB consists of two parts, the spatial feature selection unit and the channel feature selection unit, respectively. The input features $F \in R^{C \times H \times W}$ are input to the left and right units respectively. For the spatial feature selection unit in the left half, we first perform a 1×1 convolution of F to generate the feature map F'. Then the spatial vectors S_{AP} and S_{MP} are obtained by averaging pooling AP and max pooling MP respectively for the feature map F'. Upsampling UPS is performed on the two vectors respectively and finally the results are summed to obtain the spatial feature G_1. The calculation process is as follows:

$$S_{AP} = AP(Conv_{1 \times 1}(F)) \tag{6}$$

$$S_{MP} = AP(Conv_{1 \times 1}(F)) \tag{7}$$

$$G_1 = UpSampling(S_{AP})UpSampling(S_{MP}) \tag{8}$$

In the channel feature selection unit, we did not perform a 1×1 convolution on feature F because there was no need to change the number of channels in the skip-connection. Firstly, for the input feature F, Chunk by channel, the feature map is divided into $2K \times H \times W$. We set up two branches of the feature map, each with a $K \times H \times W$ feature map. One branch first performs a 3×3 depthwise separable convolution on a set of feature maps, followed by Batch Normalization (BN) and ReLU operations on the results. Another set of feature maps is set up to keep more of the original features from the encoder, which is directly stitched with the results of the other branch. Finally the 1×1 convolution and BN operations are performed in turn. The calculation process is as follows:

$$G_2 = BN(Conv_{1 \times 1}Concat(ReLU(BN(DSConv_{3 \times 3}(F_1))), F_2)) \tag{9}$$

$$G = (G_1 \otimes G_2) \oplus F' \tag{10}$$

where G_2 represents the output of the channel feature selection unit, F_1 and F_2 represent the two sets of feature maps grouped by channel respectively. Finally, the features generated by the spatial feature selection unit and the channel selection unit are element-wise multiplication. The result is summed with F' to obtain G.

4 Experiments

4.1 Datasets

To evaluate the effectiveness of IESBU-Net, we conducted extensive experiments on two public datasets for skin lesion segmentation, namely the ISIC2017 [21] and ISIC2018 [22] datasets. For the ISIC2017 dataset, we used 2000 of the skin mirror images and corresponding segmentation mask labels for training, including 18.7% of melanomas, 12.7% of seborrheic keratoses and 68.6% of nevi. Use 150 of them for validation, including 20% of melanomas, 28% of seborrheic keratoses and 52% of nevi. For the ISIC2018 dataset, there were 2694 skin mirror images and corresponding segmented mask labels. We randomly divided the dataset in a ratio of 7:3. Of these, 1886 images were used for training and 808 images were used for validation.

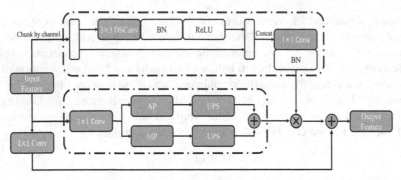

Fig. 4. Structure of the jump connection bridge, consisting of a spatial selection unit (left) and a channel selection unit (right).

4.2 Evaluation Metrics

We tested segmentation performance using five metrics: Mean Intersection over Union (mIoU), Accuracy (Acc), Recall (Rec), Dice similarity score (DSC) and Precision (Pre), where mIoU is a common metric used in competitions to compare performance between each model. In addition, Params and GFLOPs are used to represent the number of parameters and the number of complex operators respectively. Params are measured in millions (M), the model's parameters and GFLOPs are measured in 256×256 input sizes. The evaluation metrics are calculated as follows:

$$
\begin{cases}
\text{mIoU} = \frac{TP}{TP+FP+FN} \\
\text{Acc} = \frac{TP+TN}{TP+TN+FP+FN} \\
\text{Rec} = \frac{TP}{TP+FN} \\
\text{DSC} = \frac{2TP}{2TP+FP+FN} \\
\text{Pre} = \frac{TP}{TP+FP}
\end{cases}
\tag{11}
$$

where TP, FP, FN, TN represent true positive, false positive, false negative, and true negative.

4.3 Implementation Details

All experiments are implemented on a single NVIDIA GeForce RTX 2080Ti GPU. The loss function we used was the BceDice loss and an Adam [33] optimizer with a learning rate of le-4 to train all models. The number of batch sizes and epochs are set to 8 and 200 respectively. During training, we resized all images to a uniform size of 256×256. Due to the limited sample of datasets available during the training phase, acquiring and annotating images is both time consuming and expensive, we experimentally applied random vertical flips, horizontal flips, random rotations and clipping to the training set with a probability of 0.25.

4.4 Comparative Experiments

To verify the validity of our model, we will perform extensive comparison experiments on the ISIC2017 [21] and ISIC2018 [22] datasets, the results of which are shown in

Table 1. Comparative experimental results on ISIC2017 dataset.

Method	Params	GFLOP	mIoU	Acc	Rec	DSC	Pre
UNet [3]	7.75	13.74	76.52	94.33	91.83	85.86	86.21
UNet + + [5]	9.16	34.90	77.26	95.11	90.88	86.83	86.24
Attention-UNet [8]	8.62	16.58	77.32	95.13	91.63	87.93	87.86
ResUnet [9]	15.63	19.92	77.28	95.45	90.34	87.87	88.12
TransUNet [11]	27.42	8.74	78.78	95.52	91.89	87.26	87.66
TransFuse [13]	26.34	11.56	79.13	**96.71**	92.32	**88.32**	88.43
UneXt [31]	0.30	0.10	79.21	95.64	92.42	87.34	88.24
IESBU-Net	**0.24**	**0.09**	**79.54**	96.38	**92.63**	88.12	**88.89**

Table 2. Comparative experimental results on ISIC2018 dataset.

Method	Params	GFLOP	mIoU	Acc	Rec	DSC	Pre
UNet [3]	7.75	13.74	77.86	94.21	90.64	87.76	88.31
UNet++ [5]	9.16	34.90	78.34	94.13	90.68	87.90	88.93
Attention-UNet [8]	8.62	16.58	78.56	94.32	89.04	88.22	90.14
ResUnet [9]	15.63	19.92	78.22	94.48	89.13	87.68	89.53
TransUNet [11]	27.42	8.74	77.98	94.51	89.82	88.47	86.86
TransFuse [13]	26.34	11.56	80.42	**94.97**	90.24	**89.64**	90.44
UneXt [31]	0.30	0.10	79.32	94.56	**91.12**	88.78	89.76
IESBU-Net	**0.24**	**0.09**	**80.75**	94.74	90.94	89.45	**90.34**

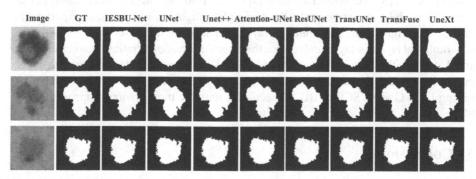

Fig. 5. Qualitative comparison results of IESBU-Net and other models in the ISIC2017 and ISIC2018 skin lesion segmentation datasets.

Tables 1 and 2. Compared with other models, the proposed model has relatively small scale and low computational complexity. In terms of performance, our proposed model is inferior to TransFuse [11] in ACC and DSC. For the ISIC2017 dataset, ACC and DSC were 33% and 20% lower, respectively. For the ISIC2018 dataset, ACC and DSC were 23% and 19% lower, respectively. But it's important to note that IESBU-Net is still superior to TransUNet in terms of mIoU, Rec and Pre metrics, with parameters and computational complexity 109× and 128× lower than TransUNet. In terms of parameters and computational complexity, our model is superior to UNeXt [27] in most of the indicators of IESBU-Net when the parameters and computational complexity are similar to UNeXt. In addition, we visualized some of the results, as shown in Fig. 5, our model achieved better segmentation results and better performance.

Table 3. Detailed ablation study of the IESBU-Net architecture.

Dataset	Method	Para	GFL	mIoU	Acc	Rec	DSC	Pre
ISIC 2017	BU	0.11	0.07	77.59	94.32	91.23	86.12	86.37
	BU + LFR	**0.09**	**0.06**	78.86	94.47	91.82	87.48	87.84
	BU + CA	0.12	0.07	78.82	94.48	91.84	87.52	87.92
	BU + SCB	0.18	0.08	**79.38**	**94.76**	**92.17**	**87.93**	**88.56**
ISIC 2018	BU	0.11	0.07	78.22	94.13	89.52	87.67	88.33
	BU + LFR	**0.09**	**0.06**	79.56	94.32	90.33	88.67	89.41
	BU + CA	0.12	0.07	79.54	94.36	90.42	88.69	89.46
	BU + SCB	0.18	0.08	**79.92**	**94.65**	**90.76**	**89.12**	**89.85**

4.5 Ablation Experiments

Based on UNet [3], we conduct ablation experiments to validate the effectiveness of our proposed module. To verify on the basis of light-weight networks, These experiments replace the original two convolutional layers per layer in the UNet network with one convolutional layer per layer, and replace the original cascade operation between encoder and decoder with element-by-element addition. We use BasicUNet (BU) as the basis for the subsequent ablation experiments. As shown in Table 3, all metrics are improved after adding LFR, CA and SCB to BU, respectively, with the most obvious improvement of SCB.

5 Conclusion

We present the IESBU-Net for skin lesion segmentation. The module consists of LFR, CA and SCB modules. The LFR module expands the receptive field for extracting original features; the CA module is used to capture denser and richer contextual information; and the SCB module smooths out the semantic gap caused by the skip-connection in terms of spatial feature selection and channel feature selection. Our model is evaluated on the ISIC2017 and ISIC2018 datasets. The results show that IESBU-Net achieves an optimal level between parameters, computational complexity and performance. Our work provides a new idea for subsequent light-weight medical image segmentation.

References

1. Hay, R.J., et al.: The global burden of skin disease in 2010: an analysis of the prevalence and impact of skin conditions. J. Investig. Dermatol. **134**(6), 1527–1534 (2014)
2. Litjens, G., et al.: A survey on deep learning in medical image analysis. Med. Image Anal. **42**, 60–88 (2017)
3. Ronneberger, O., Fischer, P., Brox, T.: U-net: convolutional networks for biomedical image segmentation. In: Navab, N., Hornegger, J., Wells, W.M., Frangi, A.F. (eds.) MICCAI 2015. LNCS, vol. 9351, pp. 234–241. Springer, Cham (2015). https://doi.org/10.1007/978-3-319-24574-4_28
4. Badrinarayanan, V., Kendall, A., Cipolla, R.: Segnet: a deep convolutional encoder-decoder architecture for image segmentation. IEEE Trans. Pattern Anal. Mach. Intell. **39**(12), 2481–2495 (2017)
5. Zhou, Z., Rahman Siddiquee, MMa., Tajbakhsh, N., Liang, J.: Unet++: a nested u-net architecture for medical image segmentation. In: Stoyanov, D., et al. (eds.) DLMIA/ML-CDS – 2018. LNCS, vol. 11045, pp. 3–11. Springer, Cham (2018). https://doi.org/10.1007/978-3-030-008 89-5_1
6. Çiçek, Ö., Abdulkadir, A., Lienkamp, S.S., Brox, T., Ronneberger, O.: 3d u-net: learning dense volumetric segmentation from sparse annotation. In: Ourselin, S., Joskowicz, L., Sabuncu, M.R., Unal, G., Wells, W. (eds.) MICCAI 2016. LNCS, vol. 9901, pp. 424–432. Springer, Cham (2016). https://doi.org/10.1007/978-3-319-46723-8_49
7. Huang, H., et al.: Unet 3+: A full-scale connected unet for medical image segmentation. In: ICASSP 2020–2020 IEEE International Conference on Acoustics, Speech and Signal Processing (ICASSP). pp. 1055–1059. IEEE (2020)
8. Oktay, O., et al.: Attention u-net: Learning where to look for the pancreas. arXiv preprint arXiv:1804.03999 (2018)
9. Xiao, X., Lian, S., Luo, Z., Li, S.: Weighted res-unet for high-quality retina vessel segmentation. In: 2018 9th international conference on information technology in medicine and education (ITME). pp. 327–331. IEEE (2018)
10. Vaswani, A., et al.: Attention is all you need. Advances in neural information processing systems 30 (2017)
11. Chen, J., et al.: Transunet: Transformers make strong encoders for medical image segmentation. arXiv preprint arXiv:2102.04306 (2021)
12. Cao, H., et al.: Swin-unet: Unet-like pure transformer for medical image segmentation. In: Computer Vision–ECCV 2022 Workshops: Tel Aviv, Israel, 23–27 Oct 2022, Proceedings, Part III. pp. 205–218. Springer (2023). https://doi.org/10.1007/978-3-031-25066-8_9
13. Zhang, Y., Liu, H., Hu, Q.: Transfuse: fusing transformers and CNNS for medical image segmentation. In: de Bruijne, M., et al. (eds.) MICCAI 2021. LNCS, vol. 12901, pp. 14–24. Springer, Cham (2021). https://doi.org/10.1007/978-3-030-87193-2_2
14. Lin, A., et al.: Ds-transunet: Dual swin transformer u-net for medical image segmentation. IEEE Trans. Instrum. Meas. **71**, 1–15 (2022)
15. Valanarasu, J.M.J., Sindagi, V.A., Hacihaliloglu, I., Patel, V.M.: Kiu-net: towards accurate segmentation of biomedical images using over-complete representations. In: Martel, A.L., et al. (eds.) MICCAI 2020. LNCS, vol. 12264, pp. 363–373. Springer, Cham (2020). https://doi.org/10.1007/978-3-030-59719-1_36

16. Chen, L.C., Papandreou, G., Kokkinos, I., Murphy, K., Yuille, A.L.: Deeplab: semantic image segmentation with deep convolutional nets, atrous convolution, and fully connected crfs. IEEE Trans. Pattern Anal. Mach. Intell. **40**(4), 834–848 (2017)
17. Gu, Z., et al.: Ce-net: Context encoder network for 2d medical image segmentation. IEEE Trans. Med. Imaging **38**(10), 2281–2292 (2019)
18. Zhao, H., Shi, J., Qi, X., Wang, X., Jia, J.: Pyramid scene parsing network. In: Proceedings of the IEEE Conference on Computer Vision and Pattern Recognition, pp. 2881–2890 (2017)
19. Chollet, F.: Xception: Deep learning with depthwise separable convolutions. In: Proceedings of the IEEE Conference on Computer Vision and Pattern Recognition, pp. 1251–1258 (2017)
20. He, K., Zhang, X., Ren, S., Sun, J.: Deep residual learning for image recognition. In: Proceedings of the IEEE Conference on Computer Vision and Pattern Recognition, pp. 770–778 (2016)
21. Berseth, M.: Isic 2017 – skin lesion analysis towards melanoma detection (2017)
22. Codella, N., et al.: Skin lesion analysis toward melanoma detection 2018: a challenge hosted by the international skin imaging collaboration (isic). arXiv preprint arXiv:1902.03368 (2019)
23. Toossi, M.T.B., et al.: An effective hair removal algorithm for dermoscopy images. Skin Res. Technol. **19**(3), 230–235 (2013)
24. Khakabi, S., Wighton, P., Lee, T.K., Atkins, M.S.: Multi-level feature extraction for skin lesion segmentation in dermoscopic images. In: Medical Imaging 2012: Computer-Aided Diagnosis, vol. 8315, pp. 130–136. SPIE (2012)
25. Sumithra, R., Suhil, M., Guru, D.: Segmentation and classification of skin lesions for disease diagnosis. Procedia Comput. Sci. **45**, 76–85 (2015)
26. He, Y., Xie, F.: Automatic skin lesion segmentation based on texture analysis and supervised learning. In: Lee, K.M., Matsushita, Y., Rehg, J.M., Hu, Z. (eds.) ACCV 2012. LNCS, vol. 7725, pp. 330–341. Springer, Heidelberg (2013). https://doi.org/10.1007/978-3-642-37444-9_26
27. Long, J., Shelhamer, E., Darrell, T.: Fully convolutional networks for semantic segmentation. In: Proceedings of the IEEE conference on computer vision and pattern recognition. pp. 3431–3440 (2015)
28. Venkatesh, G.M., Naresh, Y.G., Little, S., O'Connor, N.E.: A deep residual architecture for skin lesion segmentation. In: Stoyanov, D., et al. (eds.) CARE/CLIP/OR 2.0/ISIC -2018. LNCS, vol. 11041, pp. 277–284. Springer, Cham (2018). https://doi.org/10.1007/978-3-030-01201-4_30
29. Qamar, S., Ahmad, P., Shen, L.: Dense encoder-decoder–based architecture for skin lesion segmentation. Cogn. Comput. **13**, 583–594 (2021)
30. Jha, D., Riegler, M.A., Johansen, D., Halvorsen, P., Johansen, H.D.: Doubleu-net: A deep convolutional neural network for medical image segmentation. In: 2020 IEEE 33rd International symposium on computerbased medical systems (CBMS), pp. 558–564. IEEE (2020)
31. Valanarasu, J.M.J., Patel, V.M.: Unext: Mlp-based rapid medical image segmentation network. In: Medical Image Computing and Computer Assisted Intervention–MICCAI 2022: 25th International Conference, Singapore, 18–22 Sep 2022, Proceedings, Part V, pp. 23–33. Springer (2022). https://doi.org/10.1007/978-3-031-16443-9_3
32. Olstikhin, I.O., et al.: Mlpmixer: An all-mlp architecture for vision. Adv. Neural Inform. Process. Syst. **34**, 24261–24272 (2021)
33. Kingma, D.P., Ba, J.: Adam: A method for stochastic optimization. arXiv preprint arXiv: 1412.6980 (2014)

Molecular Structure-Based Double-Central Drug-Drug Interaction Prediction

Cheng Baitai, Jing Peng(✉), Yi Zhang, and Yang Liu

College of Computer Science and Technology, Wuhan University of Technology,
Wuhan, China
{chengbaitai,pengjing}@whut.edu.cn

Abstract. Adverse Drug-Drug Interactions(DDI) occur with drug combinations and mainly cause mortality and morbidity. The identification
of potential DDI is essential for medical health. Most of the existing
methods rely heavily on manually engineered domain knowledge, therefore, lack generalization and are inefficient. Drugs with similar molecular
structures have similar chemical properties. The molecular structures of
drugs can be obtained easily and the reactions between drugs are reactions between two molecular structures. In this paper, we proposed an
artificially intelligent DDI prediction model, Molecular Structure-based
Double-Central Drug-Drug Interaction prediction(MSDC-DDI). MSDC-
DDI utilizes a double-central encoder and a cross-dependent schema to
generate the representations of the drugs. MSDC-DDI made effective
and accurate predictions, which achieved up to more than 99% in DDI
prediction.

Keywords: Drug-Drug Interaction · Molecular structure ·
Double-central encoder

1 Introduction

Drug-drug interactions(DDI) occur with drug combinations, drugs under consideration do not always interact with each other as expected [1]. Researchers
indicated that DDIs are associated with 30% of all the reported adverse side
effects and became the major reasons for drug withdrawal from the market [2]
and resulting both in morbidity and mortality [3]. Thus, the identification of
potential DDIs is essential and became the important problem of research and
clinical studies.

The traditional method of predicting DDI is preclinical in vitro safety analysis
and clinical safety trials [4], but manpower fails to handle a large amount of DDI
data. This method can only be applied to a very small scale, and the fact that
many DDIs can not be identified during the clinical trial phase due to a large
number of interactions between drugs, blindly conducting experiments is very

© The Author(s), under exclusive license to Springer Nature Switzerland AG 2023
L. Iliadis et al. (Eds.): ICANN 2023, LNCS 14257, pp. 127–138, 2023.
https://doi.org/10.1007/978-3-031-44216-2_11

time-consuming and labor-intensive and inefficient. Computational methods can assist in DDIs identifying during clinical trials.

In the last decade, drug similarity assumption [5] based computational methods have been proposed to deal with DDI prediction tasks by exploiting drug-related similarity features such as molecular structure [5,6], side effects [7], phenotypic similarity [8] and genomic similarity [9]. [10–13] combine different drug similarity features respectively.

However, these methods highly rely on manually engineered features, which are limited by the domain expert's knowledge and need vast time to collect and construct. Therefore, these methods cannot be applied to a dataset that is relatively large in which features are often unavailable for most of the drugs.

In order to learn the drug representations automatically and utilizing the topological information of the interactions among nodes(such as drug or gene from KG), some network-based methods learn the drug representations from Knowledge Graph(KG) or DDI network. [14–19] directly derive drug node features by node embedding methods(such as TransE) or learn representations of nodes [20–22] through GNN [23] or variants of GNN from KG, which enables model capture higher-order semantics information of nodes. Though KG contains rich semantic information, KGs are large and sparse, and GNN-based methods will also introduce noise when obtaining the rich neighborhood information.

Drugs with similar molecular structures have similar chemical properties. The molecular structures of drugs can be obtained easily and the reactions between drugs are reactions between two molecular structures. [2,16] predict DDIs by generating a representation of a drug from the whole molecular structure. [24–28] consider the important role of substructures in DDI prediction. [24,26] abstract different features of substructures by GCN and GAT respectively, and represents a drug as the concatenation of these features. [25] learns representations of a drug from different-size substructures by LSTM. [27] generates the representations of drugs by treating edges(chemical bonds from molecular graph) as gates and separating the substructure in a learnable way.

Previous molecular structures-based methods implemented by GNN and variants or LSTM. These methods focus on either the node-central view or edge-central view. MPNN [29] have been proven to have a strong ability in capturing molecular substructure by aggregating the information of nodes(atoms). [30] indicate that bonds and atoms may play an equally important role in many DDI prediction scenarios. Figure 1 shows a toy example. The chemical properties of phenol and chlorobenzene are different due to the difference in atomic nodes with the same bond structure. Acetone and propen-2-ol share the same atoms with different bond structures and have different chemical properties.

[30] propose a scheme that further explores the molecular properties by combining the information of atoms and bonds and proved the superiority of the combination.

In this paper, we proposed a model: Molecular Structure-based Double-Central Drug-Drug Interaction prediction MSDC-DDI(Fig. 4) for the prediction of DDIs. MSDC-DDI utilized a node-central encoder and an edge-central

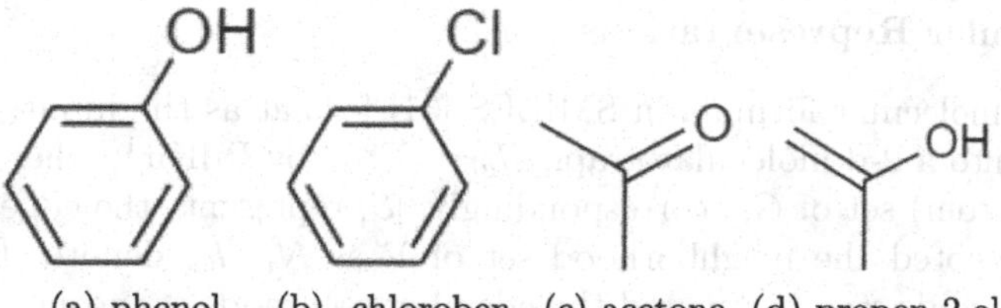

(a) phenol   (b) chloroben-   (c) acetone   (d) propen-2-ol
zene

Fig. 1. The chemical properties of phenol and chlorobenzene are different due to the difference in atomic nodes with the same bond structure. Acetone and propen-2-ol share the same atoms with different bond structures and have different chemical properties

encoder implemented by MPNN. Moreover, we pass messages between the node-central encoder and edge-central encoder by a cross-dependent scheme. For a given drug pair (d_x, d_y), this double-central encoders generates the embeddings $(n_x, e_x), (n_y, e_y)$ of d_x, d_y respectively. And then calculates the DDI scores by the predicting module. MSDC-DDI contains a node-central encoder and a edge-central encoder to capture the information from atoms and bonds. Moreover, we pass messages between node-central encoder and edge-central encoder by a cross-dependent scheme.

In the experiments, we investigated the prediction of our proposed method on DrugBank and ChCh-miner. Our method achieves 99.65% AUPRC and 98.53% AUROC on ChCh-Miner, 98.91% AUPRC, and 99.23% AUROC on DrugBank.

Compared with previous excellent works, our contributions can be summarized as follows:

– We proposed an artificially intelligent model MSDC-DDI to predict potential DDI. MSDC-DDI uses raw molecular graphs without other high-level similarities features or KGs which may be limited by expert knowledge and cannot be applied to new drugs.
– We utilized a double-central encoder focusing on atoms and bonds of molecular substructure equally, and pass messages between atoms and bonds by using a cross-dependent scheme.
– Comprehensive experiments conducted on two real-word benchmark datasets show that our method achieves SOTA performance.

2 Method

2.1 Problem Formulation

For a data set containing a drug entity set D and a drug relationship set R, a triplet in the form of (h, r, t) is given, where $(h, t) \in D$, $r \in R$, for all triplets, this prediction can be regarded as a function $f : \mathcal{D} \times \mathcal{R} \times \mathcal{D} \rightarrow [0, 1]$.

2.2   Molecular Representations

We take the molecular formula in SMILES [31] format as the input, abstract a molecular c into a 2-d molecular graph $G_c = (\mathcal{V}, \mathcal{E})$ by RdKit[1], where $|\mathcal{V}|$ refers to the node(atom) set of G_c, correspondingly, $|\mathcal{E}|$ represents the edge(bond) set of G_c. We denoted the neighborhood set of $\mathcal{V}$ as $\mathcal{N}_v$, h_v denotes the hidden embedding of node v, e_{vw} denoted the edge between node v and w.

2.3   MPNN

MPNN [29] is message passing neural network. The prevalent molecular substructure learning methods use MPNN to transmit messages between atoms, which can effectively capture the information of neighbor nodes.

$$m_v^{t+1} = \sum_{w \in N(v)} M_t \left(h_v^t, h_w^t, e_{vw} \right), \; h_v^{t+1} = U_t \left(h_v^t, m_v^{t+1} \right) \tag{1}$$

M is message passing function and U is update function. After t times of message transmission, h_v contains information of t hop neighbors, which means currently representations may contain the information of functional groups.

2.4   Cross-Dependent Message-Passing Scheme with Double-Central Encoders

We first use Cross-dependent message-passing scheme and Double-Central encoders to predict DDI. This scheme is built upon MPNN, compared with traditional MPNN, node-central encoder and edge-central encoder exchange information with each other while updating the hidden states.

- Node-central encoder: In order to enhance its expressive power, this module adds input and output layers compared with traditional MPNN, which can be illustrated as Eq. 2.

$$
\begin{aligned}
\mathbf{m}_v^{(k)} &= \mathrm{M}_{\mathrm{node}} \left(\left\{ \mathbf{h}_v^{(k-1)}, \mathbf{h}_u^{(k-1)}, \mathbf{e}_{uv} \mid u \in \mathcal{N}_v \right\} \right), \\
\mathbf{h}_v^{(k)} &= \mathrm{U}_{\mathrm{node}} \left(\left\{ \mathbf{m}_v^{(k)}, \mathbf{h}_v^{(0)} \right\} \right), \\
\mathbf{m}_v^o &= \mathrm{M}_{\mathrm{node}} \left(\left\{ \mathbf{h}_v^{(L,K_L)}, \mathbf{h}_u^{(L,K_L)}, \mathbf{x}_u \mid u \in \mathcal{N}_v \right\} \right), \\
\mathbf{h}_v^o &= \sigma \left(\mathbf{W}_{\mathrm{nout}} \, \mathbf{m}_v^o \right).
\end{aligned}
\tag{2}
$$

where $\mathbf{h}_v^{(0)} = \sigma \left(\mathbf{W}_{\mathrm{nin}} \mathbf{x}_v \right)$ is the input state of Node-Central module, $\mathbf{W}_{\mathrm{nin}} \in \mathbb{R}^{d_{\mathrm{hid}} \times d_n}$ and $\mathbf{x}_v$ is the feature of node v. The input layer can also be viewed as a residual connection. After L iterations of message passing, the node central encoder add an additional step to generate the final node embeddings $\mathbf{h}_v^{(o)} = \sigma \left(\mathbf{W}_{\mathrm{nout}} \mathbf{m}_v^o \right)$, $\mathbf{W}_{\mathrm{nout}} \in \mathbb{R}^{d_{\mathrm{hid}} \times (d_n + d_{hid})}$. The process of message passing is shown in Fig. 2a.

---

[1] https://www.rdkit.org/.

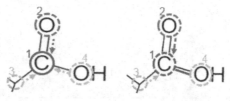

(a) node-central mes- (b) edge-central message passing   sage passing

Fig. 2. Double central message passing. (a): Take node v_1 as an example, node central encoder getting the initial edge features as the attached features from connected edge e_{21}, e_{41}, e_{31} and node features of its neighbor nodes $v_2, v_3, v_4 \in N_{v_1}$ and then updating the states of v_1 by Eq. 2. (b): Take edge e_{14} as example, $v_2, v_3 \in N_{v_1}$, edge central encoder getting the edge features of its neighbor edges e_{21}, e_{31}, and initial node information as the attached features from v_2, v_3. And then updating the message of e_{14} by Eq. 3.

- Edge-central encoder: Given an edge (v, w), edge-central encoder can be formulated as Eq. 3.

$$
\begin{aligned}
\mathbf{m}_{vw}^{(k)} &= \mathrm{M}_{\mathrm{edge}} \left(\left\{ \mathbf{h}_{vw}^{(k-1)}, \mathbf{h}_{uv}^{(k-1)}, \mathbf{x}_u \mid u \in \mathcal{N}_v \backslash w \right\} \right), \\
\mathbf{h}_{vw}^{(k)} &= \mathrm{U}_{\mathrm{edge}} \left(\left\{ \mathbf{m}_{vw}^{(k-1)}, \mathbf{h}_{vv}^{(0)} \right\} \right), \\
\mathbf{m}_{v}^{o} &= \mathrm{M}_{\mathrm{edge}} \left(\left\{ \mathbf{h}_{vw}^{(L, K_L)}, \mathbf{h}_{uv}^{(L, K_L)}, \mathbf{x}_u \mid u \in \mathcal{N}_v \right\} \right), \\
\mathbf{h}_{v}^{o} &= \sigma \left(\mathbf{W}_{\mathrm{eout}} \, \mathbf{m}_{v}^{o} \right)
\end{aligned}
\tag{3}
$$

where $\mathbf{h}_{vw}^{(0)} = \sigma \left(\mathbf{W}_{\mathrm{ein}} \mathbf{e}_{vw} \right) \left(\mathbf{W}_{\mathrm{ein}} \in \mathbb{R}^{d_{\mathrm{hid}} \times d_e} \right)$ is the input state of edge-central encoder. Edge-central encoder also adds an output layer after L iterations. $\mathbf{h}_{v}^{o}$ is the output state of output layer where $\mathbf{W}_{\mathrm{eout}} \in \mathbb{R}^{d_{\mathrm{out}} \times (d_n + d_{\mathrm{hid}})}$. Figure 2b illustrates the message-passing process of the edge central encoder.

The message passing of the cross-dependent scheme can be illustrated in Fig. 3. To enable more efficient information exchange between atoms and bonds, we adopt a cross-dependent scheme, which makes the node-central encoder and edge-central encoder cross-dependent with each other by crossing hidden states, as illustrated in Eq. 4.

$$
\begin{aligned}
\mathbf{m}_{v}^{(k)} &= \mathrm{M}_{\mathrm{node}} \left(\left\{ \mathbf{h}_{v}^{(k-1)}, \mathbf{h}_{u}^{(k-1)}, \mathbf{h}_{vu}^{(k-1)}, \mathbf{e}_{vu} \mid u \in \mathcal{N}_v \right\} \right), \\
\mathbf{h}_{k}^{(k)} &= \mathrm{U}_{\mathrm{node}} \left(\left\{ \mathbf{m}_{v}^{(k)}, \mathbf{h}_{v}^{(0)} \right\} \right), \\
\mathbf{m}_{vw}^{(k)} &= \mathrm{M}_{\mathrm{edge}} \left(\left\{ \mathbf{h}_{vw}^{(k-1)}, \mathbf{h}_{uv}^{(k-1)}, \mathbf{h}_{u}^{(k-1)}, \mathbf{x}_u \mid u \in \mathcal{N}_v \backslash w \right\} \right), \\
\mathbf{h}_{vw}^{(k)} &= \mathrm{U}_{\mathrm{edge}} \left(\left\{ \mathbf{m}_{vw}^{(k)}, \mathbf{h}_{vw}^{(0)} \right\} \right).
\end{aligned}
\tag{4}
$$

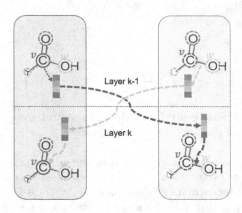

Fig. 3. Cross-dependent schema: node-central encoder and edge-central will exchange information with each other while updating the hidden states.

2.5   Prediction Modules

Double-central encoder generates embeddings (n_x, e_x), (n_y, e_y) for drug d_x, d_y and then get g_x, g_y by concatenating n_x and e_x, n_y and e_y. We use attention mechanism to capture the relevance between g_x and g_y, and then we obtain final predict score by RESCAL. The attention module illustrated as Eq. 5, where g_x and g_y are the outputs of double-central encoder of G_x and G_y respectively.

$$M_{atten} = b^T \tanh\left(W_x g_x + W_y g_y\right) \tag{5}$$

RESCAL [32] can be summarized as follows:

$$P\left(G_x, G_y, r\right) = \sigma\left(M_{atten}\, g_x \mathbf{M}_r g_y\right) \tag{6}$$

M_r is a selector of each relations, (i.e. for DrugBank, there are 86 types of relations, for each relation, we can feed it into a special binary classifier). In our method, we use the cross entropy loss function, which is computed as follows [24]:

$$\mathcal{L} = -\frac{1}{N} \sum_{i=1}^{N} \left[y_i \cdot \log\left(p_i\right) + \left(1 - y_i\right) \cdot \log\left(1 - p_i\right)\right] \tag{7}$$

2.6   Overview of MSDC-DDI

We abstract all drugs in given datasets that contain entities set V and relations set R as molecular graphs $G_v(v \in V)$. As depicted in Fig. 4, our model takes the molecular graphs of two drugs G_x and G_y as input, both G_x and G_y are represented as a 2-D molecular graph, our model obtains the feature vectors $\mathbf{x}_v$ and edge vectors $\mathbf{e}_{vw}(v, w \in V)$ of G_x, and then feed the acquired vectors to the double-central module, through which, we can get the molecular represents

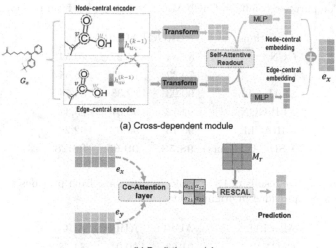

(a) Cross-dependent module

(b) Prediction module

Fig. 4. Overview of MSDC-DDI: (a) We use the molecular structure of drugs as input and then feed them into node-central encoder and edge-central encoder, respectively. Node-central encoder and edge-central encoder pass messages to each other. The outputs of the double-central encoder will be integrated(e.g. concatenation or stacking). (b) After obtaining the representations of drug pairs, MSDC-DDI uses an attention mechanism to capture the relevance between drug substructures, and then calculates the final prediction scores by RESCAL.

e_x of drug G_x. e_x contains the node-central and edge-central information, which can better represent the function groups. We use the attention mechanism to calculate correlation scores of a drug pair (e_x, e_y) and use these attention scores to calculate the prediction scores of (e_x, e_y) by RESCAL.

3 Dataset

We evaluated the MSDC-DDI on two benchmark datasets DrugBank and ChCh-Miner dataset with different scales.

- DrugBank[2]: DrugBank [33] is a widely used large-scale benchmark dataset extracted by [2]. We split it in ratio(6:2:2). DrugBank contains 1704 drugs and 191871 DDIs. All DDIs are classified into 86 relations. There are no negative samples in DrugBank, In our work, we follow the same negative sample methods [34] as baselines.
- ChCh-Miner[3]: This dataset contains 1514 drugs and 48514 DDI links. ChCh-Miner is a few labeled DDI links, there are only positive DDIs and negative DDIs in ChCh-Miner without different types of relation.

---

[2] https://bitbucket.org/kaistsystemsbiology/deepddi/src/master/.
[3] http://snap.stanford.edu/biodata/datasets/10001/10001-ChCh-Miner.htm.

134   C. Baitai et al.

Table 1. Comparative results of ChCh-Miner, results come from previous papers.

Algorithms	AUROC	AUPRC	F1
GCN	82.84	84.27	70.54
GAT	70.32	72.41	65.54
SEAL-CI	90.93	89.38	84.74
NFP-GCN	92.12	93.07	85.41
MIRACLE	96.15	95.57	92.26
MSDC-DDI(ours)	**98.53**	**99.65**	**96.28**

Table 2. Comparative results of DrugBank, results come from previous paper, - indicates that data not provided in origin paper.

Algorithms	AUROC	AUPRC	ACC
GoGNN	91.63	90.01	84.78
MHCADDI	86.33	83.98	78.50
SSI-DDI	98.95	98.69	96.33
MSAN	**99.27**	–	97.00
MSDC-DDI(ours)	99.23	**98.97**	**97.13**

DrugBank: we compare our method with baselines on DrugBank as follows.

- MIRACLE [35]: a model captured inter-view molecule structure and intra-view interactions between molecules simultaneously.
- GoGNN [26]: GoGNN proposed a model dealing with DDI prediction in two different views to capture the information from both entity graphs and entity interaction graphs.
- MHCADDI [36]: MHCADDI used a co-attention mechanism to integrate joint drug-drug information during the representation learning of individual drugs.
- SSI-DDI [24]: SSI-DDI abstracted each node hidden features as functional groups then compute interactions between these functional groups to determine the final DDI prediction.
- DeepDDI [2]: one of the early adopters of deep learning for DDI prediction. DeepDDI is a similarity-based method that designs feature structural similarity profiles for each drug based on their molecular fingerprints. Pairs of drugs' similarity profiles are then fed to a multi-layer perceptron for prediction.
- MSAN [28]: MSAN adopted a transformer-like substructure extraction module to generate the representations of molecular substructure and employs a similarity module to model the interaction between two drugs.

For this task, our method achieves up to 4.08% AUPRC, 4,02% F1, and 2.38% AUROC improvements on the ChCh-Miner dataset, and achieves up to 98.97% AUPRC, 99.23% AUROC, 97.13% ACC on DrugBank dataset. Table 1, 2 show the comparison results.

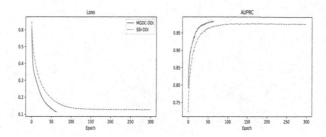

Fig. 5. Comparison of MSDC-DDI and SSI-DDI: we early stop the training phase if there are no improvements in metrics in five epochs on validation datasets.

Table 3. Comparative results of ablation study: atom and bond in this table denote we using the representations from node-central view edge-central view.

Algorithms	AUROC	AUPRC	ACC
MSDC-DDI(node only)	96.57	96.42	89.12
MSDC-DDI(bond only)	96.29	95.98	90.33
MSDC-DDI	**99.23**	**98.97**	**97.13**

Our method used a similar framework with SSI-DDI and improved on it, we performed a detailed comparison with SSI-DDI. Figure 5 shows that our model converges faster than SSI-DDI. We stop the training phase if there are no improvements of metrics while SSI-DDI set fixed epochs as 300. After 50 epochs, our model completes the training while SSI-DDI converges after 100 epochs, our model also achieves higher performance.

3.1 Ablation Study

We conducted ablation experiments to verify the effectiveness of the double-central encoder by the following methods.

- only using the representations from the node-central encoder of the given two drugs, denoted by the blue solid line.
- only using the representations from edge-central encoder of the given two drugs, denoted as yellow dashed line.

Results are shown in Table 3. Figure 6 illustrates the details of experiments. Our base model(concatenating the node-central embedding and edge-central embedding) outperforms other settings, which indicates that both atom and bond representations generated by the double-central module contribution to DDI prediction. We early stop the training phase if there are no improvements in metrics in five epochs on validation datasets.

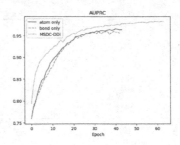

Fig. 6. Results of Ablation study: green dashed line denoted the base model, blue solid line and the yellow dashed line denotes using only node-central and edge-central encoder respectively. (Color figure online)

4   Conclusion

The identification of potential DDI is essential for medical health. In this paper, we proposed a new method MSDC-DDI to predict DDI based on molecular substructures. MSDC-DDI contains a node-central encoder and a edge-central encoder, and passes a message between node and edge by the cross-dependent schema. We use an attention mechanism to capture the relevance of substructures. Comprehensive experiment results from two real-world datasets show the advanced performance of our method. Our method is also highly interpretable, which is an attribute to the reformulating of high-level DDIs to the interaction of substructure. Our framework is possibly to be applied to cold-start scenario which requires the DDI prediction for new drugs.

References

1. Jia, J., Zhu, F., Ma, X., Cao, Z.W., Li, Y.X., Chen, Y.Z.: Mechanisms of drug combinations: interaction and network perspectives. Nat. Rev. Drug Discov. **8**(2), 111–128 (2009)
2. Ryu, J.Y., Kim, H.U., Lee, S.Y.: Deep learning improves prediction of drug-drug and drug-food interactions. Proc. Natl. Acad. Sci. **115**(18), E4304–E4311 (2018)
3. Tatonetti, N.P., Ye, P.P., Daneshjou, R., Altman, R.B.: Data-driven prediction of drug effects and interactions. Sci. Transl. Med. **4**(125), 125ra31–125ra31 (2012)
4. Whitebread, S., Hamon, J., Bojanic, D., Urban, L.: Keynote review: in vitro safety pharmacology profiling: an essential tool for successful drug development. Drug Discov. Today **10**(21), 1421–1433 (2005)
5. Vilar, S., Harpaz, R., Uriarte, E., Santana, L., Rabadan, R., Friedman, C.: Drug-drug interaction through molecular structure similarity analysis. J. Am. Med. Inform. Assoc. **19**(6), 1066–1074 (2012)
6. Vilar, S., et al.: Similarity-based modeling in large-scale prediction of drug-drug interactions. Nat. Protoc. **9**(9), 2147–2163 (2014)
7. Gottlieb, A., Stein, G.Y., Oron, Y., Ruppin, E., Sharan, R.: INDI: a computational framework for inferring drug interactions and their associated recommendations. Mol. Syst. Biol. **8**(1), 592 (2012)

8. Li, P., et al.: Large-scale exploration and analysis of drug combinations. Bioinformatics **31**(12), 2007–2016 (2015)
9. Zhou, Y., Hou, Y., Shen, J., Huang, Y., Martin, W., Cheng, F.: Network-based drug repurposing for novel coronavirus 2019-nCoV/SARS-CoV-2. Cell Discov. **6**(1), 1–18 (2020)
10. Deng, Y., Xu, X., Qiu, Y., Xia, J., Zhang, W., Liu, S.: A multimodal deep learning framework for predicting drug-drug interaction events. Bioinformatics **36**(15), 4316–4322 (2020)
11. Zhang, C., Lu, Y., Zang, T.: CNN-DDI: a learning-based method for predicting drug-drug interactions using convolution neural networks. BMC Bioinform. **23**(1), 1–12 (2022)
12. Lin, S., et al.: MDF-SA-DDI: predicting drug-drug interaction events based on multi-source drug fusion, multi-source feature fusion and transformer self-attention mechanism. Brief. Bioinform. **23**(1), bbab421 (2022)
13. Wang, F., Lei, X., Liao, B., Wu, F.X.: Predicting drug-drug interactions by graph convolutional network with multi-kernel. Brief. Bioinform. **23**(1), bbab511 (2022)
14. Celebi, R., Yasar, E., Uyar, H., Gumus, O., Dikenelli, O., Dumontier, M.: Evaluation of knowledge graph embedding approaches for drug-drug interaction prediction using linked open data (2018)
15. Karim, M.R., Cochez, M., Jares, J.B., Uddin, M., Beyan, O., Decker, S.: Drug-drug interaction prediction based on knowledge graph embeddings and convolutional-LSTM network. In: Proceedings of the 10th ACM International Conference on Bioinformatics, Computational Biology and Health Informatics, pp. 113–123 (2019)
16. Chen, Y., Ma, T., Yang, X., Wang, J., Song, B., Zeng, X.: MUFFIN: multi-scale feature fusion for drug-drug interaction prediction. Bioinformatics **37**(17), 2651–2658 (2021)
17. Yu, H., Dong, W., Shi, J.: RANEDDI: relation-aware network embedding for drug-drug interaction prediction. Inf. Sci. **582**, 167–180 (2022)
18. Feng, Y.H., Zhang, S.W., Shi, J.Y.: DPDDI: a deep predictor for drug-drug interactions. BMC Bioinform. **21**(1), 1–15 (2020)
19. Liu, Z., Wang, X.N., Yu, H., Shi, J.Y., Dong, W.M.: Predict multi-type drug-drug interactions in cold start scenario. BMC Bioinform. **23**(1), 1–13 (2022)
20. Yu, Y., Huang, K., Zhang, C., Glass, L.M., Sun, J., Xiao, C.: SumGNN: multi-typed drug interaction prediction via efficient knowledge graph summarization. Bioinformatics **37**(18), 2988–2995 (2021)
21. Lin, X., Quan, Z., Wang, Z.J., Ma, T., Zeng, X.: KGNN: knowledge graph neural network for drug-drug interaction prediction. In: IJCAI, vol. 380, pp. 2739–2745 (2020)
22. Hong, Y., Luo, P., Jin, S., Liu, X.: LaGAT: link-aware graph attention network for drug-drug interaction prediction. Bioinformatics (2022)
23. Scarselli, F., Gori, M., Tsoi, A.C., Hagenbuchner, M., Monfardini, G.: The graph neural network model. IEEE Trans. Neural Netw. **20**(1), 61–80 (2008)
24. Nyamabo, A.K., Yu, H., Shi, J.Y.: SSI-DDI: substructure-substructure interactions for drug-drug interaction prediction. Brief. Bioinform. **22**(6), bbab133 (2021)
25. Xu, N., Wang, P., Chen, L., Tao, J., Zhao, J.: MR-GNN: multi-resolution and dual graph neural network for predicting structured entity interactions. arXiv preprint arXiv:1905.09558 (2019)
26. Wang, H., Lian, D., Zhang, Y., Qin, L., Lin, X.: GoGNN: graph of graphs neural network for predicting structured entity interactions. arXiv preprint arXiv:2005.05537 (2020)

27. Nyamabo, A.K., Yu, H., Liu, Z., Shi, J.Y.: Drug-drug interaction prediction with learnable size-adaptive molecular substructures. Brief. Bioinform. **23**(1), bbab441 (2022)
28. Zhu, X., Shen, Y., Lu, W.: Molecular substructure-aware network for drug-drug interaction prediction. In: Proceedings of the 31st ACM International Conference on Information & Knowledge Management, pp. 4757–4761 (2022)
29. Gilmer, J., Schoenholz, S.S., Riley, P.F., Vinyals, O., Dahl, G.E.: Neural message passing for quantum chemistry. In: International Conference on Machine Learning, pp. 1263–1272. PMLR (2017)
30. Ma, H., et al.: Cross-dependent graph neural networks for molecular property prediction. Bioinformatics **38**(7), 2003–2009 (2022)
31. Weininger, D.: Smiles, a chemical language and information system. 1. introduction to methodology and encoding rules. J. Chem. Inf. Comput. Sci. **28**(1), 31–36 (1988)
32. Nickel, M., Tresp, V., Kriegel, H.P.: A three-way model for collective learning on multi-relational data. In: ICML (2011)
33. Wishart, D.S., et al.: DrugBank 5.0: a major update to the DrugBank database for 2018. Nucleic Acids Res. **46**(D1), D1074–D1082 (2018)
34. Wang, Z., Zhang, J., Feng, J., Chen, Z.: Knowledge graph embedding by translating on hyperplanes. In: Proceedings of the AAAI Conference on Artificial Intelligence, vol. 28 (2014)
35. Wang, Y., Min, Y., Chen, X., Wu, J.: Multi-view graph contrastive representation learning for drug-drug interaction prediction. In: Proceedings of the Web Conference 2021, pp. 2921–2933 (2021)
36. Deac, A., Huang, Y.H., Veličković, P., Liò, P., Tang, J.: Drug-drug adverse effect prediction with graph co-attention. arXiv preprint arXiv:1905.00534 (2019)

Prediction of Cancer Drug Sensitivity Based on GBDT-RF Algorithm

Yating Li(iD), Jin Gou(✉) (iD), and Zongwen Fan(iD)

College of Computer Science and Technology, Huaqiao University, Xiamen 361000, Fujian, China
goujin@hqu.edu.cn

Abstract. Accurately predicting tumor drug sensitivity is important in drug development and selection. To address this issue, we propose a novel machine learning model, called GBDT-RF, using gradient boosting decision tree (GBDT) algorithm and random forest (RF) algorithm based on the drug sensitivity IC50 correlation data from the GDSC database. Through the prediction analysis of eight drugs, compared with the GBDT, RF, logical regression (LR), and support vector machine (SVM), our GBDT-RF algorithm has the best performance for predicting cancer drug sensitivity in terms of all metrics used. This shows that the GBDT-RF algorithm has certain advantages over the conventional machine learning models. Our proposed model can also provide some reference for medical decision-makers to predict tumor drug sensitivity.

Keywords: GBDT-RF algorithm · drug sensitivity · machine-learning model · IC50

1 Introduction

Anti-tumor targeted therapies are now widely used to relieve symptoms or prolong the life of patients with certain oncological diseases. The induction of tumor cells and the spread of tumor cells are multifactorial, and the current treatment for tumors is still difficult [1]. Fortunately, the sharing of drug data and genetic data during tumor treatment provides a certain reference value for tumor treatment, drug selection, and drug development. In the context of rapidly evolving medical conditions and technologies, the selection and research, and development of tumor drugs have great potential in medical area. Therefore, in-depth studies of tumor targeting therapy and drug selection are important.

With the development of medical technology, individualized treatment of tumors can be carried out according to the genomic information, molecular characteristics, and clinicopathological characteristics of different individuals [2, 3]. Several results in modern life sciences have shown that the pathogenesis of tumors is closely related to genomic information, but it is difficult to characterize and model the relationship between genomic information and tumors by conventional means. Therefore, many machine learning techniques have been used for data analysis and research [4]. In fact, some scholars have been searching for suitable methods for related research with the goal of obtaining more

© The Author(s), under exclusive license to Springer Nature Switzerland AG 2023
L. Iliadis et al. (Eds.): ICANN 2023, LNCS 14257, pp. 139–152, 2023.
https://doi.org/10.1007/978-3-031-44216-2_12

accurate predictive models for tumor treatment through training and learning. For example, Liu et al. [5] proposed an ensemble learning method, simultaneously integrating a low-rank matrix completion model and a ridge regression model to predict anticancer drug response on cancer cell lines. Their results showed that ensemble models have promising performance. Cheng et al. [6] developed an optimal two-tier decision system model that selects optimal grid parameters to seek the highest treatment option with patient preferences for drug response and in vitro cancer cell drug screening. Model accuracy was simulated using mRNA and associated drug screens, and the results were validated for drug selection among seven drugs in 315 breast cancer patients with high accuracy. Akram et al. [7] utilized a logistic matrix factorization method for predicting cancer drug sensitivity using a regularization method. The purpose of using this method is to obtain valid features affecting drug susceptibility and to calculate the probability of susceptibility of a cell line to a drug. Noah Berlow et al. [8] established a new drug sensitivity prediction method, and compared with elastic network and random forest (RF), the data accuracy rate based on the cancer cell line encyclopedia was higher. There are also some other related research methods that have also conducted related experiments on drug sensitivity data, such as DNN (Deep Neural Networks) algorithm [9], SVM (Support Vector Machines) algorithm, and link prediction algorithm [3] for cancer drug sensitivity prediction. Michael P et al. [10] established a machine-learning model for predicting drug susceptibility, which considered genetic properties and drug properties. The model was able to predict drug sensitivity with a certain degree of accuracy. However, scholars are still working on research on the drug sensitivity of cancer cells as the prediction results are not good enough for practical use. Due to the many factors that affect cancer, it is a great challenge for us to extract important features from high-latitude datasets [11–13]. However, most of the existing studies combine the information on all cancers without considering the specificity between different cancers, which may lead to misjudgment [14, 15]. As a result, many scholars have collected and processed information on individual cancers and obtained relevant conclusions [16].

All the above studies indicate that it is of great scientific value and practical significance to use a machine-learning algorithm for predicting the drug sensitivity of cancer cells. The research of prediction method is conducive to the in-depth discussion of drug sensitivity and multi-omics information in artificial intelligence. Through intelligent algorithms, a large amount of information can be screened and used to realize the selection of cancer drugs and form accurate treatment plans [3, 17]. Cancer has a variety of triggers and sites and the mechanism of action of drugs is very complex. Therefore, the study of drug sensitivity based on cell line experiments also has great significance.

2 Data Processing

2.1 Data Sources

The drug sensitivity data involved in this study was downloaded from the Genomics of Drug Sensitivity in Cancer (GDSC, https://www.cancerrxgene.org), including 198 drug compounds and 809 cell lines and there are more than 130,000 pieces of data in this dataset. This database is one of the largest known databases of tumor drug sensitivity. Our observed data set includes various factors that affect drug sensitivity and the quantitative metric IC50 that expresses drug sensitivity. IC50 (half maximal inhibitory concentration) is an indicator of drug response half inhibitory concentration. In other words, the concentration of drug or inhibitor required to inhibit half of a given biological process (or a component in the process such as an enzyme, receptor, cell, etc.). The lower the IC50 value, the more sensitive the cells are to the drug.

2.2 Data Preprocessing

IC50 is the main piece of information we are looking at as this indicator directly indicates the resistance or sensitivity of the cell. Therefore, our normalization operation for IC50 is as follows. First, the logarithmical process of IC50 (y) can be expressed as follows:

$$y = \ln(IC50) \tag{1}$$

As shown in Fig. 1, it can be seen that y obeys a skewed normal distribution, so z-score processing is performed on y:

$$Z = \frac{y - \mu}{\sqrt{\sum_{i=1}^{n} \frac{(y-\mu)}{n}}} \tag{2}$$

In addition, the logarithmic observables are still non-normal distributions. In this case, we can see that the distribution of y ranges from -9 to 11. This wide distribution of data presents great difficulties in the classification of observations. Fortunately, we normalize the processed y such that the distribution of observed values of Z becomes smaller, ranging from -4 to 4. We normalize the distribution of the observed IC50 to eliminate the irregular distribution and make our classification more intuitive and accurate.

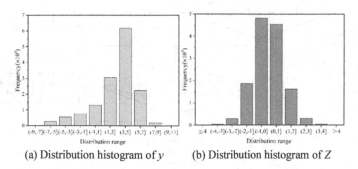

    (a) Distribution histogram of y (b) Distribution histogram of Z

Fig. 1. Distribution of observations.

2.3 Data Partition

As shown in Fig. 1, the distribution of observed data Z after processing follows a normal distribution. Depending on the actual nature of the drug, not every drug has a significant effect on tumor cells. The drug is expected to have a dramatic effect on tumor cells. But in practice, this is impossible. Also, there is more concern about whether the drug will affect tumor cells. Therefore, we need to pay more attention to whether drugs sensitize or inhibit tumor cells. According to the setting of Z in [31], we set Z less than -0.8 as the sensitive type and Z greater than 0.8 as the inhibitory type, turning this problem into a binary classification problem.

2.4 Feature Selection

In the dataset, there are 15 external features that are not related to the genes of the cell, including the name of the drug, the target of the action, the cell name, the channel of action, the maximum and minimum concentrations of the drug, etc. There are also features that are irrelevant to the results, including experimental units, cell line codes, data names, etc. To extract more effective features and reduce the time-consuming model training, we need to remove redundant and unimportant features. A flowchart for extracting important features can be found in Fig. 2.

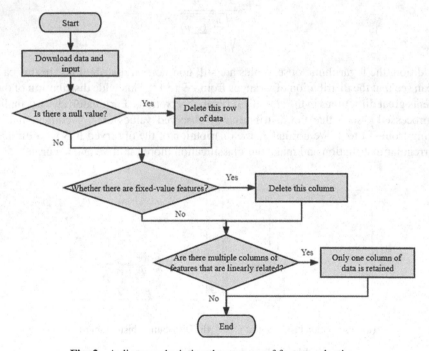

Fig. 2. A diagram depicting the process of feature selection.

In Fig. 2, after downloading the data, we first judge whether there is a null value in the table. If there is a null value, we consider the data in this row as missing and cannot guarantee its representability in the entire database, so we need to remove it. Second, we need to confirm whether the data for a column in the table is a fixed value, which is meaningless for the outcome prediction and needs to be removed. Finally, we need to judge whether there is a linear correlation between several columns of data. In this case, we only need to keep one column of data, and the remaining data is redundant and needs to be deleted. After the above operations are completed, the remaining data is retained. Ultimately, we select the cell line name, drug name, drug target, maximum drug concentration, minimum drug concentration, and gene expression. For model training, we split the data into a training set and a test set with a ratio of 8:2. We train on 80% of the data, perform prediction validation on the remaining 20%, and analyze the results.

The actual data set contains about 200 drugs. If we experimented with all the drugs, it would be very time-consuming and labor-intensive. Therefore, we selected several drugs for the experiments and verified the reliability of the algorithm. To illustrate the prediction process, we randomly selected eight kinds of drugs for the experiments. The names and codes of the eight drugs are listed in Table 1.

Table 1. Drug name and ID information.

Drug name	Drug ID	Drug name	Drug ID
Camptothecin	1003	Pictilisib	1058
Gefitinib	1010	Sorafenib	1085
Nilotinib	1013	Erlotinib	1168
Olaparib	1017	Lapatinib	1558

3   GBDT-RF Model and Evaluation Index

3.1   GBDT-RF Model

Machine learning algorithms provide a great convenience for data processing and analysis. Among them, the GBDT algorithm and the RF algorithm are widely used. The GBDT algorithm is an ensemble learning algorithm that can not only generate new classifiers through iterations but also construct new features. The feature combination represented by the path of each tree is directly used as the input feature. The constructed new feature vector is encoded as 0/1 values, and each element of the vector corresponds to a leaf node of the tree in the GBDT model. The training process of the GBDT algorithm is as follows:

Suppose that the classifier obtained after the $(t-1)$th iteration in the training process is $f_{t-1}(x)$, where x is the input feature vector. First, we define an initial model f_0 for classification.

$$f_0(x) = \arg\min \sum_{i=1}^{N} L(y_i, f_0) = \log \frac{\sum_{i=1}^{N} y_i}{\sum_{i=1}^{N} (1 - y_i)} \qquad (3)$$

$$L(y_i, f_0(x_i)) = -\sum_{i=1}^{N}(y_i \log p_i + (1 - y_i)\log(1 - p_i)) \qquad (4)$$

$$p = \frac{1}{1 + e^{-f_0(x_i)}} \qquad (5)$$

Next, the model calculates the negative gradient of the loss function for the i-th sample in the t-th round:

$$r_{ti} = -\eta\left[\frac{\partial L(y_i, f(x_i))}{\partial f(x_i)}\right]_{f(x)=f_{t-1}(x)} \qquad (6)$$

After that, the model chooses the optimal cut variable and cut point and computes χ:

$$\chi = \min_{j}\left[\min_{m}\sum_{x_i \in R_{1j}^{(m)}}\left(r_{ti} - c_{1j}^{(t)}\right)^2 + \min_{m}\sum_{x_i \in R_{2j}^{(m)}}\left(r_{ti} - c_{2j}^{(t)}\right)^2\right] \qquad (7)$$

where $x_i^{(m)}$ is the m-th feature and $s_i^{(m)}$ is the value of the feature.

$$R_{1j}^{(m)} = \left\{x_i \middle| x_i^{(m)} \le s_j^{(m)}\right\} \qquad (8)$$

$$R_{2j}^{(m)} = \left\{x_i \middle| x_i^{(m)} > s_j^{(m)}\right\} \qquad (9)$$

$$c_{tj}^{(m)} = \frac{1}{N_{tj}^{(m)}}\sum_{xi \in R_{tj}^{(m)}} r_{ti} \qquad (10)$$

We set $N_{tj}^{(m)}$ to be the number of samples of $R_{ti}^{(m)}$, if $j = J$, the iteration ends and the training process goes to the next step. Then, we calculate the optimal output value c_{tj} for the t-th iteration.

$$c_{tj} = \arg\min_{c}\sum_{x_i \in R_{tj}} L(y_i, f_{t-1}(x_i) + c) \qquad (11)$$

Next, the model is updated:

$$f_t(x) = f_{t-1}(x) + \eta\sum_{j=1}^{J} c_{tj}I\left(x \in R_{tj}\right) \qquad (12)$$

When $m = M$, the iterative process ends and the final strong classifier is obtained.

$$F(x) = f_0(x) + \eta\sum_{t=1}^{T}\sum_{j=1}^{J} c_{tj}I\left(x \in R_{tj}\right) \qquad (13)$$

Similar to the GBDT, the RF is also an ensemble model. It is implemented on top of bagging and decision trees, with improvements over both. The weak learners used in the RF are decision trees, which have no dependencies and can be generated in parallel. Ordinary decision tree selects an optimal one among all sample features on the node to split the decision tree, while the RF selects a part of the features on the node (the greater the number of selected features, the more robust the model is). After that, an optimal feature is selected from the randomly selected part of the features for tree segmentation (two-layer selection), which can further enhance the generalization ability of the model.

For the RF algorithm, it is assumed that the input sample set is P, and the number of iterations of the weak classifier is K, and the final strong classifier output is $f(x)$:

Step 1: Perform the t-th sampling on the training set and collect m times in total to obtain a sampling set D_t containing m samples, where $t = 1, 2, 3…T$.

Step 2: Use the sampling set D_t to train the t-th decision tree model $Gt(x)$ when training the nodes of decision tree model, selecting a part of the sample features from all the sample features on the node, and selecting one of these randomly selected part of the sample features The optimal features are used to divide the left and right subtrees of the decision tree.

Step 3: For classification algorithm prediction, the category or one of the categories with the most votes cast by the T weak learners is the final category.

The GBDT model can output the optimal parameter combination at each leaf node during training, and can better classify and predict according to these parameters. Therefore, according to this principle, the feature quantities of the GBDT leaf nodes are formed into a new feature set and fed into the RF algorithm for learning, which can not only avoid the confusion of the original parameters but also input the main feature parameters into the model training process.

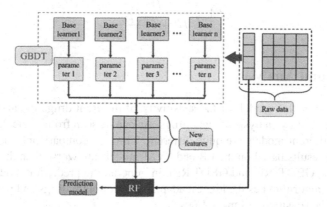

Fig. 3. Schematic diagram of the GBDT-RF model.

Figure 3 is a diagram of the experimental flow and the algorithmic process. By combining the features of RF algorithm and GBDT algorithm, we propose a classification model called GBDT-RF in this study. The main purpose of this model is to obtain the principal eigenvalues of each leaf node by the GBDT algorithm. These eigenvalues are important for the classification results. These features are fed into the RF model, and the final training prediction results are obtained through parameter adjustment.

3.2 Evaluation Indicators

For classification problems, the area under the curve (AUC) and accuracy (ACC) are generally selected for evaluation. In order to comprehensively evaluate the character-istics of the model, this study also evaluated the F1 and recall (RC) of the model. A comprehensive evaluation of the model is achieved by analyzing and comparing the four parameters. Here, the AUC represents the region directly below the receiver operating characteristic (ROC) curve after training. The higher the AUC value, the better the model performance. ACC refers to the accuracy and the closeness between the predicted results and the actual results. The higher the ACC value, the better the model. RC represents the recall rate, and the F1 score represents the harmonic average of ACC and RC. All the above evaluation indicators are related to the prediction results of the example. There are four case prediction results.

1) TP represents that the instance is positive, and the prediction result is positive.
2) TN represents that the instance is negative, and the prediction result is negative.
3) FP represents that the instance is negative, and the prediction result is positive.
4) FN represents that the instance is positive, and the prediction result is negative.

$$ACC = \frac{TP + TN}{TP + TN + FT + FN} \tag{14}$$

$$RC = \frac{TP}{TP + FN} \tag{15}$$

$$F1 = \frac{TP}{TP + \frac{FP+FN}{2}} \tag{16}$$

4 Results and Analysis

The predictions of this model for the sensitivity of different drugs to cancer cells are obtained by sensitivity analysis of eight drugs. As can be seen from Table 2, the predic-tions of the different models are quite different. Through comparison, it is found that the prediction results based on the LR and SVM models are worse than the other three algorithms (the GBDT, RF, and GBDT-RF). In general, the prediction model based on the GBDT-RF algorithm has the highest adaptability for eight drugs and performs well in predicting the sensitivity of most drugs.

First, by comparison, we find that there are three drugs with ACC greater than 80% based on the GBDT-RF algorithm, namely 1003, 1017, and 1085. However, both the GBDT algorithm and RF algorithm predict ACC lower than 80% for the sensitivity of all drugs. There are 6 drugs with ACC greater than 70% based on the GBDT-RF algorithm (including 3 drugs with ACC greater than 80%), and 6 and 5 drugs with ACC greater than 70% based on GBDT and RF, respectively. Based on the GBDT-RF algorithm, there

Table 2. Experimental results of LR, SVM, GBDT, RF, and GBDT-RF for the eight drugs.

Algorithm	Indicator	Drugs ID								
		1003	1010	1013	1017	1058	1085	1168	1558	Average
LR	ACC	0.586	0.595	0.544	0.704	0.435	0.473	0.510	0.517	0.546
	RC	0.500	0.500	0.500	0.500	0.500	0.500	0.515	0.500	0.502
	F1	0.433	0.444	0.383	0.583	0.364	0.303	0.482	0.353	0.418
SVM	ACC	0.714	0.595	0.529	0.738	0.581	0.618	0.531	0.586	0.612
	RC	0.609	0.552	0.517	0.588	0.581	0.598	0.486	0.571	0.563
	F1	0.658	0.486	0.423	0.688	0.507	0.555	0.413	0.490	0.528
GBDT	ACC	0.771	0.714	0.706	0.738	**0.661**	0.782	0.632	**0.707**	0.714
	RC	0.742	0.716	0.701	0.604	**0.682**	0.778	0.629	0.699	0.694
	F1	0.769	0.714	0.704	0.701	**0.660**	0.782	0.633	0.689	0.707
RF	ACC	0.757	0.714	0.706	0.770	0.645	0.764	**0.653**	0.672	0.717
	RC	0.740	0.707	0.707	0.628	0.673	0.757	0.643	0.579	0.679
	F1	0.758	0.712	0.707	0.727	0.640	0.763	**0.652**	0.656	0.702
GBDT-RF	ACC	**0.871**	**0.786**	**0.794**	**0.852**	0.645	**0.818**	0.633	**0.707**	**0.763**
	RC	**0.873**	**0.786**	**0.799**	**0.782**	0.673	**0.815**	**0.658**	**0.701**	**0.748**
	F1	**0.873**	**0.786**	**0.794**	**0.845**	0.640	**0.818**	0.613	**0.698**	**0.758**

are two drugs with RC greater than 80%, namely 1003 and 1085. The predicted RC of the GBDT and RF algorithms is below 80% for all drug sensitivities. There are 6 drugs with RC greater than 70% based on the GBDT-RF algorithm (including 2 drugs with RC greater than 80%), and 4 drugs with ACC greater than 70% based on the GBDT algorithm and RF algorithm. There are 3 drugs with F1 greater than 80% based on the GBDT-RF algorithm, namely 1003, 1017, and 1085. The sensitivity prediction F1 of the GBDT algorithm and the RF algorithm is less than 80% for all drugs. There are 5 drugs with F1 greater than 70% based on the GBDT-RF algorithm (including 3 drugs with F1 greater than 80%). The number of drugs with F1 greater than 70% based on the GBDT algorithm and RF algorithm is 5, but the average value of the former is larger. This shows that the GBDT-RF algorithm performs significantly better than the GBDT and RF algorithms in predicting the classification of some drugs. The fusion of the two algorithms we choose can be superior to a single algorithm in prediction performance, which also provides a method for tumor drug sensitivity prediction based on multiple features.

We also compared several approaches horizontally. Multiple algorithms are used to predict the performance of the same drug. Based on the evaluation metrics of the training results for drugs 1003, 1010, 1013, 1017, 1085, and 1558, it can be seen that the ACC, RC, and F1 scores of the GBDT-RF algorithm are higher than those of the other four algorithms for these six drugs. This indicates that the GBDT and RF algorithms can improve the predictive power of different drugs. The presented results for drugs 1058 and 1168 show that although the predictions of the GBDT-RF algorithm are not the best for these two drugs, they are generally consistent with the predictions of the GBDT and RF algorithms. This indicates that the joint algorithm does not make the prediction result worse.

Secondly, for the AUC values of different drugs in different models for drugs 1003, 1010, 1013, and 1085 (as shown in Table 3), the AUC values based on the GBDT-RF algorithm are the largest, which also reflects the advantages of the GBDT-RF algorithm from another aspect. For drugs 1017, 1168, and 1558, the AUC value based on the GBDT algorithm or the RF algorithm is the largest. The AUC value of the GBDT-RF algorithm is not the best, but very close to it.

Table 3. Experimental results of LR, SVM, GBDT, RF, and GBDT-RF of eight the drugs in terms of AUC.

Algorithm	Durg ID							
	1003	1010	1013	1017	1058	1085	1168	1558
LR	0.553	0.640	0.597	0.605	0.642	0.560	0.548	0.514
SVM	0.589	0.676	0.740	0.616	0.616	0.725	0.623	0.711
GBDT	0.836	0.782	0.791	**0.778**	0.653	0.793	**0.753**	**0.760**
RF	0.830	0.794	0.791	0.648	**0.689**	0.780	0.736	0.562
GBDT-RF	**0.845**	**0.800**	**0.800**	0.766	0.658	**0.810**	0.715	0.730

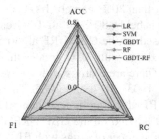

Fig. 4. Radar map of three evaluation indexes distribution of the results from Table 2.

We compared the average performance of the five algorithms on the three evaluation metrics and present them in the form of a radar map, as shown in Fig. 4. It can be seen that the GBDT-RF algorithm performs very well on all metrics and has a clear advantage over the other four algorithms. In addition, as shown in the results in Table 2, taking the mean values of ACC, RC, and F1 as the observation objects, the GBDT-RF algorithm performs the best, followed by RF and GBDT algorithms, and LR and SVM algorithm performs the worst. This indicates that GBDT, RF, and their combinations are better adapted to sensitivity prediction for multiple drugs. The average ACC based on the GBDT-RF algorithm is 76.3%, which exceeded the GBDT model by 4.9% (about 6.9%), the RF model by 4.6% (about 6.4%), the SVM model by 15.1% (about 24.7%), and the LR algorithm by 21.7% (about 39.7%). The average RC based on the GBDT-RF algorithm is 74.8%, 5.4% (about 7.8%) higher than the GBDT model, 6.9% (about 10.2%) higher than the RF model, 18.5% (about 32.9%) higher than the SVM model, and 24.6% (about 49.0%) higher than the LR model. The average F1 based on the GBDT-RF algorithm is 75.8%, 5.1% (about 7.2%) higher than the GBDT model, 5.6% (about 8.0%) higher than the RF model, 23% (about 43.6%) higher than the SVM model, and 34% (about 81.3%) higher than the LR model.

In addition, we conducted five trials for each of the eight drugs to estimate confidence intervals for predicted outcomes. Tables 4, 5, and 6, respectively, show the results of three evaluation indexes (ACC, RC, and F1) of five experiments on eight drugs based on the GBDT-RF algorithm. Then we calculated the confidence intervals of each evaluation index according to the results.

Table 4. ACC values from five experiments of eight drugs.

Drug ID	ACC				
1003	0.886	0.800	0.714	0.743	0.714
1010	0.810	0.714	0.762	0.714	0.810
1013	0.794	0.765	0.853	0.794	0.735
1017	0.774	0.839	0.774	0.742	0.774
1058	0.742	0.645	0.645	0.613	0.677
1085	0.857	0.821	0.786	0.786	0.821
1168	0.720	0.680	0.600	0.680	0.680
1158	0.759	0.793	0.689	0.724	0.689

Table 5. RC values from five experiments of eight drugs.

Drug ID	RC				
1003	0.860	0.740	0.725	0.702	0.718
1010	0.805	0.714	0.784	0.708	0.857
1013	0.794	0.753	0.853	0.816	0.742
1017	0.754	0.855	0.607	0.700	0.702
1058	0.746	0.673	0.649	0.615	0.677
1085	0.866	0.821	0.792	0.791	0.821
1168	0.718	0.695	0.570	0.673	0.677
1158	0.752	0.702	0.649	0.714	0.622

On the premise that the confidence level is 0.95, the confidence interval is calculated, and the results are shown in Table 7. Compared with the results in Table 2, it can be

Table 6. F1 values from five experiments of eight drugs.

Drug ID	F1				
1003	0.886	0.797	0.715	0.729	0.723
1010	0.807	0.714	0.765	0.714	0.815
1013	0.794	0.754	0.853	0.790	0.736
1017	0.772	0.842	0.766	0.735	0.762
1058	0.742	0.640	0.650	0.612	0.677
1085	0.859	0.819	0.787	0.788	0.821
1168	0.719	0.678	0.610	0.670	0.685
1158	0.757	0.783	0.706	0.720	0.684

seen that for drug 1003, the optimal results of the three evaluation indicators (ACC, RC, F1) based on the GBDT-RF algorithm are all greater than the upper limit of the confidence interval. For drug 1017, the optimal results of ACC and F1 based on the GBDT-RF algorithm are greater than the upper limit of the confidence interval. The results of the three evaluation indexes of other drugs based on the GBDT-RF algorithm are all within the confidence interval. This phenomenon may be due to the low number of trials. Therefore, our experimental results are normal to a large extent, which indicates that our experimental results are reliable to a certain extent. However, there are still shortcomings in our follow-up work that need to be improved.

Table 7. Confidence intervals of three evaluation indicators of eight drugs based on GBDT-RF algorithm.

Drug ID	ACC	RC	F1
1003	[0.681, 0.862]	[0.670, 0.828]	[0.680, 0.860]
1010	[0.702, 0.822]	[0.695, 0.852]	[0.703, 0.823]
1013	[0.734, 0.842]	[0.735, 0.848]	[0.730, 0.841]
1017	[0.737, 0.825]	[0.611, 0.836]	[0.726, 0.825]
1058	[0.604, 0.725]	[0.612, 0.732]	[0.603, 0.725]
1085	[0.777, 0.851]	[0.780, 0.856]	[0.778, 0.852]
1168	[0.618, 0.726]	[0.596, 0.737]	[0.623, 0.722]
1158	[0.675, 0.787]	[0.623, 0.752]	[0.681, 0.779]

5 Conclusion

Based on the drug sensitivity IC50 data in the GDSC database, we constructed an improved machine-learning model for drug sensitivity prediction based on the GBDT and RF algorithms. We used non-genetic data information to predict and analyze the sensitivity of eight drugs and showed that our proposed GBDT-RF algorithm has better prediction performance than the GBDT, RF, SVM, and LR algorithms. In summary, the proposed algorithm applied the output values of the leaf nodes of the GBDT algorithm as input values of the RF algorithm for training. By doing so, a better prediction model could be obtained by combining the optimal parameters of the GBDT algorithm output with the learning process of the RF algorithm. Experimental results showed that our combined GBDT-RF algorithm is more advantageous than a single traditional algorithm. In addition, we conducted several experiments on each drug and obtained the confidence intervals of each evaluation index, which proved the reliability of the experimental results. These confirmed that the high performance of our GBDT-RF algorithm in the practical application of tumor drug sensitivity prediction and further demonstrated the reliability of the combined algorithm. This study also provided a certain reference value for the research methods of tumor drug sensitivity prediction based on machine learning. However, our study still has room to further improve its performance. To further deepen the research, we will conduct related studies on cancer cell genome information and further reveal the underlying causes and principles of cancer cell drug sensitivity based on the results of this study.

References

1. Zhu, X., Tian, X., Ji, L., et al.: A tumor microenvironment-specific gene expression signature predicts chemotherapy resistance in colorectal cancer patients. npj Precis. Onc. **5**(1), 7 (2021)
2. Cohen, R.L., Settleman, J.: From cancer genomics to precision oncology–tissue's still an issue. Cell **157**(7), 1509–1514 (2014)
3. Tognetti, M., Gabor, A., Yang, M., et al.: Deciphering the signaling network of breast cancer improves drug sensitivity prediction. Cell Syst. **12**(5), 401–418 (2021)
4. Baptista, D., Ferreira, P.G., Rocha, M.: Deep learning for drug response prediction in cancer. Brief. Bioinform. **22**(1), 360–379 (2021)
5. Liu, C., Wei, D., Xiang, J., et al.: An improved anticancer drug-response prediction based on an ensemble method integrating matrix completion and ridge regression. Molecular Therapy - Nucleic Acids **21**, 676–686 (2020)
6. Cheng, L., Majumdar, A., Stover, D., et al.: Computational cancer cell models to guide precision breast cancer medicine. Genes **11**(3), 263 (2020)
7. Akram, E., Changiz, E.: DSPLMF: A method for cancer drug sensitivity prediction using a novel regularization approach in logistic matrix factorization. Front. Genet. **11**, 75 (2020)
8. Berlow, N., Haider, S., Wan, Q., et al.: An integrated approach to anti-cancer drug sensitivity prediction. IEEE/ACM Trans. Comput. Biol. Bioinf. **11**(6), 995–1008 (2014)
9. Turki, T., Wei, Z.: A link prediction approach to cancer drug sensitivity prediction. BMC Syst. Biol. **11**(S5), 94 (2017)
10. Menden, M.P., Iorio, F., Garnett, M., et al.: Machine learning prediction of cancer cell sensitivity to drugs based on genomic and chemical properties. PLoS ONE **8**(4), e61318 (2013). https://doi.org/10.1371/journal.pone.0061318

11. Chen, T., Sun, W.: Prediction of cancer drug sensitivity using high-dimensional omic features. Biostatistics **18**(1), 1–14 (2017)
12. Park, H., Shimamura, T., Miyano, S., et al.: Robust prediction of anti-cancer drug sensitivity and sensitivity-specific biomarker. PLoS ONE **9**(10), e108990 (2014)
13. He, N., Wang, X., Kim, N., et al.: 3D shape-based analysis of cell line-specific compound response in cancers. J. Mol. Graph. Model. **43**, 41–46 (2013)
14. Chen, B.-J., Litvin, O., Ungar, L., et al.: Context sensitive modeling of cancer drug sensitivity. PloS One **10**(8), e0133850 (2015). https://doi.org/10.1371/journal.pone.0133850
15. Bayer, I., Groth, P., Schneckener, S.: Prediction errors in learning drug response from gene expression data - influence of labeling, sample size, and machine learning algorithm. PLoS One **8**(7), e70294 (2013)
16. Turki, T., Wei, Z., Wang, J.T.L.: A transfer learning approach via Procrustes analysis and mean shift for cancer drug sensitivity prediction. J. Bioinform. Comput. Biol. **16**(03), 1840014 (2018). https://doi.org/10.1142/S0219720018400140
17. Su, R., Liu, X., Wei, L., et al.: Deep-Resp-Forest: a deep forest model to predict anti-cancer drug response. Methods **166**, 91–102 (2019)

Risk Stratification of Malignant Melanoma Using Neural Networks

Julian Burghoff[1(✉)], Leonhard Ackermann[2], Younes Salahdine[3],
Veronika Bram[3], Katharina Wunderlich[4], Julius Balkenhol[4],
Thomas Dirschka[4], and Hanno Gottschalk[5]

[1] Department of Mathematics & IZMD, University of Wuppertal, Wuppertal,
Germany
`burghoff@math.uni-wuppertal.de`
[2] BioCap GmbH, Frankfurt, Germany
`l.ackermann@biocap.de`
[3] NeraCare GmbH, Frankfurt, Germany
`{younes.salahdine,Veronika.bram}@neracare.com`
[4] CentroDerm GmbH, Wuppertal, Germany
`Katharina.wunderlich@gmx.net`, `{j.balkenhol,t.dirschka}@centroderm.de`
[5] Institute of Mathematics, TU-Berlin, Berlin, Germany
`gottschalk@math.tu-berlin.de`

Abstract. In order to improve the detection and classification of malignant melanoma, this paper describes an image-based method that can achieve AUROC values of up to 0.78 without additional clinical information. Furthermore, the importance of the domain gap between two different image sources is considered, as it is important to create usability independent of hardware components such as the high-resolution scanner used. Since for the application of machine learning methods, alterations of scanner-specific properties such as brightness, contrast or sharpness can have strong (negative) effects on the quality of the prediction methods, two ways to overcome this domain gap are discussed in this paper.

Keywords: neural nets · survival analysis · maligne melanom · domain gap

1 Introduction

Clinical and pathological staging of melanoma patients only relies on tumor size (Breslow thickness), ulceration and lymph node involvement [1]. However, the patient group with the thinnest melanomas in Tumor Stage T1 and with the most favorable prognosis resulted the most melanoma deaths in absolute numbers [2]. Additionally, patients from T3b onwards can be now offered potent adjuvant therapy [3,4]. To identify patients with small tumors but high risk of relapse or to spare patients in advanced disease but with low mortality or recurrence risk, there is a current need for biomarkers and better prognostication [5].

L. Iliadis et al. (Eds.): ICANN 2023, LNCS 14257, pp. 153–164, 2023.
https://doi.org/10.1007/978-3-031-44216-2_13

The use of digitalized histological images like H&E scans, that help pathologists to better interpret the information provided by the tissue sample under the
microscope, has been widely tried to use for improving diagnosis and prognosis
in many tumors [6]. 3D high-resolution volumetric imaging of tissue architecture from large tissue and molecular structures at nanometer resolution are new
techniques for improving early cancer detection, personalized risk assessment
and potentially identifying the best treatment strategies [7]. Deep learning has
been shown to read out additional information of these stains. These models
have shown to deliver independent prognostic information [8,9] and could also
predict the results of molecular biomarkers [10]. In melanoma, CNN networks
were shown to reach a concordance level above 80% for diagnosis compared to
human pathologists [11], could outperform histopathologists in classification [12],
and the result of the sentinel lymph node status [13].

Prognostication and predicting the risk of tumor recurrence could be shown
for combining digital analysis with the detection of tumor-infiltrating lympho-
cytes by achieving a negative predicting value (NPV) of about 85% [14]. Another
CNN approach for predicting disease specific survival in melanoma resulted in
mixed results achieving area under the curve (AUROC) values of 90% and 88%
but only NPVs of 95% and 65%, respectively, in two validation cohorts [15].

Such problems of the domain gap often arises in image recognition [16], i.e.
a method that has been optimised on a data set from a certain source, but on
data from a different source it provides unsatisfactory results. To address this
problem, we first standardise the predictions for each dataset or data source,
which already improves the accuracy. In a second approach, we add an additional
regularisation term directly to the neural network so that the results are in the
same range. This also improves the accuracy of the predictions.

The following parts of this paper are structured as follows: First, in Sect. 2
we give a description of the data in terms of its clinical and technical structure.
Section 3 provides an overview of methods that have been used in similar work
and how our method is designed and built on these. Then, in Sect. 4, we present
and classify the results of our experiments. Finally, Sect. 5 discusses the results
and considers how future work might build on them.

2   Description of Data

In this paper we consider two main sets of data:

– *Dataset A*: This dataset contains 767 images of 176 patients of the American
  Joint Committee on Cancer (AJCC) set stages IA to IIID from four different locations in Bern (Switzerland), Bochum, Bonn and Kiel, Germany. All
  images have been recorded with the H&E colouring and were created by the
  same scanner Hamatasu NanoZoomer S210, NDP Version 2.4.

  In order to obtain a data set of the highest possible quality, the data were
  first manually checked by medical experts and a total of 23 data points were
  removed from the data set, e.g. due to broken slides. This clean-up took place
  before we split the data into training, validation and test data:

The patients are assigned to train (104 patients), test (36 patients) and validation (36 patients) what results in 591 train-, 74 validation- and 102 test images. The split was chosen so that the distribution of high/low risk patients in each subset (training, validation, test) corresponds to the distribution of the full dataset A, see also Table 1, under the constraint that multiple images of one patient remain in the same subset.

– *Dataset B*: The second dataset contains 242 images of 242 patients with AJCC stages IIA to IIC from the Central Malignant Melanoma Registry (CMMR) in Tübingen, Germany, where the H&E-colored images have partly different coloring than the images of dataset A, probably caused by another scanner type Hamatasu Nanozoomer 2.0 HAT, NDP Version 2.5 and the scans are mostly disturbed by a marker pen on the slide. To see how our algorithm performs on images with a domain gap dataset B is only used as a separate test dataset.

2.1 Clinical Description

The images used represent hematoxylin-eosin (HE) stained melanoma sections. HE is a staining technique from histology that is used to better predict the disease prognosis of a melanoma patient, among other things, the mitosis rate can be determined (S3 Leitlinie Melanom).

Overall survival of dataset A (86%) is similar to dataset B (88%). However, the MSS time for dataset B with a median of 41 month was considerably lower compared to 70/73 months of dataset A. Relapse free survival differed as well with around 78% and 69% for dataset A and dataset B, respectively.

Table 1. Important features of our datasets

Characteristic	Dataset A			Dataset B
	Training	Validation	Test	Test
N(Scans)	313	36	38	242
N(Patients)	104	36	36	242
Alive/Censored	89 (86%)	31 (86%)	31 (86%)	212 (88%)
Dead/Event	15 (14%)	5 (14%)	5 (14%)	30 (12%)
MSS time (months) Mean	70.12	80.03	78.37	50
MSS time (months) Median	70	73	73	41
Relapse Free Survival Recurrence	21 (20%)	8 (22%)	7 (19%)	75 (31%)
Relapse Free Survival Non-recurrence	83 (80%)	28 (78%)	29 (81%)	167 (69%)
RFS time Mean	67	76.67	75	42
RFS time Median	70	68	73	30

2.2 Technical Description

Both datasets contain a total of 1009 images of different sizes (up to a resolution of 158720×115456 pixels) and various format ratios. Therefore, the images have to be pre-processed as neural nets on commercially available hardware are not yet able to handle images of this size at the time of writing. See Sect. 3.2 for more information on the pre-processing task. The total size of the dataset is 570,3 GB in .ndpi file format.

For every patient i, we have at least one image x_i and the information $\delta_i = 1$, indicating the death of the patient at time T_i. If the patient survived the observation period of this study, we set $\delta_i = 0$ and T_i is the time the patient has been observed.

3   Materials and Methods

3.1   Related Work

There exists abundant work on using deep neural networks for the interpretation of medical images. In this section, we focus on works with the scope of AI based prediction of survival for patients with a melanoma diagnosis.

In prior research on this topic [15] the authors use a two stage pipeline to predict risk on the basis of primary melanoma tumor images. Within this pipeline, they first use a segmentation to classify detect and crop tumor areas in the image. These small but detailed crops of 500×500px are then fed to a network of convolutional, recurrent and fully connected layers in order to predict the risk. [17] describes the approach to use a multivariable classifier that contains, besides clinical data, a score of a deep neural net, in order to predict the immunotherapy response of patients with advanced melanoma. Also here, clinical data is used for the model and a separation of segmentation and response classifier takes place.

The authors of [12] describe an experiment where a trained ResNet50 model outperforms 11 pathologists in classifying labeled histopathological images what shows that neural nets in general have high potential to improve correct melanoma diagnoses.

Similar to our approach, the authors of [18] used a VGG-based neural network architecture to detect cutaneous melanoma, although they use a binary classification for dead/alive patients instead of a survival analysis method. They evaluated their method a dataset provided by The Cancer Imaging Archive of 53 patients with a given survival status.

In [19] the authors on the one hand locate molecular biomarkers in immuno-histochemistry images using convolutional neural networks which can help enabling new cancer screenings. On the other hand they also classify the found biomarkers along their type.

However, there are not only machine learning approaches to melanoma classification based on H&E scans, but also based on topics such as dermoscopic image data [20] where the authors use a quiet small 5-layers CNN to classify the images to the corresponding tumor stage with applying the Adam optimizer on the Similarity Measure for Text Processing as loss function. This work is also based on [21] where the authors predict the melanomas thickness using a pretrained VGG-19 model on 400 × 400px preprocessed dermoscopic images.

In [22] the authors also use deep convolutional neural networks in combination with survival analysis in order to find good predictions on pathological images - here in context of lung cancer. They annotated the regions of interest of the images with help of pathologists and sampled small random high resolution crops of these regions to use in the networks whereas we used down-sampled low resolution images in our approach.

In contrast to this, in our work we extract information directly from the original image data using a VGG16-like neural network, so we don't use an additional pre-segmentation, which might be error prone by itself. In this way we also avoid labeling of the regions of interest by humans annotators, which is a time consuming process and requires highly trained annotators.

The problem of the domain gap, which is also the topic of this paper, is also addressed in other medical papers. For example, the authors of [23] present an approach for the classification of medical images that overcomes the domain gap by a combination of data augmentation and domain alignment through regularisation and thus also prevents overfitting. While the number of categories has a great influence on the regularisation term, in our work we also consider a regularisation approach, but not a classification, but determine our prediction by using a survival analysis approach. Furthermore, our regularisation term is used with the intention of bringing the output prediction values into a comparable relationship independent of their domain.

3.2 Preprocessing the Data

When pre-processed, the images are reduced from their original format by a factor of 64 in dataset A and 128 in dataset B in each dimension. The resulting image is centred in a 2500 by 2000 pixel frame which is filled with white color outside the image.

Images of patients with multiple images are seen as independent information in the training data.

3.3 Methods

Cox's Proportional Hazards Model. Survival analysis is about predicting the probability of absence of an event (e.g. the death of a patient) until time t using the parameters β of a suitable model [24]. One of the most widely used methods is Cox's Proportional Hazards Model, which predicts the hazard function $h(t|x)$ on the basis of an input vector x, see e.g., [15,22] or [25]:

$$h(t|x) = h_0(t) \cdot \exp(\beta^T x) \Leftrightarrow \log \frac{h(t|x)}{h_0(t)} = \beta^T x \tag{1}$$

The baseline hazard function $h_0(t)$ indicates how large the hazard rate would be without the influence of other parameters (like β) and is therefore only dependent on the time t, which means that for our case it is eliminated from the calculation of the loss function and therefore does not need to be calculated [25]. To estimate the parameters β of the linear model the negative log partial likelihood function

158   J. Burghoff et al.

can be minimized:

$$l(\beta) = -\sum_{i=1}^{n} \delta_i(\beta^T x_i - \log \sum_{j \in R_i} \exp(\beta^T x_j)) \qquad (2)$$

where δ is the delta-function which determines whether the data is censored or not, n the total number of data points and $R_i = \{j|y_j \geq y_i\}$ is the risk set which describes the data-subset of patients which do not had an event before timestamp y_i of the i-th event.

An adaption of linear models to non-linear models like (deep) neural nets was introduced by [26] in 1995 and applications can be found for example in [22] or [25]. The risk function $\beta^T x$ is replaced by the output of the neural net $\hat{h}_\theta(x)$ and we achieve the following loss function for each mini batch B:

$$\mathcal{L}(\theta) = -\sum_{i \in B} \delta_i \left(\hat{h}_\theta(x_i) - \log \sum_{j \in R_i} e^{\hat{h}_\theta(x_j)} \right) \qquad (3)$$

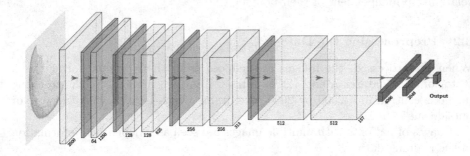

Fig. 1. Design of used neural network. Orange are convolutional layers, red are pooling layers and purple indices dense layers (Color figure online)

Neural Net Architecture and Training. Convolutional neural networks (CNN) represent the state of the art in image recognition. As neural network model, we use a modified version of a VGG16 net [27] in our experiments. Figure 1 gives an overview of the network architecture. Each convolutional layer has kernel sizes of 3×3 and each pooling layer is a maximum pooling with pooling size 2×2.

As mentioned in Sect. 3.1, we use the loss function supplied in [25] which implements a variant of the Cox's Proportional Hazards Model. In order to achieve a higher generalisability and reducing the domain gap between dataset A and dataset B, we expanded our loss function in Eq. 3 by a regularization term:

$$\mathcal{L}(\theta) \quad = \quad -\sum_{i \in B} \delta_i(\hat{h}_\theta(x_i) \; - \; \log \sum_{j \in R_i} e^{\hat{h}_\theta(x_j)}) \; + \; \lambda(\frac{1}{|B|}(\sum_{j \in B} \hat{h}_\theta(x_j))^2 \quad (4)$$

where λ is the chosen regularization strength. See Sect. 4.1 for further information why we use this additional regularization term.

In training, we employ the Adam optimizer over 50 epochs with a learning rate of $\alpha = 0.001$ and a batch size of 5.

For the implementation we used Openslide (version 1.1.2) [28] for importing the images, the GitHub repository of Sebp [25] and Tensorflow (version 2.6.1) [29] along with Keras (version 2.6.0) [30].

For the calculations, we used a workstation with a Dual Intel Xeon Gold 6248R 3.0 GHz and three Nvidia Quadro RTX 8000 graphic units with 48 GB VRAM each, whereas the different GPUs are only used for different trainings.

Concordance Index. For validation purposes of our methods we use Harrel's concordance index (CI) [31]. The CI is defined as the ratio between correctly ordered pairs and all possible rankable pairs [32]:

$$CI = \frac{\#\text{concordant pairs}}{\#\text{comparable pairs}} \quad (5)$$

A pair of observations i, j with its survival times fulfill $T_i > T_j$, is concordant if $\hat{h}_\theta(x_j) > \hat{h}_\theta(x_i)$. Also a pair i, j is not comparable if the smaller survival time is censored (i.e. $T_i > T_j \wedge \Delta_j = 0$). Otherwise this pair is comparable. Thus,

$$CI = \frac{\sum_{i,j} \mathbb{1}(T_i > T_j) \cdot \mathbb{1}(\hat{h}_\theta(x_j) > \hat{h}_\theta(x_i)) \cdot \Delta_j}{\sum_{i,j} \mathbb{1}(T_i > T_j) \cdot \Delta_j} \quad (6)$$

The CI estimates the probability of concordance $P(\hat{h}_\theta(x_j) > \hat{h}_\theta(x_i)|T_i > T_j)$ for two independent observations/predictions. It can also be interpreted as a measure of the area under a time-dependent receiver operator curve [32–34]. A value of $CI = 1$ means that all observations are correctly sequenced, $CI = 0.5$ means that the method applied is no better than guessing.

Area Under the Receiver Operating Characteristic. In the evaluation of the results our methods generate an important measurement value is the area under the receiver operating characteristic (AUROC) [35]. For a data point with $a = P(F_p)$ the probability of the data point being a false positive prediction and $b - 1 = P(T_p)$ the negative probability of the data point being a true positive prediction in a dataset D, [36] defines the AUROC as follows:

$$\text{AUROC} = \sum_{i \in D} ((1 - b_i \cdot \Delta a) + \frac{1}{2}(\Delta(1 - b) \cdot \Delta a))$$

with $\Delta(1 - b) = (1 - b_i) - (1 - b_{i-1})$ and $\Delta a = a_i - a_{i-1}$

4 Results

An overview of all the concordance indices and AUROC values of our experiments is provided in Table 2.

Table 2. Evaluation of receiver operator curve and Harrel's C-Index with and without regularization on different testsets

	Without regularization				With regularization			
	Isolated		Merged		Isolated		Merged	
	A (test)	B	Naive	Std	A (test)	B	Naive	Std
C-Index	0.677	0.612	0.569	0.644	0.795	0.615	0.646	0.676
AUROC	0.615	0.635	0.544	0.614	0.789	0.578	0.601	0.642

4.1 Results of Model Without Regularization

In our first set of experiments, we use the loss function supplied in Eq. (3). Although we achieve an AUROC value of 61.5% on the test subset of dataset A and also an AUROC value of 63.5% on the separated dataset B. We observe that the domains in which our predictions $\hat{h}_\theta(x_i)$ lay differ significantly from dataset A to dataset B.

This results in a bad overall AUROC value of 54.4% if one mixes these predictions naivly together as it would be a complete dataset from only one datasource before evaluating the whole set. One potential reason is that the net learns features that are relevant for the task, but it also is sensitive to further properties of the image like the pixel's brightness (or in general the pixel's color distribuition). While such image features do not encode meaningful medical information, they can still disturb the outcome of the network,

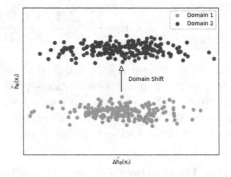

Fig. 2. Domain shift in predicting on different datasets

especially if the hazards predicted on the second data set are in a different numerical range as compared with the original training data. This in particular happens by deviation from the neutral direction $\hat{h}_\theta(x_j) \rightarrow \hat{h}_\theta(x_j) + z$ which merely leads to a redefinition of the baseline hazard function $h_0(t)$ but is not sensed in the Cox loss function. So one can imagine the predicitons $\hat{h}_\theta(x_i)$ shifted away from the total diagonal like schematically shown in Fig. 2. In our case, dataset B has a slightly other color scheme (mainly because of the use of another scanner -

see Sect. 2) and so our predictions evaluating the model trained on dataset A on this dataset leads to a significant drop in performance.

A first approach to reduce the sensitivity towards different hazards is to re-center the predicted hazards. We thus standardise (we subtract the mean and divide the result by the standard deviation) the predictions of each dataset and merge them afterwards. We display the resulting improvement in the rightest column of each approach in Table 2 (Std.).

The downside of this approach is that you need to have already a certain set of images for each source of images/scanner that is used to predict survival probabilities what will be adressed in the approach with regularization.

4.2 Results of Model with Regularization

To interdict shifting of hazard functions alltogether, we add a L2-regularization-term, see Eq. (4), to shift all predictions $\hat{h}_\theta(x_i)$ in the same domain range. This does not only lead to a higher AUROC value in evaluation on the mixed data set (60.1% instead of 54.4%), but we can improve even more if combining the regularization with the above-mentioned normalization process (64.2% instead of 61.4%)

Besides, we also achieved a significantly higher ROC value on the testdata of dataset A throughout this regularization technique. Unfortunately the overall generalizability on the isolated dataset B suffered (57.8% instead of 63.5%) from that approach.

5   Discussion and Outlook

We have shown that it is possible to make survival predictions based on simplified image information using Cox's Proportional Hazard Models on neural networks and that our domain adaptation techniques succeed in merging the predictions into one range. Compared to [18] where the authors achieved an AUROC value of 76.9% our approach with regularization slightly outperforms it with an AUROC value of 79.5%.

In future work, we will have a more detailed evaluation and we have a closer look on levels of significance and correlations to clinical variables like the Breslow depth or genetic information and demographic variables such as age or gender to evaluate and improve the clinical utility of our predictions (Table 3).

Appendix A

Table 3. Additional features of our datasets

Characteristic		Dataset A			Dataset B
		Training	Validation	Test	Test
N	Scans	313	36	38	242
	Patients	104	36	36	242
Age	Median	60	61	57.5	70
Sex	Male	55	19	19	132
	Female	49	17	17	110
AJCC Stage	IA	18 (17%)	6 (17%)	8 (22%)	0 (0%)
	IB	32 (31%)	10 (28%)	9 (25%)	0 (0%)
	IIA	11 (11%)	5 (14%)	3 (8%)	116 (48%)
	IIB	5 (5%)	4 (11%)	5 (14%)	78 (32%)
	IIC	6 (6%)	0 (0%)	0 (0%)	48 (20%)
	IIIA/B/C	2 (2%)	2 (6%)	2 (6%)	0 (0%)
	IIIA	6 (6%)	3 (8%)	2 (6%)	0 (0%)
	IIIB	7 (7%)	2 (6%)	2 (6%)	0 (0%)
	IIIC	13 (13%)	4 (11%)	5 (14%)	0 (0%)
	IIID	4 (4%)	0 (0%)	0 (0%)	0 (0%)
Breslow thickness	Mean [mm]	2.8	1.67	2.0	3.72
	Median [mm]	1.7	1.55	1.2	3
Primary Tumor	T1a	9 (9%)	4 (11%)	2 (6%)	0 (0%)
	T1b	12 (12%)	4 (11%)	8 (22%)	0 (0%)
	T2a	37 (36%)	13 (36%)	9 (25%)	0 (0%)
	T2b	5 (5%)	7 (19%)	4 (11%)	33 (14%)
	T3a	14 (13%)	1 (3%)	4 (11%)	83 (34%)
	T3b	9 (9%)	6 (17%)	6 (17%)	60 (25%)
	T4a	3 (3%)	1 (3%)	1 (3%)	18 (7%)
	T4b	15 (14%)	0 (0%)	2 (6%)	48 (20%)
Node Status	N0	67 (64%)	25 (69%)	25 (69%)	242 (100%)
	N1a	1 (1%)	1 (3%)	0 (0%)	0 (0%)
	N1b	1 (1%)	0 (0%)	0 (0%)	0 (0%)
	N2b	0 (0%)	1 (3%)	0 (0%)	0 (0%)
	N3	5 (5%)	1 (3%)	0 (0%)	0 (0%)
	N3c	3 (3%)	0 (0%)	1 (3%)	0 (0%)
	unknown	27 (26%)	9 (25%)	10 (28%)	0 (0%)
Sentinel Lymph Node Status	Negative	68 (65%)	25 (69%)	25 (69%)	194 (80%)
	Positive	30 (29%)	11 (31%)	10 (28%)	0 (0%)
	Unknown	6 (6%)	0 (0%)	1 (3%)	3 (1%)
	Not performed	0 (0%)	0 (0%)	0 (0%)	45 (19%)
Ulceration	Absent	68 (65%)	22 (61%)	23 (64%)	101 (42%)
	Present	36 (35%)	14 (39%)	13 (36%)	141 (58%)

References

1. Gershenwald, J.E., Scolyer, R.A.: Melanoma staging: American joint committee on cancer (AJCC) and beyond. Ann. Surg. Oncol. **25**(8), 2105–2110 (2018)
2. Landow, S.M., Gjelsvik, A., Weinstock, M.A.: Mortality burden and prognosis of thin melanomas overall and by subcategory of thickness, seer registry data, 1992–2013. J. Am. Acad. Dermatol. **76**(2), 258–263 (2017)

3. Luke, J.J., et al.: Pembrolizumab versus placebo as adjuvant therapy in completely resected stage IIB or IIC melanoma (keynote-716): a randomised, double-blind, phase 3 trial. Lancet **399**(10336), 1718–1729 (2022)
4. Bristol myers squibb announces adjuvant treatment with opdivo (nivolumab) demonstrated statistically significant and clinically meaningful improvement in recurrence-free survival (rfs) in patients with stage iib/c melanoma in the check-mate -76k trial. https://bit.ly/3dfAO8B. Accessed 16 Sep 2022
5. Rizk, E.M., et al.: Biomarkers predictive of survival and response to immune check-point inhibitors in melanoma. Am. J. Clin. Dermatol. **21**(1), 1–11 (2020)
6. Gurcan, M.N., Boucheron, L.E., Can, A., Madabhushi, A., Rajpoot, N.M., Yener, B.: Histopathological image analysis: a review. IEEE Rev. Biomed. Eng. **2**, 147–71 (2009)
7. Liu, Y., Jianquan, X.: High-resolution microscopy for imaging cancer pathobiology. Curr. Pathobiol. Rep. **7**(3), 85–96 (2019)
8. Qaiser, T., et al.: Usability of deep learning and H&E images predict disease outcome-emerging tool to optimize clinical trials. NPJ Precis. Oncol. **6**(1), 1–12 (2022)
9. Combalia, M., et al.: Validation of artificial intelligence prediction models for skin cancer diagnosis using dermoscopy images: the 2019 international skin imaging collaboration grand challenge. Lancet Digit. Health **4**(5), e330–e339 (2022)
10. Lee, S.H., Jang, H.J.: Deep learning-based prediction of molecular cancer biomark-ers from tissue slides: a new tool for precision oncology. Clin. Mol. Hepatol. (2022)
11. Hekler, A., et al.: Pathologist-level classification of histopathological melanoma images with deep neural networks. Eur. J. Cancer **115**, 79–83 (2019a)
12. Hekler, A., et al.: Deep learning outperformed 11 pathologists in the classification of histopathological melanoma images. Eur. J. Cancer **118**, 91–96 (2019b)
13. Brinker, T.J., et al.: Deep learning approach to predict sentinel lymph node status directly from routine histology of primary melanoma tumours. Eur. J. Cancer **154**, 227–234 (2021)
14. Moore, M.R., et al.: Automated digital TIL analysis (ADTA) adds prognostic value to standard assessment of depth and ulceration in primary melanoma. Sci. Rep. **11**(1), 1–11 (2021)
15. Kulkarni, P.M., et al.: Deep learning based on standard h&e images of primary melanoma tumors identifies patients at risk for visceral recurrence and deathdeep learning-based prognostic biomarker for melanoma. Clin. Cancer Res. **26**(5), 1126–1134 (2020)
16. Goodfellow, I., Bengio, Y., Courville, A.: Deep Learning. MIT Press, Cambridge (2016)
17. Johannet, P., et al.: Using machine learning algorithms to predict immunotherapy response in patients with advanced melanoma. Clin. Cancer Res. **27**(1), 131–140 (2021)
18. Li, A., Li, X., Li, W., Yu, X., Qi, M., Li, D.: Application of deep learning on the prognosis of cutaneous melanoma based on full scan pathology images. BioMed Research International, vol. 2022 (2022)
19. Sheikhzadeh, F., Guillaud, M., Ward, R.K.: Automatic labeling of molecular biomarkers of whole slide immunohistochemistry images using fully convolutional networks. arXiv preprint arXiv:1612.09420 (2016)
20. Patil, R., Bellary, S.: Machine learning approach in melanoma cancer stage detec-tion. J. King Saud Univ.-Comput. Inf. Sci. **34**(6), 3285–3293 (2022)

21. Jaworek-Korjakowska, J., Kleczek, P., Gorgon, M.: Melanoma thickness prediction based on convolutional neural network with VGG-19 model transfer learning. In: Proceedings of the IEEE/CVF Conference on Computer Vision and Pattern Recognition Workshops (2019)

22. Zhu, X., Yao, J., Huang, J.: Deep convolutional neural network for survival analysis with pathological images. In: 2016 IEEE International Conference on Bioinformatics and Biomedicine (BIBM), pp. 544–547. IEEE (2016)

23. Li, H., Wang, Y.F., Wan, R., Wang, S., Li, T.-Q., Kot, A.: Domain generalization for medical imaging classification with linear-dependency regularization. Adv. Neural Inf. Process. Syst. **33**, 3118–3129 (2020)

24. Harrell, F.E., et al.: Regression Modeling Strategies: With Applications to Linear Models, Logistic Regression, and Survival Analysis, vol. 608. Springer, Switzerland (2001). https://doi.org/10.1007/978-3-319-19425-7

25. Sebastian, P.: Survival analysis for deep learning, survival-cnn-estimator (2020). https://github.com/sebp/survival-cnn-estimator/blob/master/tutorial_tf2.ipynb

26. Faraggi, D., Simon, R.: A neural network model for survival data. Stat. Med. **14**(1), 73–82 (1995)

27. Simonyan, K., Zisserman, A.: Very deep convolutional networks for large-scale image recognition (2014)

28. Goode, A., Gilbert, B., Harkes, J., Jukic, D., Satyanarayanan, M.: OpenSlide: a vendor-neutral software foundation for digital pathology. J. Pathol. Inform. **4**(1), 27 (2013)

29. Abadi, M., et al.: TensorFlow: large-scale machine learning on heterogeneous systems (2015). https://www.tensorflow.org/

30. Chollet, F., et al.: Keras (2015). https://keras.io/

31. Jr Harrell, F.E., Califf, R.M., Pryor, D.B., Lee, K.L., Rosati, R.A.: Evaluating the yield of medical tests. JAMA **247**(18), 2543–2546 (1982). ISSN 0098-7484. https://doi.org/10.1001/jama.1982.03320430047030

32. Schmid, M., Wright, M.N., Ziegler, A.: On the use of Harrell's c for clinical risk prediction via random survival forests. Expert Syst. Appl. **63**, 450–459 (2016)

33. Hajian-Tilaki, K.: Receiver operating characteristic (ROC) curve analysis for medical diagnostic test evaluation. Casp. J. Intern. Med. **4**(2), 627 (2013)

34. Heagerty, P.J., Zheng, Y.: Survival model predictive accuracy and ROC curves. Biometrics **61**(1), 92–105 (2005)

35. Hanley, J.A., McNeil, B.J.: The meaning and use of the area under a receiver operating characteristic (ROC) curve. Radiology **143**(1), 29–36 (1982)

36. Bradley, A.P.: The use of the area under the ROC curve in the evaluation of machine learning algorithms. Pattern Recognit. **30**(7), 1145–1159 (1997)

Symmetry-Aware Siamese Network: Exploiting Pathological Asymmetry for Chest X-Ray Analysis

Helen Schneider[1(✉)], Elif Cansu Yildiz[1(✉)], David Biesner[1], Yannik C. Layer[2], Benjamin Wulff[1], Sebastian Nowak[2], Maike Theis[2], Alois M. Sprinkart[2], Ulrike I. Attenberger[1,2], and Rafet Sifa[1]

[1] Fraunhofer IAIS, Sankt Augustin, Germany
{helen.schneider,elif.cansu}@iais.fraunhofer.de
[2] Department of Diagnostic and Interventional Radiology, University Hospital Bonn, Bonn, Germany

Abstract. The human body shows elements of bilateral symmetry for various body parts, including the lung. This symmetry can be disturbed by a variety of diseases or abnormalities, e.g. by lung diseases such as pneumonia. While radiologists use lung field symmetry information in their radiological examinations to analyze chest X-rays, it is still under-utilized in the field of computer vision.

To investigate the potential of pathologically induced asymmetry of the lung field for the automatic detection of healthy and diseased patients, we implement a symmetry-aware architecture. The model is based on a Siamese network with a DenseNet backbone and a symmetry-aware contrastive loss function. Two different processing pipelines are investigated: first, the scan is processed as a whole image, and second, the left and right lung fields are separated. This enables an independent determination of the most important features of each lung field.

Compared to state-of-the-art baseline models (DenseNet, Mask R-CNN), symmetry-aware training can improve the AUROC score by up to 10%. Furthermore, the findings indicate that, by integrating the bilateral symmetry of the lung field, the interpretability of the models increases. The generated probability maps show a stronger focus on lung field and disease features compared to state-of-the-art algorithms like Grad-Cam++ for heat map generation or Mask R-CNN for object detection.

Keywords: Contrastive Loss · Symmetry-aware Model · Lung Abnormalities · Chest X-Ray

1 Introduction

Chest X-ray (CXR) is an important imaging technique for radiologists to analyze various cardiothoracic diseases [1]. Abnormalities can be detected and

---

H. Schneider and E. C. Yildiz—Equal contribution.

This research has been funded by the Federal Ministry of Education and Research of Germany and the state of North-Rhine Westphalia as part of the Lamarr-Institute for Machine Learning and Artificial Intelligence, LAMARR22B.

L. Iliadis et al. (Eds.): ICANN 2023, LNCS 14257, pp. 165–176, 2023.
https://doi.org/10.1007/978-3-031-44216-2_14

specific diseases can be diagnosed with the help of CXR. The procedure is time-, cost- and radiation efficient, and frequently implemented, with e.g. about 8.3 million requests solely in England 2019–2020 [1–3]. Due to this high workload, several deep learning-based computer-aided diagnosis (CAD) systems have been developed to support radiologists in the analysis of CXR and to optimize the workflow of clinics and radiology departments. Good performances have been achieved in the classification of various lung diseases and the detection of abnormalities using deep convolutional networks [1,4–6]. Automated analysis of CXR holds the potential to improve clinical workflow, e.g. patients with likely critical conditions can be grouped in a priority review to reduce processing times and potentially accelerate treatment initialization [1].

However, existing models are mainly based on a purely data-driven approach and do not consider prior medical knowledge about the use case to be analyzed. Informed machine learning has the potential to increase performance and improve the interpretability of models by adding prior domain knowledge [7]. Prior knowledge in medical image analysis may include the bilateral symmetry for specific body parts, such as the brain, the pelvis, or the lungs. This symmetry can be disturbed by various diseases and is therefore considered by experts when analyzing image data to detect abnormalities. Some studies developed architecture to specifically incorporate this prior knowledge into data-driven modeling for a variety of use cases, like the detection of mass regions in mammograms [8].

For the analysis of CXR, the bilateral asymmetry is defined as possible differences between the left and right lung fields. Symmetry-aware training has not yet been sufficiently explored in this application area. In parts, this is because CXR is a challenging image modality for symmetry-aware training, since non-pathological asymmetries, partially outside the lung field, are not relevant for the diagnosis of the diseases. Additionally, the left and right lung fields are arranged differently by anatomical circumstances. The position of the heart and the lung hila lead to non-pathological asymmetry in the lung field even for healthy patients. Nevertheless, the lung fields of a healthy person show elements of bilateral symmetry. This fact is utilized by radiologists during routine examinations to detect abnormalities that disrupt the lung field symmetry due to disease [3].

Based on this motivation, we aim to further contribute to closing the gap of symmetry-aware deep learning for lung disease analysis in CXR. In summary, the main contributions of this work are:

- implementation of a symmetry-aware architecture for the CXR use case,
- explicit integration of visual disease features into the symmetry-aware contrastive loss function,
- analysis of two different symmetry-aware processing pipelines, and
- demonstration of the interpretability of the symmetry-aware model by in-depth analysis of the visual output.

2   Related Work

In recent years, strong successes have been achieved in the development of purely data-driven CAD systems in the medical imaging field. As demonstrated in [4, 5, 9, 10] high performances are realized for the automatic diagnosis of lung diseases based on CXR. Various performance-enhancing machine learning techniques for convolutional neural networks (CNN) like transfer or ensemble learning have been investigated [6, 11].

In addition to the purely data-driven training in the medical imaging domain, few publications have investigated the incorporation of bilateral symmetry of different body regions, such as the brain or the breast [8, 12–14].

In the work of Barman et al. [15], the pathological asymmetry of the brain after a stroke is exploited to diagnose strokes more efficiently. Separate features of the brain hemispheres, extracted from computed tomography (CT) angiography scans, are fused using the L1 distance. The area under the receiver operating characteristic curve (AUROC) score is improved by up to 3% compared to a histogram feature baseline.

Pathological asymmetry can also be utilized for the classification of Alzheimer's disease to achieve a more efficient classification pipeline. In [16], the anatomical asymmetric characteristics of the brain are exploited to build symmetry-enhanced attention with improved accuracy.

In [17], Chen et al. developed a symmetry-informed deep CNN architecture to detect pelvis fractures in X-rays. This approach improved the area under the curve (AUC) score by up to 4% compared to other state-of-the-art baseline methodologies and increased the interpretability of the model.

Despite the wide variety of applications of symmetry-informed models, few publications examine the impact of bilateral symmetry for the analysis of CXRs to detect lung disease. Santosh et al. address this open research question for the diagnosis of tuberculosis disease [18]. However, no deep learning architectures are used, which presents a limiting factor for performance. In [3], symmetry-aware models can achieve an F1 score increase of up to 2% compared to a DenseNet architecture. Deep siamese networks are trained with a cross-entropy loss function, the influence of a symmetry-motivated loss is not investigated.

In general, the inclusion of the lung field symmetry represents an underexplored area of research for the analysis of CXR, despite promising prior knowledge. To the best of our knowledge, the impact of a symmetry-motivated loss has not been sufficiently investigated for deep learning architectures. With this work, we aim to fill this gap by demonstrating the performance and interpretability increase of symmetry-informed detection of abnormal CXRs.

3   Method

In this section, we provide a technical explanation of the considered classification problem and introduce the Symmetry-Aware Siamese Network (SASN) architecture.

3.1 Problem Setup

We implement a binary classification problem, with target $Y \in \{0, 1\}$, for a given CXR input I, where 0 identifies a normal and 1 identifies an abnormal scan. A scan is defined as abnormal if at least one disease is present in the CXR. More detailed information about the diseases included in the dataset used is discussed in Sect. 4.1.

In addition to the classification information, the training data provides disease bounding boxes or bounding polygons, which determine pathological asymmetric areas. We integrate these into the training of the models to increase the performance and interpretability of the networks.

Inspired by [17] considering the anatomy of the pelvis to detect any fracture, we adopted a similar approach for the symmetry-aware analysis of CXRs.

3.2 Symmetry-Aware Siamese Network

Motivated by [17], we implement the Symmetry-Aware Siamese Network as a fully convolutional end-to-end deep learning model with a DenseNet-121 [19] backbone. It consists of three different modules named siamese encoding, feature fusion, and feature comparison. The output of the network is a distance and a probability map. While distance map outputs are to observe the symmetrical awareness of the model, probability maps are used for classification.

We differentiate two distinct model architectures for the integration of symmetry awareness in the encoding, namely

- **Vanilla Symmetry-Aware Siamese Model ($SASN_{vanilla}$)**
  The model takes the entire CXR together with its flipped form as an input, denoted as I and I_f, respectively.
- **Split Symmetry-Aware Siamese Model($SASN_{split}$)**
  The left and right lung field are separated. Each lung field is processed individually by the siamese encoding, allowing an independent determination of the most important hidden features of each lung field. We denote the left and right lung field inputs as I and I_f, respectively.

See Fig. 1 for an exemplary overview of the $SASN_{vanilla}$ model architecture.

Siamese Encoding Module. The inputs are encoded in a siamese structure with two streams and shared weights [20,21]. A DenseNet-121 architecture includes 4 individual DenseNet blocks. The Siamese encoding module consists of the first 3 DenseNet blocks, which extract visual patterns and lower-dimensional feature representations, including asymmetric information. We restrict the siamese encoder to the first 3 blocks to prevent the anatomical features of the images from getting lost in the deeper layers of the DenseNet model. The calculated embeddings, denoted as F and F_f, are then processed by the two decoding modules, which are a feature fusion and feature comparison module. The siamese encoding module has the same structure for $SASN_{vanilla}$ and $SASN_{split}$.

While the inputs to SASN$_{vanilla}$ are the entire image and the flipped image, the input to SASN$_{split}$ are the left and right lung fields, obtained by splitting the image in the middle. Before processing, we additionally flip one of the split images, such that both lung fields face the same direction and asymmetries become easier to detect.

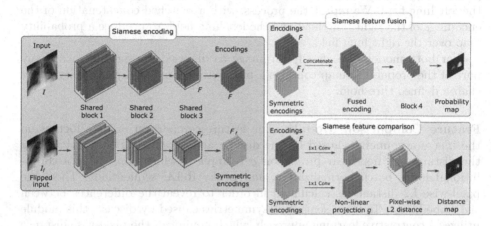

Fig. 1. Model architecture of the SASN$_{vanilla}$. A CXR image and its flipped form are given an encoding module consisting of dense blocks with shared weights. The resulting embeddings are decoded by a Siamese feature fusion module and a Siamese feature comparison module to provide a disease probability map and distance map of the features, respectively.

Feature Fusion Module. In the feature fusion module, we combine the encoded inputs by concatenation within a transition module. A transition module is located between two adjacent blocks of the DenseNet and consists of batch normalization, ReLU, a 1 × 1 convolution layer, and a 2 × 2 average pooling layer. We concatenate the embeddings after the ReLU activation function inside the transition module. Note that concatenation causes the number of convolution input channels to double. Additionally, we modify the number of kernels in the convolution layer of the transition module from 1 to 7, in order to preserve more information from the encoded embeddings. As mentioned previously, the concatenation and transition is followed by the last DenseNet block.

Finally, a 1×1 convolution layer and sigmoid function are applied to acquire the probability of disease occurrence in each pixel. In this module, the loss is calculated using pixel-wise binary cross entropy (BCE) between the predicted probability outputs $\hat{Y}$ and the ground truth Y. For an image of n pixels, we define the loss as

$$L_b = -\frac{1}{n}\sum_{i=1}^{n}(Y_i \cdot \log \hat{Y}_i + (1 - Y_i) \cdot \log(1 - \hat{Y}_i)). \qquad (1)$$

We calculate separate probability maps for each lung field with the SASN$_{\text{split}}$ model, which are concatenated into a probability map for the entire lung scan in the end. We, therefore, encode both lung fields separately with the Siamese encoder network to receive the embedded features. The encodings of the left lung field F are concatenated with the encodings of the flipped right lung field F_f and processed by the final DenseNet encoder block to produce a probability map over the left lung field. We repeat the process, with a switched concatenation of the encodings of the right lung field and the left lung field, to produce a probability map over the right lung field.

For both models, we classify an image as diseased during inference if any part of the probability map contains a pixel with a predicted probability larger than a defined threshold.

Feature Comparison Module. The feature comparison module focuses on the image asymmetry caused by the disease abnormalities. Before calculating the distances, a nonlinear projection g is applied, which consists of a convolutional layer, batch normalization, and Leaky ReLU sequentially. Then, the pixel-wise L2 distance is calculated in order to reveal the differences between the embeddings. To learn semantic asymmetries caused by disease, this module utilizes a contrastive learning approach, which minimizes the pixel-wise distance between the symmetric areas and maximizes the distance between the diseased area and its symmetric healthy part. We define the contrastive loss function as

$$L_c = \begin{cases} \sum_x \|g(F(x)) - g(F_f(x))\|^2 & \text{if } x \notin \hat{M} \\ \sum_x \max\left(0, \ m - \|g(F(x)) - g(F_f(x))\|^2\right) & \text{if } x \in \hat{M} \end{cases} \quad (2)$$

where x denotes a single pixel coordinate while F and F_f denote the embedded features of I and I_f, respectively. We denote areas annotated as diseased in the target image mask by $\hat{M}$ and define the margin m as the radius for the dissimilarity of semantic asymmetries.

We define the total loss for one input image as

$$\hat{L} = L_b + L_c \quad (3)$$

where L_b denotes binary cross entropy loss, L_c represents the contrastive loss.

To generate a distance map the for entire lung scan with the SASN$_{\text{split}}$ model, we first generate a distance map for half of the image by comparing the encodings of one lung field F and the other lung field F_f. We create a copy of the distance map, mirror it and concatenate both maps to generate a map representing the entire scan.

4   Experiments

In addition to the SASN models, we implement the CheXNet [9] and Mask R-CNN [22] models as baselines for both the binary classification performance and heatmap generation. This section describes the experimental details.

4.1 Experimental Settings

Dataset. We use ChestX-Det-Dataset released by [23], which is a subset of the ChestX-ray14 dataset [24]. This dataset consists of more bounding boxes and polygon labels annotated with 13 observations by three board-certified radiologists for selected Chest X-rays. We consider the X-rays with the observations as diseased X-rays whilst without any observations as healthy X-rays. It contains 3025 data for training (547 healthy, 2478 diseased chest X-rays) and 553 samples for testing (64 healthy, 489 diseased chest X-rays). A detailed overview of the represented diseases in the dataset is available in [23].

We remove the label Cardiomegaly and count the X-rays only affected by this label as healthy since we focus on lung disease detection. However, the label Fracture was retained as diseased, although it is not directly affecting the lung, since the detection of fractures can benefit from symmetry-aware training and the inclusion of a non-pulmonary disease can prevent overfitting.

The division after removing the Cardiomegaly observation results in 588 healthy and 2437 diseased X-rays for the training set while 71 healthy and 482 diseased X-rays for the test set. There is no patient overlap between the training and test sets. 10% of the samples from the training set are used for validation.

Implementation Details. All the models and experiments were implemented using PyTorch. The given frontal CXRs are downscaled to 512×512 and stacked to a 3-channel image. For the $\mathrm{SASN_{split}}$ model, each scan is split along the vertical center, to separately process the left and right lung fields. The image with the right lung field is mirrored, to facilitate alignment during matching [3].

The model was initialized with ImageNet [25] pre-trained weights to speed up training and improve performance. The model has been fine-tuned using Adam optimizer with a learning rate of 10^{-5} and a reduce on plateau learning rate scheduler, with a reduction factor of 0.1. The loss parameter margin is set to $m = 0.5$. The model is trained with a batch size of 16 for 300 epochs.

We compared the proposed models with two baselines. The first one is CheXNet [9] using the DenseNet-121 model. We followed the same training setup, except for setting the batch size to 256, for which we observed an improvement in performance. The second model is vanilla Mask Region-Based Convolutional Neural Network (R-CNN) [22]. We apply the same setup of our proposed models regarding batch size, optimizer, image downscaling size, and learning rate for the training of the Mask R-CNN model.

We assess the performance of the models on the test set for the binary classification task. AUROC, F1 score, and average precision (AP) are computed. We use 95% bootstrap confidence intervals (CIs) on 100 samples, 2.5th and 97.5th percentiles of the scores are taken as the 95% bootstrap CI. Non-overlapping CIs are interpreted as a significant improvement. The prediction threshold of each model is determined by the threshold of the best F1 score on the validation split and used for the AP and F1 score calculation on the test set.

5   Results

5.1   Classification Performance

It can be seen in Table 1 that the symmetry-aware models achieve the highest scores for all analyzed metrics. The AUROC score can be increased by up to 10% compared to the CheXNet model, which is a significant improvement for $SASN_{vanilla}$ as well as $SASN_{split}$. Compared to the Mask R-CNN approach, the score increases by up to 5%. The F1 score can be improved by less than 2% by symmetry-aware training compared to the CheXNet model and the Mask R-CNN. However, all CIs are in a similar range of values.

The AP of the $SASN_{split}$ model is significantly higher than the CheXNet score. Also, compared to Mask R-CNN, the symmetry-aware SASN models show higher AP. For all scores, the highest performance is achieved by $SASN_{split}$. Nevertheless, comparing the CIs of $SASN_{vanilla}$ and $SASN_{split}$, no significant difference can be detected and strong overlap of the CIs is observed. This states that separate feature extraction has no significant influence.

In summary, this score analysis shows that the presented symmetry-aware approach can significantly increase the performance of CXR analysis.

Table 1. Test classification scores and confidence intervals (CI) of symmetry-aware models $SASN_{vanilla}$ and $SASN_{split}$ compared with the two baseline models CheXNet [9] and Mask R-CNN [22]. The highest performance value per metric is highlighted in bold.

Method	AUROC (95% CI)	F1 Score (95% CI)	AP (95% CI)
$SASN_{vanilla}$	88.20 [83.54, 91.78]	93.73 [92.12, 95.26]	97.96 [97.18, 98.80]
$SASN_{split}$	**88.56** [84.79, 91.97]	**94.04** [92.65, 95.57]	**98.00** [97.08, 98.88]
CheXNet [9]	78.65 [72.56, 83.43]	93.63 [92.01, 94.84]	95.54 [93.82, 97.18]
Mask R-CNN [22]	83.51 [78.90, 88.35]	92.50 [91.01, 94.02]	96.52 [94.34, 98.28]

5.2   Interpretability

We also analyze the generated probability maps, which visualize the probability that an area is affected by a disease feature, with respect to their interpretability. Figure 2 shows the probability maps for 6 different samples. Areas that are very likely to contain diseased features are marked in red, while purple pixels indicate a very low probability.

It can be seen that the developed algorithm is interpretable. For the first four samples, the generated probability maps mark the relevant disease features. It is irrelevant whether the disease affects partially one, both, or the overall lung fields. For the fifth sample, only very few pixels are affected by the disease features. The generated probability maps indicate a healthy scan. Whether higher

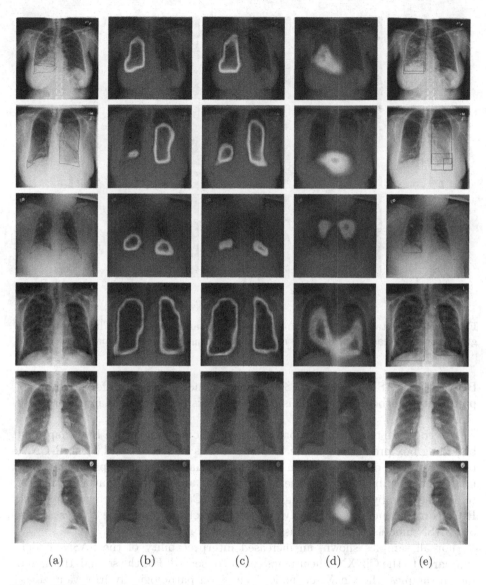

(a)   (b)   (c)   (d)   (e)

Fig. 2. Visual outputs for different models. (a) Chest X-ray with ground truth diseases, (b) probability map of SASN$_{vanilla}$, (c) probability map of SASN$_{split}$ (d), heat maps for CheXNet [9] generated with GradCam++ (e) Mask R-CNN [22] object detection boxes.

image resolutions and larger kernel sizes can support SASN models in detecting small disease features is a future research question. The last scan represents a healthy patient and illustrates that the SASN models can distinguish between pathological and non-pathological asymmetries. No diseased areas are detected in the whole scan, and non-pathological features are not recognized as diseased.

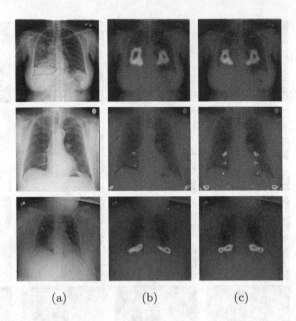

(a)   (b)   (c)

Fig. 3. Representation of the symmetry-aware distance maps. (a) Chest X-ray with ground truth diseases, (b) distance map of $SASN_{vanilla}$, (c) distance map of $SASN_{split}$.

Between the $SASN_{vanilla}$ and $SASN_{split}$ models, no significant difference in interpretability can be observed. This result is consistent with similar performance scores.

We compare the output probability maps of our models with heat maps and bounding box predictions of the baseline models (CheXNet and Mask R-CNN, respectively) as demonstrated in Fig. 2. Note that the heat maps of CheXNet, unlike the probability maps of the SASN models, are not model outputs but have to be generated by an additional algorithm GradCam++. Furthermore, the Mask R-CNN model has been explicitly trained to pixel-wise recognize objects, unlike our SASN models, which are classification networks.

For all samples shown, an increased interpretability of the SASN models compared to the CheXNet heat maps can be observed. For the second, third, and fourth samples, the CheXNet model focuses on pathologically irrelevant areas, including the heart region. Improved interpretability compared to the Mask R-CNN is observed for the same scans. Among others, the Mask R-CNN detects in contrast to the SASN models disease features in only one lung field, although both lungs are affected. In addition, for the fourth patient, the upper left lung is more strongly considered by the SASN models. These examples indicate that the interpretability of a model can benefit from symmetry-aware training.

In Fig. 3, we compare the distance map outputs of $SASN_{vanilla}$ and $SASN_{split}$ for three test samples. Distance maps are trained to measure the difference between the symmetric features of CXRs. These outputs present that the models utilize pathological asymmetry features to detect diseases.

In the first example, the disease features affect solely the right lung field. The model recognizes the pathological asymmetry between the two lung fields, which results in a stronger difference between these parts of the scan. The second example is a scan without lung disease. Both models show the strongest focus on areas outside the lung field, indicating a healthy lung. For the last row, the distance maps specify that the models notice the feature differences in the diseased regions of the lungs despite both lung fields being affected by a disease. This distance map analysis indicates that the Siamese feature comparison module appropriately encodes symmetric information into the deep neural network and that pathological asymmetries are successfully integrated into training.

6 Conclusion

We proposed the SASN model, a siamese architecture for the analysis of chest X-rays, which considers the lung field symmetry during training as prior knowledge. We adapted both the architecture and the loss function to be symmetrically motivated. An AUROC score of 88.56% was achieved, with significant improvements compared to state-of-the-art baseline algorithms. Moreover, our in depths analysis of the generated visual outputs indicates that the interpretability of the models is increased by the symmetrically motivated training. In the future, we want to further investigate the data efficiency of the presented architectures and the influence of bilateral filters on symmetric motivated training in the medical context.

References

1. Nabulsi, Z., et al.: Deep learning for distinguishing normal versus abnormal chest radiographs and generalization to two unseen diseases tuberculosis and COVID-19. Sci. Rep. **11**(1) (2021)
2. Stevens, B.J., et al.: Radiographers reporting chest x-ray images: identifying the service enablers and challenges in England, UK. Radiography **27**(4), 1006–1013 (2021)
3. Schneider, H., et al.: Towards symmetry-aware pneumonia detection on chest x-rays. In: 2022 IEEE Symposium Series on Computational Intelligence (SSCI), pp. 543–550 (2022)
4. Irvin, J., Rajpurkar, P., et al.: Chexpert: a large chest radiograph dataset with uncertainty labels and expert comparison (2019)
5. Pham, H.H., et al.: Interpreting chest x-rays via CNNs that exploit hierarchical disease dependencies and uncertainty labels. Neurocomputing **437**, 186–194 (2021)
6. Schneider, H., Biesner, D., et al.: Improving intensive care chest x-ray classification by transfer learning and automatic label generation. In: The European Symposium on Artificial Neural Networks (2022)
7. Beckh, K., et al.: Explainable machine learning with prior knowledge: an overview. ArXiv, abs/2105.10172 (2021)
8. Diniz, J.O.B., et al.: Detection of mass regions in mammograms by bilateral analysis adapted to breast density using similarity indexes and convolutional neural networks. Comput. Methods Programs Biomed. **156**, 191–207 (2018)

9. Rajpurkar, P., Irvin, J., et al.: Chexnet: radiologist-level pneumonia detection on chest x-rays with deep learning. arXiv preprint arXiv:1711.05225 (2017)
10. Biesner, D., et al.: Improving chest x-ray classification by RNN-based patient monitoring. In: 2022 21st IEEE International Conference on Machine Learning and Applications (ICMLA), pp. 946–950, December 2022
11. Kundu, R., et al.: Pneumonia detection in chest x-ray images using an ensemble of deep learning models. PLOS ONE **16**, e0256630 (2021)
12. Liang, K., et al.: Symmetry-enhanced attention network for acute ischemic infarct segmentation with non-contrast CT images. In: de Bruijne, M., et al. (eds.) MICCAI 2021. LNCS, vol. 12907, pp. 432–441. Springer, Cham (2021). https://doi.org/10.1007/978-3-030-87234-2_41
13. Liu, C.-F., Padhy, S., et al.: Using deep Siamese neural networks for detection of brain asymmetries associated with Alzheimer's disease and mild cognitive impairment. Magn. Reson. Imaging **64**, 07 (2019)
14. Yang, P., et al.: Diagnosis of obsessive-compulsive disorder via spatial similarity-aware learning and fused deep polynomial network. Med. Image Anal. **75**, 102244 (2022)
15. Barman, A., et al.: Determining ischemic stroke from CT-angiography imaging using symmetry-sensitive convolutional networks, pp. 1873–1877, April 2019
16. Wang, C., et al.: Asymmetry-enhanced attention network for Alzheimer's diagnosis with structural magnetic resonance imaging. Comput. Biol. Med. **151**, 106282 (2022)
17. Chen, H., et al.: Anatomy-aware Siamese network: exploiting semantic asymmetry for accurate pelvic fracture detection in x-ray images. In: Vedaldi, A., Bischof, H., Brox, T., Frahm, J.-M. (eds.) ECCV 2020. LNCS, vol. 12368, pp. 239–255. Springer, Cham (2020). https://doi.org/10.1007/978-3-030-58592-1_15
18. Santosh, K.C., Antani, S.: Automated chest X-ray screening: can lung region symmetry help detect pulmonary abnormalities? IEEE Trans. Med. Imaging **37**, 1168–1177 (2018)
19. Huang, G., Liu, Z., et al.: Densely connected convolutional networks. CoRR, abs/1608.06993 (2016)
20. Bromley, J., et al.: Signature verification using a Siamese time delay neural network. Adv. Neural Inf. Process. Syst. **6** (1993)
21. Koch, G.R.: Siamese neural networks for one-shot image recognition (2015)
22. He, K., et al.: Mask R-CNN. CoRR, abs/1703.06870 (2017)
23. Lian, J., et al.: A structure-aware relation network for thoracic diseases detection and segmentation. IEEE Trans. Med. Imaging **40**(8), 2042–2052 (2021)
24. Wang, X., et al.: ChestX-ray8: hospital-scale chest x-ray database and benchmarks on weakly-supervised classification and localization of common thorax diseases. In: Proceedings of the IEEE Conference on Computer Vision and Pattern Recognition, pp. 2097–2106 (2017)
25. Russakovsky, O., Deng, J., et al.: Imagenet large scale visual recognition challenge. CoRR, abs/1409.0575 (2014)

The Optimization and Parallelization of Two-Dimensional Zigzag Scanning on the Matrix

Ling Li[1,2,3], Yaobin Wang[1,2,3]([✉]), Lijuan Peng[1,2,3], Yuming Feng[1,2,3], Ning Liu[1,2,3], Guangwei Li[4], and Xiaolin Jia[1,2,3]

[1] School of Computer Science and Technology, Mianyang 621010, Sichuan, China
wangyaobin@foxmail.com
[2] Key Laboratory of Testing Technology for Manufacturing Process in Ministry of Education, Mianyang 621010, Sichuan, China
[3] Mobile Internet of Things and Radio Frequency Identification Technology Key Laboratory of Mianyang (MIOT&RFID), Mianyang 621010, Sichuan, China
[4] School of Economic and Management, Southwest University of Science and Technology, Mianyang 621010, Sichuan, China

Abstract. With the expansion of applications, such as image processing, scientific computing, numerical simulation, biomedicine, social network and so on, enormous quantities of data need to be crunched in order to get the valuable parts and discard redundant ones. For those data represented as two-dimensional digital matrix, two alternative schemes by scanning the elements of the matrix in zigzag route have been proposed. Fixed-point mode and navigation mode used in the proposed schemes are introduced. Performance comparison between the two schemes and previous works are analyzed. The experimental results show that our proposed schemes perform well with large scales of matrices. Moreover, the design of parallel programming based on our proposed scheme has been given. Finally, we have discussed the efficiency of parallelization. The speedup we get is from 3.413 to 3.996, which is stably growth with the scales of matrices.

Keywords: Application · Data · Digital matrix · Zigzag route · Parallelization

1 Introduction

With the expansion of applications and software, such as image processing, scientific computing, numerical simulation, biomedicine, social network and so on, enormous quantities of data are produced. For specific application, these data are provided with their individual characteristics. So, they need to be crunched in order to get the valuable parts that we want and discard those redundant parts. The crunching process will be beneficial for the cost of time and space.

In image processing, a specific natural image is usually represented as a two-dimensional digital matrix. The scale of the matrix is large. Then it is needed to compress the original data to another type with less quantity by detecting and removing redundant

L. Iliadis et al. (Eds.): ICANN 2023, LNCS 14257, pp. 177–189, 2023.
https://doi.org/10.1007/978-3-031-44216-2_15

ones from the original data [1]. As in [2] and [3], after discrete cosine transform (DCT) [4–7] and further quantization, a DCT coefficient matrix is formed with energy located at the top-left and some zeroes at the bottom-right. The energy should be found out for further operations and those zeroes should be removed because of redundancy. So, an efficient scanning mode to find the energy of the image and remove zeroes quickly in DCT coefficient matrix should be further discussed.

In biomedicine, medical images, such as MRI and CT, show the characteristics of various aspects of human body. It means that personal privacy information of patients are included in images and should be protected by encrypting pixels one by one [7–10]. Due to the high correlation between adjacent pixels of medical image, traditional encryptions are not suitable for protection [8]. So, in order to destroy the correlation in encryption, an efficient scanning mode to check the non-adjacent pixels should be introduced.

In numerical simulation, the solution of a system of equations is converted to multiplication between coefficient matrix and vector [11–13]. For specific application, a lot of zeroes are produced in its coefficient matrix after conversion, usually located at the upper triangle, lower triangle or dense regions. So, if these zeroes are checked at the pretreatment stage, the result of multiplication should be zero and the operations can be omitted. Then the efficiency of the solution can be significantly improved.

For those requirements mentioned above, a new scrambling mode with zigzag route was introduced in [14–18]. This mode starts scanning from the first element of the matrix at the top-left to the last element at the bottom-right in the form of zigzag. So, it is completely different from traditional way, which starts from left to right and top to bottom. Through zigzag scanning process, special parts of elements as mentioned above can be scrambled. Therefore, for special applications, zigzag scanning to the matrix at the pretreatment stage can help us to get what we want quickly, and also reduce the cost of time and space of the whole process [19–21].

In this paper, we mainly focus on the performance of zigzag scanning process base on literature [17]. Two alternative zigzag scanning schemes, named as fix-point and navigation, are proposed according to literature [17]. The details of the proposed schemes are described in pseudo code and their performances are analyzed through experiments. Finally, we discuss the parallel programming design and optimization for the proposed schemes. The rest of the paper is organized as follows. Section 2 will introduce the related concepts corresponding to our proposed schemes. In Sect. 3, we will introduce the alternative schemes and make performance analysis. Section 4 will discuss the parallelization of proposed schemes. Experimental results are shown in Sect. 5, and Sect. 6 gives conclusions and future works.

2   Related Concepts

2.1   Traditional Scanning Mode

For specific matrix, traditional scanning mode usually starts at the first element of the first row horizontally left-to-right and ends at the last element of the row, and then this process works repeatedly on the next rows until it reaches the last one. This is familiar to the scanning pattern of raster scan [22–24] shown in Fig. 1 and the reading pattern when we read books. Suppose that the order of matrix is n, then traditional scanning mode has time complexity of $O(n^2)$. So, as we learn from the literatures, it is not the effective one.

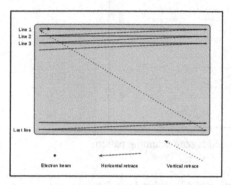

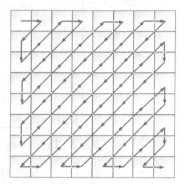

Fig. 1. Raster Scan pattern   **Fig. 2.** Zigzag Scanning pattern

2.2 Zigzag Scanning

Suppose that there is a square matrix with order n, zigzag scanning to the matrix starts from the first element of the first row. Then its neighbor, decided by the scanning direction, is scanned as the second one. The subsequent elements are scanned in zigzag route until the last one [8, 25–28]. For example, for a matrix with 8 × 8, the specific scanning process is shown in Fig. 2. As described in [18, 19, 21], this mode also has time complexity of $O(n^2)$.

2.3 Rotated Zigzag Scanning

In [17], the matrix is given a clockwise rotation with 45 degrees based on its origin of coordinate before the scanning starts, which is shown in Fig. 3. After this special transformation, we can see that the sum of X and Y coordinate of each element is just equal to the number of the layer, where it belongs to. Also, scanning direction is decided by the parity of layers. For example, in layer 1, we have two elements with coordinates (0, 1) and (1, 0). It is proved that $0 + 1 = 1 + 0 = 1$. Scanning direction is from right to left through the two coordinates. Then zigzag scanning process begins as usual from the top layer to the bottom with different scanning directions. The outputs of scanning process are just (X_co, Y_co) where "X_co + Y_co = layer number". Algorithm 1 gives the detail of the whole process mentioned above. After running Algorithm 1 in $2n - 1$ times, all layers of the matrix can be scanned (Table 1).

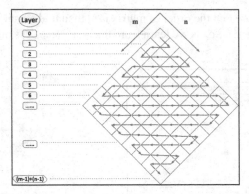

Fig. 3. The process of rotated zigzag scanning pattern

Table 1. Description of Algorithm 1

Algorithm 1: Zigzag Scanning for single layer on rotated 2D matrix

Require:
The **direction** to decide the scanning process;
The **layer** to match the scanning route though the rotated matrix;
The **matrix** to be scanned; The scale of the **rows** and **columns**.
Ensure:
All the elements in the matrix can be scanned by zigzag route.
```
 1:  get the direction by checking whether layer%2 equals to 1
 2:  If direction is false Then
 3:     exchange the value of rows and columns
 4:  Endif
 5:  For i=0 to rows do
 6:     For j=0 to columns do
 7:        If i+j equals to layer number Then
 8:           If direction is true Then
 9:              give the scanned element with its coordinate (i, j)
10:           else
11:              give the scanned element with its coordinate (j, i)
12:           Endif
13:        Endif
14:     Endfor
15:  Endfor
```

---

3 Proposed Optimization Schemes and Analysis

As described in Sect. 2.3, dual-loop is used in Algorithm 1 to find the elements in zigzag route. It means that all the elements in the matrix should be scanned and checked once. Suppose the order of square matrix is n, then Algorithm 1 has time complexity of $O(n^2)$ and the whole process has time complexity of $(2n-1)*O(n^2)$. Actually, for those elements, which are not located in current-scanning layer, it is no need to scan and check them. The related operations in Algorithm 1 could be omitted. Then, the time and space used for the operations can be saved and the corresponding time complexity would be reduced.

For the situation mentioned above, we need to change the way we find elements and try to give optimization. Our proposed schemes are mainly focus on scanning and checking the elements in zigzag route without any extra works. The efficiency of schemes with optimization will be discussed compared with Algorithm 1. In order to keep the consistency of context, the following discussions are all based on square matrix with order n.

3.1 Zigzag Scanning – Fixed Point

From Fig. 3, three important information can be considered for new algorithm design. Firstly, the number of layers of the rotated square matrix is fixed. No matter how large n is, the number of layers is equal to $2n - 1$. Secondly, the number of elements in each layer is also fixed. Layer 0 and layer $2n - 2$ contain only one element, while layer $n - 1$ contains the most ones. Thirdly, the sum of x and y coordinates of each element is equal to the layer number, in which it is located. For the convenience of algorithm design, we set layer 0 as the layer number of the first layer shown in Fig. 3.

So, we focus on each layer of the rotated matrix and change our way to scan and check those elements just only in it. The operation to other elements not in the specific layer can be totally omitted. We have "X_co + Y_co = layer number" described in Sect. 2.3, for a given layer number, if there is X_co ($0 \leq$ X_co $\leq$ rows), then "layer number-X_co ($0 \leq$ layer number-X_co $\leq$ columns)" is bound to be fixed. Then element with coordinate (X_co, layer number-X_co) or (layer number-X_co, X_co) is just the fixed point that we want. For example, we have layer 3 with odd layer number in Fig. 3. Scanning direction decided by this parity is from right to left. Only those fixed points with coordinates (0, 3–0), (1, 3–1), (2, 3–2), (3, 3–3) are scanned and checked. The process has stopped and started the next round in layer 4. Now, scanning direction decided by the parity is from left to right, just contrary to layer 3. Fixed points with coordinates (4–0, 0), (4–1, 1), (4–2, 2), (4–3 3), (4–4, 4) are scanned and checked. Next, this process goes through each layer repeatedly.

Therefore, our proposed scheme named as "Fixed-Point" starts from the layers, but no longer the rows or columns of the matrix. Table 2 gives the detail of the whole process mentioned above. After running Algorithm 2 in $2n - 1$ times, fixed points in each layer are found out through layer traversing. Finally, we concatenate these fixed points to get the zigzag scanning sequence of the matrix. As described in Algorithm 2, only one loop is used to check the fixed point in each layer without any extra works. Then algorithm 2 has time complexity of O(layer) = O($2n - 1$)$\approx$O(n) and the whole process has time complexity of ($2n - 1$)*O(n).

3.2 Zigzag Scanning – Navigation

In algorithm 2, the fixity of points in each layer has been considered. At the same time, zigzag route through points is also unchangeable. Inspired by the two basic principles, we have proposed another new scheme, which would be more efficiency than the other two.

Table 2. Description of Algorithm 2

Algorithm 2: Zigzag Scanning-Fixed Point for single layer on rotated 2D matrix

---

Require:
    The **direction** to decide the scanning process;
    The **layer** to match the scanning route though the rotated matrix;
    The **matrix** to be scanned; The scale of the **rows** and **columns**.
Ensure:
    All the elements in the matrix can be scanned by zigzag route.
 1: get the direction by checking whether layer%2 equals to 1
 2: **If** direction is false **Then**
 3:    exchange the value of rows and columns
 4: **Endif**
 5: **For** i=0 **to** layer **do**
 6:    **If** direction is true **and** i<rows **and** layer-i<columns **Then**
 7:      give the scanned element with its coordinate (i, layer-i)
 8:    **elseif** direction is false **and** i<rows **and** layer-i<columns **Then**
 9:      give the scanned element with its coordinate (layer-i, i)
10:    **Endif**
11: **Endfor**

Navigation mode, just like mobile navigation used when we drive, from the first element $(0, 0)$ to the last one has been utilized in our new scheme. Suppose the unchangeable zigzag route is the best path given by navigation. Then all the points in this path can be concatenated to get the zigzag scanning sequence of the matrix. The detail of navigation mode is described as follows.

Firstly, we set a changeable coordinate (X_Pos, Y_Pos) as the starting point of each step. Secondly, the initial value of (X_Pos, Y_Pos) is given by $(0, 0)$, where the navigation will begin. Thirdly, following the parity of layer number, navigation direction is just from left to right or on the contrary. If the coordinate of the current point is (i, j), the next point guided by navigation direction is $(i--, j++)$ from left to right or $(i++, j--)$ from right to left. Fourthly, while $(i--, j++)$ or $(i++, j--)$ reach the boundary of each layer, we should stop the navigation and turn to the new direction (bottom left with $i++$ or bottom right with $j++$ shown in Fig. 3). Then new (X_Pos, Y_Pos) is given by changed (i, j) as starting point of the next round and the navigation is continued again. Finally, we repeat the above processes until the last element.

The whole process of the new scheme is represented in Table 3. For example, in Fig. 3 we can see $(0, 0)$ is the starting point of navigation scheme. Since there is only one element in layer 0, and navigation direction is from left to right, the process reaches the boundary of layer 0. Then the navigation stops and new starting point turns to the bottom right point $(0, 1)$, where the next round of navigation on layer 1 starts. As we know in Sect. 3.1, the number of elements in each layer is fixed. Then navigation process through each layer also runs fixed times to get the points and give the new starting point of next round. Therefore, it means that for each layer algorithm 3 has $O(1)$ time complexity and the whole process has time complexity of $(2n - 1)*O(1)$.

Table 3. Description of Algorithm 3

Algorithm 3: Zigzag Scanning-Navigation for single layer on rotated 2D matrix

---

Require:
  The **direction** to decide the scanning process;
  The **layer** to match the scanning route though the rotated matrix;
  The **matrix** to be scanned; The scale of the **rows** and **columns**.
  The **initial coordinate (X_Pos, Y_Pos)** to where the scanning process starts.
Ensure:
  All the elements in the matrix can be scanned by zigzag route.
1: get the direction by checking whether layer%2 equals to 1
2: **If** direction is false **Then**
3:     exchange the value of rows and columns
4: **Endif**
5: initial (X_Pos, Y_Pos) is given to (i, j)
6: **While** 0≤i≤m-1 **and** 0≤j≤n-1 **do**
7:    **IF** i+j == layer **and** direction is false **Then**
8:       give the scanned element with its coordinate (i, j)
9:       keep scanning with rotated 2D matrix from left to right
10:   **Endif**
11:   **IF** i+j == layer **and** direction is true **Then**
12:      give the scanned element with its coordinate (i, j)
13:      keep scanning with rotated 2D matrix from right to left
14:   **Endif**
15: **Endwhile** //all elements match with the layer can be scanned
16: **IF** direction is false **Then**
17:     get the coordinate of critical point (cp_X=++i, cp_Y=--j)
18:     **IF** critical point is in the upper triangular matrix **Then**
19:        new starting point of next round turns to bottom-right(cp_Y++)
20:        (cp_X, cp_Y) is given to (X_Pos, Y_Pos) as new starting point
21:     **elseif** critical point is in the lower triangular matrix **Then**
22:        new starting point of next round turns to bottom-left(cp_X++)
23:        (cp_X, cp_Y) is given to (X_Pos, Y_Pos) as new starting point
24:     **Endif**
25: **elseif** direction is true **Then**
26:     get the coordinate of critical point (cp_X=--i, cp_Y=++j)
27:     **IF** critical point is in the upper triangular matrix **Then**
28:        new starting point of next round turns to bottom-left(cp_X++)
29:        (cp_X, cp_Y) is given to (X_Pos, Y_Pos) as new starting point
30:     **elseif** critical point is in the lower triangle matrix **Then**
31:        new starting point of next round turns to bottom-right(cp_Y++)
32:        (cp_X, cp_Y) is given to (X_Pos, Y_Pos) as new starting point
33:     **Endif**
34: **Endif**

---

4 Parallelization of the Proposed Scheme and Analysis

Parallel processing is defined as the simultaneous processing of different tasks by two or more microprocessors, as by a single computer with more than one central processing unit or by multiple computers connected together in a network [29]. OpenMP and MPI are commonly used methods in parallel processing. MPI is a communication protocol for programming parallel computers [30]. While OpenMP uses a portable, scalable model that gives programmers a simple and flexible interface for developing parallel applications for platforms ranging from the standard desktop computer to the supercomputer [31, 32]. Considering our basic experimental environment and equipment, OpenMP is chosen for parallelization based on our proposed schemes.

In Sect. 3.1, we have discussed that the number of layers of the rotated matrix is fixed. The number of points in each layer is also fixed. There is no relationship between layers and points. Then in algorithm 2, the processes which go through layers to scan and check fixed points could be executed at the same time. After each process has finished, we collect the results to make the zigzag scanning sequence of the matrix. But in algorithm 3, at the end of each process, new (X_Pos, Y_Pos) is given by changed (i, j) as new starting point of the next round. It means that there are data dependency between processes. They could not be executed at the same time. So, parallelization based on our proposed algorithm 2 has been considered.

Table 4. Design of Parallel Programming based on Algorithm 2

Steps	Description
1. Feasibility of parallelization	no relationship between layers and points in rotated matrix
2. Instruction mode	manual instruction as "#pragma omp parallel for"
3. Problem segmentation	data decomposition: layers to be allocated to different tasks
4. Task communication	embarrassingly parallel: no data sharing between tasks
5. Data dependency	use "shared(shared variables)" instruction to make shared memory structure for synchronizing read operations of matrix between tasks
6. Load balance	dynamical layers distribution for the given threads

Design of parallel programming based on algorithm 2 is organized as Table 4. Firstly, we check the feasibility of parallelization to our scheme. Secondly, instruction mode for parallel programming should be designated, as automatic parallelization or manual instruction. Thirdly, data or function decomposition decompose a program into "blocks" that can be allocated to different tasks. Fourthly, communication between tasks would be considered according to the specific problem. Fifthly, data dependency in codes, a disincentive to parallelization, should be identified and handled. Here we use "shared(shared variables)" instruction in OpenMP to make shared memory structure for synchronizing read operations of matrix between tasks. Finally, equal amounts of work between tasks should be distributed approximately for load balance. Here we use dynamical schedule instruction in OpenMP for work distribution. Then, a simple pseudocode block of parallel programming is given in Table 5.

Table 5. Description of Parallel Programming

Pseudocode block of parallel programming based on algorithm 2

Require:
  The **direction** to decide the scanning process;
  The **layer** to match the scanning route though the rotated matrix;
  The **matrix** to be scanned; The scale of the **rows** and **columns**.
Ensure:
  All the elements in the matrix can be scanned by zigzag route.
1: other codes
2: omp_set_num_threads(4)
3: #pragma omp parallel for shared(matrix) schedule(dynamic)
4:    **For** layer=0 **to** rows-1+columns-1 **do**
5:      get the direction by checking whether layer%2 equals to 1
6:      call Algorithm 2 with parameters (direction, layer, matrix, rows, columns)
7:    **Endfor**
8: other codes

Table 6. Our Computing Environment

Devices	Parameter
CPU	Intel E5 2680 v3
Memory	32G
Disk	ssd 500G
Operation System	Ubuntu 18.04 LTS

1	2	6	7	15	16	28	29
3	5	8	14	17	27	30	43
4	9	13	18	26	31	42	44
10	12	19	25	32	41	45	54
11	20	24	33	40	46	53	55
21	23	34	39	47	52	56	61
22	35	38	48	51	57	60	62
36	37	49	50	58	59	63	64

Fig. 4. Example of 8×8 filled matrix file as input for algorithms

5   Experiment and Analysis

To evaluate the proposed schemes and for comparison with previous works, two experiments are performed in our research. Our computing environment is shown in Table 6. In the first experiment, matrices with five scales used in different applications are employed [33–36]. They are DCT coefficient matrix with size 8×8 and 128×128, MRI and CT in medical image with size 256×256 and 512×512, and surface-mesh generation in numerical simulation with size 1024×1024. In the second one, three more matrices with large scales 2000×2000, 3000×3000 and 5000×5000, are employed in order to further evaluate the performance of parallelization.

Firstly, we fill in the matrix with natural number 1 to n^2 in zigzag route shown as in Fig. 4. This special design can verify the correctness of our proposed schemes through the output as sequence 1 2 3 to n^2.

Secondly, the filled matrices are employed as input for algorithm 1 to 3 to get their runtimes. For the accuracy, we get the average value of each runtime by running the programs in given times. In our experiment, we run each algorithm with same input in 10 times. Table 7 shows the average runtime of each algorithm with different scales of matrices.

Table 7. Average runtime of each algorithm with different scales of matrices (Unit: seconds)

Alg	Scale				
	8×8	128×128	256×256	512×512	1024×1024
Alg.1	4.37×10^{-3}	6.37×10^{-2}	3.56×10^{-1}	1.6861	8.941
Alg.2	4.185×10^{-3}	5.46×10^{-2}	2.522×10^{-1}	1.0307	4.305
Alg.3	3.601×10^{-3}	4.45×10^{-2}	2.31×10^{-1}	0.9535	3.986

Thirdly, performance comparison and analysis are made between the three algorithms. From Fig. 5, we can see that runtimes of all algorithms increase linearly with growing scales of matrices. Since all elements of matrix are checked, algorithm 1 always takes the most time to run. Runtime of algorithms 2 and 3 is significantly reduced, especially with large scales of matrices. But it is worth noting that, with small scales, such as 8×8 and 128×128, runtimes of the three algorithms seem to be no difference.

Finally, we discuss the efficiency of parallelization. Runtimes of algorithms both in serialization and parallelization are shown in Fig. 6. With small scale as 8×8, we can see that runtime of parallelization is almost equal to the serialization. This is because parallel algorithms take up a certain amount of time while scheduling each CPU. If the scale of the problem is small, scheduling operation takes up a large proportion of total runtime. On the contrary, with larger scale, time used in scheduling operation appears to be minimal.

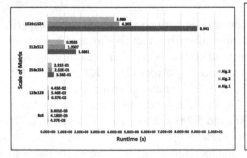

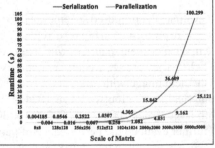

Fig. 5. Performance comparison between the three algorithms

Fig. 6. The efficiency of parallelization with 4 threads

On the other hand, we can see that runtime of parallelization for larger scales of matrices is significantly reduced compared with serialization. In order to improve the efficiency of parallelization, we employ "schedule(dynamic)", task scheduling mechanism of OpenMP, for task distribution. Through this mechanism, threads with faster execution speed request for tasks more often than slower ones. Therefore, it can better solve the problem of load imbalance caused by static mechanism. For example, layer 0 has only one element as mentioned above, if it is distributed to thread A, thread A finishes its task quickly and directly requests the next layer for scanning. At the same time, layer $n - 1$ has the most elements, if it is distributed to thread B, a relatively long time will be spent for thread B to finish its task. While thread B is working on layer $n - 1$, thread A may have scanned multiple levels due to its fewer workload and faster execution speed. As a result, the number of layers scanned by thread B will decrease, and when there are no subsequent tasks, it may be in an idle state, which will reduce the utilization of processor.

But for the last three large-scale matrices, the workload allocated to each thread (here we have 4 threads) is relatively large. No matter how quick the execution speed is, the threads are always in full-load state, so the utilization of processor is relatively higher. From Fig. 6, we can get the range of speedup is 3.413– 3.996 and the range of efficiency of parallelization corresponding to speedup is 85%–99%.

6 Conclusion and Future Work

In this paper, two alternative schemes for zigzag scanning to matrices have been proposed. Based on the idea in [17], we scan and check the elements of matrix in fixed-point mode and navigation mode in order to get the zigzag scanning sequence of the matrix. A performance comparison with the three schemes is done. Furthermore, we have presented the design of parallel programming based on algorithm 2. Finally, the efficiency of parallelization has been discussed. In the future, we will explore the feasibility of MapReduce applied in our schemes.

Acknowledgments. This work is supported financially by the National Natural Science Foundation of China (NSFC) under grant 61471306 and 61672438. The Natural Science Foundation of Sichuan Province under grant 2022NSFSC0548 and 2023NSFSC1966, Smart Education Research Fund of Southwest University of Science and Technology under grant 22ZHJYZD02 and 22SXB004, the Education and Teaching Research Project of Sichuan Provincial Education Department under grant JG2021-1414, and the Key R&D Projects of Sichuan Province under grant 2020YFS0360.

References

1. Messaoudi, A., et al.: DCT-based color image compression algorithm using adaptive block scanning. SIViP **13**(9), 1441–1449 (2019)
2. Zeng, P., Zhang, X.: Classified detection algorithm of zero-quantized DCT coefficient for H.264/AVC. J. Jiangxi Univ. Sci. Technol. **37**(1), 87–94 (2016)
3. Dolati, N., Beheshti, S.A.A., Azagegan, H.: A selective encryption for H.264/AVC videos based on scrambling. Multimed. Tools Appl. **80**, 2319–2338 (2021)

4. Hassan, E., George, L., Mohammed, F.: Color image compression based on DCT, differential pulse coding modulation, and adaptive shift coding. J. Theor. Appl. Inf. Technol. **96**(11), 3160–3171 (2018)
5. Salman, N.H., Rafea, S.: The arithmetic coding and hybrid discrete wavelet and cosine transform approaches in image compression. J. Southwest Jiaotong Univ. **55**(1), 1–9 (2020)
6. Yousif, R.I., Salman, N.H.: Image compression based on arithmetic coding algorithm. Iraqi J. Sci. **62**(1), 329–334 (2021)
7. Xue, J., et al.: 3D DCT based image compression method for the medical endoscopic application. Sensors **21**(5), 1817 (2021)
8. Li, S.S., Zhao, L., Yang, N.: Medical image encryption based on 2D zigzag confusion and dynamic diffusion. Secur. Commun. Netw. **7**, 1–23 (2021)
9. Qayyum, A., et al.: Chaos-based confusion and diffusion of image pixels using dynamic substitution. IEEE Access **8**, 140876–140895 (2020)
10. Ramasamy, P., et al.: An image encryption scheme based on block scrambling, modified zigzag transformation and key generation using enhanced logistic-tent map. Entropy **21**(7), 1–17 (2019)
11. Wei, C.C., Boon, C.N., Ahmad, N.S., et al.: Modeling and simulation for transient thermal analyses using a voltage-in-current latency insertion method. J. Electron. Sci. Technol. **4**, 383–395 (2022)
12. Partohaghighi, M., et al.: Numerical simulation of the fractional diffusion equation. Int. J. Mod. Phys. B **37**(10), 2350097 (2022)
13. Win, A.N., Li, M.M.: Numerical method based on fiber bundle for solving Lyapunov matrix equation. Math. Comput. Simul. **193**, 556–566 (2022)
14. Su, J., Zhai, A.P., Zhao, W.J., et al.: Hadamard single-pixel imaging using adaptive oblique zigzag sampling. Acta Photonica Sinica **50**(3), 0311003 (2021)
15. Guo, Y., Wang, C.: Improved Zigzag traversal and Lorenz chaotic construction of hash. Opt. Precis. Eng. **29**(2), 411–419 (2021)
16. Wen, H.P.: Cracking a color image encryption scheme based on Zigzag transformation and chaos. Comput. Appl. Softw. **36**(10), 323–333 (2019)
17. CSDN, https://blog.csdn.net/Shenpibaipao/article/details/78877294. Last accessed 20 Mar 2023
18. Wang, X., Chen, X.: An image encryption algorithm based on dynamic row scrambling and Zigzag transformation. Chaos, Solitons and Fractals **147**(C), 1–22 (2021)
19. Milosavljevic, N., Morozov, D., Skraba, P.: Zigzag Persistent Homology in Matrix Multiplication Time. In: Proceedings of the 27th annual symposium on computational geometry (SoGC'11), pp. 216–225. ACM, New York, NY (2011)
20. Zheng, J., et al.: ZM-CTC: covert timing channel construction method based on zigzag matrix. Comput. Commun. **182**(15), 212–222 (2022)
21. Rakotomalala, M., Rakotondraina, T.E., Rakotodramanana, S.: Contribution for improvement of image scrambling technique based on zigzag matrix reodering. Int. J. Comput. Trends Technol. **61**(1), 10–17 (2018)
22. Thefreedictionary, Raster Scan. https://encyclopedia.thefreedictionary.com/raster+scan. Last accessed 20 Mar 2023
23. Kinoshita, J., et al.: Nonuniformity measurement of image resolution under effect of color speckle for raster-scan RGB laser mobile projector. IEICE Trans. Electr. **E105/C**(2), 86–94 (2022)
24. Rashmi, P., Supriya, M.C.: Optimized Chaotic encrypted image based on continuous raster scan method. Global Transitions Proc. **2**(2), 589–593 (2021)
25. Chai, X., Wu, H., Gan, Z., et al.: An efficient visually meaningful image compression and encryption scheme based on compressive sensing and dynamic LSB embedding. Opt. Lasers Eng. **124**(1), 105837 (2020)

26. Wang, H., Xiao, D., Li, M., et al.: A visually secure image encryption scheme based on parallel compressive sensing. Signal Process. **155**, 218–232 (2019)
27. Cui, T., et al.: An efficient zigzag scanning and entropy coding architecture design. In: Huet, B., Ngo, C.-W., Tang, J., Zhou, Z.-H., Hauptmann, A.G., Yan, S. (eds.) PCM 2013. LNCS, vol. 8294, pp. 350–358. Springer, Cham (2013). https://doi.org/10.1007/978-3-319-03731-8_33
28. Ding, J.-J., Lin, P., Chen, H.: Generalized zigzag scanning algorithm for non-square blocks. In: Lee, K.-T., Tsai, W.-H., Mark Liao, H.-Y., Chen, T., Hsieh, J.-W., Tseng, C.-C. (eds.) MMM 2011. LNCS, vol. 6524, pp. 252–262. Springer, Heidelberg (2011). https://doi.org/10.1007/978-3-642-17829-0_24
29. Thefreedictionary, parallel processing. https://www.thefreedictionary.com/parallel+processing. Last accessed 20 Mar 2023
30. Sur, S., Koop, M., Panda, D.: High-performance and scalable mpi over infiniband with reduced memory usage: an in-depth performance analysis. In: Proceedings of the 2006 ACM/IEEE Conference on Supercomputing, pp. 105–117. ACM, New York, NY (2006)
31. Thefreedictionary, OpenMP. https://encyclopedia.thefreedictionary.com/OpenMP. Last accessed 20 Mar 2023
32. Openmp.org, OpenMP Compilers & Tools. https://www.openmp.org/resources/openmp-compilers-tools/. Last accessed 20 Mar 2023
33. An, D., et al.: A novel fast DCT coefficient scan architecture. In: Proceedings of the 27th Conference on Picture Coding Symposium, pp. 273–276. ACM, New York, NY (2009)
34. Gu, T.: Compression algorithm for electric field data based on two-dimensional lifting wavelet-discrete cosine transform. Comput. Eng. Des. **41**(6), 1652–1657 (2020)
35. Ramanjaneyulu, K., et al.: Robust and oblivious watermarking based on swapping of DCT coefficients. Int. J. Appl. Innov. Eng. Manag. **2**(7), 445–452 (2013)
36. Kong, F., et al.: Learning whole heart mesh generation from patient images for computational simulations. IEEE Trans. Med. Imaging **42**(2), 533–545 (2022)

Tooth Segmentation from Cone-Beam CT Images Through Boundary Refinement

Yiheng Xu[1], Mingkun Zhang[1], Sibo Huang[2], and Dongyu Zhang[1(✉)]

[1] School of Computer Science and Engineering, Sun Yat-sen University,
Guangzhou, China
zhangdy27@mail.sysu.edu.cn
[2] Network and Information Center, Huizhou University, Huizhou, China

Abstract. Automatic and accurate individual tooth segmentation from cone-beam computed tomography images provides important assistance for computer-aided analysis in dentistry. Many previous studies on this task employ multi-stage strategy similar to instance segmentation in natural images. Although these methods can provide considerable segmentation results, they are dependent on complex training processes, some even in need of tuning hyperparameters for clustering. Meanwhile, due to the difference of strategy from other medical image segmentation, it is difficult for these methods to be extended to the segmentation from CBCT images in other human organs. In this paper, we present a novel method to train the network in only one stage with satisfactory result. The main componets of our method are an improved U-net like network and post refinement for tooth boundary. The proposed network is designed to conduct two different works in parallel. One is to directly predict the individual tooth segmentation while the other is to generate an offset map for the refinement. Besides, in order to improve the accuracy of tooth boundary segmentation, a boundary-aware loss is also applied in our method. Comparative experiments and ablation analysis show that our approach achieves state-of-the-art segmentation performance.

Keywords: Tooth CBCT Segmentation · Boundary Refinement · Spatial Attention · Boundary-aware

1 Introduction

Recently, digital dentistry has got wide-spread attention due to the development of deep learning in medical field, which could not only enhance the efficiency for dentists' diagnosis, but also provide more accurate results for orthodontic diagnosis and treatment planning. In a system of digital dentistry, the acquisition of accurate individual tooth segmentation is an essential component. Currently, acquiring 3D tooth model from cone beam computed tomography(CBCT) images is a widely used technique in medical data processing. With high spatial resolution, CBCT could provide comprehensive 3D volumetric information, making it suitable to reconstruct tooth models. As manual labeling is a tedious and time-consuming task, the research of automatic and accurate 3D tooth segmentation methods has attracted great attention.

Segmenting teeth from CBCT images is a challenging task for the following reasons. (1) The boundary between the tooth root and its surrounding alveolar bone is unclear due to their similar intensities, which makes it difficult to separate individual tooth; (2) The above phenomenon also exists between adjacent teeth and occlusal teeth due to adhesion; (3) The presence of heavy noise.

To address the above challenges, several methods have been proposed, which can be divided into two categories: traditional methods and learning-based methods. The traditional methods include level set methods [1–4] and template-based fitting methods [5]. However, all these traditional methods, restricted either by the demand of manual initialization or the lack of robustness, cannot solve the aforementioned challenges. Meanwhile, deep learning-based methods have gained a lot of attention because of the outstanding performance of convolutional neural networks(CNN) in feature extraction [6,7] and lots of research have proved CNN practicable in medical image segmentation [8,9]. However, few of them are directly used in tooth segmentation. Miki et al. [10] exploited CNN based architecture to realize tooth type classification on 2D slices of CBCT images. More recently, Cui et al. [11] applied 3D Mask-RCNN as a base network to resolve individual tooth segmentation from CBCT images. After that, several methods [12–14] focused directly on tooth CBCT data have achieved promising results. However, these methods are all based on the two-stage strategy in instance segmentation, where the locations of teeth are firstly detected and a binary mask is generated for each one. This brings difficulty for model optimization and the performance of the final model is highly dependent on the detection on the first step. Because of limited data samples, it is possible to get over-fitting in training, leading to horrible detection and segmentation results.

In this paper, we propose a novel tooth segmentation framework based on post refinement to acquire individual tooth segmentation in one stage. Our network is designed to perform two tasks, one is for segmentation and the other for refinement. The contributions of our work are mainly reflected in three aspects. Firstly, we design an novel network to effectively utilize spatial information, which is helpful to relieve the overfitting. Secondly, in the segmentation branch, we introduce a boundary loss to optimize the segmentation result specially around the tooth boundary and refine the boundaries of overlapped teeth. Finally, the post refinement provide a further fine-grained correction on voxels near tooth boundaries. Different from [15] which is mainly for 2D natural images, we expand it to 3D and modify it to fit the tooth segmentation task. Since background voxels account for more than half of all the voxels in a CBCT image. Letting background voxels to point to background center is not a good choice. Therefore, we dilate each tooth and let the voxels outside the tooth boundary pointing to the opposite direction of the tooth centroid. The performance of our proposed framework is validated with comparisons and ablation study, which suggests the effiency of our method for tooth instance segmentation from CBCT images.

2   Related Works

2.1   Medical Image Segmentation

CNNs have been recently used for medical image segmentation. Since the seminal U-net is introduced, a number of methods on medical image segmentation [16–18] have been proposed. Inspired by U-net and DenseNet [19] architecture, Li et al. [16] proposed H-denseunet for liver and liver tumor segmentation. Roth et al. [20] proposed a multi-scale framework to obtain varying resolution information in pancreas segmentation. Tri-planar architectures [16,21,22] are sometimes used to combine three-view slices for each voxel in volume-wise segmentation while some other approaches directly utilize the full volumetric image represented by a sequence of 2D slices or modalities [23–25]. Meanwhile, Various studies have attempted to integrate self-attention mechanisms into CNNs by modeling global interactions of all pixels based on the feature maps. Wang et al. [26] introduced non-local blocks which adopts self-attention mechanisms to model the pixel-level pairwise relations. Cao et al. [27] simplyfied the non-local blocks and unified it with SE blocks [28].

2.2   Tooth Segmentation

Several studies have been conducted on individual tooth detection and segmentation based on dental images. Toothnet [11] employed a region proposal based method, utilizing Mask RCNN [29] as the pipeline and extending it to the 3D version. It introduced a similarity matrix for the classification of different types of teeth. Chung et al. [14] also employed Mask RCNN as a detector while additional training was conducted to divide the upper and lower jaws to extract the target regions. Lee et al. [13] and Wu et al. [12] both utilized a point-based method to detect tooth regions. Heatmap regression was conducted in both methods to predict the locations of tooth centroids. MWTNet [30] directly utilized the tooth boundaries to simultaneously detect and segment individual teeth in a single step. marker-controlled watershed transform was utilized in this method.

2.3   Refinement for Segmentation

Extensive studies [15,31–33] have proposed various mechanisms to refine the segmentation maps from coarse to fine. Yuan et al. [15] proposed a model-agnostic segmentation refinement mechanism where the information of boundary pixels and the offset directions were mainly concerned. Although it turns out good performance in natural image segmentation, it is not practical to directly extend it to 3D due to the difficulty in data annotation.

3   Method

This work aims to develop an automatic method to segment individual tooth in dental CBCT images. The core of our method is the utilization of the probability

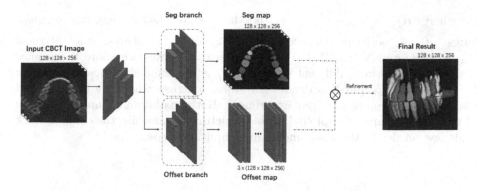

Fig. 1. The illustration of overall framework. a) Binary branch: produce a binary segmentation map, separating the voxels belonging to foreground tooth objects from the background voxels. b) Offset branch: indicating the 3D vector pointing from each foreground voxel to the centroid of the corresponding tooth. The input CBCT images are firstly fed into the two-branch network to generate the offsets maps and binary maps. Then the pointing map is generated by the outputs of the two-branch network the clustering is conducted at last

map of tooth region and the position information of foreground voxels near the boundaries. As shown in Fig. 1, a CBCT image is firstly fed into the two-branch neural network. The segmentation branch conducts a segmentation of all foreground classes, where a weighted boundary loss is proposed to enhance accuracy of tooth boundaries. While the offset branch predicts the offset from each voxel to the centroid of corresponding tooth. According to the output of offset branch, we refine the segmentation of voxels near the tooth boundaries to yield final individual tooth segmentation.

3.1 Architecture of Network

In Fig. 2 we provide a schematic representation of our convolutional neural network, which is a typical encoder-decoder architecture. Similar to 3D Unet, it consists of a contracting path and a expansive path. However, there are several differences from 3D Unet that additional attention mechanism has been applied in our network. According to [8], we add attention gates during the skip connection in order to automatically learn to focus on target structures and suppress irrelevant regions in an input CBCT image. Due to the same reason, the original convolution blocks are replaced with context blocks in the contracting path. Context blocks [27] can be represented as the following function:

$$z_i = x_i + \delta(\sum_{j=1}^{N_p} \alpha_j x_j) \tag{1}$$

where $\alpha_j = \frac{e^{W_k x_j}}{\sum_{m=1}^{N_p} e^{W_k x_m}} x_j$ is the weight factor, aggregating features of all positions to acquire global context features, and $\delta(\cdot) = W_{v2} ReLU(LayerNorm(W_{v1}(\cdot)))$ exploits feature transformation to acquire dependencies between different channels. N_p is the number of positions in the feature map, W_{v1} and W_{v2} denote transform matrices which are implemented via $1 \times 1x1$ convolutions in our experiment. Both spatial and channel relations of the feature maps are exploited in this structure. Meanwhile, the context block adds few burden to the whole model in computation cost.

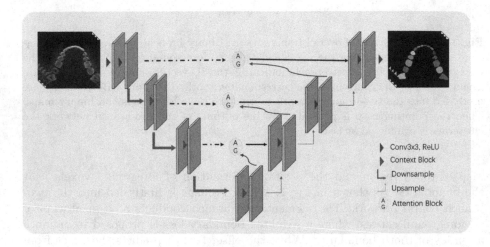

Fig. 2. Overall network of one branch

3.2   Training and Refinement

We utilized the modified U-net architecture to concurrently perform two specific prediction tasks. feature maps are firstly extracted as the CBCT images of size of $128 \times 128 \times 256$ sent in by continuous $3 \times 3 \times 3$ convolution and ReLU combinations. After that, down-sampling is conducted for three times to acquire multi-scale information. The model shares one contracting path while uses respective expansive paths to produce an all-class segmentation map and an offset map. The segmentation map provides a relatively coarse result whether a voxel belongs to a typical foreground class. The offset map is used to refine the coarse segmentation result.

On the segmentation branch, several different loss functions are applied to enhance segmentation performance. Cross entropy and dice loss is utilized to compute segmentation and classification error, which is widely used in medical image segmentation. Furthermore, an additional loss is applied to pay more attention on the tooth boundaries for individual tooth segmentation.

The loss function is formulated as follows,

$$Loss_{BD}(q,p) = \frac{1}{|N|} \sum_N ((p-q)^2 \circ (d_p^\alpha + d_q^\alpha)) \qquad (2)$$

where $|N|$ represents the number of voxels in the map. p denotes predicted probability values and q is the corresponding value on ground truth map. $d_{()}$ means the distance to the boundary, where distance transforms [34] are utilized to compute d_p and d_q. α is set as 2 in the experiment.

On the offset branch, we use smooth L1 loss for 3D offset vector regression. Since interior voxels are relatively easy to get segmented correctly, we focus on the segmentation near the tooth boundaries. The offset map of size $3 \times 128 \times 128 \times 256$ pixels indicates the 3D vector pointing from the source point to its target point. The target points of the voxels inside each tooth is the corresponding centroid while the situation of the target points of the background voxels may be a bit complex. For those near the tooth boundaries, we gave them an opposite direction to the centroid of the corresponding tooth while others were just set to point at themselves and these positions in offset map were set as zero. The optimization goal is to make voxels inside the tooth pointing to the tooth centroid while outside voxels pointing to the opposite direction. Morphological operations like dilation and erosion are utilized to acquire boundary voxels.

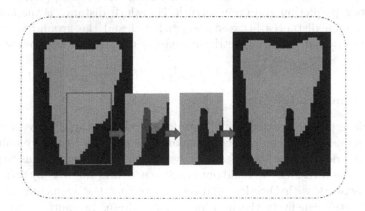

Fig. 3. Illustrating the refinement mechanism of our approach

In order to clearly describe the method we use, we use a 2D slice in Fig. 3 as a little example. The left picture is the coarse segmentation result from the segmentation branch. The voxels highlighted with dark purple are which segmented as foreground while pointing to the background and voxels highlighted with light purple are background voxels pointing to a position inside the tooth area. In the refinement phase, these voxels are redistributed and the right picture is generated in the end.

4   Experiment

4.1   Dataset and Network Training

In the experiment, we evaluate the proposed framework on 90 CBCT images in total collected from patients before or after orthodontic treatments in dental clinics. The dataset contains some undesirable cases with tooth missing or tooth crowding. The dataset is divided to three subsets randomly, 60 images for training, 10 for validation and 20 for test. Before fed to the deep network, CBCT images are firstly clipped in the intensity in the 5 to 95 percentile range and normalized to the range of [0,1] afterwards.

For training the network, CBCT images were cropped and converted to the same size of $128 \times 128 \times 256$ and then fed to the network for 500 epochs. Our network is implemented in Pytorch using AdamW optimizer with an initial learning rate at 0.0001. The training experiment is conducted on Nvidia V100 GPU and takes about 16 h to complete.

4.2   Metrics

To Comprehensively evaluate the performance of our framework, several metrics like Dice similarity coefficient (DSC), Hausdorff distance (HD) and average symmetric surface distance(ASD) are used to measure the accuracy of tooth segmentation. Dice similarity coefficient measures the overlapping between a segmentation prediction and ground truth. Hausdorff distance is the maximum of the minimum distances between the predicted and the ground truth tooth surfaces, which is an essential metric to measure the segmentation error around the tooth boundary.

4.3   Ablation Study

We have done plenty of experiments in order to validate the effectiveness of our proposed framework, including the boundary loss and the boundary refinement strategy. In order to show the differences, we set several configurations to present the segmentation results. We build our baseline network(basenet) by training the proposed network with Dice loss and directly output the segmentation results without the refinement in the post processing phase. In contrast, we replace the dice loss with proposed boundary loss and set as basenet-BD. We further demonstrate the basenet-BD with refinement in post phase as the full frame. The test result in terms of DSC, Hausdorff distance and ASD is displayed in Table 1.

Compared with Dice loss which only concerns the number of mismatch voxels, our boundary-aware loss aims to minimize the mismatch area between the ground truth image and the predicted image. Therefore, our boundary-aware loss can bring improvement to network performance in terms of Hausdorff distance. To validate its effectiveness, we compare the network with and without the boundary-aware loss and show the quantitative results in 1. It can be seen that

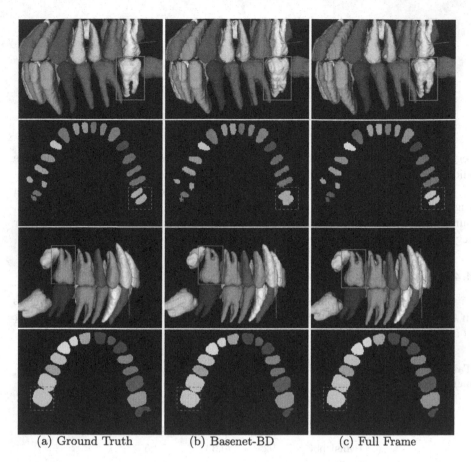

(a) Ground Truth   (b) Basenet-BD   (c) Full Frame

Fig. 4. Axial slices of CBCT image and the corresponding 3D reconstruction, comparing the segmentation result with(c) or without(b) the post refinement

basenet-BD consistently improves the segmentation performance in terms of all test metrics(0.5% Dice improvement, 0.07 mm ASD improvement and 0.22 mm HD improvement, respectively). This demonstrates that using the boundary-aware loss brings considerable benefits to capture complicated tooth shapes.

In our full framework, instead of directly using the segmentation map as the result, we add another branch to predict the offset map and conduct the refinement based on the basic segmentation map and the offset map. As shown in Table 1, compared with the basenet and basenet-BD, test result on all metrics achieves further enhancement. Especially, the Hausdorff distance of the full framework drops from 2.96 mm to 2.18 mm. Note that the Hausdorff distance measures the maximum of the minimum surface distances between the ground-truth and predicted tooth surfaces, so that the mismatch near tooth boundaries tends to lead to the large error. This indicates the offset map with the post refinement for

Table 1. Evaluation results of ablation analysis of different components

Methods	Dice[%]	ASD[mm]	HD[mm]
Basenet	94.1	0.33	3.18
Basenet-BD	94.6	0.26	2.96
Full Frame	**95.0**	**0.21**	**2.18**

segmentation helps to capture the intrinsic relation from a geometric perspective and thus improve the performance of segmentation task.

To further illustrate the effectiveness, we also provide a visual example in Fig. 4. It can be seen that, with the improvement of the refinement operation, our framework can accurately separate the tooth boundaries and acquire better segmentation results around the tooth boundaries.

4.4 Comparison with Other Methods

In this section, we will compare our method with some state-of-the-art methods in two aspects. The first one is about our training network and the second part is about the full framework.

Table 2. Network Comparison with state-of-the-art methods in medical image segmentation

Methods	Dice[%]	ASD[mm]	HD[mm]
Unet	87.3	0.54	12.51
TransUnet	92.6	0.33	7.26
Attention Unet	93.2	0.32	4.08
Ours Net	**94.6**	**0.26**	**3.04**

In order to prove the performance of our proposed network, we have compared our proposed network with several state-of-the-art methods for medical image segmentation including U-net [9], Attention U-net [8], TransUnet [35]. As is shown in Table 2, original U-net and self-attention based network does not work very well in our task while spatial attention based method can achieve a relatively better result. Additionally, the performance of TransUnet was falling short of the desired standards. It is possible that due to the symmetry of the tooth images, the local voxel-wise relations weigh more than the global information dependency. Based on such conclusion, we have made further modifications to the network. We replace the convolution blocks in contracting path with context blocks which provide extra attention in encoding phase while add few burden in computation cost. As a result, our method leads to an improvement of 1.4% Dice score and 1.04 mm HD error comparing to Attention U-net,demonstrating the effectiveness of our modified network.

Table 3. Full Framework Comparison with state-of-the-art methods in tooth segmentation

Methods	Dice[%]	ASD[mm]	HD[mm]
Toothnet	90.9	0.38	2.76
CGDNet	92.5	0.30	2.21
PBDNet	92.0	0.27	**2.12**
Ours	**95.0**	**0.21**	2.18

The overall evaluation of individual tooth segmentation is conducted by comparing our framework with several state-of-the-art deep learning based methods specially for tooth segmentation, including the anchor based detection method [11] and point based detection network [12,13]. All these compared methods are implemented in a detect-and-segment approach. As is shown in Table 3, compared with Toothnet, which only utilized bounding boxes to represent individual teeth, leading to limited detection and segmentation accuracy, our approach leads to the remarkable improvement of 4.1% Dice score and about 0.58mm HD error. CGDNet and PBDNet both used a center-based method to detect the centroids of all teeth in a tooth CBCT image and conduct semantic segmentation in detected areas. Our framework outperforms both these methods in Dice score by a large margin and comparable in other metrics, which demonstrate the feasibility of our refine-after-segment framework.

We can see that the performance of our method is comparable to other methods in tooth segmentation and get even higher score in Dice and ASD metrics, which demonstrates the performance of our work even though we only conduct a one-stage training strategy.

5   Conclusion

In this paper, we propose an one-stage automatic individual tooth segmentation method from CBCT images with post refinement. Directly using semantic segmentation methods to. Our work pay much attention on the improvements on the tooth boundary segmentation results. The boundary aware loss and post refinement are raised for higher accuracy in tooth boundary division. Furthermore, since it is a one-stage network, it allows for more flexible deployment and implementation in practice.

Acknowledgments. This work was supported part by the National Natural Science Foundation of China (NSFC) under Grant No. 61876224, and part by the 'QingTai Digital Intelligence Integration' Collaborative Innovation Project of the Science and Technology Development Center of the Ministry of Education under Grant No. 2020QT16.

References

1. Gan, Y., Xia, Z., Xiong, J., Li, G., Zhao, Q.: Tooth and alveolar bone segmentation from dental computed tomography images. IEEE J. Biomed. Health Inf. **22**(1), 196–204 (2017)
2. Gao, H., Chae, O.: Individual tooth segmentation from CT images using level set method with shape and intensity prior. Pattern Recognit. **43**(7), 2406–2417 (2010)
3. Ji, D.X., Ong, S.H., Foong, K.W.C.: A level-set based approach for anterior teeth segmentation in cone beam computed tomography images. Comput. Biol. Med. **50**, 116–128 (2014)
4. Gan, Y., Xia, Z., Xiong, J., Zhao, Q., Hu, Y., Zhang, J.: Toward accurate tooth segmentation from computed tomography images using a hybrid level set model. Med. Phys. **42**(1), 14–27 (2015)
5. Barone, S., Paoli, A., Razionale, A.V.: Ct segmentation of dental shapes by anatomy-driven reformation imaging and b-spline modelling. Int. J. Numer. Methods Biomed. Eng. **32**(6), e02747 (2016)
6. Long, J., Shelhamer, E., Darrell, T.: Fully convolutional networks for semantic segmentation. In: Proceedings of the IEEE Conference on Computer Vision and Pattern Recognition 2015, pp. 3431–3440 (2015)
7. Girshick, R.: Fast R-CNN. In: Proceedings of the IEEE International Conference on Computer Vision, pp. 1440–1448 (2015)
8. Schlemper, J., et al.: Attention gated networks: learning to leverage salient regions in medical images. Med. Image Anal. **53**, 197–207 (2019)
9. Ronneberger, O., Fischer, P., Brox, T.: U-Net: convolutional networks for biomedical image segmentation. In: Navab, N., Hornegger, J., Wells, W.M., Frangi, A.F. (eds.) MICCAI 2015. LNCS, vol. 9351, pp. 234–241. Springer, Cham (2015). https://doi.org/10.1007/978-3-319-24574-4_28
10. Miki, Y., et al.: Classification of teeth in cone-beam CT using deep convolutional neural network. Comput. Biol. Med. **80**, 24–29 (2017)
11. Cui, Z., Li, C., Wang, W.: ToothNet: automatic tooth instance segmentation and identification from cone beam CT images. In: Proceedings of the IEEE/CVF Conference on Computer Vision and Pattern Recognition, pp. 6368–6377 (2019)
12. Wu, X., Chen, H., Huang, Y., Guo, H., Qiu, T., Wang, L.: Center-sensitive and boundary-aware tooth instance segmentation and classification from cone-beam CT. In: IEEE 17th International Symposium on Biomedical Imaging (ISBI), pp. 939–942. IEEE (2020)
13. Lee, J., Chung, M., Lee, M., Shin, Y.G.: Tooth instance segmentation from cone-beam CT images through point-based detection and gaussian disentanglement. Multimed. Tools Appl. **81**(13), 18327–18342 (2022)
14. Chung, M., et al.: Pose-aware instance segmentation framework from cone beam CT images for tooth segmentation. Comput. Biol. Med. **120**, 103720 (2020)
15. Yuan, Y., Xie, J., Chen, X., Wang, J.: SegFix: model-agnostic boundary refinement for segmentation. In: Vedaldi, A., Bischof, H., Brox, T., Frahm, J.-M. (eds.) ECCV 2020. LNCS, vol. 12357, pp. 489–506. Springer, Cham (2020). https://doi.org/10.1007/978-3-030-58610-2_29
16. Li, X., Chen, H., Qi, X., Dou, Q., Fu, C.-W., Heng, P.-A.: H-DenseUNet: hybrid densely connected UNet for liver and tumor segmentation from CT volumes. IEEE Trans. Med. Imaging **37**(12), 2663–2674 (2018)

17. Dou, Q., Chen, H., Jin, Y., Yu, L., Qin, J., Heng, P.-A.: 3D deeply supervised network for automatic liver segmentation from CT volumes. In: Ourselin, S., Joskowicz, L., Sabuncu, M.R., Unal, G., Wells, W. (eds.) MICCAI 2016. LNCS, vol. 9901, pp. 149–157. Springer, Cham (2016). https://doi.org/10.1007/978-3-319-46723-8_18
18. Gibson, E., et al.: Automatic multi-organ segmentation on abdominal CT with dense v-networks. IEEE Trans. Med. Imaging 37(8), 1822–1834 (2018)
19. Huang, G., Liu, Z., Van Der Maaten, L., Weinberger, K.Q.: Densely connected convolutional networks. In: Proceedings of the IEEE Conference on Computer Vision and Pattern Recognition pp. 4700–4708 (2017)
20. Roth, H.R., et al.: Hierarchical 3d fully convolutional networks for multi-organ segmentation. arXiv preprint arXiv:1704.06382 (2017)
21. Liu, S., et al.: 3D anisotropic hybrid network: transferring convolutional features from 2D images to 3D anisotropic volumes. In: Frangi, A.F., Schnabel, J.A., Davatzikos, C., Alberola-López, C., Fichtinger, G. (eds.) MICCAI 2018. LNCS, vol. 11071, pp. 851–858. Springer, Cham (2018). https://doi.org/10.1007/978-3-030-00934-2_94
22. Xia, Y., et al.: 3D semi-supervised learning with uncertainty-aware multi-view co-training. In: Proceedings of the IEEE/CVF Winter Conference on Applications of Computer Vision, pp. 3646–3655 (2020)
23. Chen, J., Yang, L., Zhang, Y., Alber, M., Chen, D.Z.: Combining fully convolutional and recurrent neural networks for 3d biomedical image segmentation. In: Advances in Neural Information Processing Systems, vol. 29 (2016)
24. Kamnitsas, K., Chen, L., Ledig, C., Rueckert, D., Glocker, B., et al.: Multi-scale 3D convolutional neural networks for lesion segmentation in brain MRI. Ischemic Stroke Lesion Segmentation 13, 46 (2015)
25. Kamnitsas, K., et al.: Efficient multi-scale 3D CNN with fully connected CRF for accurate brain lesion segmentation. Med. Image Anal. 36, 61–78 (2017)
26. Wang, X., Girshick, R., Gupta, A., He, K.: Non-local neural networks. In: Proceedings of the IEEE Conference on Computer Vision and Pattern Recognition, pp. 7794–7803 (2018)
27. Cao, Y., Xu, J., Lin, S., Wei, F., Hu, H.: GcNet: non-local networks meet squeeze-excitation networks and beyond. In: Proceedings of the IEEE/CVF International Conference on Computer Vision Workshops (2019)
28. Hu, J., Shen, L., Sun, G.: Squeeze-and-excitation networks. In: Proceedings of the IEEE Conference on Computer Vision and Pattern Recognition, pp. 7132–7141 (2018)
29. He, K., Gkioxari, G., Dollár, P., Girshick, R.: Mask R-CNN. In: Proceedings of the IEEE International Conference on Computer Vision, pp. 2961–2969 (2017)
30. Chen, Y., et al.: Automatic segmentation of individual tooth in dental CBCT images from tooth surface map by a multi-task FCN. IEEE Access 8, 97296–97309 (2020)
31. Fieraru, M., Khoreva, A., Pishchulin, L., Schiele, B.: Learning to refine human pose estimation. In: Proceedings of the IEEE Conference on Computer Vision and Pattern Recognition Workshops, pp. 205–214 (2018)
32. Gidaris, S., Komodakis, N.: Detect, replace, refine: Deep structured prediction for pixel wise labeling. In: Proceedings of the IEEE Conference on Computer Vision and Pattern Recognition, pp. 5248–5257 (2017)
33. Islam, M.A., Naha, S., Rochan, M., Bruce, N., Wang, Y.: Label refinement network for coarse-to-fine semantic segmentation. arXiv preprint arXiv:1703.00551 (2017)

34. Karimi, D., Salcudean, S.E.: Reducing the hausdorff distance in medical image segmentation with convolutional neural networks. IEEE Trans. Med. Imaging **39**(2), 499–513 (2019)
35. Chen, J., et al.: TransuNet: Transformers make strong encoders for medical image segmentation. arXiv preprint arXiv:2102.04306 (2021)

Transformer Based Prototype Learning for Weakly-Supervised Histopathology Tissue Semantic Segmentation

Jinwen She[1], Yanxu Hu[1], and Andy J. Ma[1,2,3($\boxtimes$)]

[1] School of Computer Science and Engineering, Sun Yat-sen University,
Guangzhou, China
{shejw3,huyx69}@mail2.sysu.edu.cn, majh8@mail.sysu.edu.cn
[2] Guangdong Province Key Laboratory of Information Security Technology,
Guangzhou, China
[3] Key Laboratory of Machine Intelligence and Advanced Computing,
Ministry of Education, Guangzhou, China

Abstract. Weakly-supervised semantic segmentation for computational pathology has the great potential to alleviate the time-consuming and labor-intensive burden of manual pixel-level annotations. Existing methods relying on class activation map (CAM) to localize target objects suffer from two problems. First, most CAM-based models adopt convolutional neural networks, which cannot model the long-range dependencies of dispersed tissues. Second, CAM tends to focus on the most discriminative region of the object, resulting in incomplete segmentation results. In this paper, we propose a novel Transformer based weakly-supervised model for pixel-level tissue segmentation. The proposed model is able to capture global tissue feature relations by the self-attention mechanism in Transformer. For the issue of incomplete segmentation in CAM, we propose a patch-token prototype self-supervised learning approach to obtain more complete localization maps. Additionally, we introduce a self-refinement mechanism to dampen the falsely activated regions in the initial localization map. Extensive experiments on two histopathology datasets demonstrate that our proposed model achieves the state-of-the-art performance compared with other weakly-supervised methods.

Keywords: Histopathology image · Weakly-supervised semantic segmentation · Transformer · Prototype learning

1 Introduction

Accurate segmentation of histopathology tissue is a crucial prerequisite for the precise quantification of the tumor microenvironment [9]. With the advent of deep learning, supervised learning methods have achieved great success in the field of histopathology image segmentation [16,19]. While these methods require massive training data with pixel-wise labels annotated by expert pathologists, it

© The Author(s), under exclusive license to Springer Nature Switzerland AG 2023
L. Iliadis et al. (Eds.): ICANN 2023, LNCS 14257, pp. 203–215, 2023.
https://doi.org/10.1007/978-3-031-44216-2_17

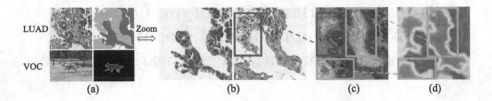

Fig. 1. (a): Examples of histopathology image (Top) in the LUAD dataset and natural image (Bottom) in the PASCAL VOC dataset with corresponding ground-truth segmentation masks. The spatial arrangement of different tissues is relatively random and dispersed compared to natural images. (b): Prototype characteristics of each pathological tissue. (c): CAM generated by CNNs. With traditional CNNs, the less discriminative tissue regions are ignored (the red box), leading to incomplete segmentation results. (d): CAM generated by our proposed model. By modeling global relations and prototype self-supervised learning, our method can generate more complete results in higher concordance with the ground truth (the yellow boxes in (c) and (d)). (Color figure online)

is time-consuming and labor-intensive to manually annotate regions of interest in histopathology images. Weakly-Supervised Semantic Segmentation (WSSS) can reduce the reliance on pixel-wise annotations by using only weak supervision. To reduce the annotation cost, it is highly desirable to develop a weakly-supervised tissue segmentation method using only image-level labels for training.

For general weakly-supervised segmentation of natural images, most methods apply the Class Activation Map (CAM) [25] technique to generate localization maps [2–4,12,13,22]. Despite the progress in weakly-supervised segmentation of natural images, there are two issues when directly applying these methods to histopathology images. First, most CAM-based methods are developed by convolutional neural networks (CNNs), in which ResNet [10] is widely employed. However, CNNs are difficult to model global relations, due to the intrinsic locality of convolution operations [5]. Thus, CNNs may not effectively capture analogous patterns among dispersed tissues in histopathology images (see the top row of Fig. 1(a)), leading to suboptimal performance. Second, CAM-based methods tend to focus on the most discriminative region of the object, which results in sparse and incomplete segmentation results. As shown in Fig. 1(c), the less discriminative tissue regions in histopathology images may not receive a large attention response, which degrades the segmentation performance.

In this paper, we propose a Transformer based model for weakly-supervised multi-class segmentation of pathological tissues. Transformer is capable of modeling global relations using the self-attention mechanism, which enables it to capture feature relations across dispersed tissues. To address the issue of incomplete segmentation in CAM, we propose a patch-token prototype self-supervised learning approach based on the observation that each pathological tissue exhibits distinct prototype characteristics in terms of its color and texture (see Fig. 1(b)). We extract tissue-specific prototype features and use them to generate a more complete localization map, as shown in Fig. 1(d). Then, it serves as a self-supervised signal of consistent regularization to push the network to focus on the less discriminative regions of the same tissue as well. Moreover, we introduce a self-refinement mechanism without additional affinity learning. As the self-attention mechanism in Transformer could capture semantic affinity, we utilize the attention matrix to refine the initial localization map, which could dampen the falsely activated regions. To the best of our knowledge, this is the first work to incorporate Transformer for weakly-supervised multi-class segmentation of pathological tissues based on CAM. Extensive experiments demonstrate that our proposed model outperforms the state-of-the-art method by 4.1% and 6% on the LUAD and BCSS test sets, respectively. The main contributions of this work are summarized as follows:

(a) We propose a novel Transformer based model to better estimate CAM for weakly-supervised multi-class segmentation of pathological tissues, which is the first attempt at this task to the best of our knowledge.
(b) We propose a novel patch-token prototype self-supervised learning approach to capture more complete localization maps. Moreover, a self-refinement mechanism is introduced to dampen the falsely activated regions in the initial localization map.
(c) Our proposed model achieves the state-of-the-art performance compared with other weakly-supervised semantic segmentation models on two publicly available histopathology datasets.

2   Related Work

2.1   Transformers

Transformers [20] were initially proposed for natural language processing tasks, and their models are primarily based on self-attention mechanism. Vision Transformer (ViT) [7], proposed for ImageNet classification, is the first model to apply Transformer in the field of computer vision. Since then, Transformers have been applied to a wide variety of medical image processing tasks, including image classification [21], image registration [6], and semantic segmentation [5,15], achieving promising results. More recently, researchers have proposed to incorporate Transformer for weakly-supervised semantic segmentation of natural images [24]. Xu et al. [24] proposed the MCTFormer model, which achieved superior performance on natural image datasets. However, no studies have applied Transformer to CAM-based weakly-supervised multi-class segmentation of pathological tissues.

2.2   Weakly-Supervised Histopathology Image Segmentation

Recently, researchers have been attempting to learn histopathology segmentation from weak labels, particularly image-level labels. Many studies are developed based on multiple instance learning (MIL) [11,17,23] for its effectiveness, which is a subset of weakly-supervised methods. However, MIL is not applicable to the multi-class segmentation task of pathological tissues. In such cases, Class Activation Map technology has emerged as a popular solution [1,8,14]. Han et al. [8] proposed a CAM-based model with progress dropout attention technique for tissue segmentation and achieved significant performance improvements compared to

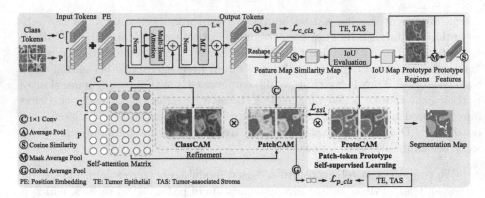

Fig. 2. Overview of the proposed method for weakly-supervised tissue segmentation. We model the global relations by using the MCTFormer [24] as the backbone. Patch-token prototype self-supervised learning is proposed to extract tissue-specific prototype features from the output patch tokens, which are then used to generate a more complete localization map called ProtoCAM. At the training stage, the entire model is optimized through two classification losses applied separately to two types of class predictions and a self-supervised loss between PatchCAM and ProtoCAM. At the inference stage, the class-to-patch attention matrix is transformed into ClassCAM, which is then fused with PatchCAM and ProtoCAM. The patch-to-patch attention matrix is used to refine the fused localization map to generate the final segmentation map.

existing methods. However, in practice, most CAM-based models for histopathology images adopt convolutional neural networks, which may not be able to effectively capture global context information. To address this issue, we design a Transformer based model for modeling the global tissue feature relations in this work.

3   Method

This section elaborates on the proposed model for weakly-supervised tissue segmentation as shown in Fig. 2. Firstly, we provide a brief introduction to the preliminary of our work. Then, we describe our proposed patch-token prototype self-supervised learning approach in detail. Additionally, we introduce the overall training loss and the inference process.

3.1   Preliminary

In this section, we briefly review the preliminary of our work. Following the setup of the MCTformer [24], each training image $X \in \mathbb{R}^{H \times W \times 3}$ is associated with only an image-level label $y \in \{0,1\}^C$ for C pre-specified categories. Given an input image, it is first split into $N \times N$ patches and transformed into P patch tokens $\mathbf{E}_p \in \mathbb{R}^{P \times D}$, where $P = N^2$ and D is the embedding dimension. Then, the patch tokens are concatenated with C class tokens $\mathbf{E}_c \in \mathbb{R}^{C \times D}$, with added position embeddings as the input tokens $\mathbf{E}_{in} \in \mathbb{R}^{(C+P) \times D}$ of the ViT [7] network. The ViT network is composed of L Transformer Encoder blocks, and each block contains Multi-Head Self-Attention, an Multi-Layer Perceptron (MLP), and two LayerNorm layers. The self-attention mechanism is formulated as:

$$\text{Attention}\,(\mathbf{Q}, \mathbf{K}, \mathbf{V}) = \mathbf{A}\mathbf{V}, \tag{1}$$

where $\mathbf{Q} \in \mathbb{R}^{(C+P) \times D}$, $\mathbf{K} \in \mathbb{R}^{(C+P) \times D}$ and $\mathbf{V} \in \mathbb{R}^{(C+P) \times D}$ are linear projection of input tokens. $\mathbf{A} = \text{softmax}\left(\mathbf{Q}\mathbf{K}^T/\sqrt{D}\right) \in \mathbb{R}^{(C+P) \times (C+P)}$ is a token-to-token attention matrix. So Eq. 1 indicates that the self-attention mechanism can model global relations across dispersed tissues in histopathology images.

To fully leverage the semantic information captured by two types of tokens, we divide the output tokens $\mathbf{E}_{out} \in \mathbb{R}^{(C+P) \times D}$ from the ViT network into the output class tokens $\mathbf{E}_{out\_c} \in \mathbb{R}^{C \times D}$ and the output patch tokens $\mathbf{E}_{out\_p} \in \mathbb{R}^{P \times D}$. Then, we use class tokens and patch tokens to generate two types of localization maps, ClassCAM and PatchCAM, respectively. ClassCAM is used to effectively localize objects, while PatchCAM is used to enhance responses on object regions.

ClassCAM [24]. Given the output class tokens $\mathbf{E}_{out\_c} \in \mathbb{R}^{C \times D}$, we apply average pooling along the feature dimension to obtain the classification score $y^c \in \mathbb{R}^C$. The classification loss $\mathcal{L}_{c\_cls}$ is computed by a multi-label soft margin loss between the image-level label y and the prediction y^c. To obtain ClassCAM $\mathbf{A}_{ClassCAM} \in \mathbb{R}^{C \times P}$, we sample the class-to-patch attention matrix $\mathbf{A}_{c2p} \in \mathbb{R}^{C \times P}$ from the token-to-token attention matrix $\mathbf{A}$, where $\mathbf{A}_{c2p} = \mathbf{A}[1 : C, C+1 : C + P]$, and then sum over L layers, i.e., $\mathbf{A}_{ClassCAM} = \sum_{l=1}^{L} \mathbf{A}_{c2p}^l$.

PatchCAM [24]. Given the output patch tokens $\mathbf{E}_{out\_p} \in \mathbb{R}^{P \times D}$, the patch tokens are reshaped to form a feature map $\mathbf{F}_p \in \mathbb{R}^{N \times N \times D}$ and then passed through a 1×1 convolutional layer to generate a classification map $\mathbf{C}_p \in \mathbb{R}^{N \times N \times C}$. Then, we apply global average pooling along the spatial dimensions to obtain the classification score $y^p \in \mathbb{R}^C$. Similarly, the classification loss $\mathcal{L}_{p\_cls}$ is computed by a multi-label soft margin loss between the image-level label y and the prediction y^p. To obtain PatchCAM $\mathbf{A}_{PatchCAM} \in \mathbb{R}^{N \times N \times C}$, we apply ReLU activation on the classification map $\mathbf{C}_p$, i.e., $\mathbf{A}_{PatchCAM} = \text{ReLU}\,(\mathbf{C}_p)$.

3.2 Patch-Token Prototype Self-supervised Learning

ClassCAM and PatchCAM tend to focus on the most discriminative region of the object, resulting in incomplete segmentation maps. Empirical observations suggest that PatchCAM demonstrates a higher response in object regions compared to ClassCAM. Therefore, we propose to leverage PatchCAM to explore the patch-token prototype, which represents the feature distribution of each tissue and helps capture more complete tissue regions.

Prototype Region Estimation. The PatchCAM of a given category can provide its approximate spatial structure within an image, where spatial structure refers to the semantic regions of the objects. Besides, a given patch token, along with other similar patch tokens, constitutes a spatial structure as well. If there is a significant similarity between these two spatial structures, it is highly probable that the patch token belongs to this category. Based on this motivation, we propose to estimate the category of each patch by exploring its spatial structure through inter-patch semantic similarity and comparing it with the PatchCAM.

First, given the feature map $\mathbf{F}_p$, we compute inter-patch semantic similarity:

$$\mathbf{S}_i(j) = \mathrm{ReLU}\left(\frac{\mathbf{F}_p(i) \cdot \mathbf{F}_p(j)}{\|\mathbf{F}_p(i)\| \cdot \|\mathbf{F}_p(j)\|}\right), \tag{2}$$

where $\cdot$ is dot product. $\mathbf{S}_i \in \mathbb{R}^{N \times N}$ is the similarity map between patch i and all other patches, capturing the spatial structure of patch i in the image.

Then, we compute the class-wise IoU between the similarity map of patch i and the PatchCAM of class c as the spatial structure similarity:

$$\mathbf{IoU}_i^c = \frac{\sum_j \mathbf{A}_{PatchCAM}^c(j)\mathbf{S}_i(j)}{\sum_j [\mathbf{A}_{PatchCAM}^c(j) + \mathbf{S}_i(j) - \mathbf{A}_{PatchCAM}^c(j)\mathbf{S}_i(j)]}, \tag{3}$$

where $\mathbf{A}_{PatchCAM}^c \in \mathbb{R}^{N \times N}$ is the PatchCAM of class c and $\mathbf{IoU}_i^c$ is the spatial structure similarity for patch i with respect to class c.

Finally, we assign each patch to the category with the highest IoU score:

$$\mathbf{R}_i^c = \begin{cases} 1, & \text{if } c = \arg\max_{c'} \mathbf{IoU}_i^{c'}, \\ 0, & \text{otherwise.} \end{cases} \tag{4}$$

And we obtain a prototype region $\mathbf{R}^c \in \{0,1\}^{N \times N}$ for each category, as shown in Fig. 2. In this way, we can fully leverage inter-patch semantic similarity to effectively explore category-specific prototype regions in the image.

Prototype Feature Estimation. With these category-specific prototype regions, we can compute a prototype feature for each category by masked average pooling:

$$\mathbf{p}_c = \frac{\sum_i \mathbf{R}_i^c * \mathbf{F}_p(i)}{\sum_i \mathbf{R}_i^c} \in \mathbb{R}^D. \tag{5}$$

ProtoCAM Estimation. With these category-specific prototype features, we can estimate the ProtoCAM of each category $\mathbf{A}_{ProtoCAM}^c \in \mathbb{R}^{N \times N}$ by computing the cosine similarity between its prototype feature and all patch features:

$$\mathbf{A}_{ProtoCAM}^c(i) = \mathrm{ReLU}\left(\frac{\mathbf{F}_p(i) \cdot \mathbf{p}_c}{\|\mathbf{F}_p(i)\| \cdot \|\mathbf{p}_c\|}\right). \tag{6}$$

The proposed ProtoCAM utilizes category-specific prototype features tailored for each image to achieve more complete object estimations, as shown in Fig. 2.

To facilitate the learning of PatchCAM, we introduce a self-supervised loss with consistent regularization that aligns PatchCAM with ProtoCAM:

$$\mathcal{L}_{ssl} = \|\mathbf{A}_{PatchCAM} - \mathbf{A}_{ProtoCAM}\|_1. \tag{7}$$

With this consistency, the ProtoCAM pushes the model to focus on the less discriminative regions of the same tissue as well. This enables the model to learn a more comprehensive feature distribution of each tissue, thereby improving the quality of localization maps.

3.3 Loss Function

The overall training loss is a weighted sum of two multi-label classification losses and a self-supervised loss, which is formulated as:

$$\mathcal{L}_{total} = \mathcal{L}_{c\_cls} + \mathcal{L}_{p\_cls} + \lambda \mathcal{L}_{ssl}, \tag{8}$$

where λ is a hyperparameter to balance classification and self-supervised losses.

3.4 CAM Fusion and Refinement for Inference

At the inference stage, ClassCAM, PatchCAM and ProtoCAM are integrated to generate the fused localization map through an element-wise multiplication:

$$\mathbf{A}_{fused} = \mathbf{A}_{ClassCAM} \otimes \mathbf{A}_{PatchCAM} \otimes \mathbf{A}_{ProtoCAM}. \tag{9}$$

To improve the accuracy of the fused localization map, we introduce a self-refinement mechanism [24] to refine $\mathbf{A}_{fused} \in \mathbb{R}^{N \times N \times C}$. Specially, we first sample the patch-to-patch attention matrix $\mathbf{A}_{p2p} \in \mathbb{R}^{P \times P}$ from the token-to-token attention matrix $\mathbf{A}$, where $\mathbf{A}_{p2p} = \mathbf{A}[C+1:C+P, C+1:C+P]$. Then we compute the sum of the patch-to-patch attention matrices of the L layers, and perform a reshape operation to obtain a patch affinity matrix $\mathbf{A}_p \in \mathbb{R}^{N \times N \times N \times N}$:

$$\mathbf{A}_p = \text{reshape}\left(\sum_{l=1}^{L} \mathbf{A}_{p2p}^l\right). \tag{10}$$

Finally, we utilize the patch affinity matrix to refine the fused localization map and derive the final segmentation map $\mathbf{A}_{seg} \in \mathbb{R}^{N \times N \times C}$:

$$\mathbf{A}_{seg}(i,j,c) = \sum_{k}^{N} \sum_{l}^{N} \mathbf{A}_p(i,j,k,l) \cdot \mathbf{A}_{fused}(k,l,c). \tag{11}$$

4 Experiment

4.1 Dataset

We evaluate our proposed model on two weakly-supervised tissue segmentation datasets, LUAD [8] and BCSS [8]. LUAD is a lung adenocarcinoma dataset with four tissue categories, including tumor epithelial (TE), tumor-associated stroma (TAS), necrosis (NEC) and lymphocyte (LYM). It consists of a training set with 16,678 images, a validation set with 300 images and a test set with 300 images. BCSS is a breast cancer dataset with four tissue categories, including tumor (TUM), stroma (STR), lymphocytic infiltrate (LYM) and necrosis (NEC). It consists of a training set with 23,422 images, a validation set with 3,418 images and a test set with 4,986 images. The size of all the images is 224 × 224.

4.2 Implementation

In our experiments, we adopt DeiT-S [18] pre-trained on ImageNet as the ViT network. We follow the data augmentation provided in [18,24]. λ in Eq. 8 is set as 0.4. The model is trained with a batch size of 64 on a NVIDIA RTX A6000 GPU. AdamW optimizer is adopted to train our model for 20 epochs, with a learning of 5e-4 and a weight decay of 0.05. At test time, we use multi-scale and horizontal flip testing to generate segmentation results. Mean intersection over union (mIoU) is used as the primary metric for evaluating segmentation results. In addition to mIoU, other metrics such as IoU for each category, frequency weighted IoU (FwIoU), and pixel-level accuracy (ACC) are also included.

Table 1. Quantitative comparison with other existing weakly-supervised semantic segmentation models on the LUAD test set. The best results are shown in bold.

Method	TE	NEC	LYM	TAS	FwIoU	MIoU	ACC
HistoSegNet [1]	0.45594	0.36302	0.58283	0.50818	0.48538	0.47749	0.65971
SC-CAM [3]	0.68286	0.64284	0.62063	0.61785	0.64743	0.64104	0.78690
OAA [12]	0.69557	0.53555	0.67181	0.62905	0.65578	0.63300	0.79251
Grad-CAM++ [4]	0.72897	0.74175	0.67933	0.66018	0.69776	0.70256	0.81967
CGNet [13]	0.71853	0.73296	0.69092	0.67262	0.69887	0.70376	0.82219
MLPS Phase 1 [8]	0.75567	0.78079	0.73694	0.69690	0.73324	0.74258	0.84508
MLPS Phase 2 [8]	0.77704	0.79321	0.73406	0.71980	0.75126	0.75603	0.85701
Ours	**0.80023**	**0.82362**	**0.79483**	**0.76709**	**0.78896**	**0.79644**	**0.88154**

Table 2. Quantitative comparison with other existing weakly-supervised semantic segmentation models on the BCSS test set. The best results are shown in bold

Method	TUM	STR	LYM	NEC	FwIoU	MIoU	ACC
HistoSegNet [1]	0.33141	0.46457	0.29047	0.01908	0.37191	0.27638	0.56410
SC-CAM [3]	0.76788	0.70606	0.58023	0.60073	0.71581	0.66373	0.83427
OAA [12]	0.75132	0.68883	0.61230	0.60600	0.70469	0.66461	0.82552
Grad-CAM++ [4]	0.66737	0.62064	0.50077	0.48053	0.62308	0.56733	0.76530
CGNet [13]	0.68215	0.61769	0.52240	0.56836	0.63390	0.59765	0.77626
MLPS Phase 1 [8]	0.72976	0.68134	0.56191	0.55989	0.68532	0.63323	0.81216
MLPS Phase 2 [8]	0.78839	0.73157	0.57295	0.66389	0.73745	0.68920	0.84832
Ours	**0.83056**	**0.76675**	**0.65246**	**0.75113**	**0.78217**	**0.75023**	**0.87664**

4.3 Comparisons

Quantitative Results. We make a comparison of our proposed model with other advanced weakly-supervised semantic segmentation models on the LUAD and BCSS test sets, respectively. As shown in Table 1 and Table 2, our model

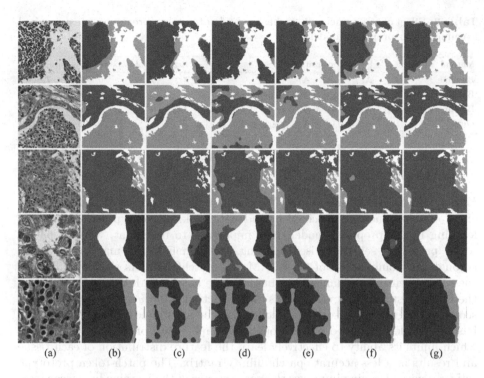

Fig. 3. Qualitative results of tissue segmentation. (a): Input Image. (b): Ground Truth. (c): MLPS Phase 2 [8]. (d): Baseline. (e): Baseline w/refine. (f): Baseline w/prototype. (g): Ours. The upper three rows are LUAD (Red: TE, Green: NEC, Blue: LYM, Yellow: TAS). The bottom two rows are BCSS (Red: TUM, Green: STR, Blue: LYM, Purple: NEC). White areas in the segmentation map refer to the background or other tissues.

consistently outperforms all existing models on both datasets across all evaluation metrics. Specifically, our proposed model achieves the state-of-the-art performance with 0.79644 mIoU on the LUAD test set and 0.75023 mIoU on the BCSS test set. This represents an improvement of 4.0% and 6.1% over MLPS Phase 2 [8], respectively. Notably, our model is designed as a single-stage and end-to-end trained model. Even the segmentation results generated from our model outperform the existing two-stage weakly-supervised model [8]. The improved segmentation performance of our model primarily stems from its ability to explicitly extract prototype features that are representative of different types of tissues within an image. This enables our model to utilize these tissue-specific prototype features to generate more complete localization maps.

Qualitative Results. Fig. 3 demonstrates qualitative visualization results of our proposed model compared to MLPS Phase 2 [8] on both datasets. As shown in Fig. 3, MLPS phase 2 fails to accurately identify certain categories of tissues, and may misclassify different categories of tissues together. In contrast, our proposed model can generate more precise and complete segmentation results, which closely align with the ground-truth labels.

Table 3. Effect of self-refinement mechanism and patch-token prototype self-supervised learning in our proposed model.

Method	Fused Localization Map	Refine	Prototype	LUAD	BCSS
Baseline	$\mathbf{A}_{ClassCAM} \otimes \mathbf{A}_{PatchCAM}$	✗	✗	0.72397	0.72806
Baseline w/refine	$\mathbf{A}_{ClassCAM} \otimes \mathbf{A}_{PatchCAM}$	✓	✗	0.73943	0.72292
Baseline w/prototype	$\mathbf{A}_{ClassCAM} \otimes \mathbf{A}_{PatchCAM} \otimes \mathbf{A}_{ProtoCAM}$	✗	✓	0.77597	0.74178
Ours	$\mathbf{A}_{ClassCAM} \otimes \mathbf{A}_{PatchCAM} \otimes \mathbf{A}_{ProtoCAM}$	✓	✓	**0.79644**	**0.75023**

4.4   Ablation Study

Effect of Main Components. We conduct an ablation study to verify the effect of self-refinement mechanism and patch-token prototype self-supervised learning in our proposed model. It is important to note that, without patch-token prototype self-supervised learning, the segmentation map is generated through the combination of ClassCAM and PatchCAM. As shown in Table 3, the self-refinement mechanism can improve the baseline mIoU score by 1.5% on the LUAD test set. However, it leads to a reduction of 0.6% in the baseline mIoU score on the BCSS test set. This decline may be attributed to the fact that the baseline model is trained only through the supervision of classification losses, which limits its ability to effectively learn the feature distribution of each tissue and results in a less accurate patch affinity matrix. The patch-token prototype self-supervised learning improves the performance of the baseline by a clear margin. By combining these two components, our full model performs significantly better than the baseline model. Furthermore, as can be seen from Table 3, the patch-token prototype self-supervised learning can enhance patch affinity learning and improve the effectiveness of the self-refinement mechanism. For example, on the LUAD test set, the self-refinement mechanism improves the performance of the model from a 1.5% increase over the baseline to a 2.0% increase over the baseline w/prototype. The visualization results in Fig. 3 further demonstrate the great benefits of combining these two essential components.

Different Values of Hyperparameter λ. We evaluate the segmentation performance of our proposed model across different values of hyperparameter λ. As shown in Fig. 4, the utilization of patch-token prototype self-supervised learning can significantly improve the performance of the model on both datasets. However, as the value of λ increases beyond a certain point, the performance of the model tends to diminish. It is possible that an excessive weight of the self-supervised loss may impede the ability of the model to learn classification objectives during training. Thus, we set $\lambda = 0.4$ in our experiments to strike a balance between classification and self-supervised losses and achieve satisfactory performance on both datasets.

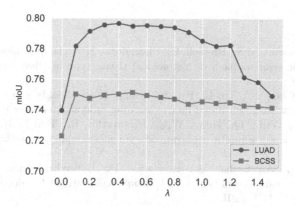

Fig. 4. Evaluation of segmentation performance with respect to different values of λ. $\lambda = 0$ implies no utilization of patch-token prototype self-supervied learning.

Table 4. Comparison of different localization map fusion strategies.

Dataset	Element-wise Maximum	Sum	Element-wise Multiplication
LUAD	0.78625	0.79336	**0.79644**
BCSS	0.73291	0.73979	**0.75023**

Different Localization Map Fusion Strategies. We evaluate the segmentation performance of our proposed model with respect to different localization map fusion strategies. As shown in Table 4, element-wise maximum has the worst performance, while element-wise multiplication is the optimal choice and achieves the best performance. This demonstrates that element-wise multiplication is more effective in integrating different localization map information.

5   Conclusion

In this paper, we propose a novel Transformer based weakly-supervised model for pixel-level tissue segmentation, which is able to capture global tissue feature relations. Considering that different tissues exhibit distinct prototype characteristics, a patch-token prototype self-supervised learning approach is presented to obtain more complete tissue segmentation results. In addition, we introduce a self-refinement mechanism to improve the initial localization map for higher segmentation accuracy. Extensive experimental results on two histopathology datasets demonstrate that our proposed model achieves the state-of-the-art performance compared with other weakly-supervised segmentation methods.

Acknowledgments. This work was supported partially by the National Natural Science Foundation of China (No. 62276281, No. 61906218), the Guangdong Basic and Applied Basic Research Foundation (No. 2020A1515011497) and the Science and Technology Program of Guangzhou (No. 202002030371).

References

1. Chan, L., Hosseini, M.S., Rowsell, C., Plataniotis, K.N., Damaskinos, S.: HistoSeg-Net: semantic segmentation of histological tissue type in whole slide images. In: ICCV (2019)
2. Chan, P.P., Chen, K., Xu, L., Hu, X., Yeung, D.S.: Weakly supervised semantic segmentation with patch-based metric learning enhancement. In: ICANN (2021)
3. Chang, Y.T., Wang, Q., Hung, W.C., Piramuthu, R., Tsai, Y.H., Yang, M.H.: Weakly-supervised semantic segmentation via sub-category exploration. In: CVPR (2020)
4. Chattopadhay, A., Sarkar, A., Howlader, P., Balasubramanian, V.N.: Grad-CAM++: generalized gradient-based visual explanations for deep convolutional networks. In: WACV (2018)
5. Chen, J., et al.: Transunet: transformers make strong encoders for medical image segmentation. arXiv preprint arXiv:2102.04306 (2021)
6. Chen, J., Frey, E.C., He, Y., Segars, W.P., Li, Y., Du, Y.: TransMorph: transformer for unsupervised medical image registration. Med. Image Anal. **82**, 102615 (2022)
7. Dosovitskiy, A., et al.: An image is worth 16 × 16 words: transformers for image recognition at scale. ICLR (2021)
8. Han, C., et al.: Multi-layer pseudo-supervision for histopathology tissue semantic segmentation using patch-level classification labels. Med. Image Anal. **80**, 102487 (2022)
9. Hanahan, D., Weinberg, R.A.: Hallmarks of cancer: the next generation. Cell **144**(5), 646–674 (2011)
10. He, K., Zhang, X., Ren, S., Sun, J.: Deep residual learning for image recognition. In: CVPR (2016)
11. Jia, Z., Huang, X., Eric, I., Chang, C., Xu, Y.: Constrained deep weak supervision for histopathology image segmentation. IEEE TMI **36**(11), 2376–2388 (2017)
12. Jiang, P.T., Hou, Q., Cao, Y., Cheng, M.M., Wei, Y., Xiong, H.K.: Integral object mining via online attention accumulation. In: ICCV (2019)
13. Kweon, H., Yoon, S.H., Kim, H., Park, D., Yoon, K.J.: Unlocking the potential of ordinary classifier: class-specific adversarial erasing framework for weakly supervised semantic segmentation. In: ICCV (2021)
14. Li, Y., Yu, Y., Zou, Y., Xiang, T., Li, X.: Online easy example mining for weakly-supervised gland segmentation from histology images. In: MICCAI (2022). https://doi.org/10.1007/978-3-031-16440-8_55
15. Li, Z., et al.: TFCNs: a CNN-transformer hybrid network for medical image segmentation. In: Pimenidis, E., Angelov, P., Jayne, C., Papaleonidas, A., Aydin, M. (eds.) Artificial Neural Networks and Machine Learning – ICANN 2022. ICANN 2022. LNCS, vol. 13532, pp. 781–792. Springer, Cham (2022). https://doi.org/10.1007/978-3-031-15937-4_65
16. Qaiser, T., et al.: Fast and accurate tumor segmentation of histology images using persistent homology and deep convolutional features. Med. Image Anal. **55**, 1–14 (2019)
17. Qian, Z., et al.: Transformer based multiple instance learning for weakly supervised histopathology image segmentation. In: Wang, L., Dou, Q., Fletcher, P.T., Speidel, S., Li, S. (eds.) Medical Image Computing and Computer Assisted Intervention – MICCAI 2022. MICCAI 2022. LNCS, vol. 13432, pp. 160–170. Springer, Cham (2022). https://doi.org/10.1007/978-3-031-16434-7_16

18. Touvron, H., Cord, M., Douze, M., Massa, F., Sablayrolles, A., Jégou, H.: Training data-efficient image transformers & distillation through attention. In: ICML (2021)
19. Van Rijthoven, M., Balkenhol, M., Silina, K., Van Der Laak, J., Ciompi, F.: HookNet: multi-resolution convolutional neural networks for semantic segmentation in histopathology whole-slide images. Med. Image Anal. **68**, 101890 (2021)
20. Vaswani, A., et al.: Attention is all you need. NeurIPS (2017)
21. Wang, X., et al.: Transformer-based unsupervised contrastive learning for histopathological image classification. Med. Image Anal. **81**, 102559 (2022)
22. Wang, Y., Zhang, J., Kan, M., Shan, S., Chen, X.: Self-supervised equivariant attention mechanism for weakly supervised semantic segmentation. In: CVPR (2020)
23. Xu, G., et al.: Camel: a weakly supervised learning framework for histopathology image segmentation. In: ICCV (2019)
24. Xu, L., Ouyang, W., Bennamoun, M., Boussaid, F., Xu, D.: Multi-class token transformer for weakly supervised semantic segmentation. In: CVPR (2022)
25. Zhou, B., Khosla, A., Lapedriza, A., Oliva, A., Torralba, A.: Learning deep features for discriminative localization. In: CVPR (2016)

A Balanced Relation Prediction Framework for Scene Graph Generation

Kai Xu, Lichun Wang$^{(\boxtimes)}$, Shuang Li, Huiyong Zhang, and Baocai Yin

Faculty of Information Technology, Beijing University of Technology,
Beijing 100124, China
{xukai,shuangli,zhyzhy}@emails.bjut.edu.cn, {ybc,wanglc}@bjut.edu.cn

Abstract. It has become a consensus that regular scene graph generation (SGG) is limited in actual applications due to the overfitting of head predicates. A series of debiasing methods, i.e. unbiased SGG, have been proposed to solve the problem. However, existing unbiased SGG methods have a tendency to fit the tail predicates, which is another type of bias. This paper aims to eliminate the one-way overfitting of head or tail predicates. In order to provide more balanced relationship prediction, we propose a new framework DCL (Dual-branch Cumulative Learning) which integrates regular relation prediction process and debiasing relation prediction process by employing cumulative learning mechanism. The learning process of DCL enhances the discrimination of tail predicates without reducing the discrimination performance of the model on head predicates. DCL is model-agnostic and compatible with existed different type of debiasing methods. Experiments on Visual Genome dataset show that, among all the model-agnostic methods, DCL achieves the best comprehensive performance while considering both R@K and mR@K.

Keywords: Scene Graph Generation · Long-tailed Problem · Cumulative Learning

1 Introduction

Scene graph generation (SGG) [18] aims to detect the relations among objects in an image and has been proved to be useful for high-level visual tasks [7, 11]. Most regular SGG methods improve the performance by optimizing the visual context fusion strategy [10,22], which has made a significant progress on metric R@K [5]. However, Visual Genome (VG) [8], the most commonly used benchmark dataset for SGG task, has an extreme long-tailed predicate distribution, that is, fewer categories (called head categories) account for a larger proportion. Therefore, the training of regular SGG model is dominated by head categories and pays less attention to tail categories with fine-grained semantics. Because the generated scene graph focuses more on head categories with coarse-grained semantics, regular SGG has great limitations in supporting high-level tasks in real-world scenarios [6,19].

© The Author(s), under exclusive license to Springer Nature Switzerland AG 2023
L. Iliadis et al. (Eds.): ICANN 2023, LNCS 14257, pp. 216–228, 2023.
https://doi.org/10.1007/978-3-031-44216-2_18

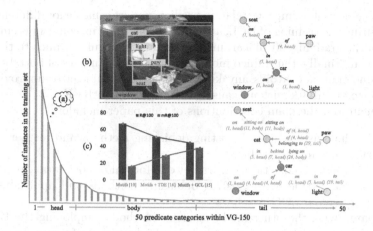

Fig. 1. Comparison of a SGG baseline and its two debiased versions. (a) Predicate distribution of VG-150. (b) A scene image and its ground truth. (c) Performance on the PredCls task and relation predictions. In the annotation (number, head/body/tail), the number represents the index of the predicates when all predicates in VG dataset are arranged in descending order according to their occurrence frequency. The larger the index, the smaller the number of instances. Best viewed in color. (Color figure online)

In order to solve the bias of regular SGG, recent works have been devoted to unbiased SGG [2,15,19], and have made a significant improvement on metric mR@K [6]. However, most unbiased SGG methods achieve the goal of debiasing by paying more attention to tail categories, that is, sacrificing the discrimination performance of head categories, which leads to another bias of the model, namely, overfitting tail categories [6]. Figure 1 illustrates the performance of baseline Motifs [22] and two corresponding debiased versions. In Fig. 1(c), the two debiased models improve on metric mR@100 while declining sharply on metric R@100. Meanwhile, the relation prediction results show that the two debiased models have the same tendency to predict predicate labels as categories with fewer instances(See Sect. 3 for details).

Comparing the performance of SGG models on metric R@K and metric mR@K, regular SGG models perform better on metric R@K but poorly on metric mR@K [5], unbiased SGG models improve performance on metric mR@K [19] but significantly decrease on metric R@K [6,15]. According to the definition of R@K [13] and mR@K [16], the former reflects the overall performance of the model for different scenes, and the latter reflects the mean performance of the model for different predicates. Therefor, it is better for a SGG model to maintain acceptable performance on both metrics.

In order to achieve better performance for different scenes and different predicates at the same time, this paper proposes a Dual-branch Cumulative Learning framework (DCL) for balanced relation prediction. The DCL includes two branches, a regular relation prediction branch is dedicated to improve relation prediction performance for different scenes, a debiasing relation prediction branch is dedicated to improve relation prediction performance for different predicates. During the training of DCL, a cumulative learning mechanism is employed to control the gradual shift of learning focus from the regular branch to the debiasing branch. Finally, the trained model retains the advantages of both branches at the same time and avoids any kind of bias, i.e. significantly improving the performance on mR@k without causing a sharp drop on R@K.

In conclusion, the main contributions of this paper include:

1) Explore the bias problem of existing debiasing methods and further analyze the reason leading to the bias.
2) Propose a model-agnostic DCL framework for balanced relation prediction, which is compatible with existing debiasing methods and applicable for a variety of regular SGG baselines.
3) Compared with the other model-agnostic methods, employing the DCL on two typical baselines achieves the best comprehensive performance while considering both R@K and mR@K.

2   Related Work

Regular Scene Graph Generation. Most regular SGG methods improve the performance of SGG by capturing richer context. Message propagation [10,18] is a kind of commonly used context fusion mechanism, for example, performing message passing between nodes [1], polymerizing contextual information between nodes and edges [10]. Another popular strategy is modeling context based on priori layout structure, the structure can be chain structure [5,22], fully-connected graph [4] or tree structure [16,21]. Although using context fusion mechanism, regular SGG models still perform poor for predicting fine-grained relation because of the long-tail predicate distribution on training data set.

Unbiased Scene Graph Generation. Unbiased SGG model is committed to solving the bias problem of regular SGG, which can be roughly divides into two types. Some methods use re-weighting strategy [19,21] or re-sampling strategy [6,10] to correct the training process of SGG model, which directly generates unbiased scene graphs. For example, PCPL [19] suggested an improved re-weighting strategy which considers the correlation among predicates. GCL [6] employed a re-sampling based group collaborative learning strategy to promote the unbiased SGG. Some other methods first generate the biased scene graphs, then recover unbiased scene graph in inference phase. For example, TDE [15] inferred and removed the effect of bias based on counterfactual causality. DLFE [3] regarded SGG as PU Learning problem and removed the bias by using label frequency. Because the debiasing strategies are usually based on reducing the impact of head categories on the model, the unbiased SGG models generally improve the prediction performance of fine-grained tail predicates while significantly reducing the prediction performance of head predicate.

Due to different emphasis of models, the existing SGG research usually focuses on a single metric (R@K or mR@K) to evaluate the effectiveness of

Table 1. Statistics of the recall results on the test set, including baseline Motifs and its debiased version Motifs+GCL [6]. "GT" denotes the number of predicate instances annotated with ground truth. "Number (proportion)" denotes the number of predictions (and its proportion in all predictions) for each category. "ΔR" represents the increment of recall on specific predicate (in %). "Δcount" represents the increment of the number of triples correctly recalled on each category. "H" and "T" denote head categories and tail categories, respectively.

		GT	Number (proportion)		Recall		ΔR (Δcount)
			Motifs	Motifs+GCL	Motifs	Motifs+GCL	
H	on	49360	1476112 (30.71%)	344175 (7.16%)	80.18%	32.14%	−48.04% (−23712)
	has	19875	534445 (11.11%)	177562 (3.69%)	80.65%	61.53%	−19.12% (−3800)
	of	16516	224195 (4.66%)	119275 (2.48%)	64.23%	48.90%	−15.33% (−2531)
T	from	95	154 (<0.01%)	817350 (17.01%)	1.41%	39.15%	+37.74% (+35)
	made of	34	284 (<0.01%)	399428 (8.31%)	0.00%	62.50%	+62.50% (+21)
	playing	25	58 (<0.01%)	100774 (2.10%)	0.00%	16.29%	+16.29% (+4)

the model, which is one-sided and insufficient. In order to achieving a trade-off between recall among different predicate categories, this paper suggests a balanced SGG framework.

3 Empirical Study

In Fig. 1(c), the debiased models tend to predict the head predicates (e.g. *on*) as the body (e.g. *sitting on*) or the tail (e.g. *to*), or predict the head predicate (like *on*) as another head predicate (e.g. *of*) with fewer instances. Therefore, the relation predictions of the two debiasing models are also biased. The bias is in the direction against that of the baseline, and is more inclined to overfit tail categories.

For the trained Motifs and its debiased version Motifs+GCL [6], we execute them on the test set of VG-150, and the metrics mR@100 on PredCls are 16.1% and 32.1% respectively. We count the prediction results of three head predicates and three tail predicates, then list the results in Table 1.

a. The debiasing method is overfitting the tail categories. Comparing "GT" and "Number (proportion)" in Table 1, there is a serious imbalance between the number of GT and the number of Motifs+GCL's prediction. For the head category *on*, ~49K instances are annotated as ground truth and ~344K predictions are generated, the number of prediction is about 7 times of that of the ground truth. For the tail category *from*, 95 instances are annotated as ground truth and ~817K predictions are generated, the number of prediction is about 8600 times of that of the ground truth. Meanwhile, the recall for the tail category *from* improves about 27.77 times, and the recall for the head category *on* decreases by 59.92%. Therefore, the improvement on metric mR@K is achieved by predicting more relation candidates as tail predicates, which is overfitting of tail predicates.

b. Only improving mR is not the best solution. Comparing ΔR and Δcount in Table 1, taking the tail category *from* as an example, Motifs+GCL improves the recall by 37.74% but the increased number of correct predictions is only 35. That means the improvement is achieved by predicting tremendous amount of instances whose ground truth labels are not *from* as predicate *from*. Because the head predicates account for a larger proportion in an image, the phenomenon also means a large number of instances whose ground truth labels are head predicate would be incorrectly predicted. The ΔR and Δcount for head categories ("H") in Table 1 can confirm the above analysis. For the image captioning task, the high-frequency ground truth relations in the VG-COCO [11] also appears more frequently in ground-truth captions [11], which means predicting head categories is also important. Furthermore, predicting the head predicates as tail predicates brings more trivial detail information in the generated scene graph, and the situation where a large number of trivial details overwhelm the key information is unfavorable to the actual task [11,20]. Therefore, for a SGG model, it is better to improve the metrics mR@K and R@K in a balanced way.

4   Methodolody

4.1   Balanced SGG

Figure 2(a) and (b) show the typical structure [22] of regular SGG and unbiased SGG respectively, where unbiased SGG uses debiasing relation prediction module to replace the regular relation prediction module of regular SGG. Without special treatment, regular relation prediction module pays little attention to the tail predicates, so regular SGG performs well on R@K and poorly on mR@K [1,5]. Through enhancing the attention to tail predicates, unbiased SGG improves mR@K but sacrifices R@K [6,19]. According to [6,15,22], the two mainstream evaluation metrics of SGG, R@K and mR@K, show a trend of confrontation in most cases, i.e., the rise of one is usually accompanied by the decline of another.

Considering the strategy for relation prediction and the performance, regular SGG and unbiased SGG are complementary, focusing on head predicates or tail predicates, higher R@K accompany with lower mR@K or lower R@K accompany with higher mR@K. In order to predict head predicates and tail predicates in a balanced way, this paper proposes balanced SGG as shown in Fig. 2(c). Using cumulative learning (CL) mechanism, balanced SGG integrates the regular relation prediction and the debiasing relation prediction to be balanced relation prediction module, which is implemented as DCL framework in Fig. 2(d).

4.2   Dual-Branch Cumulative Learning Framework

As shown in Fig. 2(d), DCL consists of two relation prediction branches, regular branch and debiasing branch. For the regular branch, the relation prediction module of Motifs [22] is selected, which is the most commonly used in regular SGG [10,16]. For the debiasing branch, the classical re-weighting strategy and re-sampling strategy are demonstrated here.

The input of DCL is the relation features F which distribution is long-tailed. In the regular branch, all the inputs are processed with a simple transformation

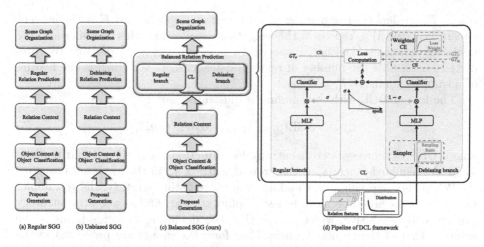

Fig. 2. Balanced SGG and DCL framework. The green components represent re-sampling and orange component represents re-weighting, which do not coexist. CL denotes cumulative learning mechanism. Note that σ is variable in the training phase and fixed at 0.5 in the test phase. Best viewed in color. (Color figure online)

without changing their dimensions: $F_r = W_r F$, where W_r represents the weights of MLP[1]. In the debiasing branch (taking re-sampling strategy as example), all the inputs pass through a sampler to change the distribution of inputs. The distribution of new features F' is relatively balanced:

$$F' = \text{re-sampler}(F), \qquad (1)$$

where F' has the same dimension as F. Similar to the regular branch, F' is transformed with another MLP: $F'_u = W_u F'$.

Then DCL employs a cumulative learning mechanism [23] to establish the connection between the two branches. In the training process, a parameter σ is used to control the learning focus of model on the two branches, and the learning focus is gradually shifted from the regular branch to the debiasing branch. In this way, the model first learns the universal expression of relations [23], then gradually focuses more on learning the tail predicates. Further, through using σ to control the parameter updating of each branch, it avoids damaging the learned universal features when emphasizing the tail data at the later periods of training. The joint output $\hat{p}$ of the two branches is formulated as:

$$\hat{p} = [\hat{p}_1, \hat{p}_2, ..., \hat{p}_C] \quad \hat{p}_i = \frac{e^{z_i}}{\sum_{j=1}^{C} e^{z_j}}, \qquad (2)$$

$$z = \sigma W_{cr} f_r + (1-\sigma) W_{cu} f'_u, \qquad (3)$$

$$\sigma = \left(\frac{E}{E_{total}} - 1\right)^2, \qquad (4)$$

---

[1] we omit additive biases of all linear layers without loss of generality.

where E_{total} denotes the number of total training epochs and E is the current epoch. W_{cr} and W_{cu} represent the weights of regular branch's classifier and the debiasing branch's classifier, respectively. $z = [z_1, z_2, ..., z_C]$ denotes the predicted logits, C is the number of relation categories. $f_r = F_r[x, :]$ is the feature of a sample, similarly $f'_u = F'_u[x, :]$.

The loss of DCL with re-sampling is illustrated as:[2]

$$\mathcal{L}_{RS} = \sigma CE(\hat{p}, y_r) + (1 - \sigma) CE(\hat{p}, y_u), \tag{5}$$

where $CE(\cdot, \cdot)$ represents cross-entropy loss function. y_r is the ground truth of f_r in the regular branch. y_u is the ground truth of f'_u in the unbiased branch.

When the debiasing branch adopts the re-weighting strategy, the re-sampler in Eq. (1) is discarded because the re-sampling strategy and re-weighting strategy are mutually exclusive, which means that the debiasing branch's input is the same as that of the regular branch. Therefore, the inputs are processed in the same as the regular branch: $F_u = W_u F$. The loss function of DCL with re-weighting strategy becomes:

$$\mathcal{L}_{RW} = \sigma CE(\hat{p}, y) + (1 - \sigma) W\text{-}CE(\hat{p}, y), \tag{6}$$

where $W\text{-}CE(\cdot, \cdot)$ represents the weighted cross-entropy loss. y is the ground truth.

5   Experiment

5.1   Datasets and Implementation Details

Dataset. We take Visual Genome [8] as our experimental dataset, and follow the most widely-used VG-150 split [18] which contains about 108K images with 150 object categories and 50 predicate categories. 70% of them are used for training and 30% for testing. Following [15], we take 5K images from the training set as validation set.

Task. The scene graph generation includes three sub-tasks [18], which are scene graph detection (**SGDet**), scene graph classification (**SGCls**) and predicate classification (**PredCls**) in order of difficulty. Specifically, the SGDet task only uses original image as input, and requires model to complete the detection of objects and relations at the same time. In addition to the original image, the SGCls takes the positions of ground truth boxes as input, the model needs to complete the object classification and relation prediction. The PreCls takes the original image together with the positions and labels of ground truth boxes into the scene graph generation model, and only needs to classify the relations.

Metrics. Currently, the mainstream evaluation metrics are Recall@K (**R@K** [13]) and mean Recall@K (**mR@K** [1,15]), in which R@K is commonly used to

---

[2] The framework should includes object classification loss. Here we only show the relation prediction loss which is related to our method.

Table 2. Comparisons with the model-agnostic methods on VG dataset. "M" denotes the **Mean** of R@50/100 and mR@50/100 scores for a subtask. The optimal result and suboptimal result of each column for the model-agnostic methods (expect for two baselines) are colored in **red** and *blue*, respectively. Best viewed in color.

Model	PredCls			SGCls			SGDet		
	R@50/100	mR@50/100	M	R@50/100	mR@50/100	M	R@50/100	mR@50/100	M
Motifs [22]	65.2/67.0	14.8/16.1	40.8	38.9/39.8	8.3/8.8	24.0	32.8/37.2	6.8/7.9	21.2
+TDE [15]	46.2/51.4	25.5/29.1	38.1	27.7/29.9	13.1/14.9	21.4	16.9/20.3	8.2/9.8	13.8
+PCPL [19]	54.7/56.5	24.3/26.1	40.4	35.3/36.1	12.0/12.7	24.0	27.8/31.7	10.7/12.6	20.7
+CogTree [21]	35.6/36.8	26.4/29.0	32.0	21.6/22.2	14.9/16.1	18.7	20.0/22.1	10.4/11.8	16.1
+DLFE [3]	52.5/54.2	26.9/28.8	40.6	32.3/33.1	15.2/15.9	24.1	25.4/29.4	11.7/13.8	20.1
+GCL [6]	42.7/44.4	**36.1/38.2**	40.4	26.1/27.1	**20.8/21.8**	24.0	18.4/22.0	**16.8/19.3**	19.1
+NICE [9]	55.1/57.2	29.9/32.3	43.6	33.1/34.0	16.6/17.9	25.4	*27.8/31.8*	12.2/14.4	21.6
+DCL(RS)	**57.7/59.6**	30.2/32.1	*44.9*	*35.4/36.3*	17.1/18.0	*26.7*	27.1/31.7	*13.2/15.5*	*21.9*
+DCL(RW)	*56.5/58.6*	*31.2/33.3*	**44.9**	**36.6/37.5**	*17.1/18.1*	**27.3**	**28.9/33.4**	12.6/15.1	**22.5**
VCTree [16]	65.4/67.2	16.7/18.2	41.9	46.7/47.6	11.8/12.5	29.7	31.9/36.2	7.4/8.7	21.1
+TDE [15]	47.2/51.6	25.4/28.7	38.2	25.4/27.9	12.2/14.0	19.9	19.4/23.2	9.3/11.1	15.8
+PCPL [19]	56.9/58.7	22.8/24.5	40.7	40.6/41.7	15.2/16.1	28.4	*26.6/30.3*	10.8/12.6	20.1
+CogTree [21]	44.0/45.4	27.6/29.7	36.7	30.9/31.7	18.8/19.9	25.3	18.2/20.4	10.4/12.1	15.3
+DLFE [3]	51.8/53.5	25.3/27.1	39.4	33.5/34.6	18.9/20.0	26.8	22.7/26.3	11.8/13.8	18.7
+GCL [6]	40.7/42.7	**37.1/39.1**	39.9	27.7/28.7	**22.5/23.5**	25.6	17.4/20.7	**15.2/17.5**	17.7
+NICE [9]	55.0/56.9	30.7/33.0	43.9	37.8/39.0	19.9/21.3	29.5	27.0/30.8	11.9/14.1	21.0
+DCL(RS)	**61.2/63.0**	27.4/29.1	**45.2**	**42.9/43.9**	18.2/19.0	*31.0*	**28.5/32.9**	11.7/13.7	**21.7**
+DCL(RW)	*57.5/59.4*	*30.6/32.6*	*45.0*	*41.1/42.2*	*21.1/22.1*	**31.6**	25.8/30.2	*12.5/15.2*	20.9

evaluate the performance of regular SGG model, mR@K is used to evaluate the debiasing performance, However, as stated in the empirical study (Sect. 3), overfitting models are likely to achieve high performance on one of the metrics and poor on another metric. Therefore, we additionally evaluate the model on **Mean** [9] which is the mean of all mR@K and R@K scores, and it is a comprehensive metric that can better reflect model performance on different predicates.

Implementation Details. Similar to [10], we adopt Faster R-CNN [14] with ResNeXt-101-FPN [12] backbone as the object detector and its parameters are frozen. The learning rate is 0.005 without decay strategy. SGD is chosen as the optimizer, where the weight decay is 1e−4. E_{total} in Eq. (4) is set to 48. Each epoch includes 1250 mini-batches and the mini-batch size is set to 12.[3]

5.2 Performance Comparison

The proposed DCL is model-agnostic, so, we select two most commonly used baselines, Motifs [22] and VCTree [16], to implement the DCL. For the debiasing branch on DCL, existing various debiasing approaches can all be integrated, we select two typical debiasing strategies here, re-sampling implemented by [6] and re-weighting implemented by [3]. The experiment results are shown in Table 2.

---

[3] the code is available at https://github.com/KAI1179/BALANCED-RELATION-PREDICTION-FRAMEWORK.

Table 3. Ablation experiment of proposed DCL. Reg. denotes only using regular branch for relation prediction. RS denotes only using re-sampling branch for relation prediction. "w/o CL" denotes that the σ in Eq. (3) is fixed at 0.5. "M" denotes the **Mean** of R@50/100 and mR@50/100 scores for a subtask.

	I. Ablation of Dual-branch structure								
Motifs	PredCls			SGCls			SGDet		
	R@50/100	mR@50/100	M	R@50/100	mR@50/100	M	R@50/100	mR@50/100	M
only Reg	65.4/67.2	15.5/16.8	41.2	38.8/39.5	8.5/9.0	24.0	32.9/37.4	7.2/8.4	21.6
only RS	42.9/45.1	35.5/37.5	40.3	25.9/26.9	21.2/22.1	24.0	18.3/22.0	16.8/19.3	19.1
DCL	57.7/59.6	30.2/32.1	44.9	35.4/36.3	17.1/18.0	26.7	27.1/31.7	13.2/15.5	21.9

	II. Ablation of Cumulative Learning								
+DCL(RS)	PredCls			SGCls			SGDet		
	R@50/100	mR@50/100	M	R@50/100	mR@50/100	M	R@50/100	mR@50/100	M
w/o CL	57.5/59.3	20.7/23.1	40.2	36.0/36.9	10.1/11.5	23.6	28.1/32.7	12.5/14.6	22.0
w/ CL	57.7/59.6	30.2/32.1	44.9	35.4/36.3	17.1/18.0	26.7	27.1/31.7	13.2/15.5	21.9

In Table 2, compared with the model-agnostic methods, +DCL(RS/RW) achieves the best comprehensive performance on all three subtasks, in which it achieves the second best performance on mR@K while keeping the best performance on R@K. Take the PredCls subtask as an example. Compared with the baseline Motifs, the mR@100 of Motifs+GCL increases by 22.1%, but its R@100 sharply decreases by 22.6%. For the proposed method, mR@100 of Motifs+DCL(RW) increases by 17.2% which is lower 4.9% than Motifs+GCL, and R@100 of Motifs+DCL(RW) only decreases by 8.4% which is higher 14.2% than Motifs+GCL. Meanwhile, the **Mean** score of Motifs+DCL(RW) is 4.5% higher than Motifs+GCL in general. The results show that DCL successfully retains the advantages of the regular branch and debiasing branch, i.e. the significant improvement of tail predicate prediction does not bring about a great sacrifice of head predicate prediction. Thus, DCL can realize a better trade-off recall of different predicate categories.

5.3   Ablation Experiments

In order to prove the effectiveness of DCL, we conduct two ablation experiments, including dual-branch structure and CL mechanism.

The ablation results of dual-branch structure is shown in the part I of Table 3. Take the PredCls subtask as an example. "only Reg. branch" has the largest R@100 value. When the regular branch is replaced by the debiasing branch ("only RS branch"), the mR@100 increases by 20.7% and the R@100 decreases by 22.1%. When two branches coexist ("DCL"), the mR@100 increases by 15.3% and the R@100 only decreases by 7.6%. In addition, Fig. 3(a) shows the recall of each predicate category for the three ablation models. For head predicates, DCL retains the advantages as the regular branch. For body predicates, DCL follows and even surpasses the debiasing branch. For tail predicates, DCL also follows the debiasing branch to a certain extent, which performs much better than the

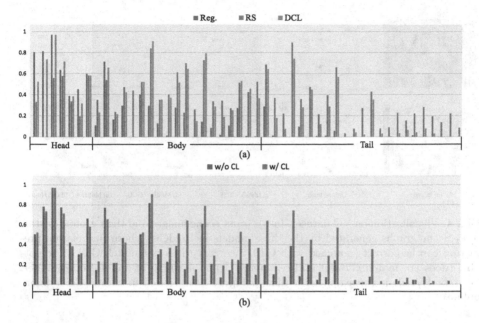

Fig. 3. R@100 of all the predicate categories under PredCls subtask. (a) The three ablation models in the part I of Table 3. (b) The two models in the part II of Table 3.

regular branch. In general, combining the advantages of the two branches, DCL eliminates the bias of regular SGG while avoids the other extreme of overfitting tail categories like debiasing branch.

The ablation of CL mechanism is shown in part II of Table 3. Take the Pred-Cls subtask as an example. For the R@100, whether to use the CL mechanism has little impact. For the mR@100, using CL mechanism increases by 9%. Figure 3 (b) shows the recall of each predicate with or without the use of CL mechanism. For head predicates, whether to use the CL mechanism has little impact. For body and tail predicates, recall can be improved by using the CL mechanism. So, an important advantage of using the CL mechanism is that the improvement on recall of tail predicates does not reduce that of head predicates.

5.4 Visualization

In order to verify the performance of the proposed DCL framework in practical relation prediction, we set up a visualization experiment for comparing with other methods. The comparison methods include typical debiasing method TDE [15], and the state-of-the-art debiasing method GCL [6].

As shown in Fig. 4, the propsoed DCL performs better for the relation prediction. Specifically, 1) Compared with TDE and GCL, DCL has higher accuracy in relation prediction. 2) By combining two relationship branches together through the cumulative learning strategy, DCL achieves optimal balance performance on

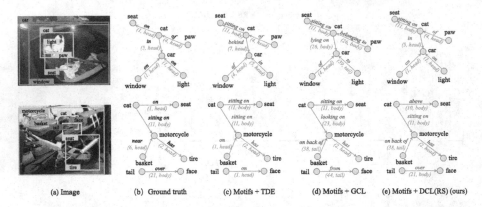

(a) Image   (b) Ground truth   (c) Motifs + TDE   (d) Motifs + GCL   (e) Motifs + DCL(RS) (ours)

Fig. 4. Visualization on VG dataset. (a-b): Input scene images and their ground truths. (c-e) Scene graphs generated by the three models in PredCls, where the relation prediction can be correct (matched with GT), incorrect (does not match GT) or acceptable (does not match GT but still reasonable). The meaning of annotation (number, head/body/tail) is consistent with that in Fig. 1. Best viewed in color. (Color figure online)

R@K and mR@K. Therefore, DCL does not excessively seek to predict the relation between objects as a fine-grained one, which keeps the key information in the scene graph from being overwhelmed by massive trivial details, and makes the scene graph well-circumscribed between important and trivial content [17]. For example, in the upper image, as a trivial information, <paw, *of*, cat> is sufficient to explain the relationship between the paw and the cat, it is unnecessary to refine it as *belong to* like GCL.

6   Conclusions

In this paper, we first analyze the bias of the unbiased SGG models, which is overfitting the tail categories. Then we propose a DCL framework which can generate scene graph in a balanced way. DCL is model-agnostic, so it can be applied to different regular SGG baselines. In addition, DCL is highly compatible with various debiasing methods. Extensive performance experiments and ablation experiments show that the proposed framework successfully retains the advantages of regular methods and debiasing methods, that is, it can realize a better trade-off recall of different predicate categories.

Acknowledgements. This work was supported in part by National Key R&D Program of China (No. 2021ZD0111902), NSFC(U21B2038, 61876012), Foundation for China university Industry-university Research Innovation (No.2021JQR023)

References

1. Chen, T., Yu, W., Chen, R., Lin, L.: Knowledge-embedded routing network for scene graph generation. In: CVPR, pp. 6163–6171 (2019)
2. Chen, Z., Rezayi, S., Li, S.: More knowledge, less bias: unbiasing scene graph generation with explicit ontological adjustment. In: WACV, pp. 4023–4032 (2023)
3. Chiou, M.J., Ding, H., Yan, H., Wang, C., Zimmermann, R., Feng, J.: Recovering the unbiased scene graphs from the biased ones. In: ACM'MM, pp. 1581–1590 (2021)
4. Dai, B., Zhang, Y., Lin, D.: Detecting visual relationships with deep relational networks. In: CVPR, pp. 3076–3086 (2017)
5. Dhingra, N., Ritter, F., Kunz, A.: BGT-Net: Bidirectional GRU transformer network for scene graph generation. In: CVPR, pp. 2150–2159 (2021)
6. Dong, X., Gan, T., Song, X., Wu, J., Cheng, Y., Nie, L.: Stacked hybrid-attention and group collaborative learning for unbiased scene graph generation. In: CVPR, pp. 19427–19436 (2022)
7. Hildebrandt, M., Li, H., Koner, R., Tresp, V., Günnemann, S.: Scene graph reasoning for visual question answering. arXiv preprint arXiv:2007.01072 (2020)
8. Krishna, R., et al.: Visual genome: connecting language and vision using crowd-sourced dense image annotations. IJCV **123**(1), 32–73 (2017)
9. Li, L., Chen, L., Huang, Y., Zhang, Z., Zhang, S., Xiao, J.: The devil is in the labels: Noisy label correction for robust scene graph generation. In: CVPR, pp. 18869–18878 (2022)
10. Li, R., Zhang, S., Wan, B., He, X.: Bipartite graph network with adaptive message passing for unbiased scene graph generation. In: CVPR, pp. 11109–11119 (2021)
11. Li, X., Jiang, S.: Know more say less: image captioning based on scene graphs. IEEE TMM **21**(8), 2117–2130 (2019)
12. Lin, T.Y., Dollár, P., Girshick, R., He, K., Hariharan, B., Belongie, S.: Feature pyramid networks for object detection. In: CVPR, pp. 2117–2125 (2017)
13. Lu, C., Krishna, R., Bernstein, M., Fei-Fei, L.: Visual relationship detection with language priors. In: Leibe, B., Matas, J., Sebe, N., Welling, M. (eds.) ECCV 2016. LNCS, vol. 9905, pp. 852–869. Springer, Cham (2016). https://doi.org/10.1007/978-3-319-46448-0_51
14. Ren, S., He, K., Girshick, R., Sun, J.: Faster R-CNN: towards real-time object detection with region proposal networks. In: NIPS (2015)
15. Tang, K., Niu, Y., Huang, J., Shi, J., Zhang, H.: Unbiased scene graph generation from biased training. In: CVPR, pp. 3716–3725 (2020)
16. Tang, K., Zhang, H., Wu, B., Luo, W., Liu, W.: Learning to compose dynamic tree structures for visual contexts. In: CVPR, pp. 6619–6628 (2019)
17. Wang, W., Wang, R., Chen, X.: Topic scene graph generation by attention distillation from caption. In: CVPR, pp. 15900–15910 (2021)
18. Xu, D., Zhu, Y., Choy, C.B., Fei-Fei, L.: Scene graph generation by iterative message passing. In: CVPR. pp. 5410–5419 (2017)
19. Yan, S., et al.: PCPL: predicate-correlation perception learning for unbiased scene graph generation. In: ACM'MM, pp. 265–273 (2020)
20. Yu, F., Wang, H., Ren, T., Tang, J., Wu, G.: Visual relation of interest detection. In: ACM'MM, pp. 1386–1394 (2020)
21. Yu, J., Chai, Y., Wang, Y., Hu, Y., Wu, Q.: CogTree: cognition tree loss for unbiased scene graph generation. arXiv preprint arXiv:2009.07526 (2020)

22. Zellers, R., Yatskar, M., Thomson, S., Choi, Y.: Neural motifs: scene graph parsing with global context. In: CVPR, pp. 5831–5840 (2018)
23. Zhou, B., Cui, Q., Wei, X.S., Chen, Z.M.: BBN: bilateral-branch network with cumulative learning for long-tailed visual recognition. In: CVPR, pp. 9719–9728 (2020)

A Graph Convolutional Siamese Network for the Assessment and Recognition of Physical Rehabilitation Exercises

Chengxian Li[1], Xichong Ling[2], and Siyu Xia[1](✉) ⬡

[1] School of Automation, Southeast University, Nanjing 210096, China
{220201816,xsy}@seu.edu.cn
[2] Department of Computing, McGill University, Montreal, Canada
xichong.ling@mail.mcgill.ca

Abstract. Recently, due to the attention of physical rehabilitation improves markedly, several researchers attempt to implement automatic rehabilitation exercise analysis. However, most of the existing methods only focus on the assessment of a single action class, which limits the application scenario of multi-type action assessment. To advance the prior work, we present a novel graph convolutional siamese network to combine action classification and action assessment task. Specifically, a test action and a standard action form a pair as input to our model, which assesses the correctness of the test action compared with the standard action. Meanwhile, our model adopts a graph convolutional network to extract a feature from the input 3D skeleton data and recognize the action. Finally, we evaluate our model on UI-PRMD and IntelliRehabDS two popular datasets. Experiments demonstrate that the proposed model reaches state-of-the-art performance on action classification and outperforms the Dynamic Time Warping algorithm and hidden Markov model method by a large margin in terms of assessment accuracy.

Keywords: Siamese Network · Action Recognition · Action Assessment · Skeleton-base

1 Introduction

Physical rehabilitation is a critical treatment approach for patients with the disease or undergoing postoperative recovery, and benefits elderly with action disorders [1,2]. In recent years, due to rapid population aging as well as a shortage of healthcare personnel, especially after the COVID-19 pandemic, people's attention to physical rehabilitation is gradually increasing, and healthcare systems undertaking a substantial burden. Recently, with the development of motion sensors, such as Kinect and Vicon sensors, carrying out rehabilitation sessions in a home-based setting has become widespread. Under these circumstances, patients need to visit physiotherapists frequently for rehabilitation assessment, causing a delay in the treatment process and becoming cumbersome. Thus, exploring effective systems capable of assessing movement quality assessment in a home-based rehabilitation setting is essential.

L. Iliadis et al. (Eds.): ICANN 2023, LNCS 14257, pp. 229–240, 2023.
https://doi.org/10.1007/978-3-031-44216-2_19

Research on human action analysis based on deep learning has laid the foundation for physical rehabilitation exercise assessment. According to [3–6], human skeletons provide a compact data form to represent the dynamics of human actions and have strong adaptability to complex backgrounds. Recent advances in depth sensing devices and human pose estimations allow human skeleton data to be easily collected. This is followed by spatio-temporal graph convolutional networks (ST-GCN) and its variants [4,7–11] to model the temporal skeleton data. Cascaded spatial and temporal graph convolution has been proven very effective in extracting the spatio-temporal features in skeleton data. Besides, researches [4,5,8] also shows that the quality of skeleton data impacts the model's performance. In our work, we employ a data preprocessing operation and follow the results of ST-GCN to encode skeleton data.

This paper aims to assess the correctness of a rehabilitation exercise and recognize the action. Earlier action assessment methods [12] treat the problem as an action classification task by analyzing the joint movement patterns. It is simple to distinguish between two actions, such as waving and kicking. However, assessing the correctness of a single action class is a more fine-grained task. Recent deep learning methods [13–17] reach great performance in action assessment but lacking in the capability of action classification. It means requiring the model to be trained individually for different action classes. To solve the task of coexisting action classification and action assessment, we design a comparative analysis strategy that assesses a test action by comparing it with a standard action template and recognizing action, respectively. Considering that the siamese network is verified by the ability to compare a pair of inputs [18,19], we propose a graph convolutional siamese network with multi-task prediction. We evaluated our proposed model on two established rehabilitation exercise datasets, namely UI-PRMD [20] and IRDS [21]. Our method outperforms existing methods on both action classification and assessment.

The main contributions of this paper are summarized as follows.

- We propose a graph convolutional siamese network based on skeleton data, which allows action assessment and recognition from a pair of physical rehabilitation exercises.
- We design a novel action assessment strategy that compares a test action with a standard action to assess the correctness of the test action.
- We conduct extensive experiments on two latest public datasets: UI-PRMD and IRDS; the proposed framework significantly outperforms the baseline and machine learning method for action assessment, and achieves better performance compared with state-of-the-art GCN-based methods for action classification.

2   Related Work

2.1   Physical Exercise Assessment

Physical exercise assessment refers to the process of evaluating and measuring an individual's physical fitness or overall health through various tests and measurements. It has been well established [22,23] that physical exercise has a high impact on the health of humans; a person may be injured when performing motions incorrectly, motivating the need for methodologies and scientific studies to evaluate the correctness of physical exercises and to provide feedback. Several previous works [24,25] by analyzing 2D human pose extracted from input images to detect abnormal posture, while our model operates on entire temporal sequences. Recently, a spatio-temporal network *Liao et al.* [13] has been proposed to encode temporal skeleton data to score an exercise. However, the method becomes dependent on many preprocessing steps that hamper the end-to-end processing of the system. *Deb et al.* [14] proposed a model consisting of GCN and LSTM to deal with variable lengths of input skeleton data and regression assessment score. Similarly, *Kanade et al.* [16] explore an attention-guided transformer-based architecture for movement quality assessment. They adopt slide windows to encode an arbitrary-length skeleton and regress an exercise score. Unlike regression-based methods, *Liu et al.* [15] merge the position and orientation feature of skeleton data and deliver a numerical exercise evaluation score by utilizing the probability results of the softmax classifier or a sigmoid function. In addition, *Zhao et al.* [17] proposed a graph convolutional network framework with a feedback module to identify mistakes and suggest personalized corrections to the user.

2.2   Skeleton-Based Action Recognition

A time series can naturally represent skeleton data of human action in the form of 3D coordinates. To model the temporal skeleton data and recognize human activities, *Yan et al.* [7] first present ST-GCN, which develops a spatial graph and temporal graph convolution to extract the spatio-temporal features from skeleton data. Each joint is regarded as a node of the graph, and its parameters are updated according to the adjacent nodes.

More follow-up work owned afterward, 2s-AGCN [4] generates a learnable adjacent matrix based on ST-GCN and leverages a two-stream ensemble with skeleton bone features. Similarly, DGNN [9] adopts multi-stream architecture and represents skeleton data as a directed acyclic graph to model the relationship between joints and bones. Nonetheless, multi-stream GCNs significantly increase the number of model parameters. *Song et al.* [8] propose ResGCN based on residual block structure to enhance the inference speed without sacrificing the accuracy. Aiming at efficiency, GCN-based methods [8,10] employ a multiple input branches strategy and add attention modules in their network. Besides, *Lee et al.* [11] propose a hierarchically decomposed graph convolutional network to decomposes all the joint nodes by hierarchy edge sets and considers the connectivity between major distant nodes.

3   Approach

Given a pair of single-person rehabilitation exercises containing a standard template and a test sample, the goal is to compare two exercises and predict the

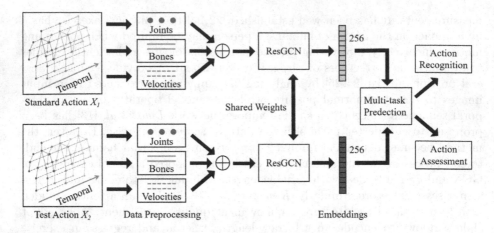

Fig. 1. Overall architecture of the proposed graph convolutional siamese network, where ⊕ means the concatenation of three skeleton feature branches.

action classification and assess whether the test sample is correct. To achieve this, we propose a novel skeleton-based Siamese network framework with multi-task prediction. The framework overview is visualized in Fig. 1 and detailed per module next.

3.1 Data Preprocessing

Our model accepts a pair of T_0 frames temporal skeleton data $\{x_1, x_2, ..., x_{T_0} \mid x_i \in \mathbb{R}^{V \times C}\}$ as input, where V, C denote the joints and 3D coordinate respectively. However, an original temporal skeleton data is a T frames sequence with arbitrary length. When $T \leq T_0$, the remaining part of the input data are all set to 0. In addition, T_0 frames are sampled averagely from original skeleton data as the model input when $T > T_0$.

According to the previous studies [4,5,8], data preprocessing is essential for a skeleton-based model. In this work, each frame of skeleton data $x_i = \{v_1, v_2, ..., v_V \mid v_i \in \mathbb{R}^C\}$ is processed by view normalization to make the two shoulders key points always horizontal, and then divided into three feature branches: 1) joint positions, 2) motion velocities and 3) bone features.

The first branch contains the original coordinate and the relative coordinate set $\mathcal{R}$. The Spine key point (n = 1) is regarded as the center joint of a skeleton.

$$\mathcal{R} = \{v_i - v_1 \mid i \in V\} \tag{1}$$

Then, the second branch is the two sets of motion velocities $\mathcal{V}$, which are calculated by x_i and x_{i-1}, x_i and x_{i-2}, respectively, and also represent the coordinate displacement of key points between frames.

$$\mathcal{V} = \{x_i - x_{i-n} \mid i \in T_0, n \in \{1, 2\}\} \tag{2}$$

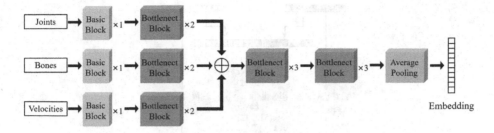

Fig. 2. Overall architecture of ResGCN backbone. The number of repeated tandem is represented behind the blocks.

Finally, the bone lengths set $\mathcal{L}$ and the bone angles set $\mathcal{A}$ as the last branch.

$$\mathcal{L} = \{v_i - v_{i_{adj}} \mid i \in V\} \tag{3}$$

$$\mathcal{A} = \{arccos(\frac{v_i - v_{i_{adj}}}{\sqrt{\sum(v_i - v_{i_{adj}})^2}} \mid i \in V\} \tag{4}$$

where i_{adj} donates the adjacent joint of the ith joint.

3.2   Siamese Network Architecture

The siamese network is always used to learn the similarity between two inputs. For our task, we propose a graph convolutional siamese network based on Res-GCN [8] architecture to encode the input skeleton data. We stipulate that the first input is always a standard action template and the second input is a test action in the same action class. The two inputs are preprocessed by Sect. 3.1 and sent to two ResGCN backbones with shared weights to extract spatio-temporal features respectively. An overview of the overall ResGCN structure is shown in Fig. 2. The blocks of ResGCN architecture are based on the ST-GCN [7] block (Basic Block) and contain a sequential execution of a spatial graph convolution and a temporal 2D convolution. Note that there are residual links added on spatial and temporal convolution. Before and after the common convolutional layer in the Basic Blocks, two 1×1 convolutional layers are inserted respectively. These blocks are named Bottleneck Blocks and can reduce the parameters of the model. After the last Bottleneck Block, an average pooling layer is followed to reduce the time and joint dimensions of extracted features. Finally, each input skeleton data $X_{1,2}$ is encoded into an embedding with a size of 256.

3.3   Multi-task Prediction and Loss Function

After obtaining latent embedding for each input, we construct a fully connected layer to predict an action classification cls. We use the cross-entropy loss function ($CELoss$) to optimize the difference between prediction and ground truth.

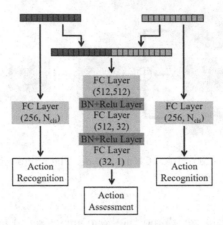

Fig. 3. Detail structure of multi-task prediction of our proposed model, where N_{cls} denotes the number of action classifications.

Besides, two embeddings are concatenated into a fusion vector, which is followed by the combination of a fully connected layer, ReLU activate layer, and batch norm layer to predict an action assessment score s. Note that $s \in [0, 1]$ and $s \geq 0.5$ indicates the test action is correct. We adopt binary cross-entropy with logits loss function ($BCELoss$) for optimization. A score greater than 0 indicates the test action is correct, and the contrary is incorrect. The overall multi-task prediction structure is shown in Fig. 3, and the total loss function is re-formulated as:

$$L = CELoss(cls, \widetilde{cls}) + BCELoss(s, \widetilde{s}) \tag{5}$$

where $\widetilde{cls}, \widetilde{s}$ are the groud-truth of the input action classification and assessment.

4   Experiment

4.1   Datasets

We experiment on two popular rehabilitation exercise datasets and only use skeleton data. Each dataset is split into a base training and a base evaluation set at a ratio of 4:1.

UI-PRMD. The UI-PRMD [20] dataset consists of 10 rehabilitation exercises (E1-10) performed by 10 healthy subjects and provides both RGB videos and skeleton data collected by Kinect v2. The subjects repeat every exercise 10 times in both correct and incorrect manners. The incorrect manner is simulating the performance of patients with musculoskeletal injuries or constraints. There are a total of 2000 samples in the dataset with action classification and assessment labels. Each correct action is considered a standard template and forms a pair

Table 1. Comparisons with the state-of-the-art action recognition methods in terms of classification accuracy (%) on UI-PRMD and IRDS dataset.

Model	UI-PRMD	IRDS
ST-GCN	98.9	96.5
2s-AGCN	99.1	96.8
Ours	**99.2**	**97.0**

of input data with other actions. Hence, there are approximately 120000 pairs, and 7800 pairs in the training and evaluation set respectively.

IRDS. The IntelliRehabDS (IRDS) [21] dataset includes 9 common rehabilitation movements (M1-9) performed by 29 subjects. The subjects consist of 15 patients and 14 healthy individuals and repeat every movement several times. The patients performed the movements comfortably, such as standing with support and sitting in a wheelchair. Hence, the movements of the dataset are more complicated and diverse than the UI-PRMD dataset. All the movements are analyzed by physiotherapists and labeled as correct or incorrect. The dataset provides 2577 samples with both RGB videos and skeleton data. Based on the same criteria in the UI-PRMD dataset, there are approximately 372000 pairs, and 23400 pairs in the training and evaluation set respectively.

4.2 Implementation Details

We implement our proposed method using PyTorch, and all experiments are conducted on a workstation with an NVIDIA GTX3060 GPU. All the input data are preprocessed by Sect. 3.1. The proposed model is trained for 50 epochs with the Adam optimizer [26] and a batch size of 32. In each epoch, the data loader feeds 6400 pairs of skeleton data randomly selected from the training set. The learning rate adopts a warm-up strategy [27] at the first 10 epochs and then decays with a cosine schedule [28]. Due to the differences between the two datasets, we employ different model parameters. For the UI-PRMD dataset, we set $T_0 = 180$ to cover all temporal lengths of skeleton data, and the num of joints V is 22. For the IRDS dataset, we set $T_0 = 128$ and $V = 25$ to format the skeleton data.

4.3 Compared with Other Methods

Action Recognition: We compared the proposed model with two state-of-the-art skeleton-based action recognition methods on both the UI-PRMD and IRDS dataset: ST-GCN [7], and 2s-AGCN [4], which are the currently most popular backbone model for skeleton-based action recognition. We retrain two models on base training sets of two datasets respectively. Note that the temporal length T_0 of the input skeleton data of these methods is the same as ours and only preprocessed by view normalization. Besides, due to these methods being single

Table 2. Comparisons with the other action assessment methods in terms of assessment accuracy (%) on UI-PRMD and IRDS dataset.

UI-PRMD	DTW [29]	HMM [30]	Ours	IRDS	DTW [29]	HMM [30]	Ours
E1	78.2	90.8	**92.4**	M1	67.2	87.2	**89.2**
E2	68.3	76.3	**97.6**	M2	52.8	**85.0**	84.4
E3	55.5	75.5	**89.1**	M3	57.0	64.8	**87.4**
E4	51.3	74.0	**88.7**	M4	78.8	86.5	**92.4**
E5	69.1	87.2	**94.0**	M5	68.4	76.9	**91.1**
E6	51.3	70.9	**95.6**	M6	64.2	86.1	**90.5**
E7	54.2	85.1	**99.9**	M7	59.4	77.5	**85.5**
E8	47.8	78.7	**98.0**	M8	79.1	89.5	**91.2**
E9	60.8	80.4	**97.8**	M9	55.8	82.1	**88.5**
E10	57.7	73.5	**94.2**	-	-	-	-
Average	59.4	79.2	**94.7**	Average	64.7	81.7	**88.9**

input, the data loader feeds twice the amount of data in each epoch to maintain a fair comparison. We use top-1 accuracy as an evaluation metric. As shown in Table 1, our proposed model outperforms ST-GCN and 2 s-AGCN by 0.3% and 0.1% on the UI-PRMD dataset, respectively. Moreover, the accuracy rate of our model on the IRDS dataset also increases by 0.5% and 0.2%, respectively. The results show that the proposed model performs at par with the comparative models and implies the effectiveness of the action recognition prediction branch of our model.

Action Assessment: For our task, a test action is compared with a standard action template to assess whether the test action is standard. First, we compare our works with Dynamic Time Warping (DTW) [29] baseline techniques for action assessment. DTW is a traditional algorithm used to compare the similarity of two sequences. As Sect. 3.1 said, a temporal action can be regarded as a sequence. To have invariant features concerning the person's height and size, angles are employed to describe the human pose. We calculate N_{ang} angles between every two connected bones. Therefore, the human pose of each frame in the action sequence can be extracted into a one-dimensional vector. Then, a T frame action sequence can be described as $Seq = \{seq_1, seq_2, ..., seq_T \mid seq_i \in \mathbb{R}^{N_{ang}}\}$. DTW uses a predefined similarity distance to deal with a pair of action sequences and generates a value. The larger value indicates the greater difference between the two action sequences. In the experimental comparison, we evaluate every pair in the evaluation set of two datasets using top1 to obtain a score set. A threshold with the highest accuracy is selected in terms of the score set to judge the correctness of an action. Moreover, we attempt three predefined similarity distances respectively: 1) manhattan distance, 2) euclidean metric and 3) cos distance to obtain the best performance of DTW.

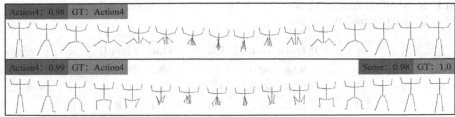

a) Input data pair from UI-PRMD dataset

b) Input data pair from IRDS dataset

Fig. 4. Examples of input data and predictions by our method from two datasets, where the first row of each input pair indicates the standard action template, while another row is the test action. The red block denotes the percent of predicted action classification and action assessment, while the green block is the ground-truth of input data. (Color figure online)

We also compared with a machine learning method hidden Markov model (HMM) [30]. According to [30], HMM trained by an action sequence in the same action class can calculate an optimal hidden sequence. When evaluating, HMM uses the optimal hidden sequence to infer a test action sequence and predict the probability of the action class. In our experimental comparison, we use the positive pairs in the training set of two datasets to train HMM respectively. We adopt the same processing as DTW to encode each frame in all action sequences into an angle vector. Then, the K-means [31] algorithm is used to cluster angle vectors into K class, which is also the number of HMM observations. Hence, an entire action sequence is represented as a one-one-dimensional action vector. Two action vectors in a positive pair are concatenated as an input of HMM. After HMM predicts all pairs in the evaluation set into a score set, similarly, the correctness of an action is assessed through a threshold. Note that the optimized solution for HMM parameters is found empirically by testing with a different number of observations and states in order to obtain the best accuracy.

Due to DTW and HMM can not predict the action classification, we experiment on each action class respectively, while our model is trained on all action classes only once. Table 2 shows the results of the evaluation on two datasets, comparing our methods with DTW and HMM. Our method outperforms DTW and HMM for all action classes by a large margin: an average accuracy of 94.7% and 88.9% on UI-PRMD and IRDS dataset, respectively. In addition, analyzed

238   C. Li et al.

Table 3. Ablation study (%) of our model w/ or w/o the multi-task prediction, where $-C$ indicates the control group.

UI-PRMD	Ours	Ours-C	IRDS	Ours	Ours-C
E1	92.4	90.0	M1	89.2	80.4
E2	97.6	95.6	M2	84.4	80.1
E3	89.1	87.2	M3	87.4	86.8
E4	88.7	91.4	M4	92.4	84.3
E5	94.0	99.9	M5	91.1	96.2
E6	95.6	91.7	M6	90.5	92.0
E7	99.9	98.5	M7	85.5	88.5
E8	98.0	90.3	M8	91.2	90.9
E9	97.8	95.8	M9	88.5	89.5
E10	94.2	84.5	-	-	-
Average	**94.7**	92.5	Average	**88.9**	87.6

from Table 2, the performance of both DTW and HMM in different action classes fluctuate greatly; there is approximately 20% accuracy difference between the best and the worst performance among action classes, while our methods only reach 11.2% and 8% on two datasets respectively. Overall, our designed network achieves better performance than DTW and HMM for almost all action classes of UI-PRMD and IRDS datasets.

An example of our experiment is also visualized in Fig. 4. These experiments demonstrate that our networks are effective enough to recognize the classification of actions and assess an action by comparing it with a standard action template.

4.4 Ablation Study

We examine the effectiveness of the proposed multi-task prediction in our model in this section by ablation study on the UI-PRMD and IRDS dataset.

We remove the multi-task prediction and construct a fully connected layer as a classifier after the concatenated fusion vector. The classifier predicts the correctness of every action class, totaling twice the number of action classifications. Therefore, the control group is considered as a pure action classification task. As shown in Table 3, the model with multi-task prediction achieves better average assessment accuracy on both UI-PRMD and IRDS datasets. This implies the performance of the model benefit from separating action assessment and action classification tasks. Besides, multi-task prediction increases the scalability of the model.

5   Conclusion

In this paper, we proposed a novel graph convolutional siamese network. The network encodes a pair of temporal skeleton data into spatio-temporal embeddings to compare a test action with a standard template and then predict the action classification and assess the correctness of the test action. We evaluate our proposed model on two popular physical rehabilitation exercises datasets UI-PRMD and IRDS. For action classification, the performance of our model and the state-of-the-art skeleton-based action recognition methods is equivalent. And for action assessment, our model achieved better results than the dynamic time-warping algorithm and hidden Markov model on two datasets. The results of the experiments confirmed the effectiveness of our model.

References

1. Burtin, C., et al.: Early exercise in critically ill patients enhances short-term functional recovery. Crit. Care Med. **37**(9), 2499–2505 (2009)
2. Langhorne, P., Bernhardt, J., Kwakkel, G.: Stroke rehabilitation. Lancet **377**(9778), 1693–1702 (2011)
3. Du, Y., Wang, W., Wang, L.: Hierarchical recurrent neural network for skeleton based action recognition. In: Proceedings of the IEEE Conference on Computer Vision and Pattern Recognition, pp. 1110–1118 (2015)
4. Shi, L., Zhang, Y., Cheng, J., Lu, H.: Two-stream adaptive graph convolutional networks for skeleton-based action recognition. In: Proceedings of the IEEE/CVF Conference on Computer Vision and Pattern Recognition, pp. 12026–12035 (2019)
5. Si, C., Jing, Y., Wang, W., Wang, L., Tan, T.: Skeleton-based action recognition with spatial reasoning and temporal stack learning. In: Proceedings of the European Conference on Computer Vision (ECCV), pp. 103–118 (2018)
6. Johansson, G.: Visual perception of biological motion and a model for its analysis. Percept. Psychophys. **14**(2), 201–211 (1973)
7. Yan, S., Xiong, Y., Lin, D.: Spatial temporal graph convolutional networks for skeleton-based action recognition. In: Thirty-Second AAAI Conference on Artificial Intelligence (2018)
8. Song, Y.F., Zhang, Z., Shan, C., Wang, L.: Stronger, faster and more explainable: a graph convolutional baseline for skeleton-based action recognition. In: Proceedings of the 28th ACM International Conference on Multimedia, pp. 1625–1633 (2020)
9. Shi, L., Zhang, Y., Cheng, J., Lu, H.: Skeleton-based action recognition with directed graph neural networks. In: Proceedings of the IEEE/CVF Conference on Computer Vision and Pattern Recognition, pp. 7912–7921 (2019)
10. Chen, H., Jiang, Y., Ko, H.: Pose-guided graph convolutional networks for skeleton-based action recognition. IEEE Access **10**, 111725–111731 (2022)
11. Lee, J., Lee, M., Lee, D., Lee, S.: Hierarchically decomposed graph convolutional networks for skeleton-based action recognition. arXiv preprint arXiv:2208.10741 (2022)
12. Lei, Q., Du, J.X., Zhang, H.B., Ye, S., Chen, D.S.: A survey of vision-based human action evaluation methods. Sensors **19**(19), 4129 (2019)
13. Liao, Y., Vakanski, A., Xian, M.: A deep learning framework for assessing physical rehabilitation exercises. IEEE Trans. Neural Syst. Rehabil. Eng. **28**(2), 468–477 (2020)
14. Deb, S., Islam, M.F., Rahman, S., Rahman, S.: Graph convolutional networks for assessment of physical rehabilitation exercises. IEEE Trans. Neural Syst. Rehabil. Eng. **30**, 410–419 (2022)

15. Liu, Y.: EGCN: an ensemble-based learning framework for exploring effective skeleton-based rehabilitation exercise assessment. In: EGCN: An Ensemble-Based Learning Framework for Exploring Effective Skeleton-Based Rehabilitation Exercise Assessment, pp. 3681–3687 (2022)
16. Kanade, A., Sharma, M., Muniyandi, M.: Attention-guided deep learning framework for movement quality assessment (2023)
17. Zhao, Z., et al.: 3D pose based feedback for physical exercises. In: Proceedings of the Asian Conference on Computer Vision, pp. 1316–1332 (2022)
18. Jain, H., Harit, G., Sharma, A.: Action quality assessment using siamese network-based deep metric learning. IEEE Trans. Circuits Syst. Video Technol. $31(6)$, 2260–2273 (2020)
19. Yucer, S., Akgul, Y.S.: 3D human action recognition with Siamese-LSTM based deep metric learning. arXiv preprint arXiv:1807.02131 (2018)
20. Vakanski, A., Jun, H.P., Paul, D., Baker, R.: A data set of human body movements for physical rehabilitation exercises. Data $3(1)$, 2 (2018)
21. Miron, A., Sadawi, N., Ismail, W., Hussain, H., Grosan, C.: IntelliRehabDS (IRDS)-a dataset of physical rehabilitation movements. Data $6(5)$, 46 (2021)
22. Anderson, E., Shivakumar, G.: Effects of exercise and physical activity on anxiety. Front. Psych. 4, 27 (2013)
23. Luan, X., et al.: Exercise as a prescription for patients with various diseases. J. Sport Health Sci. $8(5)$, 422–441 (2019)
24. Chen, S., Yang, R.R.: Pose trainer: correcting exercise posture using pose estimation. arXiv preprint arXiv:2006.11718 (2020)
25. Dittakavi, B., et al.: Pose tutor: an explainable system for pose correction in the wild. In: Proceedings of the IEEE/CVF Conference on Computer Vision and Pattern Recognition, pp. 3540–3549 (2022)
26. Kingma, D.P., Ba, J.: Adam: a method for stochastic optimization. arXiv preprint arXiv:1412.6980 (2014)
27. He, K., Zhang, X., Ren, S., Sun, J.: Deep residual learning for image recognition. In: Proceedings of the IEEE Conference on Computer Vision and Pattern Recognition, pp. 770–778 (2016)
28. Loshchilov, I., Hutter, F.: SGDR: stochastic gradient descent with warm restarts. arXiv preprint arXiv:1608.03983 (2016)
29. Bankó, Z., Abonyi, J.: Correlation based dynamic time warping of multivariate time series. Expert Syst. Appl. $39(17)$, 12814–12823 (2012)
30. Nguyen, T.N., Huynh, H.H., Meunier, J.: Skeleton-based abnormal gait detection. Sensors $16(11)$, 1792 (2016)
31. Arthur, D., Vassilvitskii, S.: K-means++: the advantages of careful seeding. Technical report, Stanford (2006)

A Graph Neural Network-Based Smart Contract Vulnerability Detection Method with Artificial Rule

Ziyue Wei⬤, Weining Zheng⬤, Xiaohong Su$^{(\boxtimes)}$⬤, Wenxin Tao⬤, and Tiantian Wang⬤

Faculty of Computing, Harbin Institute of Technology, Harbin, China
{21S003060,20B903074,21B903092}@stu.hit.edu.cn,
{sxh,wangtiantian}@hit.edu.cn

Abstract. As blockchain technology advances, the security of smart contracts has become increasingly crucial. However, most of smart contract vulnerability detection tools available on the market currently rely on artificial-predefined vulnerability rules, which result in suboptimal generalization ability and detection accuracy. Deep learning-based methods usually treat smart contracts as token sequences, which limit the utilization of structural information and the integration of artificial rules. To mitigate these issues, we propose a novel smart contract vulnerability detection method. First, we propose an approach for constructing contract graph to capture vital structural information, such as control- and data- flow. Then, we employ a Wide & Deep learning model to integrate the structural feature, sequencial feature, and artificial rules for smart contract vulnerability detection. Extensive experiments show that the proposed method performs exceptionally well in detecting four different types of vulnerabilities. The results demonstrate that integrating structural information and artificial rules can significantly improve the effectiveness of smart contract vulnerability detection.

Keywords: Smart contract · Blockchain · Graph neural network · Vulnerability detection · Wide & Deep learning model

1 Introduction

Over recent years, there has been a growing interest in blockchain technology [1]. The emergence of smart contracts signifies the evolution of blockchain technology from its initial Bitcoin-centric era of Blockchain 1.0 to the Blockchain 2.0 era, marked by the introduction of platforms like Ethereum and Enterprise Operation system (EOS) for designing commercial distributed blockchain operating systems. Smart contracts can be executed without the intervention of any party, which means that they must be executed in a trusted and peer-to-peer environment. Unfortunately, like all software, smart contracts also contain various vulnerabilities that can be exploited by attackers for financial gain. Once deployed on the blockchain, smart contracts are almost impossible to update and

© The Author(s), under exclusive license to Springer Nature Switzerland AG 2023
L. Iliadis et al. (Eds.): ICANN 2023, LNCS 14257, pp. 241–252, 2023.
https://doi.org/10.1007/978-3-031-44216-2_20

maintain, making losses irrecoverable. In June 2016, The DAO, an Ethereum project that raised $12 million was attacked, and 3.6 million ETH was stolen.

In recent years, there have been increasing successful applications of deep learning in the field of software security. However, many methods still process smart contracts by dividing them into token sequences [3,11], which may lead to a significant loss of structural information. Additionally, the vulnerability detection methods based on deep learning are difficult to combine with artificial rules. To address this problem, CGE [4] explores combining expert knowledge with graph neural network model, but does not effectively utilize sequencial feature.

In this paper, our main contributions are as follows:

1. We propose a novel method to construct a contract graph from the smart contract written in Solidity. By adding data flow information to the Control Flow Graph, a contract graph containing both control flow and data flow information is constructed. Moreover, we simulates the fallback mechanism by using special edges and nodes.
2. We propose a deep learning-based vulnerability detection methods for smart contract making full use of the sequencial and structural information of the contract code, as well as the features extracted from artificial rules. Specifically, we employ the Wide & Deep model to combine deep semantic feature with artificial features to improve the performance in vulnerability detection.
3. We evaluate our method on four types of vulnerabilities. The result shows that: (1) Using both structural and sequential feature can significantly improve the vulnerability detection performance than using one of them; (2) Artificial rules can help improve the performance of the deep learning-based vulnerability detection methods.

2   Motivation

(a) Reentrancy vulnerability 1   (b) Attack Contract   (c) Reentrancy vulnerability 2

Fig. 1. Two examples of vulnerability. (a) The first reentrancy vulnerability example; (b) Attack contract; (c) The second reentrancy vulnerability example.

Figure 1(a) and Fig. 1(c) shows two reentrancy vulnerability contracts: a) the contract will call the *call.value* function which will trigger the *fallback* function in the attack contract shown in Fig. 1(b) when *is_withdraw* is *false*, allowing attackers to steal ETH; b) the attack contract calls the *withDraw* function in Reen2, followed by the *withdrawBalances* function which calls the *call.value* function at line 12. Through the *fallback* function of the attack contract, attackers can steal ETH. For the vulnerable contract shown in Fig. 2(b), *public* permission allows all users to use the *initOwner* function to set the owner of contract, and this vulnerability can be fixed by changing the permission to *private* or using *onlyOwner*. From these two examples, we obtain the following observations:

Observation 1: Using only artificial-predefined vulnerability rules cannot detect complex vulnerabilities. Most conventional methods for smart contract vulnerability detection rely on artificial-predefined vulnerability rules, which can accurately and efficiently identify specific types of vulnerabilities. For instance, to detect reentrancy vulnerability, it is common to check whether the balance or related variables have been updated before transferring ETH. This artificial-predefined rule is insufficient to determine whether Fig. 1(c) has a reentrancy vulnerability, while it can be effective in detecting vulnerabilities in Fig. 1(a). However, we can observe a clear difference between the Call Graphs of contracts in Fig. 1(a) and Fig. 1(c), and make sure that Reen2 has a reentrancy vulnerability.

(a) Fix 1   (b) Vulnerable contract   (c) Fix 2

Fig. 2. An example of vulnerability.

Observation 2: A singular representation method is unable to capture the characteristics of multiple vulnerabilities. We can make sure that Reen2 shown in Fig. 1(c) has a reentrancy vulnerability by its Call Graph. Although graph structure can contain rich structural information, for the vulnerability shown in Fig. 2(b), using sequence-based models is better than using graph-based models: There is no obvious difference in the graph structure of the contract before and after the fix, but the sequence-based model can easily detect the difference between *public* and *private* or *onlyOwner* like Fig. 2(a) and (c).

From the examples above, we can observe that using artificial-predefined rules, sequence structures, or graph structures alone cannot accurately describe all types of vulnerabilities. However, most current smart contract vulnerability detection methods only employ a subset of features. Conventional methods rely on artificial-defined patterns. In contrast ,although deep learning-based methods for smart contract vulnerability detection have shown significant performance advantages over conventional methods, they often only utilize either sequencial or graph features and generally lack the integration with artificial rule. Therefore, it is crucial to leverage sequential feature, graph feature, and artificial rule effectively for smart contract vulnerability detection.

3   Related Work

The detection and prevention of vulnerabilities in smart contracts are key issues and significant challenges of The ongoing advancement of blockchain technology. These challenges must be overcome in order to ensure the security and stability of blockchain systems.

For Rule-based conventional vulnerability detection methods, Formal verification, such as F* [5], KEVM [6] and Isabelle/HOL [7], Symbolic execution-based tools, such as Oyente [8] and Securify [9], heavily rely on artificial-predefined rules which result in a low generalizability and a high false positive rate. Fuzzing, such as ContractFuzzer [10] and ContraMaster [10], is a widely used technique for detecting vulnerabilities, given its scalability and applicability, particularly due to its ability to be carried out without source code. However, Fuzzing is subject to path explosion, and therefore, it is not always feasible to explore all possible program paths. This issue results in a high false negative rate observed in vulnerability detection methods based on fuzzing.

Recently, an increasing number of researchers have been using deep learning techniques to detect smart contract vulnerabilities. These methods are highly scalable and adaptable to emerging security vulnerabilities. Currently, most smart contract classification approaches rely on sequence-based models, which can effectively extract deep sequencial feature from smart contracts, such as [11] which utilized the BiLSTM and attention mechanism to extract document-level features for vulnerability detection. However, sequencial-based methods cannot capture the rich structural information in the code. Previous research [12] has demonstrated that programs can be transformed into graph representations that preserve semantic relationships and retain rich structural information. Therefore, to overcome this limitation, Zhuang et al. [2] proposed a contract graph to represent the syntax and semantic structure of smart contract functions, and introduced a time message propagation network (TMP) for vulnerability detection. They also explored the integration of artificial rule with smart contract vulnerability detection [4]. However, the complexity of the contract graph construction method and normalization led to a loss of detailed information, and the sequential information was not fully exploited.

Therefore, we present a novel method for constructing a contract graph that incorporates comprehensive control-, data- flow information and the fallback mechanism. Additionally, we propose a deep learning network-based model that effectively integrates both deep semantic feature and shallow artificial feature to detect vulnerabilities in smart contracts.

4   Our Method

This section will provide a detailed description of our smart contract vulnerability detection framework shown in Fig. 3, which includes four main parts: smart

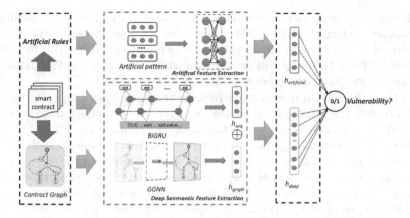

Fig. 3. The framework for smart contract vulnerability detection neural network. (Color figure online)

contract graph construction, artificial feature extraction, deep semantic feature extraction and features fusion based on Wide & Deep learning model.

4.1 Smart Contract Graph Construction

The process of contract graph construction is illustrated in Fig. 4. In the following section, we will provide a detailed description of the methodology.

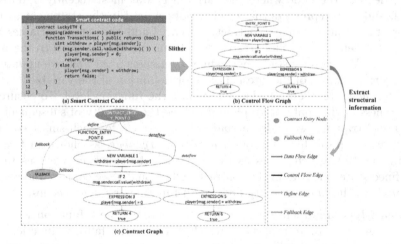

Fig. 4. The process of contract graph construction.(a) smart contract source code; (b) Control Flow Graph of (a); (c) the complete contract graph of (a).

Control Flow Graph(CFG): The control flow information is of paramount importance for detecting vulnerabilities in smart contracts, especially for the reentrancy vulnerability, which is often caused by mishandling the order of actual transfer operations and changes to balance variables. To address this challenge, we propose a contract graph construction method that leverages the Control Flow Graph as its foundation. In this study, we employ Slither [13] to extract the Control Flow Graph of functions in smart contracts as the foundation for our contract graph construction like Fig. 4(b).

For the i-th function in smart contract, there exists a *function entry node* n_0^i that represents the beginning and entrance of the function. Each node excpt n_0^i, $N^i = \{n_1^i, n_2^i, ...\}$ in CFG contain a statement of the function.

Edges in the contract graph can be represented as a triple. Specifically, an edge can be described as (V_s, V_e, l), where V_s and V_e represent the start and end of the edge, and l represents the type of the edge. In order to capture control flow, data flow, and other structural information in smart contract code, we define four types of edge, including *controlflow, dataflow, call*, and *define*.

Among them, the *call* edge represents the relationship of function calls. If statement in a CFG node calls another function in smart contract, a *call* edge will be used to connect the node to the *function entry node* of the called function.

Data Flow: Data flow represents how data moves and passes through a program during its execution. For variables $V = \{v_1, v_2, ..., v_i\}$ and nodes $N = \{n_1, n_2, ..., n_j\}$ in smart contract, we define a mapping def and a set use to capture variables defined or used in the contract:

$$def_{v \in V, n \in N} : v \to n \tag{1}$$

$$use = \{v | v \in V\} \tag{2}$$

$def(v_i)$ denotes the node where the variable v_i was most recently updated or defined, and use_j represents the set of variables used in the statement at node n_j. For statements in smart contract, we can build the set of variables used by the statement as use, and create edges from the current node to the nodes $def_{u \in use}(u)$. Whenever a statement defines or assigns a variable, we update def to reflect the location of the latest update or definition of the variable.

Slither generates Control Flow Graphs at the function level. To ensure the completeness of the contract graph and reduce the difficulty of subsequent network model training, we added a *contract entry node* for each smart contract. Each contract graph has only one *contract entry node*, as shown in the blue node in Fig. 4(c), which serves as the entry for the smart contract as well as the defined state variables in the contract. Additionally, we connect the *contract entry node* to the *function entry node* of all functions by *define* edges.

Fallback Mechanism: In smart contracts, there can be a function without a name, parameters, or return value, which is called the fallback function. Due to the existence of the fallback function in smart contracts, smart contracts' execution is more complex than other high-level programming languages, and its analysis is more difficult. To trigger the fallback mechanism, We created a *fallback node*, the green node in Fig. 4(c). If there is a transfer statement in the node's statement, this node will be connected to the *fallback* node by fallback edge, and a *fallback* edge will be added from the *fallback* node to all *function entry node*.

4.2   Artificial Feature Extraction

Similar to the approach in [4], we apply artificial-predefined rules shown in Table. reftable4 to check the smart contract code : If the code satisfies a certain artificial rule, we assign a value of 1, otherwise 0. For each smart contract, we can obtain several one-hot artificial pattern vectors based on the artificial-predefined rules. Specifically, we focus on the four types of vulnerabilities, and the artificial-predefined rules are as follow (Table 1):

Table 1. Artificial rules

Vulnerability	Artificial Rule
Reentrancy	if there is a call to *call.value* if the user's balance is deducted after the transfer if the user's balance is checked before the transfer
Timestamp Dependency	if there is a call to *block.timestamp* if the value of *block.timestamp* is assigned to other variables if *block.timestamp* is used as a conditional statement
Integer Overflow	if secure arithmetic libraries are used for arithmetic operations between variables if type conversions exist in the function if conditional statements are used to check after arithmetic operations
Dangerous Delegatecall	if there is a call to *delegatecall* in the function

Then, we concatenate all artificial pattern vectors of vulnerabilities into a single vector. Considering that different combinations of artificial vulnerability patterns have valuable vulnerability information, we made a simple transformation to obtain the artificial feature $h_{artificial}$:

$$h_{artificial} = Sigmoid(W(||_{i \in vul} x_i) + b) \qquad (3)$$

where W is the learnable parameter and b is bias. vul is the set of vulnerability types, and x_i is the artificial pattern vector of the i-th vulnerability.

4.3   Deep Semantic Feature Extraction

This part is responsible for extracting the deep features of smart contract, including the sequential feature and contract graph feature. CodeBert [15] is a model trained on a dual-modal dataset of natural language and programming language, and it has better embedding performance for programming languages. Therefore, we use CodeBert for embedding in this task. For sequential features, we divide the smart contract code into token sequence and use BiGRU to process these tokens. The process can be formulated as:

$$z_t = \sigma(W_z x_t + U_z h_{t-1} + b_z) \qquad (4)$$

$$r_t = \sigma(W_r x_t + U_r h_{t-1} + b_r) \tag{5}$$

$$\tilde{h}_t = tanh(W x_t + r_t(U h_{t-1} + b)) \tag{6}$$

$$h_t = (1 - z_t)h_{t-1} + z_t \tilde{h}_t \tag{7}$$

$$h_{seq} = \overrightarrow{h_n} || \overleftarrow{h_n} \tag{8}$$

where W and U are learnable parameters, b is bias, and $||$ denotes concatenation. Equation 3 to Eq. 6 represent the update process of a single direction of GRU. We concatenate the final hidden representations from both directions as the sequential feature h_{seq}.

Gated Graph Neural Network(GGNN) [16] is to treat the graph as a sequential data and update node states through multiple rounds of iterations, and [12] has shown that GGNN has strong potential in processing code data and has achieved good results. Therefore, we use GGNN to extract contract graph features. The process can be formulated as:

$$h_v^{(t)} = GRU \left(\sum_{u \in N(v)} W_e h_u^{(t-1)}, h_v^{(t-1)} \right) \tag{9}$$

$$h_{graph} = \frac{1}{|N|} \sum_{n \in N} h_n^i || \sum_{n \in N} h_n^0 \tag{10}$$

where W is a learnable parameter, $h_v^{(t)}$ represents the hidden representation of node v in the t-th layer, $N(v)$ denotes the neighboring nodes of v, and $||$ denotes concatenation. We take the average of the hidden representations of all nodes as the hidden representation of the contract graph. Then, we concatenate the hidden representation of the final layer with the initial hidden representation of the contract graph to obtain the smart contract graph feature h_{graph}.

Finally, we concatenate the sequential features h_{seq} with the contract graph features h_{graph} to obtain the deep semantic feature h_{deep} of the smart contract:

$$h_{deep} = h_{seq} || h_{graph} \tag{11}$$

4.4   Features Fusion Based on Wide and Deep Learning Model

The Wide & Deep model [14] improves the memory and generalization capability of the recommendation model by combining a linear model with a deep model. The deep neural network extracts and condenses the initial data features to abstract deep features h_{deep}, which tends to improve the model's generalization capability. In contrast, the artificial feature $h_{artificial}$, as a one-hot vector, is a shallow feature that summarizes and induces the past data to obtain a fixed template for specific vulnerabilities, thus tending to improve the model's memorization capability. Therefore, we use the Wide & Deep model to fuse these two features and detect vulnerability. Finally, we train this model using cross-entropy loss, where $\hat{y}$ is the ground truth:

$$y = Sigmoid(W_{wide} h_{artificial} + W_{deep} h_{deep} + b) \tag{12}$$

$$L = -\hat{y} log(y) - (1 - \hat{y}) log(1 - y) \tag{13}$$

5   Experiment

Research Questions: We will seek the answer of the following two research questions:

– **RQ1:** Can the proposed method effectively detect reentrancy, timestamp dependence, integer overflow, and dangerous delegatecall vulnerabilities? And how does it perform in terms of accuracy, precision, recall, and F1 score compared to existing smart contract vulnerability detection methods?
– **RQ2:** How do the various modules in our method affect the performance of the method?

Datasets: In our experiments, we used the open-sourced dataset from [2] which was collected from Ethereum smart contracts (ESC) and VNT Chain smart contracts (VSC), and can be obtained from [2] along with detailed descriptions. We focused on four types of vulnerabilities: reentrancy, timestamp dependency, integer overflow, dangerous delegatecall. In order to eliminate the randomness of the experiment, we randomly select 80% of them as the training set and the other 20% as the testing set for several times, and report the averaged result.

Implementation Details: We use Pytorch 1.13.1 with Cuda version 11.6 to implement our method. We ran our experiments on Nvidia GeForce RTX 3070 8GB GPU, 11th Gen Intel(R) Core(TM) i7-11800H @ 2.30 GHz.

5.1   Experiments for Answering RQ1

In order to evaluate the performance of our method in detecting multiple smart contract vulnerabilities in smart contracts, we first compare with existing methods on reentrancy vulnerabilities and timestamp dependency vulnerabilities. Table 2 presents the performance of different methods on two vulnerabilities. To ensure consistency across comparative experiments, we referred to the results of TMP and CGE from previous studies [2] and [4] as a point of reference. In the following experiments, GNN-based methods (GAT, GCN, etc.) are utilized for graph representation learning, leveraging the graph-level hidden vectors extracted from smart contract graph for binary classification. Conversely, RNN-based methods (BiLSTM, BiGRU) are employed to learn features from token sequences, utilizing the final output hidden vector for binary classification.

It is worth noting that our method still exhibits some performance gap compared to CGE in terms of performance. Both TMP and CGE normalize the graph structure to reduce training difficulty. Specifically, these two methods remove unimportant nodes from the graph structure and simplify it in a reasonable manner. Compared to our method, the graph structure proposed by these two methods are more concise. Therefore, the vulnerability detection performance of our method is slightly lower than that of the CGE method in terms of reentrancy and timestamp dependency.

Table 2. Performance comparison on the four vulnerability detection tasks.

Methods	Reentrancy				Timestamp dependency			
	Acc(%)	Recall(%)	Precision(%)	F1(%)	Acc(%)	Recall(%)	Precision(%)	F1(%)
GCN	80.79	69.23	23.08	34.62	71.75	70.97	34.92	46.81
GAT	81.92	53.85	21.21	30.43	74.57	64.52	37.04	47.06
GraphSage	63.28	53.85	10.61	17.12	81.36	83.87	48.15	61.78
GGNN	80.06	69.23	20.00	31.03	79.66	64.52	44.44	52.63
BiLSTM	94.35	69.23	60.00	64.29	85.31	77.97	56.41	62.86
BiGRU	96.61	76.82	76.92	76.89	87.57	67.74	63.64	65.62
TMP	84.48	82.63	74.06	78.11	83.45	83.82	75.05	79.19
CGE	89.15	**87.62**	**85.24**	**86.41**	89.02	**88.10**	**87.41**	**87.75**
Ours	**97.18**	76.92	83.33	80.00	**93.79**	87.10	79.41	83.08

Methods	Integer overflow				Dangerous delegatecall			
	Acc(%)	Recall(%)	Precision(%)	F1(%)	Acc(%)	Recall(%)	Precision(%)	F1(%)
GCN	75.71	75.00	23.53	35.85	84.18	46.15	22.22	30.00
GAT	89.27	18.75	33.33	24.00	86.41	42.86	23.33	32.56
GraphSage	76.24	68.75	22.92	34.38	79.10	46.15	16.67	24.49
GGNN	83.62	25.00	19.05	21.26	63.28	76.92	13.89	23.53
BiLSTM	85.88	43.75	30.43	35.90	85.88	64.51	58.83	61.54
BiGRU	92.66	78.18	56.52	66.67	88.70	**87.10**	62.79	72.97
Ours	**94.35**	**95.00**	**66.67**	**70.59**	**98.31**	84.62	**91.67**	**88.00**

Furthermore, we conducted additional experiments on integer overflow vulnerability and dangerous delegatecall vulnerability. The results demonstrate that our method outperformed the other four deep learning-based methods, i.e, our method yields 94.35% accuracy for integer overflow vulnerability and 98.31% accuracy for dangerous delegatecall vulnerability.

5.2 Experiments for Answering RQ2

By default, our method leverages both deep semantic feature extraction module (the red box in Fig. 3 which includes sequential features and contract graph features) and artificial feature extraction module (the blue box in Fig. 3). We are interested in analyzing the contribution of each module to our method's overall performance.

Table 3 presents the results of ablation experiments designed to evaluate the impact of different modules on the overall performance of the model. Specifically, in our notation, *Ours-x* indicates that feature or module x was not used in the experiment. For example, *Ours-graph* indicates that the graph feature was not used, while *Ours-deep* indicates that the deep semantic feature extraction module was not utilized.

The results demonstrate that the removal of sequential features, i.e. *Ours-seq* leads to the greatest decrease in the detection performance among all features: the accuracy of *Ours-seq* decreased by 1.13%, 6.78%, 11.30% and 12.43% com-

Table 3. Performance comparison between our method and its variants on the four vulnerability detection tasks.

Methods	Reentrancy				Timestamp dependency			
	Acc(%)	Recall(%)	Precision(%)	F1(%)	Acc(%)	Recall(%)	Precision(%)	F1(%)
Ours-graph	95.48	84.62	64.70	73.33	88.70	90.32	62.22	73.68
Ours-seq	96.05	**92.31**	66.67	77.42	87.01	**87.10**	58.70	70.13
Ours-deep	93.22	86.62	52.98	64.70	86.10	34.48	78.51	48.89
Ours-artificial	96.05	69.23	75.00	72.00	93.22	83.87	78.89	81.25
Ours	**97.18**	76.92	**83.33**	**80.00**	**93.79**	87.10	**79.41**	**83.08**
Methods	Integer overflow				Dangerous delegatecall			
	Acc(%)	Recall(%)	Precision(%)	F1(%)	Acc(%)	Recall(%)	Precision(%)	F1(%)
Ours-graph	**94.92**	76.92	62.50	68.97	97.74	76.92	90.91	83.33
Ours-seq	83.05	25.00	18.18	21.05	85.88	76.92	31.25	44.44
Ours-deep	84.75	67.50	26.09	30.77	93.79	69.23	56.25	62.07
Ours-artificial	93.79	56.25	**69.23**	62.07	97.18	82.15	78.57	80.32
Ours	94.35	**95.00**	66.67	**70.59**	**98.31**	**84.62**	**91.67**	**88.00**

pared to *Ours*. Furthermore, ours results indicate that the incorporation of graph features can enhance the performance of vulnerability detection tasks.

In contrast, the vulnerability detection performance of *Ours-deep*, which utilizes only artificial features, is relatively weak. However, the results show that the combination of artificial features with other modules can improve the vulnerability detection performance. Through our analysis, we conclude that artificial features can provide the deep learning-based model with local features and detailed information of the code, thereby improving its performance.

6   Conclusion and Future Work

In our study, we propose a method for constructing contract graph which considers the complex structural information and the fallback mechanisms. Furthermore, we propose a smart contract vulnerability detection neural network that takes advantage of contract graph feature, sequencial feature and artificial rules. Through our experiments, we conclude that: Combining sequence-based model with graph structure can enhance the performance in vulnerability detection; Additionally, relying solely on artificial rule for vulnerability detection often leads to a high false positive rate. However, integrating artificial rule can improve the performance of deep learning-based model of vulnerability detection in smart contracts. In the future, we plan to explore fine-grained vulnerability localization and consider inter-contract call during smart contracts.

Acknowledgements. This work is supported by the National Natural Science Foundation of China (Grant Nos.62272132).

References

1. Zheng, Z., Xie, S., Dai, H.N., Chen, X., Wang, H.: Blockchain challenges and opportunities: a survey. Int. J. Web Grid Serv. **14**(4), 352–375 (2018)
2. Yuan, Z., Zhenguang, L., Peng, Q., Qi, L., Xiang, W., Qinming, H.: Smart contract vulnerability detection using graph neural networks. In: Proceedings of the Twenty-Ninth International Joint Conference on Artificial Intelligence, IJCAI (2020)
3. Tann, W.J.W., Han, X.J., Gupta, S.S., Ong, Y.S.: Towards safer smart contracts: a sequence learning approach to detecting security threats. arXiv: 1811.06632 (2018)
4. Liu, Z., Qian, P., Wang, X., Zhuang, Y., Qiu, L., Wang, X.: Combining graph neural networks with expert knowledge for smart contract vulnerability detection. IEEE Trans. Knowl. Data Eng. **35**(2), 1296–1310 (2023)
5. Grishchenko, I., Maffei, M., Schneidewind, C.: A semantic framework for the security analysis of ethereum smart contracts. In: Bauer, L., Küsters, R. (eds.) POST 2018. LNCS, vol. 10804, pp. 243–269. Springer, Cham (2018). https://doi.org/10.1007/978-3-319-89722-6_10
6. Hildenbrandt, E., Saxena, M., Rodrigues, N., et al.: KEVM: a complete formal semantics of the ethereum virtual machine. In: Proceedings of the IEEE 31st Computer Security Foundations Symposium (CSF), pp. 204–217. IEEE (2018)
7. Amani, S., Bégel, M., Bortin, M., Staples, M.: Towards verifying ethereum smart contract bytecode in Isabelle/HOL. In: Proceedings of the 7th ACM SIGPLAN International Conference on Certified Programs and Proofs, pp. 66–77 (2018)
8. Luu, L., Chu, D.H., Olickel, H., Saxena, P., Hobor, A.: Making smart contracts smarter. In: Proceedings of the 2016 ACM SIGSAC Conference on Computer and Communications Security, pp. 254–269 (2016)
9. Tsankov, P., Dan, A., Drachsler-Cohen, D., Gervais, A., Buenzli, F., Vechev, M.: Securify: practical security analysis of smart contracts. In: Proceedings of the 2018 ACM SIGSAC Conference on Computer and Communications Security, pp. 67–82 (2018)
10. Jiang, B., Liu, Y., Chan, W.K.: ContractFuzzer: fuzzing smart contracts for vulnerability detection. In: Proceedings of the 33rd ACM/IEEE International Conference on Automated Software Engineering, pp. 259–269 (2018)
11. Tian, G., Wang, Q., Zhao, Y., Guo, L., Sun, Z., Lv, L.: Smart contract classification with a Bi-LSTM based approach. IEEE Access **8**, 43806–43816 (2020)
12. Allamanis, M., Brockschmidt, M., Khademi, M.: Learning to represent programs with graphs. In: International Conference on Learning Representations (2018)
13. Josselin, F., Grieco, G., Groce, A.: Slither: a static analysis framework for smart contracts. In: 2019 IEEE/ACM 2nd International Workshop on Emerging Trends in Software Engineering for Blockchain (WETSEB). IEEE (2019)
14. Cheng, H.T., Koc, L., Harmsen, J., et al.: Wide & deep learning for recommender systems[J]. ACM (2016)
15. Feng, Z., et al.: CodeBERT: a pretrained model for programming and natural languages (2020)
16. Ruiz, L., Gama, F., Ribeiro, A.: Gated graph recurrent neural networks. IEEE Trans. Signal Process. **68**, 6303–6318 (2020)

Adaptive Randomized Graph Neural Network Based on Markov Diffusion Kernel

Qianli Ma$^{(\boxtimes)}$, Zheng Fan, Chenzhi Wang, and Yuhua Qian

College of Computer and Information Technology, Shanxi University, Taiyuan, China
mymql@sxu.edu.cn

Abstract. Graph neural networks (GNNs) especially Graph convolutional networks (GCNs) GCNs, are popular in graph representation learning. However, GCNs only consider the nearest neighbor, which makes it difficult to expand the node domain, and their performance decline as the number of layers increases due to the over-smoothing problem. Therefore, this paper proposes an Adaptive Randomized Graph Neural Network based on Markov Diffusion Kernel (ARM-net) to overcome these limitations. Firstly, ARM-net designs a random propagation strategy based on Bernoulli distribution; Secondly, an adaptive propagation process based on Markov diffusion kernels is designed to separate feature transformations from propagation, expand the node domain and reduce the risk of model's over-smoothing; Finally, a graph regularization term is added to enable nodes to find more information useful for their classification results, thereby improve the generalization performance of the model. Experimental results show that the model outperforms several recently proposed semi-supervised classification algorithms in semi-supervised node classification tasks. ARM-net has better performance on multiple data sets. Through experiments, ARM-net solves the over-smoothing problem encountered during GNN propagation to some extent, and the model has better generalization performance.

Keywords: Graph convolution network · Semi-supervised learning · node classification · Markov diffusion kernel

1 Introduction

In real life, graphs are ubiquitous and can be described in various forms. They are seen as a carrier for information dissemination and are widely used in the recommendation systems, the citation networks, and the construction of protein structures in biochemistry. Recently, researches on graph data have made significant progress in the deep learning [1–3].

The semi-supervised node classification task is a popular research problem nowadays. Its objective is to predict labels of numerous unlabeled nodes in a given graph based on a small number of labeled nodes. GCN [3] and GAT [4] are basic methods used to address this problem. GCN performs well with two layers but its performance deteriorates with an increase in the number of propagation layers. GCN fails to extract effective information when the number of propagation layers exceeds two, which is the

© The Author(s), under exclusive license to Springer Nature Switzerland AG 2023
L. Iliadis et al. (Eds.): ICANN 2023, LNCS 14257, pp. 253–264, 2023.
https://doi.org/10.1007/978-3-031-44216-2_21

phenomenon known as the over-smoothing problem. Li et al. [5] shows that the reason of over-smoothing is the repeated application of Laplacian smoothing. Researchers have proposed various solutions to overcome this issue [6–12]. How to aggregate multi-order neighbors effectively is still a key focus of current research. Therefore, in order to obtain better prediction results in semi-supervised classification tasks, it is important to design a model that can collect higher-order domain information.

In the task of semi-supervised node classification, it has become one of the important research directions to obtain better classification results with fewer marked nodes. In terms of contrast learning and unsupervised graph representation learning, GRACE [13] carried out data expansion by maximizing mutual information through comparison between positive pairs and negative pairs. Cui et al. [14] proposed to use the T-distribution loss and the semantic class consistency constraints to enhance the model's ability of distinguish classes. In computer vision, PCL [15], UDA [16] try to make full use of unlabeled data to carry out consistent regularization training and improve the generalization performance of the model. These data enhancement methods have been very successful in their respective fields.

This paper proposes Adaptive Randomized Graph Neural Network based on Markov Diffusion Kernel (ARM-net) which is a simple and effective semi-supervised learning framework. In a word, it's main contributions can be highlighted as follows.

1) This paper proposes a graph data random augmentation module, which uses a Bernoulli distribution to perform random data augmentation on the feature matrix, and makes the nodes insensitive to specific neighborhoods.
2) The feature transformation and propagation are separated. The propagation is carried out first, then the feature transformation. In addition, the adaptive propagation process is defined based on Markov diffusion kernel. It extends the neighborhood of the nodes and reduces the risk of over-smoothing.
3) A graph regularization term is designed in this study to reduce overfitting and enhance the generalization performance of the model.
4) Experimental results show that ARM-net can improve the performance of semi-supervised node classification tasks and has stronger competitiveness.

The rest of this paper is structured as follows. Sect. 2 introduces related work. In Sect. 3, the proposed method is presented in detail. Sect. 4 summarizes the whole paper.

2 Related Work

2.1 Graph Concept

Given a simple undirected graph $G = (V, E)$, it consists of n nodes. A denotes the adjacency matrix, defining the interconnection between nodes, $A_{ij} = A_{ji}$. For each element in A, $A_{ij} = 1$ indicates that there is an edge between nodes v_i and v_j; $A_{ij} = 0$ means there is no edge between the two. D represents the degree matrix. The node characteristic matrix is X, $X \in R^{n \times d}$, n is the number of nodes, and d is the dimension. For the node v_i, its feature vector is X_i, and the label vector is Y_i, $Y \in R^{n \times C}$, and C represents the total class of all nodes. The definition of a semi-supervised node classification task is as follows:

Definition 1: m labeled nodes ($0 < m \leq n$), labeled as Y^L. ($n - m$) unlabeled nodes, pseudo label is Y^U. Its purpose is to learn the prediction function $f : A, X, Y^L \rightarrow Y^U$ to infer Y^U of unlabeled nodes.

2.2 Graph Convolutional Network

In recent years, the graph neural networks have become one of the hottest research topics in semi-supervised node classification tasks. GNN extends the neural network technology to graph data, such as the graph convolutional networks (GCN). The propagation rules of GCN are defined as:

$$H^{(l+1)} = \sigma\left(\hat{A} H^{(l)} W^{(l)}\right) \tag{1}$$

where $\hat{A}$ is the symmetric normalized adjacency matrix, $\hat{A} = \hat{D}^{-1/2}(A + I)\hat{D}^{-1/2}$, and $\hat{D}$ is the corresponding degree matrix of $A + I$, σ represents the ReLU operation, $H^{(l)}$ and $W^{(l)}$ is the lth hidden layer node representation and the weight matrix, $H^{(0)} = X$.

3 Model Framework

This section proposes an Adaptive Randomized Graph Neural Network based on Markov Diffusion Kernel (ARM-net), as shown in Fig. 1. In the ARM-net, a random propagation strategy using Bernoulli distribution for S times is designed first for the data augmentation (Fig. 1(a)). Then, a network structure similar to a GCN variant is devised with the aim of reducing the risk of over-smoothing. In this network structure, Markov diffusion kernel is introduced, and based on the it, K propagation steps are carried to generate K hidden layer outputs, $H^{(1)}, H^{(2)}, \ldots, H^{(K)}$ (Fig. 1(b)). The $0-K$ layers are concatenated together, and a learnable parameter S is introduced to learn the weight sizes of the $0 - K$ layers. Set $s_i \in S$, $i = 1, 2, \ldots, k$, where s_i corresponds to $H^{(i)}$ (Fig. 1(c)). As shown in Fig. 1. The output H_{out} is obtained by an aggregation function. A graph regularization term is added to improve the accuracy of predicting unlabeled nodes and enhance the generalization ability of the model in semi-supervised settings.

3.1 Random Augmentation of Feature Matrix

The random augmentation algorithm is derived from image data augmentation. In the field of image data augmentation, multiple views are generated by randomly corrupting images (i.e., randomly dropping features) to fully enhance model's generalization performance using unlabeled data. The model uses the masking feature (MF) method to randomly mask dimensions with zero in node features. Miller et al. [17] pointed out that neighboring nodes of a central node are more likely to have similar feature representations or labels. Therefore, the information lost by a node can be compensated by its neighbors, and an approximate representation can be formed in the corresponding augmentation matrix.

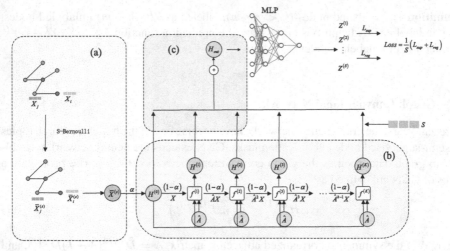

Fig. 1. ARM-net model structure

Set the MF method to Bernoulli distribution. Create a *mask* matrix and generate a binary mask ε_i for each node v_i in the graph, $\varepsilon_i \sim Bernoulli(1 - \delta)$, with δ being set as the super parameter. The corresponding ε_i for each node is placed in the *mask* matrix. For the i-th node feature X_i, let $\overline{X}_i = \varepsilon_i \cdot X_i$. The above results are repeated S times to generate multiple enhanced feature matrices for the next step.

3.2 Neural Network Structure

This section introduces two main principles of the designed neural network. Firstly, by introducing the Markov diffusion kernel, a simple and effective low-pass filter is obtained. And based on this kernel, a feature mapping function is designed. Secondly, this paper separates the traditional graph convolution into the propagation and the feature transformation, and the adjacency matrix is propagated first and then the feature matrix is transformed. Finally, the learnable parameters are set to adaptively merge information from different hidden layers.

Looking at Fig. 2, it is found that there are some differences in the structure of GCN [3], SGC [8], JKNET [6], and ARM-net. Where $f^{(k)}$ represents the classifier or the mapping function of the k-th layer. $f^{(agg)}$ denotes the aggregation function. In GCN, SGC, and JKNET, the feature transformation is performed during the propagation process. However, the APPNP [9] method separates the feature transformation from the propagation, first performing the propagation and then using a personalized PageRank method to reconstruct the graph convolution. Similar to APPNP, the proposed ARM-net first performs the propagation and then the feature transformation.

Markov Diffusion Kernel. Fouss [18] propose that when two nodes diffuse in a similar way in the graph, they are considered similar because they affect other nodes in a similar way. Markov diffusion distance can be used to measure the similarity between different

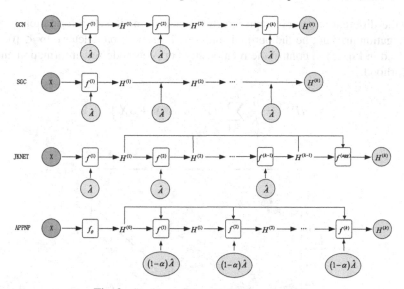

Fig. 2. Structure diagram of different models

nodes. At time T, the Markov diffusion distance between nodes v_i and v_j is defined as:

$$d_{ij}(T) = \left\| x_i(T) - x_j(T) \right\|_2^2 \tag{2}$$

assuming the transition matrix during diffusion is A, the average visitation rate of $x_i(T)$ from $T = 0$ to $T = T$ can be defined as:

$$x_i(T) = \frac{A x_i(0) + A^2 x_i(0) + \cdots + A^T x_i(0)}{T} \tag{3}$$

let T be the propagation step and $T = K$, then Eq. (3) can be simplified as follows:

$$x_i(K) = \frac{1}{K} \sum_{k=1}^{K} A^k x_i(0) \tag{4}$$

for a node v_i, the feature map of the Markov diffusion kernel in the K-th layer is denoted as $(1/K) \sum_{k=1}^{K} A^k x_i(0)$. Set $A^k x_i(0)$ as the independent variable and define the function $f(x) = (1/K) \sum_{k=0}^{K} x^k$, where setting $k = 0$ corresponds to adding self-loops in the graph. Observing Fig. 3, as K increases, small eigenvalues tend to approach 0, and the function $f(x)$ tends to preserve larger eigenvalues. Therefore, it is concluded that as K increases, the filter also maintains the node's closest position while expanding the neighborhood spaces.

Based on the Markov diffusion kernel, the traditional graph convolutional neural network can be modified as follows, where A is the symmetrically normalized adjacency matrix:

$$H^{(K)} = \frac{1}{K} \sum_{k=0}^{K} \hat{A}^k X \tag{5}$$

due to the differentiations of graph structures, adding node self-information directly in propagation may not be the optimal solution. Therefore, parameter α, $\alpha \in [0, 1]$ is introduced in Eq. (5) to control the relationship between node self-information and its neighborhood:

$$H^{(K)} = \frac{1}{K} \sum_{k=1}^{K} \left((1 - \alpha)\hat{A}^k X + \alpha X \right) \tag{6}$$

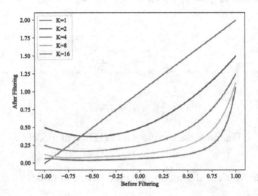

Fig. 3. Function $f(x)$ via filter

Adaptive Propagation Process. After the feature matrix is randomly propagated for S times, S matrices $\overline{X}^{(s)}$ are generated. Combining the Markov diffusion kernel proposed above, the mapping function in the propagation process is defined as:

$$H_s^{(K)} = \begin{cases} \alpha \overline{X}^{(s)}, K = 0 \\ \frac{1}{K} \sum_{k=1}^{K} \left((1 - \alpha)\hat{A}^k \overline{X}^{(s)} + \alpha H_s^{(0)} \right), K = 1, 2 \dots, K \end{cases} \tag{7}$$

When the neural network propagates to the K-th layer, the input layer $H_s^{(0)}$ and K hidden layers $H_s^{(1)}, H_s^{(2)} \dots, H_s^{(K)}$ are concatenated together using a concatenation function, which is defined as:

$$H_s = stack \left(H_s^{(0)}, H_s^{(1)}, H_s^{(2)} \dots, H_s^{(K)} \right)$$
$$T_s = \sigma(H_s t)$$
$$\hat{T}_s = reshape(T_s) \tag{8}$$
$$H_{out} = squeeze \left(\hat{T}_s H_s \right)$$

In Eq. (8), H_s contains the information from the layers $0 - K$, with a dimension of $\mathbb{R}^{n \times (K+1) \times d}$ .t is a learnable parameter, and the model can adaptively adjust the weights of $0 - K$ layers.

In Eq. (8), σ is a nonlinear activation function, and the *stack, reshape,* and *squeeze* functions are used to ensure the matrix dimensions compatible throughout the computation. $T_s \in \mathbb{R}^{n\times(K+1)\times1}$, *reshape* the dimensions of T_s to obtain $\hat{T}_s \in \mathbb{R}^{n\times1\times(K+1)}$. Finally, a weighted sum is performed to obtain the final output H_{out}, $H_{out} \in \mathbb{R}^{n\times d}$.

After deriving H_{out} using Eq. (8), the feature matrix H_{out} is transformed using an MLP to obtain the final output Z. In Sect. 4 of this paper, the effectiveness of the adaptive propagation process in the model is demonstrated.

Traditional neural network models such as GCN couple the propagation and the feature transformation together during training, and the size of the neighborhood is often difficult to expand. However, the ARM-net model separates the propagation and the feature transformation, and propagates first and then transforms features, which expands the node's neighborhood. At the same time, ARM-net balances local and global neighborhood information of each node by training the learnable parameters, and reduces the risk of over-smoothing.

3.3 Loss Function Composition

For the ARM-net model designed in this paper, the loss is specifically composed of two parts: the supervised loss and the graph regularization loss.

1) Supervised loss: After the adaptive propagation process and MLP, $Z^{(s)}$ are obtained. One graph has n nodes, where m nodes are labeled with Y^L. This paper uses cross-entropy loss to calculate the supervised loss:

$$L_{sup} = -\sum_{s=1}^{S}\sum_{i=1}^{m} Y_i^L \log\left(\text{softmax}\left(Z^{(s)}\right)\right) \tag{9}$$

2) Graph regularization loss: To improve output consistency and reduce label distribution entropy, a method called Sharpening is proposed by David [19]. Calculate the average value $\overline{Z} = (1/S)\sum_{s=1}^{S} softmaxZ^{(s)}$ of $Z^{(s)}$. After sharpening, the average prediction of node v_i in the k-th class is given by:

$$\hat{Z}_i = Sharpening\left(\overline{Z}, T\right)_i$$

$$Sharpening\left(P, T\right)_i = P_i^{\frac{1}{T}} / \sum_{k=1}^{C} P_k^{\frac{1}{T}} \tag{10}$$

in experiments, the scope of sharpening can be controlled through the super parameter "T", $0 < T < 1$. In ARM-net, in order to achieve better experimental results, it is necessary to minimize the distance between $\hat{Z}_i$ and $\overline{Z}_i$:

$$L_{reg} = \sum_{s=1}^{S}\sum_{i=1}^{n} \left\|\hat{Z}_i - \overline{Z}_i^{(s)}\right\|_2^2 \tag{11}$$

adding a regularization term and setting T to a small value can reduce the entropy of the model's output, and make the output $Z^{(s)}$ more consistent.

The final loss function includes the supervised loss function Eq. (9) and the graph regularization loss function Eq. (11). In Eq. (12), λ is the hyperparameter that controls the balance of the loss function:

$$L = \frac{1}{S}L_{\text{sup}} + \lambda\frac{1}{S}L_{reg} \tag{12}$$

4 Experiments

4.1 Datasets and Benchmark Algorithms

This study conducted experiments on three benchmark datasets: Cora, Citeseer, and Pubmed [3]. The detailed information of the datasets is shown in Table 1.

The experimental setup follows that of Yang et al. [20]. In the citation network datasets, each node represents a document, and multiple nodes form a feature matrix X. The citation links are treated as undirected edges, which constitute an adjacency matrix A. The label rate is defined as the ratio of the number of labeled nodes to the total number of nodes in the dataset. The training set consists of 20 nodes per class, a validation set of 500 nodes, and a test set of 1000 nodes.

Eight different graph neural networks are selected as benchmark algorithms, including GCN [3], GAT [4], SGC [8], APPNP [9], DropEdge [7], GPRGNN [21], SSGC [11], GCNII [22], and one GNN-based sampling method: GraphSAGE [23].

Table 1. Data set statistics

Datasets	nodes	Features	edges	classes	labeling rate
Cora	2708	1433	5429	7	0.052
Citeseer	3327	3700	4732	6	0.036
Pubmed	19717	500	44338	3	0.003

4.2 Analysis of Experimental Results

Table 2 summarizes the prediction accuracy for node classification. The results for the ARM-net model are the average of 50 random weight initialization runs.

Observing Table 2, it can be noticed that the ARM-net algorithm performs better than the compared benchmark algorithms. Specifically, the performance of the ARM-net model on the three datasets is respectively improved by 3.3%, 4.0%, and 2.7% compared to the GCN algorithm, and by 1.8%, 1.8%, and 2.7% compared to the GAT algorithm. Compared to the latest algorithm GCNII, the ARM-net model performs comparably on the Cora dataset, while the accuracy is improved by 1.4% and 1.5% on the Citeseer and Pubmed datasets, respectively.

Table 2. Classification accuracy (%) on standard split

Method	Cora	Citeseer	Pubmed
GCN	81.5	70.3	79.0
GAT	83.0 ± 0.7	72.5 ± 0.7	79.0 ± 0.3
SGC	81.0 ± 0.0	71.9 ± 0.1	78.9 ± 0.0
DropEdge	81.8 ± 0.8	71.9 ± 0.2	79.1 ± 0.3
APPNP	83.7 ± 0.5	71.5 ± 0.3	79.3 ± 0.5
GPRGNN	82.5 ± 0.4	71.1 ± 0.6	79.4 ± 0.8
GraphSAGE	81.6 ± 0.6	70.2 ± 0.7	78.3 ± 0.3
SSGC	82.6 ± 0.1	73.0 ± 0.0	80.0 ± 0.1
GCNII	84.9 ± 0.4	72.9 ± 0.5	80.2 ± 0.4
ARM-net	**84.8 ± 0.3**	**74.3 ± 0.3**	**81.7 ± 0.6**

4.3 Ablation Experiment

In this study, the ablation experiments are conducted to verify the effects of different components in the ARM-net model. The relevant components are as follows:

1) **Without mask feature (w/o Bo):** The Bernoulli distribution is not used to enhance the masking feature of data, only the dropnode is used.
2) **Without multiple graph data augmentation (w/o S_x):** the data augmentation module is not used for multiple times, and S is set to 1. Use data augmentation once, and feed it into subsequent operations.
3) **Neural network structure setting GCN (net-GCN):** the propagation process of the hidden layer is modified, and the improved GCN variant is not used, but only GCN is used.
4) **Neural network structure setting without Markov diffusion kernel (w/o Markov):** the Markov diffusion kernel is not used in the propagation process of the model, and the normalized adjacency matrix is directly used for calculation.
5) **Neural network structure setting without adaptive propagation process (w/o adaption):** the adaptive propagation process is not used in the propagation process of the model, and the propagation and the feature conversion are coupled together.
6) **Without regularization term (w/o reg):** the graph regularization term is not used, and the hyperparameter of the graph regularization term is set to 0.

Table 3 summarizes the results of all ablation experiments. After removing some components from the ARM-net, it is observed that the performance of the complete model declines, indicating that the designed components in this study help to improve the accuracy of the model.

4.4 Performance Analysis

Generalization Performance Analysis. This paper studies the effects of graph regularization terms on the generalization ability of models. To verify their effects on the

Table 3. Accuracy of ablation experiment (%)

Method	Cora	Citeseer	Pubmed
w/o Bo	84.3 ± 0.3	73.5 ± 0.4	80.4 ± 0.4
w/o S_x	83.9 ± 0.3	72.3 ± 0.6	79.6 ± 0.6
net-GCN	84.3 ± 0.3	73.5 ± 0.4	80.2 ± 0.5
w/o Markov	84.0 ± 0.2	73.3 ± 0.3	80.7 ± 1.4
w/o reg	83.1 ± 0.4	72.1 ± 0.4	79.4 ± 0.4
w/o adaption	84.6 ± 0.4	73.1 ± 0.4	79.9 ± 1.3
ARM-net	**84.8 ± 0.3**	**74.3 ± 0.3**	**81.7 ± 0.6**

models, this section analyzes the cross-entropy loss of the training set and the verification set of the model on the Cora dataset. The smaller the difference between the two models is, the better the model's generalization performance is. The generalization performance of the ARM-net model and its variant (w/o reg) is shown in Fig. 4.

After adding the graph regularization term in the ARM-net model, as shown in Fig. 4, the validation loss tends to be close to the training loss, and both become more stable.

Over-smoothing Experiment. Figure 5 displays the experimental results on the Cora dataset with varying propagation step sizes controlled by the hyperparameter k in ARM-net. For GCN and GAT, the propagation step size is adjusted by stacking different hidden layers. For SGC and SSGC, in the data preprocessing stage, the propagation depth is adjusted.

As the propagation step size increases, both GCN and GAT exhibit a significant decrease in performance metrics. ARM-net, SGC, and SSGC can alleviate some of the over-smoothing problems. However, ARM-net has better performance and wider applicability.

Robustness Analysis. This section investigates the robustness of ARM-net by generating perturbed graphs using the random attack methods. Specifically, the random attack adds pseudo edges to perturb the graph structure. Figure 5 shows the classification accuracy under different perturbation rates on the Cora dataset. The experiment shows that ARM-net consistently outperforms GCN and GAT on perturbation rates ranging from 1% to 20%. When 20% new random edges are added to Cora, the classification accuracy of ARM-net only drops by 7.3%, while those of GCN and GAT drop by 10.0% and 9.1%, respectively. This study demonstrates that ARM-net exhibits better robustness than traditional neural networks, such as GCN and GAT (Fig. 6).

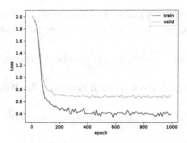
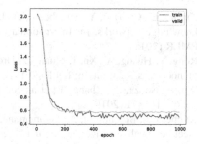

Fig. 4. Generalization performance on Cora, the left is (w/o reg), and the right is ARM-net

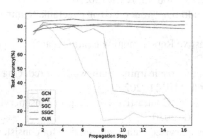
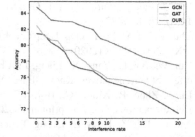

Fig. 5. Over-smoothing analysis   **Fig. 6.** Robustness analysis on Cora dataset

5 Conclusion

This paper proposes a new model for graph semi-supervised classification tasks, called Adaptive Randomized Graph Neural Network based on Markov Diffusion Kernel (ARM-net). ARM-net proposes a graph data random augmentation module using a random propagation strategy to mask features, an adaptive propagation process based on the Markov diffusion kernel, and a graph regularization term loss. Experimental results show that ARM-net has better performance and better effect of node classification. In conclusion, the proposed ideas in this paper are effective.

References

1. Grover, A., Leskovec, J.: node2vec: scalable feature learning for networks. In: Proceedings of the 22nd ACM SIGKDD international conference on Knowledge discovery and data mining, pp. 855–864 (2016)
2. Gilmer, J., Schoenholz, S.S., Riley, P.F., et al.: Neural message passing for quantum chemistry. In: International Conference on Machine Learning, pp. 1263–1272. PMLR (2017)
3. Kipf, T.N., Welling, M.: Semi-supervised classification with graph convolutional networks. In: ICLR (2017)
4. Elickovic, P.V., Cucurull, G., Casanova, A.: Graph attention networks. In: ICLR (2018)
5. Chen, D., Lin, Y., Li, W., et al: Measuring and relieving the over-smoothing problem for graph neural networks from the topological view. In: Proceedings of the AAAI Conference on Artificial Intelligence, pp. 3438–3445 (2020)

6. Xu, K., Li, C., Tian, Y., Sonobe, T., et al.: Representation learning on graphs with jumping knowledge networks. In: International Conference on Machine Learning, pp. 5453–5462. PMLR (2018)
7. Rong, Y., Huang, W., Xu, T., Huang, J.: DropEdge: towards deep graph convolutional networks on node classification. In: ICLR (2019)
8. Wu, F., Souza, A., Zhang, T., et al: Simplifying graph convolutional networks. In: ICML, pp. 6861–6871 (2019)
9. Klicpera, J.; Bojchevski, A.; Gunnemann, S.: Predict then propagate: Graph neural networks meet personalized pagerank. In: ICLR (2019)
10. Klicpera, J.; Weienberger, S.; Günnemann, S.: Diffusion improves graph learning. In: Neural Information Processing Systems (2019)
11. Zhu, H., Koniusz, P.: Simple spectral graph convolution. In: ICLR (2020)
12. Ma, Q., Fan, Z., Wang, C., et al.: Graph mixed random network based on pagerank. Symmetry. **14**(8), 1678 (2022)
13. Zhu, Y., Xu, Y., Yu, F., et al: Deep Graph Contrastive Representation Learning. arXiv preprint arXiv:2006.04131 (2020)
14. Cui, W., Bai, L., Yang, X., Liang, J.: A new contrastive learning framework for reducing the effect of hard negatives. Knowl.-Based Syst. **260**, 110121 (2023)
15. Li, J., Zhou, P., Xiong, C., Hoi, S.C.: Prototypical Contrastive Learning of Unsupervised Representations. arXiv preprint arXiv:2005.04966 (2020)
16. Xie, Q., Dai, Z., Hovy, E., Luong, T., et al.: Unsupervised data augmentation for consistency training. In: Advances in Neural Information Processing Systems. vol. 33, pp. 6256–6268 (2020)
17. McPherson, M., Smith-Lovin, L., Cook, J.M.: Birds of a feather: homophily in social networks. Ann. Rev. Sociol. **27**(1), 415–444 (2001)
18. Fouss, F., Francoisse, K., Yen, L., Pirotte, A., et al.: An experimental investigation of kernels on graphs for collaborative recommendation and semisupervised classification. Neural Netw. **31**, 53–72 (2012)
19. Berthelot, D., Carlini, N., Goodfellow, I., et al.: Mixmatch: A holistic approach to semi-supervised learning. In: NeurIPS (2019)
20. Yang, Z., Cohen, W., Salakhudinov, R.: Revisiting semi-supervised learning with graph embeddings. In: International Conference on Machine Learning, pp. 40–48. PMLR (2016)
21. Chien, E., Peng, J., Li, P., et al.: Adaptive Universal Generalized PageRank Graph Neural Network arXiv preprint arXiv:2006.07988 (2020)
22. Chen, M., Wei, Z., Huang, Z., Ding, B., et al.: Simple and deep graph convolutional networks. In: InInternational Conference on Machine Learning, pp. 1725–1735. PMLR (2020)
23. Hamilton, W., Ying, Z., Leskovec, J.: Inductive representation learning on large graphs. In: Advances in Neural Information Processing Systems. vol. 30 (2017)

Adaptive Weighted Multi-view Evidential Clustering

Zhe Liu[1]($\boxtimes$) (iD), Haojian Huang[2], and Sukumar Letchmunan[1]

[1] Universiti Sains Malaysia, Penang 11800, Malaysia
liuzhe921@gmail.com, zheliu@ieee.org
[2] Harbin Engineering University, Harbin 150001, China

Abstract. Multi-view clustering, which integrates information from different views for better performance, has gained widespread attention. However, the existing clustering methods cannot represent the uncertainty and imprecision in cluster assignment caused by the tendency of clusters to overlap and the diversity among views. To surmount this issue, in this paper, we propose an adaptive weighted multi-view evidential clustering (WMVWC) method based on the framework of belief functions. The proposed WMVEC can be viewed as a multi-view version of conventional evidential c-means clustering. We construct the objective function of WMVEC by integrating the learning of view weights and credal partition into a unified framework, and design an optimization scheme to obtain the optimal results of WMVEC. Specifically, the view weight can measure the contribution of each view in clustering. The credal partition can provide a deeper understanding of the data structure by allowing samples to belong not only to singleton clusters, but also to a union of different singleton clusters, called meta-cluster. Experiment results demonstrate the effectiveness of the proposed WMVEC with respect to other state-of-the-art methods on real-world datasets. The code can be available at link.

Keywords: Evidential clustering · multi-view learning · belief functions · credal partition

1 Introduction

Clustering, as a core paradigm of unsupervised learning, has been widely used in various domains owing to its powerful capacity in data preprocessing [13]. Many representative clustering methods like k-means and fuzzy c-means (FCM) have been invented for single-view data [10]. With the prompt development of information technology, however, single-view data can no longer meet the actual needs, and we are often faced with multi-view data represented by different sources or features. For example, an image can be expressed by multiple feature descriptors, such as LBP, SIFT and HOG. In such situations, the aforementioned classical clustering methods will no longer be applicable.

© The Author(s), under exclusive license to Springer Nature Switzerland AG 2023
L. Iliadis et al. (Eds.): ICANN 2023, LNCS 14257, pp. 265–277, 2023.
https://doi.org/10.1007/978-3-031-44216-2_22

To counter this flaw and explore multi-view data, a load of derivatives of multi-view clustering methods have been emerged. One of the most representative is hard partition-based [2,3,6,15]. For example, Cai et al. [2] suggested a $\ell_{2,1}$ norm-based multi-view k-means clustering, called RMVKM, to learn the weight of each view. Later, Chen et al. [3] developed a two-level variable-weighted k-means (TW-k-means) clustering for multi-view data by introducing two entropy regularizations to adjust the importance of the weights. Based on collaborative learning, Zhang et al. [15] presented a two-level weighted collaborative k-means (TW-Co-k-means) clustering to consider the weight of views and features. However, these multi-view clustering methods all consider that the relationship between objects and clusters is distinct, i.e., an object can only belong to a cluster completely or not.

Unlike hard partition-based clustering methods, fuzzy clustering describes the uncertainty by assigning each object to various singleton clusters with different memberships [11]. Many multi-view methods based on the idea of fuzzy clustering have been developed [4,5,7,14]. Cleuziou et al. [4] proposed collaborative fuzzy clustering for multi-view data, named Co-FKM, whereas it equally considers the contribution of each view. Jiang et al. [7] proposed a weighted view collaborative fuzzy c-means clustering to identify the contributions of different views. Recently, Yang and Sinaga [14] suggested a feature-weighted multi-view FCM based on collaborative learning (Co-FW-MVFCM), which can automatically identify the contribution of each view and feature. Although these methods have achieved reasonable results to some extent, they cannot represent the imprecision in the result. In fact, uncertain and imprecise cluster structure is very ubiquitous in applications, that is, the cluster information of some objects is difficult to distinguish.

To address such issue, a new concept of credal partition based on the theory of belief functions is introduced [8,9]. Credal partition extends the concepts of hard, fuzzy and possibilistic partitions by assigning the objects, not only to singleton clusters, but also to the union of several singleton clusters (called meta-cluster) with different masses of belief. To date, some evidential clustering methods have been developed in the framework of belief functions [9,12]. Evidential c-means (ECM) clustering [9], as the evidential counterpart of FCM, can well characterize uncertain and imprecise cluster structures and derive effective clustering results. Unfortunately, ECM is built upon the assumption of access to single-view data. Hence, how to characterize the uncertainty and imprecision of multi-view data in cluster assignment and improve the clustering performance is an open issue.

In this paper, we propose a new adaptive weighted multi-view evidential clustering (WMVEC) method. Specifically, we introduce view weights to capture the different contributions of each view in clustering and employ entropy regularization to regulate the distribution of view weights.

The main contributions are summarized as follows:

1. Inspired by the theory of belief functions, we propose a novel WMVEC method, which can characterize the uncertainty and imprecision in clustering results.

2. We design the objective function of WMVEC and obtain the weight vector, cluster prototype matrix and credal partition matrix in an alternating optimization way.
3. We conduct extensive experiments on several real-world datasets to verify the superiority of WMVEC with respect to other state-of-the-art methods.

The remainder of this paper is organized as follows. Section 2 proposes the WMVEC method and illustrates its optimization process. In Sect. 3, the effectiveness and practicability of the proposed WMVEC method are analyzed using real-world datasets. Finally, we make a brief conclusion in Sect. 4.

2   Multi-view Evidential Clustering

As mentioned earlier, many real-world applications are currently crowded with multi-view data. However, how to characterize the uncertainty and imprecision in clustering results on such data is still a challenging task. Conventional evidential clustering is no longer adequate for the situations we encounter today.

In this section, we propose a novel adaptive weighted multi-view evidential clustering (WMVEC) method to simultaneously learn the consensus credal partition and the importance of each view.

2.1   Formulation

Given a dataset $\mathcal{X} = \{\mathbf{X}_1, \mathbf{X}_2, \cdots, \mathbf{X}_{\mathcal{H}}\}$ and h-th view is expressed as $\mathbf{X}_h = \{\mathbf{x}_{1,h}, \mathbf{x}_{2,h}, \cdots, \mathbf{x}_{n,h}\} \in \mathbb{R}^{n \times \mathcal{P}_h}$. The objective function of WMVEC can be represented as follows:

$$\mathcal{J}_{WMVEC}(\mathbf{M}, \mathbf{V}, \mathbf{r}) = \sum_{h=1}^{\mathcal{H}} r_h \left(\sum_{i=1}^{n} \sum_{\substack{A_j \subseteq \Omega \\ A_j \neq \emptyset}} |A_j|^{\alpha} m_{ij}^{\beta} \|\mathbf{x}_{i,h} - \bar{\mathbf{v}}_{j,h}\|^2 + \sum_{i=1}^{n} \delta_h^2 m_{i\emptyset}^{\beta} \right) \quad (1)$$

$$+ \lambda \sum_{h=1}^{\mathcal{H}} r_h \ln r_h$$

$$s.t. \sum_{A_j \subseteq \Omega, A_j \neq \emptyset} m_{ij} + m_{i\emptyset} = 1, \quad i = 1, 2, \cdots, n; \quad \sum_{h=1}^{\mathcal{H}} r_h = 1 \quad (2)$$

with

$$\bar{\mathbf{v}}_{j,h} = \frac{1}{|A_j|} \sum_{\omega_k \in A_j} \mathbf{v}_{k,h} \quad (3)$$

where r_h is the view weight of h-th view, m_{ij} is the (i,j)-th element of credal partition matrix $\mathbf{M} \in \mathbb{R}^{n \times 2^c}$ and denotes the mass of belief of i-th object associated to cluster A_j. $\bar{\mathbf{v}}_{j,h}$ is the j-th cluster prototype of h-th view. The parameter λ is used to adjust the distribution of view weights, and parameters α, β and δ

are the same as in ECM. The objective function $\mathcal{J}_{MVEC}$ consists of two parts, the first part is similar to ECM and computes the sum of intra-cluster weighted distances in each view by assigning weights to the views. The second part is a negative weight entropy, which regulates the effect of view weight.

2.2 Optimization

In this subsection, we provide an efficient iterative method to minimize (2). More specifically, we employ the Lagrange optimization method to alternately update one variable while leaving others fixed.

Updating. **M** With **V** and **r** fixed, **M** is computed by Theorem 1.

Theorem 1. *Suppose* $\mathbf{V} = \mathbf{V}^*$ *and* $\mathbf{r} = \mathbf{r}^*$ *are fixed,* $\mathcal{J}_{WMVEC}(\mathbf{M}, \mathbf{V}^*, \mathbf{r}^*)$ *is minimized iff:*

$$m_{ij} = \frac{\left(\sum\limits_{h=1}^{\mathcal{H}} |A_j|^\alpha r_h \|\mathbf{x}_{i,h} - \bar{\mathbf{v}}_{j,h}\|^2 \right)^{-\frac{1}{\beta-1}}}{\left(\sum\limits_{A_z \neq \emptyset} \sum\limits_{h=1}^{\mathcal{H}} |A_j|^\alpha r_h \|\mathbf{x}_{i,h} - \bar{\mathbf{v}}_{z,h}\|^2 \right)^{-\frac{1}{\beta-1}} + \left(\sum\limits_{h=1}^{\mathcal{H}} r_h \delta_h^2 \right)^{-\frac{1}{\beta-1}}} \tag{4}$$

$$m_{i\emptyset} = 1 - \sum\limits_{A_j \neq \emptyset} m_{ij} \tag{5}$$

Proof. We employ Lagrange multipliers τ_i to solve the constrained minimization problem with respect to **M**. The objective function (2) can be rewritten as:

$$\mathcal{J}(\mathbf{M}, \tau_i) = \mathcal{J}_{WMVEC}(\mathbf{M}, \mathbf{V}, \mathbf{r}) - \sum\limits_{i=1}^{n} \tau_i \left(\sum\limits_{\substack{A_j \subseteq \Omega \\ A_j \neq \emptyset}} m_{ij} + m_{i\emptyset} - 1 \right) \tag{6}$$

By differentiating the Lagrangian with respect to the m_{ij}, $m_{i\emptyset}$, and τ_i and setting the derivatives to zero, we obtain:

$$\frac{\partial \mathcal{J}}{\partial m_{ij}} = \beta m_{ij}^{(\beta-1)} \sum\limits_{h=1}^{\mathcal{H}} |A_j|^\alpha r_h \|\mathbf{x}_{i,h} - \bar{\mathbf{v}}_{j,h}\|^2 - \tau_i = 0 \tag{7}$$

$$\frac{\partial \mathcal{J}}{\partial m_{i\emptyset}} = \sum\limits_{h=1}^{\mathcal{H}} \beta r_h \delta_h^2 m_{i\emptyset}^{(\beta-1)} - \tau_i = 0 \tag{8}$$

$$\frac{\partial \mathcal{J}}{\partial \tau_i} = \sum\limits_{A_j \subseteq \Omega, A_j \neq \emptyset} m_{ij} + m_{i\emptyset} - 1 = 0 \tag{9}$$

We thus have from (7):

$$m_{ij} = \left(\frac{\tau_i}{\beta}\right)^{\frac{1}{\beta-1}} \left(\frac{1}{\sum\limits_{h=1}^{\mathcal{H}} |A_j|^{\alpha} r_h \|\mathbf{x}_{i,h} - \bar{\mathbf{v}}_{j,h}\|^2}\right)^{\frac{1}{\beta-1}} \tag{10}$$

$$m_{i\emptyset} = \left(\frac{\tau_i}{\beta}\right)^{\frac{1}{\beta-1}} \left(\frac{1}{\sum\limits_{h=1}^{\mathcal{H}} r_h \delta_h^2}\right)^{\frac{1}{\beta-1}} \tag{11}$$

Using (9)–(11), we can obtain the updating (4)–(5).

Updating. r With $\mathbf{M}$ and $\mathbf{V}$ fixed, $\mathbf{r}$ is computed by Theorem 2.

Theorem 2. *Suppose* $\mathbf{M} = \mathbf{M}^*$ *and* $\mathbf{V} = \mathbf{V}^*$ *are fixed,* $\mathcal{J}_{WMVEC}(\mathbf{M}^*, \mathbf{V}^*, \mathbf{r})$ *is minimized iff:*

$$r_h = \frac{\exp\left(\frac{-\sum\limits_{i=1}^{n}\sum\limits_{\substack{A_j \subseteq \Omega \\ A_j \neq \emptyset}} |A_j|^{\alpha} m_{ij}^{\beta} \|\mathbf{x}_{i,h} - \bar{\mathbf{v}}_{j,h}\|^2 + \sum\limits_{i=1}^{n} \delta_h^2 m_{i\emptyset}^{\beta}}{\lambda}\right)}{\sum\limits_{g=1}^{\mathcal{H}} \exp\left(\frac{-\sum\limits_{i=1}^{n}\sum\limits_{\substack{A_j \subseteq \Omega \\ A_j \neq \emptyset}} |A_j|^{\alpha} m_{ij}^{\beta} \|\mathbf{x}_{i,g} - \bar{\mathbf{v}}_{j,g}\|^2 + \sum\limits_{i=1}^{n} \delta_g^2 m_{i\emptyset}^{\beta}}{\lambda}\right)} \tag{12}$$

Proof. Lagrange multiplier σ is used to solve the constrained minimization problem with respect to $\mathbf{r}$. The objective function (2) becomes:

$$\mathcal{J}(\mathbf{r}, \sigma) = \mathcal{J}_{WMVEC}(\mathbf{M}, \mathbf{V}, \mathbf{r}) - \sigma\left(\sum_{h=1}^{\mathcal{H}} r_h - 1\right) \tag{13}$$

By differentiating the Lagrangian with respect to the r_h and σ setting the derivatives to zero, we obtain:

$$\frac{\partial \mathcal{J}}{\partial r_h} = \sum_{i=1}^{n}\sum_{\substack{A_j \subseteq \Omega \\ A_j \neq \emptyset}} |A_j|^{\alpha} m_{ij}^{\beta} \|\mathbf{x}_{i,h} - \bar{\mathbf{v}}_{j,h}\|^2 + \sum_{i=1}^{n} \delta_h^2 m_{i\emptyset}^{\beta} + \lambda\left(1 + \ln r_h\right) - \sigma = 0 \tag{14}$$

$$\frac{\partial \mathcal{J}}{\partial \sigma} = \sum_{h=1}^{\mathcal{H}} r_h - 1 = 0 \tag{15}$$

We thus have from (14):

$$r_h = \exp\left(\frac{\sigma - \lambda}{\lambda}\right) \exp\left(\frac{-\sum_{i=1}^{n} \sum_{\substack{A_j \subseteq \Omega \\ A_j \neq \emptyset}} |A_j|^\alpha m_{ij}^\beta \|\mathbf{x}_{i,h} - \bar{\mathbf{v}}_{j,h}\|^2 + \sum_{i=1}^{n} \delta_h^2 m_{i\emptyset}^\beta}{\lambda}\right)$$

(16)

Using (15)–(16), we can obtain the updating (12).

Updating. **V** *while fixing* **M** *and* **r** With **M** and **r** fixed, **V** is computed by Theorem 3.

Theorem 3. *Suppose* $\mathbf{M} = \mathbf{M}^*$ *and* $\mathbf{r} = \mathbf{r}^*$ *are fixed,* $\mathcal{J}_{WMVEC}(\mathbf{M}^*, \mathbf{V}, \mathbf{r}^*)$ *is minimized iff:*

$$B_{lq,h} \triangleq \sum_{i=1}^{n} x_{iq,h} \sum_{A_j \ni \omega_l} |A_j|^{\alpha-1} m_{ij}^\beta, \ \forall l = 1, c, \ \forall q = 1, \mathcal{P}_h$$

(17)

$$H_{lk,h} \triangleq \sum_{i=1}^{n} \sum_{A_j \supseteq \{\omega_k, \omega_l\}} |A_j|^{\alpha-2} m_{ij}^\beta, \ \forall k, l = 1, c$$

(18)

$$\mathbf{H}_h \mathbf{V}_h = \mathbf{B}_h$$

(19)

where $B_{lq,h}$ *(resp.* $H_{lk,h}$*) is the* l, q*-th (resp.* l, k*-th) element of the matrix* $\mathbf{B}_h \in \mathbb{R}^{c \times \mathcal{P}_h}$ *(resp.* $\mathbf{H}_h \in \mathbb{R}^{c \times c}$*).*

Proof. The partial derivatives of $\mathcal{J}_{WMVEC}$ with respect to the cluster centers are given by:

$$\frac{\partial \mathcal{J}}{\partial \mathbf{v}_{l,h}} = \sum_{i=1}^{n} \sum_{A_j \neq \emptyset} |A_j|^\alpha r_h m_{ij}^\beta \frac{\partial D_{ij,h}^2}{\partial \mathbf{v}_{l,h}}$$

(20)

$$\frac{\partial D_{ij,h}^2}{\partial \mathbf{v}_{l,h}} = -\frac{2}{|A_j|}\left(\mathbf{x}_{i,h} - \frac{1}{|A_j|}\sum_{A_j \ni \omega_l} \mathbf{v}_{l,h}\right)$$

(21)

where

$$D_{ij,h}^2 = \|\mathbf{x}_{i,h} - \bar{\mathbf{v}}_{j,h}\|^2$$

(22)

Setting these derivatives to zero gives c linear equations that can be written as:

$$\sum_{i=1}^{n} \mathbf{x}_{i,h} \sum_{A_j \ni \omega_l} |A_j|^{\alpha-1} r_h m_{ij}^\beta = \sum_{k=1}^{c} \mathbf{v}_{k,h} \sum_{i=1}^{N} \sum_{A_j \supseteq \{\omega_k, \omega_l\}} |A_j|^{\alpha-2} r_h m_{ij}^\beta$$

(23)

The system of linear equations can be equally represented by (17) and (18).

For the convenience of implementation, the proposed WMVEC method is outlined in Algorithm 1.

Algorithm 1: Weighted Multi-View Evidential Clustering

Input: Multi-view data $\mathcal{X} = \{\mathcal{X}_1, \cdots, \mathcal{X}_{\mathcal{H}}\}$, $\mathcal{X}_h \in \mathbb{R}^{\mathcal{P}_h \times n}$, number of clusters c, and parameters α, β, λ, δ

Output: The optimal **M**, **V**, **r**

1 Initialize $\mathbf{V}^0$, and $\mathbf{r}^0$;
2 **while** *not converge* **do**
3 | Compute the prototypes of meta-clusters utilizing (3);
4 | Update the credal partition matrix **M** utilizing (4)-(5);
5 | Update the view weight vector **r** utilizing (12);
6 | Compute matrices **B** and **H** utilizing (17)-(18);
7 | Update the cluster prototype matrix **V** utilizing (19);
8 **end**

2.3 Computational Complexity

The computational complexity of ECM is $O(tn2^c)$, where t is the number of iterations, n and c represent the number of objects and clusters respectively. WMVEC is an extension of ECM in multi-view scenarios by introducing view weights. Therefore, the computational complexity of WMVEC is $O(t\mathcal{H}n2^c)$, and $\mathcal{H}$ is the number of views. It is worth noting that the number of clusters grows exponentially with the computational complexity, and the assignment of objects to high-cardinality meta-clusters is challenging to interpret in practice. Therefore, we can consider imposing constraints to limit the number of focal elements in the meta-cluster, for example, like in ECM, to keep only the meta-cluster containing two clusters. For higher cluster datasets, we can restrict the framework of discernment to consist of only singleton clusters, empty set, and Ω. By doing so, the computational complexity of WMVEC can be reduced to $O(t\mathcal{H}nc^2)$ and $O(t\mathcal{H}n(c+2))$.

3 Experiments

3.1 Experiment on Iris Dataset

In this experiment, we demonstrate the ability of credal partition in WMVEC on the Iris[1] dataset. The Iris dataset contains 150 objects with 3 clusters, where each object consists of four features (Sepal.Length, Sepal.Width, Petal.Length and Petal.Width). We split the Iris dataset into three views by different features, as shown in Fig. 1(a), (e), (i). We can see that $\{\omega_1\}$ is clearly distinguished from $\{\omega_2\}$ and $\{\omega_3\}$, whereas $\{\omega_2\}$ and $\{\omega_3\}$ are partially overlapped, and view 3 is much easier to distinguish between $\{\omega_2\}$ and $\{\omega_3\}$ than the other two views.

From Fig. 1(b)–(d), (f)–(h), (j)–(l), we can observe that WMVEC can clearly characterize the imprecision and uncertainty of cluster assignment. It carefully assigned indistinguishable objects to relevant meta-cluster (*i.e.* $\{\omega_2, \omega_3\}$). What

---

[1] https://archive.ics.uci.edu/ml/datasets/Iris/.

is more, the parameter α determines the size of the meta-cluster. A large α tends to correspond to lower imprecision and higher error, and vice versa. In applications, α should be adjusted according to the specific situation or user preferences. In the following experiments, we take $\alpha = 2$, as suggested in [9].

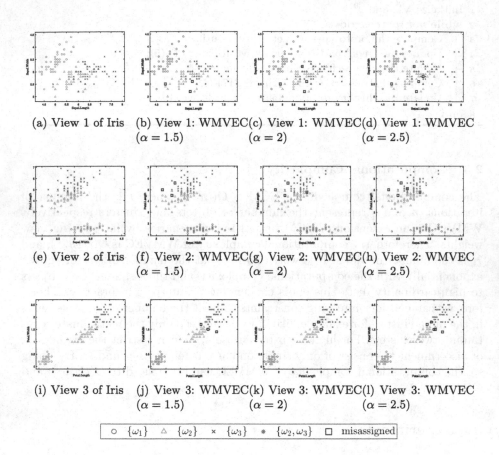

(a) View 1 of Iris   (b) View 1: WMVEC   (c) View 1: WMVEC   (d) View 1: WMVEC
                       ($\alpha = 1.5$)   ($\alpha = 2$)   ($\alpha = 2.5$)

(e) View 2 of Iris   (f) View 2: WMVEC   (g) View 2: WMVEC   (h) View 2: WMVEC
                       ($\alpha = 1.5$)   ($\alpha = 2$)   ($\alpha = 2.5$)

(i) View 3 of Iris   (j) View 3: WMVEC   (k) View 3: WMVEC   (l) View 3: WMVEC
                       ($\alpha = 1.5$)   ($\alpha = 2$)   ($\alpha = 2.5$)

| ○ $\{\omega_1\}$ | △ $\{\omega_2\}$ | × $\{\omega_3\}$ | * $\{\omega_2, \omega_3\}$ | □ misassigned |

Fig. 1. Clustering results of Iris dataset.

3.2   Experiments on Real-World Multi-view Datasets

To verify the validity of the proposed method with respect to other methods, we constructed experiments on eight public multi-view datasets, including WebKB[2], Multiple features[3], Prokaryotic Phyla [1], SensIT Vehicle[4], HumanEva 3D Motion [1] and MSRCv1 [14]. Table 1 shows the basic information of the

---

[2] http://www.cs.cmu.edu/afs/cs.cmu.edu/project/theo-20/www/data/.
[3] https://archive.ics.uci.edu/ml/datasets/Multiple+Features.
[4] https://www.csie.ntu.edu.tw/\$sim\$cjlin/libsvmtools/datasets/.

used multi-view datasets, including the numbers of objects, clusters, views and features.

Table 1. The details of the used real-world datasets

Dataset	Objects	Clusters	Views	Views name	Features
WebKB (WebKB)	203	4	3	The text on web pages	1703
				The anchor text in hyperlinks	203
				The text in the title	203
Multiple features (MF)	2000	10	6	Fourier coefficients	76
				Profile correlations	216
				Karhunen-Love coefficients	64
				Pixel averages	240
				Zernike moments	47
				Morphological features	6
Prokaryotic Phyla (ProP)	551	4	3	Gabor	393
				Wavelet moments	3
				CENTRIST	438
SensIT Vehicle (SensIT)	300	3	2	Acoustic	50
				Seismic	50
HumanEva 3D Motion (Motion)	5000	5	2	X1_person	48
				X2_person	48
MSRCv1 (MSRCv1)	210	7	4	Color moment	24
				GIST	512
				LBP	256
				CENTRIST	254

We compare the performance of the proposed WMVEC method with respect to a number of related methods, which are shown as follows: FCM [11], ECM [9], Co-FKM [4], RMVKM [2], TW-k-means [3], SMVF [6], TW-Co-k-means [15], Co-FW-MVFCM [14] and MVASM [5]. Among them, FCM and ECM are two classical single-view clustering methods, RMVKM, TW-k-means, SMVF and TW-Co-k-means are representative multi-view clustering methods based on hard partition, Co-FKM, Co-FW-MVFCM and MVASM are state-of-art methods based on fuzzy partition. In order to fully evaluate the performance of the above mentioned methods, we applied two popular performance metrics[5], namely Accuracy (ACC) and Rand Index (RI). Note that the larger values of ACC and RI correspond to better clustering performance.

Table 2 and Table 3 show the clustering results of WMVEC and other methods on real-world datasets. Specifically, several points can be drawn from the observation.

---

[5] For credal partition, we can obtain a hard or fuzzy partition by Pignistic probability transformation [9].

1. Compared with single-view clustering methods (*i.e.* FCM and ECM), WMVEC generally has obvious advantages, which indicates that it is not appropriate to use single-view clustering methods to deal with multi-view data. Besides, we can see that on the second view of the Prop dataset, FCM and ECM both achieve relatively good results, however, these results are physically meaningless.
2. Compared with the multi-view clustering method, the proposed WMVEC achieves better performance compared to other methods. In particular, the clustering methods considering view weights can often obtain better results, which further demonstrates the rationality of introducing view weights.
3. More importantly, the advantage of WMVEC is not only that it can be transformed into hard or fuzzy partition to obtain outstanding performance, but WMVEC with credal partition can also offer deeper insight into the data. It can effectively characterize the uncertainty and imprecision in cluster assignment and avoid the risk of misassignment, which is very valuable in some cautious decision-making applications.

Table 2. Clustering results with various multi-view datasets on *ACC*

Method	Dataset					
	WebKB	MF	ProP	SensIT	Motion	MSRCv1
FCM(1)	0.5110	0.2005	0.4781	0.4699	0.6785	0.2877
FCM(2)	0.4923	0.1971	0.5448	0.3687	0.4246	0.2912
FCM(3)	0.7340	0.2859	0.3354	-	-	0.3798
FCM(4)	-	0.6643	-	-	-	0.3310
FCM(5)	-	0.2027	-	-	-	-
FCM(6)	-	0.2006	-	-	-	-
ECM(1)	0.6124	0.3402	0.5384	0.5097	0.4855	0.2861
ECM(2)	0.5312	0.2766	0.5783	0.3720	0.4832	0.4204
ECM(3)	0.6158	0.3429	0.5515	-	-	0.3692
ECM(4)	-	0.3564	-	-	-	0.3418
ECM(5)	-	0.3623	-	-	-	-
ECM(6)	-	0.3190	-	-	-	-
Co-FKM	0.4709	0.5240	0.4773	0.4567	0.5288	0.4440
RMVKM	0.5418	0.7926	0.5235	0.4769	0.7994	0.5437
TW-*k*-means	0.5387	0.7609	0.5576	0.4902	0.6959	0.6052
SWVF	0.5468	0.7745	0.5620	0.5075	0.7056	0.6121
TW-Co-*k*-means	0.6109	0.8188	0.5661	0.5139	0.7124	0.6335
Co-FW-MVFCM	0.6946	0.7410	0.5408	0.5133	0.6870	0.5857
MVASM	0.7161	0.6310	0.4993	0.4796	0.7347	0.5381
WMVEC	**0.7586**	**0.8300**	**0.5789**	**0.5667**	**0.8952**	**0.7619**

3.3 Parameter Study

Finally, we also tested the parameter sensitivity of WMVEC. The ACC and RI results with different parameters β and λ are shown in Fig. 2 and Fig. 3. We take β that varies in $\{1.1, 1.2, \cdots, 2.0\}$ and λ that varies in $\{e^0, e^1, \cdots, e^{10}\}$. It can be seen that the values of β and λ have a significant impact on the performance of the WMVEC. For each dataset, the WMVEC can gain better results if appropriate β and λ can be selected. In addition, we can clearly see that the WMVEC can often obtain better results with smaller β and larger λ.

Table 3. Clustering results with various multi-view datasets on RI

Method	Dataset					
	WebKB	MF	ProP	SensIT	Motion	MSRCv1
FCM(1)	0.6206	0.5733	0.5709	0.5279	0.8217	0.6566
FCM(2)	0.5110	0.5527	0.6360	0.5121	0.6301	0.5539
FCM(3)	0.6872	0.6921	0.5449	-	-	0.7573
FCM(4)	-	0.9144	-	-	-	0.7591
FCM(5)	-	0.5718	-	-	-	-
FCM(6)	-	0.5519	-	-	-	-
ECM(1)	0.5483	0.7265	0.4242	0.5924	0.6702	0.6327
ECM(2)	0.4042	0.5622	**0.6442**	0.5287	0.6639	0.6993
ECM(3)	0.5398	0.7271	0.4121	-	-	0.6961
ECM(4)	-	0.7584	-	-	-	0.6882
ECM(5)	-	0.7701	-	-	-	-
ECM(6)	-	0.7368	-	-	-	-
Co-FKM	0.6174	0.8714	0.6041	0.5781	0.7667	0.7879
RMVKM	0.6678	0.9499	0.6151	0.5879	0.8969	0.8305
TW-k-means	0.4131	0.9453	0.6356	0.5516	0.8453	0.8500
SWVF	0.4078	0.9347	0.5411	0.5776	0.8420	0.8490
TW-Co-k-means	0.5464	0.9590	0.6374	0.5689	0.8592	0.8608
Co-FW-MVFCM	0.6410	0.9231	0.6280	0.5873	0.8313	0.8535
MVASM	0.7097	0.9059	0.5832	0.5494	0.8482	0.8345
WMVEC	**0.7361**	**0.9560**	0.6414	**0.6029**	**0.9282**	**0.8929**

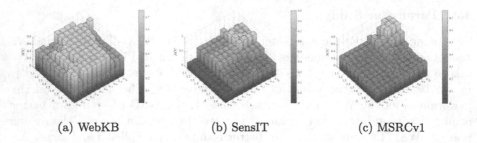

(a) WebKB   (b) SensIT   (c) MSRCv1

Fig. 2. Clustering results of multi-view datasets in terms of *ACC*.

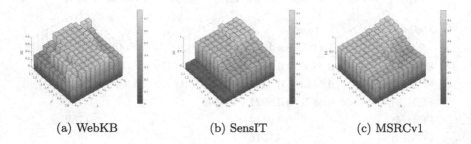

(a) WebKB   (b) SensIT   (c) MSRCv1

Fig. 3. Clustering results of multi-view datasets in terms of *RI*.

4   Conclusion

In this paper, we propose an adaptive weighted multi-view evidential clustering (WMVEC) based on the framework of belief functions. As such, WMVEC is able to handle the uncertainty and imprecision of multi-view data clustering, and provides a credal partition, which extends the fuzzy, possibilistic and rough ones, allowing the representation of the imprecision and uncertainty about the assignment of objects to clusters. What is more, WMVEC can automatically learn the importance of views. Experimental results on several real-world datasets illustrate the potential and superiority of our proposed method. In future studies, we intend to extend the proposed method to deal with mixed types of data as well as incomplete data.

References

1. Benjamin, J.B.M., Yang, M.S.: Weighted multiview possibilistic c-means clustering with L2 regularization. IEEE Trans. Fuzzy Syst. **30**(5), 1357–1370 (2022)
2. Cai, X., Nie, F., Huang, H.: Multi-view k-means clustering on big data. In: IJCAI (2013)
3. Chen, X., Xu, X., Huang, J.Z., Ye, Y.: TW-k-means: automated two-level variable weighting clustering algorithm for multiview data. IEEE Trans. Knowl. Data Eng. **25**(4), 932–944 (2013)

4. Cleuziou, G., Exbrayat, M., Martin, L., Sublemontier, J.H.: CoFKM: a centralized method for multiple-view clustering. In: ICDM, pp. 752–757 (2009)
5. Han, J., Xu, J., Nie, F., Li, X.: Multi-view k-means clustering with adaptive sparse memberships and weight allocation. IEEE Trans. Knowl. Data Eng. **34**(2), 816–827 (2022)
6. Jiang, B., Qiu, F., Wang, L.: Multi-view clustering via simultaneous weighting on views and features. Appl. Soft Comput. **47**, 304–315 (2016)
7. Jiang, Y., Chung, F.L., Wang, S., Deng, Z., Wang, J., Qian, P.: Collaborative fuzzy clustering from multiple weighted views. IEEE Trans. Cybern. **45**(4), 688–701 (2015)
8. Liu, Z.: An effective conflict management method based on belief similarity measure and entropy for multi-sensor data fusion. Artif. Intell. Rev. 1–28 (2023)
9. Masson, M.H., Denœux, T.: ECM: an evidential version of the fuzzy C-means algorithm. Pattern Recognit. **41**(4), 1384–1397 (2008)
10. Oyewole, G.J., Thopil, G.A.: Data clustering: application and trends. Artif. Intell. Rev. **56**(7), 6439–6475 (2023)
11. Ruspini, E.H., Bezdek, J.C., Keller, J.M.: Fuzzy clustering: a historical perspective. IEEE Comput. Intell. Mag. **14**(1), 45–55 (2019)
12. Su, Z., Denœux, T.: BPEC: belief-peaks evidential clustering. IEEE Trans. Fuzzy Syst. **27**(1), 111–123 (2019)
13. Xu, R., Wunsch, D.: Survey of clustering algorithms. IEEE Trans. Neural Netw. **16**(3), 645–678 (2005)
14. Yang, M.S., Sinaga, K.P.: Collaborative feature-weighted multi-view fuzzy c-means clustering. Pattern Recognit. **119**, 108064 (2021)
15. Zhang, G., Wang, C., Huang, D., Zheng, W., Zhou, Y.: TW-co-k-means: two-level weighted collaborative k-means for multi-view clustering. Knowl.-Based Syst. **150**, 127–138 (2018)

An Untrained Neural Model for Fast and Accurate Graph Classification

Nicolò Navarin[1]([✉])[iD], Luca Pasa[1][iD], Claudio Gallicchio[2][iD],
and Alessandro Sperduti[1,3][iD]

[1] University of Padua, Via Trieste 63, 35121 Padua, Italy
{nicolo.navarin,luca.pasa,alessandro.sperduti}@unipd.it
[2] University of Pisa, Largo Bruno Pontecorvo 3, 56127 Pisa, Italy
gallicch@di.unipi.it
[3] University of Trento - DISI, Trento, Italy

Abstract. Recent works have proven the feasibility of fast and accurate time series classification methods based on randomized convolutional kernels [5,32]. Concerning graph-structured data, the majority of randomized graph neural networks are based on the Echo State Network paradigm in which single layers or the whole network present some form of recurrence [7,8].

This paper aims to explore a simple form of a randomized graph neural network inspired by the success of randomized convolutions in the 1-dimensional domain. Our idea is pretty simple: implement a no-frills convolutional graph neural network and leave its weights untrained. Then, we aggregate the node representations with global pooling operators, obtaining an untrained graph-level representation. Since there is no training involved, computing such representation is extremely fast. We then apply a fast linear classifier to the obtained representations. We opted for LS-SVM since it is among the fastest classifiers available. We show that such a simple approach can obtain competitive predictive performance while being extremely efficient both at training and inference time.

Keywords: Graph Neural Network · Graph Convolution · Reservoir Computing · Structured Data · Machine Learning on Graphs · Deep Randomized Neural Networks

1 Introduction

In this paper, we develop efficient graph neural networks for graph classification. When dealing with machine learning for structured data, there are typically two distinct families of tasks that can be tackled that have to be addressed with different neural architectures. The first task is node property prediction (e.g., *node* classification) which is defined as predicting one or more values associated with each node in a graph. Graph Neural Networks (GNNs) have shown promising performance on such tasks [27]. The second task is graph property prediction (e.g., *graph* classification), in which the property that has to be predicted is a global property of a graph. In this case, the training set is composed of a set of graphs, each with the corresponding associated label. Such tasks require the inclusion of additional components in the GNN architecture, allowing the transformation of a set of node-wise representations to a single graph-level one before performing the prediction.

While many different architectures for node and graph classification have been proposed in the literature, most of the proposals have in common the end-to-end nature of their training, which results in fairly high computational complexity. Recently, in order to circumvent the need for expensive end-to-end training, a family of neural network models that are highly efficient to train have been receiving increasing attention. Most proposals along these lines so far have focused on the study of dynamic systems on discrete graphs in the area of Reservoir Computing (RC) [20,22]. In this case, a reservoir layer randomly initialized under asymptotic stability constraints, and left untrained, is responsible for computing the encoding of each node, while training is restricted only to the output *readout* layer [7,8]. However, although this approach enables learning tasks on graphs in an extremely efficient way, it involves a fixed-point convergence process of the dynamic reservoir layer on the graph. This process, in turn, requires a number of iterations that can undermine the overall efficiency of the approach. More recently, it has been shown [15,28] that the randomized approach on graphs can also be exploited without resorting to an iterative process. In particular, it is possible to perform node classification using randomized graph convolutions, i.e., without the necessity of training the convolution parameters, and still obtain competitive predictive performance when training is restricted to the readout part, as in RC-based approaches. While recently the approach has been proven feasible for tasks defined on graph nodes, it is still unclear if it also applies to graph classification tasks. This research question is not straightforward since the aggregation layer tends to lose a significant amount of information. A similar problem was already tackled in the case of randomized convolutions for time series analysis in a recent work [5].

In this paper, we show that by paying attention to some core aspects of the network architecture, it is possible to define a very efficient, randomized GNN model for graph classification tasks. Such critical components are: 1. the presence of non-linearity between graph convolution layers; 2. the adoption of a *good* aggregation scheme; 3. a wise initialization of the network weights. We analyze each one of these critical aspects in our ablation studies and show how each component influences the resulting predictive performance of the model. We refer to our proposed model as Untrained-GCN or U-GCN, acknowledging the intuitions behind it to come from the worlds of randomized neural networks and graph convolutional networks.

The rest of this paper is organized as follows. In Sect. 2 we introduce some background concepts that are necessary to present our contribution in Sect. 3. In Sect. 4 we present and discuss our experimental comparisons and ablation studies. Section 5 concludes the paper.

2   Background

In the following, we use italic letters to refer to variables, bold lowercase letters to refer to vectors, and bold uppercase letters to refer to matrices. The elements of a matrix $\mathbf{A}$ are referred to as a_{ij} (and similarly for vectors). We use uppercase letters to refer to sets or tuples.

Let $G = (V, E, \mathbf{X})$ be a graph, where $V = \{v_0, \ldots, v_{n-1}\}$ denotes the set of vertices (or nodes) of the graph, $E \subseteq V \times V$ is the set of edges and $\mathbf{X} \in \mathbb{R}^{n \times s}$ is a multivariate signal on the graph nodes with the i-th row representing the attributes of v_i. We define $\mathbf{A} \in \mathbb{R}^{n \times n}$ as the adjacency matrix of the graph, with elements $a_{ij} = 1 \iff (v_i, v_j) \in E$. With $\mathcal{N}(v)$ we denote the set of nodes adjacent to node v.

2.1   Graph Neural Networks

As a machine learning model for graph problems, graph neural networks [12,33, 34] have emerged in recent years. A Graph Neural Network (GNN) is a model that exploits the structure of the graph and the information embedded in feature vectors of each node to learn a representation $\mathbf{h}_v \in \mathbb{R}^m$ for each vertex $v \in V$. In many GNN models, the computation of $\mathbf{h}_v$ can be divided into two main steps: *aggregate* and *combine*. We can define aggregation and combination by using two functions, $\mathcal{A}$ and $\mathcal{C}$, respectively: $\mathbf{h}_v = \mathcal{C}(\mathcal{L}(v), \mathcal{A}(\{\mathcal{X}(u) : u \in \mathcal{N}(v)\}))$.

The kind of aggregation function $\mathcal{A}$ and combination function $\mathcal{C}$ determinate the type of *Graph Convolution (GC)* adopted by the GNN. The first model that relies on graph convolutions was proposed by Micheli *et al.* in 2019 [21]. Recently, many novel GCs base models have been proposed [4,13,18,19,37,39].

The model proposed in this paper is built on top of one of the most common and widely adopted GC operators: the GCN [18]

$$\mathbf{H}^{(i)} = \mathcal{F}\left(\mathbf{S}\,\mathbf{H}^{(i-1)}\mathbf{W}^{(i)}\right), i > 1 \tag{1}$$

where $\mathbf{S} = \tilde{\mathbf{D}}^{-\frac{1}{2}}(\mathbf{I} + \mathbf{A})\tilde{\mathbf{D}}^{-\frac{1}{2}}$, $\mathbf{A}$ denotes the standard adjacency matrix of the graph G and $\tilde{\mathbf{D}}$ the diagonal degree matrix with the diagonal elements defined as $\tilde{d}_{ii} = 1 + \sum_j a_{ij}$. Further, $\mathbf{H}^{(i)} \in \mathbb{R}^{n \times m_i}$ is the matrix containing the representation $\mathbf{h}_v^{(i)}$ of all nodes in the graph (one per row) at layer i, $\mathbf{W}^{(i)} \in \mathbb{R}^{m_{i-1} \times m_i}$ denotes the matrix of the layer's parameters, and $\mathcal{F}$ is the element-wise (usually, nonlinear) activation function.

2.2   Graph Neural Networks with Random Weights

In structured data domains, the models proposed in the last few years show increasing complexity, leading to novel architectures with a considerably high number of parameters. Unfortunately, this implies a high computational cost, especially in training the models.

For sequential data, many efficient architectures rely on the Reservoir Computing (RC) paradigm [20], which is based on exploiting fixed (randomized) values of the recurrent weights. The random weights are defined following the Echo State Property (ESP) [17] that ensures stability conditions of the dynamical system. In particular, the Echo State Networks (ESN) [17] are widely used when an efficient recursive model is required.

Gallicchio et al. in [7] proposed in 2010 the first model for graph domain that exploits RC framework. The proposed model, dubbed GraphESN is composed of a non-linear reservoir and a feed-forward linear readout. The reservoir computes a fixed recurrent encoding function over the whole nodes of the graph as follows:

$$\mathbf{h}_v[t+1] = f(\mathbf{W}_{in}\mathbf{x}_v + \sum_{u \in \mathcal{N}(v)} \hat{\mathbf{W}}_h \mathbf{h}_u[t]), \tag{2}$$

where $\mathbf{W}_{in} \in \mathbb{R}^{m \times s}$, and $\hat{\mathbf{W}}_h \in \mathbb{R}^{m \times m}$. For each vertex $v \in V$, $\mathbf{h}_v[0]$ is initialized to $\mathbf{0} \in \mathbb{R}^m$. The computation of the global state $\mathbf{h}_v[t^*]$ involves the iteration of Eq. (2) till $|\mathbf{h}_v[t^* + 1] - \mathbf{h}_v[t^*]| \leq \epsilon$. Then, the global state is used by the readout of the model to compute the output using a linear projection:

$$\mathbf{o} = \mathbf{W}_{out} \sum_{v \in V} \mathbf{h}_v[t^*]. \tag{3}$$

in 2020 an evolution of the GraphESN was introduced in [8]. The FDGNN (Fast and Deep GNN) model constructs a progressively more abstract neural representation of the input graph by stacking successive layers of GNN. The formulation of this model is reminiscent of the original formulation of GNN [33], but the parameters of each layer are initialized by taking into account some stability constraints and then left untrained. The GC-layer i computes, $\forall v \in V$, the following equations:

$$\mathbf{h}_v^{(i)}[0] = \mathbf{h}_v^{(i-1)}[t_v^{(i-1)*}],$$
$$\mathbf{h}_v^{(i+1)}[t] = tanh(\mathbf{W}_{in}^{(i)}\mathbf{x}_v + \sum_{u \in \mathcal{N}(v)} \mathbf{W}_h^{(i)}\mathbf{h}_u^{(i)}[t-1])$$

where $\mathbf{h}_v^{(i-1)}[t_v^{(i-1)*}]$ is the state computed by the previous layer. This equation is iterated for each node till convergence or till a maximum predetermined maximum number of iterations T is reached. Regarding the readout, the FDGNN computes a graph-level representation based only on the node representations computed on the last convolutional layer of the architecture. For k GC-layers, the output is defined as $\mathbf{o} = \mathbf{W}_{out}tanh(\mathbf{W}_n \sum_{v \in V} \mathbf{h}_v^{(k)}[t_v^{(k)*}])$. Further evolution of this kind of model is proposed in [7] where the Graph Ring-reservoir Network (GRN) is introduced. The GRN simplifies the FDGNN, based on a particular organization of the hidden neurons. In particular, it exploits a particular reservoir with a ring topology so that each neuron propagates its activation to the successive one (and is fed by the previous one) in a single cycle (ring). This is implemented by multiplying the reservoir weight matrix by a permutation matrix $\mathbf{P}$, obtaining $\mathbf{h}_v[t+1] = tanh(\mathbf{W}\mathbf{x}_v + \lambda\mathbf{P}\sum_{u\in\mathcal{N}(v)}\mathbf{h}_u[t])$, where λ is a scalar hyper-parameter and all non-zero weights are set to the same value. thank this λ can be used to contról the spectral radius of the reservoir weights matrix $\mathbf{W}_r = \lambda\cdot\mathbf{P}$. Regarding the readout, the model uses the same linear feedforward layer defined in Eq. (3).

In [7] an even more simplified model is introduced: the Minimal Graph Network (MGN). Also, in this case, the reservoir weights are arranged in a ring shape. The main difference with the GRN lies in a further architectural simplification applied to the matrix $\mathbf{W}$ where all the entries are set to the value ω, while their signs are chosen following the idea of "minimal complexity" [31].

In [28], the authors propose a model, dubbed Multi-resolution Reservoir Graph Neural Network (MRGNN) model, that exploits a Reservoir Convolutional layer for graphs able to simultaneously and directly consider all topological receptive fields up to $k - hops$. The convolutional layer relies on a multi-resolution [3,29] structure that exploits nonlinear neurons followed by a standard feed-forward readout. The multi-resolution reservoir is defined as follows: $\mathbf{H}^r = \mathbf{H}^{k,\mathcal{T}}\mathbf{W}^r$, where $\mathbf{H}^{k,\mathcal{T}} = [\underbrace{\mathbf{XW}}_{\mathbf{H}^{k,\mathcal{T}}_{(0)}}, \underbrace{\sigma(\tilde{\mathbf{A}}\mathbf{XW})}_{\mathbf{H}^{k,\mathcal{T}}_{(1)}}, \underbrace{\sigma(\tilde{\mathbf{A}}\sigma(\tilde{\mathbf{A}}\mathbf{XW})\mathbf{W}))}_{\mathbf{H}^{k,\mathcal{T}}_{(2)}}, \ldots], \sigma$ is

the $tanh$ activation function, $\tilde{\mathbf{A}}$ is is a generic transformation of the adjacency matrix that preserves its shape, $\mathbf{W}^r$ is a randomly projection matrix and $\mathbf{H}^{k,\mathcal{T}}_{(i)}$ represents the i-th column block of $\mathbf{H}^{k,\mathcal{T}}$. Note that each $\mathbf{H}^{k,\mathcal{T}}_{(i)}$ contains information only about random walks of length exactly equal to i.

Recently, Huang et al. [15] explored randomized graph convolutions for the task of node classification (differently from this paper in which we consider the more challenging setting of graph classification). The authors propose a single-layer architecture defined as $Z = \sigma(A^2XW)\beta$, where σ is the sigmoid function, $W \in \mathbb{R}^{d\times m}$ is the (random) wight matrix for m hidden neurons (that is left untrained), and β are the trained output weights. Notice that, contrarily to many graph neural networks, authors propose to adopt a single hidden layer with an increased receptive field instead of non-linearly stacking multiple layers with a smaller receptive field.

2.3 Untrained Convolutions for Time Series

The design of deep randomized neural networks represents one of the emerging topics in Deep Learning (see, e.g., [10]). The fundamental idea behind these approaches is to replace as much as possible the optimization of the parameters of a deep learning model with their randomization [30]. This usually results in a neural architecture in which hidden layers are initialized randomly and left untrained, while training algorithms operate only on the output *readout* layer. It is interesting to note how this paradigm, on the one hand, allows for the design of extremely efficient baselines while, on the other hand, allows for highlighting and exploiting the architectural biases of neural information processing models. Another advantage of this approach is its marked suitability for implementations in neuromorphic hardware [36] and, in general, in hardware with low computational resources, e.g., for AI applications of a pervasive nature [1].

When dealing with temporal information, i.e., for sequence processing, the paradigm of choice in this context is represented by Reservoir Computing (RC) [20], and in particular Echo State Networks [16,17]. Here, the crucial idea is to build an RNN whose internal connections are randomly initialized under asymptotic stability constraints. As an alternative to the RC recurrent approach, the idea of exploiting randomized convolutions has recently been explored for time series analysis in the ROCKET model [5]. ROCKET is a method based on randomized one-dimensional convolutions for efficient feature extraction on time series, performing consistently well on a diverse range of datasets. The core contributions of the ROCKET model were: 1. showing that the approach of exploiting randomized convolutional kernels (instead of learning them with backpropagation) is feasible; 2. the adoption of a new non-differentiable read-out function that being associated with the more commonly adopted global max pooling showed an improvement in the overall predictive performance. The paper also empirically identified a core set of hyper-parameters that were shown to obtain good predictive performance on heterogeneous tasks. However, the hyper-parameters of the features extraction procedure remain of utmost importance, especially considering that there is no learning involved.

3   Untrained GCN for Graph Classification

In this section, we present our model for efficient graph classification. We start in Sect. 3.1 detailing our graph convolution layers and how they are combined. Then, in Sect. 3.2 we describe the pooling operators we adopt, and finally in Sect. 3.3 we describe the readout and the possible alternatives.

3.1   Untrained GCN Feature Extraction

As previously discussed in Sect. 2.2, recent results in literature have shown that for the task of semi-supervised node classification, graph neural networks with random weights are a feasible option. However, it is known in the literature that for the problem of node classification, even simple models perform well [24–26]. In this paper, we propose a randomized architecture that is inspired by fully trained graph neural networks, including the non-linearity scheme. In particular, we instantiate multiple graph convolution layers (see Sect. 2.1), each one followed by an element-wise non-linear activation function.

Following the literature on untrained neural networks we decided to exploit the hyperbolic tangent activation function. We considered the simple and widespread GCN definition (see Sect. 2.1). The hidden node representation computed by the l-th layer is defined as:

$$\mathbf{H}^{(l)} = tanh(\mathbf{SH}^{(l-1)}\mathbf{W}^{(l)}), \tag{4}$$

where $\mathbf{S}$ is the normalized Laplacian adopted by the GCN, $\mathbf{W}^{(l)}$ are the layer parameters and $\mathbf{H}^0 = \mathbf{X}$. Note that we omit the bias terms for the sake of simplicity. The final node representations are obtained concatenating the representation computed by each graph convolution layer, i.e. $H = [H^{(1)}, \ldots, H^{(L)}]$, where L is the number of layers of the network.

While we leave as a future work the exploration of other activation functions, in our ablation studies we consider the network without activation functions between layers and show that the non-linearity has a significant effect on the overall performance of our method. Our approach is in contraposition to Huang et al. [15] that instead apply the non-linearity only after the message passing phase. Crucially, the weight values in $\mathbf{W}^{(l)}$ in Eq. 4 are initialized randomly and left untrained. For the random initialization, we resort to the widely adopted Glorot uniform approach [11]. In particular, to control the stability of the expansion of the input information through the successive layers in the architecture, we introduce a *gain* hyperparameter θ to control the effective scaling of $\mathbf{W}^{(l)}$. In the resulting process, a weight matrix of shape $n \times m$ will have entries sampled from a uniform distribution $\mathcal{U}(-a, a)$ where $a = \theta \sqrt{\frac{6}{n+m}}$. In our ablation study, we show that considering this hyperparameter significantly improves the predictive performance of the overall network.

3.2   The Global Pooling Layer

The untrained graph convolution layer presented in Eq. 4 produces node representations that include information about each node's local connectivity. To perform graph-level tasks we shall obtain a single representation for the whole graph. Usually, neural architectures for graph classification achieve this using global pooling operators, e.g. global *maximum, minimum* or *average* pooling. Notice that in the standard end-to-end training fashion, the pooling operators have to be differentiable. Instead, if no gradient has to pass through the pooling operator, we can choose also non-differentiable options. This is the case for the ROCKET model, presented in Sect. 2.3. The authors proposed a non-differentiable pooling mechanism that, in the context of randomized 1-D convolutions, was shown to consistently improve the predictive performance compared to other widespread pooling operators. This operator is referred to as *Percentage of Positive Values* (PPV) and is defined as: $PPV(\mathbf{z}) = \frac{1}{n} \sum_{i=0}^{n-1} I[z_i > 0]$, where $I[z_i > 0]$ is the indicator function which value is 1 if $z_i > 0$, 0 otherwise.

As suggested in the original paper, we used as global pooling both the *global max pooling* and *PPV*, concatenating the resulting representations. Note that this choice doubles the size of the global graph representation compared to the representations of the single nodes provided in output by the untrained graph convolution. We conducted ablation studies to show the impact of different aggregation functions on the overall performance of our proposed method.

3.3   Efficient Readout

As mentioned before, our focus in this paper is the development of efficient and effective neural network models for graph classification. As discussed in Sects. 3.1

and 3.2, the network that computes the graph-level representation does not need to be trained. This leaves the only trained parameters of the model to be those in the readout, i.e., the function mapping from the graph-level representation to the appropriate output for the task. In the case of classification tasks, one of the fastest linear classifiers in the literature is the Least Squares SVM (LS-SVM) [35] with a linear kernel (also known as Ridge Classifier). In the binary case, this classifier follows the simple idea of mapping the two possible classes in $\{-1, 1\}$, and then treats the problem as a regression task, solved with ridge regression. While other classifier choices may lead to improved results, in this paper we test only this very efficient classifier, and leave the exploration of other more complex readouts as future work.

4 Results and Discussion

In this section, we present our experimental setting. A critical point when comparing different models is the possible dataset augmentation that is applied, and the considered validation strategy. We decided to use a common setting for the chemical domain, where the nodes are labelled with a one-hot encoding of their atom type. The only exception is ENZYMES, where it is common to use 18 additional available features, and we followed this convention. Moreover, in the literature, different validation strategies have been applied, making it difficult to perform a fair comparison between the various methods. For the reported results we follow the validation strategy discussed in [6]. We estimate the performance of the U-GCN model by performing 10-fold cross-validation and repeating the whole procedure 5 times to account for the random initialization. To select the best model, we used the average accuracy of 10-fold cross-validation on the validation sets, and we used the same set of selected hyper-parameters for each fold. We did not perform an extensive hyperparameter search on the network architecture since our goal is to design an untrained GCN model whose performance is relatively stable on hyperparameter choice. For this reason, for U-GCN, we fixed the number of layers to four. As for the number of neurons, from preliminary experiments, it was clear that the more hidden neurons, the higher the predictive performance. We set the number of hidden neurons to $5,000$ per layer. Since we use four layers, and concatenate two different readouts, the resulting graph representation is of size $40,000$. Notice however that since the weights are not trained, we just have to perform the forward phase which is extremely fast. We then train an LS-SVM classifier that depends on a regularization hyper-parameter α that we choose in the set $\{10^{-4}, 10^5\}$. We also select the θ parameter for weight initialization in the set $\{0.01, 0.1, 1, 3, 5, 10, 30, 50\}$.

4.1 Datasets

We empirically evaluated U-GCN on commonly adopted graph classification benchmarks. We considered four datasets modeling bioinformatic problems: PTC [14], NCI1 [38], PROTEINS, [2], and ENZYMES [2]. Moreover, we used two large social network datasets: IMDB-B and IMDB-M [40]. PTC, and NCI1 involve chemical compounds represented by their molecular graphs, where node labels encode the atom type, and bonds correspond to edges. PROTEINS and ENZYMES involve graphs that represent proteins. Amino acids are represented by nodes and the edges connect amino acids that in the protein are less than 6Å apart. IMDB-B and IMDB-M are composed of graphs derived from actor/actress and genre information of different movies on IMDB. The target value for each movie represents its genre. IMDB-B models a binary classification task, while IMDB-M considers three different classes.

4.2   Experimental Results

In Table 1 we report the results of our experimental comparison. We considered seven datasets to allow for a comparison with many existing methods in the literature. We performed a pairwise Wilcoxon signed-rank test between our proposed *U-GCN* method and the others. We chose this test because our focus is to propose an efficient and effective alternative and we want to show that our method performs comparably to the state of the art. Thus, the absence of a statistically significant performance difference between our method and the alternatives is already a good result in our point of view. From the test, it emerges that our method performs even significantly better than some state-of-the-art end-to-end trained architectures, showing that the approach we propose is indeed promising.

In Table 2 we perform an ablation study to show the contribution of each core component of our architecture. First, we consider a version of U-GCN that only uses the global max pooling as an aggregator, thus discarding the *PPV* presented in Sect. 3.3. For this ablation, we doubled the number of neurons in the network to consider graph representations of the same size. While there is no clear winner in the comparison, notice that the feature extraction of U-GCN is faster since it requires extracting half the number of features. The second ablation we consider is the same U-GCN where the *tanh* activation function between graph convolutional layers is removed, obtaining a linear model. In this case, U-GCN performs significantly better than linear ablation. Finally, we consider the impact of the θ parameter comparing U-GCN with a version where we fix $\theta = 1$ (its default value). In this case, U-GCN performs again significantly better than the ablation. Moreover, we explored different hidden layer sizes (number of neurons) and confirmed that a higher number of neurons always corresponds to higher predictive performance (plots not reported for lack of space).

Concerning the computational times, running on CPU on a server equipped with an Intel(R) Xeon(R) CPU E5-2630L v3 @ 1.80GHz, for instance for the ENZYMES dataset with 5,000 neurons per layer the feature extraction on the whole dataset takes 33 s, while a single LS-SVM training takes on average 5 s. For NCI1, the times are 42 and 6 s, respectively. These times are orders of magnitude faster when compared to GNN models trained end-to-end with stochastic gradient descent. Concerning the test times, they correspond to the forward pass and the evaluation of the (linear) LS-SVM model, thus they are roughly equivalent to the ones of common GNN models. Notice that the forward pass could also be implemented on GPU for even faster feature extraction.

Table 1. Experimental comparison between the proposed U-GCN and many state-of-the-art methods.

Model\Dataset	PTC	NCI1	PROTEINS	D&D	ENZYMES	IMDB-B	IMDB-M
FGCNN [23]	58.8±1.8	81.5±0.4	74.6±0.8	77.5±0.9	-	-	-
DGCNN [23]	57.1±2.2	73.0±0.9	74.0±0.4	78.1±0.7	-	-	-
DGCNN [6] *	-	76.4±1.7	72.9±3.5	76.6±4.3	38.9±5.7	53.3±5.0	38.6±2.2
SGC [29] *	55.6±7.6	76.3±2.5	75.4±3.4	77.1±4.4	31.3±5.6	66.4±5.5	43.3±3.4
Cheb-Net [29]	55.2±6.5	80.9±1.9	75.8±5.1	77.9±3.7	38.1±6.2	70.6±3.8	43.9±3.4
GIN [6] *	-	80.0±1.4	73.3±4.0	75.3±2.9	59.6±4.5	66.8±3.9	42.2±4.6
DIFFPOOL [6] *	-	76.9±1.9	73.7±3.5	75.0±3.5	59.5±5.6	68.3±6.1	45.1±3.2
GraphSAGE [6]	-	76.0±1.8	73.0±4.5	72.9±2.0	58.2±6.0	69.9±4.6	47.2±3.6
Baseline [6]	-	69.8±2.2	75.8±3.7	**78.4±4.5**	65.2±6.4	50.7±2.4	36.1±3.0
FDGNN [8]	**63.4±5.4**	77.8±1.5	**76.8±2.9**	-	-	**72.4±3.6**	50.0±1.3
MGN [9]	-	78.8±2.3	-	-	-	72.7±3.2	49.5±2.2
GRN [9]	-	78.2±2.2	-	-	-	71.7±2.8	**50.5±1.4**
GESN [9]	-	77.8±2.0	-	-	-	71.7±3.6	48.7±2.1
MRGNN [28]	57.6±10.0	80.6±1.9	75.8±3.5	-	68.2±6.9	72.1±3.6	46.9±3.7
U-GCN	61.2±2.2	**82.2±0.4**	74.2±1.4	78.0±1.0	**68.8±0.6**	68.7±1.2	45.8±0.6
	($\theta = 0.1$)	($\theta = 30$)	($\theta = 10$)	($\theta = 5$)	($\theta = 3$)	($\theta = 1$)	($\theta = 1$)

Table 2. Ablation study: comparison of the proposed U-GCN with different variations.

Model\Dataset	PTC	NCI1	PROTEINS	D&D	ENZYMES	IMDB-B	IMDB-M
U-GCN	61.2±2.2	82.2±0.4	74.2±1.4	78.0±1.0	68.8±0.6	68.7±1.2	45.8±0.6
	($\theta = 0.1$)	($\theta = 30$)	($\theta = 10$)	($\theta = 5$)	($\theta = 3$)	($\theta = 1$)	($\theta = 1$)
U-GCN ablation (max aggr.)	64.1 ± 1.5	80.6 ± 0.5	74.7 ± 0.9	74.7 ± 0.8	70.1 ± 0.8	69.8 ± 1.1	45.8 ± 0.7
	($\theta = 50$)	($\theta = 30$)	($\theta = 3$)	($\theta = 30$)	($\theta = 5$)	($\theta = 1$)	($\theta = 0.01$)
U-GCN ablation (linear) *	60.6 ± 1.0	80.5 ± 0.3	73.3 ± 0.7	76.8 ± 0.5	65.7 ± 1.9	65.5 ± 1.9	45.5 ± 1.38
	($\theta = 1$)	($\theta = 30$)	($\theta = 50$)	($\theta = 30$)	($\theta = 10$)	($\theta = 30$)	($\theta = 1$)
U-GCN ablation ($\theta = 1$) *	60.8 ± 1.3	80.2 ± 0.5	73.9 ± 0.5	77.2 ± 0.6	67.6 ± 1.3	68.7 ± 1.2	45.8 ± 0.62

5   Conclusions

In this paper, we proposed a novel extremely efficient GNN model to perform graph classification. The proposed architecture, dubbed Untrained-GNN (U-GNN), is reminiscent of the models that rely on Reservoir Computing (RC). Indeed, as the name suggests, the U-GNN exploits simple stacked graph convolutional layers where the weights are randomly initialized and then left untrained. The random convolutional projections of the graph's nodes computed by the GC layers are aggregated using a global pooling operator to obtain a graph-level representation that is composed of two functions: the global max pooling and the percentage of positive values (PPV). Finally, the classification task is performed using one of the fastest linear classifiers in the literature: LS-SVM. We assessed the performance of the U-GNN on 7 datasets from different application areas, comparing our proposal both with models that exploit standard end-to-end training and with GNN based on the RC framework. The empirical results show that our approach achieved results comparable to the state-of-the-art methods.

Acknowledgements. This work was partly funded by: the SID/BIRD project *Deep Graph Memory Networks*, Department of Mathematics, University of Padua; the PON R&I 2014-2020 project *Smart Waste Treatment* founded by the FSE REAC-EU; the project "iNEST: Interconnected Nord-Est Innovation Ecosystem" funded under the National Recovery and Resilience Plan (NRRP), Mission 4 Component 2 Investment 1.5 - Call for tender No. 3277 of 30 December 2021 of Italian Ministry of University and Research funded by the European Union - NextGenerationEU, project code: ECS00000043, Concession Decree No. 1058 of June 23, 2022, CUP C43C22000340006; EMERGE, a project funded by EU Horizon research and innovation programme (grant n. 101070918).

References

1. Bacciu, D., et al.: Teaching-trustworthy autonomous cyber-physical applications through human-centred intelligence. In: 2021 IEEE International Conference on Omni-Layer Intelligent Systems (COINS), pp. 1–6. IEEE (2021)
2. Borgwardt, K.M., Ong, C.S., Schönauer, S., Vishwanathan, S., Smola, A.J., Kriegel, H.P.: Protein function prediction via graph kernels. Bioinformatics **21**(suppl_1), i47–i56 (2005)
3. Chen, L., Chen, Z., Bruna, J.: On graph neural networks versus graph-augmented MLPs. In: 9th International Conference on Learning Representations, ICLR 2021, Virtual Event, Austria, 3–7 May 2021. OpenReview.net (2021). https://openreview.net/forum?id=tiqI7w64JG2
4. Defferrard, M., Bresson, X., Vandergheynst, P.: Convolutional neural networks on graphs with fast localized spectral filtering. In: NIPS, pp. 3844–3852 (2016)
5. Dempster, A., Petitjean, F., Webb, G.I.: ROCKET: exceptionally fast and accurate time series classification using random convolutional kernels. Data Min. Knowl. Disc. **34**(5), 1454–1495 (2020). https://doi.org/10.1007/s10618-020-00701-z
6. Errica, F., Podda, M., Bacciu, D., Micheli, A.: A fair comparison of graph neural networks for graph classification. In: International Conference on Learning Representations (2020)
7. Gallicchio, C., Micheli, A.: Graph echo state networks. In: The 2010 International Joint Conference on Neural Networks (IJCNN), pp. 1–8 (2010). https://doi.org/10.1109/IJCNN.2010.5596796
8. Gallicchio, C., Micheli, A.: Fast and deep graph neural networks. In: AAAI, pp. 3898–3905 (2020)
9. Gallicchio, C., Micheli, A.: Ring reservoir neural networks for graphs. arXiv preprint arXiv:2005.05294 (2020)

10. Gallicchio, C., Scardapane, S.: Deep randomized neural networks. In: Oneto, L., Navarin, N., Sperduti, A., Anguita, D. (eds.) Recent Trends in Learning From Data. SCI, vol. 896, pp. 43–68. Springer, Cham (2020). https://doi.org/10.1007/978-3-030-43883-8_3

11. Glorot, X., Bengio, Y.: Understanding the difficulty of training deep feedforward neural networks. In: Teh, Y.W., Titterington, M. (eds.) Proceedings of the Thirteenth International Conference on Artificial Intelligence and Statistics. Proceedings of Machine Learning Research, Chia Laguna Resort, Sardinia, Italy, vol. 9, pp. 249–256. PMLR (2010)

12. Gärtner, T.: A survey of kernels for structured data. ACM SIGKDD Explor. Newsl. 5(1), 49 (2003). https://doi.org/10.1145/959242.959248

13. Hamilton, W., Ying, Z., Leskovec, J.: Inductive representation learning on large graphs. In: NIPS, pp. 1024–1034 (2017)

14. Helma, C., King, R.D., Kramer, S., Srinivasan, A.: The predictive toxicology challenge 2000–2001. Bioinformatics 17(1), 107–108 (2001)

15. Huang, C., et al.: Are graph convolutional networks with random weights feasible? IEEE Trans. Pattern Anal. Mach. Intell. 45(3), 2751–2768 (2023). https://doi.org/10.1109/tpami.2022.3183143

16. Jaeger, H.: The "echo state" approach to analysing and training recurrent neural networks. GMD Report 148, GMD - German National Research Institute for Computer Science (2001)

17. Jaeger, H., Haas, H.: Harnessing nonlinearity: predicting chaotic systems and saving energy in wireless communication. Science 304(5667), 78–80 (2004)

18. Kipf, T.N., Welling, M.: Semi-supervised classification with graph convolutional networks. In: ICLR, pp. 1–14 (2017). https://doi.org/10.1051/0004-6361/201527329

19. Li, Y., Tarlow, D., Brockschmidt, M., Zemel, R.: Gated graph sequence neural networks. In: ICLR (2016). https://doi.org/10.1103/PhysRevLett.116.082003

20. Lukoševičius, M., Jaeger, H.: Reservoir computing approaches to recurrent neural network training. Comput. Sci. Rev. 3(3), 127–149 (2009)

21. Micheli, A.: Neural network for graphs: a contextual constructive approach. IEEE Trans. Neural Networks 20(3), 498–511 (2009)

22. Nakajima, K., Fischer, I.: Reservoir Computing. Springer, Singapore (2021). https://doi.org/10.1007/978-981-13-1687-6

23. Navarin, N., Tran, D.V., Sperduti, A.: Learning kernel-based embeddings in graph neural networks. In: European Conference on Artificial Intelligence (2020)

24. Pasa, L., Navarin, N., Sperduti, A.: Compact graph neural network models for node classification. In: Proceedings of the 37th ACM/SIGAPP Symposium on Applied Computing, pp. 592–599 (2022). https://doi.org/10.1145/3477314.3507100

25. Pasa, L., Navarin, N., Erb, W., Sperduti, A.: Empowering simple graph convolutional networks. IEEE Trans. Neural Netw. Learn. Syst. 1–15 (2023). https://doi.org/10.1109/tnnls.2022.3232291

26. Pasa, L., Navarin, N., Sperduti, A.: Simple multi-resolution gated GNN. In: 2021 IEEE Symposium Series on Computational Intelligence (SSCI), pp. 1–7 (2021). https://doi.org/10.1109/ssci50451.2021.9660046

27. Pasa, L., Navarin, N., Sperduti, A.: Deep learning for graph-structured data. In: Handbook on Computer Learning and Intelligence: Volume 2: Deep Learning, Intelligent Control and Evolutionary Computation, pp. 585–617. World Scientific (2022)

28. Pasa, L., Navarin, N., Sperduti, A.: Multiresolution reservoir graph neural network. IEEE Trans. Neural Networks Learn. Syst. 33(6), 2642–2653 (2022). https://doi.org/10.1109/TNNLS.2021.3090503

29. Pasa, L., Navarin, N., Sperduti, A.: Polynomial-based graph convolutional neural networks for graph classification. Mach. Learn. **111**(4), 1205–1237 (2022). https://doi.org/10.1007/s10994-021-06098-0
30. Rahimi, A., Recht, B.: Weighted sums of random kitchen sinks: replacing minimization with randomization in learning. In: Advances in Neural Information Processing Systems, vol. 21 (2008)
31. Rodan, A., Tino, P.: Minimum complexity echo state network. IEEE Trans. Neural Networks **22**(1), 131–144 (2010)
32. Rodrigues, I.R., Neto, S.R.D.S., Kelner, J., Sadok, D., Endo, P.T.: Convolutional extreme learning machines: a systematic review. Informatics **8**(2), 33 (2021). https://doi.org/10.3390/informatics8020033
33. Scarselli, F., Gori, M., Ah Chung Tsoi, A.C., Hagenbuchner, M., Monfardini, G.: The graph neural network model. IEEE Trans. Neural Networks **20**(1), 61–80 (2009). https://doi.org/10.1109/TNN.2008.2005605
34. Sperduti, A., Starita, A.: Supervised neural networks for the classification of structures. IEEE Trans. Neural Networks **8**(3), 714–735 (1997). https://doi.org/10.1109/72.572108
35. Suykens, J., Vandewalle, J.: Least squares support vector machine classifiers. Neural Process. Lett. **9**(3), 293–300 (1999). https://doi.org/10.1023/a:1018628609742
36. Tanaka, G., et al.: Recent advances in physical reservoir computing: a review. Neural Netw. **115**, 100–123 (2019)
37. Veličković, P., Cucurull, G., Casanova, A., Romero, A., Lio, P., Bengio, Y.: Graph attention networks. arXiv preprint arXiv:1710.10903 (2017)
38. Wale, N., Watson, I.A., Karypis, G.: Comparison of descriptor spaces for chemical compound retrieval and classification. Knowl. Inf. Syst. **14**(3), 347–375 (2008)
39. Xu, K., Hu, W., Leskovec, J., Jegelka, S.: How powerful are graph neural networks? In: International Conference on Learning Representations (2019)
40. Yanardag, P., Vishwanathan, S.: Deep graph kernels. In: Proceedings of the 21th ACM SIGKDD International Conference on Knowledge Discovery and Data Mining - KDD 2015, pp. 1365–1374 (2015). https://doi.org/10.1145/2783258.2783417

BGEK: External Knowledge-Enhanced Graph Convolutional Networks for Rumor Detection in Online Social Networks

Xiaoda Wang[ID], Chenxiang Luo[ID], Tengda Guo[ID], Zhangrui Liu[ID], Jiongyan Zhang[ID], and Haizhou Wang[✉][ID]

School of Cyber Science and Engineering, Sichuan University, Chengdu 610207, China
{wangxiaoda,iridescense,guotengda,
liuzhangrui,zhangjiongyan}@stu.scu.edu.cn, whzh.nc@scu.edu.cn

Abstract. Nowadays, social media has become a dominant platform for disseminating news and information. However, it also accelerated the spread of rumors, which causes great impacts on the real world. Therefore, the detection of rumors plays a crucial role in controlling the diffusion of misinformation. Cantonese is widely spoken across the world, yet limited research has been conducted on Cantonese rumor detection. Moreover, current detection methods primarily focus on extracting textual and propagation structure characteristics without utilizing external knowledge to enhance the performance of identifying rumors. In this paper, we propose a novel model using Bidirectional Graph Convolutional Networks Embedded with External Knowledge, namely BGEK, for Cantonese rumor detection. Specifically, we first construct a directed heterogeneous knowledge graph using official statements and related entity descriptions from Wikipedia to obtain external knowledge embeddings. Secondly, we use BERT (Bidirectional Encoder Representations from Transformers) model to extract text features from source tweets and obtain the correlation vectors of external knowledge and text features through the Comparison Network. Thirdly, we utilize Bidirectional Graph Convolutional Networks to extract rumor propagation structural features. Finally, we fuse text features, structural features and comparison features to construct a Cantonese rumor detection model. To the best of our knowledge, we are the first to apply external knowledge to Cantonese rumor detection. Experimental results demonstrate that the BGEK model outperforms existing state-of-the-art detection models.

Keywords: Cantonese rumors · rumor detection · external knowledge · Bidirectional Graph Convolutional Networks · feature fusion

1 Introduction

With the rapid development of the Internet, social media has become an extremely popular source for individuals to obtain news information and express their opinions. According to the statistics in Digital 2022[1], social media users have escalated to 4.62 billion accounting for 58.4% of the global population, with an annual growth rate exceeding 10%. For instance, Facebook has emerged as the most influential social media platform, with a worldwide registration of 2.96 billion individuals[2]. At the same time, the rapid growth of social media platforms has facilitated the dissemination of rumors which can cause serious social panic [1].

Cantonese originated in Guangdong Province of China, and is presently one of the most extensively spoken languages by native and overseas Chinese. With over 82.4 million speakers[3], it has spread throughout overseas Chinese communities. The rapid dissemination of Cantonese rumors through social media has resulted in serious harm to society. Therefore, it is essential to develop an intelligent method to identify rumors automatically.

Most existing rumor detection works focus on detecting rumors in Chinese and English [1,13,16,19,21], but there are few works considering Cantonese rumors [3,7,10]. They use the textual information of tweets and feature engineering for Cantonese rumor detection [3,7]. However, Cantonese rumor detection still faces two critical challenges that still need to be resolved. **Firstly, existing studies in Cantonese rumor detection mainly rely on text and user statistic features** [3,7]. These approaches don't take into account the dissemination structures of retweets and comments, and there is no available structural Cantonese rumor dataset that includes source tweets, retweets, and comments. Therefore, the absence of a benchmark Cantonese rumor dataset makes the detection of Cantonese rumors a daunting task. **Secondly, despite the successful works achieved by current rumor detection methods, external knowledge graphs are rarely integrated into their existing methods.** Existing knowledge graph-based approaches mainly extract the structural triplets (head, relation, tail) from the tweet text to compare with faithful triples from knowledge graph to predict the truthfulness of tweets [5,14]. But they don't consider the information in the retweets, and comments and don't embed external knowledge into source tweets to assist in the judgment of rumors. Meanwhile, existing research has applied Graph Convolutional Networks for detecting rumors, but there is no research on combining external knowledge with graph convolutional networks for rumor detection.

To address the above two challenges in Cantonese rumor detection, firstly, based on Facebook, we build and label a structural Cantonese rumors benchmark dataset, including source tweets, retweets, and comments. Secondly, we propose a novel feature extraction method based on Graph Convolutional Networks for external knowledge integration. This approach involves constructing a heterogeneous graph using official statements and Wikipedia entity descriptions and utilizing BERT to capture the text features of the source tweet. To generate

---

[1] https://datareportal.com/reports/digital-2022-global-overview-report.
[2] https://www.pewresearch.org/journalism/fact-sheet/social-media-and-newfact-sheet/.
[3] https://en.wikipedia.org/wiki/Cantonese#cite_note-ethnologue23-1.

correlation vectors, a Comparison Network is employed to compare the external knowledge with source text. The Bidirectional Graph Convolutional Networks is then utilized to extract top-down and bottom-up propagation features of tweets during the rumor propagation process. Finally, these three types of features are fused to train a Cantonese rumor detection model. The main contributions of this paper are summarized as follows:

- **To the best of our knowledge, we are the first to construct a structural Cantonese rumor dataset containing source tweets, retweets and comments in social networks, which is publicly available on GitHub**[4]. Specifically, we crawled 2,721 source tweets and 91,246 comments and retweets. After data cleaning and labeling, a Cantonese rumor dataset was constructed including 1,925 source tweets, 64,221 comments and retweets.
- **We construct a novel method for extracting external knowledge features based on Graph Convolutional Networks and obtaining correlation features through Comparison Network.** First, we construct a heterogeneous knowledge graph based on official statements and entity descriptions from Wikipedia. Then, we use a Heterogeneous Graph Convolutional Networks to extract the embedded features of external knowledge. Finally, we obtain correlation vectors from external knowledge embedded and tweet text features by Comparison Network.
- **We propose a novel Cantonese rumor detection model BGEK for Cantonese rumor detection, which integrates the text features, comparison features, and structural features of tweets. To the best of our knowledge, we are the first to apply external knowledge to Cantonese rumor detection.** Our experimental results demonstrate that the BGEK detection model achieves remarkable detection results and outperforms other state-of-the-art baseline models.

2   Related Work

Traditional rumor detection methods are based on machine learning and they mainly focus on text and statistical features, aiming to train a classifier for rumor detection through supervised learning. A series of methods have been proposed [2,9,20], such as Random Forest [9], Decision Tree [2] and Support Vector Machine (SVM) [20]. The above methods rely heavily on feature engineering, which takes plenty of time, and the detection performance is not ideal.

In order to automatically extract features of rumors, a series of methods based on deep learning have been proposed [12,13,15,17,21]. They mostly use text features for rumor detection, for example, Recurrent Neural Network (RNN) [12], Convolutional Neural Network (CNN) [21], Structure Recurrent Neural Network (RvNN) [13]. Song et al. [15] proposed an adversarial awareness rumor detection framework. Sun et al. [17] applied contrastive learning to rumor detection. However, the currently available methods prove to be inefficient in their ability to learn the features of the propagation structure, and they exhibit a lack of consideration for the global structural characteristics of rumor dispersion.

---

[4] https://github.com/yiyepianzhounc/BGEK.

Compared with deep learning-based rumor detection mentioned above, Graph Convolutional Networks [8] has been applied in the field of rumor detection in recent years [1,11,19]. Bian et al. [1] used the Graph Convolutional Networks for the first time in the social network rumor detection field. Wei et al. [19] proposed an Edge-enhanced Bayesian Graph Convolutional Networks to obtain robust node feature representations. Lu et al. [11] proposed a Graph-aware Co-Attention Network (GCAN) for interpretable disinformation detection.

In recent studies, the significance of external knowledge for rumor detection has been recognized, leading to the development of rumor detection models that incorporate knowledge graph enhancement [5,6,14,16]. The methods [5,14] utilized tuples (head, relationship, tail) from the text to compare with equivalent elements in knowledge graphs. They mainly extracted the structural triplets (head, relation, tail) from the tweet text to compare with faithful triples from knowledge graph to predict the truthfulness of tweets.

Existing research on rumor detection in Cantonese [3,7,10] utilizes text and user information for rumor detection. Our previous work [3,7] combined Cantonese tweets' semantic and statistical features to detect Cantonese rumors on the Twitter platform. Lin et al. [10] proposed an annotation system that facilitates manual fact-checking. Existing Cantonese rumor detection methods mainly focus on text information and statistical features and do not use external knowledge graphs which can provide corresponding evidence for rumor detection. They also don't utilize the structural characteristics of the propagation and dispersion of rumors and limit the improvement of detection performance.

3   Methodology

In this section, we will describe the Cantonese rumor detection model based on the Bidirectional Graph Convolutional Network embedding external knowledge.

3.1   Dataset Construction

Existing Cantonese rumor datasets [3,7] mainly focus on source tweets and user information. Deep learning models can be built based on these existing datasets. However, there is no structural Cantonese rumor dataset including retweets and comments which is of great significance for the research of Graph Neural Networks based Cantonese rumor detection. Facebook has become one of the essential social media websites for users to obtain news information and a large number of Cantonese rumors spread on Facebook. So we choose Facebook social platform as the research object and construct a wholly structural Cantonese rumor dataset. To obtain the structural information, the Selenium framework is utilized to crawl data due to the Facebook's restrictions on data crawling. Then the data is manually labeled according to the method of [3]. After data cleaning and screening, we finally construct a Cantonese rumor dataset, named Facebook-C-Dataset, which contains 1,925 source tweets, 64,221 comments and retweets. The tweets are further classified into three major domains, namely society, health, and information technology, and 49 specific topics, such as cancer, chronic diseases, radiofrequency radiation, and COVID-19 vaccine. Table 1 shows the detailed composition of the dataset.

Table 1. Statistics of the Facebook-C-Dataset

	Number of Tweets	Number of Retweets and Comments	Date of Tweets	Domains	Topics
Rumor	565	20,625	01/2020-03/2023	3	49
Non-rumor	1,360	43,596			
Total	1,925	64,221			

3.2 BGEK Rumor Detection Model

The Cantonese rumor detection model BGEK is shown in Fig. 1. In order to better utilize external facts, we use a Comparison Network to embed external knowledge into the text representation of tweets. At the same time, we use a Bidirectional Graph Convolutional Networks, which fully uses the contribution of retweets and comments generated in the process of tweet dissemination to rumor detection. The specific implementation details are as follows:

Tweet Propagation Graph Construction. Given the source tweet, retweet, and comment information of a event, we can represent the total rumor dataset as $C = \{c_1, c_2, ..., c_m\}$, where c_i denotes the $i - th$ event and m is the number of events. c_i can be denoted as $c_i = \{r_i, t_1^i, t_2^i, ..., t_{n_i-1}^i, G_i\}$, where t_j^i denotes the $j - th$ responsive tweet, n_i denotes the total number of comments and retweets contained in the event c_i, G_i represents the rumor propagation graph composed of event c_i. G_i is defined as $G_i = <V_i, E_i>$, where the node set is $V_i = \{r_i, t_1^i, t_2^i, ..., t_{n_i-1}^i\}$, r_i is the root node in the propagation graph, and $E_i = \{e_{st}^i | s, t = 0, 1, ..., n_i - 1\}$ is the edge set. Each e_{st}^i represents the directed relationship among tweets, retweets, and comments. For an adjacency matrix $A_i \in \mathbb{R}^{n_i \times n_i}$, the initial value can be calculated as:

$$a_{st}^i = \begin{cases} 1, & if \ \ e_{st}^i \in E \\ 0, & otherwise \end{cases}. \tag{1}$$

For each event c_i, there is a corresponding label $y_i \in Y$, where Y represents different categories of events, our goal is to train a classifier $f : C \to Y$.

Structural Feature Extraction. Based on the relationship between source tweets, retweets, and comments, we constructed a propagation graph $G_i = <V_i, E_i>$ for each event c_i and then built the adjacency matrix $A_i \in \mathbb{R}^{n_i \times n_i}$. We constructed text features x_i for each node in the graph, and the feature matrix can be represented as $X = \{x_1, x_2, x_3, ..., x_{n_i}\}$, where n_i represents the total number of comments and retweets in the event c_i. We used a Bidirectional

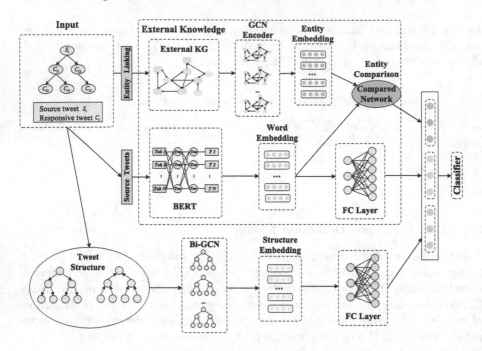

Fig. 1. BGEK rumor detection model

Graph Convolutional Networks (Bi-GCN) to calculate the node representations in the graph, which includes a top-down Graph Convolutional Networks (TD-GCN) and a bottom-up Graph Convolutional Networks (BU-GCN). The adjacency matrices for TD-GCN and BU-GCN can be represented as $A^{TD} = A$ and $A^{BU} = A^T$ respectively. The top-down and bottom-up propagation features can be obtained by two layers of GCN as follows:

$$H_1^{BU} = \sigma(\tilde{A}^{BU} X W_0^{BU}) \tag{2}$$

$$H_2^{BU} = \sigma(\tilde{A}^{BU} H_1^{BU} W_1^{BU}) \tag{3}$$

where $\tilde{A}^{BU}$ is the regularized adjacency matrix of A^{BU}, H_1^{BU}, H_2^{BU} and W_0^{BU}, W_1^{BU} are the hidden features and weight matrix respectively, and σ is the activation function. Similarly, the top-down hidden features H_1^{TD}, H_2^{TD} can be obtained by the above equation. Meanwhile, in order to make full use of the features of the source tweets, we concatenate the root node features of the $k-1$ layer with the hidden layer features of the k layer as follows:

$$\tilde{H}_k^{BU} = concat(H_k^{BU}, (H_{k-1}^{BU})^{root}) \tag{4}$$

Through the propagation and dispersion features $\tilde{H}_2^{TD}$, $\tilde{H}_2^{BU}$ obtained above, the propagation features and dispersion features can be connected to obtain the structural features:

$$T = concat(\tilde{H}_2^{TD}, \tilde{H}_2^{BU}) \tag{5}$$

External Knowledge Extraction

External Knowledge Graph Construction. We construct a heterogeneous graph $\omega = < V, E >$ for the types of source tweets, including official statements and entity descriptions. The graph contains two different types of nodes: official statements $R = \{V_1^r, V_2^r, V_3^r, ..., V_x^r\}$ and entity descriptions $D = \{V_1^d, V_2^d, V_3^d, ..., V_y^d\}$, where x represents the number of official statements and y represents the number of entity descriptions. And the set of edges E includes bidirectional connections and unidirectional connections. The construction method for the external knowledge graph is outlined as follows:

The source tweet contains M-specific aspects, which can be expressed as $S = \{s_1, s_2, s_3, ..., s_M\}$. The source tweet may belong to multiple aspects, and the content of tweets under the same aspect has a particular content similarity. First, we bidirectionally connect the official statements constructed under each aspect. Then for the entities contained in the official statement and the source tweet, we connect the entity to the entry on Wikipedia and select the content of the first paragraph as the entity description. Because the entity description and the official statement are related, we link the official statement and the entity description under the same aspect bidirectionally. Considering that the official statement corresponding to the same type of aspect has a certain similarity, we link the same type of official statement bidirectionally. Because an original tweet may belong to multiple aspects, we create an undirected connection edge between entity descriptions of the same type and other entity descriptions.

Heterogeneous Graph Convolutional Networks Construction. Through the directed heterogeneous graph $\omega = <V, E>$ constructed above, we use a Heterogeneous Graph Convolutional Networks to represent and learn official statements and entity descriptions. We use the Cantonese corpus we constructed to fine-tune the BERT model based on Chinese pre-training. Then we use BERT to obtain the node embedding feature matrix $X \in \mathbb{R}^{|V| \times D}$, where $X = \{x_1, x_2, x_3, ..., x_{|V|}\}$ includes the features of all nodes on the heterogeneous graph and x_i represents the feature of the $i - th$ node. We define A as the adjacency matrix and D as the degree matrix. Then the heterogeneous graph convolutional layer updates the $i + 1 - th$ layer clustering features by clustering the features of the $i - th$ layer adjacency matrix:

$$A' = D^{-\frac{1}{2}}(A + I)D^{-\frac{1}{2}} \qquad (6)$$

$$H^{(i+1)} = \sigma(A' H^i W^i) \qquad (7)$$

where I is the identity matrix of $|V|$ dimension, A' is the adjacency matrix after self-connection and regularization, W^i is the weight matrix of $i - th$ layer, H^i is the feature matrix of $i - th$ layer, σ is the activation function.

Comparison Feature Extraction. We get the embedded representation of external knowledge $K = \{k_1, k_2, k_3, ..., k_{|V|}\}$ through the above-mentioned Heterogeneous Graph Convolutional Networks. The text of the source tweet can be expressed as

$$T = \{t_1, t_2, t_3, ..., t_{|C|}\} \qquad (8)$$

where $|C|$ represents the number of source tweets in the dataset. We fine-tuned the BERT model based on Chinese pre-training through the constructed Cantonese corpus, and then the text features can be obtained through the features as follows:

$$B = BERT(T) . \qquad (9)$$

where $B = \{b_1, b_2, b_3, ..., b_{|C|}\}$ is the text feature of the source tweet, and then we get the comparison vector by comparing the text feature b_n of the source tweet with the knowledge embedding feature k_n:

$$C_n = f_{cmp}(b_n, k_n) \qquad (10)$$

where $f_{cmp}()$ is the comparison function. Based on [6], we designed the comparison function as $f_{cmp}(x, y) = W[x - y, x \odot y]$. Where W is the dimension transformation matrix, x and y are the text features of the source tweets and knowledge embedding feature vectors, and $\odot$ represents the Hadamard product.

Feature Concatenation. Initially, we perform concatenation of various feature sets including source tweet text features B_n, comparison features C_n and structural features T_n based on retweets and comments to obtain vector

$$F_n = concat(B_n + C_n + T_n) \in \mathbb{R}^{|B_n| + |C_n| + |T_n|} \qquad (11)$$

Then F_n is subsequently fed as input to the Softmax layer, which can be represented as

$$Z = Softmax(WF_n + b) \qquad (12)$$

Here, W is the parameter matrix of the fully connected layer, and b is the bias matrix of the fully connected layer.

4 Experiments

4.1 Experiment Settings

In our work, all experiments are conducted on an NVIDIA A100-SXM4 workstation with 80G of memory. The dataset used in the experiments is the Facebook-C-Dataset. To extract structural features, TF-IDF scores are applied to the top 5,000 words in the source tweets, retweets, and comments. In evaluating the model's performance, accuracy, precision, recall, and F1 scores are used, along with ten-fold cross-validation, to provide an average evaluation metric value.

4.2 Performance Comparison with Baselines

To assess the efficacy of our proposed BGEK model, we employ a comparative analysis approach with various state-of-the-art baselines. The results of different models for Cantonese rumor detection are shown in Table 2. Text-based features are represented by T, external knowledge-based features are represented by K, and structural features are denoted by S. Among the baseline models, BERT outperforms other models with only text information, which means text features of source tweets are important for identifying rumors. Our proposed BGEK model integrates the text features, comparison features, and structural features and achieves the best performance in terms of all metrics.

Table 2. Results of comparison among different models in Facebook-C-Dataset

Model	Features			Acc.	Non-Rumor			Rumor		
	T	S	K		Prec.	Rec.	F1	Prec.	Rec.	F1
RFC [9]	✓			0.8029	0.7915	0.9795	0.8755	0.8833	0.3759	0.5274
TextCNN [21]	✓			0.8672	0.8800	0.9642	0.9119	0.8214	0.6571	0.7302
RNN_Att [22]	✓			0.8750	0.8812	0.9570	0.9175	0.8519	0.6571	0.7419
SVM [20]	✓			0.7884	0.8405	0.8651	0.8526	0.6489	0.6028	0.6250
BERT [4]	✓			0.9135	0.9196	0.9522	0.9325	0.8448	0.7703	0.7924
Transformer [18]	✓			0.8047	0.8400	0.9032	0.8705	0.6786	0.5429	0.6032
RvNN [13]	✓	✓		0.7332	0.8099	0.8244	0.8171	0.5196	0.4953	0.5072
BiGCN [1]	✓	✓		0.7813	0.7824	0.7501	0.7635	0.6204	0.6662	0.6342
EBGCN [19]	✓	✓		0.8223	0.8679	0.8855	0.8758	0.4608	0.4230	0.4374
BGEK (Ours)	✓	✓	✓	**0.9727**	**0.9807**	**0.9792**	**0.9791**	**0.9536**	**0.9606**	**0.9528**

4.3 Ablation Experiment

Our proposed BGEK model integrates external knowledge features, text features, and propagation structure features. To assess the individual contribution of each feature on the BGEK model, we conducted ablation experiment using the variants shown in Table 3. T represents the text features extracted from the source tweets, K represents the external knowledge features, and S represents the structural features originating from the source tweets, retweets and comments.

Table 3. The description of different variants

Feature set	Features categories
BGEK	Source text feature, Structural feature, External knowledge feature
BGEK/K	Source text feature, Structural feature
BGEK/S	Source text feature, External knowledge feature
BGEK/T	Structural feature, External knowledge feature

The evaluation metrics obtained from the experiment on different variants are shown in Fig. 2. The results shows all variants perform worse than complete BGEK model integrating the text features, comparison features, and structural features. External knowledge feature plays the most important role in the identification of Cantonese rumors, which also illustrates the necessity of external knowledge information for better performance.

4.4   Embedding Visualization

To visually represent the feature embedding, Fig. 3 exhibits the embedding outcomes of diverse baselines on the Facebook-C-Dataset. From the plots, we find that our proposed BGEK model outperforms the other methods, by effectively segregating rumor and non-rumor information.

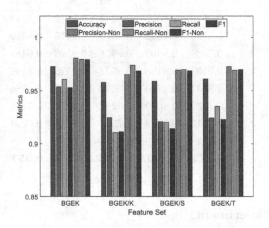

Fig. 2. Results of ablation experiment among different variants

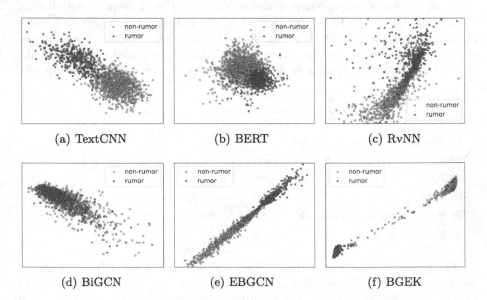

Fig. 3. Visualizing embeddings among different models

4.5   Robustness Experiment

In this experiment, a randomized portion of labels from the training set is intentionally mislabeled at varying ratios ranging from 5% to 45%. Following this, the model is re-trained on the modified training set and tested for its ability to withstand noise at different levels. The experimental results are shown in Fig. 4, which show that as the noise rate increases, the performance of all models (F1 score) decreases. Notably, our proposed model exhibits the most robust performance, displaying the smallest decline compared to other baseline models.

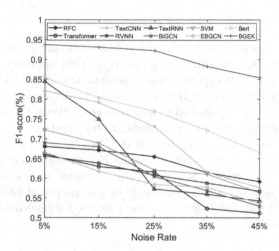

Fig. 4. Results of robustness experiment

4.6   Transferability Experiments on Twitter15 and Twitter16

To validate the efficacy of our proposed BGEK model for detecting rumors, we conducted comparative experiments on the Twitter15 and Twitter16 datasets using the aforementioned baselines.

Table 4. Results of comparison among different models in Twitter15 and Twitter16

Model	Twitter15					Twitter16				
	Acc.	NR	F	T	U	Acc.	NR	F	T	U
		F1	F1	F1	F1		F1	F1	F1	F1
DTC [2]	0.455	0.933	0.355	0.317	0.415	0.465	0.643	0.393	0.419	0.403
SVM-TS [20]	0.544	0.796	0.472	0.404	0.483	0.544	0.796	0.472	0.404	0.483
BERT [4]	0.896	0.680	0.794	0.921	0.767	0.896	0.692	0.840	0.928	0.739
RvNN [13]	0.852	0.840	0.846	0.884	0.837	0.852	0.840	0.846	0.884	0.837
BiGCN [1]	0.871	0.860	0.867	0.913	0.836	0.885	0.829	0.899	0.932	0.882
EBGCN [19]	0.892	0.869	0.897	0.934	0.867	0.915	0.879	0.906	0.947	0.910
BGEK (Ours)	**0.906**	**0.882**	**0.907**	**0.939**	**0.886**	**0.927**	**0.893**	**0.929**	**0.955**	**0.931**

Each event is labeled as Non-rumor (NR), False Rumor (F), True Rumor (T), or Unverified Rumor (U). Due to the lack of external knowledge graphs, our proposed model does not use comparison features. The experimental outcomes are presented in Table 4. Among all baseline models, BERT achieves the best accuracy in Twitter15 and EBGCN achieves the best accuracy in Twitter16. By fusing text features and structural features, our model achieves the best detection results. And it unequivocally shows the generalization ability of our model.

5 Conclusion

In this paper, we construct a structural Cantonese rumor dataset based on the Facebook platform. Additionally, we propose a novel approach for extracting embedding features that incorporate official statements and entity descriptions of external knowledge by utilizing a Heterogeneous Graph Convolutional Networks. A Comparison Network is proposed to generate comparison features by comparing external knowledge with source tweets. Subsequently, we propose a novel Cantonese rumor detection model named BGEK (Bidirectional Graph Convolutional Networks Embedded with External Knowledge) that integrates text features, comparison features, and structural features. Five main experiments are conducted to evaluate the performance of our proposed BGEK model and experimental results demonstrate that our proposed model outperforms other state-of-the-art models.

Acknowledgments. This work is supported by the National Key Research and Development Program of China under grant No. 2022YFC3303101 and Key Research and Development Program of Science and Technology Department of Sichuan Province under grant No. 2023YFG0145.

References

1. Bian, T., et al.: Rumor detection on social media with bi-directional graph convolutional networks. In: Proceedings of the 34th AAAI Conference on Artificial Intelligence, pp. 549–556 (2020)
2. Castillo, C., Mendoza, M., Poblete, B.: Information credibility on twitter. In: Proceedings of the 20th International Conference on World Wide Web, pp. 675–684 (2011)
3. Chen, X., Wang, H., Ke, L., Lu, Z., Su, H., Chen, X.: Identifying cantonese rumors with discriminative feature integration in online social networks. Expert Syst. Appl. **215**, 119347 (2023)
4. Devlin, J., Chang, M.W., Lee, K., Toutanova, K.: BERT: pre-training of deep bidirectional transformers for language understanding. arXiv preprint arXiv:1810.04805 (2018)
5. Fionda, V., Pirrò, G.: Fact checking via evidence patterns. In: Proceedings of the 27th International Joint Conference on Artificial Intelligence, pp. 3755–3761 (2018)

6. Hu, L., et al.: Compare to the knowledge: graph neural fake news detection with external knowledge. In: Proceedings of the 59th Annual Meeting of the Association for Computational Linguistics and the 11th International Joint Conference on Natural Language Processing, pp. 754–763 (2021)
7. Ke, L., Chen, X., Lu, Z., Su, H., Wang, H.: A novel approach for cantonese rumor detection based on deep neural network. In: Proceedings of 33rd IEEE International Conference on Systems, Man, and Cybernetics, pp. 1610–1615 (2020)
8. Kipf, T.N., Welling, M.: Semi-supervised classification with graph convolutional networks. arXiv preprint arXiv:1609.02907 (2016)
9. Kwon, S., Cha, M., Jung, K., Chen, W., Wang, Y.: Prominent features of rumor propagation in online social media. In: Proceedings of 13th IEEE International Conference on Data Mining, pp. 1103–1108 (2013)
10. Lin, Z.H., Wang, Z., Zhao, M., Song, Y., Lan, L.: An AI-based system to assist human fact-checkers for labeling cantonese fake news on social media. In: Proceedings of 10th IEEE International Conference on Big Data, pp. 6766–6768 (2022)
11. Lu, Y.J., Li, C.T.: GCAN: graph-aware co-attention networks for explainable fake news detection on social media. In: Proceedings of 58th Annual Meeting of the Association for Computational Linguistics, pp. 505–514 (2020)
12. Ma, J., et al.: Detecting rumors from microblogs with recurrent neural networks. In: Proceedings of the 25th International Joint Conference on Artificial Intelligence, pp. 3818–3824 (2016)
13. Ma, J., Gao, W., Wong, K.F.: Rumor detection on twitter with tree-structured recursive neural networks. In: Proceedings of the 56th Annual Meeting of the Association for Computational Linguistics, pp. 1980–1989 (2018)
14. Pan, J.Z., Pavlova, S., Li, C., Li, N., Li, Y., Liu, J.: Content based fake news detection using knowledge graphs. In: The Semantic Web-ISWC : 17th International Semantic Web Conference, pp. 669–683 (2018)
15. Song, Y.Z., Chen, Y.S., Chang, Y.T., Weng, S.Y., Shuai, H.H.: Adversary-aware rumor detection. In: Proceedings of the 59th Findings of the Association for Computational Linguistics: ACL-IJCNLP, pp. 1371–1382 (2021)
16. Sun, M., Zhang, X., Zheng, J., Ma, G.: DDGCN: dual dynamic graph convolutional networks for rumor detection on social media. In: Proceedings of the 36th AAAI Conference on Artificial Intelligence, vol. 36, pp. 4611–4619 (2022)
17. Sun, T., Qian, Z., Dong, S., Li, P., Zhu, Q.: Rumor detection on social media with graph adversarial contrastive learning. In: Proceedings of the 31st ACM Web Conference, pp. 2789–2797 (2022)
18. Vaswani, A., et al.: Attention is all you need. In: Advances in Neural Information Processing Systems, vol. 30 (2017)
19. Wei, L., Hu, D., Zhou, W., Yue, Z., Hu, S.: Towards propagation uncertainty: Edge-enhanced bayesian graph convolutional networks for rumor detection. arXiv preprint arXiv:2107.11934 (2021)
20. Wu, K., Yang, S., Zhu, K.Q.: False rumors detection on sina weibo by propagation structures. In: Proceedings of the 31st IEEE International Conference on Data Engineering, pp. 651–662 (2015)
21. Yu, F., Liu, Q., Wu, S., Wang, L., Tan, T.: A convolutional approach for misinformation identification. In: Proceedings of the 26th International Joint Conference on Artificial Intelligence, pp. 3901–3907 (2017)
22. Zhou, P., et al.: Attention-based bidirectional long short-term memory networks for relation classification. In: Proceedings of the 54th Annual Meeting of the Association for Computational Linguistics, pp. 207–212 (2016)

BIG-FG: A Bi-directional Interaction Graph Framework with Filter Gate Mechanism for Chinese Spoken Language Understanding

Wentao Zhang[1], Bi Zeng[1], Pengfei Wei[1(✉)], and Huiting Hu[2]

[1] School of Computer Science and Technology, Guangdong University of Technology, Guangzhou 510006, China
wpf@gdut.edu.cn
[2] School of Information Science and Technology, Zhongkai University of Agriculture and Engineering, Guangzhou 510006, China

Abstract. Spoken language understanding (SLU) primarily entailing slot filling and intent detection has been studied for many years with achieving significant results. However, in Chinese SLU tasks, Some models fail to take word-level information into account, and there is insufficient interaction between slot information and intent information. To address the aforementioned issues, we propose a novel bi-directional interaction graph framework with filter gate mechanism (**BIG-FG**) for Chinese spoken language understanding, which can make a fine-grained interaction directly with slot information and intent information, while also effectively fusing character-word semantic information. The model consists of two core modules: (1) bi-directional interaction graph (BIG), which is based on a multi-layer graph attention network with the bi-directional connections between intent information, slot information, and adjacent slot information, fully considering the correlation between slot filling and intent detection; (2) filter gate (FG), which enhances fusion performance by solving the problem of semantic ambiguity brought by direct fusion of character-word semantic information. Experiments on two datasets demonstrate that our model outperforms the best benchmark model by 0.39% and 2.65% in the Overall(Acc) evaluation metric, respectively, and accomplishes the state-of-the-arts performance.

Keywords: Chinese Spoken Language Understanding · Bi-directional Interaction Graph · Filter Gate · Graph Attention Network

1 Introduction

In intelligent dialogue systems, spoken language understanding (SLU) is critical, which typically includes two main subtasks: intent detection and slot filling [1].

Given an utterance for example, "play music on youtube", the intent label is "PlayMusic", and the slots are labeled in order {O, O, O, B-service}.

In the past, researchers focused mostly on English SLU and proposed different methods including gate-based methods [2–4], attention-based methods [5,6] and GATs-based methods [7,8]. In contrast to English SLU, Chinese SLU faces the difficulty of word segmentation. When there is an error in the word segmentation in Chinese SLU, it leads to error propagation, and, as a result, a slot filling error. To avoid this problem, [9] established a new collaborative memory network model based on the character to avoid the introduction of word segmentation. [10] introduced a two-stage modeling approach at the character level, exploiting the crossover effects between intent and slot information. However, it is commonly understood that Chinese word segmentation is critical for interpreting slots in an utterance. Given the utterance "我/想/听/稻香 (I want to listen to Rice Fragrance)" as an example, we use "/" to split the words in an utterance. If the model is based on character level, it is likely to wrongly predict the slot of "稻 (rice)" as "Rice_name". However, by using the information of "稻香 (rice fragrance)" in the word segmentation, the model can easily predict "稻香 (rice fragrance)" slot as "Song". To inject the word information into the Chinese SLU, [11] introduced a word adapter to combine information about characters and words. However, they did not consider the influence of redundant information in the word adapter. For example, in the example utterance mentioned above, the single word "稻香 (song)" and the single character "稻 (rice_name)" are semantically different, which causes semantic ambiguity when injecting word information, and the model lacks the guidance of slot information on intent detection.

To address these issues, we propose a unique bi-directional interaction graph framework to jointly model slot filling and intent detection, taking into account the correlation between slot information and intent information in Chinese SLU as well as alleviating the redundant information caused by the direct fusion of character-word semantic information: (1) bi-directional interaction graph, which uses slot information and intent information as feature nodes and creates bi-directionally connected edges between slot and intent information, and interacts via a multi-layer graph attention network; (2) filter gate. To fuse character-word semantic information efficiently, the redundant information caused by direct fusion is eliminated utilizing a filter gate fusion mechanism which can control the propagation of effective semantic information.

In summary, the following is the contributions of this work:

- We propose a bi-directional interaction graph for interacting with slot and intent information that takes into account the reciprocal facilitation of slot filling and intent detection.
- We propose a filter gate to limit the impact of redundant information owing to directly fusing character-word semantic information.
- Experiments on CAIS and SMP-ECDT datasets demonstrate that our model outperforms the best benchmark model and accomplishes the state-of-the-arts performance.

2   Related Works

Slot Filling and Intent Detection. The researchers proposed many implicit joint models considering the relationship between slot filling and intent detection tasks [6,12–14]. Essentially, they fail to make an explicit relationship between the two tasks. Later, some of researchers started to explore intent-augmented joint models and proposed many execellent approaches [2,3,11,15–17]. Nevertheless, these models do not account for the guiding role of slot information in intent detection. Recently, researchers have begun to explore models in which two tasks guide each other [4,10,18–21].

Graph Neural Networks. Currently, graph neural networks are performing very well in many fields. [22] applied graph attention networks to short text classification. [23] improved the performance of aspect-level sentiment classification by clarifying the dependencies between words through graph attention networks. Due to some limitations of GCN, the researcher proposed new approaches [24,25]. In SLU, [7,8] improved model performance by building effective interaction graphs. In our BIG-FG, a bi-directional interaction graph is built based on a multi-layer graph attention network to explicitly model the relationship between the two tasks, fully considering the mutual facilitation between intent detection and slot filling to enhance the performance of the model.

3   Approach

This work contributes to implementing slot filling and intent detection for Chinese SLU. In this section, the proposed approach will be introduced in detail. The overall framework of the model is shown in Fig. 1 (a). Firstly, the text encoding layer is introduced to realize the vectorized representation of characters and words in an utterance. Secondly, we propose the adaptive fusion module to obtain the slot and intent information. Next, the intent nodes and slot nodes are learned through an interrelated connection fusion using the bi-directional interaction graph. Finally, through a cooperative learning schema, slot filling and intent detection are optimized concurrently.

3.1   Text Encoding Layer

Following [11], we utilize a novel text encoding structure to obtain character-word information representation, which consists primarily of an embedding encoder, a self-attention, and a Bi-LSTM.

Character Encoding. Given a Chinese utterance $X = \{x_1, x_2, x_3, \cdots, x_T\}$, T denotes the number of characters. Firstly, each character is transformed into a character vector $E^c = \{e_1^c, e_2^c, \cdots, e_T^c\}$, and secondly, high-level semantic information is obtained by self-attention and Bi-LSTM, respectively.

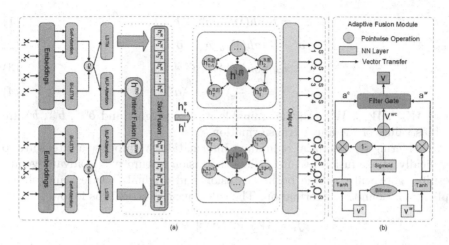

Fig. 1. The overall architecture of our proposed bi-directional interaction graph framework with filter gate fusion mechanism, where Cat denotes the concatenation operation. The internal structure of adaptive fusion module is shown in (b).

The self-attention [26] captures the features of the context of the characters in the utterance and the Bi-LSTM portrays the sequence from two directions, which can express more semantic information. We feed the characters vector E^c into self-attention and Bi-LSTM, respectively. The output vectors are $H^A = \{h_1^A, h_2^A, \cdots, h_T^A\}$ and $H^L = \{h_1^L, h_2^L, \cdots, h_T^L\}$, respectively.

Finally, the semantic information $h_t^c = [h_t^A, h_t^L]$ is obtained by concatenating self-attention and Bi-LSTM. The final output sequence of the character-level semantic information is $H^c = \{h_1^c, h_2^c, \cdots, h_T^c\}$.

Word Encoding. We use an external CWS (Chinese Word Segmentation) system. Given the Chinese utterance X, we obtain the word sequences $E^w = \{e_1^w, e_2^w, \cdots, e_M^w\}(M \leqslant T)$ by word segmentation and vectorization. The rest of the encoding part is the same as the character encoding, and the final word-level semantic encoding output is denoted as $H^w = \{h_1^w, h_2^w, \cdots, h_M^w\}$.

3.2 Adaptive Fusion Module

Fusion Module. Figure 1(b) represents the structure diagram of the adaptive fusion layer module. As one of the contribution points of this work, a filter gate mechanism is proposed based on bilinear fusion to reduce the impact of redundant information brought by character-word fusion. Following [11], with the word vector $v^w \in \mathbb{R}^d$ and character vector $v^c \in \mathbb{R}^d$ as inputs, we obtain the normalized word and character vectors a^w, a^c by $Tanh$ activation function. After that, the weights are calculated using a bilinear function, and then they are weighted and summed to obtain v^{wc}. The procedure for calculating is as follows:

$$a^w = tanh(\boldsymbol{W}_{aw}\boldsymbol{v}^w + \boldsymbol{b}^{aw}) \tag{1}$$

$$a^c = tanh(\boldsymbol{W}_{ac}\boldsymbol{v}^c + \boldsymbol{b}^{ac}) \tag{2}$$

$$\lambda = sigmoid(\boldsymbol{v}^c\boldsymbol{W}_\lambda\boldsymbol{v}^w + b^\lambda) \tag{3}$$

$$\boldsymbol{v}^{wc} = (1 - \lambda)\boldsymbol{a}^c + \lambda\boldsymbol{a}^w \tag{4}$$

where $\boldsymbol{W}_{aw}$, $\boldsymbol{W}_{ac}$, $\boldsymbol{W}_\lambda$ are the trainable matrix weights and $\boldsymbol{b}^{aw}$, $\boldsymbol{b}^{ac}$, b^λ are the bias values of the linear transformation.

Considering the potential redundant information, we propose a filter gate to specifically utilize fusion feature. When the fusion feature $\boldsymbol{v}^{wc}$ is advantageous, the filter gate will combine both the fusion and original features, and obtain explicit slot boundary information. The calculation process is as follows:

$$\boldsymbol{f}_c = \boldsymbol{W}_{fc}[\boldsymbol{a}^c, \boldsymbol{v}^{wc}] + \boldsymbol{b}^{fc} \tag{5}$$

$$\boldsymbol{f}_w = \boldsymbol{W}_{fw}[\boldsymbol{a}^w, \boldsymbol{v}^{wc}] + \boldsymbol{b}^{fw} \tag{6}$$

$$f_g = sigmoid(\boldsymbol{W}_g[\boldsymbol{f}_c, \boldsymbol{f}_w] + \boldsymbol{b}^{wc}) \tag{7}$$

$$\boldsymbol{v} = f_g * \tanh(\boldsymbol{W}_v\boldsymbol{v}^{wc} + \boldsymbol{b}^g) \tag{8}$$

where $\boldsymbol{W}_{fc}$, $\boldsymbol{W}_{fw}$, $\boldsymbol{W}_g$, $\boldsymbol{W}_v$ are the trainable matrix weights; $\boldsymbol{b}^{fc}$, $\boldsymbol{b}^{fw}$, $\boldsymbol{b}^{wc}$, and $\boldsymbol{b}^g$ are the bias values of the linear transformation, [,] represents the concatenation operation, and $\boldsymbol{v}$ is the final fusion output. The above formula for the adaptive fusion layer can be abbreviated as $\boldsymbol{v} = AFM(\boldsymbol{v}^c, \boldsymbol{v}^w)$.

Intent Fusion. We employ MLP attention to obtain an informative representation of the entire utterance $\boldsymbol{h}^{mc} \in \mathbb{R}^d$. Similarly, we can also obtain the word-level representation of the information of the whole utterance $\boldsymbol{h}^{mw} \in \mathbb{R}^d$ and get the fused intent information representation $\boldsymbol{h}^I$ through the adaptive fusion layer.

$$\boldsymbol{h}^I = AFM(\boldsymbol{h}^{mc}, \boldsymbol{h}^{mw}) \tag{9}$$

Slot Fusion. By unidirectional LSTM, we can obtain more appropriate slot information $\boldsymbol{h}_t^{sc}$, $\boldsymbol{h}_t^{sw}$. Then, through the adaptive fusion layer, the fused slot information is obtained, denoted as $\boldsymbol{h}_t^{S1}$.

$$\boldsymbol{h}_t^S = AFM(\boldsymbol{h}_t^{sc}, \boldsymbol{h}_{f_{align}(t,w)}^{sw}) \tag{10}$$

3.3 Bi-directional Interaction Graph Module

Another contribution point of this work is to carry out the interaction of slot information and intent information. We propose a bi-directional interaction graph module, as shown in Fig. 1. By constructing different edges and feature nodes, a multi-layer graph attention network is utilized to fully interact with the information between the intent and slot.

---

[1] Given a word sequence $\boldsymbol{w}$={"打","开","相机"}, $f_{align}(t,\boldsymbol{w})$ provides the index of the word that goes with the t-th character in $\boldsymbol{w}$ (e.g.,$f_{align}(1,\boldsymbol{w})$=1,$f_{align}$ $(3,\boldsymbol{w})$=3,$f_{align}(4,\boldsymbol{w})$=3).

Graph Attention Network. The GAT is a crucial network structure in the domain of deep learning which utilizes the attention mechanism to perform adaptive weighting of various neighboring edges, significantly enhancing the expressive capability. Given a series of feature nodes $Z = \{z_1, z_2, \cdots, z_N\}$, N is the total number of nodes. The graph attention network generates new node features, $Z' = \{z'_1, z'_2, \cdots, z'_N\}$ as the output.

$$\alpha_{ij} = \frac{exp(f(a^T[W_z z_i, W_z z_j]))}{\sum_{k' \in N_i} exp(f(a^T[W_z z_i, W_z z_{k'}]))} \tag{11}$$

$$z'_i = \overset{K}{\underset{k=1}{\|}} \sigma(\sum_{j \in N_i} \alpha_{ij}^k W_z^k z_j) \tag{12}$$

where α_{ij}^k denotes the attention weight at k-th head, W_z^k denotes the k-th trainable matrix weight, and $\|$ denotes the concatenation operation. In this work, the multi-headed graph attention layer is directly adopted to the bi-directional interaction graph.

Bi-directional Interaction Graph. The correlation between intent and slot is quite essential in SLU. The slot is a reflection of character-level information and the intent is a reflection of sentence-level information.

For the feature nodes of the bi-directional interaction graph, we concatenate the intent hidden layer representation h^I obtained from the intent fusion layer and the slot hidden layer representation h_t^S obtained from the slot fusion layer to be the nodes of the bi-directional interaction graph $H_g^{[l]} = \{h^{I,[l]}, h_1^{S,[l]}, h_2^{S,[l]}, \cdots, h_T^{S,[l]}\}$. $h^{I,[l]}$ denotes the intent hidden layer feature of the l-th layer and $h_t^{S,[l]}$ denotes the slot hidden layer feature of the l-th layer.

For the edges of the bi-directional interaction graph, we establish a bi-directio- nal connection between the each slot and intent node, and due to a correlation between contexts, bi-directional connections are also established between slot and slot at adjacent location.

In order to fully interact with the feature between the intent and slot, a multi-layer bi-directional interaction graph is constructed. For a bi-direction graph with $(l + 1)$ layers of interaction, a hidden layer feature of the bi-direction interaction graph at $(l + 1)$-th layer can be obtained, and this hidden layer feature is used as the final output.

$$H_g^{[l+1]} = multi\text{-}head\,GAT^{[l]}(H_g^{[l]}) \tag{13}$$

$$h^{fI}, h_t^{fs} = h^{I,[l+1]}, h_t^{S,[l+1]} \tag{14}$$

where $multi\text{-}head\,GAT^{[l]}$ represents the multi-head graph attention network at l-th layer, $h^{I,[l+1]}$ and $h_t^{S,[l+1]}$ are the intent feature and slot feature at $(l+1)$-th layer, respectively, h^{fI} is the output of the intent feature, and h_t^{fs} represents the output of the slot feature.

Through the linear layer, h^{fI} and h_t^{fs} are used for intent detection and slot filling, respectively. $y^I = softmax(W_{fI} h^{fI})$ and $y_t^S = softmax(W_{fs} h_t^{fs})$, where $\boldsymbol{W}_{fI}$ and $\boldsymbol{W}_{fs}$ are trainable parameters. $O^I = argmax(\boldsymbol{y}^I)$ is the predicted intent tags and $O^S_t = argmax(\boldsymbol{y}^S_t)$ is the predicted slot labels in an utterance.

3.4 Loss Function

In this work, cross-entropy is employed as the loss function. The training objective for combining intent and slot loss is to reduce the value of the following loss function:

$$\mathcal{L}_\theta = -\mu \sum_{i=1}^{N_I} \hat{y}_i^I log(y_i^I) - (1-\mu) \sum_{t=1}^{T} \sum_{i=1}^{N_S} \hat{y}_t^{S,i} log(y_t^{S,i}) \tag{15}$$

where N_I indicates the number of intent labels, T indicates the number of characters in an utterance, N_S indicates the number of slot labels, μ is a hyperparameter, $\hat{y}^I$ and $\hat{y}^S$ indicate the true tags of the intent and the true tags of the slot, respectively.

4 Experiment

4.1 Datasets and Evaluation Metrics

To verify the feasibility of the approach, two openly accessible Chinese datasets CAIS [9] and SMP-ECDT[2] [11] are selected to conduct experiments. The CAIS dataset contains 7995 training sets, 994 validation sets, and 1024 test sets. There are 1655 training sets, 413 validation sets, and 508 test sets in the SMP-ECDT dataset. Following [2,16], we assess the effectiveness of Chinese SLU intent prediction using precision, slot filling using F1 score, and utterance-level semantic frame parsing using overall precision. In this work, the Chinese natural language processing system (Language Technology Platform, LTP) is adopted to acquire Chinese word segmentation[3].

4.2 Implementation Details

We conduct experiments with the GPU of Tesla A100 and PyTorch framework. All of the model weights begin with a uniform distribution as the initialization. The dropout rate is 0.5. The number of layers of graph attention network is 2, and the hidden layer dimension of each layer is 128, using 8 heads. 1.0 is chosen as the value for the maximum norm of gradient clipping. The L2 norm coefficient is 10^{-6}. The Adam uses a learning rate of 5×10^{-4} to update all parameters.

---

[2] https://conference.cipsc.org.cn/smp2019/evaluation.html.
[3] http://ltp.ai/.

Table 1. Main results on CAIS and SMP-ECDT.

Models	CAIS			SMP-ECDT		
	Slot (F1)	Intent (Acc)	Overall (Acc)	Slot (F1)	Intent (Acc)	Overall (Acc)
Slot-Gated Full Atten [2]	81.13	94.37	80.83	60.91	86.02	53.75
SF-ID Network [19]	84.85	94.27	82.41	63.90	88.85	55.67
CM-Net [9]	86.16	94.56	-	-	-	-
Stack-propagation [16]	87.64	94.37	84.68	71.32	91.06	63.75
MLWA [11]	88.61	95.16	86.17	75.26	94.22	67.58
GAIR [10]	88.92	95.45	86.86	76.08	94.56	68.58
BIG-FG	89.83	95.65	87.25	76.56	95.72	71.23

4.3 Baseline Models

In order to compare with other researchers' models, some meaningful baseline models are selected including Slot-Gated [2], CM-Net [9], SF-ID Network [19], MLWA [11], Stack-Propagation [16] and GAIR [10]. We take advantage of these models' published performance data from the literature [11] on the CAIS dataset. On the SMP-ECDT dataset, we execute the published code of the comparative models utilizing the split test set, with the exception of CM-Net [9] that fails to share codes.

4.4 Main Results

Table 1 shows the primary results and some comparative baselines of the proposed model on the CAIS and SMP-ECDT datasets. From the results, we can notice that the GAIR model without injecting word information performs somewhat better than the MLWA model with injecting word information on all metrics. This result occurs since the GAIR model is two-stage and takes into account the bi-directional correlation between intent and slot information, whereas MLWA just takes into account the influence of intent information on slots, despite the addition of word information. Our proposed BIG-FG model is compared with the GAIR model. On the CAIS dataset, we accomplish a 0.91% increase in Slot (F1), a 0.20% increase in Intent (Acc), and a 0.39% increase in Overall (Acc). On the SMP-ECDT dataset, we accomplish improvements of 0.48% on Slot (F1), 1.16% on Intent (Acc), and 2.65% on Overall (Acc). From the results, we observe that our model performs better than the top baseline model and achieves state-of-the-art performance. We attribute the improvement to the following reasons: (1) Our model in this work introduces word information while using character information, which solves the problem of ambiguous word boundary; (2) Considering the mutual facilitation between slot filling and intent detection, effective interaction is carried out through the BIG module to achieve mutual communication between the two tasks and enhance the model performance; (3) The filter gate based on bilinear fusion reduces redundant information, resulting in enhanced model performance. However, the MLWA model fails to consider the influence of redundant information and the guiding role of slot information on intent detection, and the GAIR model ignores the influence of Chinese word segmentation.

Table 2. Ablation study on CAIS and SMP-ECDT datasets.

Models	CAIS			SMP-ECDT		
	Slot (F1)	Intent (Acc)	Overall (Acc)	Slot (F1)	Intent (Acc)	Overall (Acc)
w/o intent fusion	87.13	94.37	85.83	73.91	94.42	67.75
w/o slot fusion	86.85	95.27	86.01	74.91	95.55	68.67
w/o filter gate	89.80	95.45	86.75	76.36	94.97	69.84
w/o BIG	88.60	94.46	85.37	75.39	95.23	69.09
BIG-FG	**89.83**	**95.65**	**87.25**	**76.56**	**95.72**	**71.23**

4.5   Analysis

To investigate the effect of the components in the proposed model, ablation experiments are carried out to verify the effectiveness. Table 2 shows the results of the ablation experiments. In addtion, We also explore the effect of the number of BIG layers and different word segmentors on the performance of the model.

Effect of Intent Fusion Layer. To explore whether the intent fusion layer plays a role in the model, the intent fusion layer is removed in this experiment, meaning that the intent information provided by the characters and words is utilized directly, which is named as *w/o intent fusion*. From the results in *w/o intent fusion* row in Table 2, we can observe 1.28% and 1.30% drops on Intent (Acc) on the CAIS and SMP-ECDT datasets, respectively, and other evaluation metrics also decrease, which demonstrates that the intent fusion layer can efficiently fuse the intent information provided by the characters and words, and achieve improved semantic features for intent detection.

Effect of Slot Fusion Layer. Similarly, we remove the slot fusion layer to investigate whether the slot fusion layer enriches semantic knowledge of slot, which is named as *w/o slot fusion*. The experimental results are shown in *w/o slot fusion* row in Table 2. Slot (F1) decreases by 2.98% on the CAIS dataset and by 1.65% on the SMP-ECDT dataset. This indicates that directly fusing the slot information provided by characters and words is not effective, and the slot fusion layer in our model can improve the information representation of slot.

Effect of Filter Gate. The filter gate reduces the redundant information that would be produced by the direct fusion of character-word semantic information. To investigate the specific effect of the filter gate in our model, we remove the filter gate and directly fuse character-word semantic information with bilinearity, which is named as *w/o filter gate*. The *w/o filter gate* row in Table 2 shows that the Slot (F1), Intent (Acc), and Overall (Acc) decrease on both CAIS and SMP-ECDT datasets, indicating that bilinear fusion is not effective when there is no filter gate, and the filter gate plays an important role in the BIG-FG model.

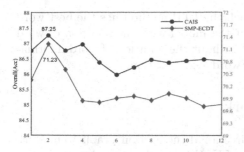 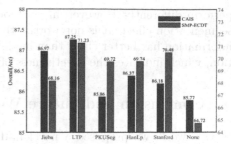

Fig. 2. Effect of the number of BIG layers and the horizontal axis indicates the number of layers of the BIG.

Fig. 3. Effect of word segmentors and the horizontal axis indicates the different word segmentors.

Effect of Bi-directional Interaction Graph. To explore the effect of the proposed bi-directional interaction graph module, we remove the bi-directional interaction graph module and directly use LSTM as the decoder. The intent detection and slot filling are modeled independently. It is named as *w/o BIG* in this experiment. The *w/o BIG* row in Table 2 shows that the evaluation metrics on two datasets drop more, which indicates that the independent modeling of intent and slot information is worse than the explicit joint modeling of intent and slot information and the BIG fully interacts with the features of intent and slot, thus enhancing the overall performance.

Effect of the Number of BIG Layers. To investigate the influence of the number of BIG layers, we plot the relationship between the Overall (Acc) and the number of layers of BIG, as shown in Fig. 2. It can be clearly seen from the figure that the model performance improves with the number of layers of the BIG, and the best performance on the CAIS and SMP-ECDT datasets is achieved when the number of layers of the BIG is 2, after which it decreases to gradually stabilize. The reason is that when there are too many layers, the model tends to exhibit excessive smoothing, resulting in the inclusion of redundant information. In general, choosing the optimal number of layers of BIG can improve the performance of the model.

Effect of Different Word Segmentors. We choose five different word segmentors for our experiments to investigate the impact of different word segmentors on the performance of our model, including Jieba[4], LTP, PKUSeg[5], HanLp[6], and Stanford[7]. Furthermore, we add an additional set of experiments without word segmentation information to validate the benefits of adding word segmentation information. Figure 3 shows the results of the experiments. We use Overall (Acc) as evaluation indice, and we can see that different word segmentation methods

---

[4] https://github.com/fxsjy/jieba.
[5] https://github.com/lancopku/PKUSeg-python.
[6] https://github.com/hankcs/HanLP.
[7] https://stanfordnlp.github.io/CoreNLP/.

perform differently. However, in our model, the LTP method has the best word segmentation effect. It is noteworthy that the model with the addition of word information has better effect than model without the addition of word information, which indicates the effectiveness of word segmentation.

5   Conclusion and Future Work

In this work, we proposed a novel bi-directional interaction graph framework with a filter gate mechanism for Chinese SLU. While reducing redundant information, we effectively fused the semantic information provided at the character level as well as word level. Furthermore, we took advantage of the correlation between intent and slot feature to enrich the semantic representations of intent and slot, thus improving the model performance. Experiments on SMP-ECDT and CAIS datasets showed that our model achieved the best performance. In the future, we will consider adding some prior knowledge and exploring a new fusion mechanism to fully fuse word information to enhance the performance of Chinese spoken language understanding tasks.

Acknowledgement. This work was supported in part by the National Science Foundation of China under Grant 62172111 and in part by the Natural Science Foundation of Guangdong Province under Grant 2019A1515011056.

References

1. Tur, G., De Mori, R.: Spoken Language Understanding: Systems for Extracting Semantic Information from Speech. Wiley, Hoboken (2011)
2. Goo, C.W., et al.: Slot-gated modeling for joint slot filling and intent prediction. In: Proc. NAACL, pp. 753–757 (2018)
3. Li, C., Li, L., Qi, J.: A self-attentive model with gate mechanism for spoken language understanding. In: Proceedings of EMNLP, pp. 3824–3833 (2018)
4. Sun, C., Lv, L., Liu, T., Li, T.: A joint model based on interactive gate mechanism for spoken language understanding. Appl. Intell. **52**, 6057–6064 (2022)
5. Chen, M., Zeng, J., Lou, J.: A self-attention joint model for spoken language understanding in situational dialog applications. arXiv preprint arXiv:1905.11393 (2019)
6. Liu, B., Lane, I.: Attention-based recurrent neural network models for joint intent detection and slot filling. In: Proceedings of Interspeech, pp. 685–689 (2016)
7. Ding, Z., Yang, Z., Lin, H., Wang, J.: Focus on interaction: a novel dynamic graph model for joint multiple intent detection and slot filling. In: Proceedings of IJCAI, pp. 3801–3807 (2021)
8. Qin, L., Wei, F., Xie, T., Xu, X., Che, W., Liu, T.: GL-GIN: fast and accurate non-autoregressive model for joint multiple intent detection and slot filling. In: Proceedings of ACL-IJCNLP, pp. 178–188 (2021)
9. Liu, Y., Meng, F., Zhang, J., Zhou, J., Chen, Y., Xu, J.: CM-Net: a novel collaborative memory network for spoken language understanding. In: Proceedings of EMNLP-IJCNLP, pp. 1051–1060 (2019)

10. Zhu, Z., Huang, P., Huang, H., Liu, S., Lao, L.: A graph attention interactive refine framework with contextual regularization for jointing intent detection and slot filling. In: Proceedings of ICASSP, pp. 7617–7621 (2022)

11. Teng, D., Qin, L., Che, W., Zhao, S., Liu, T.: Injecting word information with multi-level word adapter for Chinese spoken language understanding. In: Proceedings of ICASSP, pp. 8188–8192 (2021)

12. Guo, D., Tur, G., Yih, W.t., Zweig, G.: Joint semantic utterance classification and slot filling with recursive neural networks. In: Proceedings of SLT, pp. 554–559 (2014)

13. Hakkani-Tür, D., et al.: Multi-domain joint semantic frame parsing using bi-directional RNN-LSTM. In: Proceedings of Interspeech, pp. 715–719 (2016)

14. Xu, P., Sarikaya, R.: Convolutional neural network based triangular CRF for joint intent detection and slot filling. In: Proceedings of ASRU. pp. 78–83 (2013)

15. Ma, Z., Sun, B., Li, S.: A two-stage selective fusion framework for joint intent detection and slot filling. IEEE Trans. Neural Netw. Learn. Syst. 1–12 (2022)

16. Qin, L., Che, W., Li, Y., Wen, H., Liu, T.: A stack-propagation framework with token-level intent detection for spoken language understanding. In: Proceedings of EMNLP-IJCNLP, pp. 2078–2087 (2019)

17. Zhou, B., Zhang, Y., Sui, X., Song, K., Yuan, X.: Multi-grained label refinement network with dependency structures for joint intent detection and slot filling. arXiv preprint arXiv:2209.04156 (2022)

18. Chen, D., Huang, Z., Wu, X., Ge, S., Zou, Y.: Towards joint intent detection and slot filling via higher-order attention. In: Proceedings of IJCAI, pp. 4072–4078 (2022)

19. Haihong, E., Niu, P., Chen, Z., Song, M.: A novel bi-directional interrelated model for joint intent detection and slot filling. In: Proceedings of ACL, pp. 5467–5471 (2019)

20. Wang, J., Wei, K., Radfar, M., Zhang, W., Chung, C.: Encoding syntactic knowledge in transformer encoder for intent detection and slot filling. In: Proceedings of AAAI, vol. 35, pp. 13943–13951 (2021)

21. Zhang, C., Li, Y., Du, N., Fan, W., Yu, P.: Joint slot filling and intent detection via capsule neural networks. In: Proceedings of ACL, pp. 5259–5267 (2019)

22. Linmei, H., Yang, T., Shi, C., Ji, H., Li, X.: Heterogeneous graph attention networks for semi-supervised short text classification. In: Proceedings of EMNLP-IJCNLP, pp. 4821–4830 (2019)

23. Huang, B., Carley, K.: Syntax-aware aspect level sentiment classification with graph attention networks. In: Proceedings of EMNLP-IJCNLP, pp. 5469–5477 (2019)

24. Wang, S., Wu, Z., Chen, Y., Chen, Y.: Beyond graph convolutional network: an interpretable regularizer-centered optimization framework. arXiv preprint arXiv:2301.04318 (2023)

25. Chen, M., Wei, Z., Huang, Z., Ding, B., Li, Y.: Simple and deep graph convolutional networks. In: Proceedings of ICML, pp. 1725–1735 (2020)

26. Vaswani, A., et al.: Attention is all you need. In: Proceedings of NeurIPS, pp. 6000–6010 (2017)

Co-RGCN: A Bi-path GCN-Based Co-Regression Model for Multi-intent Detection and Slot Filling

Qingpeng Wen, Bi Zeng, and Pengfei Wei[✉]

School of Computer Science and Technology, Guangdong University of Technology,
Guangzhou 510006, China
wpf@gdut.edu.cn

Abstract. Since people's utterance usually has multiple intents, joint models of multi-intent detection and slot filling have high research value in realistic scenarios. However, the existing models lack the syntactic dependencies and semantic contextual relations of the utterance to guide the slot filling and multi-intent detection, which cannot effectively resolve word order variations and semantic dependencies in a complex utterance. Meanwhile, these models lack the fine-grained slot information to guide the multi-intent detection, fail to utilize the semantic relevance of the rich intent and slot information well. In this paper, we propose a Bi-path GCN-based Co-Regression model for Multi-intent Detection and Slot Filling (Co-RGCN), which contains two modules: (1) Bi-path GCN module, which contains SynGCN and SemGCN, guiding slot filling and multi-intent detection by extracting syntactic and semantic contextual information of the utterance; (2) Co-Regression module, which achieves bidirectional joint modeling through the co-regression operations on multi-intent information and slot information. Experiments on two datasets show that our model performs more effectively than competing models and achieves SOTA performance.

Keywords: Multi-intent Detection · Slot Filling · Bi-path GCN · Co-Regression

1 Introduction

Spoken language understanding (SLU) is an important component of task-oriented dialogue systems, especially in artificial intelligence dialogue systems, where the performance of SLU determines the system performance. The SLU task consists mainly of intent detection (ID) and slot filling (SF) [1]. In the past, studies usually focused on a single intent. Nevertheless, Kim et al. [2] discovered that a complex realistic scenarios frequently involve multiple intents in a single utterance. For instance, in Fig. 1, the ID task usually acts as a classification task [3–5] to predict the intent labels of utterance expressions, while the SF task

© The Author(s), under exclusive license to Springer Nature Switzerland AG 2023
L. Iliadis et al. (Eds.): ICANN 2023, LNCS 14257, pp. 316–327, 2023.
https://doi.org/10.1007/978-3-031-44216-2_26

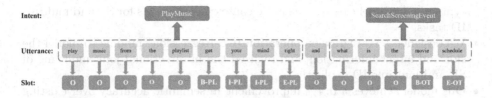

Fig. 1. An example of a multi-intent SLU utterance. Where B-PL denotes B-play_list, I-PL denotes I-play_list, E-PL denotes E-play_list, B-OT denotes B-object_type, and E-OT denotes E-object_type

acts as a sequence tagging task [6,7] to determine the slot label for each word throughout the entire utterance.

Early studies were typically applied to single intent task only, with representative approaches such as BERT-based joint ID and SF model [8], variable-length attention encoder-decoder model [9] and Wheel-Graph Attention Network model [10]. Since people's utterance usually has multiple intents, multi-intent SLU task is more practical than single-intent SLU task in realistic scenarios and have better research value. Thus, Xu et al. [11] and Kim et al. [12] started to research multi-intent SLU task. However, their model only considered single-task modeling for multi-intent detection, yet the results show that the joint dual-task modeling for ID and SF is mutually beneficial [13,14]. Subsequently, Qin et al. [15] proposed the adaptive graph interaction framework (AGIF) to extract fine-grained intent information for slot prediction via adaptive intent-slot interaction graphs. Further, Qin et al. [16] proposed a non-autoregressive graph attention-based model (GL-GIN) to improve the performance of multi-intent detection and slot filling through local and global GAT interactions. However, the above models cannot solve the problem of word order variations and semantic dependencies as they lack utterance syntactic dependencies and semantic contextual relations to guide SF and multiple ID tasks. Gangadharaiah et al. [17] introduced multi-task network with slot gating mechanism [18] to these tasks; Chen et al. [19] proposed a multi-instance learning approach and formulated multi-intent detection as a weakly supervised problem to obtain information about intent and slot decoding through multiple decoders. However, the above models only apply the intent information to the SF task and lack the explicit bi-directional joint modeling of slot information and multi-intent information.

To better implement the multi-intent SLU task, a Bi-path GCN-based Co-Regression model (Co-RGCN) is proposed in this paper. Experimental results on two publicly available datasets, MixSNIPS and MixATIS, show that our model outperforms all existing models and achieves SOTA performance.

In general, this paper's contributions are as follows:

- We proposed a Bi-path GCN-based Co-Regression model (Co-RGCN), which improves the existing joint model of multi-intent detection and slot filling.
- We firstly introduced the Bi-path GCN network, which extracts the syntactic information and semantic contextual information through the utterance

syntactic dependencies and semantic contextual relations for SF and multiple ID tasks.

- We designed a co-regression operation (Co-Regression) module to model the slot and intent information, and realized the bi-directional joint modeling of SF and multiple ID explicitly.
- Our model achieves a **0.4%** improvement in semantic accuracy over existing models on the MixSNIPS dataset and a **1.1%** improvement on the MixATIS dataset, both of which achieve SOTA performance.

The codes for this paper are publicly available at https://github.com/QingpengWen/Co-RGCN.

2   Proposed Method

In this section, we will describe in detail about the relevant modules of Co-RGCN. The general framework is shown in Fig. 2.

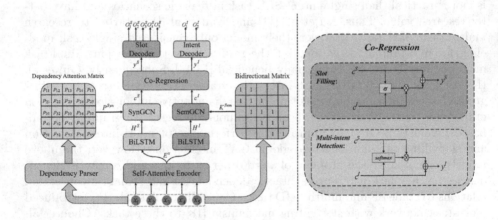

Fig. 2. The Co-RGCN model proposed in this paper. The model includes Self-Attentive Module, Bi-path GCN Module (which contains SynGCN and SemGCN) and Co-Regression Module

2.1   Self-attentive Module

In this paper, we follow the method of Qin et al. [16]. It mainly consists of an Embedding encoder, a Self-attention encoder [20] and a BiLSTM encoder [21]. For a given utterance message $x = \{x_1, x_2, ..., x_N\}$ containing N words, the Embedding encoder transforms it into vector $E_{emb}^x \in \mathbb{R}^{N \times d} = \{e_1^x, e_2^x, ..., e_N^x\}$, the BiLSTM encoder loops the input utterance forward and backward to obtain the context-aware sequence information $H^x \in \mathbb{R}^{N \times d} = \{h_1^x, h_2^x, ..., h_N^x\}$, where

$h_j^x \in \mathbb{R}^d = BiLSTM(e_j^x, h_{j-1}^x, h_{j+1}^x)$. The Self-attention encoder captures the contextual information of each token in the valid sequence as $A^x \in \mathbb{R}^{N \times d} = softmax(\frac{Q \cdot K^T}{\sqrt{d^k}}) \cdot V$, where Q, K and V are matrices acquired by the application of different linear projections to the input vectors and d^k denotes the vector dimension.

Subsequently, we concatenate the output of the BiLSTM encoder H^x and the Self-attention encoder A^x to obtain the final Self-Attentive encoding representation as $E^x \in \mathbb{R}^{N \times 2d} = \{e_1^x, e_2^x, \cdots, e_N^x\}$.

2.2   Bi-path GCN

In order to better extract effective slot information and intent information, we propose a Bi-path GCN module, which contains SynGCN and SemGCN, where SynGCN obtains slot information by extracting the syntactic dependencies of utterance and guides the slot filling task; SemGCN obtains intent information by extracting semantic contextual relations and guides the multi-intent detection task. Figure 3 shows an example of sentence transformation into the adjacency matrices for SynGCN and SemGCN.

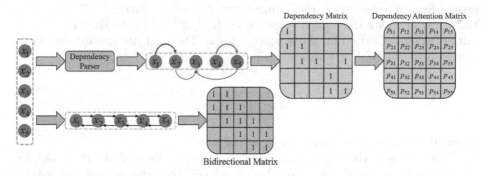

Fig. 3. An example of a sentence transformation into the adjacency matrices for Syn-GCN and SemGCN, where the Dependency Attention Matrix denotes the adjacency matrix of SynGCN and the Bidirectional Matrix denotes the adjacency matrix of SemGCN

Graph Convolutional Networks: Motivated by the traditional convolutional neural networks (CNNs) and graph embeddings, GCN is a variant of CNN that can efficiently capture contextual information. For graph embedding structures, GCN encodes local information by applying convolutional operations to neighboring nodes. Subsequently, message passing is performed by multi-layer convolution, which enables to capture more global information. A common GCN model usually has l layers, and its input graph can be built on a 0–1 adjacency matrix $A \in \mathbb{R}^{N \times N}$, where the element a_{ij} in A indicates the connection between the i-th node and the j-th node, if connected, then $a_{ij} = 1$ and otherwise $a_{ij} = 0$. Therefore, the adjacency matrix can be considered as the final discrete output of Dependency Parser. For the i-th node in the l-th layer, its hidden state is represented as h_i^l, then the update formula of GCN is:

$$h_i^l = ReLU(\sum_{j=1}^{N} a_{ij}(W^l h_j^{l-1} + b^l)) \tag{1}$$

where W^l is the weight matrix and b^l is the bias.

SynGCN: Since syntactic information can provide additional hierarchical structure and dependencies to help the model handle word order variations and enhance the node information of the slots, we use the SynGCN module to take the syntactic information of the utterance as the slot input. To encode the syntactic information, we make use of the Dependency Matrix $A^{Syn} \in \mathbb{R}^{N \times N}$ of all dependency arcs in Dependency Parser and transformed it into a Dependency Attention Matrix $P^{Syn} \in \mathbb{R}^{N \times N}$, which captures rich structural information by providing all potential syntactic structures, solves the problem of discrete output of Dependency Matrix A^{Syn} and alleviates the problem of dependency parsing errors. Subsequently, using the Dependency Attention Matrix P^{Syn}, the SynGCN module takes the hidden state vector $H^S \in \mathbb{R}^{N \times 2d}$ in the BiLSTM as the initial node information for the syntactic graph. The final slot context output is obtained as $c^S \in \mathbb{R}^{N \times 2d}$, which is computed as follows:

$$c_i^{S(l)} = ReLU(\sum_{j=1}^{N} p_{ij}^{Syn(l)}(W^l c_j^{S(l-1)} + b^l)) \tag{2}$$

where W^l is the weight matrix and b^l is the bias.

Here, we used the dependency resolution model *Spacy-Parser*[1] to obtain the Dependency Matrix A^{Syn} of all dependency arcs and convert them into Dependency Attention Matrix P^{Syn} by the following calculation:

$$p_{ij}^{Syn(l)} = \frac{a_{ij}^{Syn} \cdot exp(c_i^{S(l-1)} \cdot c_j^{S(l-1)})}{\sum_{j=1}^{N} a_{ij}^{Syn} \cdot exp(c_i^{S(l-1)} \cdot c_j^{S(l-1)})} \tag{3}$$

where $c_i^{S(l-1)} \cdot c_j^{S(l-1)}$ calculates the interaction between x_i and x_j by inner product. a_{ij}^{Syn} is an element of the Dependency Matrix A^{Syn}.

SemGCN: Unlike SynGCN, SemGCN uses the semantic relations between the adjacent words to establish a bi-directional connection to obtain the Bidirectional Matrix $K^{Sem} \in \mathbb{R}^{N \times N}$, which provides rich semantic contextual information for multi-intent detection. Furthermore, the hidden state vector $H^I \in \mathbb{R}^{N \times 2d}$ in the

---

[1] https://github.com/explosion/spaCy/tree/master/spacy.

BiLSTM is used as the initial node information of the semantic graph. Then the final intent context output is obtained as $c^I \in \mathbb{R}^{N \times 2d}$, which is calculated as follows:

$$c_i^{I(l)} = ReLU(\sum_{j=1}^{N} k_{ij}^{Sem}(W^l c_i^{I(l-1)} + b^l)) \tag{4}$$

where W^l is the weight matrix and b^l is the bias.

2.3   Co-regression

For better modeling the multiple ID and SF tasks, we propose a Co-Regression module to perform co-regression operations on the intent context information c^I and slot context information c^S to obtain the fine-grained parameter u^S and coarse-grained parameter u^I. For a given input c^I and c^S, the Co-Regression operation is computed as follows:

$$u^S = \sigma[\tanh(c^I)^T(W^S)\tanh(c^S)] \tag{5}$$

$$u^I = \frac{exp((c_i^I)^T(W_i^I)(c_i^S))}{\sum_{i=1}^{N} exp((c_i^I)^T(W_i^I)(c_i^S))} \tag{6}$$

where W^S and W^I are trainable weight matrices and σ is the activation function.

Multi-intent Detection: By fusing coarse-grained parameters and contextual information about slots and intent, the multi-intent output is obtained as $y^I \in \mathbb{R}^{N \times 2d} = \{y_1^I, y_2^I, ..., y_N^I\}$, which is calculated as follows:

$$\nu^I = c^S \cdot u^I \tag{7}$$

$$y^I = \nu^I + c^I \tag{8}$$

Subsequently, by decoding the y^I, the final intent label is obtained as $O^I = \{O_1^I, O_2^I, ..., O_k^I\}$, which is calculated as follows:

$$I_t = \sigma(w_0^I(LeakyReLU(w_1^I \cdot y_t^I + b_1^I)) + b_0^I) \tag{9}$$

$$O^I = \left\{ O_k^I \middle| (\sum_{i=1}^{N} \mathbb{I}[I_{(i,k)} > t_u]) > \frac{N}{2} \right\} \tag{10}$$

where w_0^I and w_1^I are the trainable parameter, b_0^I and b_1^I are the bias, I_t is the intent output at the t-th word, O_k^I is the output of the k-th intent label and $I_{(i,k)}$ denotes the classification result of token i for O_k^I.

During the inference, when a token receives more than half of positive predicted outcomes among all of N tokens, we declare it to be an utterance intent token. For example, if $I_1 = \{0.9, 0.7, 0.5, 0.1\}$, $I_2 = \{0.8, 0.6, 0.3, 0.3\}$, and $I_3 = \{0.9, 0.4, 0.2, 0.2\}$, we respectively received $\{3, 2, 1, 0\}$ of positive votes ($> t_u$). Therefore, the index that obtains more than half of the votes are O_1^I and O_2^I , and we predict the intent $O^I = \{O_1^I, O_2^I\}$.

Slot Filling: Similarly, by applying fine-grained parameters with contextual information about intent and slots for fusion, we obtain the slot output as $y^S \in \mathbb{R}^{N \times 2d} = \{y_1^S, y_2^S, ..., y_N^S\}$, which is calculated as follows:

$$\nu^S = c^I \cdot u^S \tag{11}$$

$$y^S = \nu^S + c^S \tag{12}$$

Subsequently, by decoding the y^S, the final slot label is obtained as $O^S = \{O_1^S, O_2^S, ..., O_N^S\}$, which is calculated as follows:

$$P(\widetilde{y}^S = i|c^S) = softmax[w^S \cdot \widetilde{y}^S] \tag{13}$$

$$O_i^S = argmax[P(\widetilde{y} = i|c^S)] \tag{14}$$

where w^S is the trainable parameter and O_i^S is the output of the i-th slot label.

2.4 Joint Loss Function

According to Goo et al. [18], we used a joint training scheme with NLLOSS for optimization to obtain the loss function for the multi-intent detection task:

$$\mathcal{L}_1 \triangleq \sum_{i=1}^{N} \sum_{t=1}^{N_I} (\hat{y}_i^{(t,I)} log(y_i^{(t,I)}) + (1 - \hat{y}_i^{(t,I)}) log(1 - y_i^{(t,I)})) \tag{15}$$

The loss function for the slot filling task is calculated as follows:

$$\mathcal{L}_2 \triangleq \sum_{i=1}^{N} \sum_{j=1}^{N_S} \hat{y}_i^{(j,S)} log(y_i^{(j,S)}) \tag{16}$$

The final joint loss function is calculated as follows:

$$\mathcal{L} = \alpha \mathcal{L}_1 + (1 - \alpha) \mathcal{L}_2 \tag{17}$$

where N_I denotes the number of single intent labels, N_S denotes the number of slot labels and α denotes the hyperparameter.

3 Experiment

3.1 Datasets and Metrics

To evaluate the effectiveness of our model, we conducted experiments on two publicly available multi-intent SLU datasets, MixSNIPS and MixATIS [16], respectively. The MixSNIPS dataset contains 39,776 training sets, 2,198 validation sets, and 2,199 test sets. The MixATIS dataset was constructed by extending the AITS dataset with 13,162 training sets, 759 validation sets, and 828 test sets. In addition, both of the above datasets are cleaned versions.

In this paper, we use F1 score and accuracy to evaluate the accuracy of SF and ID, respectively. Moreover, we use sentence-level semantic accuracy to indicate that the output of this utterance is considered as a correct prediction when and only when the intent and all slots are perfectly matched.

3.2 Experiment Setting

In this paper, the Dropout rate is set to 0.5, the initial learning rate is set to 0.001, the learning rate is dynamically adjusted using the warmup strategy [22], and the Adam optimizer [23] is used to optimize the parameters of the model. The model was trained on a Linux system using the PyTorch framework and RTX 3090, and multiple experiments were conducted using different random seeds to select the model parameters that performed best on the validation set and evaluate it on the test set.

3.3 Baseline Model

To better validate the advancedness of our model, we reproduce the following classical models, which are Bi-Model [24], a bi-directional model between SF and ID; Stack-Propagation [25], a stack-propagation framework for explicitly merging ID to guide SF; Joint Multiple ID-SF [17], a multi-tasking framework and slot gating mechanism model for multiple intent detection; AGIF [15], an adaptive interaction network model; GL-GIN [16], a non-autoregressive graph attention-based model, and SDJN [19], a Self-Distillation model. Then we compared the metrics of the above models with ours.

3.4 Main Results

The main results of the proposed model are given in Table 1, along with the baseline for comparison on the MixSNIPS dataset and the MixATIS dataset. From the results, we give the following experimental conclusions:

Table 1. The main results of the above model on the MixSNIPS and MixATIS datasets. The numbers with * indicate that the improvement of the model in this paper at all baselines is statistically significant, with p < 0.01 under t-test.

Model	MixSNIPS			MixATIS		
	Slot F1 Score	Intent Acc	Semantic Acc	Slot F1 Score	Intent Acc	Semantic Acc
Bi-Model$_{(2018)}$[24]	90.7	95.6	63.4	83.9	70.3	34.4
Stack-Propagation$_{(2019)}$[25]	94.2	96.0	72.9	87.8	72.1	40.1
Joint Multiple ID-SF$_{(2019)}$[17]	90.6	95.1	62.9	84.6	73.4	36.1
AGIF$_{(2020)}$[15]	94.2	95.1	74.2	86.7	74.4	40.8
GL-GIN$_{(2021)}$[16]	94.0	95.6	75.3	88.3	76.3	43.5
SDJN$_{(2022)}$[19]	94.2	96.1	75.5	88.2	76.6	44.4
Co-RGCN	**94.7***	**96.8***	**75.9***	**88.5***	**77.3***	**45.5***

1. Our model outperforms the baseline on both datasets and achieves competitive performance, which proves the validity of our model.

2. Compared to the model GL-GIN [16], our model improved Slot F1 Score by 0.7%, Intent Acc by 1.2%, and Semantic Acc by 0.6% on the MixSNIPS dataset. On the MixATIS dataset, our model improved by 0.2% in Slot F1 Score, 1.0% in Intent Acc, and 2.0% in Semantic Acc. These improvements indicate that the model with utterance syntactic and semantic context information achieves better performance on the multi-intent dataset compared to the model without them.

3. Compared with the current state-of-the-art model SDJN [19], our model improved Slot F1 Score by 0.5%, Intent Acc by 0.7%, and Semantic Acc by 0.4% on the MixSNIPS dataset. On the MixATIS dataset, our model improved by 0.3% in Slot F1 Score, 0.7% in Intent Acc, and 1.1% in Semantic Acc. This results indicate that our joint model achieves better performance on the multi-intent dataset compared to the joint model that does not use the explicit interaction of ID and SF.

The above results indicate that our model obtains competitive performance and proves the advancedness of the Co-RGCN model. We attribute this experimental result to the following reasons: (1) The proposed SynGCN module has a strong ability to solve the word order variations problem and improve the accuracy of the SF task. (2) The SemGCN module proposed can efficiently extract semantic contextual relations and improve the accuracy of the multiple ID task. (3) The model achieves mutual reinforcement of intent and slots through Co-Regression operations, which further improves the model's performance.

3.5 Ablation Study

In this section, to study the effect of the Co-Regression module and Bi-path GCN module on the model's performance, we conducted an ablation study in this paper. In the experiment, we ablated five important modules and used different methods for analysis. As shown in Table 2.

Table 2. Main results of ablation analysis of experiment on MixSNIPS and MixATIS datasets.

Model	MixSNIPS dataset			MixATIS dataset		
	Slot F1 Score	Intent Acc	Semantic Acc	Slot F1 Score	Intent Acc	Semantic Acc
w/o SynGCN	93.4($\downarrow$ 1.3)	95.7($\downarrow$ 1.1)	75.2($\downarrow$ 0.7)	87.5($\downarrow$ 1.0)	76.5($\downarrow$ 0.8)	44.3($\downarrow$ 1.2)
w/o SemGCN	93.7($\downarrow$ 1.0)	95.4($\downarrow$ 1.4)	75.4($\downarrow$ 0.5)	87.9($\downarrow$ 0.6)	75.8($\downarrow$ 1.5)	44.6($\downarrow$ 0.9)
SynGCN w/o P^{Syn}	93.5($\downarrow$ 1.2)	96.0($\downarrow$ 0.8)	75.5($\downarrow$ 0.4)	87.8($\downarrow$ 0.7)	76.7($\downarrow$ 0.6)	44.5($\downarrow$ 1.0)
SemGCN w/o K^{Sem}	94.0($\downarrow$ 0.7)	95.6($\downarrow$ 1.2)	75.7($\downarrow$ 0.2)	88.1($\downarrow$ 0.4)	76.4($\downarrow$ 0.9)	45.1($\downarrow$ 0.4)
w/o Co-Regression	94.1($\downarrow$ 0.6)	96.2($\downarrow$ 0.6)	75.6($\downarrow$ 0.3)	88.0($\downarrow$ 0.5)	76.8($\downarrow$ 0.5)	44.9($\downarrow$ 0.6)
Co-RGCN	**94.7**	**96.8**	**75.9**	**88.5**	**77.3**	**45.5**

Effect on SynGCN: In this experiment, we first ablated the SynGCN module. Compared to the original model, the model *w/o SynGCN* shows a significant decrease in all metrics on both datasets, we attribute this result to the fact that with the SynGCN module, the model is more powerful in extracting utterance syntactic information, thus enabling better guidance of slot filling. Subsequently, we ablated the Dependency Attention Matrix P^{Syn} in the module to discuss the impact of the dependency attention parsing results on the model's performance. That is, we use the sparse matrix A^{Syn} of Dependency Parser instead of P^{Syn}. Experimental results show that the Dependency Attention Matrix can alleviate the problem of dependency resolution errors and capture rich structural information by providing all potential syntactic structures, which leads to further improvements in model accuracy.

Effect on SemGCN: To verify the effectiveness of the SemGCN module, we first ablated it. The experimental results show that the model *w/o SemGCN* significantly degrades on both datasets, and we attribute this result to the fact that the model with SemGCN can further enhance the extraction of utterance semantic contextual information and thus enables better multi-intent classification. Subsequently, we ablated the Bidirectional Matrix K^{Sem} in the module. The experiment results show that concatenating the bi-directional relationship between adjacent words can better improve the extraction of utterance semantic contextual information by SemGCN.

Effect on Co-regression: The model *w/o Co-Regression* implies that we removed the Co-Regression module so that the slot context output by the Syn-GCN module and the multi-intent context output by the SemGCN module cannot be jointly modeled, and the experimental results demonstrate that the model accuracy without joint modeling is lower than original model, which further indicates that multiple ID and SF tasks can enhance each other.

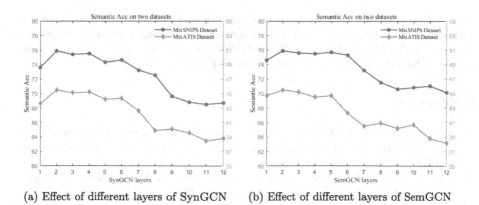

(a) Effect of different layers of SynGCN   (b) Effect of different layers of SemGCN

Fig. 4. Semantic accuracy of different Bi-path GCN layers on two datasets.

3.6 Effect of the Different Bi-Path GCN Layers

To analyze the effect on the performance of the number of the Bi-path GCN module layers, we analyzed the SynGCN and SemGCN modules with different GCN layers on two datasets using semantic accuracy. Figure 4 shows the effect of different GCN layers on the model performance.

According to the results in Fig. 4, the model reaches its maximum at a GCN layer count of 2. We attribute this to the fact that the node representation does not obtain effective propagation when the layer count is small. When there are too many layers, the model becomes unstable because of excessive smoothing and redundant information. In general, an appropriate number of layers for Bi-path GCN can effectively improve the performance of the model.

4 Conclusion and Future Work

In this paper, we propose a Bi-path GCN-based Co-Regression model for Multi-intent Detection and Slot Filling (Co-RGCN), which models the multiple ID and SF tasks by introducing dependencies and using Bi-path GCN networks. Subsequently, Co-Regression is applied for co-modeling the intent and slot information explicitly to achieve mutual enhancement of two tasks. Experimental results on two publicly multi-intent SLU datasets demonstrate that our model achieves a significant improvement over current state-of-the-art models, achieving SOTA performance.

In the future, we plan to introduce the BERT model to further improve the accuracy of our model, and we also plan to apply our approach to other multi-tasking scenarios.

Acknowledgements. This work was supported in part by the National Science Foundation of China under Grant 62172111, in part by the Natural Science Foundation of Guangdong Province under Grant 2019A1515011056, in part by the Key technology project of Shunde District under Grant 2130218003002.

References

1. Weld, H., Huang, X., Long, S., et al.: A survey of joint intent detection and slot filling models in natural language understanding. ACM Comput. Surv. **55**(8), 1–38 (2022)
2. Kim, S., D'Haro, L.F., et al.: The fourth dialog state tracking challenge. Dialogues Soc. Robots: Enablements, Anal. Eval. 435–449 (2017)
3. Haffner, P., Tur, G., Wright, J.H.: Optimizing SVMs for complex call classification. In: ICASSP (2003)
4. Lai, S., Xu, L., et al.: Recurrent convolutional neural networks for text classification. In: Proceedings of the AAAI Conference on Artificial Intelligence, vol. 29, no. 1 (2015)
5. Kim, Y.: Convolutional neural networks for sentence classification. In: EMNLP 2014, A meeting of SIGDAT, a Special Interest Group of the ACL, pp. 1746–1751

6. Raymond, C., Riccardi, G.: Generative and discriminative algorithms for spoken language understanding. In: Interspeech 2007–8th ISCA, pp. 1605–1608 (2007)
7. Yao, K., Peng, B., Zhang, Y., et al.: Spoken language understanding using long short-term memory neural networks. In: SLT, pp. 189–194 (2014)
8. Chen, Q., Zhuo, Z., Wang, W.: Bert for joint intent classification and slot filling[J]. arXiv preprint arXiv:1902.10909, 2019
9. Zhang, Z., Zhang, Z., Chen, H., et al.: A joint learning framework with BERT for spoken language understanding[J]. IEEE Access 7, 168849–168858 (2019)
10. Wei, P., Zeng, B., Liao, W.: Joint intent detection and slot filling with wheel-graph attention networks. J. Intell. Fuzzy Syst. 42(3), 2409–2420 (2022)
11. Xu, P., Sarikaya, R.: Convolutional neural network based triangular CRF for joint intent detection and slot filling. In: ASRU, pp. 78–83 (2013)
12. Kim, B., Ryu, S., Lee, G.G.: Two-stage multi-intent detection for spoken language understanding. Multimedia Tools Appl. 76, 11377–11390 (2017)
13. Ni, P., Li, Y., Li, G., et al.: Natural language understanding approaches based on joint task of intent detection and slot filling for IoT voice interaction. Neural Comput. Appl. 32, 16149–16166 (2020)
14. Tang, H., Ji, D., Zhou, Q.: End-to-end masked graph-based CRF for joint slot filling and intent detection. Neurocomputing 413, 348–359 (2020)
15. Qin, L., Xu, X., Che, W., et al.: AGIF: an adaptive graph-interactive framework for joint multiple intent detection and slot filling. In: Findings of the Association for Computational Linguistics: EMNLP, vol. 2020, pp. 1807–1816 (2020)
16. Qin, L., Wei, F., Xie, T., et al.: GL-GIN: fast and accurate non-autoregressive model for joint multiple intent detection and slot filling. In: Proceedings of the 59th ACL and the 11th IJCNLP, pp. 178–188 (2021)
17. Gangadharaiah, R., Narayanaswamy, B.: Joint multiple intent detection and slot labeling for goal-oriented dialog. In: Proceedings of the 2019 Conference of the North American Chapter of the Association for Computational Linguistics: Human Language Technologies, pp. 564–569 (2019)
18. Goo, C.W., Gao, G., Hsu, Y.K., et al.: Slot-gated modeling for joint slot filling and intent prediction. In: Proceedings of the 2018 Conference of the North American Chapter of the Association for Computational Linguistics: Human Language Technologies, pp. 753–757 (2018)
19. Chen, L., Zhou, P., Zou, Y.: Joint multiple intent detection and slot filling via self-distillation. In: ICASSP, pp. 7612–7616 (2022)
20. Vaswani, A., Shazeer, N., Parmar, N., et al.: Attention is all you need. In: Advances in Neural Information Processing Systems, p. 30 (2017)
21. Graves, A., Graves, A.: Long short-term memory. Supervised Sequence Labelling Recurrent Neural Netw. 37–45 (2012)
22. Liu, L., Jiang, H., He, P., et al.: On the variance of the adaptive learning rate and beyond. In: International Conference on Learning Representations
23. Kingma, D.P., Ba, J.: Adam: a method for stochastic optimization[J]. arXiv preprint arXiv:1412.6980 (2014)
24. Wang, Y., Shen, Y., Jin, H.: A Bi-model based RNN semantic frame parsing model for intent detection and slot filling. In: Proceedings of the 2018 Conference of the North American Chapter of the Association for Computational Linguistics: Human Language Technologies, pp. 309–314 (2018)
25. Qin, L., Che, W., et al.: A stack-propagation framework with token-level intent detection for spoken language understanding. In: EMNLP, pp. 2078–2087 (2019)

DNFS: A Digraph Neural Network with the First-Order and the Second-Order Similarity

Yuanyuan Liu and Adele Lu Jia$^{(\boxtimes)}$

College of Information and Electrical Engineering, China Agricultural University,
Beijing, China
{s20213081517,Ljia}@cau.edu.cn

Abstract. Graph Neural Networks (GNNs) have made remarkable achievements on various graph tasks such as node classification, link prediction, and graph clustering. However, most GNNs focus on undirected graphs and limited effort has been made to handle directed graphs (digraphs) due to their uniqueness and complexity.

In this article, we focus on directed graphs and propose DNFS, a Digraph Neural network model with the First-order and the Second-order similarities, which can preserve unique directional information and explore complex higher-order information in the digraphs. DNFS differentiates the in-degree and out-degree similarity matrices to carefully represent directional information of the digraphs, and it considers both the first-order and the second-order similarities to capture subtle structural information. Extensive experiments on public benchmark datasets demonstrate the effectiveness of our model compared to state-of-the-art baselines.

Keywords: Graph Neural Networks · Directed graph ·
Semi-supervised node classification

1 Introduction

Graphs are ubiquitous. Graphs normally consist of nodes and edges, representing entities and their relationships, respectively. As a special type of graphs, *digraphs*, i.e., graphs with directed edges, are widely used to model a variety of real-world applications. For instance, a directed edge of a citation graph represents a formerly published paper being cited by a later published one, and a directed edge of the Twitter social network graph indicates a user being followed by another. Directed edges imply irreversible time-series relationships [19] and edge direction alone provides important semantic information, and therefore it is worth exploring and extracting semantic information from edge directions.

Recently, GNNs have shown great powerful ability on the graphs to handle lots of practical downstream tasks such as node classification [6,9], link prediction [22], graph clustering [23], etc. Nevertheless, most methods focus on undirected graphs and methods specifically designed for digraphs are rather limited. In this article, we aim to close this gap and we focus on designing effective GNNs for digraphs. Existing GNNs can be divided into two categories: spectral-based methods [6,7,21] and spatial-based methods [4,20]. Due to the unique and complex structure of digraphs, current GNNs cannot be directly applied. There are several challenges to overcome as follows.

Firstly, most traditional spectral-based GNNs are for undirected graphs and they often require symmetric adjacency matrices while for digraphs the adjacency matrices, and hence the Laplacian matrices, are asymmetric, resulting in a violation of spectral domain definition. A few works [18,24] extend spectral-based methods from undirected graphs to digraphs. [24] learns the digraphs structure by using a complex-valued Hermitian matrix known as magnetic Laplacian [8], which does not require symmetric adjacency matrix. [18] builds the Digraph Inception Convolutional Networks, which combines digraph convolution and k^{th}-order proximity, to learn multi-scale features in the digraphs. However, these methods face the problem of scaling to large graphs.

Secondly, while spatial-based GNNs do not rely on graph spectral theory and therefore can be naturally applied to digraphs, most existing methods often simply transform the digraph into an undirected graph through symmetrizing the adjacency matrix [4,20]. Several works [12,16] intend to preserve edge direction information. They both consider two roles for each node, i.e., receiver and sender. Each node representation is obtained by combining its incoming embedding and outgoing embedding. These approaches are inadequate to the capture structure information of digraphs because of only concerning first-order relationship when convolution process.

Considerable nodes are not connected directly in digraphs, but they can still be similar because of the existence of more common neighbors. For example, in social networks, people who follow the same topic tend to become friends, but they may not follow each other. This complex and subtle relationship is difficult to capture, leading to information loss.

To address the above issues, in this article, we propose **DNFS**, a **D**igraph **N**eural network model with the **F**irst-order and the **S**econd-order similarities. DNFS can preserve directional information and at the mean time explore underlying node similarities. To be more specific, we first compute the first-order and the second-order similarity matrices with the consideration of the edge directions. Then, we apply graph convolution networks to explore the first-order and the second-order structural information from both the in-degree's and the out-degree's point of view. Finally, we concatenate all results from graph convolution networks to generate the final node representations. Extensive experiments have demonstrated that the proposed model outperforms representative baselines on benchmark datasets.

2   Related Work

In this section, we briefly introduce the graph neural networks and neural networks for directed graphs.

Graph Neural Networks. Since the graph neural network was proposed, it has developed rapidly in recent years, showing great potential in processing graph data, which makes more and more researchers focus on it. A lot of GNNs variants have been proposed. Most GNNs models can be divided by two categories: spectral-based model and spatial-based model. The spectral-based methods use spectral graph theory to explore the node's neighborhood information. GCN [6] uses a layer-wise propagation rule s based on a first-order approximation of spectral convolutions on graphs. Further, SGC [21] reduces redundant computation through successively removing nonlinearities and collapsing weight matrices between consecutive layers, which does not have a negative impact on accuracy of downstream tasks. The spatial-based methods utilize the convolution in the graph domain to aggregation node's neighborhood information. GraphSage [4] can generate effective node representation by aggregating feature information from sampled neighbors for unseen nodes or graphs, which is a general inductive method. GAT [20] leverages masked self-attentional layer to compute node different neighbors importance without costly matrix operation. Compared to above models, our method is specifically designed for digraphs.

Neural Networks for Directed Graphs. There are some works to show how to extend spectral-based methods to digraphs. Tong et al. [18] theoretically extend spectral-based graph convolution to digraphs by leveraging the connections between graph Laplacian and stationary distributions of PageRank. Besides, Tong et al. [18] further design the digraph Inception networks to learn multi-scale features. Zhang et al. [24] construct a complex-valued Hermitian matrix that encodes the asymmetric characteristic of the digraph via the complex phase of its entries.

However, these methods mentioned above are supervised. Tong et al. [17] design a directed graph data augmentation approach called Laplacian perturbation and utilize Laplacian perturbation and contrastive learning to learn from dynamic easy-to-difficult contrastive views in the unsupervised manner. Kollias, Georgios, et al. propose a new auto-encoders based on Weisfeiler-Leman algorithm to learn pairs of interpretable latent representations for the nodes of digraphs. At the same time, it is noted that several work has been done to extend the application of digraphs to action recognition [3,15]. Different from these works, our method does not require pre-build a complex Laplacian matrix, and our model can effectively capture unique directional information and complex high-order structural information.

3   Preliminary

Directed Graphs [11]. We define a directed graph $G = (V, E)$ where $V = \{v_1, v_2, ..., v_n\}$ and $E = \{e_{i,j}\}$ specify the set of nodes with the size of n and the set of directed edges, respectively. $A \in \mathbb{R}^{n \times n}$ denotes the adjacency matrix where $a_{i,j} = 1$ means that there is a directed edge from node v_i to v_j, and $a_{i,j} = 0$ otherwise. $X \in \mathbb{R}^{n \times d}$ denotes the feature matrix.

Semi-supervised Node Classification [1]. $V_L \in V$ is the labeled node set, and generally we have $|V_L| \ll |V|$. The semi-supervised node classification task is utilizing the adjacency matrix A, the feature matrix X and the labeled subset V_L to predict unknown label in $V_{UL} = V - V_L$.

4   The Proposed Method

In this section, we introduce **DNFS**, a Digraph Neural network model with the First-order and the Second-order similarities. We firstly apply graph convolution networks to conduct the first-order and the second-order similarity aggregation. Then, we concatenate all results generated by graph convolution networks to obtain final node representations. Finally, we design a regularization item to avoid the over-smoothing problem. The overall framework of DNFS is shown in Fig. 1.

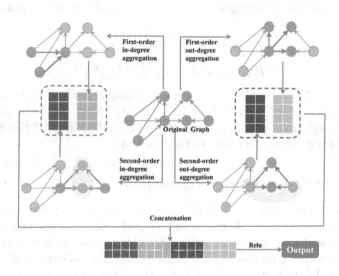

Fig. 1. The overall framework of **DNFS**

4.1   First-Order Similarity Aggregation

Due to the node's own features contributing to the aggregation process, we let $\tilde{A} = A + I$ as the adjacency matrix of the digraph with added self-loop (I is the identity matrix). We firstly define B and C as the out-degree matrix and the in-degree matrix as follows:

$$b_{ii} = \sum_i^n \tilde{a}_{ji}, \tag{1}$$

$$c_{ii} = \sum_i^n \tilde{a}_{ij}. \tag{2}$$

B and C are both diagonal matrices.

After normalization, we have $\hat{A}_{out}$ and $\hat{A}_{in}$:

$$\hat{A}_{out} = C^{-\frac{1}{2}}\tilde{A}B^{-\frac{1}{2}}, \tag{3}$$

$$\hat{A}_{in} = B^{-\frac{1}{2}}\tilde{A}^T C^{-\frac{1}{2}}. \tag{4}$$

If node u and node v are connected directly, it implies the first-order similarity between node u and node v. Otherwise, there not exist the first-order similarity between the node u and node v. The first-order similarity is very important in the digraph. For example, in social networks, people who are friends with each other tend to have similar hobbies. Also, in citation networks, authors who cite each other tend to share similar research directions.

To get the first-order similarity information in all directions, we use graph convolution networks to aggregate both in-degree and out-degree features:

$$H^l_{Ain} = \sigma(\hat{A}_{in}H^{(l-1)}_{Ain}W^l_{Ain}), \tag{5}$$

$$H^l_{Aout} = \sigma(\hat{A}_{out}H^{(l-1)}_{Aout}W^l_{Aout}), \tag{6}$$

where $H^0_{Ain} = H^0_{Aout} = X \in \mathbb{R}^{n \times d}$, σ is a non-linear activation funtion, and l is the layer number. W^l_{Aout} and $W^l_{Ain} \in \mathbb{R}^{d_{l-1} \times d_l}$ are trainable weight parameters in the l-th layer. H^l_{Ain} and H^l_{Aout} are the node embeddings of the first-order in-degree and out-degree direction in the l-th layer.

4.2   Second-Order Similarity Aggregation

Only considering the first-order similarity is not enough to fully explore the rich information of the digraphs. Some low-degree nodes may not have the first-order in-degree or out-degree neighbors, leading to information loss in the aggregation process. Therefore, we further explore the second-order in-degree and out-degree similarities of the digraphs to preserve more structural information.

If two nodes share more common neighbors, they should be more similar, even though they are not connected directly. For example, in social networks, two users share many of the same topics, but they don't follow each other. This second-order similarity relationship can explore deeper structural information compared to the first-order similarity relationship.

We consider the second-order in-degree similarity matrix S_{in} and out-degree similarity matrix S_{out}:

$$\tilde{s}_{in}(i,j) = \sum_k \frac{\tilde{a}_{k,i}\tilde{a}_{k,j}}{\sum_v \tilde{a}_{k,v}}, \tag{7}$$

$$\tilde{s}_{out}(i,j) = \sum_k \frac{\tilde{a}_{i,k}\tilde{a}_{j,k}}{\sum_v \tilde{a}_{v,k}}, \tag{8}$$

where $\tilde{a}_{k,i} \in \tilde{A}$ and k represents the common neighbors of node i and node j. v represents all the in- or out-neighbors of node k, where $k, v \in V$.

Similar to Eq. (3) and Eq. (4), we also normalize $\tilde{S}_{in}$ and $\tilde{S}_{out}$ as follows:

$$\hat{S}_{in} = \tilde{D}_{in}^{-\frac{1}{2}} \tilde{S}_{in} \tilde{D}_{in}^{-\frac{1}{2}}, \tag{9}$$

$$\hat{S}_{out} = \tilde{D}_{out}^{-\frac{1}{2}} \tilde{S}_{out} \tilde{D}_{out}^{-\frac{1}{2}}, \tag{10}$$

where $\tilde{D}_{in}$ and $\tilde{D}_{out}$ are corresponding degree matrix.

Then, we apply graph convolution to capture high-order node features from in-degree and out-degree directions.

$$H_{Sin}^{l} = \sigma(\hat{S}_{in} H_{Sin}^{(l-1)} W_{Sin}^{l}), \tag{11}$$

$$H_{Sout}^{l} = \sigma(\hat{S}_{out} H_{Sout}^{(l-1)} W_{Sout}^{l}). \tag{12}$$

Finally, we have the first-order and the second-order information in both directions. We concatenate the four matrices to obtain the node's ample embeddings:

$$H^{l} = Concat(H_{Ain}^{l}, H_{Aout}^{l}, H_{Sin}^{l}, H_{Sout}^{l}). \tag{13}$$

For the node classification task, the predict result Z becomes:

$$Z = Softmax(Linear(Relu(H))), \tag{14}$$

where H denotes the final embedding.

4.3 Loss Function

Our loss function includes two parts: classification loss and regularization, denotes as L_{class} and L_{reg}, respectively.

$$L = L_{class} + \lambda L_{reg}, \tag{15}$$

where λ is a hyper-parameter that can be used to trade off.

We adopt the cross entropy as the classification loss for the semi-supervised node classification task:

$$L_{class} = -\sum_{L \in V_L} \sum_{c=1}^{C} Y_{Lc} ln Z_{Lc}. \tag{16}$$

where $V_L \in V$ is the node subset which is labeled, C is the number of node classes, Y_{Lc} represents true labels of the nodes and Z_{Lc} represents predicted labels of the nodes.

We design a regularization item to avoid the over-smoothing problem when layer number becomes increasing. From Eq. (5) and Eq. (11), we can compute node final embedding in in-degree direction:

$$P^{l} = Mean(H_{Ain}^{l}, H_{Sin}^{l}). \tag{17}$$

Also, according to Eq. (6) and Eq. (12), we obtain node final embedding in out-degree direction:

$$Q^l = Mean(H^l_{Aout}, H^l_{Sout}).\tag{18}$$

We utilize likelyhood function as regularization item:

$$L_{reg}(P, Q) = -\frac{1}{n^2}\mathbf{1}(P^T Q \odot A - log(1 + exp(P^T Q)))\mathbf{1},\tag{19}$$

where $\mathbf{1}$ represents that the matrix entries are all ones. The algorithm DNFS is summarized in Algorithm 1.

Algorithm 1: DNFS Algorithm

Input: Directed Graph $G = (V, E)$, adjacency matrix A, feature matrix X, activation function σ, weight matrices W and hyper-parameter λ
Output: Predict class matrix Z.

1 Generate out-degree matrix B and in-degree matrix C according to the adjacency matrix via Equation (1) and Equation (2).
2 Compute the second-order in-degree and out degree similarity matrix through Equation (7) and Equation (8).
3 Normalize the first-order and the second-order similarity matrix both direction via Equation (3), Equation (4), Equation (9) and Equation (10).
4 Aggregate the first-order and high-order feature information from both in-degree and out-degree direction by Equation (5), Equation (6), Equation (11) and Equation (12).
5 Concatenate the four embedding matrices via Equation (13) and obtain output result via Equation (14).

---

5   Performance Evaluation

In this section, we first introduce public datasets and representative baselines. Secondly, we describe the experimental setup including the split of the datasets and parameter setting. Then we conduct semi-supervised node classification experiments to evaluate the effectiveness of **DNFS** against several state-of-the-art baselines on the three benchmark datasets. And the experiment results will be shown and analyzed. Finally, we carry out the ablation study to further illustrate how different components affect model performance.

5.1   Datasets and Baselines

Datasets. We select three open datasets of directed graph to evaluate our model performance, including Cora-ML [2], Citeseer [13] and AM-Photo [14]. In the Cora-ML and Citeseer datasets, nodes represent papers, and directed edges represent the citation relationship between papers. In the AM-photo dataset,

Table 1. Datasets Details.

Datasets	Nodes	Edges	Classes	Features	Train/Validation/Test
Cora-ML	2995	8416	7	2879	140/500/2355
CiteSeer	3312	4715	6	3703	120/500/2692
AM-Photo	7650	143663	8	745	160/500/6990

nodes represent goods, and directed edges represent that co-purchase relationship between the goods. The detailed information of datasets is given in Table 1.

Baselines. To evaluate the effectiveness of the proposed model, we choose the following representative models, which can be divided into three categories.

The spectral-based methods are as follows:

- **GCN** [6]: It uses an efficient layer-wise propagation rule that is based on a first-order approximation of spectral convolutions on graphs.
- **SGC** [21]: It removes GCN nonlinear layers and collapses weight matrices for reducing excess consumption.
- **APPNP** [7]: It introduces the fast approximation personalized propagation of neural predictions by considering relationship between GCN and PageRank [10].

The spatial-based methods are as follows:

- **GraphSAGE** [4]: A general inductive framework that generates effective node embeddings for unseen nodes.
- **GAT** [20]: A classical GNN model that leverages attention mechanism to compute node different neighborhood importance.

The methods specially designed for digraphs are as follows:

- **DiGCN** [18]: A spectral-based graph convolution method combined by graph Laplacian and stationary distributions of PageRank.
- **MagNet** [24]: A spectral GNN model for the directed graphs based on a complex-valued Hermitian matrix known as the magnetic Laplacian.
- **DiGCL** [17]: A directed graph contrastive learning framework to learn from contrastive views generated by Laplacian perturbation.

5.2 Experimental Setup

We conduct the semi-supervised node classification task on the three commonly used digraph datasets. We randomly split the datasets and conduct multiple experiments to obtain the stable results. In details, we choose 20 labels per class for the training set, 500 labels for the validation set regardless of class, and the rest for the test set. We calculate the mean test accuracy with standard deviation in percent (%) averaged over 20 random dataset splits with random parameters initialization.

Table 2. Results of Node Classification (accuracy, %)

Type	Method	Cora-ML	CiteSeer	Am-Photo
Spectral	GCN	53.11 ± 0.8	54.36 ± 0.5	53.20 ± 0.4
	SGC	51.14 ± 0.6	44.07 ± 3.5	71.25 ± 1.3
	APPNP	70.07 ± 1.1	65.39 ± 0.9	79.37 ± 0.9
Spatial	GraphSAGE	72.06 ± 0.9	63.19 ± 0.7	87.57 ± 0.9
	GAT	71.91 ± 0.9	63.03 ± 0.6	89.10 ± 0.7
Directed	DiGCN	76.42 ± 0.4	65.06 ± 0.4	83.91 ± 0.6
	MagNet	78.20 ± 1.1	66.23 ± 1.8	83.67 ± 1.9
	DiGCL	76.65 ± 1.8	64.76 ± 2.9	71.23 ± 1.2
This paper	**DNFS**	$\mathbf{81.57 \pm 0.6}$	$\mathbf{69.89 \pm 0.9}$	$\mathbf{89.62 \pm 0.3}$

Table 3. Results of Ablation Study (accuracy, %)

Ablation	Cora-ML	CiteSeer	AM-Photo
DNFS	$\mathbf{81.57 \pm 0.6}$	$\mathbf{69.89 \pm 0.9}$	$\mathbf{89.62 \pm 0.3}$
$A_{in} + A_{out} + S_{in} + S_{out}$	81.52 ± 0.5	68.36 ± 0.5	89.56 ± 0.3
$A_{in} + A_{out} + \text{reg}$	80.96 ± 0.6	67.74 ± 0.5	89.46 ± 0.4
$S_{in} + S_{out} + \text{reg}$	80.52 ± 0.8	66.53 ± 1.4	87.33 ± 1.1
$A_{in} + S_{in} + \text{reg}$	79.95 ± 0.5	65.86 ± 0.6	87.70 ± 0.4
$A_{out} + S_{out} + \text{reg}$	79.48 ± 0.5	67.44 ± 0.6	89.15 ± 0.3

We train our model for a maximum of 1000 epochs with early stopping if the validation accuracy does not increase for 200 consecutive epochs on the three datasets. We set the learning rate to 1e−3, the weight decay to 1e−5, the dropout to 0.6, and the hidden layer dimension to 32.

5.3 Performance Analysis

We use accuracy as evaluation metric. The experimental results are summarized in Table 2. In general, DNFS achieves the best classification accuracy.

We can see that spectral-based methods including GCN and SGC achieve less satisfactory results. The reason is that they only aggregate features of the one direction based on the asymmetric adjacency matrix. On the other hand, APPNP, which is also spectral-based method, gets relatively good performance. It allows the feature to randomly propagate with a certain teleport probability, thus breaking path limitation.

The spatial-based methods including GraphSAGE and GAT have a competitive performance, which demonstrates that these methods are more suitable for the digraphs than the spectral-based methods. GraphSAGE aims to learn a function from node's neighborhood instead of generating individual representation for every node, which is more flexible and extensible than GCN. GAT introduces attention mechanism to consider the importance of the node's neighbors in order to better learn digraph structure information, which may be the reason why GAT performs better than GCN.

The approaches specially designed for digraphs including DiGCN, MagNet, and DiGCL perform well. DiGCN preserves direction characteristic by employing digraph Laplacian matrix based on PageRank and controlling teleport chance. MagNet constructs a complex Hermitian matrix known as the magnetic Laplacian, which encodes undirected geometric structure in the magnitude of its entries and directional information in their phase. Both DiGCN and MagNet need to construct a special and symmetric Laplacian matrix to retain directed information. Our method does not require to pre-build a Laplacian matrix. We can effectively capture direction information through the first-order and the second-order similarity matrices from in-degree and out-degree perspective, which is easy to understand and calculate. DiGCL shows that contrastive learning can learn good encoders by performing a certain data augmentation in an unsupervised manner, but cannot beat our method. In the future, we will consider introducing contrastive learning into our approach in order to improve model performance.

5.4   Ablation Study

To better understand how different components affect our model performance, we conduct the ablation study and report mean test accuracy is shown in Table 3. In detail, our model can be divided by the five components including the first-order in-degree matrix (A_{in}), the first-order out-degree matrix (A_{out}), the second-order in-degree matrix (S_{in}), the second-order out-degree matrix (S_{out}) and the regularization item (reg).

By comparing the different components ablations studies, we find that all components make contributions to the model performance.

Firstly, when we remove the regularization item components, model performance becomes slightly lower, so the regularization item we design plays a positive role in the node classification task. Secondly, it is worthwhile to note that only using the first-order information can achieve reasonable performance compared to only using the second-order information, but they cannot beat DNFS. This suggests that learning both first-order and second-order information is of great importance. Also, it indicates that the first-order neighbors are more important than the second-order neighbors even in the digraphs. Finally, only using in-degree or out-degree information cannot outperform DNFS. This also suggests that model performance will become lower when ignoring any direction information. In summary, learning the first-order and second-order information in both directions is of great significance for the digraph semi-supervised node classification task.

6   Conclusion

In this paper, we propose a Digraph network model with the First-order and the Second-order similarity matrices, called DNFS, which effectively captures the first-order and high-order features information as well as direction information. Extensive experiments demonstrate the effectiveness of our model in the digraph. As one future work, we plan to explore the potential of the digraphs in the question-recommendation scenario [5,25].

References

1. Abu-El-Haija, S., Kapoor, A., Perozzi, B., Lee, J.: N-GCN: multi-scale graph convolution for semi-supervised node classification. In: Proceedings of the 35th Uncertainty in Artificial Intelligence Conference. Proceedings of Machine Learning Research, vol. 115, pp. 841–851. PMLR (2020)
2. Bojchevski, A., Günnemann, S.: Deep gaussian embedding of graphs: unsupervised inductive learning via ranking. In: International Conference on Learning Representations (2018)
3. Fu, B., Fu, S., Wang, L., Dong, Y., Ren, Y.: Deep residual split directed graph convolutional neural networks for action recognition. IEEE Multimedia **27**(4), 9–17 (2020)
4. Hamilton, W.L., Ying, Z., Leskovec, J.: Inductive representation learning on large graphs. In: NIPS (2017)
5. He, X., Deng, K., Wang, X., Li, Y., Zhang, Y., Wang, M.: LightGCN: simplifying and powering graph convolution network for recommendation. In: Proceedings of the 43rd International ACM SIGIR Conference on Research and Development in Information Retrieval, SIGIR 2020, pp. 639–648. Association for Computing Machinery (2020)
6. Kipf, T.N., Welling, M.: Semi-supervised classification with graph convolutional networks. In: International Conference on Learning Representations (2017)
7. Klicpera, J., Bojchevski, A., Günnemann, S.: Predict then propagate: graph neural networks meet personalized pagerank. In: International Conference on Learning Representations (2018)
8. Lieb, E.H., Loss, M.: Fluxes, Laplacians, and Kasteleyn's Theorem, pp. 457–483. Springer, Heidelberg (2004). https://doi.org/10.1007/978-3-662-10018-9_28
9. Ma, Y., Hao, J., Yang, Y., Li, H., Jin, J., Chen, G.: Spectral-based graph convolutional network for directed graphs (2019)
10. Page, L., Brin, S., Motwani, R., Winograd, T.: The pagerank citation ranking: bringing order to the web. In: The Web Conference (1999)
11. Poignard, C., Pereira, T., Pade, J.P.: Spectra of Laplacian matrices of weighted graphs: structural genericity properties. SIAM J. Appl. Math. **78**(1), 372–394 (2018)
12. Radmanesh, M., Ghorbanzadeh, H., Rezaei, A.A., Jalili, M., Yu, X.: Learning asymmetric embedding for attributed networks via convolutional neural network. Expert Syst. Appl. **219**(C), 119659 (2023)
13. Sen, P., Namata, G., Bilgic, M., Getoor, L., Gallagher, B., Eliassi-Rad, T.: Collective classification in network data. In: The AI Magazine (2008)
14. Shchur, O., Mumme, M., Bojchevski, A., Günnemann, S.: Pitfalls of graph neural network evaluation. CoRR abs/1811.05868 (2018)

15. Shi, L., Zhang, Y., Cheng, J., Lu, H.: Skeleton-based action recognition with directed graph neural networks. In: 2019 IEEE/CVF Conference on Computer Vision and Pattern Recognition (CVPR), pp. 7904–7913 (2019)
16. Tan, Z., Liu, B., Yin, G.: Asymmetric graph representation learning (2021)
17. Tong, Z., Liang, Y., Ding, H., Dai, Y., Li, X., Wang, C.: Directed graph contrastive learning. In: Advances in Neural Information Processing Systems, vol. 34, pp. 19580–19593. Curran Associates, Inc. (2021)
18. Tong, Z., Liang, Y., Sun, C., Li, X., Rosenblum, D.S., Lim, A.: Digraph inception convolutional networks. In: Neural Information Processing Systems (2020)
19. Tong, Z., Liang, Y., Sun, C., Rosenblum, D.S., Lim, A.: Directed graph convolutional network. ArXiv: abs/2004.13970 (2020)
20. Veličković, P., Cucurull, G., Casanova, A., Romero, A., Liò, P., Bengio, Y.: Graph attention networks. In: International Conference on Learning Representations (2018)
21. Wu, F., Zhang, T., de Souza, A.H., Fifty, C., Yu, T., Weinberger, K.Q.: Simplifying graph convolutional networks. In: International Conference on Machine Learning (2019)
22. Zhang, M., Chen, Y.: Link prediction based on graph neural networks. In: Proceedings of the 32nd International Conference on Neural Information Processing Systems, NIPS 2018, pp. 5171–5181 (2018)
23. Zhang, X., Liu, H., Li, Q., Wu, X.M.: Attributed graph clustering via adaptive graph convolution. In: Proceedings of the 28th International Joint Conference on Artificial Intelligence, IJCAI 2019, pp. 4327–4333. AAAI Press (2019)
24. Zhang, X., He, Y., Brugnone, N., Perlmutter, M., Hirn, M.: Magnet: a neural network for directed graphs. In: Beygelzimer, A., Dauphin, Y., Liang, P., Vaughan, J.W. (eds.) Advances in Neural Information Processing Systems (2021)
25. Zhao, M., Jia, A.L.: A dual-attention heterogeneous graph neural network for expert recommendation in online agricultural question and answering communities. In: 2022 IEEE 25th International Conference on Computer Supported Cooperative Work in Design (CSCWD), pp. 926–931 (2022)

Efficient Question Answering Based on Language Models and Knowledge Graphs

Fengying Li, Hongfei Huang, and Rongsheng Dong$^{(\boxtimes)}$

Guangxi Key Laboratory of Trusted Software, Guilin University of Electronic Technology, Guilin, China
{lfy,ccrsdong}@guet.edu.cn

Abstract. Knowledge graph question answering (Q&A) aims to answer questions through a knowledge base (KB). When using a knowledge base as a data source for multihop Q&A, knowledge graph Q&A needs to obtain relevant entities, their relationships and the correct answer, but often the correct answer cannot be obtained through the reasoning path because of absent relationships. Currently, using pre-trained language models (PLM) and knowledge graphs (KG) has a good effect on complex problems. However, challenging problems remain; the relationships between problems and candidate entities need to be better represented, and joint reasoning must be performed in the relationship graph based on problems and entities. To solve these problems, we expand the relational graph by adding tail entities to the list of preselected entities through reverse relations and then add the processed problems and entities to the problem subgraph. To perform inference on a relational graph, we design an attention-based neural network module. To calculate the loss of the model's inference process nodes, we use a modified Euclidean distance function as the loss function. To evaluate our model, we conducted experiments on the WebQSP and CWQ datasets, and the model obtained state-of-the-art results in both the KB-full and KB-half settings.

Keywords: Question answering · Knowledge graphs · Neural networks

1 Introduction

Question answering (Q&A) plays a central role in the field of artificial intelligence [1], and Q&A systems must be able to reason about the correct answer through the relevant knowledge base [2]. Multihop reasoning that uses knowledge bases as data sources requires subject word entities and multihop relationships from the questions and then reasons about the questions through multiple triples in the knowledge graph. For questions, it must enable an encoder that can be converted by language models (LM) to be recognized by machines [3,4], or it must have the ability to represent questions as structured knowledge graphs (KG), e.g. [5–7], For instance, the entities in Freebase [3] and YAGO [4] can be

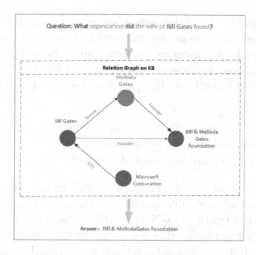

Fig. 1. A 2-hop problem on a relationship diagram, In the relationship diagram <Bill Gates, Spouse, Melinda Gates> is a pair of relationships <Melinda Gates, Spouse Bill Gates> is an inverse pair of relationships.

represented as nodes of knowledge graphs, and relations can be represented as edges. In recent years,Pre-trained language models have achieved good results in multihop Q&A. Although pre-trained language models have a very good representation of knowledge [5], they do not perform well in structural reasoning; furthermore, knowledge graphs can clearly explain the predicted results through inference paths [6], which are well suited for structural reasoning but lack the ability to provide full coverage of knowledge [7]. How to effectively combine pre-trained language models and knowledge graphs for Q&A remains an open and challenging problem.

A knowledge graph is a structured database that stores facts in the form of triples. Some of the larger publicly available knowledge graphs are Freebase [8], YAGO [9], NELL [13], Wikidata [14] built by Google in 2013, and DBpedia [15]extracted from Wikipedia entries given by Lehmann et al. In this paper, we focus on multihop Q&A on the problem relationship subgraph, which consists of entities and relationships, as shown in Fig. 1. Multihop Q&A currently has two dominant approaches: semantic parsing-based [2] and information retrieval-based approaches [16]. Both approaches first identify head entity in a question, connect them to entities in the knowledge base and then reason by executing the logical form of the parsed question or by extracting specific question subgraphs from the knowledge base to the answer in the subject entity domain. They used different working mechanisms to solve the knowledge base Q&A task, the former approach represented the problem through a logical symbolic model, and the latter approach constructed a subgraph specific to the problem, provided comprehensive relocation information to the problem and ranked the extracted entities based on their relevance to the problem [2]. In complex problems, more relations and topics increase the search space of potential logical forms used for parsing, which will increase the computational cost significantly, while more relations and entities may prevent the ranking of all entities based on information retrieval methods, leading to incorrect results. Our model outperforms all current baseline models in terms of efficiency (as shown in Fig. 3).

Currently, multihop Q&A on the problem relationship subgraph has two main challenges [7].

(1) How to form the corresponding problem-related subgraphs through incomplete knowledge graphs for the given problem text.
(2) How to reason on the problem-related subgraphs.

To address these problems, we propose an end-to-end information retrieval model using an efficient inference model consisting of a pre-trained language model and a neural network (QA-Net),[1] which has the following advantages, Effectiveness: QA-Net achieves SOTA results on all relevant data sets Transparency: QA-Net is fully attention-based, so, we can easily understand the reasoning path of the problem. We obtain the problem text by pretraining the language model and then use it for relational reasoning by constructing a structured knowledge graph. The contributions of our paper are as follows.

(1) We use the Roberta [9] model to embed the problem, expand the target entity list by reverse relationships, and embed the entity list by the TF-IDF [17] model (Renode). In question reasoning, we join the Q&A context and question relationship subgraph for reasoning, which decreases the relationship gap between questions and entities.
(2) To reason over the problem subgraph, we design an attention-based Net module for problem reasoning, add the previous problem and relation graph-generated values to the existing reasoning process by means of weights to strengthen the connection during reasoning and design a new computational function for node loss (Net).

2   Related Work

In this paper, We address multihop Q&A of a structural knowledge graph, which is constructed by extracting relevant entities and relationships from the knowledge base (as shown in Fig. 1). In previous work, PullNet [19] and QA-GNN [12] are similar to our model, with the former focusing on a hybrid form of labeled and textual relations and the latter focusing on constructing relational graph inference in multiple question and answer sessions. They first retrieve a subgraph of relations for a particular question and then use graph neural networks to reason implicitly about the answer to the question. These graph neural network-based methods are usually weak in interpretability because they cannot produce intermediate inference paths [20], which we believe is necessary in multihop Q&A.

---

[1] Source code will be made available post acceptance.

The graph form of Q&A that uses labels is called KGQA and is mainly grouped into two categories: semantic parsing [21,22] and information retrieval [1,2]. The former parses a question into logical form and queries the answer entity based on the knowledge base, while the latter retrieves subgraphs of a particular question and applies some ranking algorithm to select the most likely answer entity. Among these methods, VRN [24] and SRN [25] have good interpretability because they clarify the inference path through reinforcement learning. However, they suffer from convergence problems due to the very large knowledge base, which leads to models with very large search spaces. IRN [26] and ReifKB [27] learn the distribution of relations in the inference process but can only optimize the reasoning process through answer entities.

In single-hop problem inference, where the answers to questions can be retrieved directly from the knowledge base, pre-trained language models often outperform humans. For more challenging multihop problems, in the present work, Denis Lukovnikov et al. [28], used a transformer for a multitask model based on joint learning, but it could only handle simple Q&A tasks and used relationship prediction as a classification task. The CQA-NMT model uses a transformer for the prediction of variable-length paths in multihop Q&A but does not address the incompleteness of multihop Q&A in knowledge graphs. In this paper, we use the transformer model and TF-IDF [17] model to close the gap between the problem embedding space and the knowledge graph embedding space and add reverse relations and entities to the relationship graph to compensate for the incompleteness of knowledge graphs.

3 Methodology

We reason on a structured knowledge graph, where nodes denote entities and edges denote relationships. As shown in Fig. 1, given a question and answers, we need to reason on the knowledge graph to obtain the correct result. as shown in Fig. 3. First, we embed the problem using the Roberta model, add reverse relational entities to the list of problem-related entities and then perform entity embedding through the TF-IDF model (3.1). To find the correct inference path in the structured knowledge graph, we used the multilayer perceptron MLP for inference over the knowledge graph (3.2). To capture the relationship between the head node in the questions and other entities in the structured knowledge graph and to adjust our model, we designed the relevance score of the nodes and adjusted the calculation of the loss function (3.3) (Fig. 2).

3.1 Structured Knowledge Graph Embedding

To merge the problem and knowledge base into the same structure, we designed a joint reasoning space. We explicitly connect the problem and related entity nodes together to form a common graphical structure. Structured knowledge graphs are represented by $\mathcal{G}$, entities are represented by $\mathcal{E}$ and edges connecting entities are represented by $\mathcal{R}$. We use q to represent the problem text, e to

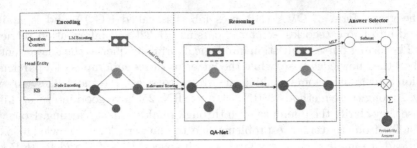

Fig. 2. The reasoning process of a 2-hop problem on QA-Net. For a two-hop problem, we start from the head entity (blue point) in the problem, and in the relationship diagram we are able to clearly know the first hop to the entity (green point) as well as the second hop entity (red point) (Color figure online)

represent the related entities, e_h to represent the head entity in the problem text, r to represent the relationship between entities, n to represent the number of entities, and $r_{i,j}$ to represent the relationship between the head entity e_i and the tail entity e_j. $r_{i,j}$ needs to be obtained from the entity relationship pairs in the knowledge base. For a multihop problem q, the correct problem path needs to be reasoned in the relational graph from the head entity e_h. The correct set of answer entities $Y = \{e_{Y^1}, \ldots, e_{Y|Y|}\}$ is found by reasoning on the path.

We encode the question q using the language model.

$$q^{LM} = Roberta(text(q)). \tag{1}$$

for each entity in all questions, in order for the model to have a better response to similar topic Q&A task, we use a TF-IDF model to quantify each entity in the knowledge base.

$$
\begin{aligned}
TF_i &= \frac{n_i}{\sum\limits_{w=0}^{k} n_w}, \\
IDF_i &= \log(D/(1+d_i)), \\
TI_i &= TF_i * IDF_i.
\end{aligned}
\tag{2}
$$

where n_i denotes the number of occurrences of word i in the knowledge base, $\sum_{w=0}^{k} n_w$ denotes the number of occurrences of all words, and TF_i denotes the word frequency of entity i. D denotes the total number of problems, and d_i denotes the number of entities i contained in the list of target entities in the problem, TI_i is the $TF - IDF$ value for the numbered word i.

3.2 QA-Net Architecture

To obtain the correct answer to a multihop question, QA-Net starts from the head entity and goes through T-step reasoning, where at each step it looks at a different part of the question and determines the most relevant content. Initially, to maintain the activation probability of the entities, QA-Net sets the head entity probability to 1 and the rest of the entity probabilities to 0. In each step, QA-Net calculates the relevance score of each node to represent its activated agent relationship, and then transmits the score of the entity in the activated relationship. Finally, we obtain the correct result by the softmax function. In each step, we use

$$h^{(t+1)} = f_t(h^t) + h^t. \tag{3}$$

to update h_t.

In the model calculation process, $h^t = [0,1]^n$ denotes the score of entities in step t. $[0,1]^n$ n-dimensional vectors have values from 0 to 1, h^0 is the initial value, and only the head entity e_h is 1.

$$
\begin{aligned}
q^{LM}(h_1, \ldots, h_n) &= f_{enc}(q), \\
c\_q^t &= f^t(q^{LM}), \\
b^t &= Softmax(c\_q^t * q^{LM}), \\
q^t &= \frac{b^t}{\sum\limits_{i=1}^{|n|} b_i^t * h_i}.
\end{aligned}
\tag{4}
$$

where f_{enc} denotes the language model of the problem embedding (Roberta), n indicates the number of words in the question, h_i denotes the vector of each word in the problem f^t denotes the MLP of $R^D \rightarrow R^D$, and $D = 768$ denotes the embedding dimension of the problem.

In addition, during the model reasoning process, we need to calculate and update the relationship between nodes, And at each step we need to calculate the midweight of the problem to achieve the best results.

$$
\begin{aligned}
p_{i,j}^t &= f^t(r_{i,j,k}^t * e_h), \\
w_{i,j,k}^t &= Sigmoid(p_{i,j,k}^t), \\
a_i^t &= e_i^{t-1} w_{i,j,k}^t.
\end{aligned}
\tag{5}
$$

where $r_{i,j,k}$ denotes the k-th relation sentence, e_h denotes the relationship vector of the head node, f^t is an MLP of $R^D \rightarrow R^R$, R denotes the number of relations, e_i^{t-1} denotes entity i, e_i^0 is the initial head node, and a_i^t is the target entity.

Finally we need to find the weighted sum of $a^1, a^2, \ldots, a^t$ in each step t to determine the final output of the target entity.

$$
\begin{aligned}
c &= Softmax(f^t(q^{LM})), \\
a^* &= \sum_{t=1}^{T} c^t * a^t.
\end{aligned}
\tag{6}
$$

where f^t is an MLP function of $R^D \rightarrow R^R$, $c \in [0,1]^T$ denotes the probability distribution of the problem jumps, and a^* indicates the final target entity answer.

3.3 Training

Assuming that the set of answer entities to the question is $Y = e_{y^1}, \ldots, e_{y^{|Y|}}$, then

$$y_i = \begin{cases} 1 & e_i \in Y \\ 0 & e_i \notin Y \end{cases} \tag{7}$$

To obtain better results, we designed an ideal equation for the model to weigh the loss between a^* and y.

$$\mathcal{L} = k * \frac{\sum_{i=1}^{|Y|} (y_i * a_i * ||a_i^* - y_i||)}{\sum_{i=1}^{|Y|} (y_i * a_i)} \tag{8}$$

where y is the answer entity, a is the target entity, and K is a constant used to adjust the size of the loss function, the training process $k = 0.8$ in the training process, and the training effect is better. $||a^* - y||$ represents the square of the two vectors Euclidean distance.

In Eq. (6), since the model may become very large in each reasoning step, the values in a_i^t values may cause the gradient to explode when the number of jumps increases, thus affecting the accuracy of the model. Therefore we need to rectify the entity fraction after each step t to ensure that the value is in the range [0, 1], while also retaining the differentiability of the operation. We have the following truncation function.

$$f(x) = \begin{cases} 1 & x \geq 1 \\ x & x < 1 \end{cases} \tag{9}$$

In step t, we use $f(x)$ to truncate each element in a^t.

4   Experiment

4.1 Dataset

WebQSP [8] is a small dataset containing 4737 Freebase-based natural language questions that can form a large-scale knowledge graph with millions of entities and triples. The questions in this dataset are one-hop and two-hop questions and can be answered by Freebase.

CompWebQ (CWQ) [9] is generated by WebQSP by extending the question entities and adding constraints to the answers with more jumps and constraints, and the questions require up to 4 jumps for reasoning in the knowledge graph. The dataset contains 34,654 questions and consists of four distinct question types: combinatorial (45%), connected (45%), comparative (5%), and top-level (5%) (Table 1).

Table 1. The training, validation and test set division of WebQSP and CWQ.

Dataset	Train	Dev	Test
WebQSP	2937	100	1569
CWQ	27623	3518	3513

4.2 Baseline

KVMemNN [29] is mainly intended to solve the problems that when Q&A applies a knowledge base, the knowledge base may be too limited, its schema for storing knowledge (schema) may not support certain types of Q&A, and the knowledge base is excessively sparse.

GraftNet [30] uses heuristics to extract a problem-specific subgraph from the entire relational graph, and then uses a neural network to reason about the answer.

PullNet [19] improves GraftNet by using a method that replaces the heuristic with a graph CNN to retrieve subgraphs.

EmbedKGQA [23] uses KGQA as a link prediction task and incorporates the knowledge graph embedding to solve the incompleteness of KGQA. Embed-KGQA embeds the questions and KG triples into the vector space, calculates the scores of the candidate answers by the score function and selects the highest scoring entity as the answer.

TransferNet [31] supports label and text relationships, and TransferNet maintains multishop relationship scores for entity score spreading. It starts from the subject entities of the problem and maintains a vector of entity scores. In each step, it processes the problem words and calculates the scores of the relationships between entities, then transforms these relationship scores into an adjacency matrix, and finally multiplies the entity score vector with the relationship score matrix. After repeating multiple steps, the target entities are obtained.

4.3 Results

In the entity set for word embedding, we perform frequency statistics on the entities in the knowledge graph, and then generate corresponding one-hot codes based on the statistical word frequencies to achieve the embedding of the entities. Moreover, we find that not only the reverse relationship will affect the experimental results. For some problems, we may need the tail entity in the knowledge graph to begin problem reasoning, so we will select some entities with the opposite relationship to add to the candidate entity list for training. On the WebQSP dataset, we set the reasoning step to T = 2, and we use Roberta as the question embedding model. We set the hidden layer size to D = 768. We optimize the model using RAdam [10] with a learning rate of 0.001, compute the final question answer by using a multilayer MLP to obtain the multihop reasoning and relations results, and finally select the final question answer by the sigmoid function. We obtained satisfactory results in less than 4 h running on a single

Table 2. Model accuracy comparison on WebQSP, QA-Net is far more efficient than other baseline models on WebQSP.

Model	WebQSP KG-full	WebQSP KG-half
KV-Mem	46.7	32.7(31.6)
GraftNet	66.4	48.2(49.7)
PullNet	68.1	50.1(51.9)
EmbedKGQA	66.6	53.2
TransferNet	71.4	–
QA-Net (ours)	74.5	59.0

Table 3. Model accuracy comparison on CWQ, QA-Net also outperforms other baseline models on the CWQ.

Model	CWQ KG-full	CWQ KG-half
KV-Mem	21.1	14.8
GraftNet	32.8	26.1
PullNet	47.2	31.5
TransferNet	48.6	–
QA-Net (ours)	47.8	33.5

NVIDIA RTX8000. CWQ contains problems that require no more than four hops of reasoning and are of different types. We set the inference step to T = 4, and other settings are the same as those for WebQSP (Table 2 and 3).

4.4 Interpretability

Table 4. QA-Net ablation experiment; Renode denotes our processes at the node and Net denotes our neural network processes; "-" means no such module is available.

	WebQSP KG-full	WebQSP KG-half
QA-Net	74.5	59.0
QA-Net(-Renode)	74.1	56.8
QA-Net(-Net)	72.4	56.7
QA-Net(-Renode/-Net)	70.3	56.1

Table 4 shows the results of our ablation experiments on the modules of QA-Net. Each module has a positive contribution to the final results of the model. During the experiments we found that when we add reverse nodes to the list of preselected entities, the effect on the one-hop Q&A is very large, and the same effect in the KG-half setting. At the same time, we find that when the knowledge graph becomes larger, the relevance score of nodes has a greater impact on the model, and it is worth considering how to better calculate the relevance between nodes.

4.5 Model Efficiency

From Fig. 3, we can see that on the WebQSP dataset, EmbedKGQA does not have a high model aggregation rate although it starts with a higher accuracy rate, instead our model has a better aggregation rate, while our model outperforms other baseline models with the same number of epochs.

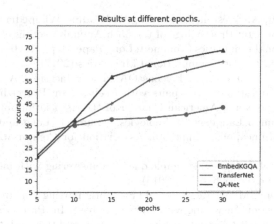

Fig. 3. Effect of different epoch numbers on model accuracy

5 Conclusion

In this paper, we propose an effective joint inference model QA-Net for knowledge graph Q&A, and we determine on how to form better subgraphs of related questions and how to combine questions and question subgraphs for reasoning. The problem embedding by pre-trained language models and TF-IDF embedding of entities are followed by joint reasoning over the problem subgraphs obtained from multilayer neural networks. The contributions of this paper are as follows: based on the Q&A problem and the knowledge graph entity relationship space, an attention-based Net module is designed for joint inference, while the information of inference in the previous step is retained by adding weights to the current inference process, and a new calculation function for node loss is designed. Our accuracy results on the WebQSP dataset surpasses the results of all baseline models to achieve state-of-the-art performance. Moreover, our model achieves good results on the CWQ dataset, proving the effectiveness of our method and illustrating the possibility of our model to be applied to larger knowledge bases.

Acknowledgements. This work is supported by National Nature Science Foundation of China (No.61762024, No.62062029) and Innovation Project of GUET Graduate Educatio (No.2022YCXS091)

References

1. Rajpurkar, P., Zhang, J., Lopyrev, K., et al.: Squad: 100,000+ questions for machine com-prehension of text. arXiv preprint arXiv:1606.05250 (2016)
2. Zhao, W., Chung, T., Goyal, A., Metallinou, A.: Simple question answering with subgraph ranking and joint-scoring. arXiv preprint arXiv:1904.04049 (2019)
3. Lan, Y., He, G., Jiang, J., et al.: A survey on complex knowledge base question answering: Methods, challenges and solutions. arXiv preprint arXiv:2105.11644 (2021)
4. Chen, D., Fisch, A., Weston, J., Bordes, A.: Reading Wikipedia to answer open-domain questions. In: Proceedings of the 55th Annual Meeting of the Association for Computational Linguistics (Volume 1: Long Papers), pp. 1870–1879, Vancouver, Canada. Association for Computational Linguistics (2017)
5. Jiang, K., Wu, D., Jiang, H.: FreebaseQA: a new factoid QA data set matching trivia-style question-answer pairs with freebase. In: Proceedings of the 2019 Conference of the North American Chapter of the Association for Computational Linguistics: Human Language Technologies, Volume 1 (Long and Short Papers), pp. 318–323, Minneapolis, Minnesota. Association for Computational Linguistics (2019)
6. Antoine, B., et al.: Large-scale simple question answering with memory networks. arXiv preprint arXiv:1506.02075 (2015)
7. Yih, S.W., Chang, M.W., He, X., et al.: Semantic parsing via staged query graph generation: question answering with knowledge base. In: Proceedings of the Joint Conference of the 53rd Annual Meeting of the ACL and the 7th International Joint Conference on Natural Language Processing of the AFNLP (2015)
8. Devlin, J., Chang, M.W., Lee, K., et al.: Bert: Pre-training of deep bidirectional transformers for language understanding. arXiv preprint arXiv:1810.04805 (2018)
9. Liu, Z., et al.: A robustly optimized BERT pre-training approach with post-training. In: Proceedings of the 20th Chinese National Conference on Computational Linguistics (2021)
10. Kassner, N., Schütze, H.: Negated and misprimed probes for pre-trained language models: birds can talk, but cannot fly. In: Proceedings of the 58th Annual Meeting of the Association for Computational Linguistics, pp. 7811–7818. Association for Computational Linguistics (2020)
11. Feng, Y., Chen, X., Lin, B.Y., Wang, P., Yan, J., Ren, X.: Scalable multi-hop relational reasoning for knowledge-aware question answering. arXiv preprint arXiv:2005.00646 (2020)
12. Yasunaga, M., Ren, H., Bosselut, A., et al.: QA-GNN: Reasoning with language models and knowledge graphs for question answering. arXiv preprint arXiv:2104.06378 (2021)
13. Mitchell, T., et al.: Never-ending learning. Commun. ACM **61**(5), 103–115 (2018)
14. Vrandečić, D., Krötzsch, M.: Wikidata: a free collaborative knowledge-base. Commun. ACM **57**(10), 78–85 (2014)
15. Färber, M., et al.: Linked data quality of dbpedia, freebase, opencyc, wikidata, and yago. Seman. Web **9**(1), 77–129 (2018)

16. Sukhbaatar, S., Weston, J., Fergus, R.: End-to-end memory networks. In: Advances in Neural Information Processing Systems, vol. 28 (2015)
17. Martineau, J., Finin, T.: Delta tfidf: an improved feature space for sentiment analysis. In: Proceedings of the International AAAI Conference on Web and Social Media, vol. 3. no. 1 (2009)
18. Yih, W., Richardson, M., Meek, C., et al.: The value of semantic parse labeling for knowledge base question answering. In: Proceedings of the 54th Annual Meeting of the Association for Computational Linguistics (Volume 2: Short Papers), pp. 201–206 (2016)
19. Sun, H., Bedrax-Weiss, T., Cohen, W.W.: Pullnet: Open domain question answering with iterative retrieval on knowledge bases and text. arXiv preprint arXiv:1904.09537 (2019)
20. Lin, B.Y., Chen, X., Chen, J., Ren, X.: KagNet: Knowledge-aware graph networks for commonsense reasoning. arXiv preprint arXiv:1909.02151 (2019)
21. Berant, J., Chou, A., Frostig, R., Liang, P.: Semantic parsing on freebase from question-answer pairs. In: Proceedings of the 2013 Conference on Empirical Methods in Natural Language Processing, pp. 1533–1544 (2013)
22. Saha, A., Ansari, G.A., Laddha, A., Sankaranarayanan, K., Chakrabarti, S.: Complex program induction for querying knowledge bases in the absence of gold programs. Trans. Assoc. Comput. Linguist. 7, 185–200 (2019)
23. Zhang, Y., et al.: Variational reasoning for question answering with knowledge graph. In: Thirty-second AAAI Conference on Artificial Intelligence (2018)
24. Qiu, Y., Wang, Y., Jin, X., et al.: Stepwise reasoning for multi-relation question answering over knowledge graph with weak supervision. In: Proceedings of the 13th International Conference on Web Search and Data Mining, pp. 474–482 (2020)
25. Zhou, M., Huang, M., Zhu, X.: An interpretable reasoning network for multi-relation question answering. arXiv preprint arXiv:1801.04726 (2018)
26. Cohen, W.W., Sun, H., Hofer, R.A., Siegler, M.: Scalable neural methods for reasoning with a symbolic knowledge base. arXiv preprint arXiv:2002.06115 (2020)
27. Lukovnikov, D., Fischer, A., Lehmann, J.: Pretrained transformers for simple question answering over knowledge graphs. In: Ghidini, C., et al. (eds.) ISWC 2019. LNCS, vol. 11778, pp. 470–486. Springer, Cham (2019). https://doi.org/10.1007/978-3-030-30793-6_27
28. Talmor, A., Berant, J.: The web as a knowledge-base for answering complex questions. arXiv preprint arXiv:1803.06643 (2018)
29. Miller, A., Fisch, A., Dodge, J., et al.: Key-value memory networks for directly reading documents. arXiv preprint arXiv:1606.03126 (2016)
30. Sun, H., Dhingra, B., Zaheer, M., et al.: Open domain question answering using early fusion of knowledge bases and text. arXiv preprint arXiv:1809.00782 (2018)
31. Saxena, A., Tripathi, A., Talukdar, P.: Improving multi-hop question answering over knowledge graphs using knowledge base embeddings. In: Proceedings of the 58th Annual Meeting of the Association for Computational Linguistics, pp. 4498–4507 (2020)
32. Shi, J., Cao, S., Hou, L., et al.: TransferNet: An effective and transparent frame-work for multi-hop question answering over relation graph. arXiv preprint arXiv:2104.07302 (2021)

Event Association Analysis Using Graph Rules

Pengyue Jiang(ID), Wenjun Wang(ID), Xueli Liu(✉)(ID), Lifei Sun(ID),
and Bowen Dong(ID)

Tianjin University, Tianjin 300350, China
610875895@qq.com, {wjwang,xueli,slf,1020201107}@tju.edu.cn

Abstract. Event association analysis is used to mine potential association relationships between different events in event data sets, and is
widely used in areas such as commodity trading and social media networks. Graph rules can be defined with different forms and expressive
capabilities according to relationships in various domains. For the event
association domain, we define an event association rule based on statistical knowledge to examine positive and negative associations between
events, and the generated patterns fuse other semantic information such
as time and location to realize the inference on event data. We innova-
tively propose a matching method for matching candidate sets, which can
further refine the rule matching results to each specific event node so that
the results can be logically interpreted. Meanwhile, based on the existing rule matching algorithms, we propose an incremental computation
method that can quickly process the incremental part of the event data,
effectively saving computational resources and time. We demonstrate the
accuracy and efficiency of the algorithm using real-life datasets.

Keywords: Event association analysis · Graph rules · Association
rules matching

1 Introduction

Discovering potential associations between events is widely used in commodity
trading, social media networks. [18]. An event is defined as a particular thing
that happens at a specific time and place, along with all necessary preconditions
and unavoidable consequences which can be represented as nodes, edges and
attributes in a network [1]. Event association analysis exists several challenges.
Firstly, it is difficult to cover the variety of associations between events. Existing
studies care more about the causal or inherited relationships [2,20]. Secondly,
existing systems for identifying event relations mainly rely on unstructured text,
human-assessed representations, and corresponding NLP techniques to extract
event data [20], which rarely focuses on graphs. Worse still, existing algorithms
can hardly explain the association between events [13]. Finally, when there is

L. Iliadis et al. (Eds.): ICANN 2023, LNCS 14257, pp. 352–363, 2023.
https://doi.org/10.1007/978-3-031-44216-2_29

a large amount of data to be updated, most of the existing algorithms need to recompute all the data, consuming a lot of time and computational resources.

Contribution. To cope with those, we develop a matching method for exploring different kinds of association between event pairs on attribute graphs. Given a structured event data set, we can obtain logically interpretable associations.

(1) Event Association Rules (Sect. 3). We define event association rules, denoted as EARs, to analyze associations between events. We define new pattern semantics $Dependency, KULC_G$, and IR_G to capture positive or negative relationships between events, which makes EARs more expressive and interpretable.

(2) Event Association Analysis Algorithms (Sect. 4). To apply $EARs$ into event associations, We provide Event Association Find(EAF), a new simulation-based method, to extract associations in graphs. EAF adds the event pairing method EventPair to the simulated candidate sets to get the association between specific events. Moreover, focusing on massive data sets, we propose an incremental algorithm $incEF$ based on $StrongSim$, which shows time efficiency.

(3) Experimental Study (Sect. 5). Using real-life data, we empirically verify the accuracy and efficiency of our algorithms. We find the following. (1) EAF algorithm outperforms most link prediction algorithms in terms of accuracy 10.2% and recall 4.4%, which shows that $EARs$ can express the vast majority of positive or negative relationships between events in the graph. (2) EAF algorithm outperforms the subgraph isomorphism algorithm in terms of efficiency (2.02 times faster). $incEF$ in calculating the incremental part is 48.1% less than the time required to recalculate the full graph when $|\Delta G|$ is 30% of $|G|$.

Related Work. We categorize related work as follows.

(1) Event Association Analysis Approaches. There has been substantial work around studying event datasets. Bhattacharjya et al. introduce Bayesian network [3] in the event model to obtain casual associations. [2] determines the causal relationship by introducing a relationship score for pairs of events. [20] defines event relationships such as inheritance, comparison, and synchronization to analyze events described in unstructured text. Detecting some specific relationship between events can be considered as a link prediction problem in machine learning. Zhang et al. [15]detect event relations by invoking machine learning algorithm to analyse the structure of sentences and build knowledge graphs. Based on knowledge graphs, some link prediction methods [5,12,19] can also be used to detect associations between event nodes by representation methods.

The novelty of this work includes: (1) We extract positive or negative relations between events while existing ML methods can only predict edges without labels between event nodes in heterogeneous attribute graphs. (2) We use association rules and pattern-matching methods for the explanation.

(2) Association Rules and Pattern Matching. Various association rules [6, 7,10,11] have been investigated for capturing topological relations on graphs, which is defined as topological pattern Q and the attribute dependency(possibly empty) $X \to Y$. They can be distinguished from each other by different complexity and expressive power. Pattern matching methods are mainly divided into simulation and isomorphism. However, isomorphism-based algorithms are too restrictive to find reasonable matches due to the noise of real data. [17] provides the first algorithm for graph simulation and is improved to quadratic time by [8], while simulation-based methods can be calculated in polynomial time. Dual simulation [16], strong simulation [16] and bounded simulation [9] are three typical extensions and cater to various occasions.

The novelty of this work consists of:(1) Our proposed EARs can express not only positive but also negative relationships between events where the negative relationships are difficult to measure with the support in existing studies. (2) Our proposed simulation-based algorithm can find specific event associations rather than candidate sets. For the event data set, our incremental approach can quickly find potentially relevant entity nodes to mine event associations.

2 Preliminaries

We start with a review of some basic notations utilized in this work. Assume alphabets Γ_1 and Θ denoting labels and attributes, respectively.

Graphs. A directed graph is defined as $G = (V, E, L, F_A)$, where (1) V is a finite set of nodes; (2) $E \subseteq V \times V$ is a set of edges, in which (v, v') denotes an edge from node v to v'; (3) each node v in V bears a label $L(v)$ in Γ_1; (4) each edge e in E bears a label $L(e)$ in Γ_1, and (5) for each node v, $F_A(v)$ is a tuple $(A_1 = a_1, \ldots, A_n = a_n)$ such that $A_i \neq A_j$ if $i \neq j$, in which a_i is a constant, and A_i is an *attribute* of v drawn from Θ, written as $v.A_i = a_i$, carrying the content of v, such as the location and event in event networks. In particular, each node $v \in V$ carries a special attribute id denoting its *node identity*.

Patterns. A connected *graph pattern* $Q[\bar{x}]$ is defined as a graph (V_Q, E_Q, L_Q, μ), where (1) V_Q is a finite set of pattern nodes; (2) $E_Q \subseteq V_Q \times V_Q$ is a set of pattern edges; (3) L_Q is a function with range in Θ that assigns a node label $L_Q(u)$ for each u in V_Q; and (4) $\bar{x}$ is a list of distinct variables, each denoting an entity in V_Q; (5)μ is a bijective mapping from $\bar{x}$ to V_Q, *i.e.*, it assigns a distinct variable to each node v in V_Q.

We adopt *pattern diameter* to show the longest length d_Q of the shortest distance $dist(v, v')$ between every two nodes in given Q. We adopt *pattern pivot* to focus on the relationship between two of the event nodes and note them as pivots, where other event nodes in the pattern are not considered.

Match Graphs. Consider a relation $S \in V_q \times V$. The match graph S is a subgraph $G[V_s, E_s]$ of G, in which (1) $v \in V_s$ if and only if in S, and (2) an edge $(v, v') \in E_s$ if and only if there exists an edge (u, u') in Q with $(u, v) \in S$ and $(u', v') \in S$.

Relevance. If the candidate set of a pivot node u is removed except v_0 , many candidates of the other pivot node(for example, v_1, v_2 are exceptions) may also be removed from S_v since they cannot compose a match of the pattern without the presence of those candidate nodes. In this situation, we can formally define the relevance set of node v_0 as $r_{v_0} = \{v_1, v_2\}$.

3   Event Association Rules

3.1   Definition of Event Association

In real-life scenarios, the relationship between two events can be various. An event may be positive or negative to another event. We now define event association rules(EAR).

Literals. A literal of pattern $Q[\bar{x}]$ is one of the following: for variables $x, y \in \bar{x}$, attributes $A, B \in \Theta$ and $\Gamma_2 = \{\text{"positive"}, \text{"negative"}\}$

(a) *attribute literal* $x.A$;
(b) *edge literal* $\iota(x, y)$, where ι is a label in Γ_1;
(c) *variable literal* $x.A = y.B$;
(d) *constant literal* $x.A = c$, where c is a constant.

EARs. An *event association rule* (EAR) φ is defined as

$$Q[\bar{x}](X \to \iota'(x, y)),$$

where $Q[\bar{x}]$ is a graph pattern, $X \to \iota'(x, y)$ is shown as dependency of φ, X is (possibly empty) conjunctions of literals of $Q[\bar{x}]$, and $\iota'(x, y)$ is the edge literal in Γ_2 which represents the relationship between two events. Note that the edge does not exist in the graph actually.

Intuitively, the pattern Q in an EAR indentifies entities in a graph, and the dependency $X \to \iota(x, y)$ is applied to the entities. However, we have to measure what associations a rule can represent exactly. We therefore introduce $KULC$ and IR statistics to assess the impact between events (see in Sect. 5).

Semantics. To interpret EAR $\varphi = Q[\bar{x}](X \to \iota'(x, y))$, we use the following notations. $R(\bar{x})$ a simulation relation of Q in a graph G, and l a literal of $Q[\bar{x}]$. We write $R(\mu(x))$ as $R(x)$, where μ is the mapping function from $\bar{x}$ to V_Q.

We say that $R(\bar{x})$ satisfies a literal l, denoted by $R(\bar{x})| = l$, if one of the following condition is met: (1) when l is an attribute literal $x.A$, each node in $R(x)$ has the attribute; (2) when l is an edge literal $\iota(x, y)$, there is an edge with label ι from a to b, where a and b come from $R(x)$ and $R(y)$ respectively; (3) when l is a variable literal $x.A = y.B$, there exist node pairs a and b in $R(x)$ and $R(y)$, attribute A and B exist at a and b respectively, and $a.A = b.B$; and (4) when l is a constant literal $x.A = c$, for each node a in $R(x)$, $a.A = c$.

For a set X of literals, we say $R(\bar{x})| = X$ if match graph $R(\bar{x})$ satisfies all the literals in X. We write $R(\bar{x})| = X \to Y$ if $R(\bar{x})$ is a simulation relation of pattern Y in G, where $\bar{x}$ is the set of nodes of Y. We say $R(\bar{x})| = X \to Y$ if $R(\bar{x})| = X$ implies $R(\bar{x})| = Y$. A graph G satisfies EAR φ, denoted by $G| = \varphi$, if for all relation $R(\bar{x})$ of X in G, $R(\bar{x})| = X \to Y$.

4 Algorithms for Event Association Match

In this section, we introduce a batch algorithm and an incremental algorithm for event association analysis.

4.1 Event Association Match

We first propose *EventAsoFind*, abbreviated as *EAF*, a batch algorithm for matching EARs.

Algorithm EAF. It takes as input a pattern graph Q, a set of literal X and a data graph $G(V, E)$, and obtain the association set of events R matched in G. First we compute the maximum relation match S_v by utilizing DualSim in the global graph G. For every matched event point v in S_v, a ball $G[v, d_Q]$ is constructed where d refers to the diameter of the pattern Q. In the scope of each ball, we verify the literal of the event nodes to eliminate some nodes that do not satisfy the condition to speed up the pairing. Then we use EventPair to pair the event nodes matched in S_v, in order to determine which two events do have positive or negative association. After verifying the literal of entity nodes, we add the relation into the set R.

EventPair. EventPair aims to find which two candidates do have association with each other, which means it pairs the candidates from the two sets of event matches. We adopt *Relevance* to help pair the candidates of two event nodes.

As is shown in Fig. 1. We first calculate relevance sets of pivot nodes in S_v by removing u_1 from S_v except for a candidate v_1 to get S_v'(line 4), performing DualSim on S_v' to determine other nodes that should be deleted(line 5). Then we use the candidate set of the other pivot node u_2 as the relevance set(line 6). Moreover, to verify the literals of other entity nodes, we eliminate all pivot

---

Procedure: EventPair
Input: The maximum match relation S_v and Pattern graph Q.
Output: The accurate pattern match S_{acc}.
1. **for each** event node $u \in V_Q$ **do**
2.   **if** (u_1, u_2) is a pair of pivot nodes in Q **then**
3.   **for each** candidate $v_1 \in sim(u_1)$ **do**
4. $S_v' := S_v \ / \ \{(u_1, v)|v \in sim(u_1)\} + \{(u_1, v_1)\}$;
5. $S_v'' := \mathsf{DualSim}(Q, S_v')$;
6. $Relevance_{v_1} := sim'(u_2)$;
7.   **for each** candidate $v_2 \in Relevance_{v_1}$ **do**
8. $S_{v_1, v_2} := S_v' \ / \ \{(u_2, v)|v \in sim'(u_2)\} + \{(u_2, v_2)\}$;
9. $S_{acc} := \mathsf{DualSim}(Q, S_{v_1, v_2})$;
10. **return** S_{acc}.

Fig. 1. Procedure EventPair

event nodes in S_v except for v_1 and v_2 and perform DualSim again to determine other entity nodes in S_{acc}(line 7–10). Notice that if the literals are unimportant, lines 7–9 can be skipped since the relationship between events has already been discovered in line 6.

4.2 Incremental Event Association Match

When a graph G is updated by ΔG, we care more about how to handle ΔG part and thus we need to propose an incremental algorithm for event association detection. However, ΔG in event graph has its speciality. Once an event happenes, it becomes a fact and events that happen later than it will have no influence on it. That is to say, ΔG only involves the addition of nodes and edges. We first propose the definition of non-isolated nodes, and then we give an incremental algorithm to efficiently save time and computational resources.

Non-isolated Node. We first introduce the notion of non-isolated nodes. A non-isolated node in a graph is shown as one of the following: (1) If an entity node in ΔG has already existed in graph G, it is then called inherent non-isolated node; (2) If an entity node is newly added by ΔG, and it has two or more edges with other nodes, it is then called new non-isolated node. However, an entity node is newly added by ΔG, and has no or only one edge with other nodes, it is then called isolated node. We are interested in these non-isolated nodes since the match result of a ball with an isolated node as its center is included by that of a ball with a non-isolated node as its center.

Corollary 1. *There is no need to perform* DualSim *with isolated nodes as the center of the ball.*

Proof: The topological relation of an isolated node has in total 4 situations. We now analyse each situation individually under the condition that the pattern is connected and conclude that there is no need to construct balls with isolated nodes as their center (Figure 2).

(1) An isolated node A has no edge or is linked with another isolated node B. (Graph 1) There is no event node linked with either of the two isolated nodes, so we cannot find any valuable event match given a connected pattern.

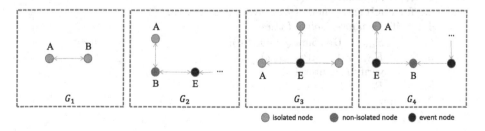

Fig. 2. Proof of isolated nodes

(2) An isolated node A is linked with a non-isolated node B. (Graph 2) Intuitively, in order to get access to other nodes(for example, event node E), the first step A has to take is $A \to B$, which restricts the search scope of the ball with node A as its center since the diameter of a pattern is fixed. However, node B can get access to any node which satisfies the ball radius without the step $A \to B$ and have a larger search scope than node A.

(3) An isolated node A is linked with an event node E, and E has only one neighbour A or all its neighbours are isolated nodes. (Graph 3) This situation is similar with (1), we cannot find the association between two events since there is only one event in the connected graph.

(4) An isolated node A is linked with an event node E, and E has at least one non-isolated neighbour B. (Graph 4) In order to get access to other event nodes, the first two steps A has to take is $A \to E \to B$. Similar with (2), taking node B as the ball center, the shared search path $A \to E \to B$ can be saved so that more nodes can be examined.

Algorithm incEF. We next propose incEventnFind, abbreviated as incEF. As is shown in Fig. 3. When given an incremental graph ΔG consisting of a few events and related entities, we first extract the non-isolated nodes to become the ball center, after initializing the association set R_Δ (line 1–3). Then we do DualSim on each non-isolated node to find potential match that may be added into the maximum relation match set $S_{\Delta v}$ (line 4–6). After pair the event candidates (line 7), we verify whether the match satisfies the rule literal (line 8) and add it into the updated set of event association match R_Δ (line 9).

nodeClassify. As is shown in Fig. 4. After extracting the non-isolated nodes, we implement DualSim only on them to release some of the calculation pressure and accelerate the incremental process. Given the definition of non-isolated nodes, a

---

Algorithm: incEventFind
Input: Pattern graph Q with diameter d_Q, previous graph $G(V, E)$, rule literal X and updated graph ΔG.
Output: The updated set R_Δ of event association match in $G \oplus \Delta G$.
1. initialize the set of event association match by previous result $R_\Delta = R$;
2. $(v, c) := \mathsf{nodeClassify}(V, V_\Delta)$;
3. **for each** entity node (v, c) involved in ΔG **do**
4.   **if** $c = non - isolated$ **then**
5. $S_{\Delta v} := \mathsf{DualSim}(Q, \hat{G}[v, d_Q])$;
6. $E_{\Delta v} := \mathsf{EventPair}(S_{\Delta v})$;
7.   verify rule literal X;
8. $R_\Delta := R_\Delta \cup \{E_{\Delta v}\}$;
9. **return** R_Δ.

Fig. 3. Algorithm incEventFind

node v is determined to be isolated (line 7–8) unless (1) it has already existed in the previous data, which means it is a member of the set of entity nodes in previous graph V (line 3–4); or (2) it has at least two edge with other nodes in the updated graph ΔG (line 5–6). The former condition represents this entity node may have closer relationship with other event nodes in the previous graph while the latter condition represents this entity node may have closer relationship with other event nodes in the updated graph. After this, DualSim is invoked to dig the potential pattern matches created by the updated graph ΔG.

5   Experimental Study

In this section, our proposed event association detection algorithm will be evaluated for accuracy, efficiency and performance on event graphs.

Experimental Setting. The machine in our experiment has 2 processors powered by Intel Xeon 2.40GHz, 2 NVIDIA GTX 1080Ti cards and 128G memory.

(1) Datasets. We use the Global Database of Events, Language and Tone (GDELT) [14] to evaluate the performance of our methods. Events in GDELT have a subject actor performing a specific action on an object actor, where actors and actions are coded by the Conflict and Mediation Event Observations (CAMEO) ontology. We use a subset of GDELT in our experiments and form it into a network, including several types of events all over the world in a month, ending up with $31k$ vertices and $133k$ edges.

(2) EAR Generator. For each graph, we generated EARs in 2 steps.

Procedure: nodeClassify
Input: updated graph ΔG, a set of entity nodes in previous graph V, a set of entity nodes in updated graph V_Δ.
Output: A set of related entity nodes with isolated or non-isolated attribute $V_{\Delta iso}$.
Declaration: Through this process, we classify all the entity nodes that are related to the newly added events.
1. $V_{\Delta iso} = \varnothing$;
2. **for each** node v in V_Δ **do**
3.   **if** $v \in V$ **then**
4. $(v, c) := (v, non - isolated)$;
5.   **elseif** there is more than 1 edge related to v in ΔG **then**
6. $(v, c) := (v, non - isolated)$;
7.   **else**
8. $(v, c) := (v, isolated)$;
9. $V_{\Delta iso} = V_{\Delta iso} \cup (v, c)$;
10. **return** $V_{\Delta iso}$.

Fig. 4. Procedure nodeClassify

(1) We first found frequent pattern which is larger than the support threshold σ, where $supp(Q, G)$ is defined as:

$$supp(Q, G) = |Q(G, x)| + |Q(G, y)| > \sigma$$

in which x, y are the two pivot event nodes, $Q(G, x)$ is the set of nodes that match event node x in graph G.

(2) We propose $KULC_G$ and IR_G to discard some rules and classify the remaining ones. Given a pair of $KULC_G$ threshold (K_{min}, K_{max}) and an IR_G threshold r, when $KULC_G < K_{min}$ and is nonzero, the rule is classified as bi-directional negative. When $KULC_G > K_{max}$ and $IR_G < r$, the rule is classified as bi-directional positive. When $KULC_G > K_{max}$ and $IR_G > r$, the rule is classified as unidirectional positive and unidirectional negative.

$$KULC_G = 1/2[(P(x|y) + P(y|x))] * Dependency$$

$$IR_G = max[P(x|y)/P(y|x), P(y|x)/P(x|y)]$$

Dependency is a boolean variable that distinguishes between no association and negative association. *Dependency* and all the probabilities involved are calculated as follows:

$$Dependency = \begin{cases} 0, & |P(xy) - P(x)P(y)| < \varsigma \\ 1, & |P(xy) - P(x)P(y)| > \varsigma \end{cases}$$

$$P(x) = \frac{|Q_{-y}(G, X_{-y})|}{N}, P(xy) = \frac{|Q(G, X)|}{N}, P(y|x) = \frac{|Q(G, X)|}{|Q_{-y}(G, X_{-y})|}$$

where $Q(G, X)$ is the set of subgraphs in G that matches pattern $Q[\bar{x}]$ and satisfies $h(\bar{x})| = X$ for all matches h of Q; $Q_{-y}(G, X_{-y})$ is the set of subgraphs in G that matches pattern $Q[\bar{x}_{-y}]$ and satisfies $h(\bar{x}_{-y})| = X_{-y}$ for all matches h of Q and $Q[\bar{x}_{-y}]$ represents a pattern $Q[\bar{x}]$ without event node y and X_{-y} represents literals X removing any literal that is related to event y. Similarly, we can get the frequency of event x. And N is denoted as the total number of events in the date set.

(3) Evaluation. We measured the accuracy by precision and recall and used assessments from human raters as ground truth. We measured the efficiency by *time* to evaluate the performance of batch algorithm and its incremental version.

(4) Baselines. We compare our methods with four link prediction baselines, including (1) a message-passing method HGT [12]; (2) relation-learning methods DistMult [19] and ConvE [5]; and (3) EAR(VF2), a method obtained by replacing the matching method with the subgraph isomorphism algorithm VF2 [4]. Note that link prediction methods based on machine learning can only predict the existence of edges and cannot infer specific association between events. In order to solve this problem, we set up two training sets to train positive and negative relations separately when using machine learning methods.

Table 1. Accuracy for GDELT

Methods	Metrics	
	Precision	Recall
DistMult	0.64	0.61
ConvE	0.60	0.58
HGT	0.69	0.68
EAR(vf2)	**0.77**	0.67
EAR(EAF)	0.76	**0.71**

Experimental Results. We next report our findings.

Exp-1: Accuracy. We first report the results of all the methods in terms of precision and recall scores in Table 1. It is shown that: (1) EAF algorithm outperformed all machine learning baselines on GDELT. In particular, our framework obtained a more significant improvement compared to the baselines of machine learning, with an average of 11.7% on precision and 8.7% on recall. This indicates that graph rules mined by statistical knowledge can better express the association between events. (2) On GDELT dataset, EAR(EAF) and EAR(VF2) have a relatively close performance, despite some slight deviations in the matching results. VF2, as an isomorphism matching algorithm, has more stringent topological requirements than homomorphism algorithm, thus causing the difference between the two methods.

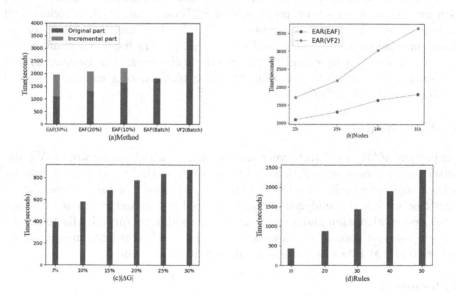

Fig. 5. Efficiency for GDELT

Exp-2: Efficiency. We next evaluated the efficiency of EAR(VF2), EAR(EAF) and its incremental version. The results are shown in Fig. 5. (1) As is shown in (a), we tested the above three methods using the same 20 rules and dataset, where we partitioned the graph into original and incremental parts to suit the incremental algorithm, *e.g.*, $EAF(30\%)$ means incrementally computing the remaining 30% of the data based on 70% of the dataset using EAF. Since the total amount of data is constant, as the original part increases and the incremental part decreases, their corresponding computational time consumptions change proportionally. The time consumed to compute the incremental part is significantly lower compared to recomputing the entire graph. This is because the incremental algorithm proposed in this paper filters out the entity nodes that play an important role in the association, which can accelerate the convergence of the incremental computation to the stable point. (2) As is shown in (b), we tested the performance of EAR(EAF) and EAR(VF2) at different graph size. The time of EAR(VF2) grows much faster than EAR(EAF) because isomorphism is a *npc* problem while the matching algorithm proposed in this paper is a *np* problem. (3) As is shown in (c), we varied $|\Delta G|$ from 5% up to 30% of $|G|$ and reported the time consumption it takes to calculate the incremental part. We find that the time required for incEF grows as $|\Delta G|$ grows, and the growth gradually slows down because of the relative slow growth rate of non-isolated nodes which need to be examined in incEF. (4) As is shown in (d), we varied the number of rules from 10 to 50 to calculate the incremental part. We can see that the more rules are used, the longer incEF takes, as expected.

Summary. We find the following. (1) EARs are effective in attribute network event association analysis. Our framework obtains a significant improvement, with an average of 11.7% on precision and 8.7% on recall. (2) EAF scales well for large graphs. The time consumption of EAF is 2.02 times lower than isomorphism on graphs with $31k$ nodes and $133k$ edges. (3) The incremental algorithm saves computational time and resources effectively. *incEF* in calculating the incremental part is 48.1% less than the time required to recalculate the full graph when $|\Delta G|$ is $30\%|G|$.

6   Conclusion

We propose EARs to detect event associations in attribute networks. We use patterns to represent connections between events so that we can make full use of their topological relations. We use literal to represent the logic of association formation so that the analyzed associations are logically interpretable. We have developed an algorithm and an incremental algorithm to apply EARs to graphs and proposed an approach to match the candidate set. Our experimental study has verified that EARs are promising in real-life applications.

References

1. Allan, J.: Topic Detection and Tracking: Event-based Information Organization, vol. 12. Springer, Cham (2002). https://doi.org/10.1007/978-1-4615-0933-2

2. Bhattacharjya, D., Gao, T., Mattei, N., et al.: Cause-effect association between event pairs in event datasets. In: Proceedings of the 29th International Conference on IJCAI, pp. 1202–1208 (2021)
3. Bhattacharjya, D., Shanmugam, K., Gao, T., et al.: Event-driven continuous time Bayesian networks. In: Proceedings of the AAAI Conference on Artificial Intelligence, vol. 34, pp. 3259–3266 (2020)
4. Cordella, L.P., Foggia, P., Sansone, C., et al.: A (sub) graph isomorphism algorithm for matching large graphs. IEEE Trans. Pattern Anal. Mach. Intell. 26(10), 1367–1372 (2004)
5. Dettmers, T., Minervini, P., Stenetorp, P., et al.: Convolutional 2d knowledge graph embeddings. In: Proceedings of the AAAI Conference on Artificial Intelligence, vol. 32 (2018)
6. Fan, G., Fan, W., Li, Y., et al.: Extending graph patterns with conditions. In: Proceedings of the 2020 ACM SIGMOD International Conference on Management of Data, pp. 715–729 (2020)
7. Fan, W., Jin, R., Liu, M., et al.: Capturing associations in graphs. Proc. VLDB Endowment 13(12), 1863–1876 (2020)
8. Fan, W., Li, J., Ma, S., et al.: Graph pattern matching: from intractable to polynomial time. Proc. VLDB Endowment 3(1–2), 264–275 (2010)
9. Fan, W., Wang, X., Wu, Y.: Incremental graph pattern matching. ACM Trans. Database Syst. (TODS) 38(3), 1–47 (2013)
10. Fan, W., Wang, X., Wu, Y., et al.: Association rules with graph patterns. Proc. VLDB Endowment 8(12), 1502–1513 (2015)
11. Fan, W., Wu, Y., Xu, J.: Adding counting quantifiers to graph patterns. In: Proceedings of the 2016 International Conference on Management of Data, pp. 1215–1230 (2016)
12. Hu, Z., Dong, Y., Wang, K., et al.: Heterogeneous graph transformer. In: Proceedings of the Web Conference 2020, pp. 2704–2710 (2020)
13. Khan, S.M., Soutchanski, M.: Diagnosis as computing causal chains from event traces. In: Proceedings of the AAAI Fall Symposium: Integrating Planning, Diagnosis, and Causal Reasoning (SIP-18). AAAI Press (2018)
14. Leetaru, K., Schrodt, P.A.: Gdelt: global data on events, location, and tone, 1979–2012. In: ISA Annual Convention, vol. 2, pp. 1–49. Citeseer (2013)
15. Liu, X., Huang, H., Zhang, Y.: Open domain event extraction using neural latent variable models. arXiv preprint arXiv:1906.06947 (2019)
16. Ma, S., Cao, Y., Fan, W., et al.: Strong simulation: capturing topology in graph pattern matching. ACM Trans. Database Syst. (TODS) 39(1), 1–46 (2014)
17. Milner, R.: Communication and Concurrency, vol. 84. Prentice hall, Englewood Cliffs (1989)
18. Spirtes, P., Glymour, C.N., Scheines, R.: Causation, Prediction, and Search. MIT press, Cambridge (2000)
19. Yang, B., Yih, W.T., He, X., et al.: Embedding entities and relations for learning and inference in knowledge bases. arXiv preprint arXiv:1412.6575 (2014)
20. Zhang, H., Liu, X., Pan, H., et al.: Aser: a large-scale eventuality knowledge graph. In: Proceedings of the Web Conference 2020, pp. 201–211 (2020)

Fake Review Detection via Heterogeneous Graph Attention Network

Zijun Ren, Xianguo Zhang$^{(\boxtimes)}$, Shuai Zhang, and Chao Yang

College of Computer Science, Inner Mongolia University, Hohhot 010021, China
2595083628@qq.com

Abstract. An approach based on a combination of semantic and non-semantic features of reviews is recognized as the most effective method for detecting fake reviews. However, existing deep learning-based fake review detection models have two main limitations. The first one is the extraction of word embedding, they only consider acquiring semantic features of text, but ignore that a good word embedding should ensure uniformity and alignment. Secondly, the non-semantic features are not effectively utilized. To solve these problems, this paper proposes a deep learning fake review detection model MFBH (Multi-feature Fusion using BERT-whitening and Heterogeneous graph attention network). It uses the BERT-whitening model in the text feature extraction part, i.e., the vectors extracted by BERT are linearly transformed into isotropic vectors conforming to the standard Gaussian distribution. In addition eight non-semantic features are extracted as entity links of meta-paths.Finally, the obtained text features are used as the node features of the graph and the adjacency matrix composed of meta-paths as the structural features of the graph, and the features are fused through a heterogeneous graph attention network. Experiments were conducted on the publicly available dataset of Yelp website, and the accuracy reached 93.81% on the restaurant dataset and 90.25% on the hotel dataset, which proved the effectiveness and generalization of the MFBH model.

Keywords: Fake review detection · BERT-whitening · Heterogeneous graph neural network · Feature fusion

1 Introduction

The amount of information in consumers' online reviews on e-commerce websites and review sites is growing rapidly, and studies have shown that consumers' consumption intentions refer more to and even rely on online reviews [1]. Some unscrupulous merchants have discovered this phenomenon and hired a large number of writers to post fake reviews to discredit or exaggerate products [2], which undermines the fairness of the market. While manual identification results are not accuracy enough [3]. The detection of reviews by a fake review detection model can improve the detection efficiency and return a fair and equitable environment to the market.

Fake review detection can be converted into a binary classification problem. Mukherjee et al. [4] found that combining meta-information for analysis gives higher accuracy

© The Author(s), under exclusive license to Springer Nature Switzerland AG 2023
L. Iliadis et al. (Eds.): ICANN 2023, LNCS 14257, pp. 364–376, 2023.
https://doi.org/10.1007/978-3-031-44216-2_30

than that obtained by using only semantic information of the comments. The main approaches to extract semantic features in the field of fake reviews are through machine learning methods such as Bag of Words (BOW), Term Frequency_Inverse Document Frequency (TF-IDF) and also through deep neural networks such as Recurrent Neural Network (RNN), Gate Recurrent Unit (GRU), BERT etc. Since the introduction of BERT [5], the development of related fields of natural language processing has also progressed a lot. A good vector representation should satisfy both alignment and uniformity, i.e., the vectors representing similarity should be similar in distance and the representation vectors should be as uniform as possible in space, preferably isotropic [6]. BERT is well used in short texts because it applies self-attention to dynamically acquire word vectors and better represent the text. However, Li et al. [7] conducted experiments to show that the semantic information in BERT word embeddings is not fully utilized.

And there are two main ways to fuse semantic and non-semantic features, the first is through machine learning methods such as Support Vector Machines (SVM) and Logistic Regression (LR) [8]. The other one is the recently emerging graph neural networks such as GCN (Graph Convolutional Network) [9, 10]. Jindal et al. constructed three types of spam reviews and extracted 36 features including review features, reviewer features and product features. Fake review detection was performed by LR [11]. Li et al. used CNN (Convolutional Neural Networks) to get text vector representations, and two features of POS and first person pronous were added on the obtained vector used to detect fake reviews [12]. The fusion of text vector representations and non-semantic features in these methods is generally performed by combining, then input the representations into a classifier for classification and recognition. After such fusion, the non-semantic features contribute a small proportion of the combined vector representations, and the computation is still performed with the text vector features as the main body, and the non-semantic features do not play their role effectively.

Based on the above shortcomings, the contributions made in this paper are mainly as follows:

(1) Eight non-semantic features were extracted by analyzing the dataset. The non-semantic features can assist the text vector representations to identify fake review. The effect of each meta-path constructed by non-semantic features on the detection results is verified by conducting experiments in a heterogeneous graph attention network constructed by a single meta-path.
(2) A deep neural network model MFBH is constructed for fake review detection. Using BERT-whitening which performs excellently in unsupervised sentence embedding [13]. The obtained text vector representations are used as node features, as well as the graph constructed by meta-paths as structural features, then the features are fused by node-level attention and semantic-level attention of heterogeneous graph attention network. The experimental results show that the performance of the model on the fake review detection task is superior compared to other comparative experiments.

2   Related Work

2.1   Text Embedding Using Neural Networks

Neural networks have been applied to fake review detection long ago, and as neural networks have evolved, the fake review detection applied to them has been improving.Word embedding have been obtained by extracting n-gram and skip-gram language models [14, 15]. Ren et al. [16] used CNN to get sentence embedding and used Bi-GRU and attention mechanism to get document embedding from sentence level. Zeng et al. [17] learned word embedding by fasttext and used Bi-directional Long Short-Term Memory (Bi-LSTM) to encode the three parts of the split as well as the whole documents, then stack two layers of attention mechanisms to get the final representation of the comment. Krishnamurthy et al. [18] used a pre-trained Word2vec model to extract the vector representation of each word in the comment, and later fused the vectors and input CNN models to get the sentence representation. Hierarchical attention networks are constructed with the idea that text is composed of sentences, and sentences are composed of words [19]. Scholars have used this idea in the phase of learning the representation of text [20]. However, the word vectors obtained by the above methods are static word vectors that do not change with the context and cannot represent the sentence semantics well. To solve this problem, dynamic word vectors are proposed.BERT can obtain dynamic word vectors, but the vectors are anisotropic in space.Li et al. [7] solved the word anisotropy by mapping the vectors extracted by BERT to standard Gaussian functions. Subsequently, Su et al. [21] found that using a simple linear variation can achieve same results to BERT-flow [7] in semantic similarity tasks, and after performing dimension reduction operations can use less memory storage and achieve faster retrieval speed.

2.2   Fake Review Detection Using Graph Neural Networks

The local graph clustering algorithm-based risky account detection system GraphRAD proposed by Ma et al. [22] is the first paper to apply graph neural networks to the fraud detection problem, by proposing the hypothesis that fraudulent users are tightly connected in the "fraud community" and sparsely connected to accounts outside the community, and using a graph-based penalty item model to score the nodes. Zhang et al. [23] selected 14 behavioral features to be used as feature vectors to score users by capturing their preference and reliability information through iterative aggregation. If the user's score differs significantly from the score from the model, the user is a fraud. Dou et al. [24] proposed a CARE-GNN model that first filters out feature-fake users by label-aware similarity metrics, filters out relationship-fake users using a similarity-aware neighbor selector approach, then uses the threshold learned by reinforcement learning as an aggregation between neighbors under different relationships. All of the above are based on aggregation of neighbor nodes under one meta-path. The Heterogeneous Graph Attention Network (HGAN) proposed by Wang et al. [25] can fuse the feature representations under all meta-paths. Scholars have made various improvements on The HGAN model and applied it to the task of fake review detection. Zhao et al. [26] constructed a heterogeneous graph network from the comment data, including the comments themselves and the non-semantic features of the comments, and finally performing Bagging framework to get the final experimental results.

3 Methodology

This section focuses on the construction process of the fake review detection model MFBH proposed in this paper. The specific architecture of the model is shown in Fig. 1. In this section, the extraction of text vector representations and the computational process of feature fusion are illustrated.

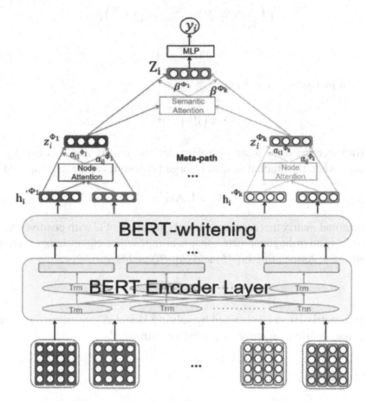

Fig. 1. Network Structure of MFBH Model.

3.1 Textual Vector Representations Extraction

Reimers et al. [27] found that the sentence embedding derived from BERT is even less effective than Glove. By projecting the word vectors derived from BERT to standard Gaussian distribution, the semantic information can be better utilized. In this paper, after averaging the first and last layer vectors of the BERT model, the word embedding are mapped to the standard Gaussian distribution space by whitening. After the following linear change, the original data X can be transformed into Y which conforms to the standard normal distribution.

$$Y = P(X - E[X]) \tag{1}$$

E[X]is the mean of sample X. The mean of the original data can be changed to 0 by Zero-centered. Let the covariance matrix of sample Y be D. The process of solving the linear change matrix P is as follows:

$$D = \frac{1}{N}YY^T = \frac{1}{N}(P(X - E[X]))(P(X - E[X]))^T \tag{2}$$

$$= P\left(\frac{1}{N}(X - E[X])(X - E[X])^T\right)P^T \tag{3}$$

$$= PCP^T = I \tag{4}$$

I is the unit matrix, so we can get:

$$C = \left(P^T\right)^{-1}P^{-1} \tag{5}$$

The covariance matrix is a semi-positive definite matrix and it is usually positive definite matrix when the amount of data is large [28], so it can be decomposed as:

$$C = U\Lambda U^T \tag{6}$$

Λ is a diagonal matrix that represents the eigenvalues of C with positive elements on the diagonal; U is an orthogonal matrix that is composed of eigenvectors corresponding to the eigenvalues. Associating Eq. (5) and Eq. (6) yields:

$$P = U\sqrt{\Lambda^{-1}}. \tag{7}$$

The linear matrix P can be obtained by solving U and Λ. , nverting the words to the standa Gaussian distribution solves the word anisotropy.

3.2 Feature Fusion

Heterogeneous graph attention network can model the features of nodes and edges, in this paper, the extracted isotropic vector representation is put into the heterogeneous graph attention network for feature fusion with meta-paths composed of other non-semantic features. The computational procedure is as follows:

(1) Node-level attention

Node-level attention allows learning the importance between nodes and their meta-path-based neighbors and obtain the node representation of aggregation between each node under a single meta-path. The calculation process is as follows:

$$h_i' = w_\phi \cdot h_i \tag{8}$$

$h_i (h_i \in \mathbb{R}^{d_1})$ is the initial node representation of node i, $h_i' (h_i' \in \mathbb{R}^{d_2})$ is the output node representation of node i, w ($w \in \mathbb{R}^{d_2 \times d_1}$)is a shareable learning parameter, ϕ. Represents the meta-path.After projection,the initial node representation can be mapped to feature space $\mathbb{R}^{d_2}$. Then the attention coefficient $e_{ij}^{\phi_k}$ between review i and first-order neighbor review j is calculated as follows:

$$e_{ij}^{\phi_k} = \mathrm{att}_{\mathrm{node}}\left(h_i', h_j'; \Phi_k\right) = \mathrm{LeakyRelu}((a^{\Phi_k})^{\mathrm{T}} \cdot \left[h_i' \| h_j'\right])$$ (9)

i is the node in the graph composed of Φ_k, j is the neighbor node of node i in the graph based on the composition of the Φ_k, , ($\|$) is the connection symbol, a^{Φ_k} is the trainable attenti weight parameter, and $(\cdot)^{\mathrm{T}}$ is the transpose operation. After obtaining the attention coefficients between node i and its first-order neighbors, normalization is performed:

$$a_{ij}^{\Phi_k} = \frac{\exp(e_{ij}^{\phi_k})}{\sum_{x \in N_i^{\Phi_k}} \exp\left(e_{ix}^{\phi_k}\right)}$$ (10)

a_{ij} is the node-level attention coefficient after normalization e_{ij}, which can reflect the importance of each neighboring node to it. $N_i^{\Phi_k}$ is the set of neighboring nodes of node i in the graph composed based on Φ_k. By aggregating the neighboring nodes, the node representation of this node based on this meta-path is obtained as follows:

$$z_i^{\Phi_k} = \delta\left(h_i' + \sum_{j \in N_i^{\Phi_k}} a_{ij}^{\Phi_k} \cdot h_j'\right)$$ (11)

To maintain the stability of the model, a multi-headed attention mechanism is used to obtain the node representation:

$$z_i^{\Phi_k} = \|_{p=1,2,\cdots,P} z_i^{\Phi_k}, z_i \in \mathbb{R}^{P \cdot d_2}$$ (12)

P is the implementation of the attention mechanism P times. Same as that, the node representations based on other meta-paths are obtained.

(2) Semantic-level attention

Different meta-paths contribute differently to the fake review detection task. The final node representation obtained by aggregating the importance of different meta-paths can be learned through semantic-level attention when the weights of each relation are calculated using the attention mechanism during fusion. The calculation process is as follows:

$$d^{\Phi_k} = \frac{1}{|V|} \sum_{i \in V}\left(q^{\mathrm{T}} \cdot \tanh\left(W \cdot z_i^{\Phi_k} + b\right)\right)$$ (13)

d^{Φ_k} is the weight coefficient based on Φ_k, V denotes the set of all nodes under Φ_k based, $|V|$ is the number of all nodes under Φ_k based, b is the bias vector, and q is the trainable attention coefficient. After obtaining the weight coefficients of each meta-path, it is normalized to obtain the importance coefficient β^{Φ_k} of different meta-paths, which are calculated as shown in Eq. (14):

$$\beta^{\Phi_k} = \frac{\exp(d^{\Phi_k})}{\sum_{k=1}^{K} \exp(d^{\Phi_k})}$$ (14)

$$Z_i = \sum_{k=1}^{K} \beta^{\Phi_k} \cdot z_i^{\Phi_k} \tag{15}$$

Z_i is the final vector representation after feature fusion. The predicted values of the reviews data labels can be obtained after classification by MLP.

4 Experiments

4.1 Dataset Introduction and Data Preprocessing

Yelp is the most famous merchant review website in the U.S. The Yelp dataset is a highly recognized dataset in the field of fake review detection. In this paper, we use the dataset containing both restaurant and hotel domains obtained from yelp.com. The statistical information of the dataset is shown in the following Table 1:

Table 1. Statistical information of the dataset.

Review	Res	Hotel
Number of fake review	4000	4000
Number of real reviews	4000	4000
Total number of reviews	8000	8000

After obtaining the review data, we first add spaces in front of the punctuation marks to ensure correct word segmentation, then pre-process the data by removing URL addresses from the text; converting uppercase letters to lowercase letters; and removing special symbols such as non-letters and numbers to make the data into a form that conforms to the model input requirements.

4.2 Extracting Non-semantic Features

The semantic features can be extracted through the text, and rich non-semantic features can also be extracted through the dataset. In this paper, the following eight features are extracted to build meta-paths, and the principles and formulas of these feature constructions are explained below.

(1) ARI [29]: Automated Readability Index. It can measure the interpretability of a text, the higher the value, the easier its content is to be understood.
(2) RD [30]: Rating Deviation. The deviation of the rating between business rating and user rating. The larger the deviation, the more it reflects the abnormal behavior of the user.
(3) RL: Review Length. Fake reviewers do not invest too long in their reviews, so the length of fake reviews is generally shorter than that of real reviews [4].

(4) Rating: Fake review publishers will have more extreme ratings, while real review publishers will have more average ratings.
(5) URD: Days of User Registration. The shorter the registration time, the more likely the user is a fake comment publisher.
(6) Count: Since the fake review publisher will often register new accounts in order to complete his tasks or not to reveal his real identity, his number of comments will be smaller than the number posted by the real comment publisher.
(7) SC: Sentiment Class. A review is highly likely to be a fake review if it describes the product with positive or negative sentiment. In this paper, we calculate review sentiment scores by using a SenticNet5 dictionary. After that, it is converted to an integer value[31] to facilitate the construction of meta-paths.
(8) UID: User ID. If a user post a fake comment, it is highly likely that he will continue to post fake comments.

4.3　Development Experiment

In order to verify the performance of the model MFBH proposed in this paper, the dataset is divided into training set, validation set, test set in the ratio of 8:1:1, and three experiments are designed to verify them separately.

(1) Experiment 1: Validation of models for the use of text vector representations. The following are the details of the seven comparison experimental methods designed in this paper:

1) BHAN: the [CLS] token vector of the BERT model is used to obtain the sentence vector of the text, followed by the paragraph representations of the text after Bi-GRU and self-attention, then use SVM to classify.
2) Word2vec: using average word embedding from Word2Vec model,then use SVM to classify.
3) LSTM: the model based on LSTM.
4) Bi-GRU: the model based on Bi-GRU.
5) HAN: the model based on Hierarchical Attention Network (HAN).
6) BERT: the model based on BERT.
7) BERT-whitening: the first and last layer vectors in the pre-training model BERT are used to average the output and then linearly transformed to use the SVM for classification.

(2) Experiment 2: Verify the effect of a single meta-path on the model.

1) RARIR (Review-ARI-Review): link reviews with readability metrics in the same interval value.
2) RrDR (Review-RD-Review): link reviews with the same rating deviation.
3) RrLR (Review-RL-Review): link reviews whose length is in the same interval value.
4) RrR (Review-Rating-Review): link reviews with the same rating.
5) RURDR (Reviewer-URD-Reviewer): link reviewers with the same interval value of registration days.
6) RCountR (Reviewer-Count-Reviewer): link the number of reviews in the same interval value of reviewers.

7) RSCR (Review-SC-Review):link reviews with sentiment scores in the same interval value.
8) RUIDR (Review-User ID-Review): link comments posted by the same user.

(3) Experiment 3: Validation of the model used for feature fusion. The node features of the graph are used with text vector representations trained by BERT-whitening. The experiments of GCN and GAT selected Φ_{RrDR} as structural features of the graph (Table 2).

4.4 Results and Analysis

Table 2. The results of Experiment 1 and Experiment 3.

Model		Res		Hotel	
		Accuracy (%)	F1(%)	Accuracy (%)	F1(%)
Exp 1	BHAN	53.87	53.88	53.37	53.65
	Word2Vec	67.25	66.51	67.09	67.17
	LSTM	61.30	71.85	70.85	70.54
	Bi-GRU	68.16	56.96	77.12	62.33
	HAN	69.25	66.21	55.62	64.86
	BERT	77.63	72.28	88.38	86.25
	BERT-whitening	**89.34**	**90.25**	**89.22**	**90.14**
Exp 3	GCN	65.56	51.67	74.81	69.09
	GATs	66.13	61.95	80.75	80.81
	MFBH	**93.81**	**93.95**	**90.25**	**90.27**

From the results of Experiment 1, it can be found that the BHAN model is not as effective as the direct extraction of Word2Vec vectors, which proves that the [CLS] token vector do not represent the semantic information of a sentence very well. The classification effect of LSTM is not good, probably because although LSTM has a gate structure that can control the information update, it still has the gradient disappearance or explosion when dealing with the real-life long sequence problem. The effect of bidirectional GRU is stronger than that of LSTM because the structure of GRU model is simpler than that of LSTM, which makes it easier to optimize and adjust the parameters during backpropagation; and with the bidirectional structure can capture the contextual information and better capture the meaning of statements. BERT works better compared to other baseline neural network models, probably because the model is more capable of extracting information and obtaining dynamic word vectors. The BERT-whitening used in this paper solves the problem of degradation of the expressiveness of words brought by BERT. As shown in Fig. 2, it can be seen that the low-frequency word vectors trained by BERT are far away from the origin and the high-frequency word vectors are close to the origin with tight distribution, while the vectors trained by BERT-whitening are more evenly distributed in space than the vectors trained by BERT. By using SVM specifically designed for the binary classification problem as a classifier, an accuracy of 89.34% was achieved on the Res dataset and 89.22% on the Hotel dataset. It shows that the text vector representations can well determine whether the reviews are fake or not.

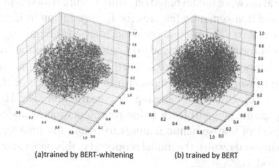

(a)trained by BERT-whitening   (b) trained by BERT

Fig. 2. Text Embedding Space Distribution Graph

From the results of Experiment 3, it can be found that the effect of the MFBH model proposed in this paper is the best on both datasets. The experimental results show that the MFBH model can perform feature fusion well, and the vectors after performing fusion can not only accurately determine fake reviews, but also have stable model performance and relatively strong generalization ability.

The results of Experiment 2 are shown in Fig. 3. Analyzing the data in the figure, the following conclusions can be drawn:

Fig. 3. Effect of Single Meta-Path on the Model Performance

The impact of each feature constituting the meta-path on the experiment is different, with the best experimental results for the meta-path consisting of the feature of rating deviation. This may be because rating deviation measures the degree to which the user rating deviates from the overall merchant rating, and fake review users generally rate products very extremely when they post reviews, so the nodes connected to the meta-path can be more easily detected as fake reviews.

5 Conclusion

In this paper, a neural network model based on multi-feature fusion is proposed to extract semantic features and non-semantic features for feature fusion to learn the final representation of comment text. The vectors obtained after BERT training are transformed into word vectors conforming to the standard Gaussian distribution by linear variation in the text part, which not only fully extracts semantic information, but also solves the anisotropy problem of words. Feature engineering was performed on the data, and eight metadata features were extracted for meta-path construction. The HGAN model was used in the fusion feature stage to learn to the representation of nodes under different meta-paths composed of non-semantic features to obtain the final text representation. Based on the experimental results, the model proposed in this paper shows that it exceeds other benchmark models.

References

1. Samha, A.K., Li, Y., Zhang, J.: Aspect-based opinion extraction from customer reviews. arXiv preprint arXiv:1404.1982 (2014)
2. Jindal, N., Liu, B.: Opinion spam and analysis. Proceedings of the 2008 international conference on web search and data mining, 219–230 (2008)
3. Ott, M., Choi, Y., Cardie, C., et al.: Finding deceptive opinion spam by any stretch of the imagination. arXiv preprint arXiv:1107.4557 (2011)
4. Mukherjee, A., Venkataraman, V., Liu, B., et al.: What yelp fake review filter might be doing? Proceedings of the international AAAI conference on web and social media 7(1), 409–418 (2013)
5. Devlin, J., Chang, M.W., Lee, K., et al.: Bert: Pre-training of deep bidirectional transformers for language understanding. arXiv preprint arXiv:1810.04805 (2018)
6. Wang, T., Isola, P.: Understanding contrastive representation learning through alignment and uniformity on the hypersphere. International Conference on Machine Learning. PMLR, pp. 9929–9939 (2020)
7. Li, B., Zhou, H., He, J., et al.: On the sentence embeddings from pre-trained language models. arXiv preprint arXiv:2011.05864 (2020)
8. Rayana, S., Akoglu, L.: Collective opinion spam detection: Bridging review networks and metadata. Proceedings of the 21th acm sigkdd international conference on knowledge discovery and data mining, pp. 985–994 (2015)
9. Ali Alhosseini, S., Bin Tareaf, R., Najafi, P., et al.: Detect me if you can: Spam bot detection using inductive representation learning. Companion Proceedings of The 2019 World Wide Web Conference, pp. 148–153 (2019)
10. Li, A., Qin, Z., Liu, R., et al.: Spam review detection with graph convolutional networks. Proceedings of the 28th ACM International Conference on Information and Knowledge Management, pp. 2703–2711 (2019)
11. Jindal, N., Liu, B.: Analyzing and detecting review spam. Seventh IEEE international conference on data mining (ICDM 2007). IEEE, pp. 547–552 (2007)

12. Li, L., Qin, B., Ren, W., et al.: Document representation and feature combination for deceptive spam review detection. Neurocomputing **254**, 33–41 (2017)
13. Huang, J., Tang, D., Zhong, W., et al.: Whiteningbert: An easy unsupervised sentence embedding approach. arXiv preprint arXiv:2104.01767 (2021)
14. Ott, M., Cardie, C., Hancock, J.T.: Negative deceptive opinion spam. Proceedings of the 2013 conference of the north american chapter of the association for computational linguistics: human language technologies, pp. 497–501 (2013)
15. Barushka, A., Hajek, P.: Review spam detection using word embeddings and deep neural networks. Artificial Intelligence Applications and Innovations: 15th IFIP WG 12.5 International Conference, AIAI 2019, Hersonissos, Crete, Greece, May 24–26, 2019, Proceedings 15. Springer International Publishing, pp. 340–350 (2019)
16. Ren, Y., Zhang, Y.: Deceptive opinion spam detection using neural network. Proceedings of COLING 2016, the 26th International Conference on Computational Linguistics: Technical Papers, pp. 140–150 (2016)
17. Zeng, Z.Y., Lin, J.J., Chen, M.S., et al.: A review structure based ensemble model for deceptive review spam. Information **10**(7), 243 (2019)
18. Krishnamurthy, G., Majumder, N., Poria, S., et al.: A deep learning approach for multimodal deception detection. Computational Linguistics and Intelligent Text Processing: 19th International Conference, CICLing 2018, Hanoi, Vietnam, March 18–24, 2018, Revised Selected Papers, Part I, pp. 87–96. Springer Nature Switzerland, Cham (2023)
19. Yang, Z., Yang, D., Dyer, C., et al.: Hierarchical attention networks for document classification. Proceedings of the 2016 conference of the North American chapter of the association for computational linguistics: human language technologies, pp. 1480–1489 (2016)
20. Jiang, C., Zhang, X.: Neural networks merging semantic and non-semantic features for opinion spam detection. Natural Language Processing and Chinese Computing: 8th CCF International Conference, NLPCC 2019, Dunhuang, China, October 9–14, 2019, Proceedings, Part I 8, pp. 583–595. Springer International Publishing (2019)
21. Su, J., Cao, J., Liu, W., et al.: Whitening sentence representations for better semantics and faster retrieval. arXiv preprint arXiv:2103.15316 (2021)
22. Ma, J., Zhang, D., Wang, Y., et al.: GraphRAD: a graph-based risky account detection system. Proceedings of ACM SIGKDD conference, p. 9. London, UK (2018)
23. Zhang, S., Yin, H., Chen, T., et al.: Gcn-based user representation learning for unifying robust recommendation and fraudster detection. Proceedings of the 43rd international ACM SIGIR conference on research and development in information retrieval, pp. 689–698 (2020)
24. Dou, Y., Liu, Z., Sun, L., et al.: Enhancing graph neural network-based fraud detectors against camouflaged fraudsters. Proceedings of the 29th ACM International Conference on Information & Knowledge Management, pp. 315–324 (2020)
25. Wang, X., Ji, H., Shi, C., et al.: Heterogeneous graph attention network. The world wide web conference, pp. 2022–2032 (2019)
26. Min, Z., Yueqin, Z., Yingtong, D.O.U., et al.: Imbalanced Fake Reviews? Detection with Ensemble Hierarchical Graph Attention Network. J. Fronti. Comp. Sci. Technol. **17**(2), 428 (2023)
27. Reimers, N., Gurevych, I.: Sentence-bert: Sentence embeddings using siamese bert-networks. arXiv preprint arXiv:1908.10084 (2019)
28. Dykstra, R.L.: Establishing the positive definiteness of the sample covariance matrix. Ann. Math. Stat. **41**(6), 2153–2154 (1970)
29. Korfiatis, N., García-Bariocanal, E., Sánchez-Alonso, S.: Evaluating content quality and helpfulness of online product reviews: The interplay of review helpfulness vs. review content. Electr. Comm. Res. Appl. **11**(3), 205–217 (2012)

30. Fei, G., Mukherjee, A., Liu, B., et al.: Exploiting burstiness in reviews for review spammer detection. Proceedings of the international AAAI conference on web and social media, **7**(1), 175–184 (2013)
31. Ren, Z., Shen, Q., Diao, X., et al.: A sentiment-aware deep learning approach for personality detection from text. Inf. Process. Manage. **58**(3), 102532 (2021)

GatedGCN with GraphSage to Solve Traveling Salesman Problem

Hua Yang[✉]

School of Software, Tsinghua University, Beijing 100084, China
yang-h17@mails.tsinghua.edu.cn

Abstract. Graph neural networks have shown good performance in many domains, as well as in combinatorial optimization. This paper proposes a new graph neural network framework to deal with the classical combinatorial optimization problem, the traveling salesman problem (TSP). The proposed framework is composed of GraphSage and GatedGCN jointly, named GGCN_GSG, where the output of GraphSage is the input of GatedGCN. With each TSP graph being used as data input, each node and its neighbors in the graph are embedded into the d-dimensional feature vector through GraphSage, and GatedGCN adds the distance information of the edge into the update function, and controls whether the TSP node enters the update function through the gated mechanism. Experimental results show that our proposed framework can get closer to the optimal solution than comparable graph neural network frameworks and other learning-based methods, achieving an optimal solution of 3.83 at 20 nodes and an optimal ratio of 30 nodes 2x increase.

Keywords: Combinatorial Optimization · GraphSage · GatedGCN · Graph Convolution Network · Deep Learning · TSP

1 Introduction

Combinatorial Optimization Problem (COP) [8,16,24,30] is a young and active branch of discrete mathematics, and the intersection of applied mathematics and computer science. Combinatorial optimization is to solve the optimal order, optimal grouping, optimal arrangement, or optimal screening of discrete events through the study of various methods of discrete mathematics [8,30]. It is developed jointly by combinatorics, linear programming and algorithm theory. In the fields of physics, chemistry, management, operations research, cybernetics, information theory, biology and computer science, combinatorial optimization theory is ubiquitous; in many aspects of the national economy, such as transportation, logistics, manufacturing, energy and social media, etc., combinatorial optimization problems have extremely important applications [8,30].

The Traveling Salesman Problem (TSP) [5,13,20] is a well-known COP. Nevertheless, the COP is an NP-complete problem [24]. In the Operation Research

L. Iliadis et al. (Eds.): ICANN 2023, LNCS 14257, pp. 377–387, 2023.
https://doi.org/10.1007/978-3-031-44216-2_31

(OR) community [1, 15, 29, 30, 37], the 2D Euclidean TSP graph has been the most intensively investigated graph issue among COPs.

Graph learning techniques for solving COPs have lately gotten a lot of press. On the other hand, graph learning can solve COPs more quickly and with greater generality and flexibility. Graph learning techniques are expected to be effective for multiple optimization projects, needing less human operations than all sorts of solvers [12, 29, 37] that only optimize for one work, thanks to heuristic ways of automatically discovering itself based on training data.

Combinatorial optimization has an important structural type of data, which is most suitable to be represented by a graph structure. The TSP, the vehicle routing problem (VRP), and the problems that are graph structures themselves, such as Maximum Cut, Minimum Vertex Cover (MVC), and Maximum Independent Set (MIS) [1, 30], are typical representative of the graph structures. The combination of graph structure and reinforcement learning [36] has achieved quite good results. There are many advantages to using graph neural networks (GNN) [32]. Graph neural networks can transmit messages according to the shape structure of the graph structure itself, rather than using it as a feature of nodes. GNNs use the weighted aggregation of neighbor nodes to update the latest state of the node, which can take into account the node information within a certain range.

The Graph Convolution Networks (GCN) [22] is an important model architecture of the GNN, has extensive application in all kinds of feilds. **However, in the field of combinatorial optimization, the GCN architecture has not been achieved on par with other learning-based methods.**

Therefore, this paper combines two important architectures of GCN, Graph-Sage [14] and GatedGCN [6], to design a new network training model GGCN_GSG to solve the TSP.

Our contributions are as follows:

- **design a new network training model GGCN_GSG to solve the TSP:** We design a new model architecture GGCN_GSG, which consists of GraphSage [14] and GatedGCN [6], to efficiently solve the TSP than other network model.
- **The validity of this model is proved by numerical experiments:** Experimental results show that our proposed framework can get closer to the optimal solution than comparable graph neural network frameworks, achieving an optimal solution of 3.83 at 20 nodes.

2   Related Works

The use of neural networks to solve combinatorial optimization problems can be traced back to Hopfield and Tank, in 1985 [17], who utilized a Hopfield-network to solve the small-scale TSP. In 1999, Smith [33] summarized the related work of using neural networks to solve combinatorial optimization problems in an online manner at the most of time. Recently, deep learning [11] usually automatically learns the features to solve the problem in an offline manner.

In 2015, Vinyals et al. [40] proposed Pointer Network (PN) architecture to solve combinatorial optimization problems, solving the mapping problem from one sequence to another [2, 35]. The network structure mainly uses the encoder-decoder [2, 35] structure. The encoder encodes the input data to obtain feature vectors, and the decoder decodes the feature vectors formed by the encoder in an autoregressive manner. At the same time, the attention mechanism is used, only one node can be selected at a time step, and the selected node is masked to ensure that it will not be selected next time until all solutions are constructed.

Bello et al. [4] use unsupervised learning to train the Pointer Network using an Actor-Critic approach, employ the tour length of a sampled solution for an unbiased Monte-Carlo estimate of the policy gradient, treating each instance as a training sample. Nazari et al. [27] use element-wise projections to replace the PN's LSTM encoder, allowing for effective computation of updated embeddings after state changes. The Vehicle Routing Problem (VRP) with split deliveries and a stochastic version is used to test this concept.

Deudon et al. [9] presented a paper in 2018 that improves on Bello et al. [4] main's notion of applying reinforcement learning to solve the TSP. Its network structure is still based on the Pointer Network's output, but it has absorbed Transformer's core component [38]. The Encoder turns all city coordinates into a corresponding number of action vectors based on the Transformer's structure. The decoder acquires the query vector with the last three actions, and the result is obtained with the Pointing mechanism and the encoder's action vector.

In a research published in 2019, Kool et al. [23] employed the Transformer [38] model. The encoder does not use positional encoding, unlike the original Transformer model, therefore node embedding is independent of input order. It provides a context node to represent the context vector during decoding, which is a significant change from earlier work. In this field in 2021, Bresson et al. [7] state that in order to overcome TSP concerns, this study preserves as much of the Transformer structure as feasible. Unlike the Transformer, the Encoder does not employ positional encoding. The Decoder receives all partly visited city nodes.

In 2009, Scarselli et al [32] proposed the concept of GNN for the first time, and proved the computational expression ability of GNN [26], and proposed a unified computing framework. Dai et al. [21] were the first to use graph neural networks [32] to solve combinatorial optimization problems. The authors used reinforcement learning [36] and graph embedding of structure2vec to construct network models. Structure2vec recursively defined the network structure of the computational model according to the input graph network structure.

The reference [25] proposes a learning-based method to compute solutions to some NP-hard problems. The network structure is a graph convolutional network (GCN) [21], which is trained to estimate whether each vertex in the graph is an optimal solution in probability. Also using graph convolutional networks, Joshi et al. [19] introduce a new learning-based method for approximately solving the traveling salesman problem on plane graphs, using graph convolutional networks [21] through highly parallel beam search to build efficient TSP graph representations and output travel distances in a non-autoregressive manner.

Experiments show that the authors reduce the average optimality gap from 0.52% to 0.01% for 50 nodes, and from 2.26% to 1.39% for 100 nodes.

The GAT (Graph Attention Network) [39] replaced the structure2vec model [21], and used an attention-based decoder to autoregressively build TSP solutions with reinforcement learning. Other works that use various variations of GCN to solve combinatorial optimization problems include GraphSage [14] and GateGCN [6], among others [3,7,10,28,31,34,41].

3   Proposed Model Architecture

We combined GatedGCN [6] and GraphSage [14] to design a new model architecture, termed GGCN_GSG, shown in Fig. 1. The content in the left box is Graph-Sage, and the right component is GatedGCN, where the output of GraphSage is the input of GatedGCN. We train a GGCN_GSG model to directly produce an adjacency matrix corresponding to a tour, using a graph as an input. For each node and edge in the graph, the network model computes d-dimensional representations. The edge representations are coupled to the ground-truth tour label through a softmax output layer, allowing the model parameters to be trained end-to-end using gradient descent to minimize cross-entropy loss. During the inference period, the adjacency matrix is transformed into a valid tour using 2opt or greedy local search.

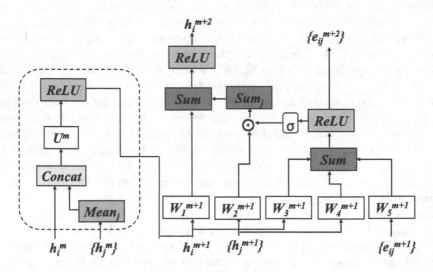

Fig. 1. The GGCN_GSG network arctecture. The dotted box on the left is the Graph-Sage component, and its output is the input of the GatedGCN component on the right. h_i^m represents the feature vector of the m-th layer node i, h_j^m represents the feature vector of the neighbor node j of the m-th layer node i, e_{ij}^m is the feature vector of edge of the node i and j connections in the m-th layer.

3.1   Input Layer

We transform the 2D node coordinates of TSP into d-dimensional embedded feature vectors by a linear transformation:

$$L_i = A_1 x_i + b_1, \tag{1}$$

where input matrix $A_1 \in \mathbb{R}^{d \times 2}$, bias $b_1 \in \mathbb{R}^{d \times 1}$.

The connection between the n nodes of TSP is a fully connected graph. In order to improve the computational efficiency, we use the k-nearest neighbor algorithm to select the k nearest neighbor nodes to node i to participate in the operation, because at node i, the optimal solution of TSP is often one of the k nodes closest to node i.

The edge e between nodes i and j is embedded as a $\frac{d}{2}$-dimensional feature vector. We also create a edge indicator function I_{ij}^{knn}, which takes the value one if nodes i and j are k-nearest neighbors, two for self-connections, and zero otherwise. The edge feature vector is:

$$O_{ij} = \text{Concat}(A_2 e_{ij} + b_2, A_3 I_{ij}^{knn}), \tag{2}$$

where vetor $A_2 \in \mathbb{R}^{\frac{d}{2} \times 1}$, bias $b_2 \in \mathbb{R}^{\frac{d}{2} \times 1}$, matrix $A_3 \in \mathbb{R}^{\frac{d}{2} \times 3}$.

3.2   Message-Passing GCN Layer

GraphSage [14] explicitly incorporates each node's own features from the previous layer, its update equation is as follows:

$$h_i^{m+1} = \text{ReLU}\left(U^m \, \text{Concat}(h_i^m, \text{Mean}_{j \in N_i} \, h_j^m) \right), \tag{3}$$

where $U^m \in \mathbb{R}^{d \times 2d}$, h_i^m represents the feature vector of the m-th layer node i, h_j^m represents the feature vector of the neighbor node j of the m-th layer node i, N_i is the neighbor node sets of the m-th layer node i.

GatedGCN [6] considers edge gates, batch normalization and residual connections to design an anisotropic GCN (Graph Convolution Network, GCN) [22]. The GatedGCN explicitly updates edge features along with node features. Let n_i^m and e_{ij}^m denote respectively the node feature vector and edge feature vector at layer m associated with node i and edge ij. For the next layer, we define the node feature and edge feature as:

$$n_i^{m+2} = n_i^{m+1} + \text{ReLU}\left(\text{BN}(W_1^{m+1} n_i^{m+1} + \sum_{j \sim i} \alpha_{ij}^{m+1} \odot W_2^{m+1} n_j^{m+1}) \right), \tag{4}$$

$$\alpha_{ij}^{m+1} = \frac{\sigma(e_{ij}^{m+1})}{\sum_{j_2 \in N_i} \sigma(e_{ij_2}^{m+1}) + \varepsilon}, \tag{5}$$

$$e_{ij}^{m+2} = e_{ij}^{m+1} + \text{ReLU}\left(\text{BN}(W_3^{m+1} n_i^{m+1} + W_4^{m+1} n_j^{m+1} + W_5^{m+1} e_{ij}^{m+1}) \right), \tag{6}$$

where $W_1, W_2, W_3, W_4, W_5 \in \mathbb{R}^{d \times d}$ is trainable parameters, $\odot$ is the Hadamard product, σ is the sigmoid function, ε is a small fixed constant, ReLU is the rectified linear unit, BN stands for batch normalization. For the input layer, we have $n_i^{m=0} = L_i$, and $e_{ij}^{m=0} = O_{ij}$.

3.3 MLP Classifier Layer

The likelihood of the edge being linked in the TSP tour of the graph is computed using the edge embedding of the previous layer. Computing a probabilistic matrix on the adjacency matrix can be used to represent this likelihood.

We first concatenate node features h_i and h_j from the final GNN layer to make a prediction for each edge e_{ij}. The edge features are then concatenated and fed into an MLP, which computes the un-normalized logits for each class, the standard cross-entropy loss is used between the logits and groundtruth TSP labels.

$$y_{ij}^{pre} = P \, \text{ReLU}(Q \, \text{Concat}(h_i^M, h_j^M)), \tag{7}$$

where $P \in \mathbb{R}^{d \times C}$, $Q \in \mathbb{R}^{d \times 2d}$.

4   Experiments

We conduct thorough tests to evaluate the effectiveness of our suggested technique. We look at five benchmark problems: TSP20, TSP30, TSP50, TSP100, and TSP200, which are Euclidean planar TSP challenges with 20, 30, 50, 100, and 200 nodes, respectively. The city node coordinates are generated at random for all jobs using a uniform distribution in the unit square [0,1]*[0,1].

4.1   Datasets and Settings

In terms of the TSP, we define a TSP instance s as a network with n nodes. Input graphs are represented as a series of n cities in a two-dimensional space $s = \{x_i\}$, with nodes $i \in \{1, 2, 3, ..., n\}$. A tour technique visits each city only once and for the shortest total tour length. A permutation π defines the length of a tour as

$$L(\pi|s) = \sum_{i=1}^{n-1} \|x_{\pi_i} - x_{\pi_{i+1}}\|_2 + \|x_{\pi_1} - x_{\pi_n}\|_2, \tag{8}$$

A tour $\pi = (\pi_1, \pi_2, \pi_3, ..., \pi_n)$ is defined as a solution with a permutation of nodes, thus $\pi_i \in \{1, 2, 3, ..., n\}$.

We followed the paradigm of Vinyals et al. [40], and used supervised learning to train the model. The validation and test sets each have 10,00 pairs of issue cases and solutions, whereas the training sets have one million pairings. Concorde [37] is used to find the best tour as the ground-truth TSP tour labels.

All our experiments are trained with a single piece of Geforce RTX 2080 Ti GPU, 11G GPU memory, CPU E5 2678v3, and 32G CPU memory [42]. Experimental language python3.8, machine learning open source framework Pytorch1.8.

The number of city nodes in the traveling salesman problem: when it is less than 100, the batch size (mini-batches) is set to 512; when it is between 100 and 200, it is set to 128. For each node we set k = 16 nearest neighbors in the adjacency matrix. In the MLP, each layer has a hidden dimension of 256 for each layer, with 50 graph convolutional layers and 5 MLP layers. We use a batch size of 64 for all TSP instances. TSP20, TSP30, TSP50, and TSP100 train for 400 epochs as convergence is faster for smaller problems, whereas TSP200 trains for 600 epochs. Our experiments use 512 hidden units and embed the two coordinates of each point in a 512-dimensional space. We train our models with the Adam optimizer and use an initial learning rate of 10^{-3} for TSP20, TSP30, TSP50, TSP100, and TSP200 that we decay every 4000 steps by a factor of 0.95. We initialize our parameters uniformly at random within $[\frac{-1}{\sqrt{d}}, \frac{1}{\sqrt{d}}]$ and clip the L2 norm of our gradients to 1.0.

4.2   Results and Analysis

In Table 1, the performance of our proposed GGCN_GSG architecture is compared with baselines: classic solvers and a variety of heuristics. In addition, we compare Cheapest, Nearest, Random and Farthest Insertion, as well as Nearest Neighbor. We also compare our proposed GGCN_GSG architecture with publicly released implementations made by the recently proposed deep learning methods [4, 18, 23, 27]. More importantly, we compare with other similar work on GNNs or GCNs [6, 9, 14, 28].

In the TSP graph, the number of city nodes that we compared is 20, 30, 50, 100, and 200. The abbreviation "ATL" stands for "Average Travel Length." The abbreviation "OGR" stands for "Optimal Gap Ratio." We chose the most commonly used solvers in combinatorial optimization: Concorde, Gurobi, and LKH3. It can be seen that various heuristic algorithms have the longest ATL and the worst performance.

We report on 20, 30, 50, 100, and 200 node graphs, respectively. In the TSP50 instances, compared with similar work by other authors, the performance of our proposed GGCN_GSG architecture is notably improved for both Bello et al. (4.36%), Dai et al. (5.16%), Kool et al. (1.53%), Nazari et al. (5.61%), Deudon et al. (1.68%), Ma et al. (1.57%), and Joshi et al. (7.87%). Compared with other similar works on GNN or GCN [6, 9, 14, 28], our proposed GGCN_GSG structure also has significant advantages. For example, in the TSP50 instances, the OGR of the GGCN_GSG is 1.55%, but GNN [28] is 4.38%, GraphSage [14] 4.34%, GatedGCN [6] 4.35%, GAT (greedy) [9] 4.45%, GAT (2opt) [9] 4.31%.

The performance of our proposed GGCN_GSG model architecture significantly outperforms other baseline models as well. In the TSP20 task, the Average Travel Length of the GGCN_GSG model architecture is 3.83, getting the optimal solution, and the Optimal Gap Ratio is 0.00%, but GNN [28], GraphSage [14], GatedGCN [6], GAT (greedy) [9], GAT (2opt) [9] is 3.85, 3.85, 3.85, 3.86 and 3.84, respectively, and the Optimal Gap Ratio is 0.38%, 0.38%, 0.38%, 0.42%, and 0.36%, respectively. Obviously, the ATL and OGR of the GGCN_GSG model

Table 1. The Comparison of the GGCN_GSG with various solvers, several heuristic algorithms and the work of other similar authors. The number of city nodes in the TSP graph are 20, 30, 50, 100 and 200. The abbreviation "ATL" stands for "Average Travel Length", "OGR" : "Optimal Gap Ratio".

method	TSP20		TSP30		TSP50		TSP100		TSP200	
	ATL	OGR	ATL	OGR	ATL	OGR	ATL	OGR	ATL	OGR
Concorde	3.83	0.00%	4.56	0.00%	5.71	0.00%	7.77	0.00%	10.53	0.00%
Gurobi	3.83	0.00%	4.56	0.00%	5.71	0.00%	7.77	0.00%	10.53	0.00%
LKH3	3.83	0.00%	4.56	0.00%	5.71	0.00%	7.77	0.00%	10.53	0.00%
Random Insertion	4.07	2.38%	4.88	3.35%	6.27	7.99%	8.54	9.44%	14.26	11.14%
Nearest Insertion	4.35	3.92%	5.28	15.69%	6.74	18.82%	9.43	21.24%	16.84	27.18%
Farthest Insertion	3.88	1.38%	4.77	3.02%	6.01	5.53%	8.35	7.71%	13.96	8.95%
Nearest Neighbor	4.46	4.85%	5.71	19.41%	6.85	22.62%	9.64	24.72%	17.80	29.85%
Cheapest insertion	4.25	3.28%	5.06	13.11%	6.36	8.48%	9.36	20.45%	15.13	25.86%
Bello et al.	3.86	1.38%	4.79	3.08%	5.88	4.36%	8.33	6.95%	13.41	7.85%
Dai et al.	3.88	1.38%	4.73	2.94%	5.97	5.16%	8.25	6.96%	15.88	16.25%
Kool et al.	3.86	1.38%	4.65	2.81%	5.77	1.53%	7.96	2.27%	13.24	6.93%
Nazari et al.	3.97	2.13%	4.85	3.22%	6.07	5.61%	8.47	9.06%	14.64	12.07%
Deudon et al.	3.84	0.36%	4.82	3.14%	5.82	1.68%	8.84	10.11%	16.97	18.11%
Qiang Ma et al.	3.84	0.36%	4.67	2.88%	5.76	1.57%	8.06	2.06%	13.87	3.54%
Joshi et al.	3.84	0.36%	4.75	2.97%	6.18	7.87%	8.07	2.08%	12.92	5.13%
GNN [28]	3.85	0.38%	4.68	2.85%	5.89	4.38%	7.98	2.27%	12.88	4.89%
GraphSage [14]	3.85	0.38%	4.65	2.73%	5.85	4.34%	7.95	2.25%	12.84	4.85%
GatedGCN [6]	3.85	0.38%	4.63	2.64%	5.86	4.35%	7.93	2.21%	12.86	4.87%
GAT(greedy) [9]	3.86	0.42%	4.69	2.88%	5.93	4.45%	7.96	2.26%	12.94	4.97%
GAT(2opt) [9]	3.84	0.36%	4.61	2.55%	5.82	4.31%	7.91	2.16%	12.77	4.78%
GGCN_GSG(ours)	**3.83**	**0.00%**	**4.58**	**1.45%**	**5.76**	**1.55%**	**7.84**	**2.13%**	**12.74**	**4.64%**

architecture are all lower than the heuristic algorithm, similar work of deep learning by other authors, and similar work of GCN or GNN by other authors. In the TSP30, TSP100, and TSP200 instances, compared with similar work of other authors, the performance of the GGCN_GSG model significantly outperforms other baseline models as well.

4.3   Greedy and 2OPT Search

Through local search [1], the heuristic technique can improve the quality of the result. The local search starts with the starting solution and swaps out the previous solution with a superior one. Local search techniques are effective for the TSP. A shorter tour is produced by the local search method k-opt, which looks for k edge swaps that will be replaced by new edges. We employed a masking strategy that reduces the log-probabilities of infeasible solutions to -10^8, allowing for speedier training and generation of feasible solutions.

The Decoder uses the projected probabilities to choose the next node at the current step either randomly or greedily based on which node is the most likely. We may acquire valid TSP tours to traverse the network beginning from a random node and masking previously visited nodes since decoders directly return probabilities over all nodes independently of one another.

A probabilistic matrix over the adjacency matrix of tour links is the model's output. The intensity of the edge prediction between nodes i and j is shown by each probability of the matrix. However, using an argmax function to directly transform the probability matrix into an adjacency matrix of the anticipated TSP tour would typically result in incorrect tours with too many or too few edges. In order to transform the probabilistic edge matrix into a valid permutation of nodes at evaluation time, we use two different search algorithms:

- greedy search: Greedy algorithms often select the local optimum solution in order to quickly approximate the global optimal solution. Starting with the initial node, we choose the neighboring node with the highest likelihood of having an edge based on our greedy selection process. When every node has been visited, the search is over. In order to build reliable solutions, we mask out nodes that have already been visited.
- 2opt search: The local search process 2opt searches for 2 edge exchanges, which will be replaced by new edges, thus resulting in a shorter tour.

5   Conclusion

This paper designs a new network model framework GGCN_GSG to solve the TSP combinatorial optimization problem. The framework is composed of two typical graph neural network models, GraphSage and GatedGCN. Through comparative experiments with other similar works, our proposed GGCN_GSG model framework achieves the optimal solution on 20 city nodes, and other nodes are closer to the optimal solution than similar works.

References

1. Arora, S.: The approximability of np-hard problems. In: Proceedings of the Thirtieth Annual ACM Symposium on Theory of Computing, pp. 337–348 (1998)
2. Bahdanau, D., Cho, K., Bengio, Y.: Neural machine translation by jointly learning to align and translate. arXiv preprint arXiv:1409.0473 (2014)
3. Barrett, T., Clements, W., Foerster, J., Lvovsky, A.: Exploratory combinatorial optimization with reinforcement learning. In: Proceedings of the AAAI Conference on Artificial Intelligence, vol. 34, pp. 3243–3250 (2020)
4. Bello, I., Pham, H., Le, Q.V., Norouzi, M., Bengio, S.: Neural combinatorial optimization with reinforcement learning. arXiv preprint arXiv:1611.09940 (2016)
5. Boese, K.D.: Cost versus distance in the traveling salesman problem. Citeseer (1995)
6. Bresson, X., Laurent, T.: Residual gated graph convnets. arXiv preprint arXiv:1711.07553 (2017)

7. Bresson, X., Laurent, T.: The transformer network for the traveling salesman problem. arXiv preprint arXiv:2103.03012 (2021)
8. Cook, W., Lovász, L., Seymour, P.D., et al.: Combinatorial optimization: papers from the DIMACS Special Year, vol. 20. American Mathematical Soc. (1995)
9. Deudon, M., Cournut, P., Lacoste, A., Adulyasak, Y., Rousseau, L.-M.: Learning heuristics for the TSP by policy gradient. In: van Hoeve, W.-J. (ed.) CPAIOR 2018. LNCS, vol. 10848, pp. 170–181. Springer, Cham (2018). https://doi.org/10. 1007/978-3-319-93031-2_12
10. Fu, Z.H., Qiu, K.B., Zha, H.: Generalize a small pre-trained model to arbitrarily large tsp instances. In: Proceedings of the AAAI Conference on Artificial Intelligence, vol. 35, pp. 7474–7482 (2021)
11. Goodfellow, I., Bengio, Y., Courville, A., Bengio, Y.: Deep Learning, vol. 1. MIT press, Cambridge (2016)
12. Google, I.: Google optimization tools(or-tools) (2018). https://github.com/google/ or-tools
13. Gutin, G., Punnen, A.P.: The Traveling Salesman Problem and Its Variations, vol. 12. Springer, Cham (2006). https://doi.org/10.1007/b101971
14. Hamilton, W., Ying, Z., Leskovec, J.: Inductive representation learning on large graphs. In: Advances in Neural Information Processing Systems, vol. 30 (2017)
15. Helsgaun, K.: An extension of the Lin-Kernighan-Helsgaun TSP solver for constrained traveling salesman and vehicle routing problems: Technical report (2017)
16. Hochba, D.S.: Approximation algorithms for NP-hard problems. ACM SIGACT News **28**(2), 40–52 (1997)
17. Hopfield, J.J., Tank, D.W.: Neural computation of decisions in optimization problems. Biol. Cybern. **52**(3), 141–152 (1985)
18. Joshi, C.K., Cappart, Q., Rousseau, L.M., Laurent, T., Bresson, X.: Learning tsp requires rethinking generalization. arXiv preprint arXiv:2006.07054 (2020)
19. Joshi, C.K., Laurent, T., Bresson, X.: An efficient graph convolutional network technique for the travelling salesman problem. arXiv preprint arXiv:1906.01227 (2019)
20. Jünger, M., Reinelt, G., Rinaldi, G.: The traveling salesman problem. Handbooks Oper. Res. Manage. Sci. **7**, 225–330 (1995)
21. Khalil, E., Dai, H., Zhang, Y., Dilkina, B., Song, L.: Learning combinatorial optimization algorithms over graphs. In: Advances in Neural Information Processing Systems. pp. 6348–6358 (2017)
22. Kipf, T.N., Welling, M.: Semi-supervised classification with graph convolutional networks. arXiv preprint arXiv:1609.02907 (2016)
23. Kool, W., Van Hoof, H., Welling, M.: Attention, learn to solve routing problems! arXiv preprint arXiv:1803.08475 (2018)
24. Li, W., Ding, Y., Yang, Y., Sherratt, R.S., Park, J.H., Wang, J.: Parameterized algorithms of fundamental np-hard problems: a survey. Human-Centric Comput. Inf. Sci. **10**(1), 1–24 (2020)
25. Li, Z., Chen, Q., Koltun, V.: Combinatorial optimization with graph convolutional networks and guided tree search. In: Advances in Neural Information Processing Systems, vol. 31 (2018)
26. Mezard, M., Montanari, A.: Information, Physics, and Computation. Oxford University Press, Oxford (2009)
27. Nazari, M., Oroojlooy, A., Snyder, L., Takác, M.: Reinforcement learning for solving the vehicle routing problem. In: Advances in Neural Information Processing Systems, pp. 9839–9849 (2018)

28. Nowak, A., Villar, S., Bandeira, A.S., Bruna, J.: A note on learning algorithms for quadratic assignment with graph neural networks. In: Proceeding of the 34th International Conference on Machine Learning (ICML), vol. 1050, p. 22 (2017)

29. Optimization, G.: Gurobi optimizer reference manual (2018). www.gurobi.com

30. Papadimitriou, C.H., Steiglitz, K.: Combinatorial optimization: algorithms and complexity. Courier Corporation (1998)

31. Prates, M., Avelar, P.H., Lemos, H., Lamb, L.C., Vardi, M.Y.: Learning to solve np-complete problems: a graph neural network for decision TSP. In: Proceedings of the AAAI Conference on Artificial Intelligence, vol. 33, pp. 4731–4738 (2019)

32. Scarselli, F., Gori, M., Tsoi, A.C., Hagenbuchner, M., Monfardini, G.: The graph neural network model. IEEE Trans. Neural Netw. 20(1), 61–80 (2008)

33. Smith, K.A.: Neural networks for combinatorial optimization: a review of more than a decade of research. INFORMS J. Comput. 11(1), 15–34 (1999)

34. Sultana, N., Chan, J., Sarwar, T., Qin, A.: Learning to optimise general TSP instances. Int. J. Mach. Learn. Cybern. 13, 2213–2228 (2022)

35. Sutskever, I., Vinyals, O., Le, Q.V.: Sequence to sequence learning with neural networks. Adv. Neural. Inf. Process. Syst. 27, 3104–3112 (2014)

36. Sutton, R.S., Barto, A.G.: Reinforcement Learning: An Introduction. MIT press, Cambridge (2018)

37. Chvatal, V., Applegate, D.L., Bixby, R.E., Cook, W.J.: Concorde TSP solver (2006). www.math.uwaterloo.ca/tsp/concorde

38. Vaswani, A., et al.: Attention is all you need. In: Advances in Neural Information Processing Systems, pp. 5998–6008 (2017)

39. Veličković, P., Cucurull, G., Casanova, A., Romero, A., Lio, P., Bengio, Y.: Graph attention networks. arXiv preprint arXiv:1710.10903 (2017)

40. Vinyals, O., Fortunato, M., Jaitly, N.: Pointer networks. Comput. Sci. 28 (2015)

41. Xing, Z., Tu, S., Xu, L.: Solve traveling salesman problem by monte Carlo tree search and deep neural network. arXiv preprint arXiv:2005.06879 (2020)

42. Yang, H.: Extended attention mechanism for TSP problem. In: 2021 International Joint Conference on Neural Networks (IJCNN), pp. 1–8. IEEE (2021)

GNN Graph Classification Method to Discover Climate Change Patterns

Alex Romanova(✉)

Melenar, LLC, McLean, VA 22101, USA
sparkling.dataocean@gmail.com
http://sparklingdataocean.com/

Abstract. Graph Neural Networks (GNN) have gained recognition as a promising method for addressing graph-based problems and modeling complex relationships in data. A notable application of GNN is graph classification, where the goal is to assign a label to an entire graph by considering its structure and features. This paper introduces a novel method for GNN graph classification to detect abnormal climate change patterns. By constructing graphs from temperature time series data and labeling them based on average cosine similarities between consecutive years, we demonstrate the effectiveness of GNN graph classification in identifying abnormal climate patterns. Outliers in the classification results, such as stable patterns in some Mediterranean cities and unstable patterns in some cities in China and Mexico, underscore the importance of regional factors and highlight the capability of GNN graph classification models in detecting and understanding such variations. Studying these outliers enhances our understanding of climate characteristics, global patterns, and contributes valuable insights to global warming research.

Keywords: Graph Classification · Climate Change · Global Warming · Graph Neural Network · Graph Topology · Deep Learning

1 Introduction

2012 was a breakthrough year for deep learning and knowledge graphs. In that year the evolutionary model AlexNet was created by Alex Krizhevsky, Ilya Sutskever, and Geoffrey Hinton [1] and Google introduced knowledge graphs. Convolutional Neural Network (CNN) image classification techniques demonstrated great success outperforming previous state-of-the-art machine learning techniques in various domains [2]. Knowledge graphs enabled machines to understand the relationships between different entities and became essential as a new era in data integration and data management that drive many products and make them more intelligent and "magical" [3].

For several years deep learning and knowledge graphs were growing in parallel. Deep learning techniques, including CNN, were highly effective for tasks that involved processing grid-structured data, such as images and text, but were less

L. Iliadis et al. (Eds.): ICANN 2023, LNCS 14257, pp. 388–397, 2023.
https://doi.org/10.1007/978-3-031-44216-2_32

effective for processing graph-structured data. Graph techniques, on the other hand, were highly effective for representing and reasoning about structured data, but did not provide the powerful pattern recognition capabilities of deep learning. This gap made it challenging to apply deep learning to graph-structured data and to leverage the strength of both approaches. In the late 2010 s, Graph Neural Network (GNN) bridged this gap and emerged as a powerful tool for processing graph-structured data and bridged the gap between deep learning and graphs [4].

CNN and GNN models have a lot in common: both CNN and GNN models are realizations of Geometric Deep Learning [4]. However GNN models are designed specifically for graph-structured data and can leverage geometric relationships between nodes and combine node features with graph topology. Before GNN was created, graph mining was mainly done using traditional graph-based algorithms, such as community detection.

GNN models were developed to address some limitations by allowing end-to-end learning of representations and features from graph-structured data. They enable deep learning algorithms to process and learn from graph data, by modeling the relationships between the nodes and edges in a graph and by capturing the underlying structure and dynamics of the graph. GNN models represent powerful tools for analyzing and modeling complex relationships and dependencies in data. They are being used for tasks related to processing and analyzing graph-structured data: node classification, link prediction, and graph classification. Node classification involves predicting the label or category of a node in a graph based on its local and global neighborhood structure. Link prediction involves predicting whether a link should exist between two nodes in a graph based on their attributes and the graph structure.

Graph classification models are classifying entire graphs into different categories based on their structure and attributes: nodes with features, edges and labels on graph level. Input data for GNN graph classification typically consists of a set of small labeled graphs and in practice GNN graph classification models are commonly used in the fields of chemistry and medicine. For example, chemical molecular structures can be represented as graphs, with atoms as nodes, chemical bonds as edges, and graphs labeled by categories.

In this study, we investigate the application of GNN graph classification models to time series data, leveraging the underlying graph structure. Our research highlights the potential of these models in diverse fields such as finance, engineering, healthcare, and environmental science.

For instance, in finance, GNN graph classification models enable the analysis of stock prices represented as time series data, facilitating the identification of patterns like bullish or bearish trends and predicting future prices.

Similarly, in neuroscience, GNN graph classification models can be applied to EEG signal data by representing brain activity as a graph. This approach allows for the classification of different brain states, such as wakefulness or sleep, and the prediction of cognitive disorders like Alzheimer's disease or schizophrenia based on the attributes of the EEG graphs.

In this paper we will introduce a novel method to classify time series graphs. We will study how to use GNN graph classification models to classify climate time series data to stable and unstable classes and detect abnormal climate change patterns.

For experiments we will explore kaggle.com dataset about daily temperature data for 40 years in 1000 most populous cities in the world [5]. For each city we will create a graph with nodes as a combination of cities and years and node features as daily temperature vectors for a city - year node. To define graph edges we will select pair of vectors with cosine similarities higher than a threshold.

To identify time changes in city daily temperature patterns we will calculate sequences of cosines between daily temperature vectors for consecutive years. Average city values of these sequences we will use as graph labels for GNN graph classification models.

The rest of the paper is organized as follows.

- We will provide a brief overview of related work.
- Clarify transformation of cosine similarity matrices to graph as input data for GNN graph classification model.
- Illustrate how to train GNN graph classification model.
- Interpret model results to identify vulnerable regions and detect abnormal climate change patters.

2   Related Work

The success of CNN started to gain significant attention and became one of the core building blocks of deep learning in various domains [2]. After it was introduced by Google [6], Knowledge Graph was adapted by many companies in order to provide more relevant and accurate information in a variety of data products [3].

GNNs have revolutionized the analysis and prediction of complex data by effectively capturing the relationships between nodes in a graph and leveraging this information to make accurate predictions and informed decisions [7,8]. Their ability to model and understand intricate graph structures has opened up new possibilities for solving challenging problems in various domains.

In medicine and biology, GNN graph classification is often used with input data that consists of small graphs representing molecules, proteins, biomolecules, brain networks, or genomic data. Researchers in medicine and biology are gaining insights into complex biological systems and develop new therapies or treatments [9–11].

Time series data are ubiquitous in many scientific and engineering fields, such as finance, health monitoring, environmental science, and speech recognition. The analysis and classification of time series have thus become increasingly important for extracting useful information and making informed decisions. In particular, the classification of groups of time series is a challenging problem that has received considerable attention in recent years. Graph classification for time series data is a complex task, as it involves representing time series as graphs and capturing the temporal dependencies between them [11].

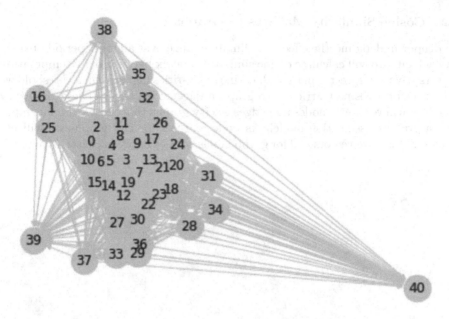

Fig. 1. Stable climate in Malaga, Spain represented in graph with high degree of connectivity.

3   Methods

In this section we will describe our novel method is the following order:

- First, to track long-term climate change trends we will calculate estimation of average daily temperature for consecutive years by city.
- Then to investigate the effects of climate change over a longer period of time we will transform cosine matrices into graph adjacency matrices and use corresponding graphs as input data into GNN graph classification models.

All these techniques are described in details in our technical blog [12].

3.1   Cosines Between Consecutive Years

To track long-term climate trends and patterns we will start with estimation of average daily temperature for consecutive years by calculating sequences of cosines between daily temperature vectors. By tracking these average values, we can identify trends and changes in the temperature patterns and determine how they are related to climate change. A decrease in the average cosine similarities between consecutive years can indicate an increase in the variance or difference in daily temperature patterns, which could be a sign of climate change and an increase in average cosine similarity could indicate a more stable climate with less variance.

3.2   Cosine Similarity Matrices to Graphs

To deeper understand the effects of climate change over a longer period of time, for each city we will calculate cosine similarity matrix between daily temperature vectors. By taking vector pairs with cosine similarities higher than a threshold we will transform cosine matrices into graph adjacency matrices. These adjacency matrices will represent nodes and edges of city graphs that will be used as input into a graph classification model. As node features for city graphs we will use daily temperature vectors and for graph labels cosines between consecutive years.

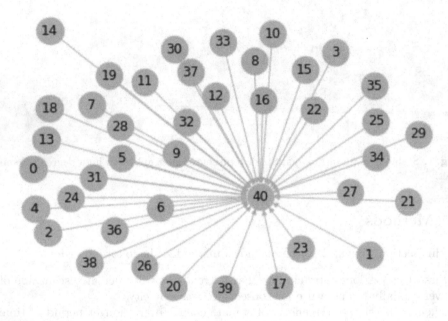

Fig. 2. Graph with low degree of connectivity at Orenburg, Russia shows that the climate patterns in that location are unstable and unpredictable.

For each graph we will add a virtual node to transform disconnected graphs into single connected components. This process makes it is easier for graph classification models to process and analyze the relationships between nodes. On graph visualizations examples in (Fig. 1, 2) virtual nodes are represented with number 40 and all nodes for other years with numbers from 0 to 39.

The city graphs, constructed from temperature time series data as described earlier, will be utilized as input data for a GNN graph classification model. This model aims to classify the graphs into two classes: stable and unstable. A city graph exhibiting a high degree of connectivity, as illustrated in Fig. 1, suggests relatively stable climate patterns in that location. On the other hand, a city graph with a low degree of connectivity, as shown in Fig. 2, implies more unstable or unpredictable climate patterns in that particular area.

3.3   Train the Model

As GNN graph classification model we used a GCNConv (Graph Convolutional Network Convolution) model from tutorial of the PyTorch Geometric Library (PyG) [13]. The GCNConv model takes the graph as input and applies graph convolutional operations to extract meaningful features from the graph structure. The extracted features are then fed into a fully connected layer to make the final prediction. The Python code for the GCNConv model is provided by the PyG library, and the code for converting data to the PyG data format is available in our technical blog [12].

4   Experiments

4.1   Data Source

As the data source for this study we used climate data from kaggle.com data sets [5] - average daily temperature data for years 1980–2019 for 1000 most populous cities in the world.

Table 1. Very high average cosine similarities indicate stable climate with less variance in daily temperature patterns.

City	Country	Cosine Scores
Malabo	Equatorial Guinea	0.999790
Hagta	Guam	0.999726
Oranjestad	Aruba	0.999724
Willemstad	Curaçao	0.999723
Monrovia	Liberia	0.999715
Mogadishu	Somalia	0.999700
Saint George's	Grenada	0.999698

4.2   Average Cosines Between Consecutive Years

For every city we calculated average cosines between vectors of consecutive years. Data in Table 1 represents cities with the highest average cosine values and data in the Table 2 - cities with the lowest average cosine values.

Temperature vectors with very high cosine similarities in Table 1 represent cities located in a tropical climate zone near the equator that tend to experience warm temperatures year-round due to the consistent exposure to direct sunlight.

Data in Table 2 represents temperature vectors for cities located in high latitude in Canada and Northern Europe that have a continental humid climate, characterized by cold winters and warm summers. The temperature vectors with low cosine similarities reflect this pattern, as these cities experience significant temperature variations throughout the year.

Average cosines between consecutive years were used as graph labels for GNN graph classification. The set of graphs was divided in half and marked with stable or unstable labels.

Table 2. A decrease in the average cosine similarity between consecutive years can indicate an increase in the variance or difference in daily temperature patterns, which could be a sign of climate change.

City	Country	Cosine Scores
Calgary	Canada	0.739156
Edmonton	Canada	0.778996
Reykjavik	Iceland	0.809576
Krasnoyarsk	Russia	0.815763
Yaroslavl'	Russia	0.827339
Perm'	Russia	0.827873
Yekaterinburg	Russia	0.830511

4.3   Prepare Data and Train the Model

In this study, the GCNConv model was used for graph classification to detect abnormal climate change patterns. The model takes the graph representation of daily temperature vectors as input data and applies graph convolutional operations to capture the structure of the graphs.

The Python code for the GCNConv model is provided by the PyG library [13], and the code for data preparation and encoding data to PyTorch Geometric data format are available on our technical blog [12].

To estimate the model results we used the same model accuracy metrics as in the PyG tutorial: training data accuracy was about 96 percents and testing data accuracy was about 99 percents.

4.4   Interpreting Model Results

The results of the GNN graph classification model correspond with observations based on average cosines in consecutive years values: most of the graphs for cities located close to the equator were classified as stable, while graphs for cities located at higher latitudes were classified as unstable.

However, the GNN graph classification model results capture some outliers: there are some cities located in higher latitudes that have stable temperature patterns and some cities located in lower latitudes that have unstable temperature patterns. Table 3 represents outliers with predictions not matching the actual temperature stability of these cities.

Table 3. Cities with stable temperature located in high latitudes and cities with unstable temperature located in lower latitudes

City	Country	Latitude	Longitude
Monaco	Monaco	43.740	7.407
Nice	France	43.715	7.265
Marseille	France	43.290	5.375
Nanning	China	22.820	108.320
Yulin	China	22.630	110.150
San Luis Potosi	Mexico	22.170	−101.000

Based on their latitude European cities Monaco, Nice and Marseille represented in Table 3, are expected to have unstable weather, but based on the model, they have very stable climate. These results correspond with the results of our previous climate time series study [14] where we showed that cities located near the Mediterranean Sea have very stable and consistent temperature patterns.

Table 4. Graph classification model outliers with probabilities that are far from classification boundary.

City	Country	Probability	Probability
Concepcion	Chile	0.0925	0.9075
Tampa	United States	0.8447	0.1553
Los Angeles	United States	0.8400	0.1600
Orlando	United States	0.8191	0.1809
Shiraz	Iran	0.1925	0.8075

As model results we received 36 outliers where the model's predictions do not match the actual temperature stability of the city. Detail data about these outliers is presented in our technical blog [12].

Table 5. Graph classification model outliers with probabilities close to the classification boundary.

City	Country	Probability	Probability
Monaco	Monaco	0.4900	0.5100
Homs	Syria	0.5117	0.4883
Marseille	France	0.5124	0.4876
Erbil	Iraq	0.4670	0.5330
Marrakech	Morocco	0.5446	0.4554

In the Table 4 you can see city outliers with the probabilities that deviate significantly from actual label and in the Table 5 outliers with probabilities close to the classification boundary.

5   Conclusions

GNN graph classification is a powerful machine learning technique that can classify objects based on small graphs by capturing complex relationships between elements. It has been successfully applied in diverse domains including molecule classification, image recognition, protein classification, social networks, brain connectivity networks, road networks, and climate data.

In this study, we presented a novel method for detecting climate change patterns using GNN graph classification models. By utilizing average cosines between consecutive years as graph labels, we classified cities into stable and unstable climate patterns, which served as input graph labels for the GNN graph classification model.

Upon applying the GNN graph classification model, we made an observation that cities located near the equator displayed more stable temperature patterns compared to those at higher latitudes. This finding aligns well with the model's classification results based on geographical location and climate stability.

The identification of outliers in the classification results revealed interesting patterns in the data. Some cities located on the Mediterranean Sea displayed highly stable temperature patterns, contrasting with some cities in China and Mexico, which exhibited a higher degree of instability or unpredictability.

These outliers highlight the importance of considering regional and local factors in climate data analysis and showcase the potential of GNN graph classification models in detecting and understanding such variations. By studying and interpreting these outliers, we can gain deeper insights into the unique climate characteristics of different regions and enhance our overall understanding of climate patterns.

Overall, our findings underscore the effectiveness of GNN graph classification as a powerful tool for solving graph-based problems and uncovering hidden patterns in data. It holds great promise for climate data analysis, providing valuable insights and contributing to a better understanding of the impacts of global warming.

References

1. Krizhevsky, A., Sutskever, I., Hinton, G.E.: ImageNet classification with deep convolutional neural networks. In: Advances in Neural Information Processing Systems (2012). https://proceedings.neurips.cc/paper/2012/file/c399862d3b9d6b76c8436e924a68c45b-Paper.pdf
2. LeCun, Y., Bengio, Y., Hinton, G.: Deep learning. Nature **521**(7553), 436–444 (2015). https://doi.org/10.1038/nature14539

3. Noy, N., Gao, Y., Jain, A., Narayanan, A., Patterson, A., Taylor, J.: Industry-scale knowledge graphs: lessons and challenges (2019). https://queue.acm.org/detail.cfm?id=3332266

4. Bronstein, M.M., Bruna, J., Cohen, T., Veličković, P.: Geometric deep learning: grids, groups, graphs, geodesics, and gauges (2021). https://arxiv.org/pdf/2104.13478.pdf

5. Temperature History of 1000 cities 1980 to 2020 (2020). https://www.kaggle.com/datasets/hansukyang/temperature-history-of-1000-cities-1980-to-2020

6. Bradley, A.: SEMANTICS 2017, Amsterdam (2017). https://2017.semantics.cc/aaron-bradley-eamonn-glass

7. Wu, Z., Pan, S., Chen, F., Long, G., Zhang, C., Philip, S.Y.: A comprehensive survey on graph neural networks (2019). https://arxiv.org/pdf/1901.00596.pdf

8. Wang, M., Qiu, L., Wang, X.: A survey on knowledge graph embeddings for link prediction. In: Symmetry (2021). https://doi.org/10.3390/sym13030485

9. Adamczyk, J.: Application of graph neural networks and graph descriptors for graph classification (2022). https://arxiv.org/pdf/2211.03666.pdf

10. Hu, W., et al.: Strategies for pre-training graph neural networks. In: ICLR 2020 (2020). https://doi.org/10.48550/arXiv.1905.12265

11. He, H., Queen, O., Koker, T., Cuevas, C., Tsiligkaridis, T., Zitnik, M.: Domain adaptation for time series under feature and label shifts (2023). https://arxiv.org/pdf/2302.03133.pdf

12. GNN Graph Classification for Climate Change Patterns (2023). https://sparklingdataocean.com/2023/02/11/cityTempGNNgraphs/

13. Pytorch Geometric Library Graph Classification with Graph Neural Networks (2023). https://pytorchgeometric.io/

14. Romanova, A.: Symmetry metrics for pairwise entity similarities. In: Pardede, E., Delir Haghighi, P., Khalil, I., Kotsis, G. (eds.) Information Integration and Web Intelligence. iiWAS 2022. LNCS, vol. 13635, pp. 476–488. Springer, Cham (2022). https://doi.org/10.1007/978-3-031-21047-1_44

GNN-MRC: Machine Reading Comprehension Based on GNN Augmentation

Sen Zhang$^{(\boxtimes)}$ and Baokui Li

Zhejiang University, Hangzhou, China
{senzhang,libaokui}@zju.edu.cn

Abstract. Inspired by recent advances in retrieval-augmented methods in NLP, in this work, we introduce GNN-MRC (Machine Reading Comprehension) framework, which extends vanilla BERT-MRC by allowing it to retrieve similar contexts in the training set. We construct the directed heterogeneous graph by taking the tokens in the input context (question + passage) and the retrieved similar contexts as nodes and the connections between nodes as edges. Graph neural networks (GNNs) are built on the graph to aggregate information from neighbor contexts to augment the distribution of answer labels. This paradigm improves the model's ability to deal with the long-tailed distribution problem and few-shot learning. We conduct comprehensive experiments to show the effectiveness of the GNN-MRC, which consistently outperforms its vanilla counterparts: we improved results on a variety of widely used MRC benchmarks SQuAD 1.1 and SQuAD2.0, and can achieve comparable results to the vanilla MRC model with 20% less amount of training data.

Keywords: Retrieval-augmented method · Machine reading comprehension · Graph neural network · Few-shot learning

1 Introduction

Machine Reading Comprehension (MRC) is a heated task in NLP [3,11,15] to evaluate the machine understanding of natural language. MRC aims to model that, given a set of documents and a question (with possible options), provides the correct answer by either retrieving a meaningful span [12,13] or selecting the correct option from a few candidates [14]. The widely employed strategy for the MRC task is to train a token classification model based on the labeled data, and this model learns to assign the probability of the starting and ending position to each token. This form of training can be viewed as a process of memorization, in which the model iterates over the training data to memorize and invoke related memory to predict the probability of the starting and ending position of each token during inference. This training strategy has two defects: (1) it is difficult to handle the long-tail problem; (2) it requires a number of training data to memorize to obtain strong generalization ability.

© The Author(s), under exclusive license to Springer Nature Switzerland AG 2023
L. Iliadis et al. (Eds.): ICANN 2023, LNCS 14257, pp. 398–409, 2023.
https://doi.org/10.1007/978-3-031-44216-2_33

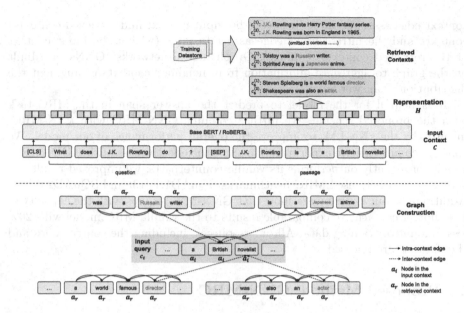

Fig. 1. An overview of the proposed GNN-MRC model pipeline. *Up*: Given an input context C (here the context is "What does J.K. Rowling do? J.K. Rowling is a British novelist, best known as the writer of the Harry Potter fantasy series."), a base BERT model encodes it into a high-dimensional representation H. We then use the representation of each token in the passage to query the training datastore to retrieve similar contexts along with the target tokens (marked in red). *Down*: A graph is formed by the tokens in the input context and the retrieved tokens, which are classified into two types of nodes: nodes belonging to the input text and those belonging to the retrieved texts. Within the same input, the tokens are linked by intra-context edges, while inter-context edges connect tokens from the retrieved contexts to the input context. After constructing the whole graph with GNNs, the updated representation of each token is used to predict the probability of the starting and ending position.

Motivated by recent research efforts in retrieval-augmented methods [8], which have been successfully employed to handle Language Modeling (LM) [7] and open-domain question answering [2,5], we propose the GNN-MRC framework for the MRC task, which provides the model with related information from the training corpus for decisions to alleviate these two problems. The related information, defined as the k retrieved similar neighbors of the input context in the training data, is served as attached references for the model to predict the probability of the starting and ending position of each token. A directed heterogeneous graph on top of the input context and the retrieved contexts is employed to integrate the references with the input context, where nodes and edges represent the tokens and the connections between them, respectively. In the heterogeneous graph, we define two types of nodes - the source nodes and neighbor nodes representing the nodes from the input context and the retrieved contexts, respectively. In addition, we define two types of edges - the inter-context edge associate inter (between the input context and retrieved contexts) contexts and the intra-context edge associate intra (within the input context or the retrieved contexts) contexts. Graph neural networks (GNNs) are built on the graph to aggregate information from neighbor contexts to augment the distribution of answer labels.

It is helpful for the model to predict the answer span in the MRC task with the proposed scheme. We further combine GNN-MRC with kNN-MRC, inspired by the kNN-LM, to improve the overall performance of our model. We conduct comprehensive experiments to show the effectiveness of the GNN-MRC, which consistently outperforms its vanilla counterparts: we improved results on a variety of widely used MRC benchmarks SQuAD1.1 [13] and SQuAD2.0 [12]. Additionally, our experiments show that GNN-MRC equips with the capacity of few-shot: it can achieve comparable results to the vanilla MRC model with 20% less amount of training data. All our resources, including the source codes and the dataset, are released.

2 Proposed Method: GNN-MRC

2.1 Overall Pipeline

We present the overall pipeline of our model in Fig. 1. In the input context, let a question be $Q = \{q_1, q_2, ..., q_m\}$, where m is the length of Q. The tokens in passage can be denoted as $P = \{w_1, w_2, ..., w_n\}$, where n is the length of P. At each iteration, a base BERT [3] model first encodes Q and P into a high-dimensional continuous representation to learn their joint representation, denoted as $\mathbf{H} \in \mathbb{R}^{T \times d}$, where T is the length of the extended input sequence, and d is the hidden dimension of BERT. $\mathbf{H}$ can be divided as $\mathbf{H}_Q$ and $\mathbf{H}_P$ to indicate question-specific and passage-specific representation. To generate the answer, we take $\mathbf{H}$ as the input to compute two probability vectors containing the starting and ending positions of the answer:

$$p_{start} = softmax(\mathbf{W}_{start}\mathbf{H}), \quad p_{end} = softmax(\mathbf{W}_{end}\mathbf{H}), \qquad (1)$$

where $\mathbf{W}_{start}, \mathbf{W}_{end} \in \mathbb{R}^{V \times d}$ are learnable parameters, and V is the size of the vocabulary. The legal spans are ranked according to the combined probabilities of their starting and ending positions, with the requirement that the former precedes the latter, and the span with the highest total value is chosen as the answer. We augment the vanilla BERT model by enabling it to reference the training set samples that exhibit similarity to the present encoded passage sequence, where $\mathbf{H}_P$ is used to query the training datastore to retrieve similar contexts. Concretely, our approach involves using a novel Graph Neural Network (GNN) for dealing with heterogeneous graphs, Heterogeneous Graph Transformer, on top of the vanilla BERT, allowing for message passing between the context C and reference tokens retrieved from the training set, which updates the representation H encoded by the vanilla BERT. The resultant updated representation is subsequently employed to estimate p_{start} and p_{end}.

2.2   Graph Construction

Our proposed framework's initial stage involves constructing a directed hetero-geneous graph that depicts the relationships between the input context tokens C and reference tokens retrieved from the training set. This graph comprises nodes consisting of input context tokens or retrieved context tokens, and edges representing distinct connections between these nodes, which will be elaborated upon below.

Formally, we define a graph as $\mathcal{G} = (\mathcal{V}, \mathcal{E}, \mathcal{A}, \mathcal{R}, \tau, \phi)$, where $\mathcal{V}$ and $\mathcal{E}$ are a collection of nodes v and a collection of edges e. We define two types of nodes $\mathcal{A} = \{a_i, a_r\}$, where a_i and a_r represent that the node is within the input context C and the node is in $\mathcal{N}(C)$, the set of contexts within the retrieved neighborhood of C. We also define two types of edges $\mathcal{R} = \{r_{inter}, r_{intra}\}$, where r_{inter} and r_{intra} represent that inter-context connection (from a_r nodes to a_i nodes) and intra-context connection (between two nodes of the same type). Each token within the input context is a node of type a_i, and edges of type r_{intra} are constructed from node w_i to w_j ($i \leq j$ or $i \geq j$). Their respective type mapping functions $\tau(v) : \mathcal{V} \rightarrow \mathcal{A}$ and $\phi(e) : \mathcal{E} \rightarrow \mathcal{R}$ are associated with both nodes and edges.

For an input context C, we retrieve k nearest neighbors $\mathcal{N}(C) = \{\mathcal{N}(c_1), ..., \mathcal{N}(c_n)\} = \{c_1^{(1)}, ..., c_1^{(k)}, ..., c_n^{(1)}, ..., c_n^{(k)}, \}$ of C from the training data as follows: we first use each token representation $\mathbf{h}_i$ of $\mathbf{H}_P$ to query the cached representations of all tokens for training samples, where the cached representa-tions are obtained by a fine-tuned BERT. The distance is measured by the cosine similarity, and we retrieve the top K tokens denoted by $\{w_i^{(j)}\}$, which means that the j-th training sample is retrieved as one of the nearest neighbors to $\mathbf{h}_i$ by the i-th token of query context. $\{w_i^{(j)}\}$ is expanded to $\{c_i^{(j)}\}$ by adding the pas-sage context, the corresponding representations $\{\mathbf{h}_1^{(1)}, ..., \mathbf{h}_1^{(k)}, ..., \mathbf{h}_n^{(1)}, ..., \mathbf{h}_n^{(k)}\}$ of which are used as the initialized node embeddings.

2.3   GNN on the Constructed Graph

The token information is now aggregated and circulated using graph neural net-works (GNNs), which rely on the graph formed in Sect. 2.2. To enable modeling of r_{intra} between node w_i and w_j in input context C, where a Transformer with self-attention is commonly employed, we extend the self-attention mechanism to r_{inter} and establish a self-attention augmented GNN as part of our study.

Specifically, the computation of the l-th layer representation of node n is as follows:

$$h_n^{[l]} = \underset{\forall s \in \mathcal{N}(n)}{Aggregate}(Attention(s, e, t) \cdot Feature(s, e, t)) + h_n^{[l-1]}. \qquad (2)$$

$Attention(s, e, t)$ estimates the importance of the source node s on target node t with relationship e, $Feature(s, e, t)$ is the information feature that s should pass to t, and $Aggregate(\cdot)$ aggregates the neighborhood message with the attention weights. Different sets of parameters are employed for various node types $\tau(\cdot)$ and edge types $\phi(\cdot)$ in order to leverage the information in the heterogeneous graph.

Attention. Our model's Attention is similar to the multi-head attention mechanism of Transformer [15] and comprises h heads that independently compute attention weights followed by concatenation to obtain the final output. We describe the single-head situation below for ease of simplicity. In the case of each edge (s, e, t), the representation of the target node t is mapped to a query vector $Q(t)$, and the representation of the source node s is mapped to a key vector $K(s)$. The attention weight between $Q(t)$ and $K(s)$ is calculated using the scaled inner-product, which is then normalized over all edges that have the same edge type.

$$K(s) = \boldsymbol{W}^k_{\tau(s)} \boldsymbol{h}^{[l-1]}_s, \quad Q(t) = \boldsymbol{W}^q_{\tau(t)} \boldsymbol{h}^{[l-1]}_t,$$

$$\text{Attention}\,(s, e, t) = \frac{1}{Z} \exp\left(K(s) \boldsymbol{W}^{\text{ATT}}_{\phi(e)} Q(t)^\top \cdot \frac{\boldsymbol{\mu}_{\langle \tau(s), \phi(e), \tau(t)\rangle}}{\sqrt{d}}\right), \quad (3)$$

$$Z = \sum_{s' \in \mathcal{N}(t), e' \in \phi(e)} \text{Attention}\,(s', e', t),$$

where d is the hidden dimensionality, and $\boldsymbol{W}^q_{\tau(s)} \in \mathbb{R}^{d \times d}, \boldsymbol{W}^k_{\tau(t)} \in \mathbb{R}^{d \times d}, \boldsymbol{W}^{\text{ATT}}_{\phi(e)} \in \mathbb{R}^{d \times d}, \boldsymbol{\mu} \in \mathbb{R}^{|\mathcal{A}| \times |\mathcal{R}| \times |\mathcal{A}|}$ are learnable model parameters.

Feature. We propagate information from the source node s to the target node t while simultaneously calculating attention weights. The single-head feature is formulated as follows:

$$Feature(s, e, t) = \boldsymbol{W}^o_{\tau(s)} \boldsymbol{h}^{[l-1]}_s \boldsymbol{W}^{\text{FEA}}_{\phi(e)} \quad (4)$$

where $\boldsymbol{W}^o_{\tau(s)} \in \mathbb{R}^{d \times d}$ and $\boldsymbol{W}^{\text{FEA}}_{\phi(e)} \in \mathbb{R}^{d \times d}$ are learnable model parameters.

Aggregate. The Aggregate function weight-sums the feature $Message(s, e, t)$ within the vicinity using $Attention(s, e, t)$, and the result is linearly projected into a d-dimensional representation:

$$\text{Aggregate}(\cdot) = \boldsymbol{W}^v_{\tau(t)} \big(\underset{\forall s \in \mathcal{N}(t)}{\oplus} (\text{Attention}(s, e, t) \cdot Feature(s, e, t)) \big) \quad (5)$$

where $\oplus$ is element-wise addition and $\boldsymbol{W}^v_{\tau(t)} \in \mathbb{R}^{d \times d}$ is model parameter. The representation of the token from the last layer is used to compute the probability of the starting and ending position.

2.4 *k*NN Based Probability

To enhance the performance of our model, we combine it with kNN, a related but orthogonal approach. This involves extending the vanilla MRC by linearly interpolating it with the k-nearest neighbors (kNN) model. Specifically, for every token c_i in the input context C, we retrieve the k nearest neighbors and calculate the kNN-based probability of the starting and ending position p^s and p^e using the following equation:

$$p^s = \lambda p^s_{\text{kNN}} + (1 - \lambda) p^s_{\text{MRC}}, \quad p^e = \lambda p^e_{\text{kNN}} + (1 - \lambda) p^e_{\text{MRC}},$$

$$p^s_{\text{kNN}} = \frac{1}{Z} \sum_{j=1}^{k} \mathbf{1}_{w_i = w_i^{(j)}} \exp\left(\cos\left(BERT(c_i), BERT\left(c_i^{(j)}\right)\right)/T\right),$$

$$p^e_{\text{kNN}} = \frac{1}{Z} \sum_{j=1}^{k} \mathbf{1}_{w_i = w_i^{(j)}} \exp\left(\cos\left(BERT(c_i), BERT\left(c_i^{(j)}\right)\right)/T\right),$$

(6)

with Z being the normalization factor, $BERT(\cdot)$ is the vanilla BERT model encoding contexts to high dimensional representations, $cos(\cdot, \cdot)$ is cosine similarity, and λ and T are hyperparameters.

3 Experiments

3.1 Metrics

The evaluation of the model's performance is based on two official metrics: Exact Match (EM) and F1-score. While EM measures an exact match between predicted and ground-truth answers, the F1-score is a more flexible metric that evaluates the average overlap between the two at the token level.

Exact Match (EM). The percentage of accurate predictions is determined by this metric, where a match with any of the true answers is considered. If the model's prediction for a question-answer pair exactly matches one of the true answers, EM is equal to 1; otherwise, EM is 0.

F1-Score. It is calculated based on the shared words between the prediction and the true answer, with precision determined by the ratio of shared words to the total number of words in the prediction and recall determined by the ratio of shared words to the total number of words in the ground truth.

3.2 Datasets

The Stanford Question Answering Dataset (SQuAD) is a reading comprehension dataset that comprises questions created by a group of crowd workers for a series of Wikipedia articles. Each question has an answer, which is a segment of text, or span, derived from the corresponding reading passage. However, some questions may not have an answer. The objective is to extract the relevant span from the context and answer the question. Our evaluation is based on two versions of SQuAD, namely V1.1 [13] and V2.0 [12]. In V1.1, the context always has an answer, while V2.0 presents more challenging questions, with some having no answer in the given context. During the evaluation, only span indices on answerable pairs are predicted.

3.3 Training Details

For all experiments, we add a 3-layer self-attention augmented GNN on top of the base BERT or RoBERTa, and use the same hidden dimension and number of heads as our base BERT or RoBERTa. We retrieve k = 64 nearest neighbors for each source token, among them the top 32 neighbors are used in the graph, and all of them are used in computing the kNN-based probability. In order to reduce memory usage and time complexity, in practice we use FAISS [6] for fast approximate kNN search.

3.4 Experiment Results

The Vanilla Models. For the vanilla MRC model, we choose BERT [3] and RoBERTa [11] for both SQuAD1.1 and SQuAD2.0 datasets. Both base and large versions of the vanilla MRC model are used in our experiments. The details of implementation can be found in the original work.

Main Results. Table 1 and Table 2 show the results on the SQuAD1.1 dataset and SQuAD2.0 dataset, respectively. GNN-MRC improves the EM and F1-score, which demonstrates the effectiveness of the GNN-MRC architecture. Especially on the SQuAD1.1 dataset, we observe an improvement of 1.13 and 1.21 respectively on EM and F1-score based on BERT-Base model. The combination of GNN and kNN further boosts the performance of BERT-Base model to 1.26 and 1.37, which is close to that of the large model. In addition, since the SQuAD1.1 dataset is simpler than the SQuAD2.0 dataset, the improvement of all models on the former outperform the latter.

Performance on Low Resource Scenario. Empirically, we also observe that GNN-MRC can achieve comparable results with much fewer training samples benefitting from direct access to the cached datastore. On dataset SQuAD1.1, we conducted experiments by varying the percentage of the training set while holding the full training set as the datastore for retrieving. Figure 2 shows that without additional training and annotation, GNN-MRC can still generate comparable results to the vanilla MRC model with 20% less amount of training data.

Table 1. EM and F1-score on the SQuAD1.1 dataset.

Model	EM	F1
Reinforced Mnemonic Reader [4]	82.28	88.53
SLQA+ [16]	82.44	88.61
QANet [20]	82.47	89.31
Base Model		
BERT-Base	80.87	88.39
BERT-Base+GNN	82.00 (+1.13)	89.60 (+1.21)
BERT-Base+GNN+kNN	**82.13 (+1.26)**	**89.76 (+1.37)**
Large Model		
BERT-Large	83.67	90.20
BERT-Large+GNN	84.75 (+1.08)	91.31 (+1.11)
BERT-Large+GNN+kNN	**84.86 (+1.19)**	**91.44 (+1.24)**
RoBERTa-Large	88.53	94.21
RoBERTa-Large+GNN	89.57 (+0.94)	95.20 (+0.99)
RoBERTa-Large+GNN+kNN	**89.64 (+1.01)**	**95.30 (+1.09)**

Table 2. EM and F1-score on the SQuAD2.0 dataset.

Model	EM	F1
SLQA+ [16]	77.00	80.21
LUKE [18]	87.43	90.16
Base Model		
BERT-Base	75.67	78.59
BERT-Base+GNN	76.69 (+1.02)	79.70 (+1.11)
BERT-Base+GNN+kNN	**76.71 (+1.14)**	**78.86 (+1.27)**
Large Model		
BERT-Large	78.88	81.69
BERT-Large+GNN	79.81 (+0.93)	82.72 (+1.03)
BERT-Large+GNN+kNN	**79.85 (+0.97)**	**82.81 (+1.12)**
RoBERTa-Large	86.54	89.41
RoBERTa-Large+GNN	87.53 (+0.99)	90.49 (+1.08)
RoBERTa-Large+GNN+kNN	**87.62 (+1.08)**	**90.60 (+1.19)**

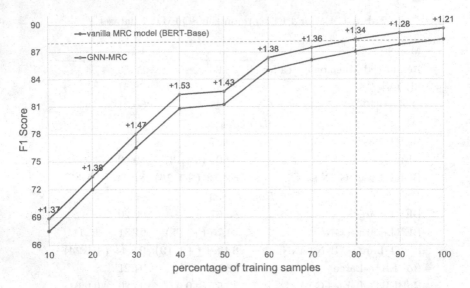

Fig. 2. F1-score on SQuAD1.1 dataset by varying the percentage of the training set.

Effectiveness and Sensitivity of K. To clearly observe the effectiveness of the hyperparameter k during kNN search, we varied k on dataset SQuAD1.1 with BERT as the vanilla MRC model. From Table 3, we observe that with the increase of k, the F1-score first increases and then decreases after k reaches 32. A larger k can retrieve more informative neighbors from the cached datastore. As k continues increasing, the newly retrieved examples are less similar to the current input example and even bring negative effects on the final performance.

4   Related Work

In this section, we will review the related work on Machine Reading Comprehension and Graph Neural Networks which play an important role in such methods. Then retrieval-augmented method in recent years will be discussed.

Machine Reading Comprehension. Machine Reading Comprehension (MRC) is a heated task in NLP to evaluate the machine understanding of natural language and various datasets and models have been proposed in recent years. According to its answer style, the MRC task can be categorized as generative and selective [1]. For the generative methods, the MRC model is required to generate answers according to the context (passage and question) [5], which is not limited to spans of the passages. While for selective methods [12–14], the MRC model is given several candidate answers to select the best one. In this paper, we only explore the method that selects the spans of the passages as answers.

Table 3. F1-score on SQuAD1.1 dataset by varying the number of retrieved neighbor.

F1-score on the SQuAD1.1 dataset	
Varying k	**F1-score**
The Vanilla MRC Model	78.59
+ by setting k=1	78.86 (+0.27)
+ by setting k=8	79.42 (+0.83)
+ by setting k=16	79.61 (+1.02)
+ by setting k=32	**79.70 (+1.11)**
+ by setting k=64	78.77 (+0.18)
+ by setting k=128	78.03 (−0.56)

Graph Neural Network. In recent years, several previous research efforts explored Graph Neural Networks (GNNs), which apply neural networks to graph learning and representation to capture the dependencies and relations between nodes connected with edges. It enjoys a wide range of natural language processing applications, including text classification [19], information extraction [9] and recommendation [17]. However, the explosive increase of graph data poses a great challenge to GNN training on large-scale datasets [10]. There are a number of research works on GNN acceleration: Graph Sampling, Graph Sparsification and Graph Partition. In this paper, we build GNNs on the graph to aggregate information from neighbor contexts to predict the probability of the start position and the end position of each input token.

Retrieval-Augmented Method. We note that recently retrieval-augmented methods have improve performance across a variety of NLP tasks, including open-domain question answering [5] and dialogue. The research of augmenting generative models with external knowledge is exploring, for example, DrQA [2] retrieve over documents to provide additional input to QA models. More recently, the RAG (Retrieval-Augmented Generation) [8] and FiD (Fusion-in-Decoder) [5] models conduct further study, which is equipped with a neural retriever and achieved superior performance. There is a growing area of research in retrieval-augmentation of language modeling, where it is used as a memory, especially using k-nearest neighbor-based cache models [7]. In this paper, we retrieve k similar neighbors of the input context in the training data, serving as additional references for the model to augment the distribution of answer labels.

5 Conclusion and Future Work

In this work, we introduce GNN-MRC framework, which extends vanilla BERT-MRC by allowing it to retrieve similar contexts in the training set. We use the high dimensional token representations of input context to retrieve k nearest neighbors as reference. We construct the directed heterogeneous graph by taking the tokens in the input context (question + passage) and the retrieved similar contexts as nodes and the connections between nodes as edges. Graph neural networks (GNNs) are built on the graph to aggregate information from neighbor contexts to augment the distribution of answer labels. Experimental results show the effectiveness of the GNN-MRC, which consistently outperforms its vanilla counterparts: we improved results on a variety of widely used MRC benchmarks SQuAD 1.1 and SQuAD 2.0, and can achieve comparable results to the vanilla MRC model with 20% less amount of training data. In the future, we will consider other ways to construct the graph to improve efficiency and performance and extend the datastore by introducing other similar datasets.

References

1. Baradaran, R., Ghiasi, R., Amirkhani, H.: A survey on machine reading comprehension systems. Nat. Lang. Eng. **28**, 683–732 (2020)
2. Chen, D., Fisch, A., Weston, J., Bordes, A.: Reading Wikipedia to answer open-domain questions. In: Association for Computational Linguistics (ACL) (2017)
3. Devlin, J., Chang, M.W., Lee, K., Toutanova, K.: BERT: pre-training of deep bidirectional transformers for language understanding. In: Proceedings of the 2019 Conference of the North American Chapter of the Association for Computational Linguistics: Human Language Technologies, vol. 1 (Long and Short Papers), pp. 4171–4186. Association for Computational Linguistics, Minneapolis, Minnesota (2019). https://doi.org/10.18653/v1/N19-1423
4. Hu, M., Wei, F., Peng, Y., Huang, Z., Yang, N., Zhou, M.: Read + verify: machine reading comprehension with unanswerable questions. ArXiv abs/1808.05759 (2018)
5. Izacard, G., Grave, E.: Leveraging passage retrieval with generative models for open domain question answering. In: Proceedings of the 16th Conference of the European Chapter of the Association for Computational Linguistics: Main Volume, pp. 874–880. Association for Computational Linguistics (2021). https://doi.org/10.18653/v1/2021.eacl-main.74
6. Johnson, J., Douze, M., Jégou, H.: Billion-scale similarity search with GPUs. IEEE Trans. on Big Data **7**(3), 535–547 (2019)
7. Khandelwal, U., Levy, O., Jurafsky, D., Zettlemoyer, L., Lewis, M.: Generalization through memorization: nearest neighbor language models. In: International Conference on Learning Representations (ICLR) (2020)
8. Lewis, P.S.H., et al.: Retrieval-augmented generation for knowledge-intensive NLP tasks. CoRR abs/2005.11401 (2020). https://arxiv.org/abs/2005.11401
9. Liu, X., Luo, Z., Huang, H.: Jointly multiple events extraction via attention-based graph information aggregation. In: Proceedings of the 2018 Conference on Empirical Methods in Natural Language Processing, pp. 1247–1256. Association for Computational Linguistics, Brussels, Belgium (2018). https://doi.org/10.18653/v1/D18-1156
10. Liu, X., et al.: Survey on graph neural network acceleration: an algorithmic perspective. In: International Joint Conference on Artificial Intelligence (2022)
11. Liu, Y., et al.: RoBERTa: a robustly optimized BERT pretraining approach. arXiv preprint arXiv:1907.11692 (2019)

12. Rajpurkar, P., Jia, R., Liang, P.: Know what you don't know: Unanswerable questions for SQuAD. In: Proceedings of the 56th Annual Meeting of the Association for Computational Linguistics (vol. 2: Short Papers), pp. 784–789. Association for Computational Linguistics, Melbourne, Australia (2018). https://doi.org/10.18653/v1/P18-2124

13. Rajpurkar, P., Zhang, J., Lopyrev, K., Liang, P.: SQuAD: 100,000+ questions for machine comprehension of text. In: Proceedings of the 2016 Conference on Empirical Methods in Natural Language Processing, pp. 2383–2392. Association for Computational Linguistics, Austin, Texas (2016). https://doi.org/10.18653/v1/D16-1264

14. Talmor, A., Herzig, J., Lourie, N., Berant, J.: CommonsenseQA: a question answering challenge targeting commonsense knowledge. In: Proceedings of the 2019 Conference of the North American Chapter of the Association for Computational Linguistics: Human Language Technologies, vol. 1 (Long and Short Papers), pp. 4149–4158. Association for Computational Linguistics, Minneapolis, Minnesota (2019). https://doi.org/10.18653/v1/N19-1421

15. Vaswani, A., et al.: Attention is all you need. In: Proceedings of the 31st International Conference on Neural Information Processing Systems, pp. 6000–6010. NIPS 2017, Curran Associates Inc., Red Hook, NY, USA (2017)

16. Wang, W., Yan, M., Wu, C.: Multi-granularity hierarchical attention fusion networks for reading comprehension and question answering. In: Proceedings of the 56th Annual Meeting of the Association for Computational Linguistics (vol. 1: Long Papers), pp. 1705–1714. Association for Computational Linguistics, Melbourne, Australia (2018). https://doi.org/10.18653/v1/P18-1158

17. Xu, C., et al.: Graph contextualized self-attention network for session-based recommendation. In: Proceedings of the 28th International Joint Conference on Artificial Intelligence, pp. 3940–3946. IJCAI 2019, AAAI Press (2019)

18. Yamada, I., Asai, A., Shindo, H., Takeda, H., Matsumoto, Y.: LUKE: Deep contextualized entity representations with entity-aware self-attention. In: Proceedings of the 2020 Conference on Empirical Methods in Natural Language Processing (EMNLP). Association for Computational Linguistics (2020). https://doi.org/10.18653/v1/2020.emnlp-main.523

19. Yao, L., Mao, C., Luo, Y.: Graph convolutional networks for text classification. In: Proceedings of the Thirty-Third AAAI Conference on Artificial Intelligence and Thirty-First Innovative Applications of Artificial Intelligence Conference and Ninth AAAI Symposium on Educational Advances in Artificial Intelligence. AAAI 2019/IAAI 2019/EAAI 2019, AAAI Press (2019). https://doi.org/10.1609/aaai.v33i01.33017370

20. Yu, A.W., Dohan, D., Le, Q., Luong, T., Zhao, R., Chen, K.: Fast and accurate reading comprehension by combining self-attention and convolution. In: International Conference on Learning Representations (2018). https://openreview.net/forum?id=B14TlG-RW

Graph Convolutional Network Semantic Enhancement Hashing for Self-supervised Cross-Modal Retrieval

Jinyu Hu, Mingyong Li$^{(\boxtimes)}$ ⓘ, and Jiayan Zhang

School of Computer Technology and Information Science,
Chongqing Normal University, Chongqing 401331, China
`limingyong@cqnu.edu.cn`

Abstract. Cross-modal hashing has gained widespread attention for its computational efficiency and reduced storage costs while achieving great success in cross-modal retrieval. However, the data information of different modalities is asymmetric, which means that we usually think of images as being much more informative than text. Currently, most previous methods have no obvious difference in feature extraction and hash function learning modules, and they do not address the semantic gap between different modalities. We propose Graph Convolutional Network Semantic Enhancement Hashing (GCSEH) approach. Specifically, We aim to let information-rich modalities further support information-poor modalities to bridge the semantic gap between different modalities. In addition, in order to more accurately capture the semantic affinity between modalities, in order to be able to discover high-level semantic information, we choose to use a self-supervised semantic network. Extensive experiments have proven that our GCSEH method can achieve excellent performance.

Keywords: Cross-modal hashing · Graph Convolutional Network (GCN) · Multi-modal retrieval

1 Introduction

In recent years the fast development of the Internet and the advent of the era of big data has led to tremendous volumes of multimedia data, which requires more efficient and accurate retrieval. Cross-modal hashing is the best solution. In our method, origin data is converted into binary code through processing, and similar binary code is finally generated. Many novel methods have been proposed in the past decade because of the efficiency of hashing methods and saving storage overhead [19,20].

Many cross-modal hashing (CMH) methods [21,22] based on convolutional neural networks (CNNs) have been proposed to enable fast retrieval between different modalities. However, most of the existing methods still have some weaknesses. First, the heterogeneity gap between different modalities [4,21,23]. For example, image data contains more information than text data. For image data,

L. Iliadis et al. (Eds.): ICANN 2023, LNCS 14257, pp. 410–422, 2023.
https://doi.org/10.1007/978-3-031-44216-2_34

it is possible to restore almost 100% of the real scene. However, for text data, it is usually not objective and specific. Second, most CNN-based methods measure the semantic similarity between different modalities using only a single label [24]. In fact, on several popular cross-modal benchmark datasets such as NUS-WIDE [10] and MS COCO [11], an image instance has labels for multiple categories [6], which is beneficial as it allows for more accurate description of semantic relatedness among different modalities. For example, SSAH [16] introduces label network and adversarial, an approach that can significantly alleviate the semantic gap between different modalities.

Graph-based hashing is also receiving widespread attention. For example, SH [15] learns binary codes by solving the graph Laplacian eigenvectors. To overcome the shortcomings of this method, a global similarity metric is needed. Hashing with graphs [5] constructs a low-rank similarity preserving algorithm in linear time. In recent years, some researchers have tried to introduce graphs into the feature extraction process to learn more semantics. Specifically, AGCH [2] uses Convolutional Neural Networks and Graph Convolutional Networks in the learning framework to learn a unique similarity matrix. GCDH [3] utilizes Graph convolutional Network as a classifier to learn a novel hash code.

In this paper, we proposed one model that has two parts, employing different methods. Specifically, the first one is we adopted two GCN based classifier Module to explore hidden information. The second one, we use a self-supervised module to mine the implicit information hidden in the label to guide the generation of the hash code. The contributions of our GCSEH are the following.

1. We proposed a novel GCN based classifier module. In this module, hidden information in labels is explored to enhance feature representation. In addition, we merge the enhanced feature and features extracted by the feature extraction module, through the semantic information can well bridge the information gap of different modalities. As a consequence, we obtain binary representations of high quality are obtained.
2. We integrate self-supervised semantic learning and graph convolutional networks to obtain hash representations of high quality are obtained, and compare two different loss functions to obtain the optimal hash code.
3. We conduct extensive experiments on the currently most popular four cross-modal retrieval datasets, proving that our proposed GCSEH outperforms other cross-modal hashing methods.

This paper is followed by the following arrangement. Related works of cross-modal hash-retrieval are briefly introduced in Sect. 1. Our method is elaborated on in Sect. 2. Section 3 introduces the optimization algorithm of our framework. Section 4 contains an extensive detailed analysis of the experiments, and Sect. 5 is a summary of our work (Fig. 1).

2   Method

2.1   Self-supervised Semantic Generation Module

Much previous research such as MLSPH [14] and MESDCH [7] proposed multiple labels and are often present in many benchmark datasets. For example, in some

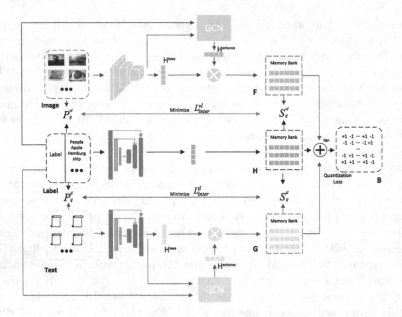

Fig. 1. An outline of our GCSEH. Generally, the proposed GCSEH integrates self-supervised semantic learning and graph convolutional networks and uses the memory library [8] to store features and save the latest hash code output of images, text, and labels.

popular, the cross-modal benchmark dataset includes an image v_i with the labels 'sky', 'birds', 'trees', 'people' and a text t_j with the labels 'people', 'flowers', and 'trees'. Over past cross-modal methods would set the $S_{ij}^{vt} = 1$ because these instances have at least one label in common such as 'trees'. To better maintain the semantic affinity between the above examples, our supervised learning of hash codes using multi-label data. Specifically, we make full use of multi-label semantic information. And use the multi-label semantic affinity preserving module [7] for the cross-modal hashing method. We also define the cosine similarity [6] to compute the multi-label semantic affinity matrix across modalities. The function is defined as:

$$P_{ij}^{vt} = \frac{L_i^v}{\|L_i^v\|_2} \cdot \left(\frac{L_j^t}{\|L_j^t\|_2} \right)^T \tag{1}$$

where $P_{ij}^{vt} \in \{0,1\}$ is the cosine similarity of multi-label semantic affinity between image V_i and text T_j, $(\cdot)^T$ represents the transpose of the vector. $\|\cdot\|_{L_2}$ denotes the L_2 norm. And $x \cdot y$ is the inner product of x and y.

Following the many cross-mode hashing methods in the previous the feature of the original instance is mapped to a common hash representation H_v^{base} and H_t^{base} by kernel-based methods or deep neural networks methods. At the same time, we map the features of the original instance to a common hash representation H_t^{base} and H_t^{enh}. We use the dot product method to fuse the information of H_v^{base} and H_v^{enh}, H_t^{enh} and H_t^{enh}, close the semantic gap between different modalities, and generate new hash codes. It should be noted that in our work, we adopt the cosine semantic similarity to denote the semantic similarity of F_i and G_j. The function is defined as:

$$S_{ij}^{vt} = \frac{F_i}{\|F_i\|_2} \cdot \left(\frac{G_j}{\|G_j\|_2}\right)^T \tag{2}$$

where $S_{ij}^{vt} \in \{-1, 1\}$ is the cosine similarity of hash representations between F_i and G_j, Obviously multilabel semantic affinity matrix P^{vt} and hash representations have different value ranges, in order to solve this problem, we use the $ReLU(\cdot)$ activation function for conversion because F_i and G_j are replacements for the hash codes B_i and B_j. If half of the bits in B_i and B_j are the same, it means that $S_{ij}^{vt} = 0$. The opposite, if $S_{ij}^{vt} < 0$, it description that B_i and B_j are not equal and the vast majority bits in B_i and B_j are different.

$$Q_{ij}^{vt} = \max(0, S_{ij}^{vt}) \tag{3}$$

2.2 Graph Convolution Semantic Enhancement Module

In each epoch, the images feature v and text feature t from the training set are first converted to the nonlinear features $f^v \in R^{d_v \times m}$ and $f^t \in R^{d_v \times m}$, Each of them is further fed into the corresponding hash layer to generate the binary representation corresponding to the modality $H_v^{enh} \in \{1, -1\}^{r \times m}$ and $H_t^{enh} \in \{1, -1\}^{r \times m}$. The process is as follows:

$$\begin{aligned} H_v^{enh} &= \text{sign}(f(v; \Phi^v)) \\ H_t^{enh} &= \text{sign}(f(t; \Phi^t)) \end{aligned} \tag{4}$$

where Φ^v and Φ^t are weight parameters of their corresponding networks, H_v^{enh} and H_t^{enh} are the image hash code and text hash code from image GCN and text GCN.

Specifically, the goal of GCN is to learn a function $f(\cdot, \cdot)$ on a graph ς, which takes feature descriptions $G^l \in R^{n \times d}$, The corresponding correlation matrix $A \in R^{c \times c}$ is used as input and the node features are updated to $G^{l+1} \in R^{n \times d'}$, and the pre-trained multi-label word embeddings are input to the GCN as the first layer. Every GCN layer can be represented as a non-linear function:

$$G^{l+1} = f(G^l, A) \tag{5}$$

According to the suggestion of [5], $f(\cdot, \cdot)$ can be represented as:

$$G_k^{l+1} = g_k(\hat{D}^{-\frac{1}{2}} \hat{A} \hat{D}^{-\frac{1}{2}} H_{k-1}^{l+1} W_k^{l+1}) \tag{6}$$

where G_k^{l+1} and G_{k-1}^{l+1} are the corresponding input and output of one layer of the GCN, $\hat{D}_{ii} = \sum_j \hat{A}_{ij}$ and $W_k^{l+1} \in R^{d \times d'}$ serve as the convolutional filters for the l-modality at the k-th layer and $\hat{A} \in \mathbb{R}^{n \times n}$ is the normalized version of correlation matrix A, and $g_k(\cdot)$ represents the activation function for the k-th GCH layer. Since using the $\text{sign}(\cdot)$ function causes problems with the gradient of the backpropagation process, we use the $\tanh(\cdot)$ function instead.

$$
\begin{aligned}
H_v^{fus} &= H_v^{enh} \odot H_v^{base} \\
H_t^{fus} &= H_t^{enh} \odot H_t^{base} \\
H^v &= \tanh(f(_v^{fus}; \theta_v^{fus})) \\
H^t &= \tanh(f(_t^{fus}; \theta_t^{fus}))
\end{aligned}
\tag{7}
$$

where $\odot$ is the matrix dot product operation, θ^{fus} denotes parameters of the sub-network. Synchronously f^v and f^t with the adjacency matrix $\hat{A}$, are fed into the corresponding GCN modules to obtain more semantic information. This method adaptively mines the information hidden in the label through the non-linear operation of the fused basic network and the graph convolutional network to enhance the hashing representation and bridge the information gap between different modalities.

2.3   Hashing Learning

We used two kinds of loss functions to prove the effectiveness of the Graph Convolution Semantic Enhancement Module. Meanwhile inter-modal loss L_{inter}, intra-modal loss L_{intra} and quantization loss Q_{quant} to constrain the similarity between instances. The following Mean Square Error is expressed as:

$$
L_{\text{inter}} = \frac{1}{n^2} \sum_{i=1, j=1}^{n} (P_{ij}^{vt} - Q_{ij}^{vt})^2
\tag{8}
$$

where Q_{ij}^{vt} is hash representation affinity. However, it is difficult to minimize the difference between P_{ij}^{vt} and Q_{ij}^{vt} converge to 0, which may be the reason for the worse training. In fact, we have not changed the value of P_{ij}^{vt} after initialization, when in the process of pulling the value between P_{ij}^{vt} and Q_{ij}^{vt}, we must force the value of to Q_{ij}^{vt} the value of P_{ij}^{vt}. This situation is the same as the previous KL loss principle. So the KL-Loss is adopted as the final intermodal loss, which is expressed as follows:

$$
L_{\text{inter}} = \frac{1}{n^2} \sum_{i=1, j=1}^{n} P_{ij}^{vt} \log \frac{\lambda + P_{ij}^{vt}}{\lambda + Q_{ij}^{vt}}
\tag{9}
$$

Correspondingly in our research, each training data input consists of image, text, and multi-label instance. To be able to deal with different inter-modal and intra-modal problems. We should maintain their semantic affinity, no matter the same modality or different modality when learning their corresponding hash representations, our formula is as follows:

$$
L_{\text{inter}} = L_{\text{inter}}^{vl} + \alpha L_{\text{inter}}^{tl}
\tag{10}
$$

L_{inter}^{vl} is used to minimize the difference between the P_{ij}^{vl} and Q_{ij}^{vl} for V_i and L_j, representing the inter-modal multi-label semantic affinity preserving loss. Where α is a hyper-parameter. The formulas for L_{inter}^{vl} and L_{inter}^{tl} are as follow:

$$
\begin{aligned}
L_{\text{inter}}^{vl} &= \frac{1}{n^2} \sum_{i=1,j=1}^{n} P_{ij}^{vl} log \frac{\lambda + P_{ij}^{vl}}{\lambda + Q_{ij}^{vl}} \\
L_{\text{inter}}^{tl} &= \frac{1}{n^2} \sum_{i=1,j=1}^{n} P_{ij}^{tl} log \frac{\lambda + P_{ij}^{tl}}{\lambda + Q_{ij}^{tl}}
\end{aligned}
\tag{11}
$$

Next, the intra-modal semantic affinity preserving loss is defined as:

$$
L_{\text{intra}} = L_{\text{inter}}^{vv} + L_{\text{inter}}^{tt} + L_{\text{inter}}^{ll}
\tag{12}
$$

where L_{intra}^{vv} is used to minimize the difference between the P_{ij}^{vv} and Q_{ij}^{vv} for V_i and V_j. Here we use superscripts to distinguish between different modalities. The formulas for $L_{\text{intra}}^{vv}, L_{\text{intra}}^{tt}$ and L_{intra}^{ll} are as follow:

$$
\begin{aligned}
L_{\text{intra}}^{vv} &= \frac{1}{n^2} \sum_{i=1,j=1}^{n} P_{ij}^{vv} log \frac{\lambda + P_{ij}^{vv}}{\lambda + Q_{ij}^{vv}} \\
L_{\text{intra}}^{tt} &= \frac{1}{n^2} \sum_{i=1,j=1}^{n} P_{ij}^{tt} log \frac{\lambda + P_{ij}^{tt}}{\lambda + Q_{ij}^{tt}} \\
L_{\text{intra}}^{ll} &= \frac{1}{n^2} \sum_{i=1,j=1}^{n} P_{ij}^{ll} log \frac{\lambda + P_{ij}^{ll}}{\lambda + Q_{ij}^{ll}}
\end{aligned}
\tag{13}
$$

Moreover, In order to measure the error between the learned binary hash code H and the real hash code, we adopt the quantization loss B, and we define the quantization loss as follows:

$$
L_{\text{quant}} = \frac{1}{nk} \left(\|F - B\|_2^2 + \|G - B\|_2^2 + \|H - B\|_2^2 \right)
\tag{14}
$$

In the formulas, F and G represent the hash code after we fused the graph convolution information, respectively, and H is the hash representation of all instances from the multi-label modality. B is the hash code matrix.

$$
\min_{B, \theta^v, \theta^t, \theta^l} L = L_{\text{inter}} + \beta L_{\text{intra}} + \gamma L_{\text{quant}}
\tag{15}
$$

where θ^v, θ^t and θ^l are the parameters for ImagNet, TxtNet and LabelNET, β and γ are hyper-parameters. Finally, in order to strengthen the learning of hash functions in the network, we construct a memory bank [8] for storing the latest hash representations of all training data, which can improve the ability to mine semantic correlations between cross-modal data.

3   Optimization

We only update one parameter while keeping other parameters constant in each epoch. This method is similar to SSAH [16].

3.1 Learning LabelNET Parameters

In the case of fixed parameters θ^t, Φ^t, θ^v, Φ^v and B, The process of learning deep neural network parameters θ^l uses stochastic gradient descent (SGD). Specifically, at each stage, we select a batch of training multi-label L_j to execute the proposed GCSEH, the algorithm computes the following gradient:

$$
\begin{aligned}
\frac{\partial L}{\partial H_j} = &-\frac{1}{n^2} \sum_{i=1,j=1}^{n} \left(\frac{P_{ij}^{vl}-Q_{ij}^{vl}}{\lambda+Q_{ij}^{vl}} + log\frac{\lambda+P_{ij}^{vl}}{\lambda+Q_{ij}^{vl}} \right) \frac{\partial Q_{ij}^{vl}}{\partial S_{ij}^{vl}} \\
&-\frac{\alpha}{n^2} \sum_{i=1,j=1}^{n} \left(\frac{P_{ij}^{tl}-Q_{ij}^{tl}}{\lambda+Q_{ij}^{tl}} + log\frac{\lambda+P_{ij}^{tl}}{\lambda+Q_{ij}^{tl}} \right) \frac{\partial Q_{ij}^{tl}}{\partial S_{ij}^{tl}} \\
&-\frac{\beta}{n^2} \sum_{i=1,j=1}^{n} \left(\frac{P_{ij}^{ll}-Q_{ij}^{ll}}{\lambda+Q_{ij}^{ll}} + log\frac{\lambda+P_{ij}^{ll}}{\lambda+Q_{ij}^{ll}} \right) \frac{\partial Q_{ij}^{ll}}{\partial S_{ij}^{ll}} + 2\gamma(H_j - B_j)
\end{aligned}
\tag{16}
$$

3.2 Learning ImageNET Parameters

In the case of fixed parameters θ^l with θ^t, Φ^t and B, The process of learning deep neural network parameters θ^v and Φ^v uses stochastic gradient descent (SGD). At each stage, we select a batch of training image V_i to execute the proposed GCSEH, the algorithm computes the following gradient:

$$
\begin{aligned}
\frac{\partial L}{\partial F_j} = &-\frac{1}{n^2} \sum_{i=1,j=1}^{n} \left(\frac{P_{ij}^{vl}-Q_{ij}^{vl}}{\lambda+Q_{ij}^{vl}} + log\frac{\lambda+P_{ij}^{vl}}{\lambda+Q_{ij}^{vl}} \right) \frac{\partial Q_{ij}^{vl}}{\partial S_{ij}^{vl}} \\
&-\frac{\beta}{n^2} \sum_{i=1,j=1}^{n} \left(\frac{P_{ij}^{vv}-Q_{ij}^{vv}}{\lambda+Q_{ij}^{vv}} + log\frac{\lambda+P_{ij}^{vv}}{\lambda+Q_{ij}^{ll}} \right) \frac{\partial Q_{ij}^{vv}}{\partial S_{ij}^{vv}} + 2\gamma(F_j - B_j)
\end{aligned}
\tag{17}
$$

3.3 Learning TextNET Parameters

In the case of fixed parameters θ^v and Φ^v and B, use stochastic gradient descent (SGD) to learn deep neural network parameter θ^t and Φ^t. At each stage, we select a batch of training text T_i to execute the proposed GCSEH, the algorithm computes the following gradient:

$$
\begin{aligned}
\frac{\partial L}{\partial G_j} = &-\frac{1}{n^2} \sum_{i=1,j=1}^{n} \left(\frac{P_{ij}^{tl}-Q_{ij}^{tl}}{\lambda+Q_{ij}^{vtl}} + log\frac{\lambda+P_{ij}^{tl}}{\lambda+Q_{ij}^{vtl}} \right) \frac{\partial Q_{ij}^{tl}}{\partial S_{ij}^{tl}} \\
&-\frac{\beta}{n^2} \sum_{i=1,j=1}^{n} \left(\frac{P_{ij}^{tt}-Q_{ij}^{tt}}{\lambda+Q_{ij}^{tt}} + log\frac{\lambda+P_{ij}^{tt}}{\lambda+Q_{ij}^{tt}} \right) \frac{\partial Q_{ij}^{tt}}{\partial S_{ij}^{tt}} + 2\gamma(G_i - B_i)
\end{aligned}
\tag{18}
$$

3.4 Learning Hash Code Matrix

In this case, fixed parameters θ^v, Φ^v, θ^t and Φ^t, B can be calculated using $\text{sign}(\cdot)$ function, B is denoted as:

$$
B = \text{sign}(H + F + G)
\tag{19}
$$

Table 1. The mAP accuracy comparisons on the MIRFLICKR-25K, NUS-WIDE, MS COCO, and IAPRTC-12 datasets based on the CNN-F as the backbone. The best performances have been displayed in boldface form.

Task	Methods	MIRFLICKR-25K			NUS-WIDE			MS COCO			IAPRTC-12		
		16bits	32bits	64bits	16bits	32bits	64bits	16bits	32bits	64bits	16bits	32bits	64bits
I→T	DCMH [13]	0.731	0.734	0.744	0.544	0.559	0.580	0.522	0.543	0.541	0.453	0.472	0.491
	PRDH [20]	0.695	0.707	0.710	0.591	0.605	0.611	0.523	0.552	0.557	0.476	0.488	0.492
	CMHH [24]	0.733	0.728	0.744	0.553	0.569	0.555	0.546	0.567	0.567	0.490	0.507	0.515
	CHN [25]	0.750	0.749	0.746	0.575	0.596	0.601	0.576	0.582	0.580	0.496	0.507	0.524
	SSAH [16]	0.774	0.788	0.799	0.616	0.627	0.614	0.512	0.525	0.506	0.534	0.561	0.578
	MLSPH [14]	0.782	0.791	0.803	0.612	0.631	0.649	0.628	0.667	0.693	0.511	0.538	0.563
	MESDCH [7]	0.796	0.812	0.824	0.631	0.651	0.666	0.668	0.698	0.720	0.553	0.589	0.608
	GCSEH	**0.879**	**0.881**	**0.889**	**0.759**	**0.769**	**0.789**	**0.717**	**0.750**	**0.778**	**0.657**	**0.718**	**0.756**
T→I	DCMH [13]	0.760	0.773	0.780	0.579	0.592	0.601	0.488	0.494	0.514	0.485	0.497	0.517
	PRDH [20]	0.762	0.771	0.775	0.615	0.628	0.634	0.512	0.519	0.540	0.511	0.528	0.540
	CMHH [24]	0.732	0.718	0.727	0.573	0.578	0.563	0.488	0.455	0.484	0.479	0.495	0.496
	CHN [25]	0.777	0.777	0.779	0.581	0.596	0.599	0.519	0.532	0.540	0.499	0.537	0.539
	SSAH [16]	0.786	0.797	0.791	0.620	0.625	0.621	0.483	0.483	0.492	0.526	0.559	0.572
	MLSPH [14]	0.757	0.776	0.788	0.612	0.629	0.641	0.613	0.655	0.682	0.506	0.525	0.551
	MESDCH [7]	0.787	0.804	0.810	0.638	0.654	0.664	0.652	0.685	0.706	0.538	0.568	0.588
	GCSEH	**0.873**	**0.870**	**0.886**	**0.751**	**0.762**	**0.787**	**0.706**	**0.732**	**0.757**	**0.590**	**0.658**	**0.694**

Table 2. The mAP accuracy comparisons on the four datasets based on the ResNet-34 as the backbone. The superscript * stands for using RESNET-50 and the best performances have been displayed in a boldface form.

Task	Methods	MIRFLICKR-25K			NUS-WIDE			MS COCO			IAPRTC-12		
		16bits	32bits	64bits	16bits	32bits	64bits	16bits	32bits	64bits	16bits	32bits	64bits
I→T	SCAHN [26]	0.816	0.831	0.834	0.642	0.651	0.663	0.630	0.648	0.659	0.542	0.576	0.590
	MLSPH [14]	0.807	0.823	0.833	0.640	0.660	0.673	0.655	0.701	0.727	0.534	0.572	0.599
	MESDCH [7]	0.819	0.834	0.844	0.645	0.670	0.683	0.684	0.734	0.759	0.539	0.579	0.607
	DADH* [1]	0.802	0.807	0.817	0.647	0.669	0.666	0.627	0.661	0.684	–	–	–
	GCDH* [3]	0.835	0.855	0.862	0.720	0.731	0.739	**0.736**	0.776	0.803	–	–	–
	GCSEH	**0.885**	**0.870**	**0.896**	**0.760**	**0.772**	**0.795**	0.730	**0.777**	**0.807**	**0.661**	**0.720**	**0.763**
T→I	SCAHN [26]	0.803	0.810	0.819	0.650	0.657	0.668	0.636	0.657	0.659	0.529	0.555	0.569
	MLSPH [14]	0.785	0.804	0.814	0.643	0.663	0.672	0.649	0.695	0.719	0.525	0.562	0.593
	MESDCH [7]	0.808	0.812	0.815	0.647	0.668	0.675	0.683	0.726	0.752	0.526	0.559	0.589
	DADH* [1]	0.792	0.795	0.806	0.650	0.667	0.680	0.582	0.619	0.639	–	–	-
	GCDH* [3]	0.815	0.822	0.832	0.736	0.745	0.751	**0.731**	**0.772**	**0.800**	–	–	–
	GCSEH	**0.885**	**0.882**	**0.896**	**0.756**	**0.767**	**0.792**	0.717	0.750	0.773	**0.596**	**0.660**	**0.704**

4 Experimental Evaluation

4.1 Evaluation Datasets

The datasets includes MIRFLICKR-25 K [9] NUS-WIDE [10] MS COCO [11] IAPRTC-12 [12], and all four of the above datasets are used to evaluate the performance of our proposed method.

4.2 Implementation Details

In our experiment, we used a three-layer feed-forward network and a multi-scale (MS) fusion model (T $\rightarrow$ MS$\rightarrow$ 4096 $\rightarrow$ 512 $\rightarrow$ N) for text data and label data and ResNet-34 [17] as the backbone network for image data. MS consists of a five-level pooling layer ($1 \times 1, 2 \times 2, 3 \times 3, 5 \times 5$, and 10×10). For the GCN in our framework, each GCN module in our architecture is composed of two graphs one fully connected layer and convolutional layers($4096 \rightarrow 2048 \rightarrow$ N).

Table 3. Ablation experiments: mAP comparison of different bits.

Task	Methods	MIRFLICKR-25K			NUS-WIDE			MS COCO			IAPRTC-12		
		16bits	32bits	64bits	16bits	32bits	64bits	16bits	32bits	64bits	16bits	32bits	64bits
I→T	GCSEH-MSE	0.864	0.867	0.876	0.744	0.760	0.771	0.672	0.733	0.745	0.555	0.608	0.636
	GCSEH-gcn	0.840	0.849	0.864	0.737	0.753	0.758	0.698	0.725	0.743	0.578	0.618	0.645
	GCSEH	**0.885**	**0.870**	**0.896**	**0.760**	**0.772**	**0.795**	**0.730**	**0.777**	**0.807**	**0.661**	**0.720**	**0.763**
T→I	GCSEH-MSE	0.815	0.836	0.826	0.725	0.731	0.745	0.658	0.715	0.728	0.516	0.565	0.587
	GCSEH-gcn	0.872	0.874	0.895	0.724	0.741	0.746	0.709	0.740	0.765	**0.654**	**0.705**	**0.735**
	GCSEH	**0.885**	**0.882**	**0.896**	**0.756**	**0.767**	**0.792**	**0.717**	**0.750**	**0.773**	0.596	0.660	0.704

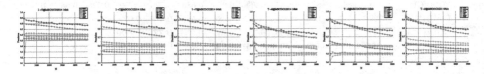

Fig. 2. TopK-precision curves on MIRFLICKR25K.

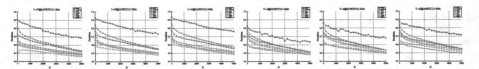

Fig. 3. TopK-precision curves on NUSWIDE.

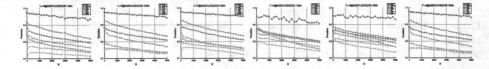

Fig. 4. TopK-precision curves on MS COCO.

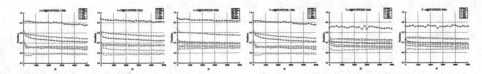

Fig. 5. TopK-precision curves on IAPRTC-12.

The enhancement module We choose to use the structure of the fully connected layer. In the above modules, only the tanh(·) activation function is used in the last layer, and we use $ReLU(\cdot)$ for the activation functions of all other layers. All the experiments are executed on an NVIDIA 3080Ti GPU and use the pytorch as the framework [18]. With regard to the settings for parameters, we set max_epoch and batch size to 200 and 128, respectively. The initial learning rate is $10^{-1.5}$, and it is gradually reduced to 10^{-6} during the iterations. We set $\alpha = 0.3$, $\beta = 1.9$, $\gamma = 0.9$ and $\lambda = 10^{-5}$ on the four datasets.

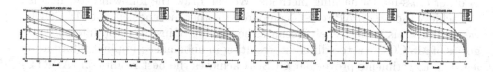

Fig. 6. Precision-Recall Curves on MIRFLICKR25K.

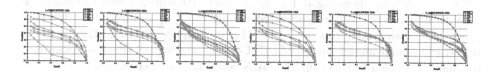

Fig. 7. Precision-Recall Curves on NUSWIDE.

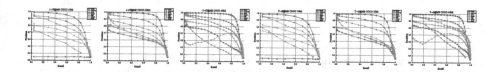

Fig. 8. Precision-Recall Curves on MS COCO.

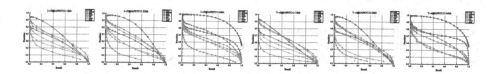

Fig. 9. Precision-Recall Curves on IAPRTC-12.

4.3 Experimental Results and Analysis

1) GCSEH-gcn: To prove that the GCN semantic enhancement module learns better hash codes, we designed it based on GCSEH without a GCN semantic enhance module, just using GCN to process text data without using a multi-scale (MS) fusion model.

420   J. Hu et al.

2) GCSEH-MSE: We compare MSE Loss (in Eq. 8) and KL Loss (in Eq. 9) to get the best loss function. From our experimental results, KL Loss is better than MSE Loss in most cases. Therefore we use KL Loss as the benchmark.

The results of the ablation study are shown in Table 3 and show that the introduction of GCN semantic enhance and KL Loss has better performance. In order to further investigate the performance of the proposed GCSEH, we evaluate GCSEH on 4 datasets based on mAP, PR-curves, and topN-precision curves are shown in Fig. 2, 3, 4, 5, 6, 7, 8 and 9. Table 1 and Table 2 show the mAP conclusions of our method and compare the mAP results of different hash codes of other cross-modal hashing methods. We can draw the following conclusions. We achieve the best mAP results compared to other methods except MS COCO, we assumed this is most likely because the number of instances of different categories of MS COCO is too different, resulting in unbalanced implicit information learned. Experiments prove that GCSEH achieves the best results on IAPRTC-12, which has more labels than the other three datasets and enables graph convolutional networks to achieve better results during learning (MIRFLICKR-25 K has 24 labels, NUS-WIDE has 10 labels, MS COCO has 80 labels and IAPRTC-12 has 275 labels). Because it has more label attributes, a more informative label-related matrix will be generated during the graph convolution learning process. Specially, we found that GCSEH-gcn outperforms our method in texts to retrieve similar images on the IAPRTC-12 but the overall effect is worse than our method. which proves that the GCN semantic enhance module can bridge the information gap between different modalities. Since GCDH and DADH did not use the IAPRTC-12 data set for top-N and PR-curves tests, this article did not include these two methods' comparisons.

5   Conclusion

In this paper, we propose the Graph Convolutional Network Semantic Enhancement Hashing for self-supervised Cross-Modal Retrieval (GCSEH) model, which has the following advantages points. We learn the information implicit in the label by using the GCN semantic enhancement module, denoted as enhancement semantic features, and merge image and text extracted features using GCN semantic enhancement module. Furthermore, we compare two different loss functions to make our method optimal, and Remove noise effects from the original data, and optimize the final hash code representation. The Extensive experiment results on four benchmark datasets show that our GCSEH method outperforms the current state-of-the-art cross-modal hashing methods.

Acknowledgment. This work was partially supported by the Chongqing Natural Science Foundation of China(Grant No. CSTB2022NSCQ-MSX1417), the Science and Technology Research Program of Chongqing Municipal Education Commission (Grant No. KJZD-K202200513) and Humanities and social science research project of Chongqing Municipal Education Commission(22SKGH100).

References

1. Bai, C., et al.: Deep adversarial discrete hashing for cross-modal retrieval. In: ICMR 2020: International Conference on Multimedia Retrieval (2020)
2. Zhang, P.F., et al.: Aggregation-based graph convolutional hashing for unsupervised cross-modal retrieval. IEEE Trans. Multimedia **24**, 466–479 (2021)
3. Bai, C., et al.: Graph convolutional network discrete hashing for cross-modal retrieval. In: IEEE Transactions on Neural Networks and Learning Systems (2022)
4. Hu, P., et al.: Unsupervised contrastive cross-modal hashing. IEEE Trans. Pattern Anal. Mach. Intell. **45**, 3877–3889 (2022)
5. Liu, W., Wang, J., Kumar, S., Chang, S.-F.: Hashing with graphs. In: Proceedings of the International Conference on Machine Learning, pp. 1–8 (2011)
6. Ranjan, V., Rasiwasia, N.: Multi-label cross-modal retrieval. In: Proceedings of the IEEE International Conference on Computer Vision (2015)
7. Zou, X., et al.: Multi-label enhancement based self-supervised deep cross-modal hashing. Neurocomputing **467**, 138–162 (2022)
8. Zhong, Z., Zheng, L., Luo, Z., Li, S., Yang, Y.: Invariance matters: exemplar memory for domain adaptive person re-identification. In: Proceedings of the IEEE Conference on Computer Vision and Pattern Recognition, pp. 598–607 (2019)
9. Huiskes, M.J., Michael, S.: The MIR Flickr retrieval evaluation. In: Proceedings of the 1st ACM International Conference on Multimedia Information Retrieval (2008)
10. Chua, T.-S., et al.: NUS-WIDE: a real-world web image database from national university of Singapore. In: Proceedings of the ACM International Conference on Image and Video Retrieval (2009)
11. Lin, T.-Y., et al.: Microsoft COCO: common objects in context. In: Fleet, D., Pajdla, T., Schiele, B., Tuytelaars, T. (eds.) ECCV 2014. LNCS, vol. 8693, pp. 740–755. Springer, Cham (2014). https://doi.org/10.1007/978-3-319-10602-1_48
12. Escalante, H.J., et al.: The segmented and annotated IAPR TC-12 benchmark. Comput. Vis. Image Underst. **114**(4), 419–428 (2010)
13. Jiang, Q.-Y., Li, W.J.: Deep cross-modal hashing. In: Proceedings of the IEEE Conference on Computer Vision and Pattern Recognition (2017)
14. Zou, X., et al.: Multi-label semantics preserving based deep cross-modal hashing. Signal Process. Image Commun. **93**, 116131 (2021)
15. Weiss, Y., Torralba, A., Fergus, R.: Spectral hashing. In: Advances in Neural Information Processing Systems, vol. 21 (2008)
16. Li, C., et al.: Self-supervised adversarial hashing networks for cross-modal retrieval. In: Proceedings of the IEEE Conference on Computer Vision and Pattern Recognition (2018)
17. He, K., Zhang, X., Ren, S., Sun, J.: Deep residual learning for image recognition, In: Proceedings of the IEEE conference on computer vision and pattern recognition, pp. 770–778 (2016)
18. Paszke, A., et al.: Automatic differentiation in PyTorch (2017)
19. Gui, J., et al.: Supervised discrete hashing with relaxation. IEEE Trans. Neural Netw. Learn. Syst. **29**(3), 608–617 (2016)
20. Yang, E., Deng, C.: Pairwise relationship guided deep hashing for cross-modal retrieval. In: Thirty-First AAAI Conference on Artificial Intelligence (2017)
21. Baltrušaitis, T., Ahuja, C.: Multimodal machine learning: a survey and taxonomy. IEEE Trans. Pattern Anal. Mach. Intell. **41**(2), 423–443 (2018)
22. Zhang, L., et al.: Optimal projection guided transfer hashing for image retrieval. IEEE Trans. Circuits Syst. Video Technol. **30**(10), 3788–3802 (2019)

23. Shen, H.T., et al.: Exploiting subspace relation in semantic labels for cross-modal hashing. IEEE Trans. Knowl. Data Eng. **33**(10), 3351–3365 (2020)
24. Cao, Y., Liu, B., Long, M.: Cross-modal hamming hashing. in: Proceedings of the European Conference on Computer Vision (ECCV), pp. 202–218 (2018)
25. Cao, Y., Long, M., Wang, J., Yu, P.S.: Correlation hashing network for efficient cross-modal retrieval. arXiv preprint arXiv:1602.06697 (2016)
26. Wang, X., Zou, X.: Self-constraining and attention-based hashing network for bit-scalable cross-modal retrieval. Neurocomputing **400**, 255–271 (2020)

Heterogeneous Graph Neural Network Knowledge Graph Completion Model Based on Improved Attention Mechanism

Junkang Shi[1,2], Ming Li[3], and Jing Zhao[1,2(✉)]

[1] Key Laboratory of Computing Power Network and Information Security, Ministry of Education, Shandong Computer Science Center (National Supercomputer Center in Jinan), Qilu University of Technology (Shandong Academy of Sciences), Jinan, China
zjstudent@126.com

[2] Shandong Provincial Key Laboratory of Computer Networks, Shandong Fundamental Research Center for Computer Science, Jinan, China

[3] School of Intelligence and Information Engineering, Shandong University of Traditional Chinese Medicine, Jinan, China

Abstract. The main purpose of knowledge graph completion is to predict the missing part of the triple. Through learning from many existing models, we found that whether it is a convolutional neural network model or a translation model, when dealing with triples, they independently treat triples and ignore the potential rich semantics and hidden information in the neighborhood of triples. Although some graph neural network models can use the structural characteristics of graph connectivity, they have not fully considered the heterogeneous graph containing different types of entities and relationships, and have updated a lot of information for the central entity. This article aims to propose a knowledge graph completion model with Improved Attention mechanism for Heterogeneous Graph Neural networks (IAHGN), which mainly uses the graph structure characteristics of heterogeneous graphs, and updates the feature representation of central entities by Adding Hierarchical Attention Mechanism (AHAM). Hierarchical attention includes entity-level attention and semantic-level attention, and then Conv-transE named convolutional network is used as decoder. Firstly, AHAM can aggregate neighbor features of different meta-paths through entity-level attention, while semantic-level attention can distinguish the importance of different meta-paths. Then AHAM can update the feature representation of central entities by aggregating neighbor features of meta-paths in a hierarchical way. Finally, the improved decoder Conv-transE can keep the translation characteristics between relations and entities, and achieve better link prediction performance. Through experiments, we prove that IAHGN proposed in this paper is effective on standard FB15k-237 and WN18RR datasets, and has relative improvement in Hits@10 and MRR values compared with other models.

© The Author(s), under exclusive license to Springer Nature Switzerland AG 2023
L. Iliadis et al. (Eds.): ICANN 2023, LNCS 14257, pp. 423–434, 2023.
https://doi.org/10.1007/978-3-031-44216-2_35

Keywords: Knowledge graph completion · Heterogeneous graph · Attention mechanism

1 Introduction

Knowledge graph completion is a task of predicting missing links based on known triplets in a knowledge graph [13]. Currently, knowledge graph completion has been successfully applied to many downstream tasks and applications, such as intelligent question-answering systems [20], information retrieval, and visual relationship detection [10]. Knowledge graph completion has always been a major research direction, and the main task is to infer missing facts more accurately from the existing facts in KG, achieve the growth of existing KG, that is, predict missing entities or relationships based on existing entities and relationships in the knowledge graph [8]. The current main task is to confirm the relationship between any two entities and the correctness of existing relationships between entities, integrate and filter existing knowledge, and conduct more accurate knowledge discovery [1], so as to improve the quality of entities in the knowledge base and solve problems such as data missing in the knowledge graph.

In existing knowledge graph completion methods, the current main research direction is to learn the distributed representations of entities and relationships in the knowledge graph, such as existing translation models (TransE [2], TransH [21], TransR [8], etc.), semantic matching models (RESCAL [12], Simple [7], etc.), and neural network models (ConvE [5], ConvR [4], ConvKB [11], etc.). However, through learning from these methods, we can easily find that translation models and semantic matching models independently treat triplets when dealing with triplets, ignoring the hidden entity information and rich semantic relationships in the surrounding neighborhood of triplets. The model structure is relatively simple and has poor expression ability. Existing neural network models are prone to ignore the overall structural characteristics of triplets and cannot capture the relationship between entities and relationships in low-dimensional space [3]. They also ignore the transformation characteristics between triplets.

The emergence of graph neural networks has achieved an extension of deep neural networks, and the addition of attention mechanisms [18] can allow a neural network to focus only on the information needed for task learning, learn the importance between entities and their neighbors, and integrate neighbor information to update the feature representation of the central entity, improving the effectiveness of training and the accuracy of testing. The amount of data that exists in reality is very large, and the attributes and associations of entities are complex. Different entities often have different features, and their features will fall into different feature spaces. Heterogeneity is an inherent property of a graph [19,24], which means that there are more than one type of entities and edges on a graph [17]. For example: an actor's features may involve gender, age, and nationality. On the other hand, the associated attributes of a movie may involve plot and actors.

In this paper, we propose a new heterogeneous graph neural network knowledge graph completion model that improves the attention mechanism [20]. We mainly use hierarchical attention mechanism (AHAM) in heterogeneous graphs, mainly at the entity level and semantic level. Attention mechanism is added to integrate effective information within multi-hop neighborhoods, so as to update the feature representation of the central entity. In particular, in order to obtain sufficient expressive power and transform input features into higher-level features, we use a weight matrix to apply parameterized shared linear transformations to each entity node. Then, entity-level attention can learn the attention values between entities and their neighbor based on meta-paths, while semantic-level attention aims to learn the attention values of different meta-paths for specific tasks in heterogeneous graphs. Based on the attention values learned in these two layers, our model can hierarchically obtain the optimal combination of neighbors and multiple meta-paths, so that the learned entity embeddings can better capture the complex structure and rich semantic information in heterogeneous graphs. Then, a convolutional network (Conv-transE) is used as a decoder. AHAM generates entity embeddings by aggregating features of neighbor based on meta-paths in a hierarchical manner. The improvement of decoder Conv-transE realizes the transformation between relations and entities, while maintaining better link prediction performance.

Our contributions are mainly as follows:

- We proposed an IAHGN model for heterogeneous graphs that introduces a hierarchical attention mechanism. In entity-level attention, a weight matrix is introduced to parameterize the linear transformation of entity nodes, which is more conducive to transforming input features into higher-level feature representations. By adding semantic-level attention mechanisms, we can distinguish the importance of the same central entity under different meta-paths and fuse entity representations under multiple different meta-paths to achieve more accurate updating of the feature representation of the central entity.
- We adopted an end-to-end model structure and used encoder AHAM and decoder Coenv-transE. The experimental results verify the superiority of this model structure.
- We used four datasets to predict links and evaluate model performance. Experimental data shows that IAHGN has good performance.

2 Related Work

2.1 TransE

The TransE model is the most representative translation model [2]. The TransE model maps the head entity h, tail entity t, and relationship r to a low-dimensional dense vector space, and regards the relationship as a translation from the head entity to the tail entity. If (h, r, t) holds, the embedding of the tail entity e_t should be close to the embedding of the head entity e_h plus the relationship embedding e_r [16]. As shown in formula (1).

$$e_t = e_h + e_r \tag{1}$$

However, the TransE model is only suitable for one-to-one models and the model structure is too simple to capture the underlying connections between entities and relationships [23].

2.2 RESCAL

The RESCALmodel, also known as the bilinear model, is the earliest semantic matching model [12]. Its representation learning process is generally completed through tensor decomposition [1]. RESCAL models the relationship r as a matrix M_r to capture pairwise interactions between entity latent factors. It can embed multiple entities and relationships into low-dimensional space for semantic matching, as shown in formula (2).

$$\mathcal{S}(h, t, r) = \boldsymbol{h}^\top M_r \boldsymbol{t} \tag{2}$$

Although the RESCAL model is easy to train, its relationship matrix cannot handle asymmetric relationships [6]. When the embedding dimension is too large, the computational complexity will increase significantly, which is a fatal disadvantage for embedding large-scale knowledge graphs.

2.3 ConvE

The ConvE model is a convolution neural network used for knowledge graph embedding, which can be applied to more complex knowledge graph completion [5]. ConvE is the simplest multi-layer convolution network used for knowledge graph completion, consisting of a single-layer convolution network, a projection layer, and an inner product layer [22]. The ConvE model not only has fewer parameters but also speeds up training through 1-N scoring [11]. However, two-dimensional convolution can only capture partial interactions, so the interaction between entities and relations is still far from enough [20]. At the same time, the ConvE model ignores the translation properties of triplets and does not pay attention to the global features of triplets.

2.4 SACN

SACN is mainly an improvement for ConvE. The author believes that ConvE ignores the graph structure information of KG [9], and its 2D convolution operation fails to retain the translation characteristics [15]. To solve these two problems, the article proposes to use a Weighted Graph Convolution Network (WGCN) to solve the problem of graph structure information not being considered, and omits the reshape operation in ConvE convolution to preserve translation characteristics. The overall model is called SACN, which is an end-to-end neural network structure [14]. However, the graph convolution network used in the SACN model does not fully consider the importance of different meta-paths for the central entity, but simply uses the connectivity structure of the graph to aggregate messages from adjacent nodes to update the feature representation of the central node.

3   Method

In this section, we will describe the IAHGN model in detail. The overall architecture of the model is shown in Fig. 3, which mainly includes the encoder AHAM and the decoder Conv-transE. The encoder mainly updates the feature representation of the entity by integrating effective information of the central entity's surrounding neighborhood under different meta-paths through hierarchical attention mechanism. The decoder Conv-transE network aims to more accurately represent the relationship by restoring the original triplets in KB. The encoder and decoder are jointly trained by minimizing the difference (cross-entropy) between the embeddings $e_s + e_r$ and e_o to maintain the translational property of $e_s + e_r \approx e_o$.

We denote the heterogeneous graph as $\mathcal{G} = (\mathcal{V}, \mathcal{E})$, consisting of entity set $\mathcal{V}$ and link $\mathcal{E}$. The heterogeneous graph is also associated with a node type mapping function $\phi : \mathcal{V} \rightarrow \mathcal{A}$ and a link type mapping function $\psi : \mathcal{E} \rightarrow \mathcal{R}$. $\mathcal{A}$ and $\mathcal{R}$ represent the sets of predefined object types and link types, where $|\mathcal{A}| + |\mathcal{R}| > 2$. For example, as shown in Fig. 2, we constructed a heterogeneous graph consisting of multiple types of objects (actors(A), movies(M), directors(D)) and relationships (shooting relationship between movies and directors, role-playing relationship between actors and movies).

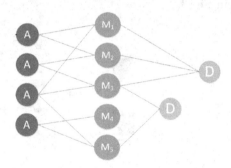

Fig. 1. An illustrative example of a heterogenous graph

In a heterogeneous graph, two objects can be connected through different semantic paths, which are called meta-paths [24]. A meta-path Φ can be described as the connection of all entities under different relationship types. For example, as shown in Fig. 1, two movies can be connected through multiple meta-paths, Movie-Actor-Movie (MAM) and Movie-Director-Movie (MDM). Different meta-paths always reveal different semantics. MAM represents a collaborative relationship, while MDM represents that they are directed by the same director. For a given meta-path Φ, each node has a set of neighbors based on the meta-path, which can reveal different structural information and rich semantics in the heterogeneous graph. For example, as shown in Fig. 2, given the meta-path of movie-actor-movie, the meta-path based on neighbors can be described as Fig. 2.

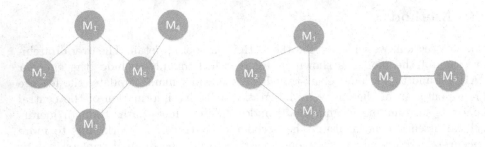

Fig. 2. Meta-path based Neighbors

3.1 Hierarchical Attention Mechanism

Entity Attention. Before aggregating the meta-path neighbor information, we should first notice the different roles played by each meta-path neighbor entity in the embedding learning of a specific meta-path and the importance they show. The addition of entity-level attention is mainly used to deepen the importance of learning the neighbors of each entity in the heterogeneous graph for each entity, while aggregating the neighbor entity information updates the embedding representation of the central entity. This part corresponds to the entity-level attention in Fig. 3.

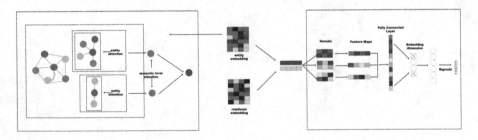

Fig. 3. The IAHGN model description is: For the encoder, the central entity's representation is updated through entity-level attention and semantic-level attention. For decoder, e_s and e_r are fed into Conv-TransE. The output embedding are vectorized and projected, and matched with all candidate e_o embeddings via inner products. A logistic sigmoid function is used to get the scores

A set of node features $\mathbf{h} = \{h_1, h_2, \ldots, h_N\}$ is used as input for our layer. Here, $h_i \in \mathbb{R}^F$ and N is the number of nodes while F is the number of features per node. The layer generates a new set of node features $\mathbf{h}' = \{h'_1, h'_2, \ldots, h'_N\}, h'_i \in \mathbb{R}^{F'}$ with potentially different cardinality as output.

In order to obtain sufficient expression ability and convert input features into higher-level features, at least one learnable linear transformation is required.

As an initial step, a shared linear transformation parameterized by the weight matrix $\mathbf{W}_{\phi_i} \in \mathbb{R}^{F' \times F}$ is applied to each node.

$$\mathbf{h}'_i = \mathbf{W}_{\phi_i} \cdot \mathbf{h}_i, \tag{3}$$

Given any pair of entities (i, j) that can be connected by a meta-path, the importance of entity j with respect to entity i can be learned through an adaptive attention mechanism. The updated node is represented by e_{ij}^{Φ}, and its formula can be expressed as:

$$e_{ij}^{\Phi} = att_{node}(\mathbf{h}'_i, \mathbf{h}'_j; \Phi) \tag{4}$$

att_{node} :represents a deep neural network that performs entity attention. It is important to note that entities i and j are asymmetric, and the importance of entity i with respect to entity j and the importance of entity j with respect to entity i are different. Therefore, the entity-level attention mechanism can maintain an asymmetric behavior, which is an important property of heterogeneous graphs. Then we need to add structural information to the attention mechanism. We only need to calculate e_{ij}^{Φ} in relation to the attention related to entity j. This can obtain the importance between entity pairs based on meta-paths, and finally normalize it through softmax.

$$\alpha_{ij}^{\Phi} = software(e_{ij}^{\Phi}) = \frac{\exp\left(\sigma(\mathbf{a}_{\Phi}^{\mathrm{T}} \cdot [\mathbf{h}'_i || \mathbf{h}'_j])\right)}{\sum_{k \in \mathcal{N}_i^{\Phi}} \exp\left(\sigma(\mathbf{a}_{\Phi}^{\mathrm{T}} \cdot [\mathbf{h}'_i || \mathbf{h}'_k])\right)} \tag{5}$$

From formula (4), we can see that the weight coefficients between entity pairs mainly depend on their features. It should be noted that the entity-level attention vector of the meta-path has different importance for different entities. This is not only because of the different connection orders in entities, but also because the neighbors of different entities are different. Therefore, the normalization term (denominator) will have a large difference. The meta-path-based embedding of vertex i can be obtained by weighting the feature mapping of its neighbors using α_{ij}^{Φ}.

$$\mathbf{z}_i^{\Phi} = \sigma\left(\sum_{j \in \mathcal{N}_i^{\Phi}} \alpha_{ij}^{\Phi} \cdot \mathbf{h}'_j\right) \tag{6}$$

Since α_{ij}^{Φ} and meta-paths are related, α_{ij}^{Φ} can capture the semantic information represented in the meta-paths. Based on the embedding of meta-paths, we can also call it semantic-related embedding. By repeating the aggregation operation K times and concatenating the vectors, multi-head attention mechanism can be realized.

$$\mathbf{z}_i^{\Phi} = \mathop{\|}_{k=1} \sigma\left(\sum_{j \in \mathcal{N}_i^{\Phi}} \alpha_{ij}^{\Phi} \cdot \mathbf{h}'_j\right) \tag{7}$$

Semantic Level Attention. Given a set of meta-paths, entity-level attention is used to learn entity representations under different semantics. This part corresponds to the semantic-level attention in Fig. 3. Furthermore, we can use semantic-level attention to learn the importance of semantics and fuse entity representations under multiple semantics. The formal description of semantic-level attention is as follows: $(\beta_{\Phi_1}, \dots, \beta_{\Phi_p}) = attt_{sem}(\mathbf{Z}_{\Phi_1}, \dots, \mathbf{Z}_{\Phi_p})$, Specifically, we use a single-layer neural network and semantic-level attention vectors to learn the importance of each semantics (meta-path) and normalize them through softmax.

In order to learn the importance of each meta-path, a linear transformation is used to transform the embedding of a specific semantics. We measure the similarity of the learned embeddings of specific semantics using a semantic-level attention vector q embedding.

$$w_{\Phi_p} = \frac{1}{|\mathcal{V}|} \sum_{i \in \mathcal{V}} \mathbf{q}^{\mathbf{T}} \cdot \tanh(\mathbf{W} \cdot \mathbf{z}_i^{\Phi_p} + \mathbf{b}) \tag{8}$$

The final entity representation can be obtained by weighted fusion of multiple semantics (fusion process as shown in Fig. 3). It should be noted that the meta-path weight here is optimized for specific tasks. Different tasks require different semantic information, and the weighted combination of meta-paths will also vary.

$$\mathbf{Z} = \sum_{p=1}^{P} \beta_{\Phi_p} \cdot \mathbf{Z}_{\Phi_p} \tag{9}$$

3.2   Conv-TransE

Based on the learning of the ConvE model, we found that the ConvE model did not merge the coherent structure in the knowledge graph into the embedding space, and because in ConvE, after the reshaping of s and r, they are concatenated into an input matrix and fed into a convolutional layer, so ConvE does not maintain translational invariance like TransE. Inspired by the model SCAN, we use Conv-transE as the decoder, remove the ConvE reshaping step, and directly operate convolution filters on the same dimension of entities and relations to maintain TransE translational invariance.

For the decoder, the input is two embedding matrices, one is the entity embedding trained by AHAM, and the other is the relation embedding, which is also trained. The convolution calculation in the decoder is as follows:

$$m_c(e_s, e_r, n) = \sum_{\tau=0}^{K-1} \omega_c(\tau, 0)\hat{e}_s(n + \tau) + \omega_c(\tau, 1)\hat{e}_r(n + \tau) \tag{10}$$

where K is the kernel width, The item in the n index output vector, $n \in [0, F^L - 1]$, and the kernel parameter ω_c is trainable, and the kernel parameter ω_c is trainable. $\hat{e}_s$ and $\hat{e}_r$ are the padded versions of e_s and e_r, respectively. If the kernel dimension s is odd, then the first $\lfloor K/2 \rfloor$ components and the last $\lfloor K/2 \rfloor$ components are padded with zeros. Here $\lfloor value \rfloor$ is the lower bound of the return value. Otherwise, the first $\lfloor K/2 \rfloor - 1$ and last $\lfloor K/2 \rfloor$ components are padded with zeros. The other components are copied directly from e_s and e_r.

Finally, the score function of the decoder after non-linear convolution is as follows:

$$\psi(e_s, e_o) = f(vec(\mathbf{M}(e_s, e_r))W)e_o \qquad (11)$$

Where $W \in \mathbb{R}^{CF^L \times F^L}$ is the matrix for linear transformation and f represents the non-linear function. The feature map matrix is reshaped into a vector $vec(\mathbf{M}) \in \mathbb{R}^{CF^L}$ and projected to an F^L dimensional space using W for linear transformation. Then the calculated embedding is matched to e_o using an appropriate distance metric. In the experiment, the score function is as follows:

$$p(e_s, e_r, e_o) = \sigma(\psi(e_s, e_o)) \qquad (12)$$

4   Experiments

4.1   Benchmark Datasets

Four benchmark datasets (FB15k, WN18, FB15k-237 and WN18RR) were selected for evaluating the performance of link prediction in this experiment. The detailed information of these datasets is shown in Table 1. FB15k is a commonly used datasets for link prediction. This datasets contains all entities mentioned more than 100 times in FreeBase, and converts the concrete n-ary relationship into a set of binary edges, which greatly affects the structure and semantics of the graph. WN18 was extracted from WordNet3. To construct WN18, the authors used WordNet3 as a starting point and then iteratively filtered out entities and relationships that were mentioned too few times. FB15k-237 is a subset of the FB15k datasets, inspired by observations of test leakage suffered by FB15k, including test data seen by the model during training. WN18RR is a subset of WN18 and was also inspired by observations of test leakage in WN18.

Table 1. Statistics of datasets

	Entities	Relations	Triples		
			Train	Valid	Test
FB15k	14951	1345	483142	50000	50971
WN18	40943	18	141442	5000	5000
FB15k-237	14541	237	272115	17535	20466
WN18RR	40943	11	86835	3034	3134

4.2   Evaluation Protocol

The knowledge graph completion evaluation adopts the same protocol as the previous article. For each test set (h, r, t), h and t are replaced with all entities in the datasets to calculate the score. Then, we apply a filter setting, where effective triples that already exist in the training, effective, and test sets are filtered out before being ranked. For knowledge graph completion tasks, processing triples with the same score is strict and fair. Three standard indicators are reported to evaluate performance, average reciprocal rank (MRR), and the proportion of ranking scores of all test triples with $N = 1$, 3, and 10 (Hits@N). MRR is the average inverse score of correctly predicted samples in all test samples. Hits@k is the proportion of scores of correctly predicted samples that are higher than or equal to the k score in all test samples.

We follow a two-step training process, that is, we first train AHAM to encode information about graph entities and relationships, and then train Conv-transE as a decoder model to perform relationship prediction tasks. The AHAM model can update the central entity by aggregating the semantic of neighboring entities through meta-path aggregation. We use Adam to optimize all parameters, and the initial learning rate is set to 0.001. The entity and relationship embeddings of the last layer are both set to 200. Table 2 shows the prediction results of some data set test sets. The results clearly show that our proposed model outperforms other models in four indicators on data set FB15k-237, and WN18RR outperforms other models in three indicators on test results. The improvement of MRR value confirms the ability of our model to correctly represent the relationship between triplets. Compared with SACN with the same model architecture in FB15k-237 data set, our model MRR has been improved by 3.5%, and the value of Hits@N is also significantly higher than other models. Compared with the convolutional network model ConvE in FB15k-237 data set, our model MRR has been improved by 6.9%, and the values of Hits@1 and Hits@3 are also significantly higher than other models. The improvement of experimental results shows that our model can better achieve knowledge graph completion.

Table 2. Link prediction for FB15k-237 and WN18RR.

Model	FB15K-237				WN18RR			
	Hits 10	3	1	MRR	Hits 10	3	1	MRR
TransE	0.465			0.279	0.501			0.243
DisMult	0.42	0.28	0.16	0.25	0.51	0.46	0.41	0.44
ConvE	0.49	0.35	0.24	0.32	0.48	0.43	0.39	0.46
SACN	0.54	0.39	0.26	0.35	**0.54**	0.47	0.43	0.47
Conv-transE	0.51	0.37	0.26	0.34	0.52	0.48	0.43	0.46
IAHGN	**0.559**	**0.398**	**0.28**	**0.363**	0.538	**0.506**	**0.455**	**0.492**

5   Conclusion and Future Work

We introduce a heterogeneous graph neural network based on an improved attention mechanism for encoder-decoder relations. By adding the attention mechanism to the heterogeneous graph neural network, the feature representation of the central entity can be updated more effectively. At the same time, the central entity can better integrate multilateral semantic information through self-attention, and use the connectivity of the knowledge graph more efficiently. properties, node attributes, and relationship types. The scoring network is a convolutional neural model called convc-transe. This method leverages convolutional networks to model relations as translation operations and captures the translational features between entities and relations. Experiments also demonstrate that using Conv-TransE has achieved more efficient performance.

In the future, we hope to incorporate the idea of neighbor selection into our training framework, taking into account the importance of neighbors when aggregating their vector representations. We also want to extend our model to have a larger knowledge graph

Acknowledgements. This work is supported in part by The Key R&D Program of Shandong Province(2021SFGC0101), The 20 Planned Projects in Jinan(202228120)

References

1. Balažević, I., Allen, C., Hospedales, T.M.: Tucker: tensor factorization for knowledge graph completion. arXiv preprint arXiv:1901.09590 (2019)
2. Bordes, A., Usunier, N., Garcia-Duran, A., Weston, J., Yakhnenko, O.: Translating embeddings for modeling multi-relational data. In: Advances in Neural Information Processing Systems, vol. 26 (2013)
3. Burstein, J., Doran, C., Solorio, T.: Proceedings of the 2019 Conference of the North American Chapter of the Association for Computational Linguistics: Human Language Technologies, vol. 1 (Long and Short Papers) (2019)
4. Çavuşoğlu, I., Pielka, M., Sifa, R.: Adapting established text representations for predicting review sentiment in Turkish. In: 2020 IEEE 7th International Conference on Data Science and Advanced Analytics (DSAA), pp. 755–756. IEEE (2020)
5. Dettmers, T., Minervini, P., Stenetorp, P., Riedel, S.: Convolutional 2D knowledge graph embeddings. In: Proceedings of the AAAI Conference on Artificial Intelligence, vol. 32 (2018)
6. Guo, L., Sun, Z., Hu, W.: Learning to exploit long-term relational dependencies in knowledge graphs. In: International Conference on Machine Learning, pp. 2505–2514. PMLR (2019)
7. Kazemi, S.M., Poole, D.: Simple embedding for link prediction in knowledge graphs. Advances in Neural Information Processing Systems, vol. 31 (2018)
8. Lin, Y., Liu, Z., Sun, M., Liu, Y., Zhu, X.: Learning entity and relation embeddings for knowledge graph completion. In: Proceedings of the AAAI Conference on Artificial Intelligence, vol. 29 (2015)
9. Liu, H., Wu, Y., Yang, Y.: Analogical inference for multi-relational embeddings. In: International Conference on Machine Learning, pp. 2168–2178. PMLR (2017)

10. Liu, X., Tan, H., Chen, Q., Lin, G.: RAGAT: relation aware graph attention network for knowledge graph completion. IEEE Access **9**, 20840–20849 (2021)
11. Nguyen, D.Q., Nguyen, T.D., Nguyen, D.Q., Phung, D.: A novel embedding model for knowledge base completion based on convolutional neural network. arXiv preprint arXiv:1712.02121 (2017)
12. Nickel, M., Tresp, V., Kriegel, H.P., et al.: A three-way model for collective learning on multi-relational data. In: ICML, vol. 11, pp. 3104482–3104584 (2011)
13. Rossi, A., Barbosa, D., Firmani, D., Matinata, A., Merialdo, P.: Knowledge graph embedding for link prediction: a comparative analysis. ACM Trans. Knowl. Discov. Data (TKDD) **15**(2), 1–49 (2021)
14. Schlichtkrull, M., Kipf, T.N., Bloem, P., van den Berg, R., Titov, I., Welling, M.: Modeling relational data with graph convolutional networks. In: Gangemi, A., et al. (eds.) ESWC 2018. LNCS, vol. 10843, pp. 593–607. Springer, Cham (2018). https://doi.org/10.1007/978-3-319-93417-4_38
15. Shang, C., Tang, Y., Huang, J., Bi, J., He, X., Zhou, B.: End-to-end structure-aware convolutional networks for knowledge base completion. In: Proceedings of the AAAI Conference on Artificial Intelligence, vol. 33, pp. 3060–3067 (2019)
16. Trouillon, T., Welbl, J., Riedel, S., Gaussier, É., Bouchard, G.: Complex embeddings for simple link prediction. In: International Conference on Machine Learning, pp. 2071–2080. PMLR (2016)
17. Vashishth, S., Sanyal, S., Nitin, V., Agrawal, N., Talukdar, P.: InteractE: improving convolution-based knowledge graph embeddings by increasing feature interactions. In: Proceedings of the AAAI Conference on Artificial Intelligence, vol. 34, pp. 3009–3016 (2020)
18. Veličković, P., Cucurull, G., Casanova, A., Romero, A., Lio, P., Bengio, Y.: Graph attention networks. arXiv preprint arXiv:1710.10903 (2017)
19. Wang, X., et al.: Heterogeneous graph attention network. In: The World Wide Web Conference, pp. 2022–2032 (2019)
20. Wang, Y., Jin, H., et al.: A new concept of knowledge based question answering (KBQA) system for multi-hop reasoning. In: Proceedings of the 2022 Conference of the North American Chapter of the Association for Computational Linguistics: Human Language Technologies, pp. 4007–4017 (2022)
21. Wang, Z., Zhang, J., Feng, J., Chen, Z.: Knowledge graph embedding by translating on hyperplanes. In: Proceedings of the AAAI Conference on Artificial Intelligence, vol. 28 (2014)
22. Wei, Y., Chaudhary, V.: The directionality function defect of performance evaluation method in regression neural network for stock price prediction. In: 2020 IEEE 7th International Conference on Data Science and Advanced Analytics (DSAA), pp. 769–770. IEEE (2020)
23. Zhang, W., Paudel, B., Zhang, W., Bernstein, A., Chen, H.: Interaction embeddings for prediction and explanation in knowledge graphs. In: Proceedings of the Twelfth ACM International Conference on Web Search and Data Mining, pp. 96–104 (2019)
24. Zhang, Z., Cai, J., Zhang, Y., Wang, J.: Learning hierarchy-aware knowledge graph embeddings for link prediction. In: Proceedings of the AAAI Conference on Artificial Intelligence, vol. 34, pp. 3065–3072 (2020)

Hierarchical Diachronic Embedding of Knowledge Graph Combined with Fragmentary Information Filtering

Kai Liu[1,2] , Zhiguang Wang[1,2](✉), Yixuan Yang[2], Chao Huang[1,2] ,
Min Niu[3], and Qiang Lu[1,2]

[1] Beijing Key Laboratory of Petroleum Data Mining, China University of Petroleum,
Beijing, China
cwangzg@cup.edu.cn
[2] Department of Computer Science and Technology, China University of Petroleum,
Beijing, China
[3] Research Institute of Petroleum Exploration and Development, Beijing, China

Abstract. Knowledge graph(KG) embedding is often used in link prediction, triplet classification, and knowledge graph completion(KGC),
which is critical to knowledge relation extraction and recommendation
algorithm design. The previous works in KG embedding have made excellent achievements in KGC, but they ignore fragment information and
the hierarchy of temporal information in KG. The hierarchy of temporal information indicates that different dimensions of information such as
year, month, and day have different degrees of influence on the fact information. Fragmentary information is usually weakly or uncorrelated with
the main information, reducing KG embedding learning efficiency. To
solve these problems, we propose two methods: Firstly, we propose word
frequency filtering to filter fragment information. Secondly, we propose
hierarchical diachronic embedding for temporal KG, which provides the
characteristics of an entity at different levels of time. We add the consideration of fragmentation filtering and hierarchical temporal embedding
to the static KG embedding model SimplE, which results in a novelty
model for KGC–HDF-ASimplE(Hierarchical Diachronic Embedding of
Knowledge Graph with Fragmentary Information Filtering for Average
SimplE). Experimental results manifest that the HDF-ASimplE model is
superior to the previous works on KGC, and the evaluation parameters
of KGC are increased by 14% on average, Hit@10 to 81.7%. It proves the
effectiveness of our method.

Keywords: Knowledge Graph Completion · Fragmentary Information
Filtering · Hierarchical Diachronic Embedding

This work is supported by National Natural Science Foundation of China
(No.61972414), National Key R&D Program of China (No. 2019YFC0312003) and
Beijing Natural Science Foundation (No. 4202066).

L. Iliadis et al. (Eds.): ICANN 2023, LNCS 14257, pp. 435–446, 2023.
https://doi.org/10.1007/978-3-031-44216-2_36

1   Introduction

KG is a collection of triples (h, r, t), where h, t denotes entities and r denotes relationships between entities. KG constructs a structured graph knowledge with complex texts in the form of directed edges and nodes, which plays a powerful role in many tasks, such as question answering [3], recommendation system [29,34], information retrieval [31] or reasoning [7].

The original text form is not suitable for computer training, even though KG is structural. However, KG embedding [30] solves this problem by representing complex texts as simple vectors. KG embedding is embedding complex high-dimensional information into a low-dimensional space by dimensional mapping, vector migration, and other forms while retaining the original KG structural information. The research significance of KG embedding is to reduce the training cost of high-dimensional semantic models as much as feasible so that the training of data can not only improve the efficiency but also improve the accuracy of the model. Inferring new facts from KG based on existing ones is a crucial problem, known as KGC [15]. A prominent approach to KGC is based on KG embedding models. The idea is to learn the embedding of entities and relations by training on the known facts, and then compute the score of the unknown points using the trained embeddings.

With the continuous development of knowledge embedding technology, people are increasingly focusing on the mode of knowledge embedding in low-dimensional space, where the quality of knowledge records and the use of dynamic knowledge play a crucial role in knowledge embedding. Most of the previous work did not evaluate the quality of the knowledge dataset and directly used the original temporal knowledge dataset for dynamic knowledge embedding. However, due to a lot of fragmented information in the original temporal KG, this may learn irrelevant or unimportant knowledge features. These fragments refer to unrelated to the central knowledge information, such as social news information in the diplomatic news KG, which is involved in the embedding training of KG and may possess an unreliable impact on data training.

To avoid weak correlation and enable stable training, we propose fragmentation information filtering in which we explicitly separate the main information from the fragmentation information of the temporal KG with word frequency filtering, as encapsulated in the algorithm flow chart in Fig. 1. Specifically as shown, among the triplet (h, r, t) that constitute the KG, we calculate the frequency values of head entity h and tail entity t, and define the triplet with head entity word frequency and tail entity word frequency lower than the threshold a as fragmented information.

Inspired by the diachronic [13] improvement of SimplE [17], we try to incorporate temporal information into entity embedding differently. To make better use of the dynamic information in temporal KG, we consider time hierarchy and reformulate the diachronic embedding method. The focus of this work is on temporal knowledge graph completion(TKGC) [5], which is the inference of missing temporal facts in temporal KG. As far as we know, no other current embedding model studies TKGC from the perspective of time hierarchy.

In this paper, we propose HDF-ASimplE, a hierarchical diachronic embedding model for TKGC. HDF-ASimplE builds on the diachronic embedding model DE-SimplE and extends it with fragment information filtering and hierarchical embeddings. In HDF-ASimplE, each level of time embedding has its corresponding embedding parameter, which represents the different connection degrees of time hierarchy to entities and relations. Moreover, this model can identify and filter the fragmented information before embedding training. Our main contributions are as follows:

We propose a method to enhance the quality of the dataset, fragment information filtering.

Following Rishab Goel et al. [13], we first use hierarchical embedding of time, which has a strong ability to capture dynamic facts.

Our proposed HDF-ASimplE is fully expressive and has a strong temporal inferential capability. We have completed comparison experiments to manifest the state-of-the-art performance of HDF-ASimplE on several TKGC baselines and demonstrated the effectiveness of our methods.

2   Related Work

2.1   Static Knowledge Graph Embedding Models

The previous KG embedding models focus on static knowledge, which can be divided into the translation model, bilinear model, and neural model. Bordes et al. propose TransE [4], a KG embedding model based on translation for the first time, which models entities and relations as point and vector displacements in the representation space. Then a slice of variant models emerged such as TransH [11], which introduces relational hyperplanes on which entities were mapped. TransR [21] maps entities to a relationship-specific space instead of a hyperplane. BoxE [1] is a spatial-translational model where fact correctness depends on absolute representation position in the embedding space. The bilinear model RESCAL [25] projects the entity as a vector and represents the relational information as an association matrix between the entity and the relation. DisMult [33] simplifies RESCAL by converting the relational matrix to a diagonal matrix. ComplEx [28] proposes the concept of ComplEx embedding and tensor decomposition techniques. TUCKER [2] demonstrates TUCKER decomposition is a generalization of the previous linear model. ROTATE [26] represents relationship information as rotations in a complex vector space. QUATE [35] captures a more flexible pattern by representing entities and relationships as quaternions on a ROTATE basis. Finally, the neural models MLP [10] and ConvE [9] use neural networks to evaluate scores for embedded triples. These researches focus on the representation and learning of static facts, without paying attention to the quality of datasets. When the quality of the dataset is poor, learning information unrelated to the main information will lead to an inefficient learning direction of the model, thus reducing the performance of KG completion. To solve this problem, we propose word frequency-based fragmentation filtering.

2.2   Temporal Knowledge Graph Embedding Models

Recently, people have begun to pay attention to temporal information in facts, and quite a few embedding models of temporal knowledge graphs are proposed. A host of methods are based on static models. TTransE [16] changes its scoring function on the basis of TransE [4], adding the consideration of time information. Ta-transe [12] uses LSTM [14] to introduce temporal features for embedding. HyTE [8] projects entities and relationships onto a time-specific hyperplane. Inspired by TransE and ROTATE [26], TeRo [32] embeds relations as translation vectors and time as rotation vectors. TNTComplEx [18] express the TKGC problem as an order 4 tensor completion problem. RotateQVS [6] represents temporal entities as rotations in quaternion vector space. HERCULES [24] uses the curvature of a manifold to coerce time-aware representation. BoxTE [23] builds on the static KG embedding model BoxE [1], and extends it with dedicated time embeddings to increase the ability of expression and induction. DE-SimplE [13] proposes diachronic embedding, which uses a specific embedding function to embed time and entity jointly. It achieves state-of-the-art performances on the temporal knowledge graph datasets ICEW14, ICEW05-15 [12] and GDELT [20].

Our work takes inspiration from the idea of diachronic embedding and generalizes hierarchical embedding into it to model the temporal-evolution pattern that DE-SimplE ignores.

3   Fragmentary Information Filtering and Processing

3.1   Definition of Fragmentary Information

In KG, there are some weakly correlated or uncorrelated information triples, which we call fragmented triples. For example, the triples (UK, located in, Europe), (Europe, located in, Eurasia) in the medical KG, are inappropriate and independent from the medical KG. Such fragment triples are fragment information in the knowledge graph.

3.2   Fragment Information Filtering

We investigate and summarize the rules of various types of KG datasets, and propose a fragment information filtering method based on entity word frequency, which can be seen in Fig. 1. The routine for calculating entities in the figure is as follows: In the knowledge graph composed of six triples, it is calculated that there are 3 blue entities and 12 entities in total, so the blue entity word frequency is 3/12. In this method, the number of entities appearing in the whole triplet sets, namely the frequency value of each entity in the KG, is used to detect the triplet sets of fragment information. As shown in Algorithm 1.

In Algorithm 1, the parameter a is the entity word frequency threshold, determined by the structure and category of the KG. Assuming that there are N entities in a KG, the word frequency value of the entity with the highest frequency is p, and the word frequency value of the entity with the lowest frequency is m, then the formulation function of a is shown in the following Eq. 1.

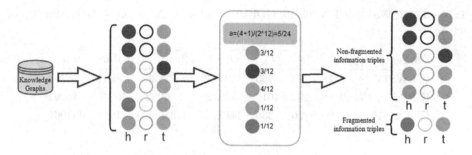

Fig. 1. Word frequency filtering.

$$a = \frac{p + m}{2N} \qquad (1)$$

According to the calculation method of entity word frequency, the orange entity word frequency value in the figure is the highest, $p = 4$, and the green and purple entity word frequency is the lowest, $m = 1$, so the parameter $a = \frac{p+m}{2N} = 3/12$. Finally, if the word frequency of the header entity or the tail entity is greater than parameter a, it is regarded as a non-fragmented triplet; otherwise, it is a fragmented triplet.

Algorithm 1. Word frequency filtering algorithm

Input: word frequency parameter a, The collection of quadruple information D, The length of quadruple information set L

Output: Fragment information set $Chips$, Non-fragment information set $Facts$.

1: Create an initial array Ent_f to store the entity frequencies.
2: **for** $i = 1$ to L **do**
3:    Separate each quadruple $D[i]$ to h, r, t, τ.
4:    For each occurrence of h and t, the corresponding $Ent_f[h]$ and $Ent_f[t]$ are accumulated by $\frac{1}{2L}$.
5: **end for**
6: i = 0, o = 0, k = 0.
7: **while** $i \neq L$ **do**
8:    Separate each quadruple $D[i]$ to h, r, t, τ.
9:    **if** $Ent_f[h] \geq a$ or $Ent_f[t] \geq a$ **then**
10:      Store the quadruple into $Facts[o]$.
11:      o add 1.
12:    **else**
13:      Store the quadruple into $Chips[k]$.
14:      k add 1.
15:    **end if**
16: **end while**
17: **return** $Chips$, $Facts$.

Table 1. ICEWS14, ICEWS05-15, GDELT's statistics($|X|$ denotes the cardinality of set X).

Dataset	$|V|$	$|R|$	$|T|$	$|D|$	$|train|$	$|valid|$	$|test|$
ICEWS14	7128	230	365	90730	72826	8941	8963
ICEWS05-15	10488	251	4017	479329	386962	46275	46092
GDELT-15	500	20	366	3419607	2735685	341961	341961

3.3 Processing of Fragmented Information

After the triplet sets are screened and classified by the word frequency filtering method, we can get the triplet sets of fragmented information and the triplet sets of non-fragmented information. Given the adverse impact of fragmented triplet sets on embedding training in the KG, two methods are adopted in this section:

The first method is to train the triplet sets of fragmented information as negative samples in negative sampling training. When the fragmented information is used as a negative sample, the matching pattern in the embedding training process will be far away from the matching pattern of the fragment information triplet.

The second method directly removes the fragment information triplet sets as junk information and uses the non-fragment information triplet sets for embedding training. This method takes into account the noise effect of the fragment information in training and uses the form of removing noise to process the fragment information.

After experimental verification, we finally chose the second method in this section due to the ineffectiveness of the first.

4 Diachronic Embedding

4.1 Hierarchical Diachronic Embedding

Based on the DE-SimplE [13], we put forward a new method of time embedding: hierarchical diachronic embedding(HDE). HDE adds corresponding time offset parameters to information of different magnitudes in temporal information to distinguish different effects of different levels of temporal information on entity and relationship information [22]. We embed different levels of time information [36], entity and relationship information in low-dimensional vector space to enhance the representation of knowledge information in the model. The diachronic entity embedding function of the model in this paper is defined as HDE(v, τ). The diachronic association between time information τ and entity v is used to embed time information into the entity vector dimension. Let Q_v^τ be the entity hierarchical diachronic embedding d-dimensional vector representation (HDEKG(v, τ)=($Q_v^\tau[0], Q_v^\tau[1], ..., Q_v^\tau[d]$)), and define Q_v^τ as shown in Eq. (2).

$$Q_v^\tau[x] = \begin{cases} \alpha_v[x]\sigma(\lambda\tau\ln|\omega_v[x]|) & 1 \le x \le \gamma d \\ \alpha_v[x] & \gamma d \le x \le d \end{cases} \tag{2}$$

α_v, ω_v is the learning parameter vector, σ is the activation function, λ is the time offset parameter, and γ is the hyperparameter controlling the percentage of time features. In the entity diachronic embedding vector, γd dimensional parameters capture the temporal information features, and the remaining $(1 - \gamma)d$ dimensions capture the static information features.

We use the HDE method in the process of entity relationship embedding, and Q_v^τ is represented as follows.

$$\overrightarrow{Q_v^\tau}[x] = \begin{cases} \overrightarrow{\alpha_v}[x]\sigma(\lambda\tau \ln|\overrightarrow{\omega_v}[x]|) & 1 \leq x \leq \gamma d \\ \overrightarrow{\alpha_v}[x] & \gamma d \leq x \leq d \end{cases} \tag{3}$$

$$\overleftarrow{Q_v^\tau}[x] = \begin{cases} \overleftarrow{\alpha_v}[x]\sigma(\lambda\tau \ln|\overleftarrow{\omega_v}[x]|) & 1 \leq x \leq \gamma d \\ \overleftarrow{\alpha_v}[x] & \gamma d \leq x \leq d \end{cases} \tag{4}$$

$\overrightarrow{Q_v^\tau}$ and $\overleftarrow{Q_v^\tau}$ are the embedding vector representations of triplet positive order (h, r, t) and triplet reverse order (t, r, h), respectively.

4.2 Scoring Function

The scoring function is an evaluation function to evaluate the effectiveness of triples in knowledge embedding training. By calculating the score of each embedding triplet, embedding training can learn the expression rules of the fact triplets, so that the model can fully express the fact information. The scoring method of semantic matching is chosen in the model, and the scoring function P is shown in Eq. (5).

$$P = \frac{h_1 \circ r_1 \circ t_1 + h_2 \circ r_2 \circ t_2 + (h_1 + r_1) \circ t_1 + (h_2 + r_2) \circ t_2}{4} \tag{5}$$

(h_1, r_1, t_1) and (h_2, r_2, t_2) represent the forward and reverse representation of a triplet, where h_1, h_2 are the head entity and tail entity embedding vectors in triples, respectively. The purpose of defining the scoring function in this way is to represent the presence of asymmetric triples in triples.

4.3 Loss Function

The loss function adopted by the model in this paper is the cross entropy loss function, whose value can be reduced to the minimum in multiple training through the optimization method of the Adam optimizer. The input of the cross entropy loss function is the set of evaluation scores obtained after the calculation of the scoring function. The loss value is obtained after the backpropagation calculation of the cross entropy loss function and the optimization parameters of the Adam optimizer, then the next iteration training is recycled.

Table 2. ICEWS14,ICEWS05-15,GDELT filtered statistics.

Dataset		$|train|$	$|valid|$	$|test|$
ICEWS14	$Facts$	50906	6343	6325
	$Chips$	21920	2598	2638
ICEWS05-15	$Facts$	248454	31076	31005
	$Chips$	138508	15199	15087
GDELT-15	$Facts$	2735685	341961	341961
	$Chips$	0	0	0

5 Experiments

5.1 Dataset

To evaluate the proposed method, we conduct experiments on two dynamic KG datasets: ICEWS [19] and GDELT [20], which are standard datasets in dynamic KG datasets. For dataset ICEWS, its data subsets ICEWS14 and ICEWS05-15 [12] are selected. ICEWS14 represents the factual information from 2014, and ICEWS05-15 contains all the factual information from 2005 to 2015. For dataset GDELT, the subset extracted by Trivedi [27] is selected, which contains all the factual information between April 1, 2015 and March 31, 2016.

The KG containing time information is represented as $G = (V, R, T, F)$, where V, R and T respectively represent the set of entity, relationship and time information. $F \in V \times R \times V \times T$ is the set of all feasible facts in the KG G. A fact s is represented as $s = (h, r, t, \tau)$, where h, r, t and τ represent head entity, relation, tail entity and time information respectively. The fact set that exists in the KG is $D \in F$, and Table 1 gives the basic information of the above data set.

We use the above word frequency filtering method to calculate the word frequency of each entity, filter according to the word frequency threshold, and finally, obtain the fragment information set $Chips$ and the non-fragment information set $Facts$. The filtered data set information is displayed in Table 2.

5.2 Evaluation Metrics

We take KGC as the evaluation task of the model. KGC needs to complete the missing head or tail entity in the fact triplet. To test the performance of the model on KGC, we convert the triplet set $\sum(h, r, t, \tau)$ of the test set with time information into the set $\sum(?, r, t, \tau)$, $\sum(h, r, ?, \tau)$ to simulate the KGC scenario [4]. We use the KGC evaluation index to evaluate the learning performance of the model.

The evaluation indexes in the KGC task are mean reciprocal ranking(MRR), Hit@1, Hit@3, Hit@10, and mean ranking(MR) is easily affected by a single error completion prediction. Compared with MR evaluation indexes, MRR is

Table 3. Results on ICEWS14, ICEWS05-15 and GDELT(Best results are in bold).

Model	ICEWS14				ICEWS05-15				GDELT			
	MRR	Hit@1	Hit@3	Hit@10	MRR	Hit@1	Hit@3	Hit@10	MRR	Hit@1	Hit@3	Hit@10
TransE	0.280	0.094	–	0.637	0.294	0.090	–	0.663	0.113	0	0.158	0.312
DistMult	0.439	0.323	–	0.672	0.456	0.337	–	0.691	0.196	0.117	0.208	0.348
SimplE	0.458	0.341	0.516	0.687	0.478	0.359	0.539	0.708	0.206	0.124	0.220	0.366
HyTE	0.297	0.108	0.416	0.655	0.316	0.116	0.445	0.681	0.118	0	0.165	0.326
TA-DistMult	0.477	0.363	–	0.686	0.474	0.346	–	0.728	0.206	0.124	0.219	0.365
DE-SimplE	0.526	0.418	0.592	0.725	0.513	0.392	0.578	0.748	0.230	0.141	0.248	0.403
F-TransE	0.319	0.120	0.460	0.671	0.334	0.120	0.388	0.707	0.113	0	0.158	0.312
HD-TransE	0.304	0.090	0.466	0.687	0.300	0.091	0.441	0.674	0.124	0	0.174	0.350
HDF-ASimplE	**0.602**	**0.486**	**0.675**	**0.817**	**0.561**	**0.440**	**0.630**	**0.795**	**0.253**	**0.164**	**0.272**	**0.426**

more stable, so in this chapter, MRR index is selected instead of MR index. The calculation formula of the above evaluation index is defined as follows.

$$\text{MRR} = \frac{1}{2 * |test|} \sum_{f=(h,r,t,\tau) \in test} (\frac{1}{k_{f,t}} + \frac{1}{k_{f,h}}) \tag{6}$$

$$\text{Hit@x} = \frac{1}{2 * |test|} \sum_{f=(h,r,t,\tau) \in test} (\delta_{k_{f,t}<x} + \delta_{k_{f,h}<x}) \tag{7}$$

In the formula of MRR index, $|test|$ represents the number of triples in the test set, $k_{f,h}$ and $k_{f,t}$ respectively represent the rankings of real head entities and tail entities in the candidate queue of predicted completion. The higher the ranking, the more accurate KGC effect of the model. In the Hit@x formula, $\delta_{k_{f,h}<x}$ and $\delta_{k_{f,t}<x}$ are the decision functions of whether the ranking of the real head entity and tail entity in the prediction completion sequence queue is less than x, respectively; if the ranking is less than x, it is 1; otherwise, it is 0.

5.3   Comparisons

In this paper, a hierarchical diachronic knowledge graph embedding model called HDF-ASimplE is proposed based on fragment filtering and processing. The experimental model was the HDF-ASimplE model, and the control group was six baseline models. In addition, the F-TransE and HD-TransE models which are the TransE models employing word frequency filtering and hierarchical diachronic embedding, respectively, were added as 7th and 8th controls. The above model uses datasets ICEWS14, ICEWS05-15, and GDELT to conduct KG embedding training and KGC task evaluation, and the evaluation results are shown in Table 3.

From the comparison of the evaluation parameters in the table and the bar Fig. 2 of the evaluation results of each model, it can be seen that the HDF-ASimplE model proposed in this paper has significant advantages in KGC. By comparing the evaluation parameters between the TransE and F-TransE models, and between the TransE and HD-TransE models, it is verified that word

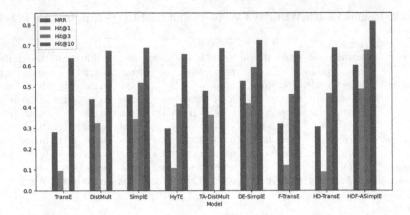

Fig. 2. HDF-ASimplE and other baseline model evaluation bar chart on ICEWS14. We show the MRR, Hit@1, Hit@3, and Hit@10 parameters for each model, which clearly showing that our approach can more accurately complete the missing triples.

frequency filtering and hierarchical diachronic embedding can improve the efficiency of the KG embedding training model.

The word frequency filtering is conducive to the knowledge representation training of the KG embedding model and solves the problem of the impact of debris information noise. Hierarchical diachronic embedding uses the hierarchical nature of the year month day time information to assign weight because the year month day information has different effects on the entity relationship information. It solves the problem of insufficient use of subsidiary information in KG and enables the trained embedding model to express knowledge more fully. Combining the two methods, we construct the HDF-ASimplE model. Compared with the DE-SimplE model, the final evaluation parameters of the HDF-ASimplE model are improved by 8% on average, and the Hit@10 parameter reaches 81.7%.

6   Conclusion

In this paper, we propose HDF-ASimplE, a temporal KG embedding model combined with fragment information filtering, and prove that the model has sufficient expressive ability, and has an efficient knowledge learning mode. The experimental comparison and evaluation of HDF-ASimplE demonstrate that the model achieves the most advanced performance compared to existing work on the TKGC, and it is stable in training. In the future, we will focus on improving the filtering efficiency of fragment information and better diachronic embedding methods to improve the performance of HDF-ASimplE.

References

1. Abboud, R., Ceylan, I.I., Lukasiewicz, T., Salvatori, T.: Boxe: a box embedding model for knowledge base completion. ArXiv abs/2007.06267 (2020)
2. Balazevic, I., Allen, C., Hospedales, T.M.: Tucker: Tensor factorization for knowledge graph completion. ArXiv abs/1901.09590 (2019)
3. Bordes, A., Chopra, S., Weston, J.: Question answering with subgraph embeddings. In: EMNLP (2014)
4. Bordes, A., Usunier, N., García-Durán, A., Weston, J., Yakhnenko, O.: Translating embeddings for modeling multi-relational data. In: NIPS (2013)
5. Cai, B., Xiang, Y., Gao, L., Zhang, H., Li, Y., Li, J.: Temporal knowledge graph completion: a survey. ArXiv abs/2201.08236 (2022)
6. Chen, K., Wang, Y., Li, Y., Li, A.: Rotateqvs: representing temporal information as rotations in quaternion vector space for temporal knowledge graph completion (2022)
7. Chen, X., Jia, S., Xiang, Y.: A review: knowledge reasoning over knowledge graph. Expert Syst. Appl. **141**, 112948 (2020). https://doi.org/10.1016/j.eswa.2019.112948
8. Dasgupta, S.S., Ray, S.N., Talukdar, P.: Hyte: hyperplane-based temporally aware knowledge graph embedding. In: Proceedings of the 2018 Conference on Empirical Methods in Natural Language Processing, pp. 2001–2011 (2018)
9. Dettmers, T., Minervini, P., Stenetorp, P., Riedel, S.: Convolutional 2d knowledge graph embeddings (2018)
10. Dong, X., et al.: Knowledge vault: a web-scale approach to probabilistic knowledge fusion. In: Proceedings of the ACM SIGKDD International Conference on Knowledge Discovery and Data Mining (2014). https://doi.org/10.1145/2623330.2623623
11. Feng, J.: Knowledge graph embedding by translating on hyperplanes (2014)
12. García-Durán, A., Dumančić, S., Niepert, M.: Learning sequence encoders for temporal knowledge graph completion (2018)
13. Goel, R., Kazemi, S.M., Brubaker, M., Poupart, P.: Diachronic embedding for temporal knowledge graph completion (2019)
14. Hochreiter, S., Schmidhuber, J.: Long short-term memory. Neural Comput. **9**, 1735–1780 (1997)
15. Ji, S., Pan, S., Cambria, E., Marttinen, P., Yu, P.S.: A survey on knowledge graphs: Representation, acquisition, and applications. IEEE Trans. Neural Netw. Learn. Syst. **33**(2), 494–514 (2022). https://doi.org/10.1109/TNNLS.2021.3070843
16. Jiang, T., Liu, T., Ge, T., Sha, L., Chang, B., Li, S., Sui, Z.: Towards time-aware knowledge graph completion. In: International Conference on Computational Linguistics (2016)
17. Kazemi, M., Poole, D.: Simple embedding for link prediction in knowledge graphs (2018)
18. Lacroix, T., Obozinski, G., Usunier, N.: Tensor decompositions for temporal knowledge base completion (2020)
19. Lautenschlager, J., Shellman, S., Ward, M.: ICEWS events and aggregations. Harvard Dataverse 3 (2015)
20. Leetaru, K., Schrodt, P.A.: GDELT: global data on events, location, and tone, 1979–2012. In: ISA Annual Convention, vol. 2, pp. 1–49. Citeseer (2013)
21. Lin, Y., Liu, Z., Sun, M., Liu, Y., Zhu, X.: Learning entity and relation embeddings for knowledge graph completion. In: AAAI Conference on Artificial Intelligence (2015)

22. Liu, K., Wu, S., Zhang, X., Wang, S.: Inter-subtask consistent representation learning for visual commonsense reasoning. In: Pimenidis, E., Angelov, P., Jayne, C., Papaleonidas, A., Aydin, M. (eds.) Artificial Neural Networks and Machine Learning - ICANN 2022. LNCS, pp. 149–161. Springer, Cham (2022). https://doi.org/10.1007/978-3-031-15934-3_13
23. Messner, J., Abboud, R., Ceylan, I.I.: Temporal knowledge graph completion using box embeddings. In: AAAI (2022)
24. Montella, S., Rojas-Barahona, L., Heinecke, J.: Hyperbolic temporal knowledge graph embeddings with relational and time curvatures (2021)
25. Nickel, M., Tresp, V., Kriegel, H.P.: A three-way model for collective learning on multi-relational data. In: ICML (2011)
26. Sun, Z., Deng, Z.H., Nie, J.Y., Tang, J.: Rotate: knowledge graph embedding by relational rotation in complex space (2019)
27. Trivedi, R., Dai, H., Wang, Y., Song, L.: Know-evolve: deep temporal reasoning for dynamic knowledge graphs (2017)
28. Trouillon, T., Welbl, J., Riedel, S., Gaussier, É., Bouchard, G.: Complex embeddings for simple link prediction. In: Proceedings of the 33nd International Conference on Machine Learning, ICML 2016. JMLR Workshop and Conference Proceedings, vol. 48, pp. 2071–2080 (2016)
29. Wang, H., et al.: RippleNet: propagating user preferences on the knowledge graph for recommender systems. In: Proceedings of the 27th ACM International Conference on Information and Knowledge Management (2018)
30. Wang, Q., Mao, Z., Wang, B., Guo, L.: Knowledge graph embedding: a survey of approaches and applications. IEEE Trans. Knowl. Data Eng. **29**(12), 2724–2743 (2017). https://doi.org/10.1109/TKDE.2017.2754499
31. Xiong, C., Power, R., Callan, J.: Explicit semantic ranking for academic search via knowledge graph embedding. In: Proceedings of the 26th International Conference on World Wide Web (2017)
32. Xu, C., Nayyeri, M., Alkhoury, F., Yazdi, H.S., Lehmann, J.: TeRo: a time-aware knowledge graph embedding via temporal rotation (2020)
33. Yang, B., Yih, W., He, X., Gao, J., Deng, L.: Embedding entities and relations for learning and inference in knowledge bases. In: 3rd International Conference on Learning Representations, ICLR 2015 (2015)
34. Zeng, W., Qin, J., Wang, X.: CKEN: collaborative knowledge-aware enhanced network for recommender systems. In: Pimenidis, E., Angelov, P., Jayne, C., Papaleonidas, A., Aydin, M. (eds.) Artificial Neural Networks and Machine Learning - ICANN 2022. LNCS, pp. 769–784. Springer Nature Switzerland, Cham (2022). https://doi.org/10.1007/978-3-031-15931-2_63
35. Zhang, S., Tay, Y., Yao, L., Liu, Q.: Quaternion knowledge graph embeddings. In: Advances in Neural Information Processing Systems, pp. 2735–2745 (2019)
36. Zhu, C., Chen, M., Fan, C., Cheng, G., Zhan, Y.: Learning from history: modeling temporal knowledge graphs with sequential copy-generation networks (2021)

K-DLM: A Domain-Adaptive Language Model Pre-Training Framework with Knowledge Graph

Jiaxin Zou[1], Zuotong Xie[1], Junhua Chen[2], Jiawei Hou[2], Qiang Yan[2], and Hai-Tao Zheng[1,3(✉)]

[1] Shenzhen International Graduate School, Tsinghua University, Shenzhen, China
{zoujx20,xiezt20}@mails.tsinghua.edu.cn, zheng.haitao@sz.tsinghua.edu.cn
[2] Department of Search and Application, Weixin Group, Tencent, China
{jeshuachen,jiaweihou,rolanyan}@tencent.com
[3] Pengcheng Laboratory, Shenzhen 518055, China

Abstract. Despite the excellent performance of pre-trained language models, such as BERT, on various natural language processing tasks, they struggle with tasks that require domain-specific knowledge. Integrating information from knowledge graphs through pre-training tasks is a common approach. However, existing models tend to focus on entity information at the word level and fail to capture the rich information in knowledge graphs. To address this issue, we propose a domain-adaptive language model pre-training framework with a knowledge graph (K-DLM). K-DLM can learn both word and lexical-semantic level entity information and relationships from the knowledge graph. It predicts entity categories and sememes for masked phrases, replaces entities in sentences according to the knowledge graph, and learns relationship information via contrastive learning. The evaluation on open-domain and domain-specific tasks demonstrates that K-DLM outperforms previous models, particularly in domain-specific contexts. Our findings highlight K-DLM as an excellent pre-training framework for knowledge-driven problems that leverage domain knowledge graphs.

Keywords: Pre-trained language model · Knowledge graph · Vertical domain search

1 Introduction

Pre-trained language models (PTMs) such as BERT [7], XLNet [26], and RoBERTa [15] have achieved promising results on various natural language processing tasks [17,22,28]. However, the domain-specific knowledge required for certain tasks is not sufficiently learned through pre-training on open-domain corpora. Incorporating external knowledge, such as knowledge graphs (KGs), can

---

J. Zou and Z. Xie—These authors contributed equally to this work.

enhance PTMs' performance on downstream tasks. Researchers have primarily focused on two approaches for integrating KGs into PTMs: embedding-based and task-based.

The embedding-based approach, such as ERNIE-Tsinghua [29], KEPLER [23] and KELM [1], employs entity embeddings or natural language descriptions of KGs for pre-training, while the task-based approach, such as LIBERT [10] and SentiLR [9], incorporates pre-training tasks to acquire factual knowledge. However, current task-based models only consider entity information at the word level, disregarding lexical-semantic level and relationship information. This limitation hampers their ability to capture comprehensive knowledge within KGs.

We introduce K-DLM, a domain-adaptive language model pre-training framework with a KG that combines embedding-based and task-based approaches. K-DLM utilizes the masked language model (MLM) from BERT, employing entity and phrase level masking to pre-train on Chinese corpora [19,20]. By integrating common sense knowledge base with the domain KG, K-DLM enhances both universal and specific knowledge. It employs soft-labeling to predict entity categories and sememes of phrases, while learning relationship information through supervised contrastive learning. Additionally, we propose a novel entity replacement strategy to create positive and negative samples for relationship learning. Our experiments demonstrate the superior performance of K-DLM over previous models, particularly on domain-specific tasks, making it an effective pre-training framework for knowledge-driven problems involving domain KGs.

In this paper, K-DLM's performance was evaluated on six tasks across 17 Chinese datasets in open and specific domains. Results show that K-DLM performs well on open-domain tasks, especially those involving sememes. Additionally, category information of entities is crucial for NER tasks. K-DLM also performs better on domain-specific tasks due to its ability to utilize relationship knowledge. Overall, the main contributions of K-DLM are as follows:

- We propose a domain-adaptive language model pre-training framework with a KG (K-DLM).
- K-DLM can fully capture word and lexical-semantic level entity information as well as relationship information in the KG.
- By incorporating external knowledge, K-DLM significantly outperforms previous models not only on all domain-specific tasks but also on most open-domain NLP tasks.

2   Related Works

2.1   Embedding-Based Approaches

KG embedding, as represented by TransE [2], models relationships by operating on low-dimensional embeddings of entities in KGs. ERNIE-Tsinghua [29] introduces the KG into pre-trained language models by combining the language and knowledge embeddings obtained by TransE. However, this approach presents a

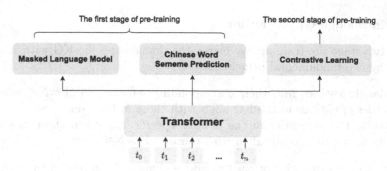

Fig. 1. Overview of the proposed Domain-Adaptive Language Model Pre-Training Framework with KG (K-DLM)

Heterogeneous Embedding Space (HES) problem where the language and knowledge embeddings are not obtained simultaneously. To address this issue more effectively, K-BERT [13] and CoLAKE [18] explicitly include knowledge triples in the training corpus to pre-train the language model and learn the knowledge representation concurrently. KEPLER [23] learns entity representation directly from entity description text and combines it with relationship embedding obtained by TransE. Furthermore, KELM [1] converts knowledge triples into fluent and natural sentences and adds them to the corpus of the pre-training model. By transforming heterogeneous KGs into text, the vector-space of knowledge representation becomes more consistent with that of language representation.

2.2 Task-Based Approaches

Since the release of BERT [7], various pre-training tasks have been proposed for different purposes, including learning external knowledge. ERNIE-Baidu [19] improved BERT's masking strategy to incorporate entity information from KGs. To overcome the limitations of predicting only single words when masked, ERNIE-Baidu masks all tokens that compose a complete phrase or entity simultaneously. SentiLR [9] extends MLM to Label-Aware MLM by adding emotional polarity to each word, while SenseBERT [11] predicts masked words and their super senses in WordNet [16] simultaneously to integrate semantic KGs into pre-trained language models. WKLM [24] replaces entities in the sentence with the same type of entities in Wikipedia and trains the model to recognize these replacements.

3 Method

In this section, we introduce K-DLM, a framework consisting of three steps: pre-processing and two-stage pre-training. The overall architecture of K-DLM is illustrated in Fig. 1.

3.1   Knowledge Graph Fusion

Before two-stage pre-training, we merge the domain-specific KG with HowNet, guided by two fundamental principles:

- We classify entities into their corresponding sememes in HowNet when the categories of entities in the KG align with those in HowNet.
- We retain the categories in the domain-specific KG when the categories of entities in the KG do not align with those in HowNet.

We refer to the categories of entities and sememes of phrases in the fused KG collectively as "sememes".

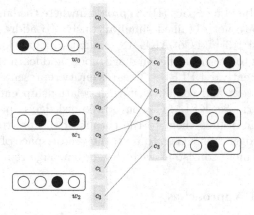

Fig. 2. Construction of mapping from characters to sememes. The set of possible sememes of each character is the union of possible sememes of all words composed of it

3.2   Masked Language Model and Chinese Word Sememe Prediction

During the first pre-training stage, K-DLM undergoes two tasks: masked language modeling and Chinese word sememe prediction. For masked language modeling, entity and phrase level masking strategies are employed. In the Chinese word sememe prediction task, K-DLM is trained to predict sememes in the fused KG. To accommodate KG integration, we modify the embedding layer and pre-training objective while utilizing the Transformer Encoder [21].

Embedding Layer. The embedding layer combines multiple embeddings to generate the input representation. We modify the input embedding E_{word} by summing four embeddings:

$$E_{word} = E_{tok} + E_{sem} + E_{seg} + E_{pos} \tag{1}$$

where E_{sem} and E_{pos} follow the original BERT. For E_{tok}, we utilize entity and phrase level masking strategies, masking entire words instead of individual Chinese characters. To capture the linguistic characteristics of Modern Chinese, we introduce a new split-and-merge mapping strategy. Let $X = (x_0, x_1, \cdots, x_n)$ denote the vocabulary index of a sentence $(c_0, c_1, \cdots, c_n)$, where n is the sentence length and $x_i \in \mathbb{R}^{D_W}$. E_{sem} is computed using a two-layer mapping:

$$E_{sem} = SMX \tag{2}$$

where $M \in \mathbb{R}^{D_S \times D_W}$ is a static mapping from characters to the union of corresponding sememes constructed with the fused KG, and $S \in \mathbb{R}^{d \times D_S}$ is a learnable mapping from sememes to the internal Transformer dimension d, where D_S is the size of the sememe vocabulary. Figure 2 illustrates an example of the construction process for M.

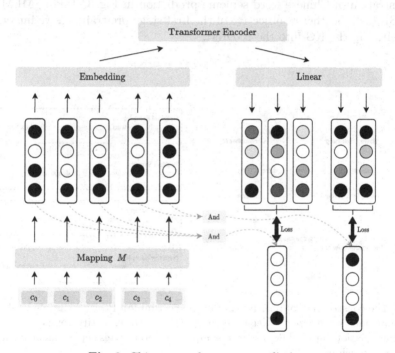

Fig. 3. Chinese word sememe prediction

Pre-Training Objective. We enhanced the original Masked Language Model (MLM) used in BERT by introducing entity and phrase level masking. Specifically, we mask all Chinese characters that belong to a complete word and require the model to recover the entire word during MLM pre-training. Besides, in our paper, we focus on predicting the allowed sememes of Chinese words, not characters. Thus, we propose $\mathcal{L}_{CSP}$ for Chinese word sememe prediction:

$$\mathcal{L}_{CSP} = -\log \sum_{s \in \bigcap_{c \in w} PS(c)} p(s|context)$$

$$- \sum_{s \in \bigcap_{c \in w} PS(c)} \frac{1}{\left| \bigcap_{c \in w} PS(c) \right|} \log p(s|context) \tag{3}$$

where c is the character-level masked token and w is the whole Chinese word which c belongs to. The second penalty term enables the model to predict the given token c as all sememes in $PS(c)$ with possibility tending to equality, which enhanced the generalization ability. The output embedding of tokens belonging to the same word can be averaged according to the word segmentation boundary and used to predict all possible sememes of the whole Chinese word. We show an illustration of Chinese word sememe prediction in Fig. 3. Taking MLM task and CSP task together as objective of the first stage pre-training, we introduced the entities in the KG into the K-DLM:

$$\mathcal{L}_{stage1} = \mathcal{L}_{MLM} + \mathcal{L}_{CSP} \tag{4}$$

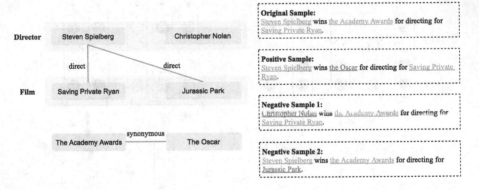

Fig. 4. The construction of positive and negative samples. Positive sample is obtained by synonymous replacement. Negative sample 1 illustrates entity replacement based on unique relationships, while negative sample 2 demonstrates replacement using non-unique relationships

3.3   Contrastive Learning

To incorporate entity relationships into K-DLM, we conduct the second stage of pre-training due to the inherent complexity of learning explicit relationships through MLM tasks. Following the contrastive framework of SimCLR [3], we introduce a novel replacement strategy for relationship types in the knowledge graph, generating positive and negative examples. Our second-stage pre-training objective employs a cross-entropy loss with in-batch negatives [4].

Replacement Strategy. In the fused KG, relationships encompass both general semantic relationships (e.g., synonyms, hypernyms, and hyponyms) and domain-specific relationships between entities. To connect corpus entities to the KG, we employ an off-the-shelf entity linking tool[1], discarding sentences without entities. For an entity e, we define positive $(P(e))$ and negative $(N(e))$ candidate sets. We propose three replacement strategies for relationships:

- **Semantic Relationship Replacement**: Synonymous replacements are considered positive samples, while hypernymous and hyponymous replacements are treated as semantic changes and used to construct negative samples. Specifically, synonyms of e are added to $P(e)$, and hypernyms and hyponyms of e are added to $N(e)$.
- **Unique Relationship Replacement**: This strategy is applied when a sentence contains multiple entities. We design a replacement strategy for each entity based on relationship uniqueness. For entities e_1 and e_2 in a sentence, assuming e_1 remains constant and e_2 is replaced, the relationship between e_1 and e_2 is denoted as r, with type t. If r is the unique relationship of type t for e_1, we select an entity of the same type as e_2 from the KG and add it to $N(e_2)$. To increase task difficulty, we calculate the edit distance between the original entity and each entity of the same type, randomly selecting from the 10 entities with the smallest edit distance as replacements.
- **Non-unique Relationship Replacement**: This strategy is employed when e_1 has relationships with other entities in the KG, excluding r, of type t. Now, r is considered a non-unique relationship for e_1. We randomly select an entity from all entities with the same relationship to e_1 and add it to $N(e_2)$.

Figure 4 illustrates the creation of positive and negative samples. The "direct" relationship between directors and films is used for comprehensibility purposes, but is not included in ServiceKG.

4   Experiments

In this section, we present the details of training setup and conduct experiments on 17 Chinese datasets, among which 13 are open-domain, and 4 are specific-domain, to answer the following research questions:

- **RQ1:** What is the role of sememes and types of phrases and entities in open-domain classification tasks?
- **RQ2:** How does our proposed method perform compared with others of introducing KG into pre-trained language model?
- **RQ3:** Could our proposed method benefit from domain KG in domain-specific tasks?

---

[1] Developed by WeChat search algorithm team.

4.1   Experiment Setup

Pre-training Corpora. To evaluate our proposed method and compare it with previous works [6,13], we pre-train our model using five Chinese corpora. These corpora include **WikiZh**, which is utilized to train **bert-base-chinese** in [7], **WebtextZh**, which is used to train **K-BERT** in [13], **Sogou baike**, **Baike QA**, and **NewsZh**. The total size of these corpora is similar to the pre-training corpus of **Chinese RoBERTa-wwm-ext** in [6], which is not publicly available. We construct our pre-training corpus, named "ext", utilizing the above five corpora about encyclopedia, QA, and news to ensure impartial comparison with the pre-training corpus of **Chinese RoBERTa-wwm-ext**.

Knowledge Graph. We utilize Hownet[2] [8] as our source of common sense knowledge. Unlike K-BERT [13], we only integrate some concepts and sememes from Hownet into the domain KG, named ServiceKG. ServiceKG is constructed from billions of search logs and contains around 60k nodes and 200k relations of ten types of nodes and five types of relations. Due to copyright reasons, we cannot publish the complete ServiceKG. The sememes and relations from Hownet are used in all our experiments, including the results marked as **ServiceKG** in Table 3. Limited by model scale and computing power, we selected the top 97 sememes out of 2196, which cover over 70% of the sememe labels in Hownet.

Baselines. We compare our proposed K-DLM with five baselines in this paper:

- **Google BERT**, the official BERT (Chinese) pretrained on **Wikizh** [7].
- **Chinese RoBERTa-wwm-ext**, the RoBERTa-like BERT pretrained on **ext** corpus [6].
- **K-BERT**, the K-BERT pretrained on **WikiZh** and **WebtextZh**, utilizing HowNet as a KG [13].
- **RoBERTa-wwm**, our implementation of RoBERTa-wwm pretrained on **Wikizh** and **WebtextZh**.
- **RoBERTa-wwm-ext**, our implementation of RoBERTa-wwm-ext pretrained on our **ext** corpus.

Evaluation Benchmarks. To evaluate the performance of our proposed K-DLM, we conducted experiments on 17 datasets belonging to six natural language understanding tasks, as follows:

- **Natural Language Inference:** CMNLI [25], XNLI [5].
- **Winograd Schema Challenge:** CLUEWSC2020 [25].
- **Semantic Similarity:** AFQMC [25], LCQMC [14], CSL [25].
- **Sentiment Analysis:** Book-Review [13], Chnsenticorp [13], Shopping [13], Weibo [13].

---

[2] https://openhownet.thunlp.org.

- **Named Entity Recognition:** MSRA-NER [12], Finance-NER [13], Medicine-NER [13].
- **Text Multi-Class Classification:** TNEWS [25], IFLYTEK [25], Affair-CLS, Service-CLS.

Out of the 17 datasets mentioned above, Finance-NER, Medicine-NER, Affair-CLS, and Service-CLS are domain-specific, while the rest are open-domain. Affair-CLS and Service-CLS are five-class datasets from two vertical search scenarios within WeChat, a platform with billions of daily active users. Affair-CLS is related to government affairs search, while Service-CLS is related to service search. In our experiments, we perform coarse-grained binary classification by grouping labels 0 to 2 as weakly relevant and labels 3 and 4 as strongly relevant.

Training Details. To clearly demonstrate the effect of introducing the KG, we used the pre-training configuration of RoBERTa-wwm [6], which employs the WordPiece encoding scheme. Our hyperparameters aligned with those of Google BERT, where model size matched the $BERT_{base}$ configuration, which is L=12, H=768, A=12, with a total of 102M parameters. Inputs were constructed as **DOC-SENTENCES** as in RoBERTa-wwm. We utilized the LAMB optimizer [27] with a batch size scaled from 512 to 32K on 128 T V100 GPUs with 32GB VRAM. Our model underwent pre-training for 15625 steps with an initial learning rate of 5e-3 and implemented a warm-up strategy for the first 20% of steps, followed by a linear decay of the learning rate.

4.2 Overall Performance

In this section, we compared our proposed K-DLM with several baseline pre-trained language models above respectively.

Table 1. Results of various models on classification tasks in CLUE benchmark (Acc.%)

Models	AFQMC	TNEWS	IFLYTEK	CMNLI	CLUEWSC2020	CSL
Google BERT	74.16	56.09	60.37	79.47	59.60	79.63
Chinese RoBERTa-wwm-ext	74.30	57.51	**60.8**	80.70	67.20	80.67
RoBERTa-wwm-ext	**74.47**	57.26	60.37	80.31	80.92	81.07
K-DLM-ext	74.40	**57.76**	59.37	**81.21**	**85.20**	**81.30**

Table 2. Results of various models on seven open-domain tasks (F1% for MSRA-NER, Acc.% for others)

Models	Book-Review		Chnsenticorp		Shopping		Weibo		XNLI		LCQMC		MSRA-NER	
	Dev	Test	Dev	Test	Dev	Test	Dev	Test	Dev	Test	Dev	Test	Dev	Test
Google BERT	88.3	87.5	93.3	94.3	96.7	96.3	98.2	98.3	76.0	75.4	88.4	86.2	94.5	93.6
K-BERT(HowNet)	88.5	87.4	**95.4**	95.6	96.9	96.9	**98.3**	**98.4**	77.2	77.0	89.2	87.1	96.3	95.6
RoBERTa-wwm	89.2	88.1	95.1	94.9	96.9	97.0	97.7	98.0	77.6	77.7	88.7	87.0	96.3	95.3
K-DLM(HowNet)	**89.3**	**88.3**	95.3	**95.6**	**97.1**	**97.1**	97.9	97.7	**78.6**	**78.1**	89.9	88.6	96.7	96.8

Classification Tasks in CLUE Benchmark (RQ1). We compare our K-DLM with Chinese RoBERTa-wwm-ext [6] to highlight the advantages of incorporating sememe and category knowledge. Table 1 presents the results on the development set of six sentence classification tasks in the CLUE benchmark [25]. The performance of Google BERT and Chinese RoBERTa-wwm-ext is obtained from the public leaderboard of the CLUE benchmark, while we use the hyperparameters provided by Chinese RoBERTa-wwm-ext without further tuning. Our observations can be categorized as follows:

– Sememes help correctly classify sentences with categories based on commonsense phrases or entities, showing a positive impact on tasks such as TNEWS, CMNLI, CLUEWSC2020, and CSL.
– In contrast, when domain-specific entities consisting of common characters impact the category (AFQMC and IFLYTEK), sememes lead to incorrect category predictions, indicating that adding these entities into the KG can solve the issue.

Other Open-Domain Tasks (RQ2). To compare our K-DLM with K-BERT, which is equipped with HowNet, we pre-trained both **RoBERTa-wwm** and our **K-DLM** on the same corpus as K-BERT (HowNet) as stated in [13]. We then evaluated the models on seven open-domain tasks, with each dataset divided into *train*, *dev*, and *test* subsets. We fine-tuned the models on the *train* subset, selected the best model based on the *dev* subset, and evaluated its performance on the *test* subset. The experimental results are presented in Table 2.

– K-DLM did not show a significant performance improvement for sentiment analysis tasks (i.e., Book-Review, Chnsenticorp, and Shopping) because sentiment mainly relies on emotion words and negations rather than knowledge. Moreover, for colloquial-style sentences from social media (i.e., Weibo), inaccurate sememe predictions impaired the model's ability to judge emotions.
– K-DLM outperforms K-BERT on common knowledge-dependent tasks (XNLI, LCQMC, and MSRA-NER) by addressing a problem encountered by K-BERT. Fine-tuning K-BERT requires word segmentation and NER, which introduce errors and restrict knowledge utilization. In contrast, our character-level sememe incorporation in K-DLM benefits downstream tasks without entity linking and improves decision-making for entities outside the KG.

Table 3. Results of various models on specific-domain tasks (%)

Models	Finance-NER			Medicine-NER			Affair-CLS			Service-CLS		
	P.	R.	F1	P.	R.	F1	P.	R.	F1	P.	R.	F1
Google BERT	84.8	87.4	86.1	91.9	93.1	92.5	97.8	91.0	94.3	**77.1**	84.9	80.8
K-BERT(HowNet)	86.3	**88.5**	87.3	93.5	93.8	93.7	-	-	-	-	-	-
K-BERT(ServiceKG)	-	-	-	-	-	-	97.8	90.9	94.2	76.8	85.2	80.8
RoBERTa-wwm	86.5	87.9	87.2	93.7	94.5	94.1	97.9	91.3	94.5	76.5	85.9	80.9
K-DLM	**86.9**	88.2	**87.5**	**94.0**	**95.0**	**94.5**	97.9	**92.2**	**95.0**	75.5	**88.7**	**81.5**

Specific-Domain Tasks (RQ3). We conduct experiments on four specific-domain tasks to assess whether domain KG benefits K-DLM. Following the experiment setup in [13] for the Finance-NER and Medicine-NER tasks, we evaluate models equipped with HowNet on these tasks. For our self-developed **ServiceKG**, we fine-tune the **RoBERTa-wwm** as described in Sect. 4.2 using the method proposed by K-BERT with this KG, and obtain **K-BERT (ServiceKG)** for comparison with our K-DLM. The results are summarized in Table 3.

- In domain-specific NER tasks, HowNet's financial and medical knowledge aids entity identification in sentences. Our K-DLM outperforms K-BERT (HowNet) in terms of precision and F1 score, indicating its successful classification of entities into correct categories with the assistance of sememes.
- For our query intention classification tasks (Affair-CLS and Service-CLS), we focus more on the relationship between entities (i.e., services offered to something) than on the types of entities in the query. Therefore, the phrase and entity mask has no significant effect. Because queries are relatively short, adding entity relation entity triples into a query using K-BERT can cause semantic drift that cannot be ignored. In contrast, our **K-DLM** introduces relations by replacement without changing the sentence length, resulting in improved performance in short text classification.

5 Conclusion

In summary, our proposed K-DLM framework utilizes a Chinese soft-label scheme, split-and-merge mapping strategy, and replacement-based relation injection strategy for short text processing. This approach enhances the utilization of sememes and category information, leading to improved model performance in vertical domain query understanding while avoiding semantic drift. Experimental results demonstrate that using sememes of Chinese words enhances the performance of open-domain classification tasks relying on common knowledge. We conducted comparisons with alternative KG introduction methods to assess efficacy and applicability. Additionally, our approach enables adaptability to tasks across diverse domains by leveraging domain-specific KGs during pre-training.

Acknowledgments. This research is supported by National Natural Science Foundation of China (Grant No.62276154), Research Center for Computer Network (Shenzhen) Ministry of Education, Beijing Academy of Artificial Intelligence (BAAI), the Natural Science Foundation of Guangdong Province (Grant No. 2023A1515012914), Basic Research Fund of Shenzhen City (Grant No. JCYJ20210324120012033 and JSGG20210802154402007), the Major Key Project of PCL for Experiments and Applications (PCL2021A06), and Overseas Cooperation Research Fund of Tsinghua Shenzhen International Graduate School (HW2021008).

References

1. Agarwal, O., Ge, H., Shakeri, S., Al-Rfou, R.: Knowledge graph based synthetic corpus generation for knowledge-enhanced language model pre-training. In: NAACL-HLT, pp. 3554–3565. Association for Computational Linguistics (2021)
2. Bordes, A., Usunier, N., García-Durán, A., Weston, J., Yakhnenko, O.: Translating embeddings for modeling multi-relational data. In: NIPS, pp. 2787–2795 (2013)
3. Chen, T., Kornblith, S., Norouzi, M., Hinton, G.E.: A simple framework for contrastive learning of visual representations. In: ICML. Proceedings of Machine Learning Research, vol. 119, pp. 1597–1607. PMLR (2020)
4. Chen, T., Sun, Y., Shi, Y., Hong, L.: On sampling strategies for neural network-based collaborative filtering. In: KDD, pp. 767–776. ACM (2017)
5. Conneau, A., et al.: XNLI: evaluating cross-lingual sentence representations. In: EMNLP, pp. 2475–2485. Association for Computational Linguistics (2018)
6. Cui, Y., Che, W., Liu, T., Qin, B., Yang, Z.: Pre-training with whole word masking for Chinese BERT. IEEE ACM Trans. Audio Speech Lang. Process. **29**, 3504–3514 (2021)
7. Devlin, J., Chang, M., Lee, K., Toutanova, K.: BERT: pre-training of deep bidirectional transformers for language understanding. In: NAACL-HLT (1), pp. 4171–4186. Association for Computational Linguistics (2019)
8. Dong, Z., Dong, Q.: HowNet - a hybrid language and knowledge resource. In: International Conference on Natural Language Processing and Knowledge Engineering, 2003. Proceedings 2003, pp. 820–824 (2003)
9. Ke, P., Ji, H., Liu, S., Zhu, X., Huang, M.: SentiLARE: sentiment-aware language representation learning with linguistic knowledge. In: EMNLP (1), pp. 6975–6988. Association for Computational Linguistics (2020)
10. Lauscher, A., Vulic, I., Ponti, E.M., Korhonen, A., Glavas, G.: Specializing unsupervised pretraining models for word-level semantic similarity. In: COLING, pp. 1371–1383. International Committee on Computational Linguistics (2020)
11. Levine, Y., et al.: SenseBERT: driving some sense into BERT. In: ACL, pp. 4656–4667. Association for Computational Linguistics (2020)
12. Levow, G.: The third international Chinese language processing bakeoff: word segmentation and named entity recognition. In: SIGHAN@COLING/ACL, pp. 108–117. Association for Computational Linguistics (2006)
13. Liu, W., et al.: K-BERT: enabling language representation with knowledge graph. In: AAAI, pp. 2901–2908. AAAI Press (2020)
14. Liu, X., et al.: LCQMC: a large-scale Chinese question matching corpus. In: COLING, pp. 1952–1962. Association for Computational Linguistics (2018)
15. Liu, Y., et al.: RoBERTa: a robustly optimized BERT pretraining approach. CoRR abs/1907.11692 (2019)
16. Miller, G.A.: WordNet: a lexical database for English. Commun. ACM **38**(11), 39–41 (1995)
17. Rajpurkar, P., Zhang, J., Lopyrev, K., Liang, P.: SQuAD: 100, 000+ questions for machine comprehension of text. In: EMNLP, pp. 2383–2392. The Association for Computational Linguistics (2016)
18. Sun, T., et al.: CoLAKE: contextualized language and knowledge embedding. In: COLING, pp. 3660–3670. International Committee on Computational Linguistics (2020)
19. Sun, Y., et al.: ERNIE: enhanced representation through knowledge integration. CoRR abs/1904.09223 (2019)

20. Sun, Y., et al.: ERNIE 2.0: a continual pre-training framework for language under-standing. In: AAAI, pp. 8968–8975. AAAI Press (2020)
21. Vaswani, A., et al.: Attention is all you need. In: NIPS, pp. 5998–6008 (2017)
22. Wang, A., Singh, A., Michael, J., Hill, F., Levy, O., Bowman, S.R.: GLUE: a multi-task benchmark and analysis platform for natural language understanding. In: EMNLP, pp. 353–355. Association for Computational Linguistics (2018)
23. Wang, X., Gao, T., Zhu, Z., Zhang, Z., Liu, Z., Li, J., Tang, J.: KEPLER: a unified model for knowledge embedding and pre-trained language representation. Trans. Assoc. Comput. Linguistics **9**, 176–194 (2021)
24. Xiong, W., Du, J., Wang, W.Y., Stoyanov, V.: Pretrained encyclopedia: weakly supervised knowledge-pretrained language model. In: ICLR. OpenReview.net (2020)
25. Xu, L., et al.: CLUE: a Chinese language understanding evaluation benchmark. In: COLING, pp. 4762–4772. International Committee on Computational Linguistics (2020)
26. Yang, Z., Dai, Z., Yang, Y., Carbonell, J.G., Salakhutdinov, R., Le, Q.V.: XLNet: generalized autoregressive pretraining for language understanding. In: NeurIPS, pp. 5754–5764 (2019)
27. You, Y., et al.: Large batch optimization for deep learning: training BERT in 76 minutes. In: ICLR. OpenReview.net (2020)
28. Zellers, R., Bisk, Y., Schwartz, R., Choi, Y.: SWAG: a large-scale adversarial dataset for grounded commonsense inference. In: EMNLP, pp. 93–104. Association for Computational Linguistics (2018)
29. Zhang, Z., Han, X., Liu, Z., Jiang, X., Sun, M., Liu, Q.: ERNIE: enhanced language representation with informative entities. In: ACL (1), pp. 1441–1451. Association for Computational Linguistics (2019)

Label Enhanced Graph Attention Network for Truth Inference

Ningjing Zhao[1,2], Xingrui Zhuo[1,2], Gongqing Wu[1,2(✉)], and Zan Zhang[1,2]

[1] Key Laboratory of Knowledge Engineering with Big Data (The Ministry of Education of China), Hefei University of Technology, Hefei 230009, Anhui, People's Republic of China
{Ningjing.Zhao,zxr}@mail.hfut.edu.cn, {wugq,zanzhang}@hfut.edu.cn
[2] School of Computer Science and Information Engineering, Hefei University of Technology, Hefei 230601, Anhui, People's Republic of China

Abstract. Crowdsourcing platforms tend to provide redundant noise labels when annotating data for machine learning, which promotes truth inference to be proposed for crowdsourced labels denoising. Existing truth inference methods have effectively improved the model's inference quality by utilizing **Graph Neural Networks** (GNNs) to mine potential crowdsourcing relationships. However, the GNN-based methods fail to reflect crowdsourcing behaviors comprehensively when mining crowdsourcing relationships in a task-worker graph, which limits their performance. To cope with this challenge, we propose a Label Enhanced Graph Attention Network for truth inference, which realizes GNN-based truth inference on complete crowdsourcing behaviors to explore latent crowdsourcing relationships between tasks and workers more effectively. Specifically, we construct an attentive label semantic propagation module based on a graph attention network, which propagates crowdsourced label semantics into the process of information aggregation to represent complete crowdsourcing behaviors. In addition, we design a label-aware graph encoder, which captures the semantics of crowdsourced labels more efficiently by reducing the difference between the predicted and the actual distribution of crowdsourced labels. Extensive experiments on eight real-world datasets demonstrate that LEGAT outperforms eight state-of-the-art methods.

Keywords: Truth inference · Crowdsourcing · Graph attention network · Label-aware propagation

1 Introduction

Crowdsourcing is a problem-solving method based on crowd intelligence which excels at some tasks that are simple for humans but difficult for computers, such as image classification [1], and recommender system [2]. Several

This work was supported by the Program for Innovative Research Team in University of the Ministry of Education under grant IRT_17R32, and the National Natural Science Foundation of China under grant 62120106008.

L. Iliadis et al. (Eds.): ICANN 2023, LNCS 14257, pp. 460–471, 2023.
https://doi.org/10.1007/978-3-031-44216-2_38

crowdsourcing platforms, such as Amazon Mechanical Turk[1], have been widely applied to large-scale data annotation tasks. Large-scale annotation tasks are distributed to crowdsourcing workers through the crowdsourcing platform to obtain crowdsourced labels; and this process usually consists of a series of **crowdsourcing behaviors**, which are quantized as crowdsourcing triples $< task, worker, label >$. Due to the openness of crowdsourcing platforms, the expertise and the annotation quality of crowdsourcing workers for different tasks vary greatly, leading to the noise of crowdsourced labels. Therefore, **truth inference** is proposed to deduce a task's truth from multiple labels that crowdsourcing workers provide.

During recent decades, many truth inference methods have been proposed. Traditional truth inference methods can be divided into two categories: methods based on distance optimization and methods based on **P**robabilistic **G**raphical **M**odels (PGM). Besides, some studies [3] have mined the **crowdsourcing relationships** (e.g., the copy relation of workers) by joint distribution. However, due to that traditional machine learning fails to comprehensively model connections among sparse crowdsourcing data, these methods have difficulty in obtaining latent crowdsourcing relationships to improve the quality of truth inference. To solve this problem, recent studies attempt to introduce GNN to capture crowdsourcing relationships effectively.

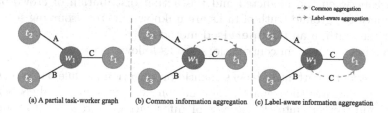

(a) A partial task-worker graph   (b) Common information aggregation   (c) Label-aware information aggregation

Fig. 1. Example of information propagation path in truth inference.

Existing GNN-based methods [4,5] utilize crowdsourced labels to initialize the representations of workers and tasks and represent crowdsourcing behaviors as an **information propagation path** from a worker to a task in a task-worker graph (as shown in Fig. 1(a), worker w_1 annotating task t_1 with label C can be represented as an information path $w_1 \xrightarrow{C} t_1$), which assists GNN-based truth inference methods perform well by mining the relationships between tasks and workers. However, it is difficult for existing GNN-based methods to effectively identify the importance of different labels' semantics in the information aggregation of a worker-task pair, which limits their performance. As shown in Fig. 1(b), although the representation of w_1 consists of the semantic information of crowdsourced labels A, B, and C (we assume that C is definitely useful for

---

[1] https://www.mturk.com/.

the aggregation between t_1 and w_1), existing GNN-based methods have difficulty in sensing the importance of the other two labels A and B (A and B are not provided by w_1 for t_1) when propagating the information of w_1 to t_1, which may cause the model to propagate noisy information to t_1, thereby disturbing with the model's inference. The reason causing the above result is that related methods lack a label-aware propagation mechanism to enhance the role of crowdsourced label semantics in the aggregation of worker-task pairs, that is, failing to completely reflect the crowdsourcing behaviors, which leads to information inductive bias when aggregating crowdsourced labels' semantic information.

To cope with this problem, we propose a **L**abel **E**nhanced **G**raph **A**ttention network (LEGAT) for truth inference, which realizes GNN-based truth inference on complete crowdsourcing behaviors to explore latent crowdsourcing relationships between tasks and workers more effectively. Specifically, we construct an attentive label semantic propagation module based on a **G**raph **A**ttention network (GAT) [6], which propagates the semantics of crowdsourced labels between worker-task pairs into the process of information aggregation to represent complete crowdsourcing behaviors. As shown in Fig. 1(c), we regard the semantic information of label C as path information of $w_1 \xrightarrow{C} t_1$ to make the model aware of the importance of the semantics of different labels in w_1 for inferring the truth of t_1. In addition, we design a label-aware graph encoder, which captures the semantics of crowdsourced labels more efficiently by reducing the difference between the predicted and the actual distribution of crowdsourced labels. Since the ground truth of tasks are unknown in crowdsourcing scenarios, we infer the truth in an **unsupervised** method.

In summary, our main contributions are as follows:

- We construct an attentive label semantic propagation module based on GAT, which propagates the semantic information of crowdsourced labels between tasks and workers into the process of information aggregation to represent complete crowdsourcing behaviors.
- We design a label-aware graph encoder that captures the crowdsourcing label semantics efficiently by reducing the difference between the predicted and the actual distribution of crowdsourced labels.
- We conduct extensive experiments on eight real datasets and compare our model with eight state-of-the-art algorithms. Experimental results show that our method outperforms these compared algorithms in truth inference.

2   Related Work

Existing studies on truth inference are mainly divided into three categories: distance optimization methods, PGM-based methods and crowdsourcing relationship-based methods.

Distance Optimization Methods. Conflict **R**esolution on **H**eterogeneous Data (CRH) [7] is a typical algorithm based on distance optimization. Some existing studies observe that if a worker annotates more tasks, then the worker is more confident. Thus, [8] also considers worker confidence in modeling a worker's quality, which depends on the number of tasks annotated by the worker. In addition, the MinMax algorithm proposed by Zhou et al. [9] leverages the idea of minimax entropy [10].

PGM-Based Methods. There are also a part of truth inference algorithms that are based on PGM. Gianluca et al. [11] proposed the **Z**en**C**rowd algorithm (ZC) to complete large-scale entity linking. As an extension of ZC, the **G**enerative model of **L**abels, **A**bilities and **D**ifficulties (GLAD) [12] considers both task difficulty and worker probability. Unlike ZC, GLAD adopts a gradient descent method to optimize the objective function. Due to that [11] and [12] use point estimate, Karger et al. [13] first introduced the belief propagation technology for truth inference. The **D**awid and **S**kene algorithm (DS) [14] constructs a confusion matrix for each worker, which denotes the probability that the worker will give the correct label when the truth is known. Li et al. [15] proposed a **B**ayesian **W**eighted **A**verage (BWA) to infer the truth from highly redundant data, which uses a bayesian graphical model with conjugate priors.

Crowdsourcing Relationship-Based Methods. Although traditional truth inference methods have achieved good performance, these methods fail to consider the latent crowdsourcing relationship. [16] and [17] try to mine relationships between tasks by manually constructing task features. Wu et al. [4] constructed a heterogeneous task-worker graph and inferred the truth from task representations. But the semi-supervised training paradigm is not applicable to most crowdsourcing scenarios. Besides, Wu et al. [5] proposed a **R**eliability-driven **M**ulti-view **G**raph **E**mbedding framework for **T**ruth inference (TiReMGE).

3 Preliminaries

Problem Setup. In general, we consider crowdsourcing tasks as multi-class single-choice tasks. Assuming that the task has K label classes, the label set of tasks is $C = \{c_k\}_{k=1}^{K}$. We use $U = \{u_i\}_{i=1}^{M}$ to denote a set of M tasks, and $V = \{v_j\}_{j=1}^{N}$ to denote a set of N workers. Since a task is assigned to several workers, we use V^{u_i} to denote a set of workers that have annotated task u_i, and similarly, U^{v_j} to denote a set of tasks annotated by worker v_j. $L = \{l_{ij} \mid l_{ij} \in C, u_i \in U, v_j \in V^{u_i}\}$ is used to denote all labels collected from workers on the crowdsourcing tasks, where l_{ij} is a label annotated by worker v_j to task u_i and $l_{ij} \in C$.

Constructing Task-Worker Graph. We define a task-worker graph $\mathcal{G} = \{U, V, \Phi\}$ to mine crowdsourcing relationships between tasks and workers. U, V represent a set of task nodes and a set of worker nodes respectively, and Φ represents a set of graph edges, which is expressed as $\Phi = \{(u_i, v_j) \mid u_i \in U, v_j \in V^{u_i}\}$.

4 Method

In this section, we elaborate the design schema of LEGAT according to the three modules that shown in Fig. 2.

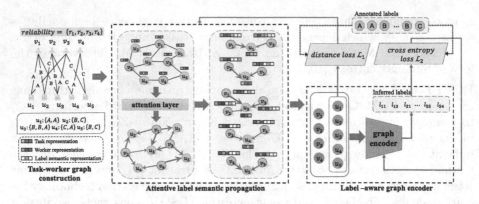

Fig. 2. Overall framework of LEGAT. It includes (1) a task-worker graph construction module, (2) an attentive label semantic propagation module, and (3) a label-aware graph encoder.

4.1 Initialization of Node Representation

We now describe the node initialization criterion for graph $\mathcal{G}$. Since tasks and workers are difficult to be represented by randomly initialized representation, we initialize node representations with worker reliabilities. Usually, when the present reliabilities of all workers are known, we can obtain the weight of a label by aggregating the reliabilities of workers who provide this label for a task.

$$x_{u_i}^* = \sum_{v_j \in V^{u_i}} r_j l_{ij}, \tag{1}$$

where $\{r_j\}_{j=1}^N$ represent the reliabilities of crowdsourcing workers, l_{ij} is the one-hot vector of label l_{ij}, $l_{ij} \in \mathbb{R}^K$, and K is the number of label classes. If $l_{ij} \in C$ and $l_{ij} = c_k$, it implies that the kth element in l_{ij} is 1. Obviously, the t-th element in $x_{u_i}^*$ represents the weight of the t-th class label that corresponds to x_{u_i}. Since l_{ij} is a sparse vector, vector $x_{u_i}^*$ multiplied by l_{ij} and r_j is also sparse. Therefore, we regularize the initialized node representation with softmax to obtain dense representations.

$$x_{u_i} = \text{softmax}(x_{u_i}^*), x_{u_i} \in \mathbb{R}^K. \tag{2}$$

Similarly, we initialize the worker node representations with the worker reliabilities and annotated labels.

$$x_{v_j}^* = \sum_{u_i \in U^{v_j}} r_j l_{ij}, \ \ x_{v_j} = \text{softmax}(x_{v_j}^*), x_{v_j} \in \mathbb{R}^K. \tag{3}$$

4.2 Attentive Label Semantic Propagation

To propagate label semantic information while mining crowdsourcing relationships, we propose an attentive label semantic propagation module based on GAT.

Then, we aggregate adjacent node feature and label semantic information based on these coefficients.

To enhance the representation ability of the nodes, we need to convert the input vector into a high dimensional representation. Based on that, we use linear transformation to transform the representations of task nodes and worker nodes separately:

$$h_{u_i}^T = W_u x_{u_i}^T + b_u, h_{v_j}^T = W_v x_{v_j}^T + b_v, \tag{4}$$

where h_{u_i} and h_{v_j} denote the transformed task u_i representation and worker v_j representation respectively, $W_u, W_v \in \mathbb{R}^{D \times K}$ denote two trainable weight matrices, and $b_u, b_v \in \mathbb{R}^D$ denote trainable biases. D is the dimensionality of the transformed representations after the linear transformation. Besides, $\cdot^T$ denotes a transposition operation.

Then, we use a sharing mechanism of GAT to compute α_{ij}, which is denoted as the importance coefficient between u_i and v_j.

$$\alpha_{ij} = \frac{\exp(f([h_{u_i}||h_{v_j}]\Theta^T))}{\sum\limits_{v_z \in V^{u_i}} \exp(f([h_{u_i}||h_{v_z}]\Theta^T))}, \tag{5}$$

where f denotes the LeakyRelu function, Θ denotes the shared weight matrix, and $||$ denotes a concatenation operation.

After obtaining the important coefficients between adjacent nodes, we can dynamically aggregate the adjacent node information and label semantic information through the message propagation mechanism [4] to update node representations. As crowdsourcing labels are mapped to semantic representation of the edges in $\mathcal{G}$, the edge can be represented by one-hot vectors of labels, e.g., the edge representation between task node u_i and worker node v_j is l_{ij}. Therefore, the updated node representation is formulated as:

$$h'_{u_i} = \sigma(\sum\limits_{v_j \in V_{u_i}} \alpha_{ij}[h_{u_i}||l_{ij}]), h'_{u_i} \in \mathbb{R}^K, \tag{6}$$

where σ denotes the ReLU function, a non-linear activation function, and W_a denotes a weight matrix for dimensional change.

[7] argues that workers with higher reliability are more likely to provide the truth, and the truth is closer to the label annotated by the worker with higher reliability. Based on this idea, we design the objective function to minimize the weighted distance between the task representations and one-hot vectors of crowdsourced labels, where the weights refer to the worker reliabilities.

$$\mathcal{L}_1 = \sum\limits_{v_j \in V} r_j \sum\limits_{u_i \in U^{v_j}} \| h'_{u_i} - l_{ij} \|_2. \tag{7}$$

In addition, if the label annotated by the worker is close to the ground truth, the reliability of the worker is high. Therefore, we use the distance between task representations and crowdshourcing label's one-hot vectors to update the reliability. Similarly, the updated worker reliability will be involved in the next iteration.

$$r_j = -\log\left(\frac{\sum\limits_{u_i \in U^{v_j}} \| \boldsymbol{h}'_{u_i} - \boldsymbol{l}_{ij} \|_2}{\sum\limits_{v_j \in V} \sum\limits_{u_i \in U^{v_j}} \| \boldsymbol{h}'_{u_i} - \boldsymbol{l}_{ij} \|_2}\right). \tag{8}$$

4.3   Label-Aware Graph Encoder

In this section, we design a label-aware graph encoder to improve the model ability to capture label semantic information by reducing the difference between the predicted and the actual distribution of crowdsourced labels.

We design a two-layer **Graph Convolutional Networks (GCN)** as a graph encoder to encode node representations learned by attentive label semantic propagation module. We denote representation matrix $\boldsymbol{H}$ which joins all node representations learned by the label semantic propagation module as the input:

$$\boldsymbol{E}^{(1)} = \sigma(\tilde{\boldsymbol{A}}\boldsymbol{H}\boldsymbol{W}_1), \boldsymbol{E}^{(2)} = \sigma(\tilde{\boldsymbol{A}}\boldsymbol{E}^{(1)}\boldsymbol{W}_2), \tag{9}$$

where $\tilde{\boldsymbol{A}}$ denotes a symmetric normalized adjacency matrix transformed by the adjacency matrix of $\mathcal{G}$, and $\boldsymbol{W}_1, \boldsymbol{W}_2 \in \mathbb{R}^{K \times K}$ denote two weight matrices of the encoder. $\boldsymbol{e}^{(2)}_{u_i}, \boldsymbol{e}^{(2)}_{v_j}$ are the representations of task u_i and worker v_j, which are the row vectors in $\boldsymbol{E}^{(2)}$. Thus, we compute the Hadamard product of $\boldsymbol{e}^{(2)}_{u_i}$ and $\boldsymbol{e}^{(2)}_{v_j}$ which is denoted by $\hat{\boldsymbol{y}}_{ij}$ to obtain the predicted label distribution of task u_i annotated by worker v_j.

$$\hat{\boldsymbol{y}}_{ij} = \boldsymbol{e}^{(2)}_{u_i} \odot \boldsymbol{e}^{(2)}_{v_j}. \tag{10}$$

We use $\hat{\boldsymbol{y}}_{ij} = \{y_{ij}^{(k)}|k = 1, ..., K\}$ to represent the probability vector of task u_i belonging to each label class. For example, $\hat{y}_{ij}^{(k)}$ denotes the probability that the truth of u_i is label c_k. To make the predicted label distribution approximate the actual crowdsourced label distribution, the loss function is defined as the cross-entropy over all tasks:

$$\mathcal{L}_2 = -\sum_{u_i \in U} \sum_{v_j \in V^{u_i}} \sum_{k=1}^{K} l_{ij}^{(k)} \log \hat{y}_{ij}^{(k)}, \tag{11}$$

where $\boldsymbol{l}_{ij} = \{l_{ij}^{(k)}|k = 1, ..., k\}$.

Considering the attentive label semantic propagation method and the label-aware graph encoder, the final loss function is defined as:

$$\mathcal{L} = \mathcal{L}_1 + \lambda \mathcal{L}_2, \tag{12}$$

where λ indicates the penalty coefficient. Updating the node representation and optimizing multiple weight matrices are difficult to convert to a convex optimization problem for solution [5]. Therefore, we use the **Adaptive motion estimation (Adam)** gradient descent method to minimize the loss function $\mathcal{L}$.

4.4 Truth Inference

In the previous sections, we introduce an attentive label semantic propagation method for aggregating label semantic information and obtaining the representations of tasks and workers. Thus, we can infer the truth according to the learned task representations. For task u_i, truth inference of h'_{u_i} is formulated as:

$$\hat{l}_i = \mathrm{argmax}(\mathrm{softmax}(h'_{u_i})), \tag{13}$$

where $\mathrm{argmax}(\cdot)$ indicates the index with maximum of a vector, and $\hat{l}_i$ denotes the inferred label for task u_i, $\hat{l}_i \in C$.

5 Experiment

5.1 Experiments Setup

Datasets. The eight crowdsourcing datasets are selected from different application scenarios. The tasks of FEJ2013[2] are to identify whether 576 facts are true according to the labels annotated by 48 workers. The Sentiment[3] distributes 1000 tweets to 85 workers and asks them to determine whether the sentiment in tweets is positive or negative. The tasks in SP[4] consist of 500 sentences extracted from film reviews, and 143 workers judge the sentences in the reviews to be positive or negative. Trec2011[5] makes 10 workers determine whether 16785 texts are relevant to a special topic. The tasks in Temporal[2] are 462 binary files representing events, which are assigned to 76 workers to determine if the sequence of events in a file is correct. ZC_all[4], ZC_in[4] and ZC_us[4] [11] employ 78, 25 and 74 workers to determine whether a uniform resource location is relevant to a name entity. Besides, ZC_all combines ZC_in and ZC_us, and all ZC datasets share the same tasks.

Baselines. To verify the effectiveness of LEGAT, LEGAT is compared with eight state-of-the-art methods. MV is a simple and fast way to obtain the truth of tasks, which only takes the majority votes as the truth. CRH [7] is an iterative, distance-optimized truth inference algorithm. GLAD [12] is based on PGM that models both worker reliability and task difficulty. DS [14] models each worker as a confusion matrix, which represents the probability distribution of worker's possible answers for a task. BWA [15] is a bayesian graphical model with conjugate priors to infer truth in the case of high redundancy. GTIC [16] is a clustering-based inference model. TILCC [17] builds on GTIC by considering the label confidence of workers and incorporating label confidence into the feature extraction process. TiReMGE [5] considers the relationships between tasks and workers from multiple perspectives and proposes a reliability update strategy.

---

[2] https://github.com/lazyloafer/TiReMGE/tree/main/data.
[3] https://github.com/yuanli/truth-inference-at-scale/tree/master/data.
[4] https://github.com/orchidproject/active-crowd-toolkit/tree/master/Data.
[5] https://sites.google.com/site/treccrowd/2011.

Parameter Settings. Our algorithm is implemented on TensorFlow 2.5.0 and the tf_geometric library. In the overall experimental setup, the number of iterations and the learning rate are set to 100 and 0.01. For attentive label semantic propagation module, the dimension of the trainable weight matrix is initialized to $D = 256$. For the label-aware graph encoder, a dropout layer is added to the two-layer GCN and the dropout rate is set to 0.1. For the final loss function, the penalty coefficient λ is set to 0.01.

Settings of Ablation Experiments. Ablation experiments are designed to demonstrate the effect of the two proposed methods.

- Exp-1 tends to mine crowdsourcing relationships without label-aware propagation mechanism, which only considers the aggregation of adjacent information based on a GAT module. At the same time, Exp-1 does not contain a label-aware graph encoder.
- Exp-2 removes the label-aware graph encoder from LEGAT, and the loss function only contains $\mathcal{L}_1$.

Evaluation Metrics. *accuracy* is used to demonstrate the performance of LEGAT. *accuracy* is calculated by the truth inferred over all labels:

$$accuracy = \frac{\sum_{i=1}^{M} \mathbb{I}(\hat{l}_i, l_i^*)}{M},$$

where $\hat{l}_i$ denotes the inferred truth and l_i^* denotes the ground truth. $\mathbb{I}$ is an indicator function, and if $\hat{l}_i = l_i^*$, $\mathbb{I}(\hat{l}_i, l_i^*) = 1$; otherwise, $\mathbb{I}(\hat{l}_i, l_i^*) = 0$.

5.2   Overall Performance Analysis

By analyzing the performance of LEGAT and baselines on multiple datasets in Table 1, we can find that the average precision of LEGAT is about 2.1% higher than the other baselines on the eight datasets.

Although LEGAT does not achieve the best accuracy on several datasets, LEGAT performs best overall on the eight datasets. In addition, we also analyze the performance of other mainstream algorithms. The first is the MV, which achieves moderate inference accuracy by counting the most annotated labels. CRH performs poorly on some datasets (e.g., FEJ2013, ZC_in and ZC_us), which is caused by only relying on crowdsourcing workers' reliability to infer truth. DS obtains the best accuracy on Sentiment, but the overall result of DS does not surpass MV; in addition, GLAD and BWA also perform less well. These methods based on PGM are difficult to find prior parameters suitable for most crowdsourcing scenarios, resulting in poor model universality.

When the ground truth has a specific relationship with the content of a task, GTIC and TILCC can infer the truth based on task feature clustering. TiReMGE proposes a strategy of updating reliability and mining second-order

Table 1. Accuracy (mean% ± std.%) of algorithms on various datasets

Dataset	MV	CRH	GLAD	DS	BWA	GTIC	TILCC	TiReMGE	LEGAT
FEJ2013	90.19 ±0.09	90.10 ±0.00	90.10 ±0.00	86.46±0.00	92.18 ±0.00	87.5 ±0.00	86.46 ±0.00	90.28 ±0.00	**92.48**±0.68
Sentiment	93.40 ±0.42	95.20 ±0.00	95.20 ,±0.00	**96.00**±0.00	85.40 ±0.00	93.20 ±0.00	95.50 ±0.00	93.50 ±0.17	95.30 ±0.00
Trec2011	68.99 ±0.23	68.87 ±0.00	62.90 ±0.00	69.27 ±0.00	67.00 ±0.00	**69.60** ±0.00	69.00 ±0.00	69.40 ±0.25	**69.60** ±0.00
Temp	93.57 ±0.37	94.13 ±0.29	93.27 ±0.00	94.14±0.00	92.86 ±0.00	93.94 ±0.00	94.10 ±0.25	93.94 ±0.00	**94.16** ±0.00
SP	94.33 ±0.17	93.46±0.18	**94.80**±0.00	94.40±0.00	87.18±0.00	94.40±0.00	94.26±0.14	94.32±0.10	94.46±0.10
ZC_all	83.21±0.26	83.07±0.02	81.47±0.00	79.60±0.00	81.76±0.00	77.01±0.00	78.25±0.12	82.85±0.06	**83.81**±0.10
ZC_in	74.10±0.15	75.00±0.00	76.96±0.00	75.88±0.00	**78.38**±0.00	73.63±0.00	71.54±0.10	77.57±0.74	77.41±1.20
ZC_us	86.14±0.20	84.6±0.00	83.58±0.00	82.25±0.00	80.78±0.00	79.85±0.00	78.19±0.00	86.71±0.00	**87.02**±0.24
Avg.	85.49±0.24	85.67±0.06	84.79±0.06	84.75±0.00	83.19±0.00	83.64±0.00	83.41±0.08	86.07±0.27	**86.78**±1.54

relations of the graph, and achieves second place on all datasets. However, their models lack the label-aware propagation mechanism to complete reflect crowd-sourcing behaviors, which leads to information induction bias and limits their performance. By comparing the performance of GTIC, TILCC and TiReMGE, we conclude that mining crowdsoucing relationships on complete crowdsourcing behaviors can significantly improve the inference accuracy.

5.3 Detailed Performance Analysis

In this section, we conduct comparative experiments based on the above variant experiment settings.

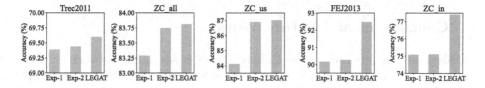

Fig. 3. Accuracy of variant experiments on multiple datasets

First, we compare the *accuracy* of Exp-1 and Exp-2 on multiple datasets and observe from Fig. 3 that Exp-2 is 0.05%, 0.46% and 2.75% higher than Exp-1 on Trec2011, ZC_all and ZC_us. Thus, we can conclude that the useful crowd-sourced label semantic information between worker-task pairs is aggregated to task representations when label semantic information is propagated along the information propagation path.

Then, the comparison of LEGAT and Exp-2 in Fig. 3 also demonstrates the validity of the label-aware graph encoder. For FEJ2013 and ZC_in, LEGAT is 2.21% and 2.30% higher than Exp-2 respectively, while the accuracy between Exp-1 and Exp-2 is less variable. However, we find that on some datasets the inference accuracy is significantly improved when both methods work together. There are some datasets that have an unbalanced distribution of label classes (e.g., FEJ2013) or a disproportionate number of wrong labels. At this point, if the wrong labels are propagated to the task representations, the label-aware graph encoder will also feed back to the loss function.

5.4   Parameter Sensitivity Analysis

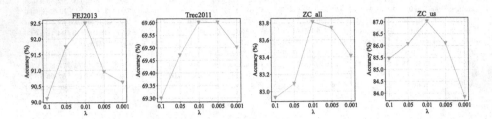

Fig. 4. Accuracy of different λ on multiple datasets

We apply the penalty coefficient λ in the final loss function to make the influence of label-aware graph encoder in a controllable way. As shown in Fig. 4, LEGAT has achieved the best accuracy on four datasets while λ reaches 0.01. For some datasets with a higher quality annotation, inference accuracy have an obvious change on the different values of λ. Therefore, we draw the following conclusion: If λ is too large, our method may overfit the predicted label attribute and is affected by the noisy crowdsourced labels. But λ with a small value also leads to the invalidation of label-aware graph encoder.

6   Conclusions and Future Work

In this paper, we propose a Label Enhanced Graph Attention Network for truth inference, which realizes GNN-based truth inference on complete crowdsourcing behaviors to explore latent crowdsourcing relationships between tasks and workers more effectively.

In the future, we will focus on improving LEGAT from the following aspects: 1) LEGAT does not perform well on some datasets with poor label quality. For example, there are some difficult tasks in Sentiment and Temporal, which receive little truth. 2) We will try to extend LEGAT in some crowdsourcing scenarios where task features or worker features are available.

References

1. Balayn, A., Soilis, P., Lofi, C., Yang, J., Bozzon, A.: What do you mean? Interpreting image classification with crowdsourced concept extraction and analysis. In: Proceedings of WWW, pp. 1937–1948. ACM (2021)
2. Shi, Z. R., Lizarondo, L., Fang, F.: A recommender system for crowdsourcing food rescue platforms. In: Proceedings of WWW, pp. 857–865. ACM / IW3C2 (2021)
3. Qi, G.J., Aggarwal, C.C., Han, J., Huang, T.: Mining collective intelligence in diverse groups. In: Proceedings of WWW, pp. 1041–1052. ACM (2013)

4. Hanlu, W., Ma, T., Lingfei, W., Fangli, X., Ji, S.: Exploiting heterogeneous graph neural networks with latent worker/task correlation information for label aggregation in crowdsourcing. ACM Trans. Knowl. Discov. Data **16**(2), 1–18 (2021)
5. Wu, G., Zhuo, X., Bao, X., Hu, X., Hong, R., Wu, X.: Crowdsourcing truth inference via reliability-driven multi-view graph embedding. ACM Trans. Knowl. Discov. Data, **17**(5), 65:1–65:26 (2023)
6. Velickovic, P., Cucurull, G., Casanova, A., Romero, A., Lio, P., Bengio, Y.. Graph attention networks. In: Proceedings of ICLR. OpenReview.net (2018)
7. Li, Q., Li, Y., Gao, J., Zhao, B., Fan, W., Han, J.: Resolving conflicts in heterogeneous data by truth discovery and source reliability estimation. In: Proceedings of SIGMOD, pp. 1187–1198. ACM (2014)
8. Gao, Q.L.Y.L.J., Lu, S., Zhao, B., Demirbas, M., Fan, W., Han, J.: A confidence-aware approach for truth discovery on long-tail data. Proc. VLDB Endow. **8**(4), 425–436 (2014)
9. Zhou, D., Basu, S., Mao, Y., Platt, J.: Learning from the wisdom of crowds by minimax entropy. In: Proceedings of NeurIPS, pp. 2204–2212. Curran Associates Inc., (2012)
10. Zhu, S., Yingnian, W., Mumford, D.: Minimax entropy principle and its application to texture modeling. Neural Comput. **9**(8), 1627–1660 (1997)
11. Qi Li, Yaliang Li, Jing Gao, Bo Zhao, Wei Fan, and Jiawei Han. ZenCrowd: leveraging probabilistic reasoning and crowdsourcing techniques for large-scale entity linking. In: Proceedings of WWW, pp. 1187–1198. ACM (2014)
12. Whitehill, J., Wu, T.F., Bergsma, J., Movellan, J., Ruvolo, P.: Whose vote should count more: optimal integration of labels from labelers of unknown expertise. In: Proceedings of NeurIPS, pp. 2035–2043. Curran Associates Inc., (2009)
13. Karger, D., Oh, S., Shah, D.: Iterative learning for reliable crowdsourcing systems. In: Proceedings of NeurIPS, pp. 1953–1961. Curran Associates Inc., (2011)
14. Dawid, A.P., Skene, A.M.: Maximum likelihood estimation of observer error-rates using the EM algorithm. J. R. Stat. Soc. C-appl. **28**(1), 20–28 (1979)
15. Li, Y., IP Rubinstein, B., Cohn, T.: Truth inference at scale: a Bayesian model for adjudicating highly redundant crowd annotations. In: Proceedings of WWW, pp. 1028–1038. ACM (2019)
16. Zhang, J., Sheng, V.S., Jian, W., Xindong, W.: Multi-class ground truth inference in crowdsourcing with clustering. IEEE Trans. Knowl. Data Eng. **28**(4), 1080–1085 (2016)
17. Wu, G., Zhou, L., Xia, J., Li, L., Bao, X., Wu, X.: Crowdsourcing truth inference based on label confidence clustering. ACM Trans. Knowl. Discov. Data **17**(4), 46:1–46:20 (2023)

LogE-Net: Logic Evolution Network for Temporal Knowledge Graph Forecasting

Yuxuan Liu[1], Yijun Mo[1], Zhengyu Chen[2], and Huiyu Liu[1]([✉])

[1] Huazhong University of Science and Technology, Wuhan, China
{m202173652,moyj,liuhuiyu}@hust.edu.cn
[2] Carnegie Mellon University, Pittsburgh, PA, USA

Abstract. In recent years, research on predicting future events using temporal knowledge graphs by leveraging their rich structural and historical information has just begun. Due to their interesting application potential, they have gained more attention from researchers. Existing methods mainly focus on using evolution representation learning to aggregate and propagate recent graph structural information or integrate historical memory to infer the future. However, simply considering the historical repeated facts during reasoning is insufficient. Therefore, we propose a novel model called LogE-Net (Logic Evolution network) that simultaneously considers short-term facts and logical rules. Additionally, we propose a mutual-information control mechanism based on contrastive learning to control the freedom of temporal evolution. Finally, experiments on two public datasets demonstrate that our model consistently outperforms the state-of-the-art baseline on entity prediction and relation prediction tasks.

Keywords: Knowledge graph · Logic rule · Evolution representation learning

1 Introduction

Since Google proposed Knowledge Graph, it has been widely used in fields such as intelligent question-answering [1] and fault diagnosis [2], due to its ability to intuitively express relations between entities. In recent years, Knowledge Graphs have shown a trend toward vertical industry development. Along with the development of GNNs(Graph Neural Networks), static representation learning of Knowledge Graphs has also achieved rapid progress and has achieved great success in the fields of Knowledge Graph completion and reasoning. In recent years, as static Knowledge Graphs are insufficient to model the changes in real-world events, a lot of researchers have begun to focus on the temporal evolution of Knowledge Graphs.

This work is supported by Key Research and Development Project in Hubei Province (2021BAA171), and Hubei Specialized Institute of Intelligent Edge Computing.

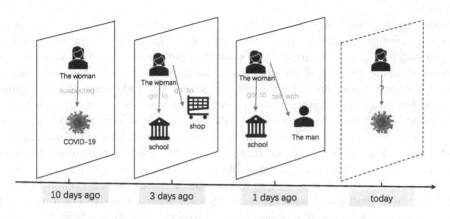

Fig. 1. An example of temporal knowledge graph.

The representation learning methods for static knowledge graphs have become an important topic. Given the unique structure of graphs, representing an entity node can directly capture and utilize its surrounding neighbors and relation structure information. These representations can be applied to various areas, such as drug molecule graphs [3], social networks [4], and knowledge graph completion [5]. However, not all scenarios can be modeled using static graphs. For example, the relations between two entities in a news event may change dynamically, and entities may also participate or withdraw from the event as it progresses, just like Fig. 1. As a result, knowledge graphs constantly evolve over time, generating new entities and relations. To address these issues, temporal knowledge graphs composed of static graph snapshots have emerged. Different from static graph representation, temporal knowledge graphs need to incorporate time information properly to represent the states of the same entity at different timestamps by leveraging historical facts and potential trend evolution.

The representation learning of temporal knowledge graph nodes is extremely challenging due to the complexity and variability of their graph structures. Good node representation methods can be used to complete or predict temporal knowledge graphs. Completion methods have been extensively explored in previous work [5], while the prediction task of predicting completely unknown moments based on historical knowledge graph sequences is currently less studied. Recently, many methods such as RE-NET [6], RE-GCN [7], first use R-GCN [8] as a structural encoder to obtain the representation of the same entity at different timestamps, then use RNN-based architecture to integrate historical entity embedding sequences, extract temporal evolution information, and finally obtain the final entity embedding matrix to predict subsequent events. However, this modeling method can only integrate short-term facts within a period of the time window, and cannot fully utilize historical factual information throughout the entire cycle. CyGNet [9],TiRGN [20] use a copy generation mode to intuitively and easily find historical repetitive facts that exactly match the same facts for each query, using the skill that the same facts are easily repeated. But not all facts follow this rule.

Therefore, it is not comprehensive to rely solely on this simple rule to assist in the judgment of the model. And both of the above methods lack interpretability.

In order to make the model more interpretable and take into account the actual thinking process of humans when making forecasting, it is not simply to repeat facts based on historical scenarios to assist judgment. Rather, while comprehensively considering all concurrent events in the short term, we also learn some basic logic rules based on global historical information. We simulate the reasoning process of the human brain based on logical chains [22], and further obtain more logical answers based on them, thereby assisting the human brain in making judgments and reasoning to obtain correct answers. Therefore, in order to use short-term historical memory in the time window and full-cycle long-term memory from multiple perspectives, we introduce a contrastive learning-based mutual information control mechanism to control the evolution freedom of short-term memory. Angle control based on this method is limited for only considering similarity in term of angle [8], contrastive learning has been proven to be a good multi-view representation learning technique in many works. Therefore, based on contrastive learning, we maximize the mutual information between history embedding and current embedding, design a time decay mechanism to maximize the near mutual information, and minimize the far mutual information, to evolve better next step embedding. At the same time, the logic memory module is introduced to assist reasoning based on long-term memory.

In general, the contributions of our work are as follows:

1. Aiming at scenarios in temporal knowledge graph forecasting, a logic rule-based reasoning model, logE-Net, is proposed to assist evolution embedding representation in making decisions, making the model more interpretable.
2. The introduction of dynamic embedding contrastive learning mechanisms, using contrastive learning to simulate the evolution process of entities, overcomes the direct limitations of using angles, and the problem of only calculating similarity in the same dimension while ignoring differences in different dimensions.
3. We have verified the accuracy of our model on two public datasets. LogE-Net can outperform the existing SOTA baseline in entity prediction and relation prediction tasks, with a stable improvement of about 1%.

2   Related Work

Temporal knowledge graph reasoning can be divided into two categories: completion (interpolation) and forecasting (extrapolation). Completion means completing missing entities or relations on known historical timestamps. Forecasting refers to predicting upcoming events on a future timestamp based on the facts that occur on the historical timestamps. Our work focuses on forecasting.

2.1 Temporal Knowledge Graph Completion

The original completion methods mainly extended classic methods such as TransE [10] to the temporal domain, proposing TTransE [11], which initializes an embedding for each timestamp. The sum of time and relations is considered a translation from the head entity to the tail entity. HyTE [12] regards time as a hyperplane that can project head entities, relations, and tail entities into this time-space. The above methods use time information alone and do not incorporate it into the representation of relations or entities. TA-DistMult [13] integrates temporal information into relations, and LSTM is used to encode timestamped relations. On the contrary, DE-Simple [14] attempts to combine time with entities and split a complete entity representation into static and dynamic parts.

2.2 Temporal Knowledge Graph Forecasting

Know-Evolve [15],GHNN [16], Dyrep [17] using the time point process, time is modeled as a random variable, and the intensity function is fitted by a neural network. Therefore, the probability of the occurrence of a specific event at a specific timestamp can be obtained. RE-NET [6] captures local features obtained by aggregating node information through R-GCN, and ultimately, the embedding of the queried entity can be obtained through RNN. CyGNet [9],TiRGN [20] use copy generation mode, taking advantage of the high probability that historical events will recur, that is, the periodicity of events. The advantage of CyGNet is its simplicity, but it relies heavily on historical information, but not all queries follow the simple rule of recurrence. They may require two or even three steps of logical reasoning, or one step of indirect relational reasoning, to obtain more likely candidate answers. In order to solve the unseen entity problem in the model, a static knowledge graph is constructed in RE-GCN [7], using the category information of the entities themselves in the dataset, and the unseen entities can get suitable initial embedding. Reinforcement learning is used in TITer [18], Cluster [19]. Unlike embedding-based methods, path-based methods have better interpretability. In xERTE [21] graph sampling is introduced and reasoning is performed on the sampled subgraphs. TLogic [22] has learned relevant laws based on historical facts but is powerless to handle occasional queries that have no rules to follow.

3 Preliminary

3.1 Problem Statement

A temporal knowledge graph can be expressed as $\mathbf{G} = \{g^1, g^2, g^3, \cdots, g^T\}$, which respectively denotes knowledge graph structure of T different time steps in the dataset. The g^t of these different steps can be represented by $\{E, P, F_t\}$. E is the entity set, P is the predicate set, F_t denotes the collection of events that occurred at time t. If an event occurred at time t: e_s and e_o have a relation p_1, then it is expressed as (e_s, p_1, e_o, t) by quads.

Because there are hundreds of T in a dataset, our model should specify a part of it as the input sequence. If the length of this part (time window) is L, then the input sequence is $\{g^{t-L}, g^{t-L+1}, \cdots, g^{t-1}\}$. Our task is to use this part of the information to predict events in the knowledge graph at t. Given $\{g^{t-L}, g^{t-L+1}, \cdots, g^{t-1}\}$ and $(e_s,p,?,t)$, to predict tail entity is the entity prediction task. Given $(e_s,?,e_o,t)$, to predict relation is the relation prediction task.

3.2   TLogic

TLogic [22] is an association rule mining algorithm based on confidence and support for the prediction task of the temporal knowledge graph. It is based on time random walk. According to the facts that the training set occurs, it extracts the temporal logic rule chains that conform to the non-increasing time, and attempts to provide one-step, two-step, three-step logical rule sets $\{r_1 \Rightarrow r, r_1 \rightarrow r_2 \Rightarrow r, r_1 \rightarrow r_2 \rightarrow r_3 \Rightarrow r\}$ for each relation r, and apply the learned temporal logic rules to each query $q=(e_s, r, ?, t)$ to obtain candidate answers with scores. If there are no corresponding rules, there will be no answers. It can automatically mine cyclic time logic rules by extracting time random walk from the graph, and achieve high prediction performance and time-consistent interpretation in the form of temporal rules, which is consistent with the actual observation that new events are triggered by previous events.

4   The Proposed Method

4.1   Model Architecture

The model architecture proposed by us is composed of three components, including a short-term memory reasoning module, a logic memory reasoning module, and a decoder module. The short-term memory reasoning module uses the evolution units in RE-GCN to recursively integrate events that occur in a short period of time and provide knowledge storage for reasoning. The logic memory reasoning module first preprocesses the data and is responsible for learning logical rules from the training set, and applying these rules to the training set, validation set, and test set, in order to obtain candidate entities that more conform to logical rules for each query. Based on the candidate entities obtained in the preprocessing stage, the short-term memory is assisted in making reasoning. Finally, the decoder module scores the candidate answers and trains the embedding representation using a contrastive learning loss function.

4.2   Short-Term Memory Reasoning Module

In this component, we want to make full use of both static knowledge graph representations and temporal knowledge graph representations at the same time. To solve the problem that entity embedding in RE-GCN depends on the angle, it is necessary to continuously adjust the angle to obtain the appropriate embedding position. We introduce the contrastive learning loss function Barlow Twins [23], as far as we know, this is the first time that contrastive learning has been introduced in the field of temporal knowledge graph forecasting to restrict evolution embedding representations at different timestamps.

The static knowledge graph is constructed in the same way as in RE-GCN by extracting entity type information and constructing a static graph G_s for temporal knowledge graph at different time steps. By the following formula:

$$H_s = RA - GCN(H, G_s) \tag{1}$$

We can get static graph embedding representation $H_s \in \mathbb{R}^{N \times d}$, $H \in \mathbb{R}^{N \times d}$ is initial entity embedding, G_s is static graph topological structure.

The representations of entities and relations at different timestamps follow the following formula:

$$H_{t-L}, P_{t-L} = EU(H_s, P, g^{t-L}) \tag{2}$$

$$H_{t-L+i}, P_{t-L+i} = EU(H_{t-L+i-1}, P_{t-L+i-1}, g^{t-L+i})(i \neq 0) \tag{3}$$

where EU is an evolution unit in RE-GCN, and its main structure is a dual feedback mechanism. Firstly, the predicate embedding P is updated by the entity embedding, and then the entity embedding is updated by the predicate embedding. TimeGate is used to obtain the next time entity embedding. Equation 2 denotes that at the first moment of the memory window, by inputting H_s and P, we can get the output $H_{t-L} \in \mathbb{R}^{N \times d}$ and $P_{t-L} \in \mathbb{R}^{N_r \times d}$ at the first step. Equation 3 denotes the entity embeddings $H_{t-L+i} \in \mathbb{R}^{N \times d}$ and predicate embedding $P_{t-L+i} \in \mathbb{R}^{N_r \times d}$ for subsequent moments except the first one, both are obtained after being processed by the evolution unit.

Inspired by contrastive learning, we use the contrastive learning loss function Barlow Twins, which is different from directly using angles to restrict the angle of static graph features and temporal graph features at different timestamps. It performs joint learning on static graph node features and initial temporal graph node features, and designs two loss functions respectively:

$$L_{c1} = BL(H_s, H_{t-L}) \tag{4}$$

$$C_r = H_s^T \cdot H_{t-L} \tag{5}$$

$$BL(C_r) = \sum_i (1 - C_{rii})^2 + \alpha \sum_i \sum_{j \neq i} C_{rij}^2 \tag{6}$$

Equation 4 calculates the loss by comparing the static embedding with the temporal embedding output at the t-L. Equation 5 calculates the correlation matrix between the two matrices first. Then in Eq. 6, the diagonal elements of it are all 1, and the non-diagonal elements are all 0, α is the hyperparameter. Above allow the static representation of the same entity to be as similar as the temporal graph representation obtained at the first moment in the same dimension as possible, while the features in different dimensions are as independent as possible, thereby enhancing the representation ability of each dimension. Instead, the cosine similarity is directly used to calculate the angle, without restricting the different dimensional features. However, the above loss function cannot simulate the evolution process of entity embedding at different timestamps. Therefore, the second loss function is designed:

$$L_{c2} = \sum_{k=t-L+1}^{L} BL\left(\left(\sum_{j=t-L}^{k-1} (j-t+L/n)\, H_j\right), H_k\right) \tag{7}$$

$$n = \sum_{i=t-L}^{k-1} i \tag{8}$$

Equations (7-8) denote comparing the k-th moment entity representation with the sum of all previous moments' time-decay factors representations to calculate Barlow Twins loss. BL(·) is the same as that of formula (5–6), which makes the output at each moment both relevant and different from all previous moments, the design of the time decay factor can maximize the mutual information of the current entity embedding and more recent entity embedding, thus simulating the evolutionary representation process of entities.

For the matrix obtained at the last moment H_{t-1}, P_{t-1}, and the query(e_s, p, t), we have:

$$score_e = ConvTransE(e_s, p, H_{t-1}, P_{t-1}) \tag{9}$$

For the query(e_s, e_o, t), we have:

$$score_r = ConvTransR(e_s, e_o, H_{t-1}, P_{t-1}) \tag{10}$$

where $score_r \in \mathbb{R}^{1 \times N_r}$, $score_e \in \mathbb{R}^{1 \times N}$ denote the scores for relation prediction and entity prediction tasks. ConvTransE [24] is the convolutional TransE [10] restriction for triples in static knowledge graph.

4.3   Logic Memory Reasoning Module

In the data preprocessing stage, we use TLogic to find all the logical rule sets R in the training set, and for each given query (e_s, p, t):

$$C_{(e_s, p, t)} = R_{p,t}(e_s) \tag{11}$$

where $R_{p,t}(\cdot)$ denotes all rule paths in the rule set R that are related to predicate p and comply with time constraints. e_s denotes the subject entity itself, $C_{(e_s, p, t)}$ is the set of all candidate entities that meet the logic rules obtained. From $C_{(e_s, p, t)}$, we can get $M_{(e_s, p, t)} \in \mathbb{R}^{1 \times N}$, where N is the number of entity if the i-th entity $e_i \in C_{(e_s, p, t)}$, the i-th dimension of $M_{(e_s, p, t)}$ is 1, otherwise is 0. Finally, we stack all $M_{(e_s, p, t)}$ of entity-predicate pair, then we can get $M_t \in \mathbb{R}^{N \times P \times N}$, where P is the number of predicates.

For a given query $(e_s, p, ?)$, we have:

$$score_{et} = ConvTransE(e_s, p, H_{t-1}, P_{t-1}) \tag{12}$$

$$score_l = M_{(e_s,p,t)} \times score_{et} \tag{13}$$

where $score_{et} \in \mathbb{R}^{1 \times N}$ is the score of entity prediction, $score_l$ is the product of candidate entity scores and mask, which keep only the results of candidate entities that meet logical rules.

For the relation prediction task r, there is no logic memory reasoning module processing for relations because no logical rule reasoning to obtain suitable candidate relations.

4.4   Training Objective

The final entity and relation score of the model is obtained through comprehensive reasoning of short-term memory and logic memory:

$$S_e = \varepsilon \times score_e + (1 - \varepsilon) \times score_l \tag{14}$$

$$S_r = score_r \tag{15}$$

Finally entity and relation prediction loss are:

$$L_e = \sum_{(s,r,o) \in g^t} \mathbf{y}_t^e \log S_e \tag{16}$$

$$L_r = \sum_{(s,r,o) \in g^t} \mathbf{y}_t^r \log S_r \tag{17}$$

$$L = \gamma L_e + (1 - \gamma)L_r + \beta L_{c1} + \mu L_{c2} \tag{18}$$

where γ, β, μ are hyperparameters.

5   Experiments

5.1   Setup

Datasets. We use two public temporal knowledge graph datasets, ICEWS14 (Integrated Crisis Early Warning System 14), ICEWS18. The former records some news events that occurred in 2014, with a total number of 7128 entities and 230 relations. Its interval is 24 h, and the whole dataset contains 365 timestamps, that is, a year's events. ICEWS18 has 23033 entities and 256 relations, covering a total of 304 d at 24-hour intervals per day. Due to the background of the prediction task, they are divided into training sets, validation sets, and test sets based on a timeline of 80%, 10%, and 10% from early to last. The training set timeline is earlier than the validation set timeline and earlier than the test set timeline.

Evaluation Metrics. The evaluation metric MRR (mean reciprocal rank), can measure the rank of the overall prediction results. However, for a prediction model, the higher the ranking of the correct prediction results, the more accurate and effective they are. The metrics Hits@$\{1,3,10\}$ can be used to measure the probability of the correct results ranking within the first, third, and tenth places. In this article, we adopt the time filter MRR and Hits @ $\{1,3,10\}$ just like TITer for both entity prediction and relation prediction tasks.

Baselines. For entity prediction, the models we compare are all designed for temporal knowledge graph forecasting tasks, including RGCRN, RE-NET, and RE-GCN with graph neural networks as the core modules, xERTE with graph sampling and attention propagation as the core ideas, TITer uses reinforcement learning, CyGNet is the model with copy generation mode, and TLogic uses logic rule mining for our logic memory reasoning module. For entity prediction, we compare our model with the above baselines. For relation prediction, since most methods cannot perform the task, we only compare with RE-GCN.

Implementation Details. The embedding dimension d of both entity and relation is 200, the number of R-GCN layers is 2, and the dropout of each layer is 0.2. Adam is used as the optimizer, with a learning rate of 0.001. ε is 0.7, γ is 0.7, β is 0.01, μ is 0.1. The input graph sequence length is 3 for ICEWS14 and 6 for ICEWS18. The step of logic rules found by TLogic is 1 for ICEWS14, and 3 for ICEWS18. All experiments are conducted on Nvidia GeForce RTX 3090 GPU.

5.2   Results

The results of entity prediction and relation prediction tests are shown in Table 1 and Table 2, respectively. In the entity prediction task, the results of LogE-Net

Table 1. Entity prediction results on two public datasets.

Model	ICEWS14				ICEWS18			
	MRR	Hits@1	Hits@3	Hits@10	MRR	Hits@1	Hits@3	Hits@10
RGCRN	38.48	28.52	42.85	58.10	28.02	18.62	31.59	46.44
RE-NET	39.86	30.11	44.02	58.21	29.78	19.73	32.55	48.46
CyGNet	37.65	27.43	42.63	57.90	27.12	17.21	30.97	46.85
TANGO	-	-	-	-	28.97	19.51	32.61	47.51
xERTE	40.79	32.70	45.67	57.30	29.31	21.03	33.51	46.48
TITer	41.73	32.74	46.46	58.44	29.98	22.05	33.46	44.83
TLogic	43.04	**33.56**	48.27	61.23	29.82	20.54	33.95	48.53
RE-GCN	42.00	31.63	47.20	61.65	32.45	22.17	36.59	52.53
LogE-Net	**43.72**	33.35	**48.69**	**63.72**	**32.69**	**22.32**	**36.89**	**53.00**

are significantly higher than CyGNet because CyGNet only uses historical repetitive facts as candidate answers to provide more historical information when reasoning, without considering the huge amount of information that short-term memory can bring, and only considering the way to find candidate answers based on repetitive patterns is relatively simple, Through summarizing laws and logical reasoning in a large number of historical events, people not only refer to recent events when predicting events but also further find answers through logical rules. LogE-Net is also higher than RGCRN, RE-NET, and TANGO, mainly due to the evolution features of static knowledge graph and temporal knowledge graph representations used in logE-Net. Entities and relations evolve alternately during the evolution process. At the same time, contrastive learning is used to ensure the similarity between the evolved representations of each step and the previous time steps, enabling entity representations to obtain stronger evolutionary representation capabilities under suitable constraints. LogE-Net has a stronger effect than xERTE and TITer, both of which are path-based multi-hop reasoning methods, without using R-GCN for neighborhood information aggregation, nor transferring short-term memory information from the perspective of embedding and evolution. Moreover, for unseen entities, or entities that occur less frequently, it is difficult to obtain answers through their path information, which affects their effect. Although TITer attempts to solve the unseen entity problem, it dose not achieve very good results. LogE-Net is start-of-the-art on ICEWS14 except for TLogic Hits@1 in all metrics, and Hits@10 has an improvement of nearly 2% due to the wider coverage of candidate answers found through TLogic compared to those found directly through historical repetitive facts, which is more helpful for the logic memory module to make broader and comprehensive choices among all entities. LogE-Net is significantly superior to TLogic in all metrics on ICEWS18 because the dataset is relatively large and it is relatively difficult to search for appropriate rules. However, experiment results show that better results can be obtained by using the rules learned to assist short-term memory in reasoning. LogE-Net is better than RE-GCN in all metrics, not only due to the contribution of logic memory but also due to the use of contrastive learning to evolutionarily represent entities from the perspective of mutual information, resulting in better representation capabilities for entity embedding.

Table 2. Relation prediction results on two public datasets.

Model	ICEWS14				ICEWS18			
	MRR	Hits@1	Hits@3	Hits@10	MRR	Hits@1	Hits@3	Hits@10
RE-GCN	45.34	32.84	50.27	73.03	46.19	33.46	51.22	**74.50**
LogE-Net	**45.98**	**33.67**	**50.63**	**73.34**	**46.26**	**33.51**	**51.53**	74.40

In the relation prediction task, LogE-Net outperforms RE-GCN in all ICEWS 14 metrics. Since the relation prediction task can not introduce a logic memory module, the improvement in this task is brought by contrastive learning. From the relation prediction results, it is not difficult to see that the entity evolutionary embedding obtained through contrastive learning is more conducive to improving relation prediction performance, which is particularly evident in the dataset ICEWS14 with a small number of entities and relations. Due to the large number of entities and relations on ICEWS18, it still brings some performance improvements.

5.3 Ablation Study

To further demonstrate and analyze the role of each module in the model, we conduct ablation experiments on the ICEWS14 dataset for the model, and the results are shown in Table 3. The metrics we use here are the time filter of the entity prediction task. First, we remove the short-term memory module and use only the logic memory module and contrastive learning, resulting in a significant decrease in results. Short-term memory is necessary for modeling concurrent facts. It is not sufficient to rely solely on candidates that conform to logical facts to make judgments, which can have a significant inducing effect on the results, leading to insufficient consideration when making reasoning and incorrect choices.

Table 3. Ablation study on ICEWS14 for entity prediction.

Model	MRR	Hits@1	Hits@3	Hits@10
LogE-Net w.o. short-term memory module	40.33	31.39	45.53	57.41
LogE-Net w.o. logic-memory module	42.24	31.84	47.43	62.17
LogE-Net w.o. static graph limitation	43.03	32.45	48.25	63.45
LogE-Net w.o. evolution contrastive learning	43.40	32.90	48.42	63.69
LogE-Net	**43.72**	**33.35**	**48.69**	**63.72**

In order to prove the necessity of the short-term memory module, we remove the logic memory module, making it degenerate to only use the RE-GCN evolution unit and contrastive learning, which reduces its performance by about 1.5%. The experiment results show that the candidate entities obtained after using TLogic preprocessing that comply with logical rules can assist the short-term memory in making better decisions, thereby demonstrating the importance of introducing this module.

Then, in order to demonstrate the necessity of static graph components, and the importance of information limitations on static graphs for entity prediction tasks, in LogE-Net w.o. static graph limitation, we did not take any restrictive measures on the evolution process of entities. The results indicate that it is necessary to apply certain restrictions on the evolution process of entities, This makes the coming moments somewhat dependent on all the preceding moments and does not deviate too much during evolution.

Finally, we explore the impact of the design of contrastive learning on entity prediction performance. In LogE-Net w.o. evolution contrastive learning, we use angle constraints to replace our comparative evolutionary learning mechanism and find that there is a slight decrease in performance. Although the decrease is not significant, there is still a negative impact, which demonstrates the effectiveness of our design. Due to a large number of entities, the performance improvement is not significant, However, its effect can be more clearly demonstrated on relation tasks.

5.4 Parameter Analysis

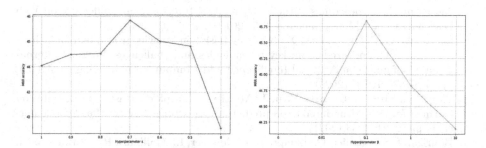

Fig. 2. The MRR results with different hyperparameter setting on validation dataset.

On the ICEWS14 validation set, we explore the impact of different hyperparameter settings on the metrics MRR. As shown in Fig. 2, the left one is the results when hyperparameter ε in the range of $\{0, 0.1, 0.2, 0.3, 0.4, 0.5, 1\}$. In order to ensure the fairness of the comparative experiment, we fix other parameters and only change its values within the above range. It can be found that when it is 0.7, the best effect is achieved on the validation set. The metrics that the impact of short-memory results on the overall prediction results is greater than that of logic memory, and the results of logic memory play an auxiliary role in the overall effect.

The right one is hyperparameter β when $\{0, 0.01, 0.1, 1, 10\}$ is selected, it is easy to see that the best effect can be achieved when the value is 0.1, and the value of the hyperparameter has a greater impact on the results, which also verifies the effectiveness of our contrastive learning design from this view.

6   Conclusions

In this paper, we propose a framework called LogE-Net based on logical rules and contrastive learning to assist in evolution representation learning, which addresses the issues of lack of logicality and consideration of correlation with previous representations in the reasoning process of temporal knowledge graph forecasting scenarios. LogE-Net can accomplish both entity prediction and relation prediction tasks through multi-task learning. On the public datasets ICEWS14 and ICEWS18, we verified the accuracy of our model in these two tasks, and further prove the role of our modules through ablation study and hyperparameter analysis.

Acknowledgements. This work is supported by Key Research and Development Project in Hubei Province (2021BAA171), and Hubei Specialized Institute of Intelligent Edge Computing.

References

1. Huang, X., Zhang, J., Li, D., Li, P.: Knowledge graph embedding based question answering. In: Proceedings of the Twelfth ACM International Conference on Web Search and Data Mining, pp. 105–113 (2019)
2. Su, L., Wang, Z., Ji, Y., Guo, X.: A survey based on knowledge graph in fault diagnosis, analysis and prediction: key technologies and challenges. In: 2020 International Conference on Artificial Intelligence and Computer Engineering (ICAICE), pp. 458–462. IEEE (2020)
3. Wang, Y., Min, Y., Chen, X., Wu, J.: Multi-view graph contrastive representation learning for drug-drug interaction prediction. In: Proceedings of the Web Conference, pp. 2921–2933 (2021)
4. Bourigault, S., Lagnier, C., Lamprier, S., Denoyer, L., Gallinari, P.: Learning social network embeddings for predicting information diffusion. In: Proceedings of the 7th ACM International Conference on Web Search and Data Mining, pp. 393–402 (2014)
5. Chen, Z., Wang, Y., Zhao, B., Cheng, J., Zhao, X., Duan, Z.: Knowledge graph completion: a review. IEEE Access **8**, 192435–192456 (2020)
6. Jin, W., Qu, M., Jin, X., Ren, X.: Recurrent event network: autoregressive structure inference over temporal knowledge graphs. In: Proceedings of the 2020 Conference on Empirical Methods in Natural Language Processing (EMNLP), pp. 6669–6683 (2020)
7. Li, Z., et al.: Temporal knowledge graph reasoning based on evolutional representation learning. In: Proceedings of the 44th International ACM SIGIR Conference on Research and Development in Information Retrieval, pp. 408–417 (2021)
8. Schlichtkrull, M., Kipf, T.N., Bloem, P., Van Den Berg, R., Titov, I., Welling, M.: Modeling relational data with graph convolutional networks. In: ESWC, pp. 593–607 (2018)
9. Zhu, C., Chen, M., Fan, C., Cheng, G., Zhang, Y.: Learning from history: modeling temporal knowledge graphs with sequential copy-generation networks. In: Proceedings of the AAAI Conference on Artificial Intelligence, pp. 4732–4740 (2021)
10. Bordes, A., Usunier, N., Garcia-Duran, A., Weston, J., Yakhnenko, O.: Translating embeddings for modeling multi-relational data. In: Advances in Neural Information Processing Systems, vol. 26 (2013)
11. Jiang, T., et al.: Towards time-aware knowledge graph completion. In: Proceedings of COLING 2016, the 26th International Conference on Computational Linguistics: Technical Papers, pp. 1715–1724 (2016)
12. Dasgupta, S.S., Ray, S.N., Talukdar, P.: HyTE: hyperplane-based temporally aware knowledge graph embedding. In: Proceedings of the 2018 Conference on Empirical Methods in Natural Language Processing, pp. 2001–2011 (2018)

13. Garcia-Duran, A., Dumančić, S., Niepert, M.: Learning sequence encoders for temporal knowledge graph completion. In: Proceedings of the 2018 Conference on Empirical Methods in Natural Language Processing, pp. 4816–4821 (2018)
14. Goel, R., Kazemi, S.M., Brubaker, M., Poupart, P.: Diachronic embedding for temporal knowledge graph completion. In: Proceedings of the AAAI Conference on Artificial Intelligence, pp. 3988–3995 (2020)
15. Trivedi, R., Dai, H., Wang, Y., Song, L.: Know-evolve: Deep temporal reasoning for dynamic knowledge graphs. In: International Conference on Machine Learning, pp. 3462–3471 (2017)
16. Han, Z., Ma, Y., Wang, Y., Gunnemann, S., Tresp, V.: Graph hawkes neural network for forecasting on temporal knowledge graphs. In: Automated Knowledge Base Construction (2020)
17. Trivedi, R., Farajtabar, M., Biswal, P., Zha, H.: DyRep: learning representations over dynamic graphs. In: International Conference on Learning Representations (2019)
18. Sun, H., Zhong, J., Ma, Y., Han, Z., He, K.: TimeTraveler: reinforcement learning for temporal knowledge graph forecasting. In: Proceedings of the 2021 Conference on Empirical Methods in Natural Language Processing, pp. 8306–8319 (2021)
19. Li, Z., et al.: Search from history and reason for future: two-stage reasoning on temporal knowledge graphs. In: Proceedings of the 59th Annual Meeting of the Association for Computational Linguistics and the 11th International Joint Conference on Natural Language Processing, pp. 4732–4743 (2021)
20. Li, Y., Sun, S., Zhao, J.: TiRGN: time-guided recurrent graph network with local-global historical patterns for temporal knowledge graph reasoning. In: IJCAI, pp. 2152–2158 (2022)
21. Han, Z., Chen, P., Ma, Y., Tresp, V.: Explainable subgraph reasoning for forecasting on temporal knowledge graphs. In: International Conference on Learning Representations (2020)
22. Liu, Y., Ma, Y., Hildebrandt, M., Joblin, M., Tresp, V.: TLogic: temporal logical rules for explainable link forecasting on temporal knowledge graphs. In: Proceedings of the AAAI Conference on Artificial Intelligence, pp. 4120–4127 (2022)
23. Zbontar, J., Jing, L., Misra, I., LeCun, Y., Deny, S.: Barlow twins: self-supervised learning via redundancy reduction. In: International Conference on Machine Learning, pp. 12310–12320 (2021)
24. Shang, C., Tang, Y., Huang, J., Bi, J., He, X., Zhou, B.: End-to-end structure-aware convolutional networks for knowledge base completion. In: Proceedings of the AAAI Conference on Artificial Intelligence, pp. 3060–3067 (2019)

LTNI-FGML: Federated Graph Machine Learning on Long-Tailed and Non-IID Data via Logit Calibration

Dongqi Yan[1,2,3], Jinyan Wang[1,2,3](✉), Qingyi Huang[3], Juanjuan Huang[3], and Xianxian Li[1,2,3]

[1] Key Lab of Education Blockchain and Intelligent Technology, Ministry of Education, Guangxi Normal University, Guilin 541004, China
wangjy612@gxnu.edu.cn
[2] Guangxi Key Lab of Multi-Source Information Mining and Security, Guangxi Normal University, Guilin 541004, China
[3] School of Computer Science and Engineering, Guangxi Normal University, Guilin 541004, China

Abstract. Federated Graph Machine Learning (FGML) is an emerging field that combines graph neural networks and federated learning to learn from distributed graph-structured data while preserving the privacy of data owners. Dealing with non-IID data is a major challenge in the field of FGML, and existing methods have been proposed to address the negative impawct of non-IID data, but they only consider the case where the class distribution of client nodes is balanced. However, in many real-world scenarios, the class distribution of client nodes is long-tailed, which can lead to significant bias in the model. To address this issue, this paper proposes a novel framework called LTNI-FGML, which addresses the joint problem of non-IID and long-tailed data in FGML. The framework comprises two main stages. In the first stage, we introduce Graph-Sage combined with the Mixup model on the client side to utilize the graph structure information and achieve feature anonymization. In the second stage, we propose a hybrid mechanism that incorporates a layer-wise attention mechanism and logit adjustment to address the challenges of long-tailed and non-IID data. Finally, we validate our proposed approach on several benchmark datasets to demonstrate its effectiveness in scenarios of long-tailed and non-IID data distribution.

Keywords: Federated learning · Graph · Non-IID · Long-tail data distribution

1 Introduction

In recent years, graph neural networks [1] have been proven effective in processing graph-structured data. However, due to the limited availability of data from individual clients and the need for data privacy, the demand for distributed graph-structured data learning has gradually increased. Direct data sharing can

L. Iliadis et al. (Eds.): ICANN 2023, LNCS 14257, pp. 486–498, 2023.
https://doi.org/10.1007/978-3-031-44216-2_40

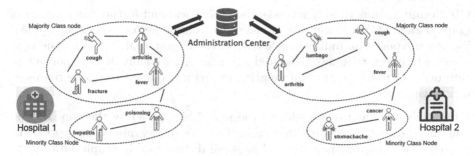

Fig. 1. A toy example of a distributed storage healthcare system. In this scenario, there are two hospitals and a medical administration center. Medical data can be represented as a graph, where nodes represent patients, nodes attributes represent illness (e.g. cough and fever) and an edge between two patients may indicate that they have the same chronic disease, have undergone similar surgeries, or have been treated by the same doctor.

lead to privacy leaks, so privacy-preserving methods for centralized graph neural networks [2,3] have received much attention. However, these methods often introduce too much noise, which may severely affect the model's accuracy and makes data sharing meaningless.

Federated learning (FL) is a promising solution to the challenge of privacy-preserving machine learning, as it allows multiple data owners to participate in the training process without sharing their raw data [4–7]. However, FL was originally designed for image data and its application to graph data is not straightforward due to the unique features of graph data, such as its topology and node attributes.

FGML is a distributed graph machine learning method that enables learning on distributed graph-structured data without compromising the privacy of client data [8,9]. However, FGML is faced with challenges such as non-independent and identically distributed (non-IID) and long-tail distribution data. Non-IID data refers to the differences in topological structure, node attributes, or edge attributes of graph data among clients in a distributed setting. The long-tailed data refers to the issue where the number of samples for certain categories is much larger than others in the clients, which leads to imbalanced data distribution. These issues often lead to significant model bias among clients, particularly in graph mining tasks.

Motivating Scenario. Taking the healthcare system as an example, as shown in Fig. 1. The graph is inherently long-tailed, and some diseases may be rarer than others in a hospital. Additionally, the data are non-IID, because each institution may have a different patient population, leading to variations in the distribution of medical conditions and outcomes. The purpose of this medical system is to obtain a globally powerful graph mining model.

Federated graph learning with long-tailed distribution and non-IID data offers several benefits for medical applications. However, this new and practical scenario presents two distinct technical challenges that have been rarely investigated previously.

Challenge 1: How to fully leverage the topological and feature information of graph data in FGML to improve model generalization performance? As topological information is an indispensable component of graph mining, it is crucial to seamlessly integrate it into federated learning. Additionally, it is important to consider how to use feature information to further enhance the node representation capability.

Challenge 2: How can we address the model bias posed by the non-IID and long-tailed distribution of graph data in the federated learning framework? The existence of significant non-IID and long-tail distribution in graph data due to various perspectives on the real dataset presents a formidable obstacle for naive federated learning algorithms to attain optimal performance.

These challenges inspired us to propose LTNI-FGML, a novel federated graph machine learning system that addresses the aforementioned difficulties and exhibits strong model performance.

To Address Challenge 1: LTNI-FGML uses GraphSage [1] combined with Mixup [10] model (GraphSage-Mixup) to make full use of structure and feature information. By randomly mixing node features, the GraphSage-Mixup model generates mashed embeddings that enhance the representation power of the original embeddings. Moreover, the random mixing process adds an extra layer of privacy protection, making it more challenging for potential attackers to deduce sensitive information. Consequently, this approach improves both privacy protection and generalization performance of graph machine learning.

To Address Challenge 2: we train a global model on a central server. To train this global model, we begin by generating the global node embedding using the concatenation strategy, which combines all mashed node embeddings uploaded by the clients. Then, we design the layer-wise attention algorithm to aggregate the model parameters and generate the microbalance logits, which are trained on the combined global embeddings. Additionally, the adjusted logits can be obtained by adjusting the ensemble model's logits based on meta-learning, which helps to further improve the model's performance. Finally, an adaptive calibration algorithm is applied to efficiently fuse the microbalance and adjusted logits, leading to better performance in federated graph machine learning

We validate LTNI-FGML on the four real-world datasets in non-IID and long-tail settings to better simulate the application scenarios. Experimental results show that LTNI-FGML significantly outperforms baselines, which verifies the effectiveness of LTNI-FGML. We summarized our main contribution as follows:

- We introduce a GraphSage-Mixup model in LTNI-FGML, which utilizes the structure and feature information of graph data to enhance node representations. Meanwhile, we generate mashed embeddings using this model and upload them to the server to avoid direct sharing of local data.
- We propose a novel method for server-side joint learning that utilizes a three-layer modeling technique, including an Attention Layer, a Logit Adjustment Layer, and an Adaptive Calibration Layer. This approach can enhance the robustness of the global model on both non-IID and long-tailed data.

- We conducted extensive experiments on four datasets with different modalities and the results demonstrate the superior performance of LTNI-FGML over existing state-of-the-art federated learning algorithms.

2   Related Work

In the recent past, there was a growing interest in federated learning on graphs, and several frameworks were proposed to combine the power of federated learning and graph neural networks. These frameworks included GraphFL [11], D-FedGNN [12], FedSage+ [9], FedGL [13], FedEgo [8], and FedGCN [6]. GraphFL was a meta-learning approach designed for few-shot learning, while D-FedGCN was a distributed federated graph framework that allowed collaboration among clients without a centralized server. FedSage+ trained a missing neighbor generator to recover the missing edges across clients, mainly targeting distributed subgraph systems. FedEgo addressed the challenges posed by data heterogeneity by designing personalization layers both locally and on the server. However, FedGL and FedGCN suffered from severe privacy problems, as they revealed whether a specific node was in a certain client's local dataset. The above-mentioned methods mainly focused on dealing with non-IID data, but they did not consider the challenges posed by both non-IID and long-tailed data distributions.

3   Problem Definition

In this paper, we consider a global graph $G = \{V, E, X\}$, where V is the set of nodes and $E \subseteq V \times V$ is the set of edges. X represents the node feature matrix, where x_i is the input attribute vector of node i, and the neighborhood of node i is defined as $N(i) = \{j \in V | (i, j) \in E\}$, which is known as node i's receptive field. In the federated learning system, we have a central server S, and K clients with distributed subgraphs $G_n = \{V_n, E_n, X_n\}$ owned by D_n for $n \in [K]$. We set the data distribution for D_n to be drawn from a long-tailed distribution (X, Y), where Y belongs to one of the C classes. The task for each client is to perform node classification training on their local data.

4   Proposed Method: LTNI-FGML

In LTNI-FGML, the main objective is for the server to capture the structure and feature information of non-IID and long-tailed distributed graph data from clients. To achieve this, the training process of LTNI-FGML can be divided into two stages: the local stage and the global stage. The framework of LTNI-FGML is illustrated in Fig. 2.

4.1   Local Stage

In a federated learning framework, data distribution among clients is often severely non-IID and long-tailed, which makes training a centralized model challenging. However, even with varying labels, these heterogeneous data may share

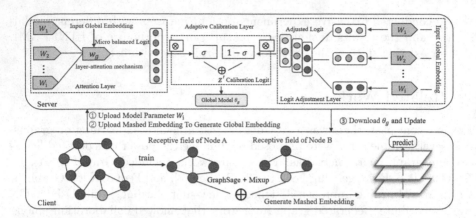

Fig. 2. The detailed framework of LTNI-FGML

a common representation [14]. To capture this representation, we can introduce
a powerful model to generate node embeddings.

The specific implementation described above is as follows. Since the inductive and scalable nature of the GraphSage model facilitates the training of
long-tail distribution data under heterogeneous queries. Therefore, we propose
a GraphSage-Mixup local client model for the downstream task of node classification. To perform the Mixup of nodes i and j and generate their mashed
embedding, mixing up their receptive field subgraphs is a usual technique. However, this may introduce unnecessary extra noise leading to excessive perturbation of the input features, such as mixing up information outside the receptive
field. During the local training phase, the local data is fed to the two-stage
GraphSage-Mixup model to obtain the mashed embedding. In the first stage,
hidden representations of the nodes without Mixup are obtained as follows:

$$\mathbf{h}_v^{(l)} = \sigma\left(W^{(l)} \cdot \mathbf{h}_v^{(l-1)} + W^{(l)} \cdot \text{MEAN}\left(\left\{\mathbf{h}_u^{(l-1)}, u \in N(v)\right\}\right)\right), \quad (1)$$

where the hidden representation $\mathbf{h}_v^{(l)}$ of a node v at layer l by applying a non-
linear activation function σ to the sum of two terms. The first term is the product
of the weight matrix $W^{(l)}$ and the hidden representation $\mathbf{h}_v^{(l-1)}$ of the same
node at the previous layer. The second term is the product of the weight matrix
$W^{(l)}$ and the mean value of the hidden representations of the 1-hop neighbors
$u \in N(v)$ of node v at the previous layer. Next, in the second stage, we randomly
pair the nodes in the mini-batch to conduct the Mixup of node attributes and
label by as follows:

$$\widetilde{\mathbf{x}_{ij}} = (1 - \lambda)\mathbf{x}_i + \lambda\mathbf{x}_j \quad and \quad \widetilde{\mathbf{y}_{ij}} = (1 - \lambda)\mathbf{y}_i + \lambda\mathbf{y}_j, \quad (2)$$

where the node $\widetilde{\mathbf{x}_{ij}}$ is a mixture of node $\mathbf{x}_i$ and node $\mathbf{x}_j$, where the mixing weight
is determined by the random variable λ sampled from a beta distribution. Finally,
we conduct the GraphSage as an aggregate function based on nodes i and j's

topologies separately at each layer l as:

$$\begin{cases} \hat{\mathbf{h}}_{ij,i}^{(l)} = \text{AGGREGATE}(\hat{\mathbf{h}}_{ij}^{(l-1)}, \{\mathbf{h}_k^{(l-1)}|k \in N(i)\}, W^{(l)}), \\ \hat{\mathbf{h}}_{ij,j}^{(l)} = \text{AGGREGATE}(\hat{\mathbf{h}}_{ij}^{(l-1)}, \{\mathbf{h}_k^{(l-1)}|k \in N(j)\}, W^{(l)}), \end{cases} \quad (3)$$

where $\hat{\mathbf{h}}_{ij}^{(0)} = \widetilde{\mathbf{x}_{ij}}$, and mix the aggregated features from the two topologies together before the next layer as:

$$\hat{\mathbf{h}}_{ij}^{(l)} = \lambda\hat{\mathbf{h}}_{ij,i}^{(l)} + (1-\lambda)\hat{\mathbf{h}}_{ij,j}^{(l)}. \quad (4)$$

The mashed node embedding $\hat{\mathbf{h}}_{ij}$ was obtained by applying Eq. 2, 3, and 4 to all nodes in the mini-batch graph. The $\hat{\mathbf{h}}_{ij}$ have the same dimension as the number of classes passed through a SOFTMAX classifier to perform multi-class node classification training by:

$$\mathbf{Z}_{ij} = \text{SOFTMAX}(\hat{\mathbf{h}}_{ij}) = \frac{\hat{\mathbf{h}}_{ij}}{\sum_i exp(\hat{\mathbf{h}}_{ij})} \quad and \quad L = -\sum_{v_i \in V_l} \sum_{j=1}^{c} Y_{ij} \ln \mathbf{Z}_{ij}, \quad (5)$$

to compute the cross-entropy error of classification results, where V^l is a set of labeled training nodes and $Y \in R^{n \times c}$ is the one-hot label indicator matrix of graph nodes (n being the number of nodes and c being the number of classes). Particularly, our method generates mashed node embeddings by using Eq. 2 and 4 to provide privacy protection. As a result, potential attackers find it difficult to infer sensitive information from these node embeddings.

4.2 Global Stage

Logit Adjustment Layer. To train a global model, the server combines the local node embeddings from each client to obtain the global node embedding $\mathbf{h_g}$. To better preserve the local node embeddings learned from the clients, we use a combined strategy [15] of concatenation, which involves concatenating the local node embeddings from each client to generate the global node embedding $\mathbf{h_g}$ as:

$$\mathbf{h_g} \leftarrow \text{CONCAT}(\mathbf{h_1}, \mathbf{h_2}, ..., \mathbf{h_K}). \quad (6)$$

Due to the long-tail distribution of local data, the number of samples in the minority classes is often small or even as few as only a few. The lack of training samples for these classes can result in the poor performance of the model. Some minority classes may be ignored, which can affect the overall performance of the model. Therefore, an ensemble model integrates multiple models and increases the weight of the minority classes to ensure that each class is fully considered. Specifically, on the server, we can define an ensemble model as:

$$\mu^e(\mathbf{h_g}) = \sum_{k=1}^{K} p_k \mu_{w_k}(\mathbf{h_g}). \quad (7)$$

To calculate the ensemble weights p_k for client k's local model, we use the function $\mu(\cdot)$ to refer to each client model. Since each local model is trained on data with different distributions, they may perform differently on the tail classes. Thus, it is reasonable to assign a higher ensemble weight to the local model that performs well on the tail classes to improve the ensemble model's generalization ability. First, we calculate the logits of the local models $\mu_{w_k}(\mathbf{h_g})$ on the server. Then, we calculate the ensemble weights p_k using a non-linear transform as follows:

$$\mathbf{p_k} = \text{SIGMOID}\left(\alpha_p^T \mu_{w_k}\left(\mathbf{h_g}\right) + \mathbf{b_p}\right), \tag{8}$$

where $a_p \in R^C$ and b_p is a learnable parameter. p_k is then normalized to make its sum equal to 1. Subsequently, the weighted logits of the local model can be computed, as shown in Eq. 7. However, if none of the clients are able to handle the tail classes effectively, the weighted ensemble may still exhibit bias towards the head classes. To address this issue, we propose a meta-network logits calibration method based on meta-learning, which can be implemented as follows:

$$\mathbf{scaled\_logits} = \frac{\mathbf{logits}}{\tau} \quad and \quad \mathbf{corrected\_logits} = \mathbf{scaled\_logits} - \alpha, \tag{9}$$

$$\mathbf{correction} = f(\text{MEAN}(\text{SIGMOID}(\mathbf{scaled\_logits}))), \tag{10}$$

$$\mathbf{z^{cl}} = \mathbf{corrected\_logits} \odot \mathbf{correction}. \tag{11}$$

Firstly, the $\mathbf{logits} \in \mu^e(\mathbf{h_g})$ are scaled to a smaller range by dividing them by a learnable temperature parameter τ in Eq. 9. Then, the $\mathbf{scaled\_logits}$ are calibrated by subtracting a learnable offset parameter α in Eq. 9. Afterward, the sigmoid function is applied to the $\mathbf{scaled\_logits}$ and their mean is taken along the first dimension to obtain a calibration factor $\mathbf{correction}$ in Eq. 10, where the function f is a multi-layer perceptron. Finally, the $\mathbf{corrected\_logits}$ are multiplied element-wise by the $\mathbf{correction}$ factor to obtain the adjusted logit $\mathbf{z^{cl}}$ in Eq. 11, where the symbol $\odot$ represents the hadamard product.

Attention Layer. The effectiveness of the logit adjustment layer relies on the assumption that the features have been properly extracted. Since the feature extractors of local models are severely affected by non-IID and long-tailed local data, simply manipulating the logits may not be sufficient to address the underlying issues of poor feature extraction capability of the model. Therefore, we propose to update the feature extractor to complement logit adjustment. Specifically, The layer-wise attention scheme introduced in model aggregation in the server can be represented by the following formula.

$$w_g = \sum_{k=1}^{K} w_k \quad and \quad w_k = \left(\alpha_k^0 w_k^0 \,||\, \alpha_k^1 w_k^1 \,||\, \cdots \,||\, \alpha_k^l w_k^l\right), \tag{12}$$

where w_g represents the parameters of the global server model and w_k represents the parameters of the client's model. For each layer l of the k-th client models, α_k^l and w_k^l represent the attentive weight and model parameter, respectively.

|| is an operator that concatenates multiple vectors in sequence. The attention weight is computed using a softmax function as follows:

$$\alpha_k^l = \frac{\exp(w_k^{(l)})}{\sum_{k=1}^{K} \exp(w_k^{(l)})}. \tag{13}$$

Specifically, we can define a model $\mu_{w_g}(\mathbf{h_g})$ on the global embedding $\mathbf{h_g}$. Since $\mathbf{h_g}$ is global embedding, w_g is adjusted to obtain an unbiased feature extractor. Then, we can obtain the micro balanced logits $\mathbf{z^{mb}} = \mu_{w_g}(\mathbf{h_g})$ for the input $\mathbf{h_g}$.

Adaptive Calibration Layer. The logits $\mathbf{z^{cl}}$ and $\mathbf{z^{mb}}$ serve the same purpose of addressing the long-tailed data, but they are produced using different methods. The logits $\mathbf{z^{cl}}$ are generated through the proposed meta-network method based on meta-learning, which adapts the model ensemble with fixed feature extractors. On the other hand, the logits $\mathbf{z^{mb}}$ are obtained from a single global model with fine-tuned feature extractors using a layer-wise attention mechanism. Building on the inspiration from [16], we introduce an adaptive calibration layer to balance the trade-off between $\mathbf{z^{mb}}$ and $\mathbf{z^{cl}}$, enabling effective integration of adjusted and micro balanced logits and leveraging their complementary strengths. As mentioned above, we then define a confidence score function $\sigma(x)$ to adaptively combine the original and the transformed class scores:

$$\mathbf{z'} = \sigma(x) \cdot \mathbf{z^{mb}} + (1 - \sigma(x)) \cdot \mathbf{z^{cl}}. \tag{14}$$

This equation represents the adaptive calibration layer that controls the balance between $\mathbf{z^{mb}}$ and $\mathbf{z^{cl}}$ by using a sigmoid function $\sigma(x)$, where x is a learnable parameter. The sigmoid function outputs a value between 0 and 1 that determines the trade-off between $\mathbf{z^{mb}}$ and $\mathbf{z^{cl}}$. If the output of the sigmoid function is close to 1, then the calibrated logits $\mathbf{z^{cl}}$ will have a greater contribution to the final output $\mathbf{z'}$. Conversely, if the output of the sigmoid function is close to 0, then the fine-tuned logits $\mathbf{z^{mb}}$ will have a greater contribution. By adjusting the value of x during training, the model learns to effectively integrate the calibrated and fine-tuned logits and make them complement each other.

$$L_{CE} = -\frac{1}{N} \sum_{i=1}^{N} \sum_{j=1}^{C} y_{ij} \log(\hat{\mathbf{z}}_{\mathbf{ij}}). \tag{15}$$

After obtaining the calibrated logits $\mathbf{z'}$, we train the global model using cross-entropy loss and obtain the updated global model parameters θ_g, which are then sent back to each client for parameter update. This way, the global model can continuously gain new logits from local models of various participating parties, thereby constantly improving its performance and generalization ability.

5   Experiment

5.1   Datasets and Experimental Settings

We conduct our experiments on four real datasets: Cora, Citeseer, CoraFull, and Wiki. Table 1 shows the details of the datasets and the relevant settings. In our experiments, we created a local dataset for each client and a global dataset for final testing. We used Adam optimizer with a momentum of 0.9 for local updates and GraphSage as the backbone network. By default, we ran 200 global communication rounds. We used Pareto distribution to generate long-tailed distribution for majority and minority class nodes and used Dirichlet distribution with a concentration parameter of $\alpha = 0.1$ to generate data for the remaining class nodes, thus generating non-IID and long-tailed distributed data in clients. This ensures that the data distribution of each client has certain differences, simulating the federated learning scenarios in the real world.

Table 1. The statistics and relevant setting of four datasets. Nodes and Edges show the number of nodes and edges, respectively. C denotes the number of classes. N indicates the number of clients, lr is the learning rate of the optimizer.

Dataset	Nodes	Edges	C	N	lr
Cora	2708	5049	7	5	0.01
Citeseer	3312	4715	6	5	0.01
Wiki	17716	52867	4	10	0.003
CoraFull	19763	63421	70	10	0.01

Table 2. F1 score (%) for LTNI-FGML and compared FL methods on four datasets with different Imbalance Ratio (IR) $= max_c \sum_k N_c^k / min_c \sum_j N_c^K$. On every local client device k, and the number of samples for each class c, is denoted by N_c^k.

Dataset	Cora		Citeseer		Wiki		CoraFull	
IR	10:1	20:1	10:1	20:1	10:1	20:1	10:1	20:1
Local training	69.01	62.71	63.41	55.43	70.14	66.45	50.41	44.50
FedAvg	75.40	68.71	70.01	62.43	77.50	73.45	54.41	48.50
FedProx	77.01	71.04	70.15	63.74	78.40	72.37	54.90	47.30
GraphFL	73.90	64.40	64.90	57.00	67.71	63.43	35.01	30.10
D-FedGNN	77.60	70.20	70.92	65.32	79.05	65.77	57.60	52.40
FedGCN	68.10	63.28	65.52	58.10	43.90	65.03	48.60	43.21
LTNI-FGML	**78.31**	**72.84**	**71.54**	**66.89**	**81.80**	**74.65**	**58.08**	**54.01**

5.2 Comparison Methods

We compare LTNI-FGML with the following state-of-the-art methods:

- **Local Training**. Each client trains its own model separately using its own local data, without any interaction or sharing with other clients.
- **FedAvg** [4]. Federated averaging: Each client trains a model on local data and the server averages the model updates to obtain a global model.

- **FedProx** [5]. Regularizes updates with a proximal term to prevent client overfitting in Federated Learning.
- **GraphFL** [11]. GraphFL is a few-shot learning method using model-agnostic meta-learning, addressing non-IID graph data between clients.
- **D-FedGNN** [12]. Decentralized federated learning on graph data, utilizes graph partitioning and asynchronous communication to overcome the challenges of heterogeneous and non-IID data.
- **FedGCN** [6]. To improve the accuracy of GNN models trained on decentralized graph data by incorporating both node and edge features. FedGCN employs a message-passing mechanism and utilizes a graph convolutional network as the base model.

Generalization Ability. The comparison results presented in Table 2 show that LTNI-FGML outperforms other methods consistently, and enhances the generalization ability of the client's local models. At different imbalance rates (IR), LTNI-FGML achieved a performance improvement of around 10% compared to local training by incorporating attention layers, logit adjustment layers, and adaptive calibration layer. This significant improvement suggests that LTNI-FGML successfully enables collaboration among clients and addresses the challenges posed by non-IID and long-tailed distribution graph data.

FedProx and FedAvg also show some improvements but still fall short of LTNI-FGML. D-FedGNN performs slightly better than FedAvg due to its unique aggregation feature. On the other hand, GraphFL and FedGCN perform poorly in all cases, indicating that they are vulnerable to non-IID and long-tailed distribution data. Overall, LTNI-FGML's personalized model and logit calibration methods are more effective than the naive averaging method used in FedAvg and D-FedGNN, especially in the case of severe non-IID and long-tailed data.

5.3   Model Validation

Ablation Study on Server. In Fig. 3(a), an ablation study is conducted to evaluate the necessity of the three modules in LTNI-FGML. We designed three experiments. The first one was "w/o mixup". The experimental results show that compared to LTNI-FGML and LTNI-FGML w/o Mixup, LTNI-FGML with Mixup achieves a 1% increase in accuracy. This indicates that Mixup enhances both the generalization ability and the node representation capability, improving its robustness even in the presence of severe non-IID and long-tailed data distribution among clients. The second experiment was "w/o attention layer". The experimental results showed that even without the attention layer, the logit adjustment layer was able to correct biased logits, and this is because the logit adjustment takes into account the distribution of the training data and effectively reduces the impact of biased data on model training. As a result, the model accuracy was still better than the baseline model. The third experiment was "w/o logit adjustment layer". The results indicated that although the attention mechanism could successfully address the non-IID problem, it failed to solve the long-tailed data problem. The global model still tended to favor the head class. Only by combining the attention layer with the logit adjustment layer in LTNI-FGML, the non-IID and long-tailed data problems could be effectively addressed.

The Effect of the Degree of Non-IIDness. Figure 3(b) illustrates the test accuracy of five methods at varying degrees of non-IIDness. As the degree of non-IIDness increases, the performance of all methods declines. However, compared to the other methods, LTNI-FGML shows a relatively smaller decrease in performance as α decreases from 1.0 to 0.01.

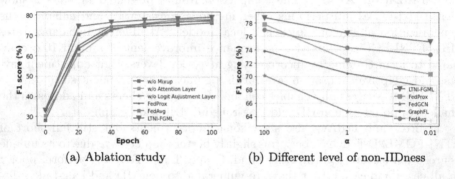

(a) Ablation study   (b) Different level of non-IIDness

Fig. 3. Experimental Evaluation of LTNI-FGML with IR of 10:1 on Cora Dataset

Graph Visualization. Figure 4 shows the 2-D node embedding visualization results on the Wiki dataset. Compared with FedAvg, we can observe that LTNI-FGML learns more discriminative node embeddings, especially for minority classes, such as L1 and L6, which account for 9% and 7% node population, respectively.

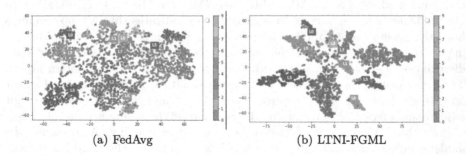

(a) FedAvg   (b) LTNI-FGML

Fig. 4. Graph Visualization On the Wiki dataset.

6   Conclusion

This work aims at obtaining a generalized node classification model in a distributed system without direct data sharing. To solve the joint problem of non-IID and long-tailed data in FGML, we propose a novel framework called LTNI-FGML. The framework incorporates a GraphSage-Mixup model on the client side and a hybrid mechanism with layer-wise attention and logit adjustment on the server side to overcome the challenges of long-tailed and non-IID data. Extensive experiments on several benchmark datasets demonstrate the superiority of LTNI-FGML over state-of-the-art FL methods. Finally, similar to existing FL methods, future work needs to be done to address the communication cost of LTNI-FGML.

Acknowledgment. This paper was supported by the National Natural Science Foundation of China (Nos. 62162005 and U21A20474), Guangxi Science and Technology Project (GuikeAA22067070), Guangxi "Bagui Scholar" Teams for Innovation and Research Project, and Guangxi Collaborative Innovation Center of Multisource Information Integration and Intelligent Processing.

References

1. Hamilton, W.L., Ying, Z., Leskovec, J.: Inductive representation learning on large graphs. In: Advances in Neural Information Processing Systems, pp. 1024–1034 (2017)
2. Wei, Y., et al.: Heterogeneous graph neural network for privacy-preserving recommendation. In: International Conference on Data Mining, pp. 528–537 (2022)
3. Wang, J., Li, Q., Hu, Y., Li, X.: A privacy preservation framework for feedforward-designed convolutional neural networks, neural networks. Neural Netw. **155**, 14–27 (2022)
4. McMahan, H.B., et al.: Communication-efficient learning of deep networks from decentralized data. In: Proceedings of the 20th International Conference on Artificial Intelligence and Statistics (2017)
5. Li, T., Sahu, A.K., Zaheer, M., Sanjabi, M., Talwalkar, A., Smith, V.: Federated optimization in heterogeneous networks. In: Proceedings of Machine Learning and Systems, pp. 429–450 (2020)
6. Yao, Y., Joe-Wong, C.: FedGCN: convergence and communication tradeoffs in federated training of graph convolutional networks. arXiv preprint arXiv:2201.12433 (2022)
7. Kang, J., Xiong, Z., Niyato, D., Xie, S.: Incentive mechanism for reliable federated learning: a joint optimization approach to combining reputation and contract theory. IEEE Internet Things J. **6**, 10700–10714 (2019)
8. Zhang, T., Chen, C., Chang, Y., Shu, L., Zheng, Z.: FedEgo: privacy-preserving personalized federated graph learning with ego-graphs. arXiv preprint arXiv (2022)
9. Zhang, K., Yang, C., Li, X., Sun, L., Yiu, S.M.: Subgraph federated learning with missing neighbor generation. In: Advances in Neural Information Processing Systems (2021)
10. Wang, Y., Wang, W., Liang, Y., Cai, Y., Hooi, B.: Mixup for node and graph classification. In: The International Conference of World Wide Web, pp. 3663–3674 (2021)

11. Wang, B., Li, A., Pang, M., Li, H., Chen, Y.: GraphFL: a federated learning framework for semi-supervised node classification on graphs. In: International Conference on Data Mining, pp. 498–507 (2022)
12. Pei, Y., Mao, R., Liu, Y., Chen, C.: Decentralized federated graph neural networks. In: International Workshop with IJCAI (2021)
13. Chen, C., Hu, W., Xu, Z., Zheng, Z.: FedGL: federated graph learning framework with global self-supervision. arXiv preprint arXiv:2105.03170 (2021)
14. Collins, L., Hassani, H.: Exploiting shared representations for personalized federated learning. In: International Conference on Machine Learning (2021)
15. Chen, C., Zhou, J., Zheng, L., Wu, H., Lyu, L.: Vertically federated graph neural network for privacy-preserving node classification. In: International Joint Conference on Artificial Intelligence (2021)
16. Zhang, S., Li, Z., Yan, S., He, X., Sun, J.: Distribution alignment: a unified framework for long-tail visual recognition. In: CVPR (2021)

Multi-Granularity Contrastive Learning for Graph with Hierarchical Pooling

Peishuo Liu[1], Cangqi Zhou[1(✉)], Xiao Liu[1], Jing Zhang[2], and Qianmu Li[1]

[1] Nanjing University of Science and Technology, Nanjing, China
cqzhou@njust.edu.cn
[2] Southeast University, Nanjing, China

Abstract. Graph contrastive learning is an unsupervised learning method for graph data. It aims to learn useful representations by maximizing the similarity between similar instances and minimizing the similarity between dissimilar instances. Despite the success of the existing GCL methods, they generally overlook the hierarchical structures of graphs. This structure is inherent in graph data and can facilitate the organization and management of graphs, such as social networks. Therefore, the representation results learned from previous methods often lack important hierarchical information in the graph, resulting in suboptimal performance for downstream tasks. In this paper, we propose a Multi-Granularity Graph Contrastive Learning (**MG2CL**) framework that considers the hierarchical structures of graphs in contrastive learning. This method enables effective learning of better graph representations by combining view information at different resolutions. In addition, we add a cross-granularity contrast module to further improve the accuracy of representations. Extensive experiments are conducted on seven graph classification datasets to demonstrate the effectiveness of MG2CL in learning unsupervised graph representations.

Keywords: Graph Contrastive Learning · Unsupervised Learning · Graph Neural Networks · Graph Pooling · Graph Classification

1 Introduction

Graph-structured data, including interpersonal networks, biological structures, and financial networks, is everywhere in the real world. Learning graph representation is a fundamental problem in various areas and tasks, such as community analysis in social networks [16], biological networks [2], and molecular properties prediction in drug discovery [7]. The mainstream methods for this task are learning representation by using Graph Neural Networks (GNNs). The majority of the current GNN models are mostly constructed in a supervised way [11], which requires abundant labeled data for training. However, in many practical scenarios, labeled data is very finite and costly to acquire. So, learning the representations of entire graphs in an unsupervised way becomes more significant.

Lately, motivated by success in natural language processing and computer vision, considerable interest has been shown in unsupervised contrastive learning

L. Iliadis et al. (Eds.): ICANN 2023, LNCS 14257, pp. 499–511, 2023.
https://doi.org/10.1007/978-3-031-44216-2_41

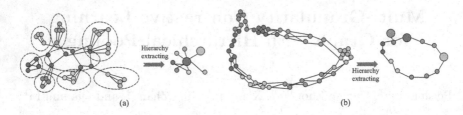

Fig. 1. The PROTEINS datasets consist of graphs with unique hierarchical structures, such as the star-like structure in graph (a) and the ring structure with a tail in graph (b). However, these structures may contain redundant information, as seen in graph (b) with two overlapping ring structures. Thus, removing nodes from one of the rings does not affect the graph's overall evaluation but can improve the clarity of its structural characteristics and facilitate representation. To achieve this, we extract the hierarchical structures of graphs (a) and (b) to obtain coarsened versions.

based on graph representation. Graph contrastive learning has advanced to the SOTA on a variety of problems, including node classification, graph classification, applications to recommender systems [8] etc. These methods' fundamental premise is to encourage augmentations (views) of the same input to have more similar representations compared to augmentations of different inputs.

However, current approaches do not explicitly consider the hierarchical structures of graphs. As is known to all, graph naturally has this significant attribute, as shown in Fig. 1. The hierarchical structure of graphs is essential in many applications. For example, in a knowledge graph, hierarchical relationships between concepts represent subsumption, while in social networks, the hierarchical structure of users reflects relationship strength and social influence. Nevertheless, most graph contrastive learning methods only consider the fine grained node level features of the original graph; they learn node representations in a single graph and then construct a graph representation in a single step, mostly by averaging or summing all node embeddings. This approach does not consider the hierarchical structure of graphs, which misses critical hierarchical information during the learning process and thus misses the best results. Moreover, in graph contrastive learning, leveraging multiple granularity views can offer diverse levels of abstraction in terms of information and structures, enabling models to gain a deeper understanding and analysis of the structures and properties of graphs. This is an aspect that has received relatively less attention in existing research.

In this study, we propose the **Multi-Granularity Graph Contrastive Learning** (**MG2CL**) framework to learn representations of graphs by considering hierarchical structure. Specifically, we generate two correlated graph views via data augmentation of the input graph. We then employ hierarchical pooling to obtain a coarse-grained view and augment it in the same manner as the original graph. The resulting coarsened graph includes node clustering and edge connectivity information. We utilize a contrastive loss to train our model, which maximizes mutual information between the graph representations of the two augmented views of the input graph and the two views of the coarsened graph. Thus, we simultaneously apply the contrastive loss to both granularities to improve the model's accuracy. In addition, we add a cross-granularity contrast module to further improve the accuracy of representations. Our model outperforms SOTA unsupervised graph representation learning techniques in overall performance.

The core contribution of this paper is three-fold:

- Firstly, we make the first attempt to study the hierarchical structure of the graph in contrastive learning. This hasn't been done much in the past, but it is important for effective unsupervised graph representation learning.
- Secondly, we propose a general contrastive framework for unsupervised graph representation learning called MG2CL. The proposed MG2CL framework trains the model on both node attributes and node clustering attributes at the same time. This makes the results more accurate.
- Thirdly, we conduct extensive studies using 7 public benchmark datasets on the graph classification task. MG2CL consistently surpasses existing methods and even outperforms some supervised methods on several tasks.

2   Related Work

In this section we introduce some relevant technical background:

Graph Representation Learning. Thanks to the development of GNNs, many graph representation learning methods now utilize powerful GNNs as encoders. These methods adopt an iterative neighborhood aggregation strategy with message passing, where each node aggregates its neighbors' feature vectors to generate its own new feature embedding [7]. A node's representation is described by its newly created feature vector, which combines the data information of the node's k-hop neighbors after k iterations of aggregation. To obtain the whole graph's representation, a pooling mechanism can be used, such as denoting the representation embeddings of every node in the graph.

Graph Pooling. Graph-level tasks require comprehensive representations of input graphs, which can vary in size and structure. To achieve robust and effective graph-level representations, pooling operations are necessary. These operations compress input graphs with node representations learned by GNN into smaller graphs or single embeddings. There are two main types of graph pooling designs: flat pooling and hierarchical pooling. Flat pooling creates a graph representation in a single step using the average [4] or sum of all node embeddings. On the other hand, hierarchical pooling coarsens the graph step-by-step, mainly through node dropping pooling [5] and node clustering pooling [23]. Node dropping pooling selects a subset of nodes from the input graph to form a coarsened graph, leading to information loss [6]. In contrast, node clustering pooling fuses nodes into clusters and treats the process as a node clustering problem, preserving the hierarchical structure of graphs.

Graph Contrastive Learning. Contrastive learning promotes proximity between views derived from the same instance, and distance between views from

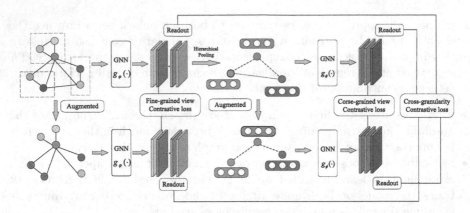

Fig. 2. The Overview of the Proposed Method.

distinct instances. This approach has been widely adopted in recent studies of graph-structured data. For instance, deep graph Infomax (DGI) [20] applies the Infomax criterion to graph data for node classification. Similarly, InfoGraph [18] maximizes mutual information (MI) between graph-level representations and patch-level representations to improve graph-level representations. GraphCL [24] employs view augmentation techniques such as node dropping, edge perturbation, subgraph sampling, and attribute masking, and contrasts hidden layer representations of two types of augmented graphs to learn graph representation. MVGRL [10] focuses on classification tasks at both the graph and node levels by maximizing MI between graph representation and node representations. It transforms the adjacency matrix into a diffusion matrix, treating the two matrices as two congruent perspectives, then learns node and graph representations.

3   Our Proposed Model: MG2CL

Figure 2 illustrates the proposed framework. Given a graph $\mathcal{G}$, we first use data augmentation to obtain positive pairs $\mathcal{G}$ and $\bar{\mathcal{G}}$. We select other graphs from the training set as negative samples. Next, we utilize GNNs to learn representations $z_{\mathcal{G}}$ and $z_{\bar{\mathcal{G}}}$ for the two views, respectively. We then employ a shared MLP layer to project the graph representations from both views into a low-dimensional embedding. We use hierarchical pooling to obtain the coarse-grained graph G, which includes both topological structure and node representations. We use the same approach to obtain the augmented view $\bar{G}$ and their representations z_G and $z_{\bar{G}}$ for the coarsened graph, but with a different encoder than the one used for the original graph. Finally, we optimize the encoder by minimizing the loss function, which comprises four parts: 1) mutual information between the two views of the original graph; 2) mutual information between the two views of the coarse-grained graph; 3) clustering loss; 4) cross-granularity contrastive loss.

3.1 Data Augmentations

Data augmentation aims at creating realistic and reasonable data through trans-formation methods that do not alter the semantic label. In contrast to aug-mentation in other areas, graph data augmentation must consider the graph's structural information, including nodes, edges, and subgraphs. We classify four different types of data augmentation strategies for graph data using defini-tions akin to those in [24]. **Node dropping** produces a new graph view by removing a subset of nodes as well as their edges from the original graph. **Edge perturbation** affects the graph's connectivity information by adding or deleting fractional edges. **Attribute masking** hides some of the node attributes. **Subgraph sampling** samples section of the input graph. These methods are jus-tified by the fact that the semantic meaning of a network is rather resilient to graph disturbance.

We use the same strategy for obtaining the augmentation views of original graphs and coarse-grained graphs. We apply [24] to carefully choose data aug-mentations for different datasets. The given graph $\mathcal{G}$ and coarse graph G are subjected to graph data augmentations to gain their related views $\bar{\mathcal{G}}$, $\bar{G}$, where $\bar{\mathcal{G}} \sim q(\cdot \mid \mathcal{G})$ is the augmentation distribution constrained by the input graph.

3.2 Graph Encoder

We utilize any GNN as the encoder, which is not particularly limited, just depending on the specific experimental datasets. After that structure and attribute information are conserved in the generated representations. $\mathcal{G} = \{\mathcal{V}, \mathcal{E}\}$ represents an undirected graph with $X \in \mathbb{R}^{|\mathcal{V}| \times N}$ denoting its node feature matrix where $x_n = X[n, :]^T$ is the N-dimensional feature vector of the node $v_n \in \mathcal{V}$. The propagation of the lth layer in a GNN $f(\cdot)$ is shown as:

$$h_n^{(l)} = \text{COMBINE}^{(l)}(h_n^{(l-1)}, \text{AGGREGATION}^{(l)}(\{h_{n'}^{(l-1)}\})) \tag{1}$$

where $n' \in \mathcal{N}(v)$, $h_n^{(l)}$ denotes the embedding of the node v_n at the lth layer with $h_n^{(0)}$, $\mathcal{N}(v)$ is a collection of nodes adjacent to v_n. $\text{AGGREGATION}^{(l)}(\cdot)$ and $\text{COMBINE}^{(l)}(\cdot)$ are component functions of the GNN layer. Following L-layer propagation, the READOUT function is used to summarize the output embedding $f(\mathcal{G})$ for $\mathcal{G}$ on layer embeddings. The downstream task at the graph level is then implemented using a multi-layer perception (MLP):

$$f(\mathcal{G}) = \text{READOUT}(\{h_n^{(l)} : v_n \in \mathcal{V}, l \in L\}); \quad z_{\mathcal{G}} = \text{MLP}(f(\mathcal{G})) \tag{2}$$

3.3 Contrastive Learning of Multi-Granularity Views

To better conserve the hierarchical structure of the graph, we use the node clustering pooling method within it. This method regards graph pooling as a node clustering problem, which maps the nodes into a collection of clusters. The clusters are subsequently handled as new nodes in the newly coarsened graph.

To improve the effectiveness of obtaining the graphs' hierarchical structure, we are inspired by the DMoN: Deep Modularity Networks [19], which combines knowledge from spectral modularity maximization with regularization to make sure that informative clusters are created to maximize the assignment S:

$$\mathcal{L}_s = -\frac{1}{2m} \cdot \text{Tr}(S^T B S); \quad \mathcal{L}_c = \frac{\sqrt{C}}{n} \left\| \sum_i S_i^T \right\|_F - 1; \quad \mathcal{L}_o = \left\| \frac{S^T S}{\|S^T S\|_F} - \frac{I_C}{\sqrt{C}} \right\|_F \quad (3)$$

where $S \in \mathbb{R}^{n \times c}$ indicates the learnt cluster assignment matrix; n is the number of nodes. And c is the number of cluster. We obtain S through the output of a softmax function: $S = \text{softmax}(H)$. Where H is the graph node feature representation generated by the GNN. $\mathcal{L}_s$ is the spectral loss, B is the modularity matrix, $\mathcal{L}_c$ is the cluster loss, C is the number of clusters, $\|\cdot\|_F$ is the Frobenius norm. The modularity matrix B defined as $B = A - \frac{dd^T}{2m}$, d be the degree vector, m is the number of edges, the spectral loss $\mathcal{L}_s$ is the opposite number of the modularity $\mathcal{Q} = \frac{1}{2m} \cdot \text{Tr}(S^T B S)$. Moreover, we designate the orthogonality loss $\mathcal{L}_o$ which guarantees the assignment matrix is orthogonal. The final loss of node cluster pooling is: $\mathcal{L}_P = \mathcal{L}_s + \mathcal{L}_c + \mathcal{L}_o$. By training the overall model, we can get good clustering results, which is also the node assignment matrix S. To obtain the coarse-grained graph, which contains structural information with the node-level clustering features and the topology, we use the following methods:

$$X' = \text{softmax}(S)^T \cdot X; \quad A' = \text{softmax}(S)^T \cdot A \cdot \text{softmax}(S) \quad (4)$$

X', A' represent the node features and connectivity matrices of the coarse-grained graph, respectively. And then we employ another GNN encoder that has different parameters from the previous encoder, but the principle is the same. Thus, we acquire the representations of the coarse-grained graph's nodes, namely the node clustering of input graphs. And the readout of the graph is:

$$H' = \text{GNN}'(X', A'); \quad z_G = \text{MLP}(f(H')) \quad (5)$$

where G is a coarse-grained graph from N graphs in a batch. We generate four graphs based on the process described: the original fine-grained graph $\mathcal{G}$, its augmentation graph $\bar{\mathcal{G}}$, the coarse-grained node clustering graph G, and its corresponding augmentation graph $\bar{G}$, each with its respective representation $(z_{\mathcal{G}}, z_{\bar{\mathcal{G}}}, z_G, z_{\bar{G}})$. Our goal is to train our encoders and effectively learn graph representations through the construction of positive and negative examples for contrastive learning. We define the first two embeddings as a positive pair, representing different views of the same input graph that should be comparable, and minimize their distance as an unsupervised learning objective. Similarly, for the next two embeddings, we aim to minimize the distance between the positive pair in the two granularity graphs and increase the distance or reduce the agreement between the negative pair, accomplished through our defined objective:

$$\mathcal{L}_{oss}(z, \bar{z}) = -\sum_{i=1}^{N} \log \frac{\exp(sim(z_i, \bar{z}_i)/\tau)}{\exp(sim(z_i, \bar{z}_i)/\tau) + \sum_{i'=1, i' \neq i}^{N} \exp(sim(z_i, \bar{z}_{i'})/\tau)} \quad (6)$$

Table 1. Datasets Description.

Name	Graphs	Classes	Avg. Nodes	Avg. Edges	Domain
PTC_MR	344	2	14.29	14.69	Molecule
MUTAG	188	2	17.93	19.79	Molecule
PROTEINS	1113	2	39.06	72.82	Bioinf.
NCI1	4110	2	29.87	32.30	Molecule
COLLAB	5000	3	74.49	2457.78	Social
RDT-B	2000	2	429.63	497.75	Social
RDT-M5K	4999	5	508.52	594.87	Social

Table 2. Average 10-fold cross-validation accuracy for unsupervised methods on graphs.

Datasets	PTC_MR	MUTAG	PROTEINS	NCI1	COLLAB	RDT-B	RDT-M5K
WL	58.0±0.5	80.7±3.0	72.9±0.6	80.0±0.5	-	68.8±0.4	46.1±0.2
DGK	60.1±2.6	87.4±2.7	**73.3±0.8**	**80.3±0.5**	-	**78.0±0.4**	41.3±0.2
MLG	**63.3±1.5**	87.9±1.6	41.2±0.0	80.8±1.3	-	63.3±1.5	**57.3±1.4**
GCKN	-	87.2±6.8	50.8±0.8	70.6±2.0	54.3±1.0	58.4±7.6	**57.3±1.4**
GRAPHSAGE	63.9±7.7	85.1±7.6	75.9±3.2	77.7±1.5	-	-	-
GCN	64.2±4.3	85.6±5.8	76.0±3.2	80.2±2.0	79.0±1.8	50.0±0.0	20.0±0.0
GIN-0	**64.6±7.0**	**89.4±5.6**	**76.2±2.8**	**82.7±1.7**	**80.2±1.9**	**92.4±2.5**	**57.5±1.5**
GIN-ϵ	63.7±8.2	89.0±6.0	75.9±3.8	**82.7±1.6**	80.1±1.9	92.2±2.3	57.0±1.7
sub2vec	60.0±6.4	61.1±15.8	53.0±5.6	52.8±1.5	55.3±1.5	71.5±0.4	36.7±0.4
graph2vec	60.2±6.9	83.2±9.6	73.3±2.16	73.2±1.8	71.1±0.5	75.8±1.0	47.9±0.3
InfoGraph	61.7±1.4	89.0±1.1	74.4±0.3	76.2±1.1	70.7±1.1	82.5±1.4	53.5±1.0
MVGRL	62.5±1.7	89.7±1.1	-	77.0±0.8	-	84.5±0.6	-
GraphCL	61.3±2.1	86.8±1.3	74.3±0.5	77.9±0.4	71.4±1.2	89.5±0.8	56.0±0.3
MG2CL	**63.8±0.8**	**90.9±1.0**	**76.2±0.7**	**79.0±0.2**	**73.9±0.4**	**90.8±0.7**	**56.7±1.2**

where τ denotes the temperature parameter. So the two different granularity contrastive losses are: $\mathcal{L}_{fine} = \mathcal{L}_{oss}(z_{\mathcal{G}}, z_{\tilde{\mathcal{G}}})$ and $\mathcal{L}_{coarse} = \mathcal{L}_{oss}(z_G, z_{\tilde{G}})$.

3.4 Cross-Granularity Contrast

In addition, we conducted cross-granularity comparisons between the original graph fine-grained view representation and the augmented view coarse-grained view representation. The contrastive loss is presented as:

$$\mathcal{L}_{cross} = \mathcal{L}_{oss}(z_{\mathcal{G}}, z_{\tilde{G}}) + \mathcal{L}_{oss}(z_{\tilde{\mathcal{G}}}, z_G) \tag{7}$$

Finally, by combining all contrastive losses and the cluster loss mentioned in the last section, the multi-level loss of our model that needs to be optimized can be described as $\mathcal{L} = \mathcal{L}_{fine} + \lambda \mathcal{L}_{coarse} + \mu \mathcal{L}_p + \delta \mathcal{L}_{cross}$. Where λ, μ and δ are the hyper-parameters to control the impact of contrastive learning on the model.

4   Experiment

4.1   Datasets and Configuration

We performed experiments on seven benchmark datasets [14], including four bioinformatics datasets (MUTAG, PTC_MR, PROTEINS, and NCI1) and three social network datasets (COLLAB, REDDIT-BINARY, and REDDIT-MULTI-5K), with dataset statistics summarized in Table 1. The MUTAG dataset comprises nitroaromatic chemicals, PTC-MR consists of 344 chemicals evaluated for carcinogenicity in rats, PROTEINS represents protein structures, and NCI1 depicts chemical compounds with vertices representing atoms and edges representing bonds. The COLLAB dataset represents scientific collaborations, while REDDIT-BINARY and REDDIT-MULTI-5K are balanced datasets with each graph representing an online discussion thread and nodes representing users.

Table 3. Types of encoders and values of other hyper-parameters in training.

Datasets	GNN1	GNN2	hidden layers	cluster number	hidden dim	batch size
PTC_MR	GIN	GCN	3	7	128	80
MUTAG	GIN	GCN or GAT	3	10	64	80
PROTEINS	GAT	GIN	2	3	64	64
NCI1	GIN	GCN	3	10	64	80
COLLAB	GIN	GIN	3	30	64	64
RDT-B	GIN	GCN	3	30	64	64
RDT-M5K	GIN	GCN	3	30	64	64

We use evaluation metrics employed by SOTA graph contrastive learning methods, repeating experiments five times. We report the mean 10-fold cross-validation accuracy after five runs using a linear SVM trained on the training data folds, and select the best mean accuracy. To ensure a fair comparison, we employ GraphCL's default configuration for graph classification. Our experiments vary the GNN type, number of hidden layers, number of clusters, batch size, epoch size, and SVM parameters in sets of $\{GCN, GIN, GAT\}$, $\{2, 3, 5, 8\}$, $\{3, ..., 30\}$, $\{32, 64, 128, 256\}$, $\{10, 20, 50, 80, 100\}$, and $\{10^{-3}, 10^{-2}, ..., 10^{2}, 10^{3}\}$.

4.2   Comparison Results

We validate the efficacy of our model's graph representation learning by comparing it with SOTA methods, including four graph kernel methods (Weisfeiler-Lehman Sub-tree Kernel (WL) [17], Deep Graph Kernels (DGK) [22], Multi-Scale Laplacian Kernel (MLG) [13], and Graph Convolutional Kernel Network (GCKN1) [3]), four supervised GNNs (GraphSAGE [9], GCN [12], GIN-0, and GIN-ϵ [21]), and five unsupervised methods (sub2vec [1], Graph2Vec [15], Info-Graph [18], MVGRL [10], and GraphCL [24]). Our comparison focuses on unsupervised learning for graph classification.

Table 4. Single-grained graph contrastive learning.

$\mathcal{L}_{fine}$	$\mathcal{L}_{coarse}$	$\mathcal{L}_p$	$\mathcal{L}_{cross}$	PTC_MR	MUTAG	PROTEINS	NCI1	RDT-B
✓				61.3 ± 2.1	86.8 ± 1.3	74.3 ± 0.5	71.4 ± 1.2	89.5 ± 0.8
	✓	✓		60.4 ± 0.3	87.7 ± 2.1	73.9 ± 0.9	70.4 ± 2.2	84.0 ± 1.3
✓	✓	✓		63.5 ± 0.2	90.0 ± 0.7	75.6 ± 1.3	73.4 ± 0.2	88.7 ± 1.0
✓	✓	✓	✓	$\mathbf{63.8 \pm 0.8}$	$\mathbf{90.9 \pm 1.0}$	$\mathbf{76.2 \pm 0.7}$	$\mathbf{73.9 \pm 0.4}$	$\mathbf{90.8 \pm 0.7}$

Table 2 presents the results of our unsupervised graph-level representation for graph classification tasks. Overall, the table demonstrates that our method outperforms existing unsupervised models and achieves state-of-the-art performance across all seven datasets. Specifically, our model improves the accuracy of state-of-the-art unsupervised methods by 1–2% points. For instance, on the PROTEINS dataset, our model achieves 76.2% accuracy, which is a 2.0% absolute improvement over GraphCL, and on the COLLAB dataset, it achieves 73.9% accuracy, a further 3% improvement over GraphCL. Notably, our model outperforms graph kernel techniques on four out of seven datasets. On the PROTEINS dataset, for example, it outperforms the cutting-edge graph kernel approach (DGK) by an absolute margin of 3.0%. For the three social network datasets, our model outperforms all the aforementioned graph kernels. In comparison to supervised baselines, our model surpasses GraphSAGE on two datasets and GCN on three, such as a 5.5% improvement over GCN on the MUTAG dataset. It is worth mentioning that MG2CL narrows the gap with the supervised baseline of GIN, with a performance difference of less than 3% on four datasets.

4.3 Ablation Study

Table 2 illustrates that in the majority of graph classification tasks that use unsupervised representation learning, GraphCL outperforms other methods. To encode the graphs and aggregate the processed node features, GraphGL employs a default setting of the Graph Isomorphism Network (GIN), which is known for its advanced representation learning capabilities. To obtain graph embeddings in the first module, our MG2CL also adopts GIN and a Multi-Layer Perceptron (MLP). We use this approach to obtain the embeddings of fine-grained graphs in most datasets, with the exception of the PROTEINS dataset, where we found that using Graph Attention Network (GAT) works better.

In this study, we take into account the hierarchical structure of graphs and leverage the varying levels of granularity to learn graph representations. Unlike GraphCL, we employ a hierarchical pooling operation to obtain a coarse-grained graph in the second module. Additionally, we use various GNN models, such as GAT, GIN, and GCN, in the third module to adapt to different datasets. Specifically, we use different combinations of GNN models, such as GIN-GIN for COLLAB, GAT-GIN for PROTEINS, and GIN-GCN for NCI1. Our experimen-

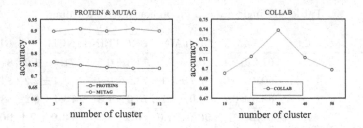

Fig. 3. The impact of the number of clusters on accuracy.

tal results demonstrate that MG2CL outperforms GraphCL, underscoring the effectiveness of contrastive learning in multi-granularity graph datasets.

We conducted ablation experiments on contrastive learning using different granularity views and five graph classification datasets as shown in Table 4. Firstly, we compared the performance of fine-grained views only, using a similar configuration to GraphCL. Then, we compared the performance of coarse-grained views only, where we applied hierarchical pooling to obtain the target view and conducted data augmentation. The contrastive loss included the clustering loss induced by the pooling operation and the contrastive loss between the coarse-grained and augmented views. The results suggest that multi-granularity contrastive learning is more effective than single-granularity contrastive learning. However, we found that the performance of MG2CL-coarse-grained was worse than that of MG2CL-fine-grained due to the significant reduction in the number of nodes and edges after pooling. This resulted in less effective augmentation of the coarse-grained views and a slight decrease in contrastive learning accuracy. In conclusion, coarse-grained contrastive learning can complement fine-grained contrastive learning in clustering-level features. Multi-granularity contrastive learning, which considers structural information at different levels of the graph, improves accuracy and precision of representation learning, especially for graphs with complex structures.

4.4   Analysis

In this part, we analyze the other factors that affect the learning effect:

Hierarchical Pooling Operation. As shown in Fig. 1, we utilized hierarchical pooling to extract the hierarchical structure from PROTEINS dataset graphs, resulting in two distinct granularity views. The fine-grained view contains highly informative node features, while the coarse-grained view represents node class features, with each node encapsulating all cluster information. Unlike non-hierarchical pooling, these nodes fuse information from nodes within the same class rather than being mere representatives. Our approach enables joint graph representation learning across different granularity views, especially for graph-level representation. The coarse-grained view facilitates better understanding and analysis of the graph's structure and properties by dividing the network

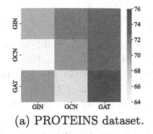

(a) PROTEINS dataset.

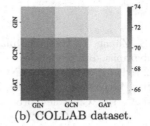

(b) COLLAB dataset.

Fig. 4. MG2CL's performances with different pairs of graph encoders on two datasets.

into several communities. Each community represents a low-resolution summary node with finer-grained high-resolution nodes and edges, resulting in richer information and enhanced representation accuracy.

Number of Clusters. In this study, we find the number of clusters must be different between different datasets, which depends on the size of nodes and edges in the datasets. The number of clusters is an important factor affecting the accuracy of the results, as shown in Fig. 3. We select different values according to the average number of nodes. The datasets' nodes range from 10 to 500; thus, we set the clustering number varying from 3 to 50. We select appropriate values through multiple experiments. All hyper-parameters are summarized in Table 3.

Encoder Combination. Using appropriate graph encoders can improve the semantics of contrastive examples and enhance the effectiveness of the MG2CL approach. To fully leverage the advantages of MG2CL, it is crucial to select encoder pairs that are suitable for various granularity graphs and datasets. GIN is a versatile encoder that can be applied to almost any dataset and is particularly useful as the first encoder for fine-grained graphs, where it can extract node features to capture hierarchical structures. The second encoder is typically either GIN or GCN to encode coarse-grained graph representations. By selecting different encoders for fine-grained and coarse-grained graphs, it is possible to create contrasting views that can facilitate graph contrastive learning Fig. 4.

5 Conclusion

In this paper, we present a novel framework for unsupervised graph representation learning, called Multi-Granularity Graph Contrastive Learning (MG2CL), which leverages the hierarchical structure of graphs. MG2CL contrasts the embeddings of graphs at different granularity, as well as their augmented views obtained through hierarchical pooling operations. Through extensive experiments, we demonstrate the effectiveness of our method in enhancing performance.

Acknowledgements. This work was supported by the National Natural Science Foundation of China (No. 61902186 and 62076130), and the National Key Research and Development Program of China (No. 2020YFB2104200).

References

1. Adhikari, B., Zhang, Y., Ramakrishnan, N., Prakash, B.A.: Sub2Vec: feature learning for subgraphs. In: Phung, D., Tseng, V.S., Webb, G.I., Ho, B., Ganji, M., Rashidi, L. (eds.) PAKDD 2018. LNCS (LNAI), vol. 10938, pp. 170–182. Springer, Cham (2018). https://doi.org/10.1007/978-3-319-93037-4_14
2. Alvarez, M.A., Yan, C.: A new protein graph model for function prediction. Comput. Biol. Chem. **37**, 6–10 (2012)
3. Chen, D., Jacob, L., Mairal, J.: Convolutional kernel networks for graph-structured data. In: International Conference on Machine Learning, pp. 1576–1586. PMLR (2020)
4. Duvenaud, D.K., et al.: Convolutional networks on graphs for learning molecular fingerprints. In: Advances in Neural Information Processing Systems, vol. 28 (2015)
5. Gao, H., Ji, S.: Graph U-nets. In: International Conference on Machine Learning, pp. 2083–2092. PMLR (2019)
6. Gao, X., Dai, W., Li, C., Xiong, H., Frossard, P.: iPool-information-based pooling in hierarchical graph neural networks. IEEE Trans. Neural Netw. Learn. Syst. **33**(9), 5032–5044 (2021)
7. Gilmer, J., Schoenholz, S.S., Riley, P.F., Vinyals, O., Dahl, G.E.: Neural message passing for quantum chemistry. In: International Conference on Machine Learning, pp. 1263–1272. PMLR (2017)
8. Guo, N., et al.: HCGR: hyperbolic contrastive graph representation learning for session-based recommendation. arXiv preprint arXiv:2107.05366 (2021)
9. Hamilton, W., Ying, Z., Leskovec, J.: Inductive representation learning on large graphs. In: Advances in Neural Information Processing Systems, vol. 30 (2017)
10. Hassani, K., Khasahmadi, A.H.: Contrastive multi-view representation learning on graphs. In: International Conference on Machine Learning, pp. 4116–4126. PMLR (2020)
11. Hu, F., Zhu, Y., Wu, S., Wang, L., Tan, T.: Hierarchical graph convolutional networks for semi-supervised node classification. arXiv preprint arXiv:1902.06667 (2019)
12. Kipf, T.N., Welling, M.: Semi-supervised classification with graph convolutional networks. arXiv preprint arXiv:1609.02907 (2016)
13. Kondor, R., Pan, H.: The multiscale laplacian graph kernel. In: Advances in Neural Information Processing Systems, vol. 29 (2016)
14. Morris, C., Kriege, N.M., Bause, F., Kersting, K., Mutzel, P., Neumann, M.: Tudataset: a collection of benchmark datasets for learning with graphs. arXiv preprint arXiv:2007.08663 (2020)
15. Narayanan, A., Chandramohan, M., Venkatesan, R., Chen, L., Liu, Y., Jaiswal, S.: graph2vec: learning distributed representations of graphs. arXiv preprint arXiv:1707.05005 (2017)
16. Newman, M.E., Girvan, M.: Finding and evaluating community structure in networks. Phys. Rev. E **69**(2), 026113 (2004)
17. Shervashidze, N., Vishwanathan, S., Petri, T., Mehlhorn, K., Borgwardt, K.: Efficient graphlet kernels for large graph comparison. In: Artificial Intelligence and Statistics, pp. 488–495. PMLR (2009)
18. Sun, F.Y., Hoffmann, J., Verma, V., Tang, J.: Infograph: unsupervised and semi-supervised graph-level representation learning via mutual information maximization. arXiv preprint arXiv:1908.01000 (2019)

19. Tsitsulin, A., Palowitch, J., Perozzi, B., Müller, E.: Graph clustering with graph neural networks. arXiv preprint arXiv:2006.16904 (2020)
20. Velickovic, P., Fedus, W., Hamilton, W.L., Liò, P., Bengio, Y., Hjelm, R.D.: Deep graph infomax. ICLR (Poster) **2**(3), 4 (2019)
21. Xu, K., Hu, W., Leskovec, J., Jegelka, S.: How powerful are graph neural networks? arXiv preprint arXiv:1810.00826 (2018)
22. Yanardag, P., Vishwanathan, S.: Deep graph kernels. In: Proceedings of the 21th ACM SIGKDD International Conference on Knowledge Discovery and Data Mining, pp. 1365–1374 (2015)
23. Ying, Z., You, J., Morris, C., Ren, X., Hamilton, W., Leskovec, J.: Hierarchical graph representation learning with differentiable pooling. In: Advances in Neural Information Processing Systems, vol. 31 (2018)
24. You, Y., Chen, T., Sui, Y., Chen, T., Wang, Z., Shen, Y.: Graph contrastive learning with augmentations. Adv. Neural. Inf. Process. Syst. **33**, 5812–5823 (2020)

Multimodal Cross-Attention Graph Network for Desire Detection

Ruitong Gu, Xin Wang, and Qinghong Yang[✉]

Beihang University, Beijing, China
yangqh@buaa.edu.cn

Abstract. The study of human desire is significant in gaining a better understanding of human behavior and emotions, as desire is one of the most fundamental instincts of human beings. With the development of multimodal algorithms, there have been many recent research tasks using both text and visual information for sentiment classification. However, human desires underlying emotions are still relatively underdeveloped. In this paper, we propose a novel multi-modal approach that combines both visual and textual information to provide a more comprehensive and accurate representation of human desires. Specifically, we first use text and visual encoders that can contain more information to extract features. To better connect the contextual relationships of the same modality and the associations of objects between different modalities, we construct a cross-modal graph and use the cross-attention method for graph representation learning. We evaluate our model on a public multimodal dataset of human desires. Extensive experimental results and in-depth analysis demonstrate that our model achieves state-of-the-art performance in desire detection tasks (Our code can be found at https://github.com/guruitong/-MCAGN.git).

Keywords: multi-modal desire detection · sentiment analysis · graph networks

1 Introduction

Sentiment analysis and recognition has been a popular research topic. Since the 1990s, researchers gradually focused on leveraging computers to automatically detect and analyze human emotions [8]. As computer processing speed has improved and machine learning algorithms have advanced, this field has become increasingly important in natural language processing. However, understanding the underlying human desires that drive emotions remains a relatively underdeveloped area. In recent years, the emergence of large language models has reignited interest in the impressive performance of artificial intelligence, as well as its potential future directions. Exploring and learning the motivations behind human emotions can greatly enhance artificial intelligence's ability to understand human emotions and behavior.

© The Author(s), under exclusive license to Springer Nature Switzerland AG 2023
L. Iliadis et al. (Eds.): ICANN 2023, LNCS 14257, pp. 512–523, 2023.
https://doi.org/10.1007/978-3-031-44216-2_42

(a) Boyfriend proposing marriage to girl- (b) African American girl reading in liv-
friend while kneeling at beach against sea. ing room.

Fig. 1. Two examples of multimodal emotion data, with objects in the image and mentioned in the text labeled in the same color. (Color figure online)

Desire embodies the profound yearning that humans possess towards a particular object or entity, eliciting a diverse range of emotional responses. It serves as an internal driving force that compels individuals to take action and pursue their goals. In the field of sentiment research, desire is a crucial topic as it can significantly impact our emotions. A strong desire for a particular object or experience can evoke excitement and anticipation, while the inability to satisfy that desire can result in disappointment and frustration. Therefore, studying desire is of utmost importance in the field of sentiment research.

Previously, research in the field of artificial intelligence primarily focused on emotions and sentiments. Human emotion recognition research can be categorized into unimodal and multimodal methods, depending on the number of modalities. Unimodal data can be classified into four types, namely text, images, videos, and physiological signals [2,22,23,26], These methods rely on features such as word frequency, facial expressions, body movements, and physiological responses to identify emotions. However, the problem with unimodal methods is that there are many ways to induce emotional fluctuations, and different people have varying expressions of emotions. This is where the advantages of multimodal research lie. Multimodal research involves the fusion of various unimodal data sources, such as combining EEG with eye movements or sound with text or images [27]. Nevertheless, as research requires a significant amount of data to support it, selecting readily available and effective data is essential for the development of emotion classification and recognition models. Explicitly represented data such as text and images are easier to analyze and extract, while hidden features like sound and physiological signals require multiple feature extractions and are harder to validate. Therefore, research on exploring emotional information in text and images has become increasingly popular, and similar research methods can be employed to study desire.

This paper presents the Multimodal Cross-Attention Graph Network (MCAGN). In order to capitalize on the connections between different types of features, the MCAGN builds a cross-modal graph for each instance by linking significant words in the text and image patches that represent specific objects. Specifically, our objective, as illustrated in Fig. 1[1], is to boost emotion and desire recognition performance by connecting object information from both modalities. To enhance visual information capture, we utilize a DINO-pretrained ViT and employ cross-attention for graph representation learning [1,5]. This enables us to assign edge weights based on token relatedness, further improving our approach's effectiveness. Our main contributions are as follows: (1) To the best of our knowledge, we are the pioneers in utilizing graphs to model multi-modal affective data, including sentiment, emotion and desire, in our research. (2) We utilize a graph learning approach with cross-attention to connect textual and visual modalities, which contain richer information. (3) Through experiments on the MSED [9] dataset and comparisons with other mainstream models, our model achieves the best performance.

2 Related Work

Traditional unimodal sentiment analysis research in the natural language processing field has primarily focused on word representation methods for text [23]. However, with the advancement of multimodal algorithms, it has become clear that relying solely on textual modality for sentiment analysis is inadequate. There have been various advancements in multimodal sentiment analysis, including research that utilizes human physiological data. In one study, Hassan et al. used unsupervised deep belief networks (DBN) to extract deep-level features from fused sensor signals of electrodermal activity (EDA), photoplethysmography (PPG), and zygomatic electromyography [7]. However, collecting datasets for this type of research is challenging. Fortunately, with the development of networked information, large amounts of image and text data can be gathered to train sentiment recognition models [3,14]. Researchers have used this data to conduct special task-related research on emotions, such as humor analysis [6] and sarcasm detection [25].

Several studies have explored graph models to handle multimodal tasks. For instance, Yang et al. proposed the Multichannel Graph Neural Network with Sentiment Perception (MGNNS) for image-text sentiment detection [24], while Xiao et al. combined self-attention mechanisms with a densely connected graph convolutional network to learn the dynamics between modalities [21]. While prior research has achieved some successes, these tasks did not incorporate cross-attention to automatically learn how text and image features interact and construct a graph that integrates both modalities. Additionally, the majority of research has primarily concentrated on sentiment or emotion analysis, overlooking the exploration of desire, which is a fundamental motivation that underlies human behavior.

---

[1] The data is from the publicly available dataset MSED.

3   Methodology

In this section, we first formulate our research problem and then present the Multimodal Cross-Attention Graph Network (MCAGN) architecture for multimodal desire detection. As shown in Fig. 2, The MCAGN consists of three modules: the textual modality representation module, the visual modality representation module, and the cross-modal graph module.

3.1   Problem Formulation

Sentiment recognition, desire recognition, and emotion recognition tasks can all be viewed as n-class classification tasks. Given a dataset $\mathcal{D}$ of N data samples, $\mathcal{D} = \{(T_i, I_i, Y_i) | i = 1, ..., N\}$, where $T_i = (t_i^1, \cdots, t_i^{m_i})$ represents the i-th textual description, which is composed of m_i tokens, I_i represents the i-th image, and Y_i represents the ground-truth label of the i-th training sample. We target at learning a model $\mathcal{F}$ that can predict the sentiment, desire, and emotion of given data samples as follows,

$$\hat{Y}_i = \mathcal{F}(T_i, V_i | \Theta), \tag{1}$$

where Θ represents the set of learnable parameters in the model $\mathcal{F}$, and $\hat{Y}_i$ represents the predicted classification probabilities of the given input data. For clarity, we temporally omit the subscript i of the training samples.

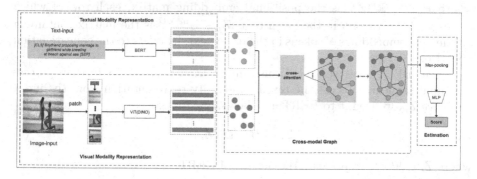

Fig. 2. The architecture of the proposed MCAGN framework is depicted in the figure.

3.2   Textual Modality Representation

Recently, BERT has been applied to various language understanding tasks [4, 16, 17, 20] and achieved massive success. Because of its powerful language modeling capability, we adopt BERT to drive the textual representation. We first get the embedding of the input sentence, and then feed it to the encoder layers in BERT to obtain the final textual modality representation.

Following the original setting of BERT, we first add $[CLS]$ and $[SEP]$ tokens to the beginning and end of the input sequence, respectively. Formally, we have

$$\hat{T} = ([CLS], T, [SEP]), \tag{2}$$

where $\hat{T}$ denotes the merged token sequence. Furthermore, to obtain the embedding of the input text, we then use the embedding layer of BERT to encode the merged text modality of the product. To be specific, we embed each token of $\hat{T}$ with a linear transformation as follows,

$$\mathbf{e}^j = \mathbf{W}^T \mathbf{t}^j, j = 1, \cdots, U, \tag{3}$$

where $\mathbf{W} \in \mathbb{R}^{|\mathcal{V}| \times D}$ is the token embedding matrix to be fine-tuned, which is initialized according to the pre-trained BERT. Intuitively, the i-th row of $\mathbf{W}$ refers to the representation of the i-th token in the token vocabulary $\mathcal{V}$. $|\mathcal{V}|$ refers to the size of the token vocabulary. $m' = m + 2$ is the total number of tokens in $\hat{T}$. $\mathbf{e}^j \in \mathbb{R}^{|\mathcal{V}|}$ is the one-hot vector indicating the index of the j-th token of $\hat{T}$ in the token vocabulary, while $\mathbf{e}^j \in \mathbb{R}^D$ denotes the embedding of the j-th token in $\hat{T}$. D is the dimensionality of the token embeddings.

To encode the order of information among input tokens, position encodings [4] are further inserted as follows,

$$\mathbf{Z}_p = [\mathbf{e}^1; \cdots; \mathbf{e}^U] + \mathbf{P}_{pos} \tag{4}$$

where $\mathbf{P}_{pos} \in \mathbb{R}^{m' \times D}$ is the positional embedding matrix, each row of which corresponds to a token in the given text. $\mathbf{Z}_p \in \mathbb{R}^{m' \times D}$ is the matrix containing all the final embeddings of tokens in the input text. $[;]$ refers to the concatenation operation.

Then, BERT uses several Transformer encoder layers to further process the input sequence. To get the textual modality representation from the input sequence $\mathbf{Z}_p$, we feed it to BERT as follows,

$$\mathbf{Z}_t = BERT(\mathbf{Z}_p) \tag{5}$$

where $\mathbf{Z}_t \in \mathbb{R}^{m' \times D}$ represents the output of BERT.

3.3   Visual Modality Representation

Object-level information is vital for sentiment analysis because it contains abstract high-level semantics. Therefore, we extract object information from the visual modality. We used the pre-trained Vision Transformer (ViT) model [5] trained by DINO [1], which has shown great success in language processing tasks [10,19]. DINO is a self-supervised pre-training algorithm, which can be applied to pre-train ViT models. The DINO-ViT can extract features containing more object information. In terms of extracting object information from images, compared to traditional object detection tasks, DINO does not require an additional region proposal network and can directly learn features from the image, thus improving feature extraction efficiency and achieving faster speed. The processes of using DINO-ViT to extract visual features are as follows.

Firstly, the input image I with a size of $L_i \times L_i$ is split into a set of image patches, where the length and width of each patch are both L_p. Therefore, we can represent an image as follows,

$$I = \{\mathbf{p}_j\}_{j=1}^r, \tag{6}$$

where $\mathbf{p}_j \in \mathbb{R}^{L_p \times L_p}$ is the j-th patch of the input image and $r = L_i/L_p \times L_i/L_p$ is the total number of patches. Following the original setting of ViT, after obtaining the patches, we use a trainable Linear Projection to flatten each patch into a feature vector,

$$\mathbf{x_j} = \mathbf{p}_j\mathbf{E}, \tag{7}$$

where $\mathbf{x_j} \in \mathbb{R}^{d^I}$ is the vector representation of j-th patch, $\mathbf{E} \in \mathbb{R}^{L_p^2 \times d^I}$. Later, at the beginning of the image, the $[CLS]$ token embedding $\mathbf{x}_{[cls]} \in \mathbb{R}^{d^I}$ is added to represent the entire image. Similar to the Transformer model, ViT adds a positional encoding vector to each patch vector. This positional encoding vector includes position information for the patch in the input image, allowing the model to use positional encodings to understand the relationships between pixels at different locations. In this way, the ViT model leverages positional encodings to capture spatial information and extract meaningful features from image patches. Therefore, the image embedding can be represented as,

$$\mathbf{X} = [\mathbf{x}_{[cls]}; \mathbf{x_1}; \mathbf{x_2}; \cdots; \mathbf{x_r}] + \mathbf{P}, \tag{8}$$

where $\mathbf{X} \in \mathbb{R}^{r' \times d^I}$ is a matrix containing the encoded information of image patches, and $\mathbf{P} \in \mathbb{R}^{r' \times d^I}$ is a matrix of position embedding. $r' = r + 1$.

Then we feed the concatenated matrix $\mathbf{X}_i$ into the ViT, which is composed of the Multi-Head Attention Mechanism and FeedForward Neural Network. The ViT outputs the feature vector for each patch.

$$\mathbf{Z}_i = ViT(\mathbf{X}), \tag{9}$$

where the outputs $\mathbf{Z}_i \in \mathbb{R}^{r' \times D}$ as the representation for the visual modality, where D represents the dimensionality of the output vectors from ViT.

3.4 Cross-Modal Graph

To achieve the detection task, we need to fuse visual and textual modalities so as to obtain a multimodal representation. Motivated by previous research [11–13,17], we use graph to model this correlation is an effective approach. After extracting features from both text and visual modality, we represented each token and patch as a node in the graph and learned the representation of the entire graph using cross-attention. Cross-attention is a method for calculating the relevance of a node to its neighboring nodes. By utilizing cross-attention, the model can automatically learn the interplay between textual and visual modalities, generating more informative and precise feature representations.

In order to better express the relationships between nodes, we use attention scores as edge weights, which means that nodes with higher attention scores are more closely connected. We represent the graph as $\mathbf{G} = (\mathbf{V}, \mathbf{A})$. $\mathbf{V} = [\mathbf{Z}_t; \mathbf{Z}_i] = [\mathbf{v}_1; \cdots; \mathbf{v}_{m'+r'}] \in \mathbb{R}^{(m'+r') \times D}$, and the adjacency matrix $\mathbf{A} \in \mathbb{R}^{(m'+r') \times (m'+r')}$ can be represented as:

$$\mathbf{A}_{i,j} = \begin{cases} k_{i,j}, if \ k_{i,j} > K \ and \ i < m' + r', j < m' + r', \\ 0, \quad otherwise, \end{cases} \quad (10)$$

where $k_{i,j} = Att(\mathbf{q}_i, \mathbf{k}_j) = \mathbf{q}_i \mathbf{k}_j / \sqrt{D}$ is the cross-attention score, $K = p \times \max(k_{i,j})_{i,j \in (1,m'+r')}$, and p is a proportion that we can set to filter edges. Because of the powerful structural modeling ability [13,21], we use the graph neural network to learn the sentiment information involved in the input data.

When using cross-attention to update graph representations, we first need to calculate the attention weights between each node and its neighboring nodes. Then, we obtain the weighted representations of each node's neighbors by summing the weighted attention weights. Finally, we concatenate this weighted representation with the node's original representation to obtain the new representation of the node. The overall process can be formulated as follows,

$$\mathbf{v}'_i = [\mathbf{W}^m (1/|\mathcal{N}(i)| \sum_{j \in \mathcal{N}(i)} \mathbf{A}_{i,j} \mathbf{v}_j); \mathbf{v}_i], \quad (11)$$

where $\mathcal{N}(i)$ represents the set of neighboring nodes of the i-th node, $\mathbf{W}^m \in \mathcal{R}^{D \times D}$ represents a trainable parameter, and $[;]$ represents concatenation.

After obtaining the graph, in order to get the classification results from it, we add a Max-pooling layer, which helps to reduce the dimension of the graph while preserving important features, and then use Multilayer Perceptron (MLP) to get the classification result as follows,

$$\hat{Y} = softmax(ReLU(M_{pool}([\mathbf{v}'_1, \cdots, \mathbf{v}'_{m'+r'}])\mathbf{W}^1 + \mathbf{b}^1)\mathbf{W}^2 + \mathbf{b}^2), \quad (12)$$

where M_{pool} is the max pooling operation. $W^1 \in \mathbb{R}^{D \times h'}$ is the weight matrix, $\mathbf{b}^1 \in \mathbb{R}^{h'}$ is the bias vector, h is the dimension of the hidden layer and $ReLU(x) = \max(0, x)$.where $W^2 \in \mathbb{R}^{h' \times K}$ is the weight matrix, $\mathbf{b}^2 \in \mathbb{R}^K$ is the bias vector and softmax$(\cdot)$ is the softmax activation function. To optimize our model, we use cross-entropy loss function $CE(\cdot)$ to train our model as follows,

$$\mathcal{L} = -\sum_{i=1}^{N} CE(\hat{Y}_i, Y_i). \quad (13)$$

4 Experiment

4.1 Dateset

We performed experiments on the MSED dataset [9], which is a publicly available dataset consisting of 9,190 English text-image pairs and is the first multi-modal dataset for sentiment, emotion, and desire recognition. It contains three classes of sentiment, six classes of emotion, and six classes of desire. Each example in this dataset consists of a textual description and a corresponding image. The dataset is split into three subsets for training, validation, and testing, respectively, with a ratio of 70%, 10%, and 20%. The training subset contains 6,127 examples, while the validation and testing subsets comprise 1,021 and 2,042 examples, respectively.

Table 1. Comparison of different models. The results shown in the figure are the average values obtained after conducting the experiments at least five times.

Model	Text	Image	Desire Detection			Sentiment Analysis			Emotion Recognition		
			P	R	M_a-F1	P	R	M_a-F1	P	R	M_a-F1
Text	BiLSTM [18]	-	73.20	67.82	69.14	78.43	78.75	78.58	73.49	72.17	72.73
	BERT	-	81.74	80.39	80.88	84.43	84.28	84.35	81.76	80.57	81.10
Image	-	AlexNet	51.47	49.33	50.07	68.76	68.21	68.45	56.42	53.29	54.66
	-	ResNet	49.97	49.35	49.20	70.85	70.61	70.64	58.74	54.67	56.40
	-	ViT	52.61	53.42	52.91	69.65	65.47	67.28	55.55	55.43	55.52
Text+Image	BiLSTM	AlexNet	67.80	68.00	67.67	78.73	79.22	78.89	71.17	70.70	70.89
	BiLSTM	ResNet	54.97	49.94	51.99	75.89	75.27	75.25	63.63	60.80	61.98
	BERT	AlexNet	80.84	75.50	77.17	83.22	83.11	83.16	78.06	78.19	78.10
	BERT	ResNet	83.42	82.43	82.28	85.83	85.79	85.81	83.54	81.51	82.42
Multimodal Model	CMGCN [15]		87.22	83.03	87.03	87.59	83.49	86.60	88.82	88.64	87.56
	MCAGN		**88.21**	**88.23**	**88.26**	**91.70**	**89.27**	**90.01**	**90.35**	**91.86**	**90.71**

4.2 Experimental Details

In our experiments, we utilize precision (P), recall (R), and macro-F1 (Ma-F1) as evaluation metrics. We modeled the textual modality using the pertrained bert-base-uncased from HuggingFace[2] and the word embedding dimension D is 768. For the image modality, we preprocessed input images to resize them to 224×224 and used DINO pre-trained ViT provided by HuggingFace[3] to embed each patch to a 768-dimension vector. Each patch's resolution was set to 8×8. L_p and r are set to 8 and 784, respectively. The cross-graph had 6 layers, with 8 attention heads used in each cross-graph layer, and the MLP had a hidden layer size of 1,536. The final classifier used a $2-$layer MLP with a hidden layer size of 1,536 and an output layer size of number of classes, where number of classes was 7, for example, for the 'desire' task. We set the dropout rate to 0.1 to randomly drop some neurons during training and applied weight decay $= 0.001$ to reduce overfitting. We used adam as the optimizer with alpha $= 0.001$, beta1 $= 0.9$, beta2 $= 0.999$, a starting learning rate $= 0.0005$ for BERT/ViT, and 0.006 for cross-graph. We used fixed-step decay as the learning rate scheduler, with a decay rate $= 0.5$ per epoch. Early stopping patience was set to 1, and the model was trained for a total of 8 epochs, with a batch size of 128.

---

[2] https://huggingface.co/bert-base-uncased.
[3] https://huggingface.co/facebook/dino-vitb8.

4.3 On Model Comparison

The main experimental results show the performance of models in unimodal and multimodal scenarios in Table 1[4]. The best performing models in a single modality, either text or image, are BERT and ViT, respectively. For the Text+Image part, the features of the two modalities are directly concatenated. The CMGCN model is currently known as a high-performing multimodal sentiment model in previous works. Based on the results, it is evident that our MCAGN outperforms other models, which demonstrates the effectiveness of our proposed model in sentiment, desire, and emotion recognition tasks. Furthermore, the model trained solely on image data performs relatively poorly compared to text and multimodal models, indicating that text modality contributes more emotional information to the model. Overall, the multimodal approach combining both image and text modalities shows superior performance compared to the single modality baseline, which suggests that utilizing multimodal information for sentiment recognition is meaningful.

Table 2. Experimental results of ablation study.

Model	Desire Detection			Sentiment Analysis			Emotion Recognition		
	P	R	M_a-F1	P	R	M_a-F1	P	R	M_a-F1
MCAGN	88.2	88.2	88.2	91.7	89.2	90.0	90.3	91.8	90.7
w/o-D	87.6	88.0	87.9	86.5	85.4	85.8	87.1	86.8	86.7
w/o-C	82.3	81.2	81.6	84.8	84.9	84.9	83.2	81.3	82.6
w/o-G	82.9	81.9	82.6	85.2	86.0	82.4	83.9	81.5	82.9

4.4 On Ablation Study

In order to investigate the impact of different components of our proposed model, we conducted ablation experiments, and the results are shown in Table 2. The experiments indicate that using either the text or image modality alone leads to a significant decrease in performance. This suggests that multimodal fusion of visual and textual information is meaningful for emotion and desire recognition. Directly concatenating the two modal features without using the graph fusion (w/o-G) method does not yield satisfactory results. Removing cross-attention (w/o-C) also results in a performance drop, demonstrating that using the cross-attention mechanism for graph representation learning of emotional text and image data enables learning of the connection between the two modalities. Removing the DINO (w/o-D) pretraining information also affects the model's

---

[4] To facilitate the implementation of all baselines, we get results of all baselines from [9].

performance, indicating that the DINO pre-trained ViT, which employs self-supervised learning, can contain more visual information. Based on these results, we conclude that using the DINO pre-trained ViT model to extract image features, graph fusion to fuse the two modalities, and cross-attention mechanism for graph representation learning can achieve relatively good performance in emotion recognition tasks.

4.5 On Case Study

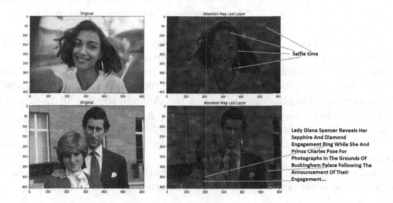

Fig. 3. Visualized cross-attention mechanisms for two testing samples.

The Fig. 3 presented illustrates a comparison of original images and last-layer attention maps side by side. The model demonstrated its ability to harness complementary information from both image and text modalities without focusing too much on redundant information. For example, in the first image, the vision transformer focuses on the subject's bright eyes, uplifted brow, and sunny background, which predict positive emotion. This information is not available from the textual input, which only reads "selfie time". The cross attention then focuses on the outline of the face and sunny background, which evokes feelings of joy. The attention in the image is not on the cheeks and smile because this redundant information is already in the text. On the other hand, the image attention pattern in the bottom image focuses on the rosy uplifted cheeks, which signal positive information that is not contained in the corresponding text input. Cross attention further focuses on the keywords "engagement", "palace", and "ring", which all indicate positive emotions. These are linked to image patches of the background and hand over the shoulder, indicating the closeness of the two subjects. However, note that this attention map is only for the last layer, and each layer may focus on a different aspect.

5   Conclusion

In this paper, we present a novel approach for multi-modal desire detection that combines text and visual data through a cross-modal graph. Our method differs from previous models in that we employ cross-attention in the cross-modal graph to learn token connections between modalities, capturing long-range dependencies between them by computing similarity between nodes.

References

1. Caron, M., et al.: Emerging properties in self-supervised vision transformers. In: Proceedings of the IEEE/CVF International Conference on Computer Vision, pp. 9650–9660 (2021)
2. Chang, C.Y., Chang, C.W., Zheng, J.Y., Chung, P.C.: Physiological emotion analysis using support vector regression. Neurocomputing **122**, 79–87 (2013)
3. Chauhan, D.S., Dhanush, S., Ekbal, A., Bhattacharyya, P.: Sentiment and emotion help sarcasm? A multi-task learning framework for multi-modal sarcasm, sentiment and emotion analysis. In: Proceedings of the Annual Meeting of the Association for Computational Linguistics, pp. 4351–4360 (2020)
4. Devlin, J., Chang, M.W., Lee, K., Toutanova, K.: BERT: pre-training of deep bidirectional transformers for language understanding. arXiv preprint arXiv:1810.04805 (2018)
5. Dosovitskiy, A., et al.: An image is worth 16x16 words: transformers for image recognition at scale. In: International Conference on Learning Representations (2020)
6. Hasan, M.K., Rahman, W., Zadeh, A., Zhong, J., Tanveer, M.I., Morency, L.P., et al.: UR-FUNNY: a multimodal language dataset for understanding humor. arXiv preprint arXiv:1904.06618 (2019)
7. Hassan, M.M., Alam, M.G.R., Uddin, M.Z., Huda, S., Almogren, A., Fortino, G.: Human emotion recognition using deep belief network architecture. Inf. Fusion **51**, 10–18 (2019)
8. Hearst, M.A.: Automatic acquisition of hyponyms from large text corpora. In: COLING 1992 Volume 2: The 14th International Conference on Computational Linguistics (1992)
9. Jia, A., He, Y., Zhang, Y., Uprety, S., Song, D., Lioma, C.: Beyond emotion: a multi-modal dataset for human desire understanding. In: Proceedings of the Conference of the North American Chapter of the Association for Computational Linguistics: Human Language Technologies, pp. 1512–1522 (2022)
10. Jing, L., Li, Y., Xu, J., Yu, Y., Shen, P., Song, X.: Vision enhanced generative pre-trained language model for multimodal sentence summarization. Mach. Intell. Res. **20**, 1–10 (2023)
11. Jing, L., Song, X., Lin, X., Zhao, Z., Zhou, W., Nie, L.: Stylized data-to-text generation: a case study in the e-commerce domain. ACM Trans. Inf. Syst. (2023)
12. Jing, L., Song, X., Ouyang, K., Jia, M., Nie, L.: Multi-source semantic graph-based multimodal sarcasm explanation generation. arXiv preprint arXiv:2306.16650 (2023)
13. Jing, L., Tian, M., Chen, X., Sun, T., Guan, W., Song, X.: CI-OCM: counterfactual inference towards unbiased outfit compatibility modeling. In: Proceedings of the 1st Workshop on Multimedia Computing towards Fashion Recommendation, pp. 31–38. Association for Computing Machinery (2022)

14. Li, X., et al.: EEG based emotion recognition: a tutorial and review. ACM Comput. Surv. **55**(4), 1–57 (2022)
15. Liang, B., et al.: Multi-modal sarcasm detection via cross-modal graph convolutional network. In: Proceedings of the Annual Meeting of the Association for Computational Linguistics (Volume 1: Long Papers), pp. 1767–1777 (2022)
16. Nie, L., Jia, M., Song, X., Wu, G., Cheng, H., Gu, J.: Multimodal activation: awakening dialog robots without wake words. In: The 44th International ACM SIGIR Conference on Research and Development in Information Retrieval, pp. 491–500. ACM (2021)
17. Qiao, Y., Jing, L., Song, X., Chen, X., Zhu, L., Nie, L.: Mutual-enhanced incongruity learning network for multi-modal sarcasm detection. In: Proceedings of the AAAI Conference on Artificial Intelligence, vol. 37, pp. 9507–9515 (2023)
18. Schuster, M., Paliwal, K.K.: Bidirectional recurrent neural networks. IEEE Trans. Signal Process. **45**(11), 2673–2681 (1997)
19. Song, X., Jing, L., Lin, D., Zhao, Z., Chen, H., Nie, L.: V2P: vision-to-prompt based multi-modal product summary generation. In: The International ACM SIGIR Conference on Research and Development in Information Retrieval, pp. 992–1001. ACM (2022)
20. Sun, T., Wang, W., Jing, L., Cui, Y., Song, X., Nie, L.: Counterfactual reasoning for out-of-distribution multimodal sentiment analysis. In: The ACM International Conference on Multimedia, pp. 15–23. ACM (2022)
21. Xiao, L., Wu, X., Wu, W., Yang, J., He, L.: Multi-channel attentive graph convolutional network with sentiment fusion for multimodal sentiment analysis. In: IEEE International Conference on Acoustics, Speech and Signal Processing, pp. 4578–4582. IEEE (2022)
22. Xu, B., Fu, Y., Jiang, Y.G., Li, B., Sigal, L.: Video emotion recognition with transferred deep feature encodings. In: Proceedings of the ACM on International Conference on Multimedia Retrieval, pp. 15–22 (2016)
23. Xu, G., Meng, Y., Qiu, X., Yu, Z., Wu, X.: Sentiment analysis of comment texts based on BiLSTM. IEEE Access **7**, 51522–51532 (2019)
24. Yang, X., Feng, S., Zhang, Y., Wang, D.: Multimodal sentiment detection based on multi-channel graph neural networks. In: Proceedings of the Annual Meeting of the Association for Computational Linguistics and the International Joint Conference on Natural Language Processing, pp. 328–339 (2021)
25. Zhang, Y., et al.: CFN: a complex-valued fuzzy network for sarcasm detection in conversations. IEEE Trans. Fuzzy Syst. **29**(12), 3696–3710 (2021)
26. Zhao, S., Yao, H., Yang, Y., Zhang, Y.: Affective image retrieval via multi-graph learning. In: Proceedings of the ACM International Conference on Multimedia, pp. 1025–1028 (2014)
27. Zheng, W.L., Liu, W., Lu, Y., Lu, B.L., Cichocki, A.: Emotionmeter: a multimodal framework for recognizing human emotions. IEEE Trans. Cybern. **49**(3), 1110–1122 (2018)

Negative Edge Prediction for Attributed Graph Clustering

Zhenhao Zhang, Yibo Hu, and Bin Wu[✉]

Beijing University of Posts and Telecommunications,
No. 10, Xitucheng Road, Beijing, China
{zzhpro,huyibo,wubin}@bupt.edu.cn

Abstract. Modern methods for attributed graph clustering typically use the (variants of) adjacency matrix as a filter to generate smooth graph signals. However, the existence of negative edges (i.e., edges connecting nodes with different labels) can make the adjacency matrix noisy and harm clustering performance. Therefore, we propose an unsupervised negative edge prediction problem, which aims to recognize negative edges using node attributes and graph topology, without the supervision of node labels. A good solution for negative edge prediction can also help clustering models achieve better results. In this paper, we introduce CRNet, a neural network that utilizes a Contrastive and Reconstruction loss for supervision. CRNet extracts node representations from raw features and scores edges using the cosine similarity of the learned node representations. Low-scored edges are considered predicted negative edges. Clustering models can then be trained on the denoised graph to achieve performance gains. Extensive experimentation on common datasets showed that CRNet achieved state-of-the-art performance on negative edge prediction and helped improve the performance of various backbone models on graph clustering.

Keywords: Graph structure learning · Graph clustering · Denoising

1 Introduction

An attributed graph is a powerful abstraction of the real world. Social networks [1], citation networks [2], and recommendation systems [3] can all be efficiently represented using attributed graphs. Attributed graph clustering (AGC) is the task of partitioning nodes into clusters without any labels. Due to the prevalence of network-structured data and the lack of accurate labels, AGC is an important and ubiquitous task.

The key ingredient of graph neural networks is aggregation, which involves gathering information from a node's neighborhood. A node's representation is derived by aggregating its attributes and those of its neighbors. Aggregation is beneficial because it elegantly combines the information in graph topology and node attributes, and the adjacency matrix can serve as a low-pass filter [4] to generate smooth signals. This procedure can be seen as the denoising of

L. Iliadis et al. (Eds.): ICANN 2023, LNCS 14257, pp. 524–536, 2023.
https://doi.org/10.1007/978-3-031-44216-2_43

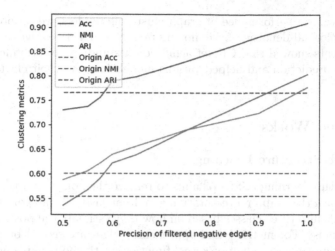

Fig. 1. Clustering metric growth with the percentage of correctly filtered negative edges. Dashed lines represent the corresponding metric when the original adjacency matrix was used.

node attributes. However, what if the filter itself is noisy? Potentially harmful and task-irrelevant information may be introduced during aggregation. Thus, topological denoising is a necessary tool to improve the performance of learning methods on graphs.

As in [5], we define the concept of negative edges as edges connecting nodes with different labels. If the final purpose is to assign the correct label to each node, information passed through the negative edges is probably harmful. [5] showed that with the removal of negative edges, GCN obtains significant performance gain on node classification on Cora. In Fig. 1, we conducted experiments in which a fixed-size set of edges were removed with a controlled percentage of true negative edges and randomly chosen positive edges. The performance was obtained by running AGE [6] on Cora. It can be seen that, even in this non-optimal setting, as long as the precision of predicted negative edges is above about 57%, the clustering performance can be improved.

To effectively identify negative edges, we propose CRNet, a feed-forward neural network trained by contrastive and reconstruction loss. Edges are scored and ranked by the cosine similarity between the nodes' representations produced by CRNet. Edges whose score is lower than a threshold will be remove from the original graph. We suggest tuning threshold based on the corresponding DBI.

In conclusion, our contributions can be summarized as:

- We formally propose the task of unsupervised negative edge prediction. A competitive baseline model CRNet is also proposed for this task.

- To improve the performance of graph clustering models, we propose to conduct topological denoising by removing predicted negative edges.
- Experiments showed that CRNet achieved outstanding performance in negative edge prediction and helped various models improve their clustering performance.

2 Related Works

2.1 Graph Structure Learning

Graph structure learning (GSL) [7] aims to remove the noisy and task-irrelevant edges and learn the graph representation simultaneously. [7] categorizes existing GSL methods into three classes based on how they estimate the possibility of an edge being noisy. For metric-based approaches, edges are scored by a pairwise metric function (inner product or kernel function) of the node pair's embedding. Whereas for neural approaches: edges are weighted by a neural network. Finally, there are direct approaches where the adjacency matrix is optimized as a variable directly. However, these methods generally need to entangle the process of refining graph structure and training task-specific models, which may be unsuitable for complicated task-specific algorithms. Our method decouples the graph structure refining process and the downstream task training process, making it applicable to almost all graph clustering algorithms.

2.2 Attributed Graph Clustering

Since both node attributes and graph topology exist in the input of AGC task, classic machine learning algorithms like KMeans [8] and spectral clustering [9] could apply. In recent years, with the fast development of deep learning techniques, the enriched toolkit has profound impact on AGC algorithms. VGAE (Variational Graph Auto-Encoder) [10] learns node representations with GCN (Graph Convolutional Network) supervised by an adjacency matrix reconstruction loss. Many later works [11,12] followed this paradigm with optimizations towards graph clustering.

Another line of research started at PPNP [13], who focus on the disentanglement of aggregation and transformation in GNNs. Similarly motivated, AGE [6] uses a Laplacian filter to generate smoothed node features. Then the smoothed features are transformed by a learnable weight matrix into node embedding. The weight matrix is optimized to minimize a self-training loss. Experiments showed that AGE is one of the state-of-the-art methods in graph clustering.

It can be seen that, although various advanced deep learning techniques are applied in the field of attributed graph clustering, almost all of them involve neighborhood feature aggregation. So adjacency matrix denoising technique can be easily and widely applied to different models.

3   Methodology

In this section, we first formally define the concept of "negative edge" and then propose a self-supervised model called CRNet which can detect negative edges efficiently and effectively. The overall structure of CRNet is shown in Fig. 2.

3.1   Problem Formulation

We use $\mathcal{G} = (\mathcal{V}, \mathcal{E}, \mathbf{X})$ to denote an attributed graph, where $\mathcal{V} = \{v_1, v_2, ..., v_N\}$ is the set of vertices with $|\mathcal{V}| = N$, $\mathcal{E}$ is the set of edges, $\mathbf{X} \in \mathbb{R}^{N \times F}$ is the attribute matrix, the ith row of which represents the attribute vector of v_i, and F is the dimension of one node's attribute vector. The topological structure of $\mathcal{G}$ can be represented by the adjacency matrix $\mathbf{A} \in \{0, 1\}^{N \times N}$, where $a_{ij} = 1$ if and only if $(v_i, v_j) \in \mathcal{E}$ and $a_{ij} = 0$ otherwise. We further assume that every vertex v_i is attached with a label $y_i \in \{1, 2, ..., K\}$ where K is the number of classes. This assumption is reasonable in scenarios like graph clustering.

Definition. In an attributed graph $\mathcal{G}$, we define a *negative edge* as an edge that connects nodes that belong to different classes. In other words, for $v_i, v_j \in \mathcal{V}$, (v_i, v_j) is a negative edge iff $y_i \neq y_j$ and $(v_i, v_j) \in \mathcal{E}$.

To avoid the potential harm caused by negative edges, we need to identify them first. In scenarios like graph clustering, all the labels are missing during training, so identifying negative edges from the definition is not feasible. We thus introduce the task of *unsupervised negative edge prediction*: given a graph $\mathcal{G}$ represented by its adjacency matrix $\mathbf{A}$ and attribute matrix $\mathbf{X}$, identify the negative edges out of all edges.

3.2   Base Model

In our solution, we divide the problem of unsupervised negative edge prediction into two phases. To begin with, we train a self-supervised model to learn the similarity of any pair of nodes. Then the threshold is tuned as a hyperparameter based on the clustering performance of the downstream model. If the nodes connected by an edge have a similarity score below the threshold, the edge is considered negative by our model.

Since the adjacency matrix is considered noisy, we utilize the node attributes **only** as the input feature. The normalized embedding of vertex v_i is calculate as

$$\mathbf{z}_i = \frac{f_\theta(\mathbf{x}_i)}{||f_\theta(\mathbf{x}_i)||_2} \tag{1}$$

where f_θ is a neural encoder parameterized by θ and $\mathbf{x}_i \in \mathbb{R}^F$ is the feature vector of node v_i. A simple implementation can be a multi-layer perceptron (MLP):

$$f_\theta(\mathbf{x}_i) = \mathrm{MLP}(\mathbf{x}_i) \tag{2}$$

Since the concept of negative edges is closely related to the unknown node classes and we aim to improve the performance of backbone models on graph clustering,

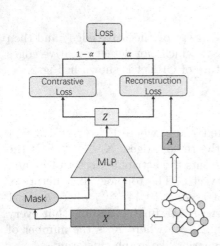

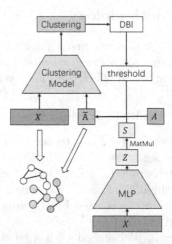

(a) The forward pass of CRNet during training.

(b) Training downstream model using denoised graph. The threshold is selected based on the corresponding DBI.

Fig. 2. Overall structure of CRNet and the denoising process. Node colors represent the node labels. Positive and negative edges are distinguished by colors (Color figure online)

we'd like to add pseudo-label information as an additional input feature. We obtain the pseudo-labels by running K-Means with node attributes as input. We use $\mathbf{e}_i \in \{0,1\}^K$ as the one-hot row representation of node i's pseudo-label. Then the node embedding from enhanced input feature can be computed as:

$$f_\theta(\mathbf{x}_i) = \text{MLP}(\mathbf{x}_i \mathbf{W}^{(x)} \| \mathbf{e}_i \mathbf{W}^{(e)}) \tag{3}$$

where $\mathbf{W}^{(x)} \in \mathbb{R}^{F \times D}$ and $\mathbf{W}^{(e)} \in \mathbb{R}^{K \times D}$ are learnable parameters and $\|$ represents concatenation. It should be noticed that, in practice, Eq. (3) may perform worse than Eq. (2) when then node attributes are noisy. An intuitive heuristic is Eq. (3) perform better only when K-Means can produce a rather reasonable clustering.

The cosine similarity matrix between all pairs of nodes can be easily calculated as

$$\mathbf{S} = \mathbf{Z}^T \mathbf{Z} \tag{4}$$

3.3 Contrastive and Reconstruction Loss

What we are facing is a fine-grain classification problem, without direct supervision. "Fine-grain" comes from the observation that negative edges, although noisy, are still edges. If two nodes are connected by a negative edge, their similarity probably is still higher than two random nodes from the graph. We thus encourage the model to form multiple similarity levels by a carefully designed loss function. For $(v_i, v_j), (v_i, v_k) \in \mathcal{E}, y_i = y_j \neq y_k$ and $(v_i, v_h) \notin \mathcal{E}$, we expect the continued inequality

$$\text{sim}(v_i, v_i) > \text{sim}(v_i, v_j) > \text{sim}(v_i.v_k) > \text{sim}(v_i, v_h) \qquad (5)$$

to hold. When the ground truth labels are missing, we can at most encourage the model to learn:

$$\text{sim}(v_i, v_i) > \text{sim}(v_i, v_{j|k}) > \text{sim}(v_i, v_h) \qquad (6)$$

At first glance, it may seem confusing how the first part of Eq. (6) may help the learning of model parameters. We address this problem by express the first part of Eq. (6) as a contrastive loss as in [14]. We denote two random data augmentation by $\mathcal{H}$ and $\mathcal{G}$. Suppose $\mathbf{z}_i = f_\theta(\mathcal{H}(\mathbf{x}_i))$ and $\mathbf{z}_i' = f_\theta(\mathcal{G}(\mathbf{x}_i))$, we formulate the contrastive loss as:

$$\mathcal{L}_{con} = -\frac{1}{B} \sum_{(i,k)\in[B]} \log \sigma(\mathbf{z}_i^T \mathbf{z}_i' - \mathbf{z}_i^T \mathbf{z}_k') \qquad (7)$$

where $[B]$ is a batch of sample edges of size B. $\mathcal{L}_{con}$ takes the form of Bayesian Personalized ranking [15], which is a well-known loss function in the field of recommender systems. It makes positive pairs have higher scores than negative pairs. We defer the detailed description of data augmentation methods to the next section and focus on loss functions here.

The second part of Eq. (6) can be seen as the reconstruction of graph adjacency matrix, which is the way we inject the information in $\mathbf{A}$ into our model. There is no need to use data augmentation in this part. We simply use BPR loss to force connected nodes to score higher than the unconnected nodes:

$$\mathcal{L}_{rec} = -\frac{1}{B} \sum_{(i,k)\in[B]} \sum_{h\notin\mathcal{N}(i)} \log \sigma(\mathbf{z}_i^T \mathbf{z}_k - \mathbf{z}_i^T \mathbf{z}_h) \qquad (8)$$

Finally, the total loss function is given by the weighted sum of contrastive loss and reconstruction loss, with some level of L2 regularization:

$$\mathcal{L} = (1 - \alpha)\mathcal{L}_{con} + \alpha\mathcal{L}_{rec} + \lambda||\theta||_2^2 \qquad (9)$$

3.4   Data Augmentation

Random Feature Masking(RFM) means to randomly divide the features into two disjoint sets with roughly equal sizes. In this case, the indexes of masked features are defined by $M = \{i_0, i_1, ...\}$ with $|M| \approx F/2$.

As stated in [14], random masking of node features allows the model to exploit the shortcut of highly correlated features, which would make the contrastive learning task too easy. Following [14], we split the features according to their mutual information. The mutual information of two discrete features is calculated as:

$$MI(F_i, F_j) = \sum_{f_i \in F_i, f_j \in F_j} P(f_i, f_j) \log \frac{P(f_i, f_j)}{P(f_i)P(f_j)} \qquad (10)$$

where F_i and F_j denote the sets of all possible values of the ith and jth component of the feature vector. For each dataset, the mutual information matrix between all pairs of features can be precomputed.

When sampling data augmentation functions $\mathcal{H}$ and $\mathcal{G}$ during training, we first choose a seed feature randomly, whose index is denoted by $seed$. Then the index of masked features set M is defined by

$$M = \{seed\} \bigcup \{i | \text{argsort}(MI(F_{seed}))_i > F/2\} \qquad (11)$$

which means the seed feature and its most correlated features are masked together to force the model to learn high-level semantic information. This technique is called Correlated Feature Masking(CFM) in [14].

At last, for an input node attribute vector $\mathbf{x}$, the sampled h and g can be defined as:

$$h(\mathbf{x})_j = \begin{cases} x_j, & j \in M \\ 0, & else \end{cases}, \ g(\mathbf{x})_j = \begin{cases} x_j, & j \notin M \\ 0, & else \end{cases} \qquad (12)$$

3.5 Determining the Threshold

Recall that in our method, an edge whose corresponding similarity score is above the threshold is considered a positive edge and vice versa. In other words, for $(v_i, v_j) \in \mathcal{E}$,

$$(v_i, v_j) \in \begin{cases} positive \ edges, & s_{ij} > threshold, \\ negative \ edges, & else \end{cases} \qquad (13)$$

However, determining the optimal value of the threshold is hard in unsupervised scenario. Since we aim to improve the performance of backbone models on AGC, we score the threshold by its contribution to the downstream task. Because of the lack of ground truth labels, so we need to find a surrogate metric: a metric whose computation doesn't involve true labels and whose value is highly correlated with the real performance of the backbone model. As in [6], we found the Davies-Bouldin index [16] a suitable surrogate metric. Due to the way it is defined, as a function of the ratio of the within-cluster scatter, to the between-cluster separation, a lower value will mean that the clustering is better. The computation of DBI only requires a feature vector and a predicted label for each data point, which is applicable.

3.6 Time Complexity

In each epoch, we visit every edge once on average. And we sample random node pairs as negative sample, whose size is proportional to the size of true edges. We use symbol k to denote the ratio of size of negative samples to that of the positive samples. The computation time complexity can be represented as $O(k|\mathcal{E}|)$.

Table 1. Datasets

Dataset	#Nodes	#Features	#Classes	#Edges	#Negative Edges	%Negative Edges
Cora	2708	1433	7	5278	1003	19.00
CiteSeer	3327	3703	6	4552	1204	26.45
PubMed	19717	500	3	44324	8759	19.76

4   Experiments

The experiments were designed to answer the following research questions:

RQ1: How do transferred baselines and CRNet perform on the newly proposed unsupervised negative edge prediction task?

RQ2: To what extent can the predicted negative edges help downstream backbone models improve their performance on graph clustering?

RQ3: Ablation study: how do different parts of the loss function affect the performance of negative edges prediction? And is CFM really better than RFM in our scenario?

4.1   Datasets

We conduct negative edge prediction and attributed graph clustering experiments on three widely used network datasets (Cora, CiteSeer and PubMed [17]). All three datasets are citation networks where nodes are papers and an edge connects two nodes when one of the corresponding papers cited the other. For Cora and CiteSeer, the node attributes are the bag-of-word vectors of the papers. For PubMed, the node attributes are the tf-idf word vectors of the papers. Basic statistics and the number of negative edges are listed in Table 1.

4.2   Experiments on Negative Edge Prediction

Although the concept of negative edges has been mentioned in [5], the task of unsupervised negative edge prediction is first seriously treated as a new task in this paper. We will first introduce the appropriate performance metrics for this task and then describe the ways we transfer classic graph clustering models to our new task as baselines. At last, we show experimental results that demonstrated the superior performance of CRNet.

Metrics. As Table 1 shows, for most datasets, there is a severe class imbalance problem: positive edges generally outnumbered negative edges by a large margin. Area Under the Receiver Operating Characteristic Curve(ROC AUC) is an appropriate choice for class imbalance tasks with two classes. ROC AUC can be intuitively interpreted as the possibility of a positive sample being scored higher by a model than a negative sample. F1 score, the harmonic mean of precision and recall, is also known as a suitable metric for class imbalance tasks. Intersection over Union(IoU) measures the similarity of two sets by the cardinality of their intersection divided by the cardinality of their union. The IoU between the predicted negative edges and true negative edges is a natural reflection of the quality of prediction.

Transferred Baselines. Graph clustering methods can be directly transferred to predict negative edges. An edge is predicted as negative when it connects two nodes with different predicted labels. We name this kind of transfer "from *label*". All graph clustering methods can be transferred this way. For some baseline methods like AGE [6] and VGAE [10], there exists another way of transfer, which is named "from *similarity*". These methods can produce similarity scores for all pairs of nodes, so we can recognize the edges with low node pair similarity as negative edges. Since we are evaluating, we assume the number of true negative edges is known and pick the same number of predicted negative edges.

Betweenness centrality [18] of an edge is the sum of the fraction of all possible shortest paths that pass through this edge. Very roughly speaking, negative edges can be seen as edges connecting different communities, so their betweenness centrality scores may be higher than positive edges. Betweenness centrality can serve as a very trivial baseline. KMeans [8] and spectral clustering [9] are classic clustering algorithms that use node attributes or graph topology only.

VGAE [10] combines graph convolutional network with variational autoencoder to produce latent representations for each node in the graph. AGE [6] first perform Laplacian smoothing on node features and then learn a node embedding based on the smoothed node features using self-training techniques. These two methods can be easily transferred in both "from label" and "from similarity" ways.

SEComm [19] combine the principle of self-expressiveness with the framework of self-supervised graph neural network for graph clustering. ROD [20] is a novel reception-aware online knowledge distillation approach for sparse graph learning. ROD can be applied to many graphs learning tasks including link prediction, node classification, and graph clustering.

Experimental Results. The experimental results are listed in Table 2. We can see that CRNet consistently performed better than all baseline methods on all datasets when measured by AUC, F1, and IoU. AGE also performed well because it's the state-of-the-art graph clustering algorithm and gave the most accurate label prediction. Spectral clustering made its prediction merely based on the graph structure, which is inconsistent with the task, so the bad performance is reasonable.

4.3   Experiments on Graph Clustering

In this section, we applied the CRNet-denoised **A** to representative graph clustering models to verify the performance improvement. For SEComm, AGE and

Table 2. Experimental results on negative edge prediction

Methods	From	Cora			CiteSeer			PubMed		
		AUC	F1	IoU	AUC	F1	IoU	AUC	F1	IoU
Betweenness	Sim	0.587	0.331	0.198	0.538	0.320	0.190	0.530	0.246	0.140
KMeans	Label	0.531	0.319	0.190	0.589	0.437	0.279	0.601	0.357	0.217
Spectral-G	Label	0.499	0.000	0.000	0.500	0.000	0.000	0.517	0.082	0.043
SEComm	Label	0.632	0.409	0.257	0.539	0.193	0.107	0.513	0.267	0.154
ROD	Label	0.586	0.314	0.186	0.528	0.158	0.085	0.515	0.222	0.125
VGAE	Label	0.684	0.318	0.189	0.523	0.174	0.095	0.514	0.182	0.100
	Sim	0.667	0.356	0.216	0.567	0.319	0.189	0.544	0.232	0.131
AGE	Label	0.592	0.321	0.191	0.532	0.153	0.083	0.537	0.166	0.090
	Sim	0.761	0.427	0.271	0.658	0.423	0.268	0.561	0.288	0.168
CRNet	Sim	**0.787**	**0.481**	**0.316**	**0.689**	**0.446**	**0.287**	**0.660**	**0.373**	**0.229**

ROD, their official PyTorch implementation, and recommended parameters were used. For VGAE, the implementation in PyG [21] was used. GAT [22] was used as the encoder and spectral clustering was used to convert the reconstructed adjacency matrix to clustering results. For all models, no other hyperparameters were tuned except the threshold.

Table 3. Experimental results on attributed graph clustering

Methods	A	Cora			CiteSeer			PubMed		
		ACC	NMI	F1-macro	ACC	NMI	F1-macro	ACC	NMI	F1-macro
VGAE	Original	0.648	0.455	0.649	0.535	0.278	0.489	0.666	0.244	0.666
	Denoised	**0.687**	**0.500**	**0.685**	**0.587**	**0.351**	**0.560**	**0.685**	**0.290**	**0.691**
SEComm	Original	0.732	0.536	0.716	0.535	0.329	0.419	0.419	0.007	0.310
	Denoised	**0.743**	**0.554**	**0.730**	**0.641**	**0.371**	**0.555**	**0.717**	**0.337**	**0.713**
ROD	Original	0.735	0.555	0.682	0.629	0.385	0.608	0.644	0.245	0.607
	Denoised	**0.760**	**0.593**	**0.705**	**0.652**	**0.386**	0.608	**0.674**	**0.298**	**0.664**
AGE	Original	0.768	0.607	0.701	0.702	0.448	**0.648**	**0.711**	0.316	0.700
	Denoised	**0.782**	**0.617**	**0.729**	**0.705**	**0.454**	0.644	0.703	**0.373**	**0.704**

Experimental results are shown in Table 3. Rows labeled "original" are the performance of the backbone models with the original adjacency matrix while rows labeled "denoised" show the performance of backbone models with a denoised adjacency matrix. It can be seen that improvement was achieved for almost all metrics on almost all datasets. In addition, when the denoised adjacency matrix was used, AGE achieved state-of-the-art clustering performance on Cora.

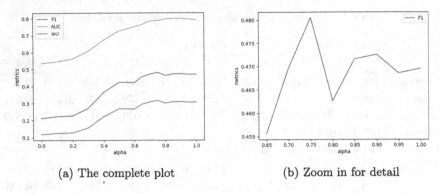

(a) The complete plot   (b) Zoom in for detail

Fig. 3. The impact of α on negative edge prediction performance.

Table 4. Ablation Study: difference between CFM and RFM

DA	Cora			CiteSeer		
	AUC	F1	IoU	AUC	F1	IoU
RFM	**0.793**	0.470	0.307	**0.690**	0.436	0.279
CFM	0.787	**0.481**	**0.316**	0.689	**0.446**	**0.287**

4.4 Ablation Study

Here we demonstrate the difference between CFM and RFM data augmentation strategies. The results of the ablation study are shown in Table 4. Experimental results indicate when measured by AUC, RFM was slightly better but when measured by all other metrics, CFM outperformed RFM by a rather large margin. In conclusion, we consider CFM a more suitable data augmentation strategy.

α is the weight of reconstruction loss while $1 - \alpha$ is the weight of contrastive loss. To demonstrate their influence on CRNet's performance, the relationship between α and negative edge prediction metrics is shown in Fig. 3. According to the plots, all metrics reached their best value when α was somewhere between 0 and 1. In Fig. 3a, the peak of the curve may be vague; so we zoom in on the plateau part of the F1 curve and get Fig. 3b. Then it's clear that F1 was best when $\alpha = 0.75$, which proves that both contrastive loss and reconstruction loss are necessary.

5 Conclusion

In this paper, we formally define the concept of negative edges and then propose the task of unsupervised negative edge prediction. CRNet, a neural network under the supervision of a contrastive and reconstruction loss, is proposed as a competitive baseline model for this task. We also show that, by removing rather accurately predicted negative edges, the performance of graph clustering models can be improved.

Regarding future work, we propose using subgraph GNNs [23] to replace the current MLP for better edge ranking quality, and consequently, further improving the performance of AGC models. Additionally, for the node classification task, some node labels are available, which makes the negative edge prediction task semi-supervised and requires a different approach.

References

1. Hastings, M.B.: Community detection as an inference problem. Phys. Rev. E **74**(3), 035102 (2006)
2. Kipf, T.N., Welling, M.: Semi-supervised classification with graph convolutional networks. In: 5th International Conference on Learning Representations, ICLR 2017, Conference Track Proceedings. OpenReview.net (2017)
3. Ying, R., He, R., Chen, K., Eksombatchai, P., Hamilton, W.L., Leskovec, J.: Graph convolutional neural networks for web-scale recommender systems. In: Proceedings of the 24th ACM SIGKDD International Conference on Knowledge Discovery & Data Mining, KDD 2018, pp. 974–983. ACM (2018)
4. Li, Q., Han, Z., Wu, X.: Deeper insights into graph convolutional networks for semi-supervised learning. In: Proceedings of the Thirty-Second AAAI Conference on Artificial Intelligence, (AAAI-18), the 30th innovative Applications of Artificial Intelligence (IAAI-18), and the 8th AAAI Symposium on Educational Advances in Artificial Intelligence (EAAI-18), pp. 3538–3545. AAAI Press (2018)
5. Luo, D., et al.: Learning to drop: robust graph neural network via topological denoising. In: WSDM 2021, The Fourteenth ACM International Conference on Web Search and Data Mining, Virtual Event, Israel, 8–12 March 2021, pp. 779–787. ACM (2021)
6. Cui, G., Zhou, J., Yang, C., Liu, Z.: Adaptive graph encoder for attributed graph embedding. In: Proceedings of the 26th ACM SIGKDD International Conference on Knowledge Discovery & Data Mining, pp. 976–985 (2020)
7. Zhu, Y., et al.: A survey on graph structure learning: Progress and opportunities, arXiv e-prints, pp. arXiv-2103 (2021)
8. Arthur, D., Vassilvitskii, S.: K-means++: the advantages of careful seeding. In: Proceedings of the Eighteenth Annual ACM-SIAM Symposium on Discrete Algorithms, ser. SODA 2007, pp. 1027–1035. Society for Industrial and Applied Mathematics, USA (2007)
9. von Luxburg, U.: A tutorial on spectral clustering. Stat. Comput. **17**(4), 395–416 (2007)
10. Kipf, T.N., Welling, M.: Variational graph auto-encoders. In: NIPS Workshop on Bayesian Deep Learning (2016)
11. Pan, S., Hu, R., Long, G., Jiang, J., Yao, L., Zhang, C.: Adversarially regularized graph autoencoder for graph embedding. In: Proceedings of the Twenty-Seventh International Joint Conference on Artificial Intelligence, IJCAI 2018, pp. 2609–2615. ijcai.org (2018)
12. Wang, C., Pan, S., Long, G., Zhu, X., Jiang, J.: MGAE: marginalized graph autoencoder for graph clustering. In: Proceedings of the 2017 ACM on Conference on Information and Knowledge Management, CIKM 2017, pp. 889–898. ACM (2017)
13. Klicpera, J., Bojchevski, A., Günnemann, S.: Predict then propagate: graph neural networks meet personalized pagerank. In: 7th International Conference on Learning Representations, ICLR 2019. OpenReview.net (2019)

14. Yao, T., et al.: Self-supervised learning for large-scale item recommendations. In: Proceedings of the 30th ACM International Conference on Information & Knowledge Management, pp. 4321–4330 (2021)
15. Rendle, S., Freudenthaler, C., Gantner, Z., Schmidt-Thieme, L.: BPR: Bayesian personalized ranking from implicit feedback. In: UAI 2009, Proceedings of the Twenty-Fifth Conference on Uncertainty in Artificial Intelligence, Montreal, QC, Canada, 18–21 June 2009, pp. 452–461. AUAI Press (2009)
16. Davies, D.L., Bouldin, D.W.: A cluster separation measure. IEEE Trans. Pattern Anal. Mach. Intell. **1**(2), 224–227 (1979)
17. Sen, P., Namata, G., Bilgic, M., Getoor, L., Gallagher, B., Eliassi-Rad, T.: Collective classification in network data. AI Mag. **29**(3), 93–106 (2008)
18. Brandes, U.: A faster algorithm for betweenness centrality. J. Math. Sociol. **25**(2), 163–177 (2001)
19. Bandyopadhyay, S., Peter, V.: Unsupervised constrained community detection via self-expressive graph neural network. In: Proceedings of the Thirty-Seventh Conference on Uncertainty in Artificial Intelligence, ser. Proceedings of Machine Learning Research, vol. 161, pp. 1078–1088. AUAI Press (2021)
20. Zhang, W., et al.: ROD: reception-aware online distillation for sparse graphs. In: KDD 2021: The 27th ACM SIGKDD Conference on Knowledge Discovery and Data Mining, pp. 2232–2242. ACM (2021)
21. Fey, M., Lenssen, J.E.: Fast graph representation learning with PyTorch geometric. In: ICLR Workshop on Representation Learning on Graphs and Manifolds (2019)
22. Velickovic, P., Cucurull, G., Casanova, A., Romero, A., Liò, P., Bengio, Y.: Graph attention networks. In: 6th International Conference on Learning Representations, ICLR 2018, Conference Track Proceedings. OpenReview.net (2018)
23. Zhang, M., Chen, Y.: Link prediction based on graph neural networks. In: Advances in Neural Information Processing Systems, vol. 31 (2018)

One-Class Intrusion Detection with Dynamic Graphs

Aleksei Liuliakov$^{(\boxtimes)}$ ⓘ, Alexander Schulz ⓘ, Luca Hermes ⓘ,
and Barbara Hammer ⓘ

Machine Learning Group, Bielefeld University, Bielefeld, Germany
{aliuliakov,aschulz,lhermes,bhammer}@techfak.uni-bielefeld.de

Abstract. With the growing digitalization all over the globe, the relevance of network security becomes increasingly important. Machine learning-based intrusion detection constitutes a promising approach for improving security, but it bears several challenges. These include the requirement to detect novel and unseen network events, as well as specific data properties, such as events over time together with the inherent graph structure of network communication.

In this work, we propose a novel intrusion detection method, *TGN-SVDD*, which builds upon modern dynamic graph modelling and deep anomaly detection. We demonstrate its superiority over several baselines for realistic intrusion detection data and suggest a more challenging variant of the latter.

Keywords: Temporal dynamic graph · One class classification · Intrusion detection

1 Introduction

The field of anomaly detection deals with detecting rare observations, sometimes also referred to as outliers or novelties, that differ substantially from the majority of samples. This is approached (mostly) in a fully unsupervised fashion with only regular samples being available. The interest in this problem has been increasing in recent years due to a growing potential impact in different areas, such as security, medicine or finance. A variety of successful models for this problem has been proposed, ranging from shallow approaches like the One-Class Support Vector Machine (OCSVM), the Support Vector Data Description (SVDD), Isolation Forest (IF) or Local Outlier Factor (LOF) [2,7,16,19], over deep methods like Deep SVDD or Deep OCSVM [3,15], to graph based ones like the Temporal Hierarchical One-Class (THOC) network or Event2Graph [18,22]. Several more have been discussed in survey articles focusing on specific aspects, such as deep or graph based models [6,9,14]. This field has been investigated from different areas, including automated machine learning based approaches [8].

We gratefully acknowledge funding by the BMBF within the project HAIP, grant number 16KIS1212.

L. Iliadis et al. (Eds.): ICANN 2023, LNCS 14257, pp. 537–549, 2023.
https://doi.org/10.1007/978-3-031-44216-2_44

In the present work we want to focus on the subfield of intrusion detection in computer networks. Specifically, we aim to detect abnormal network traffic that constitutes an attack by an intruder. This is a relevant topic, because the size and abundance of computer networks keeps increasing. Accordingly, the dependence of the public and the private sector on the former is ever-growing. This makes the potential danger and costs of attacks on such networks, such as network intrusion attacks, evident. In this domain, specific properties of the data are present that are not necessarily typical for classical anomaly detection: First, network communication appears sequentially over time, making dynamical data structures promising candidates; second, communication has the structure of a sender, a recipient and a communication message [17], which can be most naturally represented as graphs. For this purpose, Dynamic Graph Neural Networks are a promising model class, including the approaches [5,13,20,21,23]. In a recent study [12], the Temporal Graph Network (TGN) [13], has shown to be particularly successful in modelling dynamical network data. However, empirically, the TGN is not sufficient for intrusion detection. Hence, we propose an extension of this model and evaluate it in the context of intrusion detection.

Our contributions are the following:

- We propose a new fully unsupervised end-to-end trainable intrusion detection model, that we call *TGN-SVDD*, which utilizes dynamic graph modelling and combines the two approaches TGN and Deep SVDD.
- We demonstrate that the vanilla TGN is not sufficient for intrusion detection in realistic benchmark data [17], while performing better than shallow models. Both are outperformed by our proposed TGN-SVDD.
- We analyze the dataset [17] in depth and detect a potential easy workaround that could be used by models for intrusion detection. We suggest a solution to this problem making the dataset more challenging and show that our proposed method still achieves a high performance level.

2   Fundamentals

Network traffic and more specifically internet traffic refers to the collective flow of data packets transmitted, received, and routed between interconnected devices and systems. This traffic encompasses various data types, including text, multimedia, and control information exchanged through a diverse set of application-layer protocols such as HTTP, FTP, SMTP, etc. Internet traffic can be represented as a set of network flows, where each is a sequence of data packets that share common attributes, such as the source IP address, destination IP address, source port, destination port, and protocol. It can be further conceptualized as dynamic temporal graphs. In this representation, source and destination are represented as nodes and identified by their respective IP address and the connections between these nodes, defined by network flows, act as the edges or links. Note that each edge is associated with a timestamp that reflects when that particular network flow appeared.

2.1 Continuous-Time Dynamic Graphs (CTDG)

Continuous-time dynamic graphs (CTDG) are represented as timed event lists, including edge or node addition/deletion and feature transformations. Temporal (multi-)graphs are sequences of time-stamped events $G = \{x(t_1), x(t_2), ...\}$, with events $x(t)$ adding/changing nodes or interactions. There are two event types: 1) node-wise events $\mathbf{v}_i(t)$ such as creating a node i or updating its features, and 2) interaction events in the form of directed temporal edges $\mathbf{e}_{ij}(t)$.

Denote $V(T) = \{i : \exists\, \mathbf{v}_i(t) \in G, t \in T\}$ and $E(T) = \{(i,j) : \exists\, \mathbf{e}_{ij}(t) \in G, t \in T\}$ as temporal vertex and edge sets, and $\mathcal{N}_i(T) = \{j : (i,j) \in E(T)\}$ as node i's neighborhood in time interval T. $\mathcal{N}_i^\nu(T)$ is the ν-hop neighborhood. A snapshot of graph G at time t is the (multi-)graph $G(t) = (V([0,t]), E([0,t]))$.

2.2 Temporal Graph Network (TGN)

One popular framework to model dynamic graphs is the TGN [13]. TGN model with graph attention mechanism consists of an encoder-decoder pair for dynamic graph analysis. The TGN encoder for continuous-time dynamic graphs generates node embeddings that capture long-term dependencies. The decoder uses the embeddings to make task-specific predictions.

The model maintains a vector for each node as memory which represents the compressed history. Messages are computed for each node participating in the event. Separate message functions for source, target, and node-wise changes are used. After each event node memory is updated by means of a learnable memory function (e.g. GRU) with messages and previous memory states as inputs respectively. This enables the model to capture long-term dependencies.

In a given interaction event between nodes i and j at time step t, a Temporal Graph Attention Module effectively incorporates the historical events of either node. For node i, the module retrieves its current representation along with its previous interactions with other nodes. These past interactions are then weighted according to the attention mechanism and subsequently aggregated to provide a representation of the node's temporal dynamics. The output of this module results in an embedding vector for a particular node i in time t.

To define the model we use the same notation as above for CTDG. $G = \{x(t_1), ..., x(t_D)\}$ is a sequences of time-stamped and time-ordered interaction events $x(t)$, where D is the number of events in the data. For every t_k with $k \in \{1, .., D\}$, we have certain source and destination nodes pairs $(i,j) \in E(t_k)$, and corresponding event feature vectors $\mathbf{e}_{ij}(t_k)$. We denote a TGN memory state $\mathbf{s}_i(t_k^-)$ of the node i at the time $t_k^- < t_k$, which gets updated every time when node i appears in an event. We denote TGN encoder functional module $\mathbf{z}(i, \mathbf{s}_i(t_k^-), \mathcal{N}_i(t_k), \mathbf{W})$, which provides a vector representation of the node i in embedding space $\mathcal{F} \subseteq \mathbb{R}^p$ with respect to the past temporal events at time t_k^-, the history of this node $s_i(t_k^-)$ and with respect to its temporal neighborhood $\mathcal{N}_i(t_k)$. $\mathbf{W}$ are TGN's encoder model parameters.

In the original work, a multi-layer perceptron (MLP) decoder is employed by the authors for self-supervised next edge (event) prediction task. In our work we only utilize TGN's encoder part to obtain node embeddings that we complement with a decoder specialized for one-class classification (s. Sect. 3).

2.3 Deep Support Vector Data Description (Deep SVDD)

One-Class classification focuses on learning the target class representation to identify novel or outlier instances. Traditional shallow methods like OCSVM and SVDD [16,19] face scalability issues and struggle in complex high-dimensional scenarios. Deep SVDD [15] addresses these limitations by learning a feature space representation in an end-to-end setting with a deep network. It also improves performance and scalability in one-class classification and anomaly detection tasks. Deep SVDD can be integrated with various deep learning encoder architectures, leveraging recent successes in deep representation learning.

For a given input space $\mathcal{X} \subseteq \mathbb{R}^d$ and output space $\mathcal{F} \subseteq \mathbb{R}^p$, let $\phi(\cdot; \mathbf{W}) : \mathcal{X} \to \mathcal{F}$ represent a deep neural network with parameters $\mathbf{W}$. For any test point $\mathbf{x} \in \mathcal{X}$, an anomaly score $\mathbf{s}$ is defined by calculating the squared distance between the point and the center of a hypersphere $\mathbf{c}$. This can be expressed as:

$$s(\mathbf{x}) = \| \phi(\mathbf{x}; \mathbf{W}) - \mathbf{c} \|^2 \qquad (1)$$

The training data is represented as $\mathcal{D}_\mu = \{\mathbf{x}_1, \dots, \mathbf{x}_\mu\}$, where $\mathbf{x}_i \in \mathcal{X}, \forall i \in \{1, \dots, \mu\}$. Where $\mu \in \mathbb{N}$ is a number of data points. The objective of Deep SVDD can be formulated as following:

$$\min_{\mathbf{W}, \mathbf{c}} \frac{1}{\mu} \sum_{i=1}^{\mu} \| \phi(\mathbf{x}_i; \mathbf{W}) - \mathbf{c} \|^2 + \lambda \|\mathbf{W}\|^2, \qquad (2)$$

aims to minimize the sum of the squared distances between the network representations of input data points $\phi(\mathbf{x}_i; \mathbf{W})$ and the center $\mathbf{c} \in \mathcal{F}$ of the hypersphere, along with a weight decay regularizer term for model parameters $\mathbf{W}$, which is controlled by the hyperparameter λ. Note that $\mathbf{c}$ is optimized jointly with the network parameters.

3 Our Proposed Model: TGN-SVDD

In the application case of cybersecurity and Network Intrusion Detection Systems (NIDS) usually only normal/benign data is available. At the same time attacks exhibit a wide range of characteristics and new attack types may be found. Thus, training data cannot be assumed to cover all possible attacks. This makes standard supervised Machine Learning techniques suboptimal for such data and applications. We introduce a novel end-to-end trainable unsupervised approach which is best suited for, but not limited to, cybersecurity and NIDS applications.

For the TGN encoder functional module, from Sect. 2.2, we will use the notation $\mathbf{z}_i(t_k, \mathbf{W})$ for brevity. The rest of the notation remains unchanged.

We apply a modified Deep SVDD decoder to compute an anomaly score for each given interaction event $x(t_k)$ as follows:

$$s(\mathbf{x}(t_k)) = \| (\mathbf{z}_i(t_k, \mathbf{W}) \oplus \mathbf{z}_j(t_k, \mathbf{W})) - \mathbf{c} \|^2, \tag{3}$$

where $\mathbf{z}_i$ and $\mathbf{z}_j$ are the temporal node embeddings of nodes i and j that participate in event $x(t_k)$, $\oplus$ denotes concatenation, and, as in Deep SVDD, $\mathbf{c}$ is a trainable vector that points to the center of a hypersphere. At initialization time, the node's memory states are set to zero-vectors. The end-to-end training objective is defined as

$$\min_{\mathbf{W},\mathbf{c}} \frac{1}{D} \sum_{k=1}^{D} \| (\mathbf{z}_i(t_k, \mathbf{W}) \oplus \mathbf{z}_j(t_k, \mathbf{W})) - \mathbf{c} \|^2 + \lambda \| \mathbf{W} \|^2, \tag{4}$$

which aims to minimize the sum of the squared distances between the concatenated TGN encoder representations of source node i and destination node j and the center $\mathbf{c} \in \mathbb{R}^{2 \times p}$ of the hypersphere, along with a weight regularization term for TGN encoder model parameters $\mathbf{W}$, and corresponding trade-off hyperparameter λ.

4 Experiment

In the following, we describe our performed experimentation, including the setup, the utilized data and pre-processing as well as the final results.

4.1 Dataset and Experimental Setup

Dataset. To evaluate our proposed model, we employed the CIC-IDS2017 dataset [17], which was created by the University of New Brunswick. This publicly available dataset offers realistic intrusion detection scenarios for evaluation. The dataset was generated by designing two separate networks: the Victim-Network and the Attack-Network. The authors proposed a B-profile system to replicate background traffic, capturing the abstract behavior of 25 users based on HTTP, HTTPS, FTP, SSH, and email protocols for normal traffic. The attack traffic incorporates six attack profiles, including Brute Force, Heartbleed, Botnet, DoS, DDoS, Web, and Infiltration attacks. Data collection encompasses data gathering over five working days Monday to Friday, with Monday featuring only benign traffic and the other days containing various attacks.

To format the raw PCAP files provided by the authors for compatibility with the model, we pre-processed the data. As dynamic temporal graphs require a sequence of timestamped events as input data, it is common to use a temporal adjacency list table format. This table includes columns for source node ID, destination node ID, timestamp, and a vector of features corresponding to the event. If applicable, an additional column for event labels may be included. We choose Network Flows (NetFlow) as source of the timestamped sequence of events, with source and destination IP addresses as unique node IDs.

Table 1. Statistics of the resulting data for the days that includes attacks.

Name	Events	Nodes	Features
Tuesday	572087	12972	61
Wednesday	597202	13595	61
Thursday	614336	13611	61
Friday	753468	13314	61

To convert raw traffic into an adjacency list of timestamped NetFlow events, we utilised the NFStream framework [1]. This allows us to extract a list of timestamped NetFlows along with 61 custom statistical 'core' and 'postmortem' features. Raw IP addresses are enumerated to unique IDs, and the timestamp is set to the first appearance of the first flow's packet. All continuous features are scaled to the [0, 1] interval. We labeled the data according to the attacker IP, victim IP, and time frame during which each attack was conducted, resulting in timestamped NetFlow event lists for each working day of the experiment.

Our model requires a strict sequential order, with normal data streams occurring earlier in the training phase and actual attacks appearing later in the testing phase. To accomplish this, we modified the data as follows. Since Monday only included normal traffic activities, we concatenated Monday's event list with one of the other working days (Tuesday, Wednesday, Thursday, or Friday) while respecting the timestamps. This resulted in four temporal dynamic graphs, each starting with Monday's events and continuing with malicious traffic from one of the subsequent working days.

We subtracted the largest timestamp from every event's timestamp in both parts of each data day-pair and added the largest timestamp from the first part (Monday) to the second part (one of the malicious days). This eliminates temporal discontinuity in the data (night gap between working days activity), and results in timestamps starting at 0 and monotonically increasing up to the end of the dataset. This modification is considered valid without significantly affecting the data pattern, as we are interested in intraday activity rather than intra -week, -month, or -year scales. We assume that events within days are similarly distributed over time. Details about the data are provided in Table 1.

In this study, we partitioned the data into train, validation, and test subsets for each day, adhering to a consistent split criterion across all four datasets. The train subset comprises the initial 200,000 events, while the validation subset encompasses the subsequent 70,000 events. The remaining events constitute the test subset. The data splitting was conducted with respect to the timeline to ensure that the train and validation subsets contain only normal events, with all attacks appearing only in the test set.

Experimental Setup. The proposed model was implemented in Python 3.9 using the Pytorch [10] and PyG [4] packages.

The baselines LOF and IF are provided in the sckit-learn package [11], the vanilla TGN baseline algorithm by the PyG package example implementations.

For our model implementation we use the TGN's encoder part from PyG, with the following parameters: time embedding dimension 200, memory and node embedding dimensions both 200. The remaining parameters are chosen as they were provided by the default model. TGN-SVDD was trained over 25 epochs.

The number of neighbors in LOF was 20, the remaining parameters default. For IF default parameters are employed. We ran a vanilla TGN model as an additional baseline using the default parameters provided in PyG.

4.2   Results

In this section, we present the evaluation results of our TGN-SVDD model and the baseline models: Vanilla TGN, LOF (novelty), LOF (outlier) and IF. The evaluation metrics, including precision, recall, F1-score and ROC AUC, are provided in the Table 2; Figs. 1 and 2 illustrate the performance of our model.

We conducted the evaluation under two different scenarios. In the first scenario, we used temporal event data *with* features as input for our TGN-SVDD model and the baseline vanilla TGN model. In the second scenario, we set all event-related features to 0, which is equivalent to the case *without* features at all. In this scenario TGN-SVDD and vanilla TGN rely solely on the temporal graph dynamics of the data.

The other baseline models, LOF (novelty), LOF (outlier), and Isolation Forest, were evaluated on the exact same data, including source/destination node IDs and timestamps, both with and without features. The LOF (novelty) model, as a novelty detector, was trained on the training data, and inference was performed on the testing data. LOF (outlier) and Isolation Forest, as outlier detectors, were evaluated directly on the testing data. The *contamination* parameter was computed from the data as the ratio of inliers and outliers and explicitly passed to both models.

For LOF (novelty), LOF (outlier), and Isolation Forest, we used default inference settings from the scikit-learn library. For the TGN-SVDD model and the baseline vanilla TGN model, we applied a 0.99 percentile threshold obtained on the training set and used this threshold to infer labels on the test set.

ROC AUC metrics require the model to output scores for inference. For LOF (novelty), LOF (outlier), and Isolation Forest, we used local outlier factor and Isolation Forest anomaly score as measures of data point anomaly. As TGN-SVDD directly computes anomaly scores, we were able to compute ROC AUC directly. For the baseline vanilla TGN model, we chose score $= 1 - p$, where p is the probability of the event to occur, meaning the higher this score, the more likely the event is an outlier.

Results are shown in the Table 2. Proposed TGN-SVDD model outperforms all baseline models in both scenarios and on all datasets. In the scenario with features, Isolation Forest performed remarkably close to our method in terms of ROC AUC metric on the Wednesday dataset. LOF (novelty) for Friday showed the second-best result, significantly outperforming other baseline models. In the

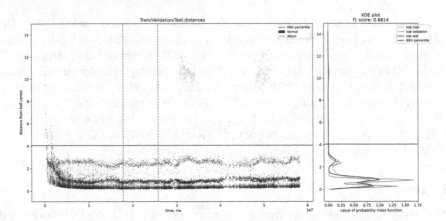

Fig. 1. Tuesday working hours. Illustration of TGN-SVDD performance. Left: On the y-axis, the anomaly score is depicted as it described in the model description. The two vertical lines imply the separation between training, validation and testing data. The red line shows the 99th percentile from the train set as a threshold. Right: Density estimation. (Color figure online)

scenario without features, remarkable second-best ROC AUC results were shown by LOF (novelty) on Friday and Isolation Forest on Monday and Thursday.

The Attack class in the CIC-IDS2017 dataset comprises multiple specific attacks. To demonstrate the performance of our model across different Attack classes, we present the confusion matrix in Table 3. Given that TGN-SVDD is a novelty detector, it only predicts 'Normal' or 'Attack' classes for each network event. As evident from the table, the model accurately predicts the majority of Attacks, with the exceptions of 'Bot' on Friday and 'Infiltration' on Thursday.

4.3   Deeper Dive into Data

The dataset is structured such that the majority of malicious activities originate from a single source IP, often targeting the same destination IP - these nodes ids are 32 and 11, respectively, in our dataset's nodes enumeration. Upon further investigation, it was found that while node 11 participated in numerous normal events, node 32 was exclusively present during the testing phase, potentially serving as a strong feature that could lead the model to a trivial solution.

To examine this potentially trivial model behavior, we modified the dataset to include node 32 during training while mapping events with node 32 as normal. We randomly selected 500 events from the training set with the source node 31 and created 500 additional identical events, replacing the normal source node 31 with our suspicious node 32. These 500 modified events were then injected into the training data. If this alteration does not significantly reduce performance or produce significantly different results, while simultaneously mapping injected events closely to the enclosed ball centre in the training phase, our hypothesis regarding the undesirable trivial model behavior would be refused.

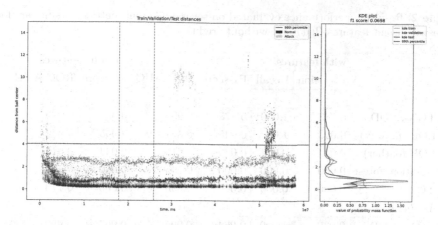

Fig. 2. Thursday working hours. Illustration of TGN-SVDD performance. Left: On the y-axis, the anomaly score is depicted as it described in the model description. The two vertical lines imply the separation between training, validation and testing data. The red line shows the 99th percentile from the train set as a threshold. Right: Density estimation. (Color figure online)

As illustrated in Fig. 3 (left), the model successfully learned to map injected events indistinguishably from the remaining normal activities, maintaining a good performance, as shown in Table 4.

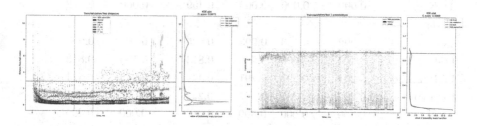

Fig. 3. Friday dataset. Left: TGN-SVDD with additional 500 events with the node 31 as a source injected in train data and labeled with orange. Right: Vanilla TGN with 1-p on the y-axis, where p is the probability of the event to occur. (Color figure online)

Similarly to TGN-SVDD we provide visualisation of vanilla TGN in the Fig. 3 (right). The results look noisy with many events assigned to a low probability. This does not allow to properly distinguish attack events from normal ones. One possible explanation is the strong assumption over negative sampling, which is made originally at random in the TGN paper and may lead to suboptimal solutions. More discussions about that can be found in the article [12].

Table 2. Resulting performance evaluated on several different metrics. Results are for data with event features (left) and without (right).

	with features				without features	
	Precision	Recall	F1-score	ROC AUC	F1-score	ROC AUC
Tuesday						
TGN-SVDD	0.783	1.000	0.878	0.999	0.931	0.999
LOF (novelty)	0.023	1.000	0.045	0.484	0.045	0.484
LOF (outlier)	0.044	0.044	0.044	0.615	0.044	0.615
Isolation Forest	0.000	0.000	0.000	0.760	0.000	0.701
TGN	0.000	0.000	0.000	0.690	0.000	0.173
Wednesday						
TGN-SVDD	0.930	1.000	0.964	0.999	0.967	0.999
LOF (novelty)	0.072	1.000	0.134	0.354	0.134	0.354
LOF (outlier)	0.027	0.027	0.027	0.346	0.031	0.347
Isolation Forest	0.588	0.588	0.588	0.946	0.000	0.167
TGN	0.000	0.000	0.000	0.268	0.000	0.390
Thursday						
TGN-SVDD	0.035	0.997	0.068	0.994	0.056	0.992
LOF (novelty)	0.005	1.000	0.011	0.209	0.011	0.209
LOF (outlier)	0.000	0.000	0.000	0.680	0.000	0.679
Isolation Forest	0.006	0.006	0.006	0.626	0.000	0.796
TGN	0.000	0.000	0.000	0.459	0.000	0.072
Friday						
TGN-SVDD	0.992	0.993	0.993	0.995	0.991	0.994
LOF (novelty)	0.424	1.000	0.596	0.813	0.596	0.813
LOF (outlier)	0.291	0.291	0.291	0.449	0.244	0.411
Isolation Forest	0.237	0.237	0.237	0.222	0.006	0.005
TGN	0.000	0.000	0.000	0.613	0.000	0.295

Table 3. The confusion matrix for all attack classes is presented, corresponding to the same experimental setup as previously described. To threshold the scores from TGN-SVDD, we selected the 99th percentile from the training set.

		True Class				
		Wednesday				
		Normal	Golden Eye	Hulk	Heartbleed	Slowloris	Slow http test
Predicted Class	Normal	301788	0	0	0	0	0
	Attack	1764	2996	1	4217	3898	12538

	Friday				*Tuesday*	
	Normal	Bot	DDoS	PortScan	Normal	ssh/ftp-Patator
Normal	276697	1247	0	0	293213	0
Attack	1471	0	44927	159126	1920	6954

	Thursday			
	Normal	Brute Force	XSS	SQL Injection	Infiltration
Normal	287108	0	0	0	6
Attack	55184	1365	661	12	0

Table 4. Friday working hours. With additional 500 events with the node 31 as a source in train data. In the table established TGN-SVDD performance applying simple 99 percentile from train set on test set.

Friday	Precision	Recall	F1-score	ROC AUC %
TGN-SVDD	0.995	0.999	0.997	0.999

5   Conclusion

In this contribution, we presented a novel unsupervised model for intrusion detection, TGN-SVDD, making explicit use of the dynamic graph based behaviour of the data, by modelling network communications as a temporal dynamic graph.

For the evaluation, we pre-processed the public CIC-2017 dataset, which consists of 4 different attack days which we treated as different datasets and various modern attacks. We demonstrated that our method significantly outperforms classical techniques, as well as the vanilla TGN model. We demonstrated that our model can accurately identify the majority of specific attacks present in the datasets, while maintaining a moderate level of false positives.

In our experiments, we investigate potential limitations of the utilised dataset and suggest a possible remedy by including the attacker IP in the normal dataset, making the dataset more challenging. Our proposed model, however, still obtains high performance values as measured by our metrics. Future work includes the evaluation of data from other domains of anomaly detection. Also, investigating a semi-supervised approach such as the Deep semi-supervised SVDD, is a promising direction.

References

1. Aouini, Z., Pekar, A.: NFStream: a flexible network data analysis framework. Comput. Netw. **204**, 108719 (2022). https://doi.org/10.1016/j.comnet.2021.108719. https://www.sciencedirect.com/science/article/pii/S1389128621005739
2. Breunig, M.M., Kriegel, H.P., Ng, R.T., Sander, J.: LoF: identifying density-based local outliers. In: Proceedings of the 2000 ACM SIGMOD International Conference on Management of Data, pp. 93–104 (2000)
3. Erfani, S.M., Rajasegarar, S., Karunasekera, S., Leckie, C.: High-dimensional and large-scale anomaly detection using a linear one-class SVM with deep learning. Pattern Recogn. **58**, 121–134 (2016)
4. Fey, M., Lenssen, J.E.: Fast graph representation learning with pytorch geometric. arXiv preprint arXiv:1903.02428 (2019)
5. Kumar, S., Zhang, X., Leskovec, J.: Predicting dynamic embedding trajectory in temporal interaction networks. In: Proceedings of the 25th ACM SIGKDD International Conference on Knowledge Discovery & Data Mining, pp. 1269–1278 (2019)
6. Kwon, D., Kim, H., Kim, J., Suh, S.C., Kim, I., Kim, K.J.: A survey of deep learning-based network anomaly detection. Clust. Comput. **22**, 949–961 (2019)
7. Liu, F.T., Ting, K.M., Zhou, Z.H.: Isolation forest. In: 2008 Eighth IEEE International Conference on Data Mining, pp. 413–422. IEEE (2008)
8. Liuliakov, A., Hermes, L., Hammer, B.: AutoML technologies for the identification of sparse classification and outlier detection models. Appl. Soft Comput. **133**, 109942 (2023)
9. Pang, G., Shen, C., Cao, L., Hengel, A.V.D.: Deep learning for anomaly detection: a review. ACM Comput. Surv. (CSUR) **54**(2), 1–38 (2021)
10. Paszke, A., et al.: Pytorch: an imperative style, high-performance deep learning library. In: Advances in Neural Information Processing Systems, vol. 32 (2019)
11. Pedregosa, F., et al.: Scikit-learn: machine learning in python. J. Mach. Learn. Res. **12**, 2825–2830 (2011)
12. Poursafaei, F., Huang, S., Pelrine, K., Rabbany, R.: Towards better evaluation for dynamic link prediction (2022)
13. Rossi, E., Chamberlain, B., Frasca, F., Eynard, D., Monti, F., Bronstein, M.: Temporal graph networks for deep learning on dynamic graphs. arXiv preprint arXiv:2006.10637 (2020)
14. Ruff, L., et al.: A unifying review of deep and shallow anomaly detection. Proc. IEEE **109**(5), 756–795 (2021)
15. Ruff, L., et al.: Deep one-class classification. In: International Conference on Machine Learning, pp. 4393–4402. PMLR (2018)
16. Schölkopf, B., Platt, J.C., Shawe-Taylor, J., Smola, A.J., Williamson, R.C.: Estimating the support of a high-dimensional distribution. Neural Comput. **13**(7), 1443–1471 (2001)
17. Sharafaldin, I., Lashkari, A.H., Ghorbani, A.: Toward generating a new intrusion detection dataset and intrusion traffic characterization. In: ICISSP (2018)
18. Shen, L., Li, Z., Kwok, J.: Timeseries anomaly detection using temporal hierarchical one-class network. Adv. Neural. Inf. Process. Syst. **33**, 13016–13026 (2020)

19. Tax, D.M., Duin, R.P.: Support vector data description. Mach. Learn. **54**, 45–66 (2004)
20. Trivedi, R., Farajtabar, M., Biswal, P., Zha, H.: Dyrep: learning representations over dynamic graphs. In: International Conference on Learning Representations (2019)
21. Wang, Y., Chang, Y.Y., Liu, Y., Leskovec, J., Li, P.: Inductive representation learning in temporal networks via causal anonymous walks. arXiv preprint arXiv:2101.05974 (2021)
22. Wu, Y., Gu, M., Wang, L., Lin, Y., Wang, F., Yang, H.: Event2graph: event-driven bipartite graph for multivariate time-series anomaly detection. arXiv preprint arXiv:2108.06783 (2021)
23. Xu, D., Ruan, C., Korpeoglu, E., Kumar, S., Achan, K.: Inductive representation learning on temporal graphs. arXiv preprint arXiv:2002.07962 (2020)

Sequence-Based Modeling for Temporal Knowledge Graph Link Prediction

Lijie Li[1], Wenqiang Liu[1], Zuobin Xiong[2], and Ye Wang[1]($\boxtimes$)

[1] Harbin Engineering University, Harbin 150006, China
{lilijie,lwq,wangye2020}@hrbeu.edu.cn
[2] Department of Computer Science, Georgia State University, Atlanta, GA 30303, USA
zxiong2@gsu.edu

Abstract. Currently, the majority of research in temporal knowledge graph link prediction focuses on completing missing facts. Nevertheless, the utilization of knowledge graphs to forecast future facts has garnered significant scholarly attention. The attainment of efficient future fact prediction for time-series data hinges primarily on an in-depth exploration of both past historical facts and concurrent facts in the present. Presently, the majority of research in this domain lacks an all-encompassing integration of temporal points and durations in factual features, thereby hindering the effective management of two distinct types of facts with varying chronologies and ultimately disregarding their latent influence on future facts. This paper introduces an advanced representation model - the Progressive Representation Graph Attention Network (PRGAN) - which harnesses the potential of Graph Convolutional Neural Network and Recurrent Neural Network. PRGAN aims to ameliorate the existing shortcomings and augment the efficacy of future event prediction through attention-based learning of progressive representations of entities and relations in time series. We evaluated our proposed method with five event datasets. Extensive experimentation revealed that, in comparison with other baseline models, the PRGAN model displayed remarkable performance and efficiency in temporal reasoning tasks, thereby demonstrating its outstanding superiority.

Keywords: Graph Representation Learning · Knowledge Representation · Temporal Knowledge Graph · Event Prediction

1 Introduction

A Knowledge Graph (KG) [1] is a structured information management and knowledge representation system designed to integrate data in a human-readable and computer-friendly way. However, current research has primarily focused on using static KGs to reason with this data. In reality, however, multi-relational data is generated over time, making static KGs unsuitable for describing the dynamic nature of the world, such as the continuous changes in social networks.

© The Author(s), under exclusive license to Springer Nature Switzerland AG 2023
L. Iliadis et al. (Eds.): ICANN 2023, LNCS 14257, pp. 550–562, 2023.
https://doi.org/10.1007/978-3-031-44216-2_45

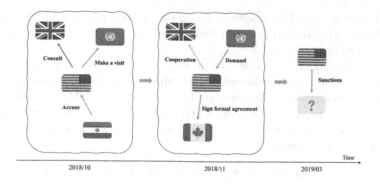

Fig. 1. Diagram of inference on TKG.

To address this issue, researchers have introduced Temporal Knowledge Graphs (TKGs). TKGs can be seen as a sequence of multiple KGs, each representing facts occurring at the same timestamp, as illustrated in Fig. 1. Yet, similar to static KGs, TKGs also face the problem of incompleteness or lack of information, which makes the task of completing TKGs a critical challenge.

Typically, Temporal Knowledge Graph (TKG) reasoning involves time stamps that vary from t_0 to t_T and can be classified into two types: internal reasoning and external reasoning. The internal reasoning approach aims to predict new facts that occur within the time period $t_0 < t < t_T$, while the external reasoning approach focuses on predicting new facts that occur after time t_T $(t > t_T)$. In this area, researchers have made few attempts to infer future facts, which makes it still under-researched. Know-Evolve [2] predicts future facts by evolving embeddings of entities, while RE-Net [3] encodes past event sequences using embeddings of the original entities. However, RE-Net mainly focuses on entities in the aggregation process and ignores the relationships. Therefore, the best practice is to locally model the facts that occur in each time window as concurrent facts and then represent the historical facts across the entire time series to infer future facts.

In this article, we propose a novel network model called the Progressive Representation Graph Attention Network (PRGAN) for predicting future facts in a Knowledge Graph (KG). PRGAN models the entire sequence of KG to learn progressive representations of entities and relationships. Its main contribution is summarized in the following aspects:

- Progressive representation: PRGAN uses graph convolutional neural networks and recurrent neural networks to learn progressive representations of entities and relationships throughout the entire KG sequence.
- Historical event attention mechanism: The attention mechanism is used to dynamically select and linearly combine different historical facts, allowing the model to emphasize the importance of different historical facts for the current query.

- Flexible structure: The modeling based on graph structure and the decoder is a flexible plug-in part and can be replaced/integrated with other models if there is better ones.
- Effective model: We conducted extensive experiments and evaluations of PRGAN on five temporal knowledge graph datasets, using various metrics to assess its performance. We compared our model with several baseline models commonly used in this area of research, where the results demonstrate that PRGAN outperforms most of the baseline models in terms of accuracy, efficiency, and robustness.

The remaining of this work is organized as follows. We introduce the related works of knowledge graph in Sect. 2. In Sect. 3, we formulate the studied problem of this work and then detail our proposed model in Sect. 4. Our experiments in Sect. 5 illustrate the performance of our model over selected baselines. Finally, this work is concluded in Sect. 6.

2   Related Work

2.1   Knowledge Graph Embedding

Knowledge graph embedding (KGE) [5] maps each entity $e \in E$ and each relation $r \in R$ to a low-dimensional continuous vector. Currently, there are two types of knowledge graph embeddings: static knowledge graph embedding and temporal knowledge graph embedding.

Static Knowledge Graph Embedding. Static knowledge graph embedding do not consider temporal information and has been widely studied. Typically, their embedding methods fall into three categories: (i) translation-based models, such as TransE [6]; (ii) bilinear models, such as RESCAL [7], DistMult [8], and SimplE [9]; and (iii) neural network models, such as graph convolutional network (GCN) [10]. However, these knowledge graph embedding methods are not suitable for temporal knowledge graphs (TKGs) as they cannot capture the rich dynamic temporal information of TKGs.

Temporal Knowledge Graph Embedding. Temporal Knowledge Embedding (TKE) methods aim to capture both temporal and relational information. To achieve this goal, each method either embeds discrete timestamps into a vector space or learns time-aware representations for each entity. Some popular TKE models include: TTransE [11], which extends the traditional TransE [6] model to the temporal domain by embedding time information into the scoring function; HyTE [12], which extends TransH [13] by associating each timestamp with a corresponding hyperplane and projecting entity and relation embeddings onto hyperplanes specific to the timestamp; RE-Net [3], which aggregates entity neighborhoods as historical information and models the temporal dependencies of facts using a recursive neural network; DE-SimplE [14], which extends SimplE [9] by exploring temporal functions to combine entities and timestamps to generate time-specific representations; TPmod [15], which is a trend-guided prediction model based on attention mechanisms developed to predict missing facts in TKGs; and TempCaps [16], which is the first model that applies capsule networks [17] to temporal knowledge graph completion. Although these models perform well in their tasks, they do not capture long-term temporal dependencies of real-world facts.

2.2 Graph Representation Learning

Graph representation learning aims to transform graph data into low dimensional dense vectors either at the node level or the whole graph level. The primary goal of graph representation learning is to map nodes to vector representations while preserving as much topological information of the graph as possible. And, if the representation of graph data can contain rich semantic information, it can obtain good input features and directly use linear classifiers for classification tasks. Graph Convolutional Networks (GCN) are a type of neural network architecture that is primarily used in graph representation learning and is similar to Convolutional Neural Networks (CNN) but designed for graph data structures. GCN features can be used to perform various tasks such as node classification, link prediction, community detection, and network similarity detection, demonstrating the broad range of applications of GCN.

3 Problem Formulation

A event-based Temporal Knowledge Graph (TKG) can be viewed as a series of static Knowledge Graphs (KGs) sorted by event timestamp. Therefore, the TKG G can be formally represented as a sequence of KGs with timestamps, i.e., $G = \{G_1, G_2, ..., G_t, ..., G_T\}$ (that is $G = G_1 \cup G_2 \cup ... \cup G_t ... \cup G_T$), where each $G_t = (V, R, F_t)$ is a directed multi-relational graph at timestamp t. Any event in G_t can be represented as a timestamped quadruple, i.e., (subject, relation, object, time), and is dented by the quadruple $(s, r, o, t) \in G_t$. The important mathematical symbols used in this paper are shown in Table 1.

Table 1. Important symbols and their descriptions.

Symbol	Descriptions
G, G_t	TKG, the KG of the timestamp t
V, R, F_t	Entity set, relationship set, and fact set in TKG (at timestamp t)
E_t, R_t	Embedding matrix of entities and relationships at time t
H, R	Embedding matrix of random initialized entities and relationships

In extrapolation prediction tasks, facts are sorted based on their timestamps. Given an incomplete event (missing either the object entity $(s, r, ?, t)$, or the subject entity $(?, r, o, t)$, or the relation $(s, ?, o, t)$), we should predict the missing object, entity or relation based on the historical facts before time t. For each event $(s, r, o, t) \in F_t$, we can obtain three sub-prediction tasks: $(s, r, ?, t)$, $(?, r, o, t)$ and $(s, ?, o, t)$. Therefore, the overall joint probability is calculated as follows:

$$P(F_t) = \frac{(P_o(F_t) + P_s(F_t) + P_r(F_t))}{3}, \tag{1}$$

where $P_o(F_t)$, $P_s(F_t)$, and $P_r(F_t)$ represent the joint probability of $(s, r, ?, t)$, $(?, r, o, t)$ and $(s, ?, o, t)$. Applying the division rule in Eq. (1) ensures that the resulting probability $P_o(F_t)$ is normalized to the range of $[0, 1]$.

Suppose that the prediction of future facts at time stamp t depends on the facts of its previous k time steps, i.e., $G_{t-k}, G_{t-k+1}, ..., G_{t-1}$. We use $E_t \in R^{|V| \times d}$ to represent the entity embedding matrix modeled in the historical KG sequence and $R_t \in R^{|R| \times d}$ to represent the relation embedding matrix modeled in the historical KG sequence (where d is the embedding dimension). The problem of predicting future facts can be formalized into two categories: entity prediction and relation prediction, both of which can be ultimately formulated as a ranking problem.

The prediction of subject entities is defined as follows:

$$P_s(F_t) = P(s|G_{t-k:t-1}, r, o) = P(s|E_t, R_t, r, o). \tag{2}$$

The prediction of object entities is defined as follows:

$$P_o(F_t) = P(o|G_{t-k:t-1}, s, r) = P(o|E_t, R_t, s, r). \tag{3}$$

The prediction of relations is defined as follows:

$$P_r(F_t) = P(r|G_{t-k:t-1}, s, o) = P(r|E_t, R_t, s, o). \tag{4}$$

4   The PRGAN Model

PRGAN is a novel network model proposed by this work for predicting future facts in Temporal Knowledge Graphs (TKGs). As shown in Fig. 2, the framework of PRGAN consists of an encoder and a decoder. PRGAN utilizes a relation-aware graph neural network [4] to encode concurrent facts at each timestamp and capturing structural dependencies. It further models the historical KG sequence via an autoregressive approach using a time-gated recurrent module and a recurrent neural network based on an attention mechanism to obtain a progressive representation of entities and relations over time.

4.1   Concurrent Dependency Modeling Module

To predict future facts, the concurrent facts that occur at the same time can have a significant impact. Therefore, PRGAN utilizes a relation-aware graph neural network (RGCN) to model concurrent facts at each timestamp and uses a w-layer relation-aware GCN to model structural dependency relationships. Specifically,

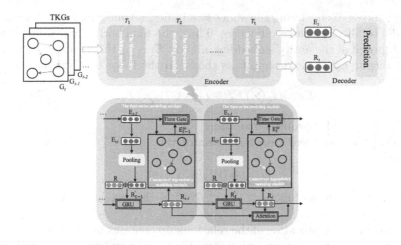

Fig. 2. The framework of proposed PRGAN.

for each graph with a timestamp, the embedding of the object entity o at layer $l \in [0, w - 1]$ is considered to obtain representation learning information under a messaging framework with l layers. Its embedding in layer $l + 1$ is obtained using the following formula:

$$Z_o^l = \frac{1}{k} \sum_{(s,r),\exists(s,r,o)\in G_t} W_1^l \left(e_{s,t}^l + r_t\right) + W_2^l e_{0,t}^l \qquad (5)$$

$$e_{o,t}^{l+1} = \sigma \left(Z_o^l\right) \qquad (6)$$

where, $e_{s,t}^l$, r_t, and $e_{0,t}^l$ represent the l layer embeddings of subject entity s, relationship r and object entity o at timestamp t. W_1^l and W_2^l are the parameters for aggregating features and self-looping in l layer. k is a normalization constant equal to the in-degree of object entity o. σ is the ReLU activation function.

4.2 The Time-Series Modeling Module

For predicting future facts, the potential impact behind all the facts that occurred at every time is also significant. Therefore, PRGAN utilizes a time-gated recurrent unit (GRU) [18] with an attention mechanism to model the historical facts of the entire knowledge graph (KG) time sequence. The latent time sequence problem of historical facts is solved by stacking the ω-layer RGCN. However, it should be considered that, firstly, if the same entity pairs appear with repeated relationships at adjacent timestamps, the obtained entity embeddings may converge to the same value, resulting in the problem of excessive smoothing in the graph. Secondly, considering the length of the time sequence, a large number of stacked RGCNs may eventually encounter the problem of gradient disappearance, causing the model's weights to remain unchanged during the training process. Considering the above two issues, a time-gated unit is added to the model to alleviate these influences. Thus, the final entity embedding matrix E_t is composed of the entity embedding matrix E_{t-1} at timestamp $t-1$ and the current output E_t^ω at timestamp t, as shown in the following formula:

$$E_t = G_t \bigotimes E_t^\omega + (1 - G_t) \bigotimes E_{t-1}, \tag{7}$$

where $\bigotimes$ denotes dot product operation.

Besides, the non-linear transformation of time gate $G_t \in R^{d \times d}$ is performed as follows:

$$G_t = \alpha \left(W_3 E_{t-1} + b \right) \tag{8}$$

where α is the sigmoid function, $W_3 \in R^{d \times d}$ is the weight matrix of the time gate.

Meanwhile, the embedding of the relationship contains information about the entities involved in the corresponding fact. That is, the embedding of relationship r_t at timestamp t is influenced by two factors: (i) the progressive representation of the relevant entities $C_{r,t} = e| (e, r, o, t) \, or \, (s, r, e, t) \in F_t$ of relationship r at timestamp t in the time series; (ii) the embedding representation of relationship r itself at timestamp $t-1$.

In addition, in order to better capture the progressive representation of historical facts, we use an attention mechanism for historical facts, allowing the model to dynamically select and linearly combine different historical facts of the relationship, namely:

$$e_\tau = \nu_e^T tanh(W_e R_t + U_e R_\tau) \tag{9}$$

$$\alpha_\tau = \frac{exp(e_\tau)}{\sum_{\tau=1}^t exp(e_\tau)} \tag{10}$$

$$R_t = \sum_{\tau=1}^t \alpha_\tau R_\tau \tag{11}$$

where ν_e^T, W_e and U_e are parameters that determine the importance of different historical facts when making predictions for a given query.

4.3   Loss Calculation

Predicting future facts based on the historical KG sequence can be viewed as a multi-classification task for predicting the object entity given (s, r, t), where each class corresponds to a possible object entity. Similarly, predicting the relationship given (s, o, t) and predicting the subject entity given (r, o, t) can also be viewed as multi-classification tasks. For the sake of simplicity, we omit the symbols for previous facts here. Therefore, the loss function can be formulated as follows:

$$\mathcal{L}^e = \sum_{t=1}^T \sum_{(s,r,o,t) \in G_t} \sum_{i=0}^{|V|-1} y_{t,i}^e log[p_i \left(o | E_{t-1}, R_{t-1}, s, r \right)]. \tag{12}$$

$$\mathcal{L}^r = \sum_{t=1}^{T} \sum_{(s,r,o,t)\in G_t} \sum_{i=0}^{|R|-1} y_{t,i}^r log[p_i\,(r|E_{t-1}, R_{t-1}, s, o)]. \tag{13}$$

where $p_i\,(o|E_{t-1}, R_{t-1}, s, r)$ and $p_i\,(r|E_{t-1}, R_{t-1}, s, o)$ represents the probability score of entity i and relationship i, respectively. $y_{t,i}^e$ represents the i-th vector in y_t^e. $y_{t,i}^r$ represents the i-th vector in y_t^r. If $y_{t,i}^e$ and $y_{t,i}^r$ correspond to a true fact, their values are 1, otherwise 0. T represents the total number of KG timestamps in the training dataset. It is worth noticing that $y_t^e \in \mathbb{R}^{|V|}$ represents the label vector representation of entity prediction task at timestamp t; $y_t^r \in \mathbb{R}^{|R|}$ represents the label vector representation of relationship prediction task.

The final loss can be represented sum of two tasks as follows.

$$\mathcal{L}_{final} = \lambda_1 \mathcal{L}^e + \lambda_2 \mathcal{L}^r, \tag{14}$$

where λ_1 and λ_2 are weighted parameters that control the weight of each loss term. λ_1 and λ_2 can be selected based empirically based on the tasks. If the task is to predict the object entity o given (s, r), we can set relatively small values for λ_1. And visa versa for λ_2.

5 Experiments

5.1 Experimental Setup

Datasets. To evaluate the performance of our PRGAN model, we conducted experiments on five commonly used datasets, namely WIKI [19], YAGO [20], GDELT [21], ICEWS05-15 [22], and ICEWS18 [22]. To ensure fairness and accuracy, we split each dataset into training, validation, and test sets in a ratio of 80%, 10%, and 10%, respectively. Table 2 presents the statistical information of the experimental datasets.

Table 2. More about datasets.

Datasets	$|\mathcal{V}|$	$|\mathcal{R}|$	$|Train|$	$|Valid|$	$|Test|$	Time Gap
WIKI	12,554	24	539,286	67,538	63,110	1 year
YAGO	10,623	10	161,540	19,523	20,026	1 year
GDELT	7,691	240	1,734,399	238,765	305,241	15 min
ICEWS05-15	10,094	251	368,868	46,302	46,159	24 h
ICEWS18	23,033	256	373,018	45,995	495,45	24 h

Decoder. For knowledge graph link prediction tasks, we usually use specific scoring functions to measure the plausibility of quadruples. Previous research has shown that some GCNs with convolutional scoring functions perform well in knowledge graph link prediction tasks. In order to better reflect the translation property of the progressive embedding of entities and relationships implied in Eq. (5), we chose ConvTransE [23] as our decoder. As we mentioned in previous section, ConvTransE decoder can also be replaced by other scoring functions.

Optimizer. In our model, we used the latest AI optimizer proposed by Google Brain - VeLO [24]. It is constructed entirely based on AI and does not require manual adjustment of any hyperparameters, which can be applied on different tasks and has an acceleration effect on training 83 tasks, surpassing a series of currently available optimizers.

Metrics. We use four evaluation metrics to measure our model, namely MRR and Hits@1/3/10.

Baselines. The PRGAN model is mainly compared with two types of models: the SKG reasoning model and the TKG reasoning model. The SKG reasoning model includes DistMult [8], RGCN [4], ConvTransE [23], and RotatE [25]. The TKG reasoning model includes TA-DistMult [26], HyTE [12], R-GCRN [27], and RE-Net [3].

5.2   Experimental Results

We conducted a detailed comparison of our proposed method with the above baseline models. The best score of each column is represented in bold black, and the second-best score is represented with an underline notation.

Results of Entity Prediction Task. The results of the entity prediction task are presented in Table 3 and Table 4.

As we can see, SKG reasoning methods perform much worse than PRGAN, mainly because they cannot capture the temporal information in facts. Moreover, the experimental results on the WIKI and YAGO datasets show a more significant improvement. This is mainly because the time intervals in these two datasets are much larger than the other two datasets. Therefore, we can conclude that at each timestamp, PRGAN can capture more structural dependencies between concurrent facts, which also justify that modeling complex structural dependencies between concurrent facts is necessary.

However, PRGAN did not achieve the best results on the GDELT dataset. Through our analysis, we found that in the GDELT dataset, most entities are abstract concepts. Thus, when PRGAN models the entire KG sequence, these abstract concept entities might affect the progression representation of other concrete entities.

Results of Relation Prediction Task. The results of the relation prediction tasks are presented in Table 5.

Since currently most models are mainly focused on entity prediction, we selected two typical baseline models, ConvTransE [23] and R-GCRN [27] for comparison. In Table 5, we only selected the MRR metric to analyze the results. After analysis, we found that the performance gap of PRGAN in relation prediction tasks is much smaller than in entity prediction tasks. This is mainly

Table 3. Results of entity prediction task on WIKI, YAGO, GDELT.

Model	WIKI			YAGO			GDELT			
	MRR	H@3	H@10	MRR	H@3	H@10	MRR	H@1	H@3	H@10
DistMult	27.96	32.45	39.51	44.05	49.70	59.94	8.61	3.91	8.27	17.04
R-GCN	13.96	15.75	22.05	20.25	24.01	37.30	12.17	7.40	12.37	20.63
ConvTransE	30.89	34.30	41.45	46.67	52.22	62.52	19.07	11.85	20.32	33.14
RotatE	26.08	31.63	38.51	42.08	46.77	59.39	3.62	0.52	2.26	8.37
TA-DistMult	26.44	31.36	38.97	44.98	50.64	61.11	10.34	4.44	10.44	21.63
HyTE	25.40	29.16	37.54	14.42	39.73	46.98	6.69	0.01	7.57	19.06
R-GCRN	28.68	31.44	38.58	43.71	48.53	56.98	18.63	11.53	19.80	32.42
RE-NET	30.87	33.55	41.27	46.81	52.71	61.93	**19.60**	**12.03**	**20.56**	**33.89**
PRGAN	**38.44**	**44.09**	**53.21**	**58.46**	**64.11**	**74.78**	19.11	11.80	20.41	32.08

Table 4. Results of entity prediction task on ICEWS05-15, ICEWS18.

Model	ICEWS05-15				ICEWS18			
	MRR	H@1	H@3	H@10	MRR	H@1	H@3	H@10
DistMult	19.91	5.63	27.22	47.33	13.86	5.61	15.22	31.26
R-GCN	27.13	18.83	30.41	43.16	15.05	8.13	16.49	29.00
ConvTransE	30.28	20.79	33.80	49.95	23.22	14.26	26.13	41.34
RotatE	19.01	10.42	21.35	36.92	14.53	6.47	15.78	31.86
TA-DistMult	27.51	17.57	31.46	47.32	16.42	8.60	18.13	32.51
HyTE	16.05	6.53	20.20	34.72	7.41	3.10	7.33	16.01
R-GCRN	35.93	26.23	40.02	54.63	23.46	14.24	26.62	41.96
RE-NET	36.86	26.24	41.85	57.60	26.17	16.43	29.89	44.37
PRGAN	**38.16**	**27.23**	**42.87**	**60.03**	**27.29**	**18.62**	**30.22**	**47.10**

Table 5. Results of relation prediction task.

Model	WIKI	YAGO	GDELT	ICEWS05-15	ICEWS18
ConvTransE	86.64	90.98	**18.97**	38.26	38.00
R-GCRN	88.88	90.18	18.58	38.37	37.14
PRGAN	**93.57**	**93.11**	18.82	**38.40**	**38.94**

because in the dataset, the number of relations is much smaller than the number of entities. At the same time, the improvement on the WIKI and YAGO datasets is slightly larger than on the other three datasets because they contain fewer relations. In summary, the analysis of the results on the relation prediction task once again confirms the superiority of our model against baselines.

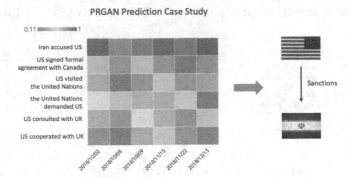

Fig. 3. Case Study - Heat Map.

5.3   Case Study

To further evaluate the performance of our PRGAN model, we conducted a case study on a selected subset of the test dataset's event-based Temporal Knowledge Graph (TKG). The subset was chosen based on its relevance to real-world events and the potential impact of predicting future facts accurately. As shown in Fig. 3, we obtained historical facts from the TKG at the timestamps of October 2018 and November 2018 and attempted to predict which country the United States would sanction at the timestamp of March 2019. Our hypothesis was that the United States and the United Kingdom had established a good relationship due to their "cooperation", while the United States and Iran had a hostile relationship due to "accusation". Since "sanction" is a hostile relationship, we predicted that "Iran" was more likely to be the entity that the United States would sanction based on the relationships between the entities in the TKG.

We conducted a heatmap analysis on this prediction, and as shown in Fig. 3, PRGAN successfully obtained the correct answer - Iran. This indicates that our model has good performance as expected.

6   Conclusion

In this paper, we proposed PRGAN. The model reduces the event prediction problem to an extrapolation reasoning problem in the temporal knowledge graph by learning the temporal and structural information of facts from the perspectives of historical facts and concurrent facts, and obtaining the progressive representation of entities and relations in the time series to make future predictions. The experimental results on five datasets demonstrate that PRGAN outperforms the baseline models in predicting future facts in Temporal Knowledge Graphs (TKGs), as measured by various metrics. Moreover, the use of the VeLO optimizer developed by Google Brain greatly improved the speed and effectiveness of training, enabling PRGAN to achieve state-of-the-art performance in predicting future facts in TKGs.

Acknowledgment. This work was supported by the National Key R&D Program of China under Grant No. 2020YFB1710200, China Higher Education Innovation Fund No. 2021ITA05010.

References

1. Nickel, M., Murphy, K., Tresp, V., Gabrilovich, E.: Knowledge graphs: a survey of techniques and applications. IEEE Trans. Knowl. Data Eng. **29**(12), 2724–2743 (2016)
2. Trivedi, R., Dai, H., Wang, Y., Song, L.: Know-evolve: deep temporal reasoning for dynamic knowledge graphs. In: Proceedings of the 34th Proceedings of the International Conference on Machine Learning, vol. 70, pp. 3462–3471. ACM (2017)
3. Jin, W., Zhang, C., Szekely, P., Ren, X.: Recurrent event network for reasoning over temporal knowledge graphs. In: Proceedings of the 7th International Conference on Learning Representations (2019)
4. Schlichtkrull, M., Kipf, T.N., Bloem, P., van den Berg, R., Titov, I., Welling, M.: Modeling relational data with graph convolutional networks. In: Gangemi, A., et al. (eds.) ESWC 2018. LNCS, vol. 10843, pp. 593–607. Springer, Cham (2018). https://doi.org/10.1007/978-3-319-93417-4_38
5. Wang, Z., Zhang, J., Feng, J., Chen, Z.: Knowledge graph embedding: a survey of approaches and applications. IEEE Trans. Knowl. Data Eng. **29**(12), 2724–2743 (2018)
6. Bordes, A., Usunier, N., Garcia-Duran, A., Weston, J., Yakhnenko, O.: Translating embeddings for modeling multi-relational data. In: NeurIPS (2013)
7. Nickel, M., Tresp, V., Kriegel, H.-P.: A three-way model for collective learning on multi-relational data. In: ICML (2011)
8. Yang, B., Yih, W., He, X., Gao, J., Deng, L.: Embedding entities and relations for learning and inference in knowledge bases. In: ICLR (2015)
9. Kazemi, S.M., Poole, D.: Simple embedding for link prediction in knowledge graphs. In: NeurIPS (2018)
10. Kipf, T.N., Welling, M.: Semi-supervised classification with graph convolutional networks. arXiv preprint arXiv:1609.02907 (2016)
11. Jiang, T., Liu, T., Ge, T., Sha, L., Chang, B., et al.: Towards time-aware knowledge graph completion. In: Proceedings of the COLING, Osaka, Japan, pp. 1715–1724 (2016)
12. Dasgupta, S.S., Ray, S.N., Talukdar, P.: HyTE: hyperplane-based temporally aware knowledge graph embedding. In: Proceedings of the EMNLP, Brussels, Belgium, pp. 2001–2011 (2018)
13. Wang, Z., Zhang, J., Feng, J., Chen, Z.: Knowledge graph embedding by translating on hyperplanes. In: Proceedings of the AAAI, Quebec City, Quebec, Canada, pp. 1112–1119 (2014)
14. Goel, R., Kazemi, S.M., Brubaker, M., Poupart, P.: Diachronic embedding for temporal knowledge graph completion. In: Proceedings of the AAAI, New York, New York, USA, pp. 3988–3995 (2020)
15. Bai, L., Ma, X., Zhang, M., Wenting, Yu.: TPmod: a tendency-guided prediction model for temporal knowledge graph completion. ACM Trans. Knowl. Discov. Data **15**(3), 17 (2021). Article 41
16. Fu, G., et al.: TempCaps: a capsule network-based embedding model for temporal knowledge graph completion. In: Proceedings of the Sixth Workshop on Structured Prediction for NLP, pp. 22–31 (2022)

17. Sabour, S., Frosst, N., Hinton, G.E.: Dynamic routing between capsules. In: Advances in Neural Information Processing Systems, pp. 3859–3869 (2017)
18. Chung, J., Gulcehre, C., Cho, K., Bengio, Y.: Empirical evaluation of gated recurrent neural networks on sequence modeling. arXiv preprint arXiv:1412.3555 (2014)
19. Yasseri, T., Bright, J., Margetts, H.: Wikipedia as a data source for political scientists: accuracy and completeness of coverage. PS: Polit. Sci. Polit. **45**(04), 711–716 (2012)
20. Mahdisoltani, F., Biega, J., Suchanek, F.: YAGO3: a knowledge base from multilingual Wikipedias. In: 7th Biennial Conference on Innovative Data Systems Research. CIDR Conference (2014)
21. Leetaru, K., Schrodt, P.A.: GDELT: global data on facts, location, and tone, 1979–2012. In: ISA annual convention, vol. 2, 1–49. Citeseer (2013)
22. King, G., Lam, P., Roberts, M.: The integrated crisis early warning system (ICEWS)-a framework for the automated analysis of societal-level crisis early warning. J. Peace Res. **50**(2), 275–285 (2013)
23. Shang, C., Tang, Y., Huang, J., Bi, J., He, X., Zhou, B.: End-to-end structure-aware convolutional networks for knowledge base completion (2019)
24. Lample, G., Sablayrolles, A., Ranzato, M., Larochelle, H.: Vector-Less objectives for neural machine translation. arXiv preprint arXiv:1902.01370 (2019)
25. Sun, Z., Deng, H., Nie, L., Tang, L., Yang, Y., Liu, Z.: RotatE: knowledge graph embedding by relational rotation in complex space. In: Proceedings of the AAAI Conference on Artificial Intelligence, vol. 33, pp. 4602–4609 (2019)
26. Du, X., Dai, H., He, M., Zhang, Y.: Temporal attentive knowledge graph embedding for predicting social facts. In: Proceedings of the 2020 Conference on Empirical Methods in Natural Language Processing (EMNLP), pp. 7488–7498 (2020)
27. Seo, Y., Defferrard, M., Vandergheynst, P., Bresson, X.: Structured sequence modeling with graph convolutional recurrent networks. In: Cheng, L., Leung, A.C.S., Ozawa, S. (eds.) ICONIP 2018. LNCS, vol. 11301, pp. 362–373. Springer, Cham (2018). https://doi.org/10.1007/978-3-030-04167-0_33

Structure-Enhanced Graph Neural ODE Network for Temporal Link Prediction

Jinlin Hou[1,2], Xuan Guo[1], Jiye Liu[1], Jie Li[1], Lin Pan[3],
and Wenjun Wang[1,2(✉)]

[1] College of Intelligence and Computing, Tianjin University, Tianjin 300350, China
{houjinlin,guoxuan,jayliu7319,jieleo}@tju.edu.cn
[2] Georgia Tech Shenzhen Institute, Tianjin University, Shenzhen 518055, China
wjwang@tju.edu.cn
[3] School of Marine Science and Technology, Tianjin University, Tianjin 300072,
China
linpan@tju.edu.cn

Abstract. Temporal link prediction aims to predict future links by
learning the structural information and temporal evolution of a network. However, existing methods are heavily dependent on the latest
snapshots, which hinders their power to reveal the essential evolutionary
patterns based on and leverage them for dynamical inference. As a result,
they generally achieve better predictions for the closest future snapshots
than remote ones. Moreover, most methods do not take into account the
effects of higher-order and global structure. To address these issues, we
propose Structure-Enhanced Graph Neural Ordinary Differential Equation (SEGODE), a framework effectively performing dynamic inference
by neural ordinary differential equation incorporating attention mechanisms and empowering to capture higher-order and global structure. To
validate the proposed model, we conduct multiple experiments on a total
of seven real datasets. The experimental results show that the SEGODE
not only achieves good performance in link prediction but also maintains
excellent results even under data-scarce conditions.

Keywords: Temporal Network · Link Prediction · Network
Representation Learning · Neural Ordinary Differential Equation

1 Introduction

The real world is full of ever-changing systems, and temporal networks are used
to describe these complex systems in various fields, including social networks [9],
academic networks [17] and viral distribution networks [12]. Link prediction,
which involves predicting future links based on the structural information already
available in the network, is a crucial problem in temporal networks. Frequently,
temporal networks may be portrayed as a sequence of snapshots. Investigating

---

J. Hou and X. Guo—contribute equally.

L. Iliadis et al. (Eds.): ICANN 2023, LNCS 14257, pp. 563–575, 2023.
https://doi.org/10.1007/978-3-031-44216-2_46

how to derive from these snapshots the evolutionary principles of the network structure that buttress link prediction is a worthwhile conundrum.

Temporal network representation learning (TNRL) is now mainstream for learning the evolving network structure and solving the link prediction problem due to its eminent expressive ability and efficiency. The primary objective of temporal network representation is to generate low-dimensional embeddings which preserve the major information of the temporal network. This process typically involves two stages, i.e., snapshot structure encoding and temporal evolution learning.

To encode the structure information of each snapshot, deep learning methods employing graph neural networks (GNNs) have gained widespread popularity recently. However, most of these approaches primarily focus on capturing node proximity to achieve good link prediction results, and only a few algorithms consider the impact of the higher-order and global structure (**Challenge 1**). Ignoring the role of higher-order and global structure in temporal link prediction may limit the effectiveness of the learned embeddings. The higher-order structure can provide a simple and effective means of characterizing specific rules that can enhance link prediction, such as Triadic Closure [1]. In addition, the global structure can capture the inclination of nodes to be linked in the graph based on metrics such as node degree and PageRank (PR) [13].

The route to capturing temporal information in the deep learning manner has three main branches. The first category involves recurrent neural network (RNN) approaches. Dyngraph2vec [5] proposes inputting the structural information of each snapshot obtained by the encoder into Long Short-Term Memory (LSTM) to learn the temporal information. EvolveGCN [14] combines static structure learning with a static GNN and LSTM/Gate Recurrent Unit (GRU) to encode the temporal information. The second category involves attention mechanisms. DySAT [16] uses attention mechanisms at both static and dynamic scales to learn the representation of the temporal graph, while STGSN [11] globally constrains the model by taking into account the historical topology and incorporating global information in the computation of attention weights. However, these two categories of methods are highly dependent on the latest snapshots and generally perform better for the closest future snapshots than remote ones. They lack dynamical inference uncovering the true evolutionary patterns (**Challenge 2**). Furthermore, obtaining the most immediate training data is usually not feasible in the real world. Moreover, the above methods flounder in this situation as they cannot directly predict snapshots for multiple future moments (**Challenge 3**). Real-world temporal networks may also suffer from snapshot loss due to data corruption, which we call scarce data in this paper. Similarly, the above methods also flounder in this situation as they cannot handle missing snapshots (**Challenge 4**). Recently, the third category of methods leveraging neural ordinary differential equations (ODEs) [3] has been proposed. On the one hand, the dynamic rules of most real-world systems can be elucidated by ODEs. On the other hand, by solving ODEs in a neural network framework, neural ODEs can learn opaque dynamic patterns underlying extremely complex systems like the social network. Through dynamic inference step by step, it can directly predict multiple future moments while maintaining the ability to handle snapshot missing. NDCN [20] is the first approach that combines neural ODEs with graph neural networks to obtain low-dimensional representations of temporal graphs. While NDCN can solve Challenges 2, 3, and 4, its simple structural encoding cannot effectively learn structural features, and the fixed ODE function limits its ability to handle the temporal network with varying topologies.

To overcome the limitations mentioned above, this paper proposes a novel framework for temporal link prediction called **S**tructure-**E**nhanced **G**raph Neural **O**rdinary **D**ifferential **E**quation (**SEGODE**). In order to address Challenge 1, SEGODE introduces the Graphlet Degree Vector (GDV) [7] method and PR [13] for learning the snapshot features from the perspective of higher-order and global structure, respectively. To tackle Challenges 2, 3, and 4, we incorporate the neural ODE with an attention mechanism to characterize dynamical systems. The proposed method in this paper effectively refines the snapshot graph structure encoding and captures the dynamic rules of temporal evolution. In summary, our contributions are as follows:

1. This article points out that learning dynamic rules and being able to infer based on them are necessary for learning temporal network representations. Meanwhile, higher-order and global structure information are needed for better dynamic inference. However, contemporary approaches are inadequate in both aspects.
2. We propose SEGODE, a framework for temporal link prediction, that effectively captures the evolving rules of temporal patterns through the use of a neural ODE with an attention mechanism and the enhancement via multiscale structure encoding.
3. We compare our proposed model with the baselines on real networks and conduct experiments on single-step link prediction, multi-step prediction, and data-scarce link prediction. The results demonstrate that our model not only exhibits excellent link prediction performance but also performs exceptionally well on multi-step link prediction and data-scarce link prediction.

2 Related Work

2.1 Temporal Network Representation Learning

TNRL has received significant attention recently, owing to its relevance in various domains. Some of the previous approaches are through matrix factorization. This technique exploits the correlation between the node embeddings of different snapshots to learn the dynamics of temporal graphs. They generally go through different optimization rules to reconstruct the adjacency relations and learn the dynamics of the network through snapshot smoothing. For instance, LIST [19] employs a multi-step label propagation method on each snapshot and models the dynamic topology as a function of temporal correlation. MLjFE [10] learns higher-order approximation by multi-label learning and handles network dynamics through a temporal smoothing term.

In recent years, several researchers have explored deep learning-based methods to tackle the problem of learning temporal network representation. These approaches typically leverage neural networks to learn both adjacency relationships and temporal evolution between multiple snapshots. For example, DynGEM [6] employs an auto-encoder to learn the structural information of each snapshot, and it initializes each snapshot using the parameters of the last one, which accelerates convergence while maintaining embeddings stability between snapshots. Dyngraph2vec [5] considers the impact of multiple moments on the current state, capturing highly nonlinear interactions between multiple snapshots. GNNs are commonly utilized to learn the structural information of snapshots and are combined with mechanisms learning temporal information to jointly accomplish temporal networks. EvolveGCN [14] updates the graph convolutional network (GCN) [8] parameters at each moment through RNNs, allowing the model parameters to adapt to more recent snapshots. DySAT [16] leverages the extended graph attention network and Transformer to incorporate temporal information, enabling the model to capture more salient information. In addition to learning adjacencies using GCN and attention layers in each snapshot individually, STGSN [11] improves graph structure learning by stacking global temporal adjacencies obtained from the entire historical snapshot. The latest approach ROLAND [18] extends static GNNs to achieve dynamic representation learning by fusing the hidden representations of neighboring snapshot GNNs to learn the evolutionary laws. The above approach can be summarized as the graph-then-time approach. Relatively, the time-then-graph model [4] can also be used for network representation learning. It is no less capable than the graph-then-time approach, which is proved by both theoretical analysis and a typical representative of this type of method GRU-GCN experimentally.

3   Preliminaries

3.1   Problem Definition

Temporal Network. We define a temporal network as $G = \{\mathcal{G}^0, \mathcal{G}^1, ..., \mathcal{G}^T\}$, where $\mathcal{G}^t = (\mathcal{V}^t, \mathcal{E}^t)$ denotes a network snapshot at time t. $\mathcal{V}^t$ is a set node at time t, and we denote by $\mathcal{V} = \mathcal{V}^0 \cup \mathcal{V}^1 \cup ... \cup \mathcal{V}^T = \{v_0, v_1, ..., v_{N-1}\}$ the set of N nodes among all the historical snapshots. The structure of each snapshot can be represented by the binary adjacency matrix $\boldsymbol{A}^t \in \mathbb{R}^{N \times N}$. The attributes of all nodes in $\mathcal{V}^t$ are represented by $\boldsymbol{X}^t \in \mathbb{R}^{N \times F}$, where $F \ll N$ is the number of attributes. In this paper, we leverage GDV and PR separately to measure the higher-order and global structure of each snapshot. $\boldsymbol{L}^t$ and $\boldsymbol{P}^t$ denote the GDV matrix and PR matrix of the snapshot at time t, respectively.

Temporal Network Representation Learning. Given a temporal network G, the goal of TNRL is to obtain a low-dimensional representation $\boldsymbol{z}_i^t$ for each node v_i at time t based on the adjacencies and attributes of each snapshot. The representations of all nodes at time t are given by the matrix $\boldsymbol{Z}^t$. The learned representations would be used for downstream tasks.

Link Prediction. Set the current time as τ. The single-step link prediction task aims to predict the adjacency matrix A^τ of the network at time τ using the historical snapshot $\{\mathcal{G}^0, \mathcal{G}^1, ..., \mathcal{G}^{\tau-1}\}$. In this paper, we also extend the single-step task to multi-step link prediction, i.e., predicting the adjacencies of the future l snapshots from A^τ to $A^{\tau+l-1}$. We also define a data-scarce link prediction task, which involves simulating missing data by deleting some historical snapshots by a certain percentage, based on the single-step link prediction. The latter two tasks require a more powerful ability of the proposed model to learn the dynamics.

3.2 Neural Ordinary Differential Equations

Neural Ordinary Differential Equations can model continuous dynamics and solve Initial Value Problems (IVP) by giving initial values [3]. For a future state $z(t_1)$, it can be obtained by solving from the initial state $z(t_0)$:

$$z(t_1) = z(t_0) + \int_{t_0}^{t_1} f(z(t), t, \boldsymbol{\theta}) \mathrm{d}t, \tag{1}$$

where $f(z(t), t, \boldsymbol{\theta})$ is a neural network used to fit the differential $\frac{\mathrm{d}z(t)}{\mathrm{d}t}$, which is a mapping to control changes in the dynamical system, often referred to as the ODE function. $z(t_i)$ represents the state of the system at time t_i and $t_i \in [0, T]$ refers to a time-point. $\boldsymbol{\theta}$ is the set of parameters. The entire ordinary differential equation is computed by a black-box ODE solver, with adjoint sensitivity method [15] used to compute the gradient. By providing a time series and the initial state of the system, the solution for the time series can be obtained. Due to the advantages of memory efficiency, adaptive training, and continuous time series modeling, neural ODEs are worth being introduced to TNRL.

4 The Proposed Model

4.1 Overview

In this section, we proffer SEGODE, a framework for the dynamic inference of temporal graphs. Figure 1 presents the overview of SEGODE which comprises three fundamental modules including (a) Structure Encoding, (b) Evolution Learning, and (c) Representation Decoding. Preprocessing is carried out on the temporal network, obtaining local, higher-order, and global structural information by the adjacency matrix, GDV matrix and PR matrix for each network snapshot. After inputting them into the Structure Encoding module, they are encoded separately through the three corresponding encoders to acquire the structural embedding of each snapshot. In the evolution learning module, we create the ODE function using the attention mechanism on obtained structural embeddings and then temporally update the node hidden embeddings via the ODE solver. Finally, after transmitting the hidden embeddings through the representation decoding model, we get the final node representations and train them via both snapshot reconstruction and snapshot smoothness.

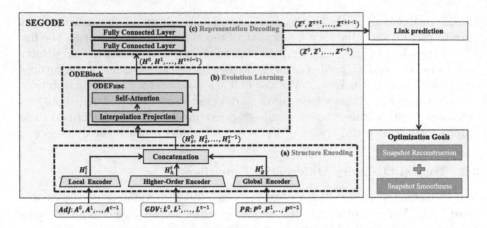

Fig. 1. An overview of the SEGODE framework. SEGODE consists of three modules: structure encoding, evolution learning, and representation decoding. Optimization is performed through two objectives: snapshot reconstruction and snapshot smoothness.

4.2   Structure Encoding

This module aims to comprehensively learn structural information from different perspectives, which is the basis of learning evolutionary dynamics. We construct three encoders to learn the local, higher-order, and global structure of each snapshot graph respectively.

To learn the local proximity among the nodes, we employ two GCN [8] layers as the local encoder f_l on $\boldsymbol{A}^t$ and $\boldsymbol{X}^t$. Through this process, we obtain the local structural embedding $\boldsymbol{H}_l^t$ at time t:

$$\boldsymbol{H}_l^t = f_l^{(1)}(\boldsymbol{A}^t, f_l^{(0)}(\boldsymbol{A}^t, \boldsymbol{X}^t)), \quad f_l(\boldsymbol{A}, \boldsymbol{X}) = \mathrm{Tanh}(\widetilde{\boldsymbol{D}}^{-\frac{1}{2}}\widetilde{\boldsymbol{A}}\widetilde{\boldsymbol{D}}^{-\frac{1}{2}}\boldsymbol{X}\boldsymbol{W}_l), \quad (2)$$

where $\widetilde{\boldsymbol{A}} = \boldsymbol{A} + \boldsymbol{I}$ and $\widetilde{\boldsymbol{D}}$ is the degree matrix of $\widetilde{\boldsymbol{A}}$. $\boldsymbol{W}_l$ represent the learnable parameters. For graphs without attributes, the node degree is leveraged to construct the attribute matrix.

In the higher-order and global encoder, two distinct mapping functions are employed to map GDV [7] matrix $\boldsymbol{L}^t$ and PR [13] matrix $\boldsymbol{P}^t$ into the hidden space. The mapping functions $f_h(\boldsymbol{L}^t)$ and $f_g(\boldsymbol{P}^t)$ are characterized by nonlinear layers, which result in higher-order embedding $\boldsymbol{H}_h^t$ and global embedding $\boldsymbol{H}_g^t$:

$$\boldsymbol{H}_h^t = f_h(\boldsymbol{L}^t) = \sigma(\boldsymbol{L}^t\boldsymbol{W}_h + \boldsymbol{b}_h), \quad \boldsymbol{H}_g^t = f_g(\boldsymbol{P}^t) = \sigma(\boldsymbol{P}^t\boldsymbol{W}_g + \boldsymbol{b}_g). \quad (3)$$

σ is sigmoid activation and $\boldsymbol{W}_h$, $\boldsymbol{W}_g$, $\boldsymbol{b}_h$ and $\boldsymbol{b}_g$ are the learnable parameters.

Ultimately, the three aforementioned embeddings are merged by a fusion function denoted as f_{con} to acquire $\boldsymbol{H}_s^t$:

$$\boldsymbol{H}_s^t = f_{con}(\boldsymbol{H}_l^t \| \boldsymbol{H}_h^t \| \boldsymbol{H}_g^t), \quad (4)$$

where $\|$ denotes the concatenation operation. f_{con} is defined by a multi-layer perceptron (MLP) comprised of two layers with Tanh activation function.

4.3   Evolution Learning

To use the neural ODE to compute the final embeddings of the desired snap-shot, we need to transform the discrete-time embeddings $\{H_s^0, H_s^1, ..., H_s^{\tau-1}\}$ obtained from the structural encoding into continuous-time embeddings. Thus by interpolation projection, the continuous representation H_{ip}^t is obtained as:

$$H_{ip}^t = \frac{\lceil t \rceil_e - t}{\lceil t \rceil_e - \lfloor t \rfloor_e} H_s^{\lfloor t \rfloor_e} + \frac{t - \lfloor t \rfloor_e}{\lceil t \rceil_e - \lfloor t \rfloor_e} H_s^{\lceil t \rceil_e}, \tag{5}$$

where $\lfloor t \rfloor_e$ is crafted to explore downwards up to a non-negative integer, and the embedding at time $\lfloor t \rfloor_e$ ought to be non-empty. This process can effectively address data-scarce cases. If the data is complete, $\lfloor t \rfloor_e$ means rounding down. Correspondingly, the $\lceil t \rceil_e$ explores upwards. If $t = 0$, then $H_{ip}^0 = H_s^0$. Moreover, when t is larger than $\tau - 1$, $H_{ip}^t = H_s^{\tau-1}$.

We utilize the attention mechanism to construct the ODE function:

$$f_{ode}(H^t, t, \theta) = \text{softmax}(\frac{Q^t K^{t^\top}}{\sqrt{d_k}}) V^t, \tag{6}$$

$$Q^t = H_{ip}^t W_q, \quad K^t = H_{ip}^t W_k, \quad V^t = H^t, \tag{7}$$

where lies the task of fitting the t moment hidden embedding, denoted as H^t, through the utilization of a neural ODE. H^t denotes the state matrix of the system at time t. d_k is the embedding dimension. θ includes the weight matrices W_q and W_k. We obtain the input to the neural ODE in time t_0 by a single-layer MLP i.e., $f_{mlp}(H_{ip}^0)$. Finally, the neural ODE can be expressed as:

$$H^{t_1} = f_{mlp}(H_{ip}^0) + \int_0^{t_1} f_{ode}(H^t, t, \theta) dt. \tag{8}$$

By designating $\mathcal{T}$ as a series of discrete moments $\mathcal{T} = \{0, 1, ..., \tau + l - 1\}$ and $t_1 \in \mathcal{T}$, we are able to procure the hidden embeddings at each of these specific instances through Eq. (8). Specifically, we use Runge-Kutta of order 5 of Dormand-Prince-Shampine [2] as the ODE solver to implement Eq. (8).

4.4   Model Optimization

After obtaining H^t through the evolution learning module, we proceed to pass it through the representation decoding module prior to conducting model optimization. The final representation set $\{Z^0, Z^1, ..., Z^{\tau+l-1}\}$ used for optimization and link prediction is generated by the module via two fully connected layers. Optimization is performed on $\{Z^0, Z^1, ..., Z^{\tau-1}\}$. Our approach to optimizing the model is two-fold: snapshot reconstruction and snapshot smoothness.

Snapshot Reconstruction. To enable the node representation to preserve information pertaining to its adjacent nodes, we utilize the binary cross-entropy function identical to that of DySAT [16] for every individual time step:

$$\mathcal{L}_r = \sum_{t=0}^{\tau-1} \sum_{i \in \mathcal{V}} (\sum_{j \in \mathcal{P}_i^t} -\log\sigma(<z_i^t, z_j^t>) - \alpha \sum_{j' \in \mathcal{N}_i^t} \log(1 - \sigma(<z_i^t, z_{j'}^t>))), \qquad (9)$$

where $z_i^t = Z_{i,:}^t$ and $< a, b >$ denotes the inner product of a and b. $\mathcal{P}_i^t$ represents the set of positively sampled neighbors of node v_i at time t_i that are obtained through random walks. The degree distribution $\mathcal{N}_i^t$ is utilized for negative sampling. The hyperparameter α serves the purpose of regulating the respective contributions of positive and negative sampling.

Table 1. Dataset statistics.

Dataset	$|\mathcal{V}|$	$|\cup_t \mathcal{E}^t|$	Min. $|\mathcal{E}^t|$	Max. $|\mathcal{E}^t|$	#Snapshots
Email	1,891	5,870	102	2,861	6
UCI	1,899	15,675	291	9,015	7
Bitcoin	3,783	14,380	945	3,113	8
Reality	6,809	16,623	607	1,351	18
Wiki	8,227	32,856	1,045	2,744	14
Reddit	10,985	292,222	9,015	11,869	27
Math	24,740	230,956	4,899	13,162	26

Snapshot Smoothness. Maintaining the smoothness of two adjacent snapshot representations is a crucial optimization objective. Using snapshot smoothness can impose penalties on mutated node representations within the network. Our objective function for snapshot smoothness using L1-norm is as follows:

$$\mathcal{L}_s = \sum_{t=1}^{\tau-1} \sum_{i \in \mathcal{V}} \|z_i^t - z_i^{t-1}\|_1. \qquad (10)$$

By leveraging a hyperparameter β, we ultimately obtain the final objective function which facilitates the adjustment of the respective contributions of both snapshot reconstruction and snapshot smoothness:

$$\mathcal{L} = \mathcal{L}_r + \beta\mathcal{L}_s. \qquad (11)$$

5   Experiments

5.1   Experimental Setup

Datasets and Baselines. The seven used real-world datasets include Email-dnc (shortly as Email), UCI, Bitcoinalpha (shortly as Bitcoin), Reality-call (shortly as Reality), Wikipedia (shortly as Wiki), Reddit, and Math. Statistical details of these datasets are given in Table 1.

We apply seven temporal graph link prediction algorithms for comparison. For the RNN-based methods, we choose Dyngraph2vec [5] (best version: DynAERNN), EvolveGCN [14] (best version: EvolveGCN-H) and ROLAND [18] (best version: ROLAND-GRU). We also use attention mechanism-based approaches DySAT [16] and STGSN [11], an ODE-based method NDCN [20], and an implementation of the time-then-graph paradigm, namely the GRU-GCN [4].

Table 2. AUC (%) on the inductive single-step link prediction.

Methods	Email	UCI	Bitcoin	Reality	Wiki	Reddit	Math
Dyngraph2vec	97.6 ± 0.9	87.0 ± 1.1	89.6 ± 0.7	96.4 ± 0.4	93.4 ± 0.2	**96.7 ± 0.1**	91.9 ± 1.5
EvolveGCN	96.9 ± 1.2	85.9 ± 2.1	92.2 ± 0.4	92.9 ± 0.9	88.7 ± 0.8	91.9 ± 0.7	90.4 ± 0.5
DySAT	95.9 ± 1.3	87.3 ± 1.8	87.8 ± 1.7	96.5 ± 0.3	89.3 ± 0.2	96.5 ± 0.3	93.3 ± 0.9
NDCN	95.4 ± 1.2	80.4 ± 3.3	85.3 ± 1.4	96.7 ± 31.3	88.2 ± 1.5	95.3 ± 2.7	92.3 ± 0.8
STGSN	97.9 ± 0.2	89.3 ± 2.7	82.9v2.5	93.0 ± 1.2	94.1 ± 2.5	94.3 ± 1.3	95.6 ± 0.4
GRU-GCN	95.0 ± 2.5	83.6 ± 1.6	91.0 ± 0.8	96.4 ± 0.6	88.7 ± 1.7	92.9 ± 1.1	91.1 ± 1.1
ROLAND	96.5 ± 1.8	88.5 ± 0.9	94.7 ± 1.6	93.1 ± 0.4	92.7 ± 1.4	95.0 ± 0.9	91.6 ± 1.3
SEGODE	**98.3 ± 0.6**	**89.8 ± 1.0**	**96.6 ± 0.7**	**97.9 ± 0.4**	**94.5 ± 1.3**	96.6 ± 0.3	**95.7 ± 0.2**

Parameter Setting and Evaluation Metric. We set the size of node representations to 256. For optimization, we use the Adam algorithm with a learning rate of 0.01, weight decay of 0.0005, and a dropout rate of 0.05. We set the random walk length to 20 in the snapshot reconstruction loss and the number of negative samples to 10 for each positive edge. The positive and negative sampling contribution hyperparameter α is set to 1. The regulation value β for Email, UCI, Bitcoin, Reality, Wiki, Reddit, and Math are 10, 10, 10, 10, 1, 0.0001, and 0.00001, respectively. We report the average results over 10 repeated times. The evaluation metric chosen is the area under the ROC curve (AUC).

More details of the datasets and implementation of our model are available at https://github.com/Houl1/SEGODE.

5.2 Single-Step Link Prediction

For single-step link prediction, the model is trained on the set $\{\mathcal{G}^0, \mathcal{G}^1, ..., \mathcal{G}^{\tau-1}\}$. SEGODE and NDCN generate node embedding predictions directly for $\mathcal{G}^\tau$, while the others rely on the embeddings of $\mathcal{G}^{\tau-1}$ for prediction on $\mathcal{G}^\tau$. For evaluation, we use a downstream Logistic Regression (LR) classifier with equal numbers of connected and unconnected node pairs (non-links) randomly sampled from $\mathcal{G}^\tau$. We split the links into training, validation, and test sets in a 1:1:2 ratio. The results for ten runs expressed as mean ± standard deviation are presented in Table 2, where the best results are in bold, and the runner-ups are underlined. Our method performs the top results on all the datasets.

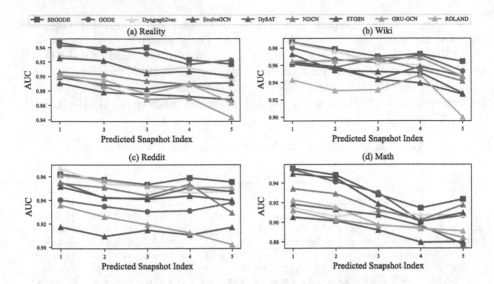

Fig. 2. AUC on the multi-step link prediction.

Table 3. AUC (%) on the data-scarce link prediction.

Methods	Email	UCI	Bitcoin	Reality	Wiki	Reddit	Math	Avg. Drop
Dyngraph2vec	<u>97.3</u>	82.1	87.9	94.6	<u>92.2</u>	<u>95.3</u>	88.3	<u>1.99</u> ↓
EvolveGCN	96.0	84.3	75.7	91.6	88.6	90.3	88.0	3.49 ↓
DySAT	88.2	82.3	87.3	<u>96.2</u>	85.6	95.0	91.3	2.96 ↓
NDCN	94.4	79.2	81.5	88.9	82.8	94.2	91.2	3.06 ↓
STGSN	68.1	<u>88.5</u>	75.5	87.5	87.2	91.1	<u>93.4</u>	7.97 ↓
GRU-GCN	95.1	78.2	81.4	95.5	86.5	90.9	86.5	3.51 ↓
ROLAND	96.2	86.5	<u>91.9</u>	92.9	86.8	94.3	88.1	2.20 ↓
SEGODE	**97.4**	**88.7**	**94.5**	**97.9**	**92.6**	**96.5**	**95.4**	**0.91** ↓

5.3   Multi-step Link Prediction

Here we conduct the multi-step link prediction. To test the usefulness of our model design, we add GODE (SEGODE without higher-order and global encoder) as a baseline. We use the same inductive manner as before, training the model on $\{\mathcal{G}^0, \mathcal{G}^1, .., \mathcal{G}^{\tau-1}\}$. While SEGODE, GODE, and NDCN directly output node embeddings of $\{\mathcal{G}^\tau, \mathcal{G}^{\tau+1}, ..., \mathcal{G}^{\tau+4}\}$, other methods predict links in these 5 snapshots using node embedding of $\mathcal{G}^{\tau-1}$. For each snapshot, we use the same way to implement the evaluation mentioned in Sec. 5.2. The experimental results, presented in Fig. 2, show that SEGODE consistently performs at a high level on multi-step prediction. GODE shows top or competitive results on three datasets, indicating that the implemented neural ODE using the attention mechanism, can effectively learn the dynamics. On Reddit with a larger average node degree, GODE has a significant decrease in performance, indicating that the learned structural information via the structure encoding module is critical for dynamic inference in this situation.

5.4   Data-Scarce Link Prediction

To verify whether SEGODE can get rid of the strong dependence on history recent snapshots and really capture the temporal pattern of the network, we remove 20% of recent (rounding up) snapshots for each dataset. We directly apply SEGODE with the scarce data. For baselines, we use the weighted combination of adjacent undeleted snapshots to fill the gaps made by snapshot deletion, where we keep the common edges of adjacent snapshots and sample non-common edges in proportion to their temporal distance. Our results are shown in Table 3. There is instability in the effect of baselines on this experiment, with a substantial decrease in effect on several datasets. In contrast, SEGODE can still achieve relatively high results on all the datasets.

Table 4. AUC (%) for ablation study.

Methods	Email	UCI	Bitcoin	Wiki
SEGODE	**98.3 ± 0.6**	**89.8 ± 1.0**	**96.6 ± 0.7**	**94.5 ± 1.3**
SEGODE w/o f_h	97.3 ± 1.4	87.8 ± 3.2	95.3 ± 1.5	93.1 ± 1.8
SEGODE w/o f_g	97.5 ± 1.0	87.3 ± 2.3	95.3 ± 1.1	91.1 ± 2.3
SEGODE w/o ODE	93.8 ± 1.9	86.4 ± 1.1	90.6 ± 2.7	86.8 ± 2.9
SEGODE w/o $\mathcal{L}_s$	96.8 ± 1.4	87.8 ± 1.4	94.8 ± 1.1	87.7 ± 2.2
GODE	96.4 ± 1.9	87.3 ± 1.4	93.1 ± 0.8	91.5 ± 3.3

5.5   Ablation Study

To investigate the individual impact of the different components in SEGODE, we perform an ablation study via single-step link prediction with four variants: SEGODE w/o f_h, SEGODE w/o f_g, SEGODE w/o $\mathcal{L}_s$, GODE, SEGODE w/o ODE (where the ODE-based Evolution Learning module is replaced with RNN-based model). The results of our experiments are presented in Table 4. We observe the neural ODE component is the most crucial element for effectively learning temporal features compared with the RNN-based model. The absence of the snapshot smoothness loss $\mathcal{L}_s$ also substantially reduces the experimental effect, which reflects the loss $\mathcal{L}_s$ can facilitate model training. Furthermore, removing one of the structure encoders f_h and f_g reduces AUC values significantly, and removing both of them reduces the AUC values more, indicating all kinds of structural information are needed for enhancing the dynamic inference.

6 Conclusion

In conclusion, our proposed framework, SEGODE, effectively captures the temporal evolution pattern of graphs by using neural ODE with an attention mechanism. Additionally, SEGODE captures higher-order and global structural information to enhance evolution learning compared with classic methods. SEGODE performs well in multi-step link prediction and data-scarce link prediction tasks, indicating that the model effectively learns the dynamics of networks. Overall, our proposed framework provides a powerful tool for analyzing the temporal evolution of graphs and has significant potential for applications in various fields.

Acknowledgment. In this work, we were supported by the Shenzhen Sustainable Development Project (KCXFZ20211020172544004) and the Natural Science Foundation of Inner Mongolia Autonomous Region of China (2022LHMS06008).

References

1. Bianconi, G., Darst, R.K., Iacovacci, J., et al.: Triadic closure as a basic generating mechanism of communities in complex networks. Phys. Rev. E **90**, 042806 (2014)
2. Calvo, M., Montijano, J., Randez, L.: A fifth-order interpolant for the Dormand and prince Runge-Kutta method. J. Comput. Appl. Math. **29**(1), 91–100 (1990)
3. Chen, R.T., Rubanova, Y., Bettencourt, J., et al.: Neural ordinary differential equations. In: Advances in Neural Information Processing Systems, vol. 31 (2018)
4. Gao, J., Ribeiro, B.: On the equivalence between temporal and static equivariant graph representations. In: International Conference on Machine Learning (2022)
5. Goyal, P., Chhetri, S.R., Canedo, A.: dyngraph2vec: capturing network dynamics using dynamic graph representation learning. Knowl.-Based Syst. **187** (2020)
6. Goyal, P., Kamra, N., He, X., Liu, Y.: DynGEM: deep embedding method for dynamic graphs. In: IJCAI International Workshop on Representation Learning for Graphs (2018)
7. Hočevar, T., Demšar, J.: A combinatorial approach to graphlet counting. Bioinformatics **30**(4), 559–565 (2014)
8. Kipf, T.N., Welling, M.: Semi-supervised classification with graph convolutional networks. In: International Conference on Learning Representations (2017)
9. Kumar, S., Zhang, X., Leskovec, J.: Predicting dynamic embedding trajectory in temporal interaction networks. In: Proceedings of the 25th ACM SIGKDD International Conference on Knowledge Discovery & Data Mining (2019)
10. Ma, X., Tan, S., Xie, X., et al.: Joint multi-label learning and feature extraction for temporal link prediction. Pattern Recognit. **121** (2022)
11. Min, S., Gao, Z., Peng, J., et al.: STGSN–a spatial-temporal graph neural network framework for time-evolving social networks. Knowl.-Based Syst. (2021)
12. Murphy, C., Laurence, E., Allard, A.: Deep learning of contagion dynamics on complex networks. Nat. Commun. **12**(1), 4720 (2021)
13. Page, L., Brin, S., Motwani, R., Winograd, T.: The PageRank citation ranking: bringing order to the web. Technical report, Stanford InfoLab (1999)
14. Pareja, A., Domeniconi, G., Chen, J., et al.: EvolveGCN: evolving graph convolutional networks for dynamic graphs. In: Proceedings of the Thirty-Fourth AAAI Conference on Artificial Intelligence (2020)

15. Pontryagin, L.S.: Mathematical Theory of Optimal Processes. CRC Press, Boca Raton (1987)
16. Sankar, A., Wu, Y., Gou, L., et al.: DySAT: deep neural representation learning on dynamic graphs via self-attention networks. In: Proceedings of the 13th International Conference on Web Search and Data Mining (2020)
17. Tang, J., Zhang, J., Yao, L., et al.: ArnetMiner: extraction and mining of academic social networks. In: Proceedings of the 14th ACM SIGKDD International Conference on Knowledge Discovery and Data Mining (2008)
18. You, J., Du, T., Leskovec, J.: ROLAND: graph learning framework for dynamic graphs. In: Proceedings of the 28th ACM SIGKDD Conference on Knowledge Discovery and Data Mining (2022)
19. Yu, W., Cheng, W., Aggarwal, C.C., et al.: Link prediction with spatial and temporal consistency in dynamic networks. In: International Joint Conference on Artificial Intelligence (2017)
20. Zang, C., Wang, F.: Neural dynamics on complex networks. In: Proceedings of the 26th ACM SIGKDD International Conference on Knowledge Discovery & Data Mining (2020)

Supervised Attention Using Homophily in Graph Neural Networks

Michail Chatzianastasis[✉], Giannis Nikolentzos, and Michalis Vazirgiannis

LIX, École Polytechnique, IP Paris, Palaiseau, France
mixalisx97@gmail.com

Abstract. Graph neural networks have become the standard approach for dealing with learning problems on graphs. Among the different variants of graph neural networks, graph attention networks (GATs) have been applied with great success to different tasks. In the GAT model, each node assigns an importance score to its neighbors using an attention mechanism. However, similar to other graph neural networks, GATs aggregate messages from nodes that belong to different classes, and therefore produce node representations that are not well separated with respect to the different classes, which might hurt their performance. In this work, to alleviate this problem, we propose a new technique that can be incorporated into any graph attention model to encourage higher attention scores between nodes that share the same class label. We evaluate the proposed method on several node classification datasets demonstrating increased performance over standard baseline models.

Keywords: Graph Neural Networks · Graph Attention Networks · Supervised Attention

1 Introduction

Graph neural networks (GNNs) have recently emerged as a general framework for learning graph representations and have been applied with great success in different domains such as in bioinformatics [21], in physics [9] and in natural language processing [28], just to name a few. Among others, GNNs have been used to generate molecules with specific chemical characteristics [23], to predict compound-protein interactions for drug discovery [33] and to detect misinformation in social media [16].

While different types of GNNs have been proposed, most of these models follow an iterative message passing scheme, where each node aggregates information from its neighbors [12]. One of the most popular classes of this kind of models are the graph attention networks (GATs) [3,6,34]. GATs employ an attention mechanism which can capture the importance of each neighbor, and are thus considered state-of-the-art models in various graph learning tasks. These models are also highly interpretable since the learned attention scores can provide information about the relevance of the neighboring nodes.

Unfortunately, real-world graphs often contain noise, as there usually exist edges between unrelated nodes. In such a setting, once multiple message passing

L. Iliadis et al. (Eds.): ICANN 2023, LNCS 14257, pp. 576–586, 2023.
https://doi.org/10.1007/978-3-031-44216-2_47

steps are performed, nodes will end up receiving too much noisy information from nodes that belong to different classes, thus leading to indistinguishable representations. This problem is known as oversmoothing in the graph representation learning literature [4, 7], and can dramatically harm the performance of GNNs in the node classification task. Several approaches have been proposed to address the issue of oversmoothing such as normalization layers [11, 38], generalized band-pass filtering operations [24], and approaches that change the graph structure [7]. However, most of them are computationally expensive or require extensive architectural modifications.

In this work, we focus on removing the noisy information from the graph using an attention mechanism. Specifically, we propose a new loss function that encourages nodes to mainly attend to nodes that belong to the same class, and to a lesser extent to nodes that belong to different classes by supervising the attention scores. To motivate our approach, we first experimentally verify that GNNs perform better as the edge homophily in the graph increases, i.e., as we remove inter-class edges. Therefore, it is important to learn attention scores close to 0 for the inter-class edges. Furthermore, we demonstrate that the proposed method outperforms various baselines in real-world node classification tasks. Our approach is computationally efficient, and it can be applied to any graph attention model with minimal modifications in the architecture. Finally, we visualize the distribution of the learned attention scores of our proposed model and of vanilla graph attention networks, for the intra- and the inter-class edges. We verify that our proposed model learns higher attention scores for the intra-class edges, leading to high quality node representations.

Our contributions can be summarized as follows:

- We show experimentally that GNNs perform better as the edge homophily in the graph increases, and that it is important to learn attention scores close to 0 for the inter-class edges.
- We propose a novel loss function for attentional GNNs that encourages nodes to attend mainly to nodes that belong to the same class, and to a lesser extent to nodes that belong to different classes.
- We show that our approach outperforms various baselines in real-world node classification tasks.

The rest of the paper is organized as follows. Section 2 presents the related work. Section 3 introduces the proposed loss function. Finally, Sects. 4 and 5 present the experimental results and conclusions, respectively.

2 Related Work

Graph Neural Networks (GNNs) have received significant attention in the past years, with a growing number of research works proposing novel methods and applications. The first GNN models were proposed several years ago [29, 32], however with the rise of deep learning, GNNs have gained renewed interest in

the research community [15,20]. The majority of GNN models can be reformulated into a single common framework known as Message Passing Neural
Networks (MPNNs) [12]. These models iteratively update a given node's representation by aggregating the feature vectors of its neighbors. Graph attention
networks (GATs) correspond to one of the major subclasses of MPNNs [3,6,34].
GATs employ an attention mechanism which allows them to incorporate explicit
weights for each neighbor. One of the main advantages of these models is that
they are highly interpretable due to the learned attention scores. Numerous
studies have proposed several enhancements and expansions to the message passing mechanism of MPNNs. These include among others, works that use more
expressive or learnable aggregation functions [6,10,25,31], schemes that operate
on high-order neighborhoods of nodes [1,17,27], and approaches that operate in
the hyperbolic space [5,22,26]. However, a common issue that affects the performance of various MPNNs is oversmoothing. Several studies have investigated
the causes and effects of oversmoothing, as well as potential solutions to mitigate this problem, including normalization techniques [11,37] and graph rewiring
methods [7,18].

3   Methodology

3.1   Preliminaries

Let $G = (V, E)$ be an undirected graph where V is a set of nodes and E is a
set of edges. We will denote by N the number of vertices and by M the number
of edges, i.e., $N = |V|$ and $M = |E|$. Then, we have that $V = \{v_1, v_2, \ldots, v_N\}$.
Let $A \in \mathbb{R}^{N \times N}$ denote the adjacency matrix of G, $X = [x_1, x_2, \ldots, x_N]^\top \in$
$\mathbb{R}^{N \times d}$ be the matrix that stores the node features, and $Y = [y_1, y_2, \ldots, y_N]^\top \in$
$\{1, \ldots, C\}^N$ the vector that stores the nodes' class labels where C is the number
of classes. Let $\mathcal{N}(i)$ denote the indices of the neighbors of node v_i, i.e., the
set $\{j \colon \{v_i, v_j\} \in E\}$. We denote the features of the neighbors of a node v_i by
the multiset $X_{\mathcal{N}(i)} = \{x_j \colon j \in \mathcal{N}(i)\}$. We also define the neighborhood of v_i
including v_i as $\overline{\mathcal{N}}(i) = \mathcal{N}(i) \cup \{i\}$ and the corresponding features as $X_{\overline{\mathcal{N}}(i)}$.
Given a training set of nodes, the goal of supervised node classification is to
learn a mapping from the node set to the set of labels, $f : V \to \{0, 1, \ldots, C\}$.

3.2   Graph Neural Networks

GNNs typically use the graph structure A along with the node features X to
learn a representation h_i for each node $v_i \in V$ [14]. As already discussed, most
GNNs employ a message-passing scheme [12] where every node updates its representation by aggregating the representations of its neighbors and combining
them with its own representation. Since there is no natural ordering of the neighbors of a node, the aggregation function needs to be permutation invariant, and
usually has a significant impact on the performance and the expressiveness of
the GNN model [36]. Common aggregation functions include the sum, mean,
max, and min operators, but also attention-based pooling aggregators [15,20].

In this work, we mainly focus on attention-based aggregators, where the representation of each node v_i is updated using a weighted sum of the representations of its neighbors:

$$h_i = \sigma \left(\sum_{j \in \mathcal{N}(i)} \alpha_{ij} W h_j \right) \tag{1}$$

where $h_i \in \mathbb{R}^d$ denotes the hidden representation of node v_i, $W \in \mathbb{R}^{d_o \times d}$ is a weight matrix and α_{ij} is the learned attention score (e. g., how much node v_i attends to node v_j). Equation (1) is applied iteratively, however, for ease of notation, we have dropped the superscript (that denotes the iteration number). Among the different attention models that have been proposed in the past years, the Graph Attention Network (GAT) [34] computes the attention scores by applying a single-layer feedforward neural network in the concatenated node features of the two nodes, while GATv2 [3], an improved version of GAT, computes more expressive and dynamic attention. In our experiments, we use GATv2 as the backbone network, but our approach can be easily applied to any graph attention model. Specifically, we compute the un-normalized attention score between two nodes v_i, v_j using the following equation:

$$e_{ij} = a^\top \text{LeakyReLU} \left(W_2 \left[h_i \| h_j \right] \right) \tag{2}$$

where $a \in \mathbb{R}^{d_o}$ is a weight vector and $W_2 \in \mathbb{R}^{d_o \times 2d}$ a weight matrix. Then, we apply the softmax function to normalize the attention scores across all neighbors of v_i:

$$\alpha_{ij} = \frac{\exp\left(e_{ij}\right)}{\sum_{k \in \mathcal{N}(i)} \exp\left(e_{ik}\right)} \tag{3}$$

3.3   Problem of Information Mixing

Definition 1 (Edge Homophily). *Given a graph $G = (V, E)$ with a vector of node class labels Y, the edge homophily ratio is the fraction of intra-class edges in the graph, i. e., the fraction of edges that connect nodes with the same labels.*

$$h(G, Y) = \frac{\left| \left\{ (v_i, v_j) : (v_i, v_j) \in E \wedge y_i = y_j \right\} \right|}{|E|} \tag{4}$$

The problem of information mixing or oversmoothing [7,35] occurs mainly in cases where there are edges between nodes that belong to different classes (i. e., inter-class edges). In each message passing iteration, information will be exchanged through these "noisy" edges, leading nodes that belong to different classes into obtaining highly non-separable representations. Therefore, the node classification task is becoming extremely challenging. Ideally, we would like to identify and eliminate those "noisy" edges, such that nodes will only aggregate information from intra-class edges.

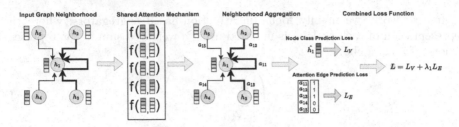

Fig. 1. An illustration of our proposed method (**HS-GATv2**). We combine the loss L_V from the node classification task and the loss L_E from the attention scores based on the training edges, to push neighbor nodes with the same class to have large attention scores and nodes from different classes to have small attention scores. Our approach is applicable to any graph attention model, by setting accordingly the attention function **f**.

In this paper, we leverage graph attention networks in order to alleviate this issue. Specifically, we encourage the network to learn attention scores that minimize information mixing in the graph. Note that a node v_i receives noisy information as follows:

$$\text{noise}(i) = \sum_{j \in \mathcal{N}_{\text{inter}}(i)} \alpha_{ij} \boldsymbol{W} \boldsymbol{h}_j \tag{5}$$

where $\mathcal{N}_{\text{inter}}(i)$ is the set of indices of the inter-class neighbors of node v_i. Therefore, we would like our attention scores to satisfy the following equation:

$$\left\{ \alpha_{ij}^* : j \in \mathcal{N}_{\text{inter}}(i) \right\} = \underset{\left\{ \alpha_{ij} : j \in \mathcal{N}_{\text{inter}}(i) \right\}}{\arg\min} \sum_{j \in \mathcal{N}_{\text{inter}}(i)} ||\alpha_{ij} \boldsymbol{W} \boldsymbol{h}_j|| \tag{6}$$

The solution of the above equation gives us $\alpha_{ij} = 0$ for all the inter-class edges $\{v_i, v_j\}$.

3.4   Supervised Attention Using Homophily (HS-GATv2)

Based on the previous analysis, we propose a new loss function for training graph attention networks that deals with the information mixing problem. Specifically, we propose to supervise the attention scores between the edges, by providing labels that indicate if the edge is an intra- or an inter-class edge. Let V_{train} denote a set that contains the indices of the nodes that belong to the training set. Let also E_{train} denote the training edge set which consists of all the edges where both source and target nodes belong to the training node set, i.e., $E_{\text{train}} = \left\{ \{v_i, v_j\} : \{v_i, v_j\} \in E \land i \in V_{\text{train}} \land j \in V_{\text{train}} \right\}$. Formally, the proposed loss function combines the following two terms: (1) the cross-entropy loss between model predictions and class labels of nodes (denoted by L_V); and (2) the supervised attention losses for the edges between nodes of the training set (denoted by L_E) with mixing coefficient λ:

$$L = L_V + \lambda L_E$$

$$L_V = -\frac{1}{|V_{\text{train}}|} \sum_{i \in V_{\text{train}}} \sum_{c=1}^{C} y_{i,c} \log(\boldsymbol{p}_{i,c})$$

$$L_E = -\frac{1}{T|E_{\text{train}}|} \sum_{t=1}^{T} \sum_{e \in E_{\text{train}}} \left(y_e \log\left(\sigma(e_e^{(t)})\right) \right.$$

$$\left. + (1 - y_e) \log\left(1 - \sigma(e_e^{(t)})\right) \right)$$

(7)

where $y_{i,c}$ indicates if node v_i belongs to the class c (i.e., $y_{i,c} = 1$ if v_i belongs to class c, and 0 otherwise), $\boldsymbol{p}_{i,c}$ is the predicted probability of node v_i belonging to class c, $e_e^{(t)}$ is the un-normalized attention score of edge e in the t-th message passing layer, and y_e is the label of the edge (i.e., 1 if source and target nodes belong to the same class, and 0 otherwise). An illustration of the proposed method is given in Fig. 1.

4   Experiments

In this section, we extensively evaluate our method on synthetic as well as standard node classification datasets, and compare it against state-of-the-art GNNs. As already mentioned, we apply the proposed method to the GATv2 model.

4.1   Adjusting Homophily in Graphs

Our method is based on the assumption that node classification is easier in homophilic graphs, since nodes from the different classes will have separable representations. In this experiment, we try to verify this claim. Therefore, we test the performance of various GNNs by adjusting the edge homophily in various graph datasets. Specifically, we remove $k|E_{\text{inter}}|$ inter-class edges from each dataset, where $|E_{\text{inter}}|$ is the number of inter-class edges in a graph. Setting $k = 0$ corresponds to the original graph and $k = 1$ corresponds to a fully homophilic graph. We report the results for Cora, Citeseer and Disease datasets in Fig. 2. We observe that the performance increases for all the models, as the homophily of the graph increases. Our approach is strongly motivated by this observation, since the proposed loss function encourages the attention scores of inter-class edges to be close to 0, thus generating a more homophilic-like setting.

4.2   Node Classification Benchmarks

Baselines. We compare our approach (HS-GATv2) against the following state-of-the-art GNN models: Graph Convolutional Network (GCN) [20], Graph-SAGE [15], Graph Attention Network (GAT) [34], GATv2 [3], and Principal Neighbourhood Aggregation (PNA) [8].

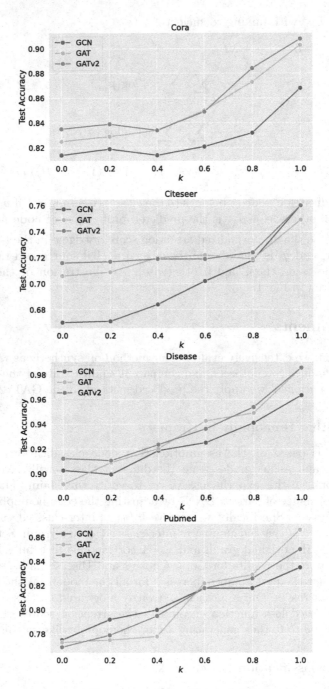

Fig. 2. Test performance of GNNs by removing $k|E_{\text{inter}}|$ inter-class edges. Setting $k = 0$ corresponds to the original graph and $k = 1$ corresponds to a fully homophilic graph. Performance improves as the ratio of homophilic edges increases.

Table 1. Test accuracy in the node classification benchmarks.

Method	Cora	Citeseer	Disease	Pubmed
MLP	43.8	52.9	79.1 ± 1.0	74.2 ± 0.2
GCN	81.4	67.5	89.0 ± 2.2	77.8 ± 0.3
GraphSAGE	77.2	65.3	88.8 ± 2.0	77.9 ± 0.6
PNA	76.4	58.9	86.8 ± 1.9	75.8 ± 0.6
GAT	82.5	70.6	88.1 ± 2.5	78.1 ± 0.6
GATv2	83.5	71.6	89.2 ± 1.7	78.5 ± 0.4
HS-GATv2 (ours)	**85.3**	**73.5**	$\mathbf{89.3} \pm 3.3$	$\mathbf{79.1} \pm 0.3$

Datasets. We utilize four well-known node classification benchmark datasets to evaluate our approach in real-world scenarios. We use three citation network datasets: Cora, CiteSeer and Pubmed [30], where each node corresponds to a scientific publication, edges correspond to citations and the goal is to predict the category of each publication. We follow the experimental setup of [20] and use 140 nodes for training, 300 for validation and 1000 for testing. We further use one disease spreading model: Disease [5]. It simulates the SIR disease spreading model [2], where the label of a node indicates if it is infected or not. We follow the experimental setup of [5] and use 30/10/60% for training, validation and test sets and report the average results from 10 different random splits.

Experimental Setup. We use the Adam optimizer [19] with the Glorot initialization [13]. We search the layers from $\{1, 2\}$ and the attention heads from $\{1, 4, 8\}$. We set the weight decay equal to 5e−5. We fix the mixing coefficient λ to 0.1. We search the hidden dimensions from $\{8, 16, 32, 64, 128\}$, the learning rate from $\{0.001, 0.005\}$ and the dropout rate from $\{0.0, 0.2, 0.5\}$.

Results. Table 1 illustrates the obtained test accuracies. We observe that the proposed HS-GATv2 method outperforms the baselines on all three datasets. This highlights the ability of the proposed approach to use the attention mechanism to reduce the noisy information that each node receives from its neighbors, thus producing high-quality node representations.

4.3   Distribution of Attention Scores

In this experiment, we compute the distribution of the un-normalized attention scores produced by HS-GATv2 and GATv2 for edges whose endpoints are not in the training set. The results for the Cora dataset are illustrated in Fig. 3. Attention scores obtained from GATv2 have the same distribution for the intra- and inter-class edges. On the other hand, we observe that HS-GATv2 produces higher attention values for the intra-class edges even though it has not seen them during training. This allows our model to reduce the noisy information in the message passing procedure, and to focus mainly on the homophilic edges.

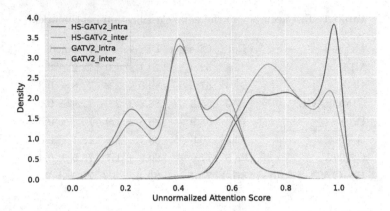

Fig. 3. Distribution of attention scores averaged across the eight attention heads in Cora for intra and inter class edges that were not presented in the training set.

5   Conclusion

In this paper, we introduced a new type of graph attention model that uses supervision in the attention scores by exploiting the network homophily. Our proposed loss function contains a loss term that encourages attention scores to be high between nodes that share the same label and therefore alleviates the problem of information mixing in GNNs. Our extensive experiments demonstrate an increase in the performance of the proposed method over state-of-the-art GNNs such as GAT and GATv2 in node classification tasks.

Acknowledgements. G.N. is supported by the French National research agency via the AML-HELAS (ANR-19-CHIA-0020) project.

References

1. Abu-El-Haija, S., et al.: MixHop: higher-order graph convolutional architectures via sparsified neighborhood mixing. In: Proceedings of the 36th International Conference on Machine Learning, pp. 21–29 (2019)
2. Anderson, R.M., May, R.M.: Infectious Diseases of Humans: Dynamics and Control. Oxford University Press, Oxford (1992)
3. Brody, S., Alon, U., Yahav, E.: How attentive are graph attention networks? In: 10th International Conference on Learning Representations (2022)
4. Cai, C., Wang, Y.: A note on over-smoothing for graph neural networks. arXiv preprint arXiv:2006.13318 (2020)
5. Chami, I., Ying, Z., Ré, C., Leskovec, J.: Hyperbolic graph convolutional neural networks. In: Advances in Neural Information Processing Systems (2019)
6. Chatzianastasis, M., Lutzeyer, J., Dasoulas, G., Vazirgiannis, M.: Graph ordering attention networks. In: Proceedings of the 37th AAAI Conference on Artificial Intelligence, pp. 7006–7014 (2023)

7. Chen, D., Lin, Y., Li, W., Li, P., Zhou, J., Sun, X.: Measuring and relieving the over-smoothing problem for graph neural networks from the topological view. In: Proceedings of the 34th AAAI Conference on Artificial Intelligence, pp. 3438–3445 (2020)
8. Corso, G., Cavalleri, L., Beaini, D., Liò, P., Veličković, P.: Principal neighbourhood aggregation for graph nets. In: Advances in Neural Information Processing Systems, pp. 13260–13271 (2020)
9. Cranmer, M., et al.: Discovering symbolic models from deep learning with inductive biases. In: Advances in Neural Information Processing Systems, pp. 17429–17442 (2020)
10. Dasoulas, G., Lutzeyer, J., Vazirgiannis, M.: Learning parametrised graph shift operators. In: 9th International Conference on Learning Representations (2021)
11. Dasoulas, G., Scaman, K., Virmaux, A.: Lipschitz normalization for self-attention layers with application to graph neural networks. In: Proceedings of the 38th International Conference on Machine Learning, pp. 2456–2466 (2021)
12. Gilmer, J., Schoenholz, S.S., Riley, P.F., Vinyals, O., Dahl, G.E.: Neural message passing for quantum chemistry. In: Proceedings of the 34th International Conference on Machine Learning, pp. 1263–1272 (2017)
13. Glorot, X., Bengio, Y.: Understanding the difficulty of training deep feedforward neural networks. In: Proceedings of the 13th International Conference on Artificial Intelligence and Statistics, pp. 249–256 (2010)
14. Gori, M., Monfardini, G., Scarselli, F.: A new model for learning in graph domains. In: Proceedings of the 2005 IEEE International Joint Conference on Neural Networks, vol. 2, pp. 729–734 (2005)
15. Hamilton, W., Ying, Z., Leskovec, J.: Inductive representation learning on large graphs. In: Advances in Neural Information Processing Systems, pp. 1024–1034 (2017)
16. Han, Y., Karunasekera, S., Leckie, C.: Graph neural networks with continual learning for fake news detection from social media. arXiv preprint arXiv:2007.03316 (2020)
17. Jin, Y., Song, G., Shi, C.: GraLSP: graph neural networks with local structural patterns. In: Proceedings of the 34th AAAI Conference on Artificial Intelligence, pp. 4361–4368 (2020)
18. Karhadkar, K., Banerjee, P.K., Montufar, G.: FoSR: first-order spectral rewiring for addressing oversquashing in GNNs. In: 11th International Conference on Learning Representations (2022)
19. Kingma, D.P., Ba, J.: Adam: a method for stochastic optimization. In: 3rd International Conference on Learning Representations (2014)
20. Kipf, T.N., Welling, M.: Semi-supervised classification with graph convolutional networks. In: 5th International Conference on Learning Representations (2017)
21. Li, M.M., Huang, K., Zitnik, M.: Graph representation learning in biomedicine and healthcare. Nat. Biomed. Eng. 6(12), 1353–1369 (2022)
22. Liu, Q., Nickel, M., Kiela, D.: Hyperbolic graph neural networks. In: Advances in Neural Information Processing Systems, pp. 8230–8241 (2019)
23. Mahmood, O., Mansimov, E., Bonneau, R., Cho, K.: Masked graph modeling for molecule generation. Nat. Commun. 12(1), 1–12 (2021)
24. Min, Y., Wenkel, F., Wolf, G.: Scattering GCN: overcoming oversmoothness in graph convolutional networks. In: Advances in Neural Information Processing Systems, pp. 14498–14508 (2020)

25. Murphy, R., Srinivasan, B., Rao, V., Ribeiro, B.: Relational pooling for graph representations. In: Proceedings of the 36th International Conference on Machine Learning, pp. 4663–4673 (2019)
26. Nikolentzos, G., Chatzianastasis, M., Vazirgiannis, M.: Weisfeiler and leman go hyperbolic: learning distance preserving node representations. In: Proceedings of the 26th International Conference on Artificial Intelligence and Statistics, pp. 1037–1054 (2023)
27. Nikolentzos, G., Dasoulas, G., Vazirgiannis, M.: k-hop graph neural networks. Neural Netw. **130**, 195–205 (2020)
28. Nikolentzos, G., Tixier, A., Vazirgiannis, M.: Message passing attention networks for document understanding. In: Proceedings of the 34th AAAI Conference on Artificial Intelligence, pp. 8544–8551 (2020)
29. Scarselli, F., Gori, M., Tsoi, A.C., Hagenbuchner, M., Monfardini, G.: The graph neural network model. IEEE Trans. Neural Netw. **20**(1), 61–80 (2008)
30. Sen, P., Namata, G., Bilgic, M., Getoor, L., Galligher, B., Eliassi-Rad, T.: Collective classification in network data. AI Mag. **29**(3), 93–93 (2008)
31. Seo, Y., Loukas, A., Perraudin, N.: Discriminative structural graph classification. arXiv preprint arXiv:1905.13422 (2019)
32. Sperduti, A., Starita, A.: Supervised neural networks for the classification of structures. IEEE Trans. Neural Netw. **8**(3), 714–735 (1997)
33. Tsubaki, M., Tomii, K., Sese, J.: Compound-protein interaction prediction with end-to-end learning of neural networks for graphs and sequences. Bioinformatics **35**(2), 309–318 (2019)
34. Veličković, P., Cucurull, G., Casanova, A., Romero, A., Lio, P., Bengio, Y.: Graph attention networks. In: 6th International Conference on Learning Representations (2018)
35. Wang, G., Ying, R., Huang, J., Leskovec, J.: Improving graph attention networks with large margin-based constraints. arXiv preprint arXiv:1910.11945 (2019)
36. Xu, K., Hu, W., Leskovec, J., Jegelka, S.: How powerful are graph neural networks? In: 7th International Conference on Learning Representations (2019)
37. Yang, C., Wang, R., Yao, S., Liu, S., Abdelzaher, T.: Revisiting over-smoothing in deep GCNs. arXiv preprint arXiv:2003.13663 (2020)
38. Zhao, L., Akoglu, L.: PairNorm: tackling oversmoothing in GNNs. In: 8th International Conference on Learning Representations (2020)

Target-Oriented Sentiment Classification with Sequential Cross-Modal Semantic Graph

Yufeng Huang[1], Zhuo Chen[2], Jiaoyan Chen[3], Jeff Z. Pan[4], Zhen Yao[1], and Wen Zhang[1(✉)]

[1] School of Software Technology, Zhejiang University, Hangzhou, China
{huangyufeng,yz0204,zhang.wen}@zju.edu.cn
[2] College of Computer Science and Technology, Zhejiang University, Hangzhou, China
zhuo.chen@zju.edu.cn
[3] Department of Computer Science, The University of Manchester, Manchester, UK
jiaoyan.chen@manchester.ac.uk
[4] School of Informatics, The University of Edinburgh, Edinburgh, UK
j.z.pan@ed.ac.uk

Abstract. Multi-modal aspect-based sentiment classification (MABSC) is an approach aimed at classifying the sentiment of a target entity mentioned in a sentence using images. However, previous methods failed to account for the fine-grained semantic association between the image and the text, which resulted in limited identification of fine-grained image aspects and opinions. To address these limitations, a new approach called SeqCSG has been proposed in this paper. SeqCSG enhances the encoder-decoder sentiment classification framework using sequential cross-modal semantic graphs. SeqCSG utilizes image captions and scene graphs to extract both global and local fine-grained image information and considers them as elements of the cross-modal semantic graph along with tokens from tweets. The sequential cross-modal semantic graph is represented as a sequence with a multi-modal adjacency matrix indicating relationships between elements. Experimental results have shown that the approach outperforms existing methods and achieves state-of-the-art performance on two standard datasets. Further analysis has demonstrated that the model can implicitly learn the correlation between fine-grained information of the image and the text with the given target.

Keywords: Cross modal · Scene graph · Sentiment classification

1 Introduction

Multi-modal aspect-based sentiment classification (MABSC) is an emerging task that focuses on classifying the sentiment of a given target such as a mentioned entity in data with different modalities. Specifically, MABSC seeks to identify the sentiment polarities of a target when given a text-image pair.

Recent years have witnessed increasing attention on the MABSC task and many methods are proposed for this challenging task. Some studies [7] fuse

L. Iliadis et al. (Eds.): ICANN 2023, LNCS 14257, pp. 587–599, 2023.
https://doi.org/10.1007/978-3-031-44216-2_48

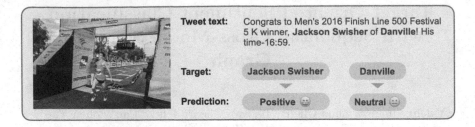

Fig. 1. Examples of MABSC.

caption and tweet to achieve model alignment. Yu et al. [24] proposes a multi-task learning model to capture the image-target matching relations. Zhao et al. [28] leverages the adjective-noun pairs to align text and image. Other works like [10] model aspects, opinions and their alignment through task-specific visual language pre-training (VLP-MABSA). These methods mainly relied on coarse-grained information extracted from images, such as the features of the entire image, and achieved alignment between images and texts to a certain extent. However, it is very common to have the same image and text but different targets in the MABSC task. While coarse-grained features are insufficient for accurately classifying two tasks with the same image-text pair but different targets and sentiments, as shown in Fig. 1. Therefore, it is crucial to model both the global and local fine-grained information from the image, while also leveraging text that takes into account the target and the fine-grained information from the image in a cross-modal manner.

With the objective of achieving this aim, we extract global and local features as fine-grained image information by utilizing image captions and scene graphs, respectively. We then propose a method to construct a sequential cross-modal semantic graph for each image-text pair, which is represented as a sequence with a multi-modal adjacency matrix. This representation enables us to obtain a high-level structured representation of the visual context. Specifically, the elements of the sequential cross-modal semantic graph include tokens of the input text and the image caption, as well as triples that indicate relationships between fine-grained images and objects in the scene graph. Then we transform all these elements into a sequence and construct the structure of the semantic graph through a multi-modal adjacency matrix indicating the connections between different elements. Meanwhile, we built a manual prompt template that guides the model to connect the target and the other information. To make effective use of the sequential cross-modal semantic graph, we introduce an encoder-decoder framework that incorporates a target prompt template.

To demonstrate the effectiveness of our approach, we experimentally evaluate the model on two benchmarks, Twitter2015 [26] and Twitter2017 [13]. Results show that our approach achieves better performance. Furthermore, the ablation study shows that the sequential cross-modal semantic graph with the multi-modal adjacency matrix can effectively facilitate MABSC.

In summary, our main contributions are as follows: We propose a sequential cross-modal semantic graph construction method, which can crossly utilize fine-grained information from images and text. Besides, we propose an encoder-decoder method with a prompt template that could effectively utilize the sequential cross-modal semantic graph considering the target. We perform comprehensive experiments and extensive analysis on two datasets illustrating that SeqCSG can effectively and robustly model the multi-modal representations of descriptive texts and images and achieves state-of-the-art performance. Our code is available at https://github.com/zjukg/SeqCSG.

2   Related Work

Text-based Target-oriented Sentiment Classification. This task aims to predict the sentiment polarities of the target, which is a mentioned entity in the text. Dai et al. [2] leveraged RoBERTa to reconstruct dependency trees, Yan et al. [20] proposed a generative framework that achieves competitive performance.

Multi-modal Sentiment Classification. The goal of this task is to discover the sentiment expressed in multi-modal samples. Yu et al. [25] proposed the task of multi-modal joint training and learning multi-modal and unimodal representation; Yang et al. [21] extended the BERT model to cross-modal scenarios and proposed a multi-modal BERT for sentiment analysis; Wu et al. [18] designed a multi-modal emotion analysis model based on multi-head attention; Keswani et al. [6] used BERT's multi-modal Bitransformer and ResNet to model text and visual features. There were also some existing works that used LXMERT and ViLT [8] as the backbone for multi-modal sentiment analysis.

Multi-modal Aspect-Based Sentiment Classification. Xu et al. [19] and Yu at el. [23] used LSTM to effectively model the target-text and target-image interactions. [7,17,22,27] explored the usefulness of the BERT and proposed TomBERT, SaliencyBERT, ModalNet-BERT and EF-CapTrBERT. Yu et al. [24] proposed a multi-task learning model to leverage two auxiliary tasks to capture the image-target matching relations. Zhao et al. [28] leveraged the adjective-noun pairs to align text and image. The work most related to ours is VLP-MABSA [10], which is a task-specific vision-language pre-training framework.

3   Methodology

Given a target entity mention t, a sentence s where t is located, and an image v which is associated with s, MABSC aims to predict the sentiment label y for t, where $y \in \{negative, neutral, positive\}$. s is composed of a sequence of words, denoted as $\{w_1, w_2, w_3, \ldots, w_{|N|}\}$, where N is the sequence length, and t can consist of multiple words. In the example shown in Fig. 1.

Given a sample $m = \{s, v, t, y\}$, there are two steps in our method. First, we construct a sequential cross-modal semantic graph in order to represent the input of multi-modal information in the form of text. Our sequential cross-modal semantic graph elements consist of the tweet text, the caption, and the triples in the scene graph. For the input image $v \in \mathbb{R}^{3 \times H \times W}$, we generate a caption of the image v, while a scene graph is extracted from the image v via the scene

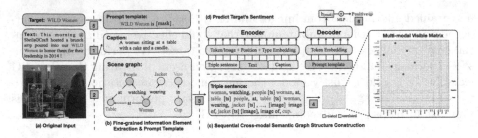

Fig. 2. Overview of our proposed approach.

graph generation method. Then, we input the semantic graph and multi-modal adjacency matrix into an encoder-decoder framework. We introduce the graph construction in Sect. 3.1 and the encoder-decoder architecture in Sect. 3.2.

3.1 Sequential Cross-Modal Semantic Graph Construction

The components of our sequential cross-modal semantic graph consist of scene graphs, image captions, and tweet text, which were carefully selected for their ability to provide a comprehensive representation of the visual content.

Semantic Graph Element Extraction. There are three elements in our semantic graph: image caption, tweet text and scene graph. We generate a caption of the image v via caption transformers, the image captions serve to encapsulate global visual information while tweet text is already in the form of text. In contrast to prior studies [14] that rely on visual knowledge sourced from object representations extracted from the image, we use scene graph, which consists of the Recall@5 $(subject, predicate, object)$ triples from a pre-trained scene graph generator to represent the object-level image context, e.g., $(car, behind, man)$, as well as Recall@5 ([img], $image\ of, object$) triples to represent the relation between the sub-image and the object. Particularly, [img] is a special token, which represents the relevant sub-image. The scene graphs were employed to depict local fine-grained image features.

Element-to-Sequence Transformation. The merging of the caption, tweet text, and triple sentence is facilitated through the utilization of the separator token [/s]. This unified input is subsequently employed as the encoder input within the sequence-to-sequence model [1], conforming to the specified template:

$$S_{in} = [\text{s}] \ \textbf{triple sentence} \ [/\text{s}] \ \textbf{caption} \ [/\text{s}] \ \textbf{tweet} \ [/\text{s}]. \quad (1)$$

The objective of our research is to establish a uniform sequence from the three elements in order to act as input to an encoder-decoder framework. Given that the tweet text and image caption are already presented in a sequential format, the primary objective of our transformation efforts centers on the integration of the scene graph into a textual format. Specifically, two types of triples include object-to-object and object-to-image are extracted from the image, which are converted into serialized sentences separated by "," and then connected via the special token [ts] to construct those final triple sentences. For example, given triples of the scene graph: $(train, has, seat)$, $(person, watching, man)$, $(img_1, image\,of, train)$, $(img_2, image\,of, person)$, $(img_3, image\,of, man)$. We convert them into the following serialized form:

$$[\text{s}]\ \texttt{train, has, seat}\ [\text{ts}]\ ...\ [\text{ts}]\ [\text{img}]\,, \texttt{image of, man}\ [/\text{s}]. \tag{2}$$

Semantic Graph Structure Construction. Our representation of a set of triples $\mathcal{T}_{in}$ entails the conversion of the set into a sequence of tokens. Despite the fact that the serialized triple sentence presently contains a significant amount of information concerning the triples, this serialization process is prone to damaging the inherent structure of the triple itself and compromising the implicit information that exists between entities. Notably, one potential issue that arises with knowledge is the possibility that it may result in an alteration of the meaning conveyed within the original sentence. Consequently, our objective is to ensure that the model enhances the internal connections present within the triples, while concurrently extracting additional valid information from the same entity within the serialized triple sentence.

Inspired by K-BERT [12], we build a adjacency matrix to establish the inter-relatedness between elements presented within the sequence of the semantic graph. Formally, the adjacency matrix M is defined as Eq. (3),

$$M_{ij} = \begin{cases} 1 & \text{if } w_i, w_j \in (e_1, r_1, e_2), \\ 1 & \text{if } w_i \in K \text{ or } w_j \in K, \\ 1 & \text{if } (w_i \in S \cup C) \text{ or } (w_j \in S \cup C), \\ 1 & \text{if } (w_i \in e_1) \cap (w_j \in e_2) \cap (e_1 = e_2), \\ 0 & \text{otherwise,} \end{cases} \tag{3}$$

where w_i and w_j are tokens in sentences; e_1 and e_2 are entities; r_1 is a relation; K is special tokens; S denotes the tweet text and C denotes the image caption.

Concretely, (i) for input triple sentences S_{in}, we make elements in the same triple visible to each other. The shared entities within various triples are visible to each other while the rest of is invisible. Through this approach, we mitigate the influence of extraneous information and effectively model implicit information present between entities; (ii) the tweet, caption, and other special tokens in the encoder should be visible to each other so that the text information can interact with the triple information extracted from the image. To some degree, the adjacency matrix M contains the structural information of the triple sentence.

3.2 Model Architecture

Our study employs a sequence-to-sequence architecture to implement a generative model, intended to classify the target's sentiment for MABSC. This approach is structured two integral components, the encoder and the decoder. The overview of the model is shown in Fig. 2.

Encoder. The input of the encoder is composed of the sequential cross-modal semantic graph, which consists of three elements: scene graph, caption, and tweet text. For sentence S_{in} in the encoder, we tokenize it into a sequence of tokens $S_{in} = \{s_1, s_2, ..., s_n\}$. The encoder is to encode sentence S_{in} and adjacency matrix M_{ij} into the hidden representation space as a vector H_{en},

$$H_{en} = Encoder(S_{in}, M_{ij}), \tag{4}$$

where $H_{en} \in \mathbb{R}^{n \times d}$ and d is the hidden state dimension.

To utilize the adjacency matrix, we make the encoder transformer layer aware of the relatedness between elements defined in M in the self-attention module. The vanilla transformer layer includes a self-attention module and a position-wise feed-forward network. Suppose the input of self-attention module is $H = [s_1, ..., s_n]^\top \in \mathbb{R}^{n \times d}$ with the ith row as the d dimensional hidden state for the ith element. The self-attention operation is

$$Q = HW_Q, K = HW_K, V = HW_V, \tag{5}$$

$$A = \frac{QK^\top}{\sqrt{d_K}}, Attn(H) = softmax(A)V, \tag{6}$$

where $W_Q \in \mathbb{R}^{d \times d_Q}$, $W_K \in \mathbb{R}^{d \times d_K}$, $W_V \in \mathbb{R}^{d \times d_V}$ is the projection matrix to generate the query, key, and value representation of H respectively; A is the matrix capturing similarity between the query and the key. To inject adjacency matrix, we modify the self-attention module into

$$A_{ij} = \frac{M_{ij} \times (h_i W_Q) (h_j W_K)^\top}{\sqrt{d}} + (1 - M_{ij}), \tag{7}$$

$$Attn(h_i) = \sum_{j=1}^{n_s} softmax(A_i)_j \times (e_j W_V), \tag{8}$$

where δ is a large negative number to make values after the softmax function $softmax()$ near 0.

The primary purpose of the embedding layer is to transform the sentence into an embedding representation that can be subsequently fed into the Transformers. Our proposed model adopts an approach similar to that of BERT [3], wherein the embedding representation is calculated as a sum of three distinct embeddings, namely the element embedding, position embedding, and type embedding.

Our model contains language tokens and sub-image tokens. Therefore, the embedding process for our input is crucial in order to preserve its structural information. Considering the input of multi-modal information, token/image embedding distinguishes input tokens. For text tokens, the vocabulary provided by BART [9] is adopted. Each token in the sentence tree is mapped to an embedding vector with a dimension of H through a trainable lookup table. In addition, image tokens are encoded using ResNet and transformed into an embedding vector of the same dimension through a linear layer.

Following ViLT [8], we set the image token embedding as 1 and the text token embedding as 0. In the context of transformer models, the absence of position embedding can cause the loss of structural information, leading to a bag-of-words model with unordered tokens. To avoid this issue, we adopted the position embedding technique used in the BART model for encoding purposes.

Decoder. At the t-th time of decoding, the decoder takes the encoder's output H_{en} and the decoder's previous output $y_1, y_2, ..., y_{t-1}$ as inputs. Then the decoder outputs y_t, where i in y_i indicates the token index. Existing studies [11] have shown that answer engineering has a strong influence on the performance of prompt-tuning. The basis for classification in the MABSC is not solely reliant on textual and visual inputs, but also on the target being evaluated. For example, given the tweet text "Congrats to Men's 2016 Finish Line 500 Festival 5K winner, Jackson Swisher of Danville! His time-16:59." and its corresponding image, the sentiment tendency of "Jackson Swisher" is "Positive" but "Danville" is "Neutral". Therefore, it is crucial to consider the target during the integration and fusion of text and image information. To this end, we propose transforming the target information in the input into a prompt template. This approach enables the establishment of a connection between the target and sentiment orientation, resulting in a more accurate classification outcome.

Taking "Congrats to Men's 2016 Finish Line 500 Festival 5K winner, Jackson Swisher of Danville! His time-16:59." as an example, the input content of the encoder remains the same and is composed of three elements: serialized triple sentence, caption, and tweet text. We transform the target "Jackson Swisher" in this sentence into the form of "Jackson Swisher is [mask].", input it to the decoder end, and then input the vector $H_{[m]}$ corresponding to the [mask] in the last layer of the decoder into a MLP for sentiment classification.

Then for each target x_{in} and the prompt template $\mathcal{T}$, let the manipulation $X_{prompt} = \mathcal{T}(x_{in})$ be a masked language modeling (MLM) input which contains one [mask] token. In this way, we can treat our task as a MLM, and model the probability of predicting class $y \in \mathcal{Y}$ as:

$$p\left(y \mid H_{[m]}\right) = softmax\left(\theta_{Linear} Dropout\left(H_{[m]}\right)\right), \qquad (9)$$

where $H_{[m]}$ is the hidden vector of [mask]. $\theta_{Linear} \in \mathbb{R}^{3 \times 768}$ is learned by back propagation. We learn θ_{Linear} by fine-tuning the BART alongside Eq. (9) using the standard cross-entropy loss.

4   Experiments

In this section, we compared with one image-only, five text-only and several text-image baselines to demonstrate the effectiveness of our method by answering the following questions: **Q1:** How does SeqCSG perform compared with state-of-the-art methods for MABSC? **Q2:** Do image captions and scene graphs help capture the fine-grained information of images better? **Q3:** Whether the multi-modal adjacency matrix help crossly utilize image and text information?

4.1 Experiment Setting

Datasets. We conduct experiments on two benchmarks Twitter2015 and Twitter2017 [22].

Implement Details. We employ BART [9], a denoising and simple encoder-decoder PLM. The image caption is obtained by the transformer-based caption model [7]. We utilize a pre-trained scene graph generator [16] to extract a scene graph. Note that we freeze the ResNet parameters to decrease the learnable parameters hence avoiding overfitting. Specifically, we fix all the hyperparameters after tuning them on the development set and fine-tune for 30 epochs. The batch size is set to 16; the learning rate is set to 2e−5. We implement all the models with PyTorch, and run experiments on a RTX3090 GPU.

Table 1. The property prediction performance of our method (SeqCSG), compared with image-only (first group), text-only (second group) and multi-modal methods (third group) baselines on Twitter2015 and Twitter2017 datasets.

Modality	Method	Twitter2015		Twitter2017	
		Acc	Macro-F1	Acc	Macro-F1
Visual	Res-Target	59.9	46.5	58.6	54.0
Text	MGAN [4]	71.2	64.2	64.8	61.5
	BERT [3]	74.3	70.0	68.9	66.1
	BERT+BL [3]	74.3	70.0	68.9	66.1
	BERT-Pair-QA [15]	74.4	67.7	63.1	59.7
	BART [9]	76.0	67.6	69.5	67.0
Text + Visual	Res-MGAN	71.7	63.9	66.4	63.0
	Res-BERT+BL	75.0	69.2	69.2	66.5
	mPBERT (CLS) [22]	75.8	71.1	68.8	67.1
	TomBERT [22]	77.2	71.8	70.5	68.0
	MIMN [19]	71.8	65.7	65.9	63.0
	ViLBERT [14]	73.8	69.9	67.4	64.9
	ModalNet-BERT [27]	79.0	72.5	72.4	69.2
	CapTrBERT [7]	78.0	73.2	72.3	70.2
	JML-MASC [5]	78.7	–	72.7	–
	SaliencyBERT [17]	77.0	72.4	69.7	67.2
	VLP-MABSA [10]	78.6	73.8	73.8	71.8
	ITM [24]	78.3	74.2	72.6	72.0
	KEF-SaliencyBERT [28]	78.2	73.5	71.9	69.0
	KEF-TomBERT [28]	78.7	73.8	72.1	70.0
	Multi-BART [9]	77.2	72.6	70.5	69.0
	SeqCSG (Ours)	**79.3**	**75.0**	**74.6**	**73.2**

4.2   Main Results (Q1)

Table 1 shows the results of different methods on both Twitter2015 and Twitter2017. Based on the results of our experiments, SeqCSG has demonstrated superior performance compared to other baseline models across all benchmark datasets. Notably, our model achieves a greater F1-score by 1.2 and 1.4 absolute percentage points, respectively, and accuracy that is 0.7 and 0.8 absolute percentage points higher, respectively, than the VLP-MABSA system.

Our approach stands out due to the utilization of image captions and scene graphs, which allow for the modeling of both global and local fine-grained information present in the original image. By processing these elements through a multi-modal adjacency matrix alongside the tweet text, we are able to extract a significant amount of auxiliary information from the image, including the relationship between entities and relevant sub-images. This enables our model to learn an implicit correlation representation of the target, fine-grained information, and tweet text during training, which leads to superior performance compared to other methods. In our approach, we aim to mitigate the negative impact of triple knowledge noise. To achieve this, we set a limit on the number of triples, while also taking care to ensure that the serialized triple knowledge only interacts with each other when a connection exists through the multi-modal adjacency matrix. This analysis indicates **SeqCSG performs good for MABSC compared with other methods (Q1).**

We observe that the performance of single-modal methods, either based on image or text alone, is inferior to that of their multi-modal counterparts. Specifically, the image-based methods exhibit much lower accuracy than the multimodal approaches, while the text-based methods also suffer from a certain performance gap. Our findings suggest that there is still considerable potential for improving the processing of visual features as well as enhancing the interaction between modalities to achieve better results.

From the results, we can observe that Multi-BART also achieves a good performance, even better than some multi-modal methods. This observation serves as evidence of the effectiveness of the proposed framework as a solid foundation. In the context of multi-modal methods, VLP-MABSA outperforms its predecessors due to its design of pre-training tasks tailored to specific tasks, thereby facilitating alignment and interaction between textual and visual features.

4.3   Ablation Study (Q2 and Q3)

Component Analysis. We perform an ablation study to evaluate the efficacy of each component on Twitter2015. Results are shown in Table 2.

An important distinction between BART and Multi-BART lies in the latter's inclusion of image caption information as input. Upon removing the caption and using only triple sentences and text, we observe a decrease of [2.3, 2.2] points in [acc, F1] performance. These comparative results suggest that the image caption serves as a valuable global representation. As an essential component, it is evident that the experimental results show a significant decrease without the

Table 2. Ablation Study on Twitter2015 dataset.

Method	Acc	Macro-F1
Multi-BART (CLS)	77.2	72.6
w/o {caption}	76.0	67.6
SeqCSG (Ours)	**79.3**	**75.0**
w/o {caption}	77.0	72.8
w/o {adjacency matrix}	78.9	74.7
w/o {adjacency matrix & scene graph}	78.2	74.4
w/o {prompt}	78.4	74.2
w/o {freeze}	78.6	74.3

presence of scene graphs, as compared to the SeqCSG model. All these observations verify that **both image captions and scene graphs help capture fine-grained information of image better (Q2)**.

Our results prove that the incorporation of the multi-modal adjacency matrix enhances the performance, indicating the efficacy of serializing the sequential cross-modal semantic graph in conjunction with the adjacency matrix. Therefore we can draw the conclusion that the **multi-modal adjacency matrix can make crossly utilize image and text information usefully (Q3)**.

Instead, SeqCSG optimizes the input structure of the model and converts the problem into a classification problem under a generation-based paradigm. We observe that our model exhibits a performance decay in the absence of other components, i.e., prompt template, parameter frozen, indicating the efficacy of all the modules. Concretely, we observe that taking the sequence-to-sequence model as the base comparison, our model achieves significant improvement (4.3% on accuracy and 10.9% on f1-score), which verifies its effectiveness. The performance rises sharply when taking the prompt template built for the target as the input to the decoder side of the model. We argue that the design of prompt templates, along with aspect-based sentiment classification using embeddings corresponding to the [mask], highly appropriate for this specific scenario. By utilizing the prompt template, we are able to establish an implicit association between the multi-modal corpus and the target, thereby enabling targeted classification predictions for multiple targets in a sentence.

Impact of the Triple Numbers. Upon conducting an analysis of the triple numbers with Fig. 3. We draw the following conclusions: Feeding the triples into the model has a certain performance gain. The performance of SeqCSG is highly influenced by both the quantity and quality of triples. The model performs best when the number of recalled triples is controlled to five triples A lower number of triples may limit the availability of detailed image information contained in the triples. Conversely, an excessively high number of triples may impede the efficiency of the training process and increase the risk of noisy data.

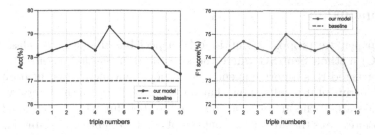

Fig. 3. Performance of SeqCSG with different triple numbers on Twitter2015.

Image				
Text	(a) @ MissAmerica 2014 Nina Davuluri working with @ TonyBowls at @ MAO-Teen in Orlando . # MissALovesTony	(b) RT @ graphure : Marie is serious business.	(c) This morning @ SheilaGCraft hosted a brunch amp poured into our WILD Women to honor them for their leadership in 2014 !	(d) Forbes Magazine Real insights from the business world . # MarketingMonday # Advertising
Target	**Nina Davuluri**	**Marie**	**WILD Women**	**Forbes Magazine**
Caption	A man and a woman posing for a picture.	A television with a tv screen and a movie on it.	A woman sitting at a table with a cake and a candle.	A man in a suit and tie standing in a room with a piano.
Scene Graph				
GT	Positive 😊	Neutral 😐	Positive 😊	Neutral 😐
Prediction	Multi-BART : neutral ✗ CapTrBERT : neutral ✗ w/o scene graph&visible matrix: neutral ✗ w/o Visible matrix: neutral ✗ Ours : positive ✓	Multi-BART : positive ✗ CapTrBERT : positive ✗ w/o scene graph&visible matrix: positive ✗ w/o Visible matrix: positive ✗ Ours : neutral ✓	Multi-BART : neutral ✗ CapTrBERT : positive ✓ w/o scene graph&visible matrix: neutral ✗ w/o Visible matrix: neutral ✗ Ours : positive ✓	Multi-BART : positive ✗ CapTrBERT : positive ✗ w/o scene graph&visible matrix: neutral ✓ w/o Visible matrix: neutral ✓ Ours : neutral ✓

Fig. 4. Predictions of different approaches.

4.4 Case Study

To further analyze the robustness of SeqCSG for error sensitivity, we visualize some predictions from different methods. The compared methods include BART, CapTrBERT, our model using the same inputs without scene graph and adjacency matrix, and our model using scene graph without adjacency matrix, respectively. As illustrated in Fig. 4, BART outputs wrong predictions in all these four cases. CapTrBERT outputs correct prediction in the third case but makes mistakes in the first, second and fourth cases, where the caption can not provide enough information from images. In contrast, our full model, which combines the scene graph and the adjacency matrix, makes correct predictions in those cases. Among all the cases, we notice that SeqCSG obtains more fine-grained image representation, which is essential for reducing error sensitivity. We can further reveal that the model lacking a scene graph and adjacency matrix has a poor prediction effect, which shows the superiority of our framework and the multi-modal adjacency matrix crossly utilizes image and text information.

5   Conclusion

In this paper, we propose a multi-modal aspect-based sentiment classification (MABSC) method SeqCSG where the sequential cross-modal semantic graphs are constructed to support our encoder-decoder sentiment classification framework. Experimental results show that our proposed approach generally outperforms the state-of-the-art methods on standard benchmarks. As a unified model, SeqCSG integrates the advantages of prompts and sequential cross-modal semantic graphs to effectively model global and local fine-grained image information and crossly utilize image and text information.

References

1. Chen, Z., et al.: LaKo: knowledge-driven visual question answering via late knowledge-to-text injection. CoRR abs/2207.12888 (2022)
2. Dai, J., Yan, H., Sun, T., Liu, P., Qiu, X.: Does syntax matter? A strong baseline for aspect-based sentiment analysis with RoBERTa. In: NAACL-HLT, pp. 1816–1829. Association for Computational Linguistics (2021)
3. Devlin, J., Chang, M., Lee, K., Toutanova, K.: BERT: pre-training of deep bidirectional transformers for language understanding. In: NAACL-HLT (1), pp. 4171–4186. Association for Computational Linguistics (2019)
4. Fan, F., Feng, Y., Zhao, D.: Multi-grained attention network for aspect-level sentiment classification. In: EMNLP, pp. 3433–3442. Association for Computational Linguistics (2018)
5. Ju, X., et al.: Joint multi-modal aspect-sentiment analysis with auxiliary cross-modal relation detection. In: EMNLP (1), pp. 4395–4405. Association for Computational Linguistics (2021)
6. Keswani, V., Singh, S., Agarwal, S., Modi, A.: IITK at SemEval-2020 task 8: unimodal and bimodal sentiment analysis of internet memes. In: SemEval@COLING, pp. 1135–1140. International Committee for Computational Linguistics (2020)
7. Khan, Z., Fu, Y.: Exploiting BERT for multimodal target sentiment classification through input space translation. In: ACM Multimedia, pp. 3034–3042. ACM (2021)
8. Kim, W., Son, B., Kim, I.: ViLT: vision-and-language transformer without convolution or region supervision. In: ICML. Proceedings of Machine Learning Research, vol. 139, pp. 5583–5594. PMLR (2021)
9. Lewis, M., et al.: BART: denoising sequence-to-sequence pre-training for natural language generation, translation, and comprehension. In: ACL, pp. 7871–7880. Association for Computational Linguistics (2020)
10. Ling, Y., Yu, J., Xia, R.: Vision-language pre-training for multimodal aspect-based sentiment analysis. In: ACL (1), pp. 2149–2159. Association for Computational Linguistics (2022)
11. Liu, P., Yuan, W., Fu, J., Jiang, Z., Hayashi, H., Neubig, G.: Pre-train, prompt, and predict: a systematic survey of prompting methods in natural language processing. CoRR abs/2107.13586 (2021)
12. Liu, W., et al.: K-BERT: enabling language representation with knowledge graph. In: AAAI, pp. 2901–2908. AAAI Press (2020)
13. Lu, D., Neves, L., Carvalho, V., Zhang, N., Ji, H.: Visual attention model for name tagging in multimodal social media. In: ACL (1), pp. 1990–1999. Association for Computational Linguistics (2018)

14. Lu, J., Batra, D., Parikh, D., Lee, S.: ViLBERT: pretraining task-agnostic visiolinguistic representations for vision-and-language tasks. In: NeurIPS, pp. 13–23 (2019)
15. Sun, C., Huang, L., Qiu, X.: Utilizing BERT for aspect-based sentiment analysis via constructing auxiliary sentence. In: NAACL-HLT (1), pp. 380–385. Association for Computational Linguistics (2019)
16. Tang, K., Niu, Y., Huang, J., Shi, J., Zhang, H.: Unbiased scene graph generation from biased training. In: CVPR, pp. 3713–3722. Computer Vision Foundation/IEEE (2020)
17. Wang, J., Liu, Z., Sheng, V., Song, Y., Qiu, C.: SaliencyBERT: recurrent attention network for target-oriented multimodal sentiment classification. In: Ma, H., et al. (eds.) PRCV 2021. LNCS, vol. 13021, pp. 3–15. Springer, Cham (2021). https://doi.org/10.1007/978-3-030-88010-1_1
18. Wu, T., et al.: Video sentiment analysis with bimodal information-augmented multi-head attention. Knowl. Based Syst. **235**, 107676 (2022)
19. Xu, N., Mao, W., Chen, G.: Multi-interactive memory network for aspect based multimodal sentiment analysis. In: AAAI, pp. 371–378. AAAI Press (2019)
20. Yan, H., Dai, J., Ji, T., Qiu, X., Zhang, Z.: A unified generative framework for aspect-based sentiment analysis. In: ACL/IJCNLP (1), pp. 2416–2429. Association for Computational Linguistics (2021)
21. Yang, K., Xu, H., Gao, K.: CM-BERT: cross-modal BERT for text-audio sentiment analysis. In: ACM Multimedia, pp. 521–528. ACM (2020)
22. Yu, J., Jiang, J.: Adapting BERT for target-oriented multimodal sentiment classification. In: IJCAI, pp. 5408–5414. Ijcai.org (2019)
23. Yu, J., Jiang, J., Xia, R.: Entity-sensitive attention and fusion network for entity-level multimodal sentiment classification. IEEE ACM Trans. Audio Speech Lang. Process. **28**, 429–439 (2020)
24. Yu, J., Wang, J., Xia, R., Li, J.: Targeted multimodal sentiment classification based on coarse-to-fine grained image-target matching. In: IJCAI, pp. 4482–4488. Ijcai.org (2022)
25. Yu, W., Xu, H., Yuan, Z., Wu, J.: Learning modality-specific representations with self-supervised multi-task learning for multimodal sentiment analysis. In: AAAI, pp. 10790–10797. AAAI Press (2021)
26. Zhang, Q., Fu, J., Liu, X., Huang, X.: Adaptive co-attention network for named entity recognition in tweets. In: AAAI, pp. 5674–5681. AAAI Press (2018)
27. Zhang, Z., Wang, Z., Li, X., Liu, N., Guo, B., Yu, Z.: ModalNet: an aspect-level sentiment classification model by exploring multimodal data with fusion discriminant attentional network. World Wide Web **24**(6), 1957–1974 (2021)
28. Zhao, F., Wu, Z., Long, S., Dai, X., Huang, S., Chen, J.: Learning from adjective-noun pairs: a knowledge-enhanced framework for target-oriented multimodal sentiment classification. In: COLING, pp. 6784–6794. International Committee on Computational Linguistics (2022)

Author Index

Printed in the United States
by Baker & Taylor Publisher Services